JETHRO TULL - THE A
Volume

by

DAVID REES and MARTIN WEBB

First published August 2012

Published by A NEW DAY

ISBN 978-0-9573533-0-5

Printed by the MPG Books Group, Bodmin and King's Lynn

This book is dedicated to

Rebecca Carter

and

Bonnie Mai, Niamh and Fionnuala Webb

CONTENTS

FOREWORD

David Rees, Martin Webb and the group of foolish but merry diehards at "A New Day Magazine" have come up trumps with a collection of over 25 years-worth of scandalous, scurrilous, rambling and occasionally coherent interviews from Ian Anderson, various band members and associates.

Hours of effort, gallons of British beer and hundreds of litres of various European brews have disappeared into the cavernous maw of intellectual and disciplined journalistic enquiry. Midnight lamps have burned into the wee sma' hours. Biros and qwerty keys have been worn to the nub. Heads scratched and options tossed like an overstuffed omelette to bring you the best and the worst of blah and blether.

And don't believe a word that Barriemore Barlow says. He's a softie, really.

Ian Anderson
July 2012

PREFACE

The history of A NEW DAY magazine through the eyes of Dave Rees

A NEW DAY was born on October 22nd 1985 with the launch of a black & white photocopied collection of old press cuttings and musings from yours truly, Dave Rees.

I had no pretensions of journalism, and certainly no expectations of a long-term project. As a Tull fan since 1972 I had become increasingly frustrated by the total lack of press coverage given to my favourite band, and having noticed the abundance of "fanzines" cropping up for all manner of bands and artists I thought it was about time that Jethro Tull had a point of focus for the fans. I hoped that by publishing a few little fanzines myself I might encourage someone, somewhere, to pick up the mantle and press on with a more professional version. Something that I could look forward to reading....

I placed a small ad in "Sounds", ran off 50 copies of A New Day, carefully hand-folding each page, collating and stapling them together, all the while thinking that I might be left with 49 copies for recycling. But to my surprise orders came flooding in, I ran off more copies, and it soon achieved massive sales of....well, a couple of hundred. But it was an encouraging start.

By issue #2 Martin Webb (aka Old Webby) had come onboard as a contributor, then 'staff photographer' and subsequently my usual companion when interviewing almost everyone that has played in Jethro Tull. It was a mere 20 years or so before he got himself a decent camera and therefore some half-decent photos for A New Day, but his stoic and dedicated approach to the "art or mystery of photography" was always appreciated. Old Webby was in the fortunate position of 'working' for the Civil Service and thus had very little to do with his time other than write articles for AND, and indeed in the last few years, whilst I have been overrun by other, more pressing matters, his enthusiasm helped keep AND afloat almost single-handedly.

There have been occasions when it looked like AND might not last the distance. Very early on it became clear to me that I could no longer carry on with the hand-written/badly typed photocopied approach but the circulation was too small to warrant a properly printed publication. Enter one Tommy Vance, rock-loving DJ at the BBC and a huge Tull fan. In July 1986 he gave AND a great plug on his Radio 1 Rock Show, and the jump in sales allowed for a properly produced (but still defiantly amateurish) publication.

The real boost however came in 1987 with the release of "Crest Of A Knave". Ian Anderson kindly offered to print the details of AND on the sleeve of the album, which consequently became Tull's biggest seller for many years and won the band a Grammy in the process. The response from Tull fans was incredible; a few days after the release I came home after the post had arrived and was almost unable to open the door due to the amount of mail I had received!

The strength of A New Day lies in the respect that it has been given by Ian Anderson and the other band members. Always fiercely independent, and never afraid to criticise, perhaps the finest compliment came when Ian Anderson announced onstage "I like the guys from A New Day because if they think we are shit, they say we are shit..... in the nicest possible way!"

At its peak AND had approximately 4,500 subscribers, and an estimated readership of over 12,000. In the days before the internet AND was practically the only source of Tull information for the huge worldwide following, and it is a source of great pride for me that many people still believe this humble little magazine helped to keep the band going in the late 80's. I'm not sure I agree with that, but I do know that through the pages of AND hundreds of Tull fans made new friends - friendships that have endured ever since. Other magazines sprang up around the world, fan clubs, fan conventions etc etc, and many are still going strong. That is the real and lasting legacy of A New Day, and that is what pleases me more than anything.

On a personal note, AND has given me and Old Webby the chance to do things we would never have dreamed of as we watched the mighty Tull way back in the early days. Earlier for Old Webby of course, but then he is much, much older than me..... (Well ok, just three years older, but he looks much older). We have travelled (much) of the world following our favourite band, been privileged to meet and chat to and often drink the night away with the band, many of whom we are honoured to call friends. We have been asked to write tour programmes, album sleeve notes etc, and were consultants for the highly praised "20 Years Of" box set and other album/DVD releases. And in 1998 I was commissioned by Firefly to write "Minstrels In The Gallery", the very first full-length biography of the band.

And of course we too have made many good friends on our travels, most notably our drinking companions in the *"A New Day Team"*, Terry The Innocent and Frank The Snowman. Our many enjoyable outings with "the team" and other friends throughout the world will one day make for another book, an undoubted best-seller, although I'm sure I shall have to change all the names and locations and pitch it in the 'fiction' genre – because nobody would ever believe it!

Of course there have been downs as well as ups. The miserable week endured in Athens, staying in Hotel Hell in Ammonia Square surrounded by prostitutes, pimps, murderers, passport thieves and corrupt police officers, all to witness Tull performing just TWO songs with a Greek superstar that we'd never heard of. The everyday touring ritual (in pre satnav days) of driving out of city centres only to drive past our hotel again an hour later. The bizarre way we always ended up in Brussels city centre no matter where we were supposed to be going. Having to endure Terry and Frank constantly complaining about my choice of music on our five hour car journeys (I thought everybody liked Nusrat Fateh Ali Khan?) Old Webby whinging on about five of us being crammed into my Capri/Probe/Puma or whatever 4 seater car I was driving at the time (it was always comfortable in the driver's seat 😊) .... Frank setting fire to the car while I was driving it. Frank falling asleep in the shower and flooding the room. Frank sleeping on an After Eight mint and waking with an earful of chocolate, convinced he had gone deaf. Frank proposing to a young lady called Potato in a bar in Germany whilst she was sitting on her boyfriend's knee. Good old Frank!..... And then there was Terry – but decency and possible legal complications prevent any detailed revelations I'm afraid.

In these modern times cyberspace is the medium for information, and Tull fans now consult the various websites and forums for the latest news, but for many there is still a place for the warmth and comfort of the printed word. The hardcore readership of A New Day remains intact, and we shall continue to intersperse our feeble ramblings and opinions with lengthy, interesting and exclusive interviews with the boys (and girls) in the band for as long as they are making music.

I find it incredible that (as I write) the 104th issue of A New Day is out, and even more incredible that it has features on the NEW album! Back in 1985 it seemed unlikely that Tull would be around for too much longer. Now, some 27 years later, it seems unlikely again..... but you never know, do you?

This first volume of the collected interviews from A New Day is a long overdue response to demand from the readers, and it has been a pleasure for me to revisit them. I hope you enjoy reading the Tull story as recalled by the band members themselves. Volume 2 will be out early in 2013.

Dave Rees, July 2012

The history of A NEW DAY magazine through the eyes of Martin Webb

In the mid-1970s Jethro Tull were massive news. Every tour was heralded on the front pages of *Melody Maker* and *NME*, and each annual (hah! - remember that??) album warranted a 5-page interview with Ian Anderson. Less than a decade later, in the days before monthly magazines like *Q* and *Mojo* and way before the internet, *MM* and *NME* had shifted their fickle focus to the next cool newbies, and it was becoming increasingly difficult to get hold of any information about Jethro Tull's activities.

One man, a not-yet-portly printer from the rock'n'roll wastelands of Farnborough, Hampshire, decided that if you want something done you might as well do it yourself. Thus, David Rees decided to start a magazine devoted entirely to Jethro Tull. Now, DR – as he is universally known by his family, workmates, music biz associates, drinking buddies, creditors and teenage girl entourage – knew that I dabbled in the odd bit of writing. I can't remember now how we first got in touch with each other, but I do recall that we used to swap copies of those dodgy live cassettes which were advertised in the back pages of *Sounds*. Anyway, DR rang me up one day in early 1985, announced that he was thinking of starting a Jethro Tull magazine, and asked if I'd like to write for it. My response was, "Let me see what the first issue looks like and then I'll decide whether to write for you." That was the only time I ever heard DR mutter "pompous tosser" under his breath – all subsequent occasions have been out loud, to my face, and not necessarily as polite as "tosser". And, let's face it, he had a point…

Looking back, that first issue was a rather scrubby, amateur, speculative, affair. But, in the absence of anything similar, I was impressed with both the content and aims of the magazine – and it did offer a platform for my barely latent hankerings to waffle on in print about my beloved Jethro Tull. (And in retrospect I applauded DR for the title of the mag, which not only drew upon a phrase that had cropped up in a couple of Tull songs, but also reflected a forward-looking rather than nostalgic approach – unlike, for example, the subsequent and now defunct American fanzine *Living In The Past*. Not us, mate…) So I jumped on board as first mate to DR's captain, little dreaming of the unchartered waters into which generally fair winds would blow us over the next quarter of a decade in what is, frankly, an already overstretched nautical analogy.

Early Days

Although issue 2 contained an interview with Dave Pegg, DR hadn't met him face-to-face – he'd sent Peggy a list of questions, and the ever-obliging and fan-friendly Peggy had sent a cassette back with his answers. It was not until issue 10, after the inevitable fanzine staple articles about bootlegs and unreleased songs, peppered with DR's thankfully short-lived obsession with the Oz band Mara, that we bagged our first 'proper' interview, the seeds for which were sown after a trip to Bedfordshire.

Up until then, although *AND* had been in existence for 18 months, I still hadn't met DR. Indeed, in those pre-email days, I would write an A4-sized article on a battered old typewriter, stuff it in an envelope and post it off to DR, who would reduce it to A5 to print it as per in the mag. But then in March 1987 I got a call from DR, asking if I fancied going to a Mick Abrahams gig in a pub Dunstable. I did, of course, and we agreed to meet at the entrance to

Uxbridge tube station. Ho, ho – Uxbridge tube station has two entrances, and inevitably we were each waiting at the other. Standing in the cold at Uxbridge station consulting my watch and cursing DR's tardiness was to become a distressingly large part of my life – but that was all to come. In this instance DR eventually found me and we headed north on the M1. For the next hour all my attempts at conversation were met with either monosyllabic grunts or just silence. Blimey, I thought – the bloke's a nutter. It was not until we'd got to the pub and had downed a couple of pints that I mentioned the magic word "football", whereupon DR suddenly came to life and started talking. And, 25 years later, not much has changed…

Anyway, Mick played a storming gig, and we had a few words with him afterwards at the bar, in the course of which it became clear that he was a diamond geezer. My suggestion to DR was that we write down what Mick had told us and present it in *AND* as an interview – but to his credit DR showed the vision that had made him start *AND* in the first place and counter-suggested that we ask Mick for a proper interview. And Mick, being indeed a diamond geezer, readily agreed - the results of which appeared in issue 10, which is kind of the point where I think *AND* came of age. We interviewed Mick at length in his office, and then he took us off for lunch – which was the conversation that we *should* have taped. Also in issue 10 was an interview which I had conducted with Clive Bunker in the cramped dressing room of the late lamented Mean Fiddler club in north west London, where Clive was playing with the late lamented Poor Mouth. I went along on spec, blagged my way backstage and found Clive flat on his back relaxing before the gig. An equally diamond geezer, without any warning or preparation he willingly chatted away about his time before, during and after Tull, and our second interview was in the bag. Nowadays I wouldn't dream of approaching an interview like that, partly because DR and I enjoy doing them together if practicable, and partly because it's unfair on the interviewee to spring it upon them. But hey, we were only learning…

Enter Ian Anderson, stage right
Although it had always been an ambition of mine to interview Ian Anderson, I don't think either DR or I ever really thought it would happen; indeed neither did we even dream that he was aware of our humble little fanzine. Not so. Ian Anderson knows everything – and not only did he know about *AND*, he had been quietly monitoring its progress. Thus it was that in April '87 DR was somewhat startled to get a message via Kenny Wylie that, if we were interested, Ian would be available for interview. If????

The resultant interview filled the whole of issue 11, having been conducted in the oak-panelled study of Ian's 16th century 'Pophleys' house near the village of Radnage, Buckinghamshire – the very same room where the *Heavy Horses* back cover band photo was taken. (He's since moved to Wiltshire, so I haven't just given his address away…) We were nervous of course, but Ian was relaxed on his own patch and with no other commitments that day, so it all went swimmingly well. On reflection, I suspect that whilst Ian recognised that a Jethro Tull magazine would be a good publication to which to chat about Jethro Tull stuff, equally he was keen to check us out to ascertain which side of the fine line between fans and fanatics we lay. He must have recognised that we weren't nutters or stalkers and did have some sort of serious amateur journalistic aspirations. And so began the start of an incredible journey into unchartered waters… oh, done that one.

The Jethro Tull family
Since those first interviews with Mick and Clive, we've conducted innumerable interviews with past and present Tull members, plus associates like Anna Phoebe, Ann-Marie Calhoun and Lucia Micarelli. And I am delighted to report that, absolutely without exception, they have all been really top blokes and blokesses (and, in the case of David/Dee Palmer, both). There is no real reason why any musician should be obliged to talk to us, but no-one has ever

turned us down, and all have been most engaging and accommodating company. It would appear that, aside from being a bit of a whizz on your chosen musical instrument, the two prerequisites for joining Jethro Tull are a keen intelligence and a sharp sense of humour – the combination of which makes the task of chatting with these fascinating people, often over a beer, nothing less than a pleasure. The only Jethro Tull members that have not been interviewed by *AND* are the late John Glascock, Eddie Jobson and Peter-John Vettese. In the latter two cases, it's actually simply because we haven't got round to asking them yet. We will.

The other bunch of people that we've had great pleasure in meeting, and drinking with, are Jethro Tull fans around the world. Too many to mention them all, but of legendary status in the *A New Day* annals are Terry The Innocent and Frank The Snowman. Our adventures around Europe over two decades would fill a book: Frank accidentally setting fire to the car at 80mph on a German autobahn, Terry trying to strangle driver DR at 90mph on a German autobahn – a lot of stuff happens on German autobahns – and a whole raft of hazier incidents fogged by a surfeit of beer and the lateness of the hour. We've also become good friends with the chaps from the German fanzine *Beggar's Farm News*, the wittily-titled Italian fanzine *Itullians*, the Spanish *Tullianos* mob, the Czech Fan club, the Dutch Fan Club, and a host of Americans. Not many French, though.

DR, MW & *AND*

A question asked – oft of ourselves – is how on earth have a couple of loafers like me and DR managed to last 27 years without being banished from the Jethro Tull kingdom? The answer I think lies partly with our mostly managing to remember to show the kind of professionalism expected by Ian Anderson of his band and crew, and not make bleedin' nuisances of ourselves backstage, but also with our showing a healthy degree of both honesty and irreverence. Our independence from the band is very important – we're not an official fan magazine. Jethro Tull is by some way our favourite band ever – but *A New Day* has for the most part shunned sycophancy. If we don't like an album, or feel that a stage performance hasn't met the standards we've come to expect, we'll say so, hopefully constructively. And with interviews, we can be cheeky but on the right side of respectful, and equally certainly not obsequious.

And of course, we're useful, not only in our expansive (but not complete – blimey, some people do know some trivia) knowledge of JT, but in our ability to translate that knowledge and understanding into words and sentences with commas and full stops. Hence our being wheeled out every few years to contribute towards tour programmes and box sets etc. So whilst *A New Day* is independent, occasionally DR and I do find ourselves working "for" Jethro Tull. And that's never been anything but a pleasure – although I must admit it still feels a little surreal when the 'phone rings and it's Ian Anderson on the other end…

Finale

Why me, I sometimes think? How come I, a humble civil servant from Nowheresville, am in this amazing position of being on drinking terms with my favourite band, writing their tour programmes and taking 'phone calls from their one-legged flute-playing leader? The answer is that DR had the gumption to start *A New Day*, and I had the energy and commitment to join him. It could have been any two fans, really; but we got there first – and stayed there.

And finally, if you bump into either of us at a bar at a Tull gig, do buy us a Guinness, do engage us in learned discourse on the season's chances of Tottenham Hotspur and West Ham, but never, ever ask us about the variety of catalogue numbers of the multiple CD and vinyl versions of the *Aqualung* album (Germany 2001, still a painful memory for us both…)

Old Webby, July 2012

Introducing Dave Rees (DR)

Born in 1957 (many years after Old Webby) in Woking, Surrey. Endured an education at the Salesian College for boys in Chertsey, Surrey and left with eleven "O" levels and a special request from the headmaster not to return for further education.

Foolishly declined a job offer from the GLC in favour of an apprenticeship in printing, and wasted the next 39 years in a dying profession, gaining 1st Class C&G's on the way in Letterpress, Letterset, Lithographic, Gravure, Flexographic, Collotype and God knows what other methods of printing. Still not sure why.

Started "A New Day" magazine in October 1985, which in turn led to the offshoot record company, cunningly called "A New Day Records" in 1990. We released many CDs both Tull related and not, very few of which made any money.

In 1998 I wrote *Minstrels In The Gallery*, the first full length biography of Jethro Tull, published by Firefly. It went to #1 in the music book charts and was also translated for publication in Poland, Germany and the Czech Republic. The follow-up has been in the planning stages for the past eight years – I'll get there in the end!

In 2007 became a partner in *Weyfest* music festival in Surrey

First Jethro Tull album purchased was *Stand Up* and first saw Tull at the Rainbow in London in 1974. I have absolutely no idea how many times I've seen them since...
My favourite Tull albums are *A Passion Play, Thick As A Brick* and *Stand Up.*

Most memorable Jethro Tull / A New Day moments? (a) getting the call inviting me to interview Ian Anderson for the first time in 1987: (b) Ian saying onstage in Ipswich how "the next song was saved from obscurity by Dave Rees" before playing *Jack-a-Lynn*: (c) being asked by Ian to get just 20 Tull fans to a pub in Leamington for the filming of the reunion of the original Tull line-up (d) Ian onstage in Prague dedicating *From Birnam Wood to Dunsinane* to "a good friend of ours, Dave Rees, who is seriously ill at the moment. I know he loves this tune" after I had slagged it off in AND! I was in the audience at the time, in good health. Well, as good as it gets.... (e) anything involving Terry The Innocent.

Other favourite artists include: The Stranglers, Talk Talk, The The, Stevie Ray Vaughan, Al Hodge & The Mechanics, Feeder, Jackie Leven, Jackie Lynton, Muddy Waters, John Lee Hooker, Tommy Justice, It Bites, Francis Dunnery, The Smiths, New Model Army, Kate Bush, Dr Feelgood, Nine Below Zero, The Tea Party..... could go on forever.

Favourite non-Tull albums: Gorecki *3rd Symphony*: This Mortal Coil *Blood*: This Mortal Coil *Filigree & Shadow*: Talk Talk *Colour Of Spring.*

Non-Tull interests: Weyfest, West Ham United FC, not even bothering to think of excuses for not doing the gardening.

Dave now lives in the frozen wastes of the North Pole, aka Newcastle upon Tyne, with his partner Rebecca Carter.

Introducing Martin Webb (MW)

Born in 1954 in Worcester (England), and grew up in Winchester where he attended Peter Symonds Grammar School. Spent five years at Bangor University, where he got a BA (Hons) and post-graduate Diploma in Drinking Beer and Playing Football. Won the 1974 North Wales AAA 800 metres championship before switching back to his first love of football and spending several years chasing shadows in the Welsh League and the Caernarfon & District League. On moving to London he became a footballing legend in his own head in the Southern Amateur League before injury forced his premature retirement at the age of 43.

Joined the civil service in 1979, taking in the Ministry of Defence, the Parliamentary Commissioner for Administration, the Department of the Environment, the Government Office for London, The Department for Transport, Local Government and the Regions, the Office of the Deputy Prime Minister, and the Department for Communities and Local Government, and spent the entire 33 years looking forward to retirement (and the last 27 writing for *A New Day*) – achieved in July 2012 on a pension much smaller than the media would have you believe.

First Jethro Tull album purchased was *This Was*, and first saw Tull live on 20 October 1969 at Southampton Guildhall. Hasn't missed a UK tour since and has seen Tull live in 18 different countries (so far), not entirely co-incidentally the same as DR. Likewise has no idea how many Jethro Tull/Ian Anderson concerts he's been to, but undoubtedly 250+. Favourite obscure Tull song is *Summerday Sands*, favourite Tull 'hit' is *Living In The Past*, and – controversially - favourite Tull albums are *This Was*, *A Passion Play* and *Minstrel In The Gallery*. Most memorable Jethro Tull/A New Day moments have been: (a) being invited by Ian Anderson at a gig in Germany in 2007 to take photos of the whole show from on the stage rather than just the first three songs from the photographers' pit; (b) Frank The Snowman accidentally setting fire to the car at 80mph on an autobahn; and (c) anything involving Terry The Innocent.

Writing/photography credits other than *A New Day*, fellow Jethro Tull fanzines and tour programmes include *Record Collector, Mojo, Q, Rock'n'Reel, R2, Classic Rock, Prog, RARO!, TNT, the Daily Express, the Evening Standard* (plus too many publications to mention which have used his 'promo' photos from the official Jethro Tull website) and 20+ album/CD covers/booklets.

Other favourite artists include: John Otway, The Inmates, Nine Below Zero, Dead Can Dance, Blodwyn Pig, The Beatles, Nick Drake, Mogwai, The Cramps, U2, The Powders, Snow Patrol, Anna Phoebe, Francis Dunnery, The Saints, The Pogues, Beirut, Helen Andrews, Tommy Justice, Karma Control and far too many others to mention.

Non-Tull obsessions… er hobbies… include the history of Colditz Castle as Oflag IVc, the trials and tribulations of Tottenham Hotspur FC, and inventing excuses for not doing the gardening.

Martin lives in London with his wife Bonnie Mai and daughters Niamh (TV/stage actress) and Fionnuala (fashion PR).

14

WHO'S WHO OF INTERVIEWEES

(in *almost* alphabetical order)

Mick Abrahams (1967-1968) (Guitar)
*Born Luton, 1943. Founder member of Jethro Tull, having previously played
with McGregor's Engine, The Toggery Five, Neil Christian's Crusaders and
a host of others. Post-Tull had great success with Blodwyn Pig and then The
Mick Abrahams Band. Effectively retired from the music biz during the late
70s/early 80s, but re-entered the fray in 1987 with a revamped Blodwyn Pig.
Published his autobiography 'What Is A Wommet' in 2008. See
www.squirrelmusic.com*

Don Airey (1987) (Keyboards)
Born Sunderland, 1948. A heavy-rock legend who has played with everyone from Deep Purple, Cozy Powell, Rainbow, Gary Moore, Whitesnake, Judas Priest, Black Sabbath and Ozzy Osbourne to, er, Katrina and the Waves (he orchestrated their Eurovision Song Contest winning entry). Released a new solo album in 2011. See www.donairey.com

Martin Allcock (1988-1991) (Keyboards, guitar & mandolin)
Born Manchester, 1957. The man who introduced darts and the heavy-metal broomstick to the Jethro Tull live show, Maart was in Fairport Convention from 1985 to 1996, and has played with absolutely everybody on the folk scene, including Mike Harding, The Bully Wee Band, Dave Swarbrick, Kieran Halpin, Beth Nielsen Chapman, Ralph McTell, Yusuf Islam and Billy Connolly, plus non-folkies such as Beverley Craven, Robert Plant and The Mission. He tours and records constantly (over 200 album sessions to date), and has two solo albums under his belt. See www.maartinallcock.com

Ian Anderson (1967-current) (Flutes, whistles, guitars, saxes, vocals, tambourine etc)
Born Dunfermline, 1947. Founder member of The Blades, The John Evan Band and Jethro Tull. You know the rest... See www.jethrotull.com

Barriemore Barlow (1971-1980) (Drums & percussion)
Born Birmingham, 1949. Previously played with Ian Anderson, John Evans and Jeffrey Hammond in The Blades and The John Evan Band. Appeared on ten Tull albums. After leaving Tull formed Tandoori Cassette, and subsequently played with the likes of Robert Plant, John Miles, Yngwie Malsteem and Jimmy Page. Has his own recording studio, and has produced and managed a number of bands. See www.thedoghousestudio.co.uk

Martin Barre (1968-current) (Guitars, mandolin, bouzouki, flute & recorder)

Born Birmingham, 1946. Has been Jethro Tull's guitarist for all but their first year, having joined Tull from Gethsemane. Previous bands included The Moonrakers, The Motivation, the Dwellers and the Penny Peeps. Has released three solo albums.

In 2012 Martin launched his own band, Martin Barre's New Day. See www.martinbarre.com

Clive Bunker (1967-1971) (Drums & percussion)

Born Luton, 1946. Founder member of Jethro Tull, along with his ol' mate Mick Abrahams, with whom he had previously been in McGregor's Engine and The Toggery Five. After leaving Tull he played with Jude, Aviator, Manfred Mann, Jack Bruce, Gordon Giltrap, Steve Hillage, Poor Mouth, Solstice, Uli Jon Roth and hundreds of others. Recorded a solo album in 2000 with guests Ian Anderson and Martin Barre. Recent ventures have included the Wild Turkey reunion with Glenn Cornick and folk-rock supergroup The Gathering.

Glenn Cornick (1967-1970) (Bass guitar)
Born Barrow-in-Furness 1947. Founder member of Jethro Tull having stuck it out with Ian Anderson after the demise of the John Evan Band. Was previously in The Vikings, Formula One, The Wild Violets, and The Hobos. Post-Tull had considerable success with Wild Turkey, and then Karthago and Paris. Now lives in Los Angeles where he divides his time between business and music. Reformed Wild Turkey in 2006 and released a new CD. See www.cornick.org

Mark Craney (1980-1981) (Drums & percussion)
Born Minneapolis, 1952. Jethro Tull's first American member. Previously played and recorded with Jean Luc Ponty, Tommy Bolin, Gino Vanelli, and Eddie Jobson. Recorded the "A" album with Tull, and played on the "A" tours. Subsequently hooked up again with Gino Vanelli, and toured with Tower of Power, but suffered severe health problems requiring a kidney transplant in 1988. Battled back to play with the likes of Dweezil Zappa and Eric Burdon, but suffered a brain stem stroke and passed away in November 2005.

21

John Evans (1970-1980) (Keyboards)

Born Blackpool, 1948. Founder member of The Blades and The John Evan Band with Ian Anderson, Jeffrey Hammond and Barrie Barlow. Played on twelve Tull albums. Later played with David Palmer in Tallis, but then retired from the music biz completely to concentrate on running his own business. Now living in Australia.

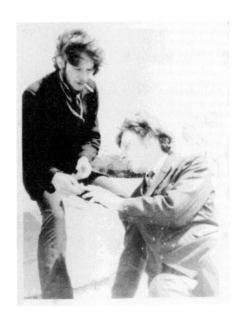

Andrew Giddings (1991-2006)
(Keyboards, accordion &
recorder)
*Born Pembury, 1963. Played with
Eric Burdon, Leo Sayer and Sniff
'n' the Tears before joining Tull to
become their longest-serving
keyboard player. Collaborated
with Ian Anderson on the 'solo'
"Divinities" album, and has
produced several other artists'
albums. Released a solo CD in
2010. Downloads of his new solo
work are available at
www.myspace.com/andrewgidding
smusic*

Jeffrey Hammond-Hammond (1971-1975) (Bass guitar)
Born Blackpool, 1946. Founder member of The Blades and The John Evan Band with Ian Anderson, John Evans and Barrie Barlow. Was a Jethro Tull legend even before he joined the group. Left the music biz behind completely when he left Tull to become a full-time painter. (Artist, not decorator...)

Tony Iommi (1968) (Guitar)
Born Birmingham, 1948.
Founder and ever-present
member of Black Sabbath.
Only appearance with Jethro
Tull was on the Rolling
Stones' infamous Rock'n'Roll
Circus. Published his
autobiography 'Iron Man' in
2011, and reformed the
original Black Sabbath in
2012. See www.iommi.com

Matt Pegg (1992-1994) (Bass
guitar)
Born Birmingham, 1971. Son of
Dave, for whom he depped on
several Jethro Tull tours when Dad
was otherwise engaged. Recorded
with Tull on the Catfish Rising
album. Since then is best known for
his work with Francis Dunnery,
Procol Harum, Ian Brown and
Chris Difford.

David/Dee Palmer (1976-1980)
(Keyboards & arrangements)
*Born London, 1937. Studied at The
Royal Military School of Music and
then The Royal Academy of Music.
Was involved with Jethro Tull as an
arranger right from the first album in
1968, and eventually became an
onstage member in1976, playing
keyboards, the portative pipe organ
and occasional saxophone. Post-Tull
formed the short-lived group Tallis
with John Evans, and continued to
work occasionally with Ian Anderson
as well as releasing a series of albums
of orchestrations of rock groups'
works. In 2003 underwent a gender
change and became Dee. Still writes,
orchestrates and performs music
worldwide.*

Dave Pegg (1979-1995) (Bass guitar & mandolin)
Born Birmingham, 1947. First recorded in 1965/66 with The Crawdaddies and The Uglys. Played in The Band Of Joy with Robert Plant and John Bonham before joining The Ian Campbell Folk Group. Has been a stalwart member of Fairport Convention since 1969, including at the same time as his lengthy tour of duty with Tull, and on Fairport's nights off he tours with The Dylan Project and with PJ Wright. Has played too many sessions to even begin to attempt to list; released a solo album in 1998. See www.fairportconvention.com

Doane Perry (1984-current) (Drums & percussion)

Born New York, USA, 1954. Tull's longest-serving drummer, has played with a multitude of artists in a variety of genres, notably Lou Reed, Bette Midler, Phyllis Hyman, Todd Rundgren, Dave Mason, Pat Benatar, Jim Messina, Martha and the Vandellas, Pete Cetera, Dweezil Zappa, Stan Getz, Laura Branigan, Dionne Warwick, Liza Minelli, Patty Scialfa, Charles Aznavour, Maxus, Hunter/Dragon and his own band Thread. Continues to work voraciously outside of Tull, and mysteriously claims to be writing a book.

Doane with Mark Craney and Clive Bunker

David Rees

Born under a bad sign. Editor and publisher of A New Day and author of "Minstrels In The Gallery"
Since 2007 has been a partner in Weyfest Music Festival.
A printer by trade but hoping never to see a Heidelberg again!
"What in blazes," I hear you say, "Is he doing in this list?" All is revealed in Chapter 15.

Tony Williams (1978-1979) (Bass guitar)

Born Blackpool, 1947. Played in numerous Blackpool groups, including Requiem with Barrie Barlow, but somehow managed to avoid joining the John Evan Band. Earned a gold disc with Stealers Wheel before answering an SOS call from Tull in 1978 to deputise for the unwell John Glascock. Played on the famous Madison Square Gardens 'satellite TV' gig. Still has his own band in Blackpool, where he is Deputy Leader of the Conservative Group on Blackpool Borough Council.

Chris Riley (-) (Guitar)
Born Blackpool, 1946. Guitarist with The John Evan Band, having previously played with The Atlantics, The Hobos (with Glenn Cornick), and others. Now retired and living in Spain after a music teaching career.

Neil "Chic Murray" Smith (-) (Guitar)
Born Aberdeen, 1947. Guitarist with The John Evan Band. Retired from the music biz to pursue a number of careers, culminating in social work back in his native Scotland.

Tony Wilkinson (-) (Saxophone)
Born Blackpool, 1948. Saxophone player with The John Evan Band, his only group. Later ran his own building firm. Tragically killed in a motor accident in 1990.

Martin Skyrme (-) (Saxophone)
Born Bath, 1948. Saxophone player with The John Evan Band. Session work includes – extraordinarily – Jethro Tull's A Passion Play. Has his own jazz ensemble which plays in the north-west of England. See www.martinskyrme.co.uk

JOHN EVANS BAND

Chapter 1

DAVE PEGG

(Published in Issue #2, December 1985)

When DR started A New Day *the notion of meeting and interviewing the various members and ex-members of Jethro Tull was still at the wildest-dream stage.*
However, one chap who was readily accessible even in those early days, usually at the bar of a Fairport Convention gig, was bass player Dave Pegg. 'Honest' Dave is everybody's friend, and always ready to offer help and support to fans of both Tull and Fairport, and so it was that he had the honour of becoming our first interviewee.
Not that it was quite that easy, as the plans of mice, men and DR repeatedly fell through and, through nobody's fault, the intended face-to-face interview did not materialise. The logistical problems were eventually overcome by DR sending Dave a list of questions, and Dave sending a tape back with his spoken replies. AND's series of exclusive interviews was underway...

Dave, how did you come to join Jethro Tull? Were you invited or did you approach them?
Well, I got a call around July of 1979 while I was out doing Fairport's farewell tour, as we split in '79 officially. John Glascock was very poorly and the band had just finished recording the *Stormwatch* LP and were to do an American tour in September. And luckily I went along to an audition and was asked to do the tour, which was great and of course I was delighted to be asked. The only unfortunate thing was while we were in San Francisco, the last but one gig of the tour, we got word that John had passed away, so it was a very sad occasion for everybody.

Were you a fan of Tull from the early days, or did you get into them when they started to 'dabble' in folk music?
I was a bit of a fan from the early days. I think I bought Living In The Past – I remember buying the single. And also Fairport had played three nights at the Filmore West in 1970 so I had seen the band in the early days, and I was aware of some of their records. I did have the first album on Island, but I tended to lose touch when I started playing with Fairport because we were so busy.

Do you and Martin Barre have much say as to what goes into a Tull record?
Everybody has a chance of putting their ideas into a new LP. In fact, on *Under Wraps* both Martin and Peter Vettese feature quite a lot. Peter, in fact, must have written about half the music for it. I am not a writer as such so my input is fairly minimal in terms of a Tull album.

Have you ever recorded a song with Tull that you can't bear?
There have been several times when... I mean, the last album we probably recorded about 20 or 25 backing tracks, purely instrumental pieces, and then Ian would put his bits on after all the backing tracks were finished. So 90% of the time songs are created in the studio as backing tracks and we don't really have an idea what the lyrics are going to be, or indeed what the song may be about. So there are times when there are backing tracks that you really don't like, but by the time it is finished with the vocals etc on it you really enjoy what you have done. Conversely, the stuff that you really liked as a backing track, by the time it's finished may not work, in your opinion. The only track I really didn't like on the last album was *Lap Of Luxury*, which I don't think any of us were too fond of. It was just unfortunate that Chrysalis decided to put that out as a single, thinking it to be commercial.

What is your favourite Tull track or LP?
I think my favourite track off the last album is the acoustic version of *Under Wraps*. My favourite album that I have played on, which is only three, or four if you include *A Classic*

Case – incidentally, the drummer on *A Classic Case* is Paul Burgess, even though there is no credit on the record – my particular favourite is *The Broadsword And The Beast*. My other favourite Tull albums are I think *Songs From The Wood* and *Heavy Horses*. I like that kind of 'English' period that the band went through.

Are you happier playing with Tull or Fairport? If you HAD to make a choice which one would you leave?
Well, Fairport don't really exist at all – although as you'll see from the list of dates, which I hope you will print in case any Tull fans want to come along and see us, we have a new Fairport line-up with some very good players in it, including a wonderful violinist called Ric Sanders. Er, no, we don't really exist. We only get together when everyone is available; it is very much a secondary thing to Tull. My obvious commitment is with Jethro Tull, but 1985 was always going to be a year off for Tull. It kind of goes in phases because we'll do an album which we will probably spend nine months in total time-wise doing – *Under Wraps* took nine months to make – and then we spend a couple of months rehearsing for touring followed by three months on tour. So it really is over something like a 14-month work period, so you do need some time off after that, I can assure you! That is why '85 has been time off for everybody, and everybody in the band has other interests. But I enjoy playing with Tull, I love doing those big halls in the States or Germany, and the fact that we can obviously put much more into a live show in terms of production and effects. It's a totally different thing from just playing in a club or a small concert hall with Fairport. They both have their advantages; it's nice to play a very small venue and in fact I did that last June with Fairport when we did an American tour with Steeleye Span and we played some fairly small venues. And when we weren't playing with Steeleye we were doing what were more or less coffee houses – I mean, one venue we played had a total capacity of 85 people! It's great doing places like that where you can have a good time... I enjoy playing with both bands but my priorities are obviously with Jethro Tull.

Do you agree with critics that Gladys Leap is one of the finest LPs Fairport have ever made?
I'm very pleased with the reaction that Gladys Leap has got. Woodworm Records is our own little company and we are very much a cottage industry. My wife Chris and I run Woodworm records as well as the Fairport reunion at Cropredy on the second weekend in August every year. We are pleased that a lot of Tull fans have started to come along to that. We are delighted with the reaction to Gladys Leap because it was made by Simon Nicol, myself and Dave Mattacks, which is really the group's rhythm section, in a couple of months. We wanted some new material and it's going to be fun going out and playing the music from *Gladys Leap*. Yes, I think it is a very good album. I also really like *Fairport 9* and I love *Rising For The Moon* because it has got some great Sandy Denny songs on it.

Did you ask Ian Anderson to write a song for the album?
We've asked Ian to write stuff for us in the past. By the way, *Jack Frost And The Hooded Crow* was not written specifically for me – it was recorded for the *Broadsword* album but it wasn't used. We are hoping that Chrysalis will bring it out this Christmas but, er, you know, [laughing] I have my doubts with, er...their activities. We did ask Ian to play whistle on one of the songs on *Gladys Leap*, *A Bird From The Mountain*, which he would have done, time permitting, but unfortunately we ran out of time. But I'm sure he would have played on it because he did offer to.

Have you any plans to follow up your *Cocktail Cowboy* LP?
I do have plans for another album but I don't know when it will be. My *Cocktail Cowboy* LP was done on an 8-track which we bought here. It was difficult doing everything myself just having 8 tracks, but now we're 16-track and we've got a few more toys so I think the next one will be a great improvement and certainly will be fun to make. So I will do another one, yes.

I heard you say in a radio interview in 1982 that you would love to see Ian Anderson make a solo LP, as you were sure that a lot of people would like a set of songs with Ian

just singing and playing acoustic guitar. Were you disappointed when *Walk Into Light* sounded more like Ultravox than Jethro Tull? Do you think it would have been more successful had it been a simple acoustic set?

Yes, I would have enjoyed a lot more acoustic-type songs on it, I musty confess. Er, I wasn't disappointed with *Walk Into Light*. I thought there were some very good songs on it, like *Made In England* which I though was a great song, and also *Fly By Night* I enjoyed. I don't know if it would have been more successful had it been an acoustic set. I think it would have pleased Tull fans a lot more if it had more acoustic things on it – certainly,. It would have been my preference. But I think for a first kind of solo album it did very well...sorry, I'll rephrase that... it was a good first solo album but I think it would have benefitted from more variety in the choice of material that went onto it. I was very disappointed with the reaction that it got from the music press, and also with the amount of effort that was put behind marketing it.

At about that time there was also talk of a 'Jethro Tull' LP without Ian. Has that idea now been scrapped or is it still a possibility?

You must have imagined the possibility of Jethro Tull without Ian. Obviously that would be totally impossible!

Do you go to other people's gigs? Who do you listen to at home?

Yes, we've been to see quite a few bands. We saw Genesis at the NEC and David Bowie at the NEC last year or the year before. I have seen Joni Mitchell, and Martin Barre and I saw The Stones at Wembley. Martin goes to quite a few gigs, and Peter Vettese and Ian Anderson went to an awful lot of gigs when we were rehearsing for the Under Wraps tour, checking out lighting and P.A..

I listen to lots of things at home – lots of different things, really. You know, everybody's got fairly wide tastes in music.

Is there anybody outside the Tull/Fairport circle that you would like to play or record with?

I'd love to play with Steve Winwood. I'm a great fan of his and I would love to go on one of his tours. Obviously he does most of the stuff on his albums himself, but I would really enjoy that I think.

What do you think of the "punk-folk" fad, e.g. The Pogues and The Men They Couldn't Hang?

I'm not a great Pogues fan, I'm afraid. I've seen them twice, and I must confess to being very unimpressed, although obviously they are fairly exciting; but I think musically they are...pretty dire! I can't comment on The Men They Couldn't Hang because I have not seen them. I quite like Billy Bragg but, um, not a fan of the Pogues!

Have you heard of the Australian group Mara! who toured here recently, taking various folk festivals by storm?

Yes I have, and I think they are very good. I've only heard one tape, and I haven't seen them live. They would be good for Cropredy and if they are over in England perhaps we might have them one year.

Will Tull be touring in 1986 as far as you know?

If we do another album, of which there is talk, obviously if we get it finished and released in time we would of course be doing a tour. The group never tour, as you probably know, unless there is an album to promote. I hope we can tour. On our last tour we did an awful lot of dates in England – well, not an awful lot more than the group normally do - and it was most enjoyable. It was great starting off in England because the band were fresh and had lots of energy. It is often better at the beginning than it is at the end of 76 dates! In fact, the UK audiences were very lucky in the fact that we did do all those dates, because by the end of the tour Ian had a very serious throat problem and we had to cancel a lot of dates in America. So sure, we will be doing the UK. We are very grateful for the loyal support that we get from the Tull British audiences – they are probably the best in the world to play to.

Did you play at Sun City last month as I heard you might?
We didn't play at Sun City, although we have had offers to play there. Last September we were offered a charity show in Johannesburg along with about four other English acts. But because of the political situation it didn't happen, so we didn't go to South Africa – although I got a letter the other day from a long-standing Jethro Tull fan John Belville who did actually go out there just to see us. John has done an awful lot of tours – he must be the most travelled Tull fan. He has done about five European tours and five US tours.

Finally, why do you think Chrysalis Records are so very unhelpful? (n.b. This question has been severely edited in the cause of decency, not to mention the risk of libel...)
Yes, I know you don't get much help from them. They are obviously a big company and they have got other acts apart from us to worry about who probably sell a lot more records than we do, and who are a lot younger and not so much of a hassle! I think your Tull magazine is a great idea because it gives Tull fans a chance to communicate with each other and swap tapes from gigs which I know you all do! And often videos as well. I myself get stuff through the post from Tull fans which I am very grateful for. I can't help you with Chrysalis, but now people will have somewhere to write to. Good luck with it!

Chapter 2

MICK ABRAHAMS

(Published in Issue #10, May 1987)

In November 1986 DR and MW made their first acquaintance with Tull's founder-member guitarist Mick Abrahams, at a rare gig in Dunstable. We had a chat with Mick at the bar after a truly storming set, and he seemed such an affable chap that we took the plunge and asked him whether we could do a proper interview for AND.

Mick readily agreed, and a couple of months later we met up with him at his office, where he was working as a financial consultant. We nattered for so long that we ended up finishing the interview over lunch at a local restaurant. Mick spoke very frankly and openly about a number of subjects, and the eventual transcript printed in AND was suitably edited to dilute some highly colourful language and to omit some names to protect the guilty! Mick is a born raconteur and mimic, and our first "proper" interview was hugely entertaining as well as informative. And, as it transpired, our own enthusiasm for Jethro Tull, Blodwyn Pig and The Mick Abrahams Band provided a small catalyst for Mick's return to making records and playing live more often - including several guest appearances with Jethro Tull and Ian Anderson, with whom he has long buried any hatchets.

What were the real reasons behind your leaving Jethro Tull?
Well, you know I got the boot…

That is the question really – did you jump or were you pushed?
Well, I jumped – but when they found out I was about to, they pushed me, which I thought was a real shit. I've never forgiven Terry Ellis for that.
The black and white of it was that I was getting severely pissed off with not having a say any more with song writing with Ian Anderson. They just pushed me aside, made no bones about it, and I saw no reason for them to do so. If my contribution to the band had been lacking in some way I think I would have been aware of it, but I didn't feel it was. I think it was a little bit of jealousy on Ian's part because I was getting as much attention as he was. Whether that is true or not I don't know – maybe I'm looking back on it from an emotional viewpoint rather than from a business one. I think in the end I had to leave whatever happened because I just couldn't stand Anderson any more. I mean, I would have ended up docking him on stage – it got nearer and nearer to that every night. And the fact that my nose was put out I thought I'd rather go the way I wanted to go. There was nothing to stop me. I'd already spoken to Chris Wright and he said, well, if you have to go you've got plenty of contacts, why don't you form your own band? I said OK, but I didn't want to let Jethro Tull down, so I was quite happy to stay with them until they found a replacement and worked it all out. So I gave them that information, I said that's what I'm gonna do, you'd better look around for someone else. And within 48 hours of me saying that Terry Ellis called me into the office and told me I was fired! I mean, he fired me because I had quit, which was an arsehole thing to do, just a piece of childish bullshit. And obviously he and Ian Anderson were party to that – not as a big conspiracy thing, but of course they were close business partners anyway.

Ian has always said in interviews since that… I mean, he has never put you down as a musician, he praises you as a guitarist, but…
Well, I would never put Ian down as a musician. Now, I don't really bear the guy any grudges you know… I just joke about it really because it's expected of me. Funnily enough when we formed Blodwyn Pig there was such an anti-Ian Anderson feeling around that I had to try to play it down. People used to come up to me and say: "Gee, that Ian Anderson - what a mother******, don't you hate him? Isn't he an asshole?", and so I had to say, like, no, he's a great bloke you know. But of course to some people it was fairly plain that there was some aggro there.

But he has always maintained that it was because you did not want to be a "full time" musician - lack of commitment to touring, going abroad, etc.
Well, I don't know… he may well have a point. I've never been one for being away from home for a long time I must admit.

You didn't want to go to America?
Yeah, I wanted to go to America. I wanted to go and do the business, so it wasn't a question of that - I think it was just not wanting to do it with him. Of course I went there with Blodwyn Pig - I know I did have this thing about flying for a while, which was not helpful at times, but I think that is something that can be worked around. Pig were a hell of a big band over there, and my views are that if Bowie, who at the time was at the same stage as Blodwyn Pig were, and Alan Price and other guys could get it on by working on the road then so could we. The unfortunate thing about it all - I don't mean unfortunate for me because, well, I'm alright - but it was unfortunate that we never seemed to be able to get it quite straight exactly who was who. I could never quite work out who was trying to shaft who, and so I used to just try to keep myself in the background and just get on with being a guitar player, which I considered to be my prime role.

Within Jethro Tull, you mean?
With Tull and with all the bands I've been in. I know I'm a front man, not perhaps in the same way as Ian Anderson but I suppose on the opposite end of the track. My approach is a bit more… wearing my heart on my sleeve sort of thing, I suppose.

How would you describe Ian Anderson in 1968?
In what way?

Well, as a person.
[*Long pause*]… Initially as a guy I liked very much actually.

Easy to get on with?
No, not by any stretch of the imagination, but a guy that I initially had a lot of admiration for, and a lot of trust in. And really, the hurtful part, the emotional part of what happened to that band was the fact that there was no trust between either of us, and I think that was caused more by him than me. The only thing that he would ever have against me, and I don't know if he's ever mentioned it, is that I actually refused to go to a gig once. I had to put my foot down because I was so pissed off with the bullshit and the whole attitude that I just said right, bollocks, I'm just not going - which was really the worst, the most wrong thing I've ever done in my life. And I tell you, that one thing got me branded with a lot of other things.

At what stage was that?
Um…it was after Sunbury but before the album. I suppose it's just one of those things, but you know there was so much pissing around and so much nonsense going on - and a lot of the bad feeling was caused by Anderson. It was the only way I could think of at the time to fight back, but it was a pretty nasty way of doing it - I should have just belted him and done the gig. But then belting people doesn't get you anywhere either, does it?

Were there musical differences as well as personality clashes?
No, I don't think so. From his point of view there were musical problems. I think he wanted to go in a completely different direction from me: I AM a blues guitarist.

The Blodwyn Pig albums sound more like *This Was* than do any other Tull albums.
Yeah, the same feel, I still maintain, and without any prejudice to Tull whatsoever, that *This Was* was the best album they ever made. It has much more of a raw feel about it, and I think all the rest of the albums, unfortunately because Ian is a talented musician… the albums and songs I felt were more contrived and too specifically put together, and so neat, and yet somehow they never really came across to me. And yet when I listen, and I do listen every

couple of years to *This Was*, some of the flute playing that Ian did on that album was just magic. Real, warm flute playing and a genuine heartfelt bit of musicianship. His musicianship in technical terms has improved beyond recognition but it never comes over to me in the same way. It happens to a lot of groups, you become processed, machines – I guess you have to. I know that from being in other bands.

But when we had a poll in *A New Day, This Was* got hardly any votes.
Yeah, it's hard to know whether modern fans would like that kind of stuff. The real change in Jethro came after *Aqualung*. I thought *Thick As A Brick* was a diabolical album, although I did listen and TRY to like all the other stuff.

Have you ever looked back and regretted leaving Jethro Tull?
A frequent question that. I regret not having a quarter of a million in the bank! But as I've never had it I suppose I don't miss it.

Do you still get royalty cheques from Tull records?
Yeah, I still get four or five cheques a year, but not a fortune.

Do you think that if you had stayed with Tull and Ian had left instead, Tull would have continued in the style of Blodwyn Pig?
Yes, I suppose so. Blodwyn Pig in fact had a flute player who I think was every bit as good as Ian Anderson, although in a different style of course.

Why did you pack it all in? Have you not had a band since '74?
Yeah, I've had various bands but, you know, I just take it the way I want it. I do what I do now because I enjoy it – it's like old times again.

You have no desire to get back to music full-time?
[*Pause*]… I have moments when I think yes, it would be nice, and I can't turn round and say I'm knocking 44 years old and so shouldn't be on the road because that's just bullshit; age has got nothing to do with it at all. I suppose in a lot of ways I am fairly settled, but if a situation arose where it was financially feasible for me to do it, then yes, I would. But I have never seen a situation yet that would initially be viable for me to do so. I have got a situation where I've got what some people would consider to be horrendous commitments, and like there's no way I could go sloping off every night. I've got a family that I do like seeing – I've always been that way anyway, I've never had wanderlust, and I've been round the world anyway so I am not particularly bothered about it now. We do get trips to exotic places with the firm occasionally but really I would rather go to Clacton!

How did Jethro Tull come together?
Well the whole thing started in a place called The Beachcomber, which was a disco in a part of a bowling alley in Luton. I think it was Ladbrokes Casino downstairs and upstairs was The Beachcomber where we played gigs. I was with a three-piece called McGregor's Engine, in which Andy Pyle was the bass player and Clive Bunker was the drummer, and we just happened to play opposite the John Evan Smash one night, which comprised of Ian Anderson, Glenn Cornick, John Evan, Chic Murray on guitar – he's now a tax inspector, by the way – Neil and a big guy called Tony on tenor sax, and Barrie Barlow. Ian Anderson wasn't even playing the flute then, just a harmonica. And they liked us and we liked them. They had an interview with Chris Wright from the Ellis/Wright agency in Regent Street, and because he'd got Ten Years After he saw the blues thing as becoming a big scene, you know, in the middle and late sixties. He said he liked the band but not the guitarist, and he told them that if they got a screaming good guitarist they would crack it. It was purely coincidence that Chris Wright used to be the social secretary of the Manchester University Union, and he used to book bands for a club in Manchester, and as we all lived in Manchester we all knew him. He mentioned my name and they asked me to go up there and see them. McGregor's Engine was on the point of splitting up – Andy Pyle just turned round one night, when we had about three months of commitments, and said: "I'm going to Malta – bye bye!". So that was me and Clive

left without a band. Clive was going back to work for Commer Cars because his Mum wanted him to – you know [*laughing*] he looks just like his Mum; the whole family look exactly the same! I haven't seen him now for…ooh… [*calls to his secretary Kate, who we now discover to be his wife, who replies*: "Must have been about four months ago".] Well, I don't know when it was but I do know he went home well pissed.

He is playing in a band now.
[*Surprised*] Is he??

According to *Record Collector* magazine last month he is in a band called Poormouth with an ex-member of Them, gigging and recording.
Well, that's interesting. I've tried 'phoning him a couple of times but I can't get hold of him.

Presumably he is working full-time?
The last I'd heard he had got himself a truck and an HGV licence and was shooting up and down the country stuffing Yorkie bars in his mouth!

In the mid-'70s didn't he own a factory or something?
He did, yes, but he was completely ripped off. I only see him about once a year at a business meeting, but I generally convince him to take the rest of the day off and we get legless.

Does he play the occasional gig with you?
He has done on occasions, but not usually. I think our drummer John is more suited to the type of gigs we play in pubs. We don't rehearse or anything – on the day we rehearse while we are having a drink and when we are all pissed we just convince ourselves that we've had a good rehearsal. And it all goes right on the night anyway – nobody gives a fuck. God, that sounds dreadfully complacent, doesn't it? Well, you've been, so you know what I mean.

It sounded great.
Well, we enjoy ourselves. I don't ever recall doing a bad gig as such.

Your enthusiasm certainly shows through – it's not a question of "stars" and "audience".
Well, yes; the only time I use myself in that way is if it's gonna give the charity I work for some financial advantage. Then I kick some arse and pull some weight.

Is it always the same charity you work for?
My soft spot is children, because I am a family man. I really got serious about it three or four years ago when I was in Cannes supporting a hospice for dying children. There was this incredibly beautiful lady, this nun – um, I don't know how you take that, it is not meant in a sexual way; like, I've never shagged a nun in my life. Alright, I lied – but only once! But this lady came and showed us round the place and it just broke my heart. We were sitting there weeping and I thought I've just got to do something about it, so that is why we do it.

How often do you play?
At the moment, about six times a year, which is not enough. And again that depends on my commitments at work. I try not to see people in the evenings if I can help it, but if people do need to see me late in the day I like to consider myself flexible enough to be able to do so.

Have you any gigs coming up?
No, nothing planned at the moment. Things are a bit hectic so I haven't arranged anything yet this year – I'll have to jump on that. Actually, you guys could help with that, if you advertised the gigs in aid of the charity.

Fine - people are always writing to *A New Day* asking what you are doing. You mentioned earlier some demo tapes you have recorded with a view to releasing an LP in aid of the charity…

Yeah, the basic idea was... [*breaks off to speak to his wife, who is leaving*] ...I'll tell you what, that is the best thing that has ever happened to me in my life. She is absolutely magic – turned me right round, she has. You know, not forcefully but she has just been a great support, a great friend. We have been married for ten years. [*Then followed a lengthy discussion on marriage, kids etc*]

It's funny, you know – I was just thinking about what you said earlier. Ian Anderson's comment that I was like a part-timer. I've never heard him say that.

It was not that you were a part-timer as such, but that you didn't want to play more than three of four nights a week.
I think I might have even said that at the time. I don't know; I used to have a habit of saying things I didn't really mean.

Come to think of it, you play more gigs than Tull these days.
Ha ha! Give him my regards and say Abrahams says you're the part-timer now!
But going back to when I was playing full-time, I eventually got so frustrated with record company stuff and finances and band politics and stuff that in the end I just said fuck it and walked out. I went to manage a swimming pool.

So it was the business that you left rather than the music?
Never the music. I will play that forever; it's timeless. Music never rips people off. I had a spell of very severe Christianity. I still am a Christian but I am not a bible puncher, as you can clearly tell! But I was very serious about it because I'd got really pissed off with the whole thing, and so I went through the whole thing of like searching for, I don't know... the truth? That was something that I'd always adhered to as a child so it came back in that form. But unfortunately when you get into something don't you always get into the excess situation? Everywhere I went I had a bible handy so that I could refer to it, and I ended up like a real pious arsehole.

It's hard to imagine you like that...
Yes I know, but under all the gags I am fairly serious. I worry about my family now, in as much as my kids are being brought up in a society that doesn't even relate to anything I knew. I was brought up to look after myself, try to look reasonable. I don't mean the clothes you wear, just basic cleanliness. It is important to have some self- respect, otherwise how can people respect you?

[*At this point we adjourned to the pub. On the way Mick played us some demos he had recorded which sounded fantastic. He mentioned that he intended to upgrade his home studio from 4- to 8-track eventually.*]

How did you arrive at the name "Jethro Tull"?
When we were gigging it started off as Ian Anderson's Blues Band, then it was going to be Ian Anderson's Bag O'Nails. But we went into the studio and did this thing for Derek Lawrence. I had a song called *Sunshine Day* and Ian and Glenn had written a song called *Aeroplane* which went on the B-side of that record. Derek Lawrence was crazy about *Sunshine Day* and that got released on MGM, but under the name "Jethro Toe".

Was that a genuine mistake?
Yes it was. The stupidity of it was the night we actually recorded that song there was a guy called Dave somebody who was a booking agent for Ellis/Wright and who had studied history. We were all looking for a name, and he said: "Jethro Tull's a great name". He told us where it came from and we all agreed on it, but I assume Derek misheard it and thought: "Yeah, great, Jethro Toe" and that was it.

How did you come to be in the studio with Derek Lawrence?
I'm not sure actually, I can't remember how it came about.

Was *Sunshine Day* a number you were playing on stage?
No, we never did play that on stage, in fact. It was just something I'd put together and we did it for the record.

Did the finished thing sound to you the way you expected it to? It sounds 'poppy' rather than a blues thing.
I suppose on reflection it didn't – Derek Lawrence did what he wanted to do with it.

Was *Sunshine Day* recorded at the same time as *Aeroplane*?
No, *Aeroplane* had been recorded in a studio in Manchester some time before. There was no time to do another track so we used that one. So *Aeroplane* was actually by The John Evan Smash.

What did The John Evan Band sound like? Was it a blues band?
Yes, they were great – a good blues/jazz band. I suppose it would have been called at the time "funk", but it was more a bluesy soul type of band really, bloody good as well.

Were any live recordings made of you with Jethro Tull?
No, there's nothing of that nature around at all. I don't know, maybe radio – Peely had us on a couple of times, but they were sessions rather than live,

It is a shame, because *This Was* is so enjoyable it would be great to hear the live versions of some of those songs.
Oh, I'll tell you what you might be able to get hold of through the BBC Archive – do you remember a show called *Colour Me Pop*?

We have been trying to get that.
I tried as well, but had no luck. I just wanted a copy of it, but they wouldn't let it go.

What blues standards were you playing in those days?
A couple of Alexis Korner things. *I Wonder Who Baby* was one I used to sing. *So Much Trouble*, which I still do now. *Rock Me Baby*, which I'll probably be playing until I die…

Alexis Korner was your 'hero' then? [*Mick has a son called Alexis.*]
Yes, I was very fond of Alexis – in fact, I was with him the day before he died. I was sad that I couldn't go to his funeral, but it was a private thing for his close family. And I missed the benefit gig, which really pissed me off. I was away on business the day Bobby rang, and she thought I was on holiday, so I missed it. It was a bloody shame. He was a great guy, a really warm person, and it really annoyed me to hear people slag him as a musician, whereas because of his rawness all the real warmth and sincerity of his music was missed by all the real technical bods. Hi tech counts for shit when you really mean it.

Who else inspired you?
Pre-Tull? Bo Diddley, Chuck Berry, Jerry Reed, early Scotty Moore, Mel Travis… I've always admired Albert Lee… and Chet Atkins. I don't know a guitarist who doesn't like him.

You must have started playing when you were very young then?
I was ten years old. My first public performance was at the Royal Ancient Buffalo Club of which my uncle was a member. I played *Oh Mary Don't You Weep, Rock Island Line* and *Don't You Rock Me Daddy-o*. Played it two or three times and copped myself two bob and a pint of orange juice. I thought right, if this is stardom I've gotta go for it! One must realise one's calling in life. So yes, I've been at it a long time.

You mentioned earlier a band called The Hustlers.
That was a local band I was in, originally called The Jesters. We graduated from mohair jumpers to suits and became The Hustlers because we started playing at the US air bases. £10 a night and free hamburgers, which was good money in those days.

Did you make any records before Tull?
No, but I did play with Neil Christian And The Crusaders, and a few times with Lord Sutch And The Savages. With Neil Christian I took over from Jimmy Page. And I missed by hours the gig with Johnny Kidd, one of my idols from the early days. They offered me the job and I went home and had a serious think about it and decided to take it. I went in the next day and they told me he had been killed in a car crash – I've never forgiven him for that!

How did you meet Clive Bunker?
I've known him for years, through youth clubs and things like that. The Toggery Five was one of the bands we played in, with Paul Young of Sad Café.

What sort of places did Tull play in the early days?
The usual places, you know – pub gigs etc. The Marquee came as a real bonus – John Gee liked us, and if John Gee liked you, you were in!

After playing in other bands with little success, did you ever suddenly think, "This is the band to make it" when Tull were formed?
I never really gave it much thought. I guess you must always feel that deep down, but I never consciously thought we were bound for stardom.

Do you listen to much "modern" music?
No. Some of it really annoys me. Kate and I went out with friends the other night, and next to the restaurant there was this flash wine bar type thing with video screens all over the place. All the time I was there, about 20 minutes, everything sounded exactly the same. Maybe it's age creeping up on me, but I actually made a point of watching it and none of it was good. It is all based purely on the video and it was just shit! I think someone who has got it today is Paul Young – I think he is great, although he is getting a bit mellow and laid-back these days. I can accept that to a degree as long as it is not done purely for commercial reasons, because then it bears no relation to the original concept of being a musician. It's more like being a prostitute.

Getting back to the demo tapes, are you going to make another record?
I'm open to offers. If anybody thinks what I have got there is any good, of any value, then yes, I'd be quite happy to go and do it, the idea being that I'd have 50% of the action and 50% would go to a kids charity.

It is down to you to tout it round the record companies then?
That's right. I went to, would you believe, Chrysalis. I played it to Chris Wright, and he thought it was magic. He's always thought a lot of me and I knew he was pissed off about the Blodwyn Pig split because that was down to Ellis and a certain band member. And yet, we did set the band up again in '74 with Clive Bunker.

You didn't make a record with Blodwyn Pig that time around?
No, it only lasted about three months – four gigs, although we did a radio session and an *In Concert*.

Why did the second Blodwyn Pig fizzle out?
Tragically, our manager June Whyton topped herself. It just seemed the whole thing was doomed to failure from the very beginning, you know.

You recorded an album with a band called The Mighty Flyers...
Yes, with a guy called David Rees [*no relation...*], a good mate of mine who died in 1980. Believe it or not, he was my very first death claim when I got into life insurance. He died about three days after my son was born and of course it was very sad. In fact Dave was instrumental in my going through my religious period – although whatever I say about that, don't take it that I am being too flippant. I am and always have been a Christian person but, you know, I don't want to end up sounding like James Alderton. [*We then entered into*

another lengthy discussion covering the police, striking miners, football hooligans and Stonehenge, but we'll spare you our words of wisdom.]

It seems Chrysalis are planning to celebrate Tull's 20th Anniversary this year and it is possible that they might play a 'reunion' gig. If they asked you would you do it?
Yes, sure. But I would be MOST surprised if that happened. I've always had the impression that decisions… like when compilations come out with my tracks excluded…

Well, we think that is probably Chrysalis rather than Ian Anderson. *Original Masters* was released without any support from Tull.
Hmm, maybe; but I would have thought it might have changed now that Ellis has been bought out and gone.

[*The conversation then turned, for some reason, to Billy Connolly, Mick's mate from way back. Mick met him again recently in Dunstable and Mick was rather chuffed that Connolly had mentioned the meeting on a television show afterwards – much to the delight of Mick's young son. Apparently Connolly has a pig called Blodwyn!*]

Why did you call the band Blodwyn Pig?
Again, some lunatic gave us the name, a fella called Graham at the rehearsal studio who had just come back after four years as a Buddhist monk – really, one of the best jazz keyboard players I've ever heard, went totally potty, shaved his head, took too much LSD. He couldn't become a Christian because they are too pious, so he became a Buddhist, which was the more acceptable, hippy version of religion. He left because the monks would not let him have Kellogg's Corn Flakes! Anyway, we asked him if he had a name for the band and he just came out with Blodwyn Pig.

Who thought of the record cover with the smoking pig?
I did. I've got a ceramic tile at home with that picture on it, with the legend, "Mick Abrahams Relaxed"!

Were you disappointed that the band only lasted for two albums?
I was in a way, because I was booted out of my own band.

I thought you had left the band voluntarily, leaving them with the name?
No, I just wasn't doing it their way and they kicked me out.

What about Wommet?
Ah, Wommet turned into The Mick Abrahams Band, which was alright. I always had the shout, and from day one I was able to do it my way.

The way you tell it, you always seem to be the casualty.
No, not a casualty. I was in one case, with Blodwyn, but not with Jethro Tull.

Before they became "Jethro Tull", when they were "The Ian Anderson Blues Band" and so on, surely it was already the idea that Ian was the leader and focal point?
That was the original thing, but when the name Jethro came along that seemed to be the commercial way to do it, under the guise of a four-man collective partnership.

I've always had the impression that you and Ian were 'joint leaders' of the band.
It's funny you should say that – that was my impression too! But my view of it was not having people employed by me and Ian, but rather having people to negotiate and be constructive with. But when we started getting heavy with the public it became more and more apparent that Ian wanted to take everything over.

You co-wrote *Beggar's Farm*. Was it a case of sitting down together to write it?

I forget how we did it. Probably in rehearsal. You know, the guy would come up with something on the flute and I'd work around it. Song writing should be like that. I am not a songwriter in the sense that I read and write music. I can read it, but hellishly slow. I know what it all means, but... I've done sessions where I've been longing to hear the backing track so that I could copy it, which I can do straightaway once I've heard it. Obviously the sort of sessions I do don't require reading – I've recorded with Gary Wright, Spooky Tooth, The Hollies, etc.

Do you still get asked to do sessions?
No, not now. I think most people assume that I'm resting on my laurels and living off the fat of the land. You thought I was, didn't you – but I hope you'll be seeing a lot more of me in the future.

Do you still write songs?
Yes – I'll play you some later on, see what you think.

If you release another album will you tour in some way?
I could do some limited touring, but I'm not about to go flying round the world or anything like that.

Have you thought of putting the album out yourself?
No, I have not got the funds to do it. We worked it out and to make it viable we would have to lay out about 35 grand and I haven't got that sort of money to splash out, so I am happier to let somebody else sort it out.

But you have your own little studio – you get these indie bands making albums on a shoestring hoping to sell a thousand or so. If they make a profit, and you would obviously sell more than that...
Well, if I had 16-track I'd be alright; I could do the mastering then. I suppose it might be possible. You reckon I'd sell a few then?

There is a hard-core of Tull fans who would want it, and of course blues fans. How would you deal with it if it really took off again?
I'd take some time off work! Actually I saw Chris Wright last December and he listened to a few things I'd done. I don't know if he was really interested or not but he reckons I'm playing better than ever, and I actually do think I am. It sounds daft but it is because I am more relaxed now. He said, "There is still a place for you", but I'm trying to work it so that there is a place for me on my own terms. I want to be able to continue doing what I do now because I am committed to my work and to my customers, and I feel that I should maintain the personal commitment I have made to those people. I am happy to go half way with that and my music.

Surely Chrysalis is the wrong place to look for a record deal? It is not like it was, when the music came first.
Hmm... Max Headroom! Mind you, I quite like that.

Did Tull contact you in '83 when they were talking of a reunion gig at The Marquee? It was said that it never happened because they could not find the original members.
No, nobody called me at all. It can't be that difficult. If I wanted to contact Ian I could do it, and it wouldn't be hard for him to find me if he wanted to.

When did you last see Ian?
The last time was when I went to Maison Rouge Studios with Bob Wilson, around '77 of '78. He said that Ian wanted to hear some stuff that I had done.
How did the meeting go?
It was OK, you know – we shook hands and so on, there is no real animosity there. But it was a weird meeting. He was really upset at the time because he thought his father was dying; he was obviously very affected by it. It was horrible, really, you know...

Were there any tracks left over from *This Was*?
No, all the stuff we recorded was put out.

I think the sessions you did for the BBC sound even better than the album – the sound is more dynamic.
I've never heard them, actually – I'd like a tape of them if you could manage it as it would be very interesting to hear them.

When Tommy Vance played some of the tracks a few years ago he said he thought that Tony Iommi played on one session.
No, Tony only did the Rolling Stones' *Rock'n'Roll Circus* TV thing. He phoned me up afterwards and told me he couldn't stand it – he quit straight after that.

Chapter 3

CLIVE BUNKER

(Published in Issue #10, May 1987)

Little had been heard of Tull's first drummer Clive Bunker for a number of years when, in 1987, news filtered through that he was playing in an Irish rock band called Poormouth, led by Jackie McAuley, formerly of Them. To MW's excitement they were booked to play The Mean Fiddler, just down the road from his north-west London home, and so the chance was not to be missed.

Sneaking into the dressing-room prior to the show, MW found Clive stretched out on a bench, taking the expression "laid-back" to its extreme. Clive was quite happy to do the interview there and then – his first, apparently, for some five years. It turned out that he had kept in close touch with Jethro Tull and Ian Anderson, and his continuing love of the band shone through throughout the interview.

The obvious one to start with – why did you leave Tull?
To get married, funnily enough. We were just about to do the first world tour – I think we had one American tour to do, and then we were starting to do a world thing, and then going to live in Switzerland…

For tax reasons?
Yeah. And it was in the gap prior to the tour to that that I'd met what is now my wife, and decided through the tour to get married and knock it all on the head. But I didn't know exactly what to do. So I had regular chats with Eric Brooks, who was then like a father to us all, about what I should do over this, and at the death he just said, "Well, tell Terry Ellis and get it all sorted out." Terry was flying out just at the end of the tour, so I thought I'll cop him one day and get it all sorted out. I didn't! So I arranged with Eric to get me a seat next to him on the plane on the way home. Terry Ellis didn't come over, he went somewhere else on holiday, so it all got a little bit "like that" [*shaking hand*]. Eventually we got back to England and it was Eric who told Ian, I think, and Ian came round to my place, and we sat and chatted it through, as it were. It was a right sort of a… traumatic time if you want, y'know, 'cos it was about as big as it was going to get, almost – just I'd say a little bit further to go. But oh no, I've no regrets about it, it was great.

It wasn't musical differences, or…
No, no. I mean, that's one thing you can say when you leave the band is what a genius Anderson is – wonderful.

He did't put pressure on you to stay, it was just chatted through, was it?
No, we just had a very long chat that evening, and Barrie, who was from The John Evan Smash anyway, and was a friend of the band and knew most of the material – he should have done, anyway! – he just sort of stepped in and he did the next tour. And then he had that unfortunate thing with, er, what was it called, the opera one, what I class as the opera one anyway, the ballet one…

A Passion Play?
Passion Play, yes. He sort of stepped straight in and then got that terrible slating, and I felt really sorry for him. But I think it worked out better in the end, because it probably made him a bit more determined, getting all that hassle.

How much input did you have into Jethro Tull's music, or how much did you want even?
We had all that we wanted. Because it was the original band, the formation of it, it was a lot freer than it is now, as it were. Ian just used to come in with acoustic guitar and play through a

song, and then we'd tap on knees and stuff, and then take it into a hall, have a little blow through electrically, and work out whatever worked, or we'd change it around a little bit. Then there were some things that Ian had… I think he must have had an idea for everything in his mind, but he'd let everything go and take its course. And then there were a few songs – one of them I can remember was *A Song For Jeffrey* – where he had the idea for everything, and it didn't work out the way we were doing it, so Ian said: "Can we try it the way I've got it in my mind?" It was a good way of learning.

Do you write music yourself?
I do, yes, but [*modestly*] y'know, a good laugh!

Why is *Dharma For One* so called? Was it anything to do with Ritchie Dharma?
No, no, it's not. It's something from the Jack Kerouac books, actually, that dharma thing. Ian will tell you about that, actually, 'cos he came up with the title.

Did he? It tends to be thought of as your song obviously, because of the drum solo…
Yeah, but it was Ian's title for that one.

A passing roadie: "'Dharma' is an Indian word – it means 'enlightenment' or something."
Yeah, it was something that Jack Kerouac used in his books…
Roadie: 'On The Road' was the one.

[Suitably ashamed of my ignorance] **Perhaps Ritchie Dharma took his name from that!**
[*Laughing*] Yes!

What was Ian like to work with? Did he change much between 1968 and when you left, in his approach to work?
He went into himself more, which is only understandable really. I would hate to have been in his position where he was the front man and the key man. Really, a lot of the responsibility he took on anyway, and so virtually all the pressures of the band were on his shoulders, and so he introverted himself a lot. A lot of it, as I say, was self-imposed because of the writing. On a tour he'd be the one that would supposedly go to bed early, but he'd go back to his hotel room and sit there writing so that we'd have a store of stuff ready for when we got back. But he was great to work with - I never had any problems with him at all. When I left there were a lot of people saying, "Nudge nudge, wink, wink, know what you mean," and I could never understand it, 'cos he'd always been great with me.

It's funny, because you read so much in the whole press about how he's arrogant and difficult to work with, but people who've actually been in the band say what you say, that he's quite fair in the way he works.
Oh, he's brilliant, yeah. That band, and the material obviously that Ian wrote, was the most enjoyable, not just because it was a big band or anything like that, but the actual material was wonderful to play. It was the most enjoyable period of playing really, apart from other blows I've had with other brilliant musicians that ARE blows; but to get down to serious work and do something properly, there's so much in it that you could do. I mean, I used to play it through, a lot of the arrangements that could have gone on… in fact, it did in parts when Barrie was in. Barrie was keen to 'go' and all that, and was putting in arrangements with everything, and some of it was to me just a little bit overbearing, because I like more to keep it going. It's like the weird timing ones we had – if I could make it feel like a 4/4, even though it wasn't, that was what I thought was good… it seemed to work, anyway.

You came into the group because you knew Mick Abrahams, or you and Mick joined up together, I should say, with Ian and Glenn. When Mick left, did you feel any divided loyalty, that maybe you should go with him?
No. Actually what happened was that there was a bit of resentment going on between Ian and Mick. Mick I think felt that Ian didn't want to know about Mick's writing, which up to that point was shared, I found. And then, as I say, Ian's writing just got incredibly good…

And away from the blues as well...
Yes. And Mick was the problem because he went a bit moody and stuff like that. He didn't create problems as such, but the 'mood' thing was going on, and everyone was feeling bad about it, and we just had a meeting, in the van funnily enough, at Watford Gap Service Station I think it was. Mick went in to get something to eat, and the others just sort of held back for a minute. I think Ian was more worried about what I was going to say, obviously, and I said, "Fair enough, he's causing problems, let him go," y'know. I mean, I'm still good mates with Mick – I was out with him a couple of days ago.

How did you meet Mick?
He was in the biggest local band there was in the area, and I first met him at a talent competition, funnily enough. They were, like, the biggest band. They'd been professional and got there early in the afternoon and done a soundcheck. And poor little us, our first little band, set up on the floor. I had one of those cheapo drumkits, and how he noticed me was that I was playing away, and because this kit was useless, every time I hit the bass drum it moved forwards and I ended up half way down the hall in the middle of the audience, and the band were miles behind me! And of course they were laughing their heads off at me! And afterwards we went out for a drink and had a right good laugh. Then not long after that we had a lot better band, and I went round to Mick's and said, "Do you fancy joining this one?" and he did. And then on and off we were in loads of bands together.

The Toggery Five...
The Toggery Five in Manchester, yes.

And McGregor's Engine...
McGregor's Engine! Oh, they were great days! In fact it was after McGregor's split up I think that Mick and myself used to knock around up at what is now Caesar's Palace thing – it used to be a gambling casino with a disco above it, and that was when The John Evan Smash used to play up there, and we got friendly with them. They were going to move to London; we said the rents are cheaper in Luton, so they moved down. And then they couldn't make it work – they started filtering back to Blackpool and they said they were going to knock it on the head. That's when Ian, Mick, myself and Glenn thought we might as well finish off the gigs they had, which were soul gigs! We were a 4-piece blues band in soul places. Brilliant! And then it was Terry Ellis, he couldn't believe the band reports he was getting, and one night he said, "I'm going to come and see you," so it was own-up time. It worked out really well, because Chris Wright had Ten Years After, and he wanted something to get off on. So it was one of those old clichés, really, everybody was in the right place at the right time.

What about Glenn Cornick, do you ever hear from him nowadays?
No – the last time I saw Glenn was when we went over there to do that picture for the compilation album...

The reunion dinner thing?
Yes. We all went to Los Angeles for a week for about an hour's lunch – amazing! 'Cos he's living in Los Angeles now. I was over there last year and that was weird. I went into a studio – there was a mate of mine producing an album there, and I went into the studio; and they're all English people there, and I was chatting away and said about Glenn, and one of them said, "Ah, he's doing a session in so-and-so studio." So I went down to this other studio and walked in, and there was his guitar case and everything – brilliant, I've found him! But they said, "Oh, he's finished here," and they didn't know when he was coming back, and they didn't have an address or 'phone number or anything, so I didn't get to see him. But apparently he's a bit of a punk and everything – coloured hair and that!

Really? What happened to the headband?!
I think he probably designer cut it up or something!

What was he like?

49

Glenn? Brilliant. He was two different people. One in the studio, excellent bass player; every note you played was… you couldn't play anything rough. And just sort of chatting, and quiet and stuff. Bung him on a stage and he was like a freaky lead guitarist…

Yes, I saw him in those days – incredible.
Yeah, that was one of the reasons why I kept it sort of simple or, when it got a bit hectic, a lot of rumble with the bass drums, because the bass wasn't doing anything like what we did on the record. I just kept a rumble going at the back there. Oh, but he was great, a superb bass player. Superb. And a great image as well.

Mick Abrahams described him as a Christmas tree with Pifco lights.
[*Collapses laughing*] Yes, right! Could well be!

What about the name Jethro Tull? We've heard so many different stories as to how you finally landed on "Jethro Tull" – what's your version?
The truth of the matter [*laughing*] is that we had done a first single, *Sunshine Day*, and there was a guy producing it called Derek Lawrence. We'd done it, and gone through loads of group names like "Bag of Blues", things like that, and one of the bookers from Chrysalis came up with "Jethro Tull" from a history thing that he'd done, because he looked like Ian somehow. And the guy said: "Oh, Jethro Toe would be better," and so he put that on the single.

So that was deliberate – it wasn't a misprint?
No – he thought it would be a better name. Mind you, you've heard the production, so you know what he was like! But that's how it all came about. I forget who it was – one of the bookers from Chrysalis. It's one of those, actually, where you go through so many names that at the end you just get anything. I mean, we weren't overawed with it, we just settled on that and it seemed to stick a treat. In fact, everyone used to call Ian "Jethro".

Did you feel any resentment that Ian was labelled "Mr Jethro Tull"?
Oh no, no – it was wonderful! That was why I bought so many cymbals, to hide myself. It was great!

Were you disappointed that your subsequent bands didn't achieve the same level of success?
No. It was only to be expected really. You can't expect to be in a band that big and then go into another one, unless you walk straight out of it into things with mates. No, no. I've really enjoyed a lot of the stuff that I've done since, and I don't think I would have enjoyed it as much if I'd done it with a permanent thing. And then again, there aren't that many people who are as good as Ian. That's a very rare talent, that guy, so you can't really hope to. I could probably have been in bands as big-ish, but it wouldn't have been as enjoyable as the material he writes. I've always said to the guy that he should make an album of just acoustic guitar and him singing.

I agree!
When I left he was saying, "Ooh, I'll be standing on one leg for the rest of my life," and I said to him: "Do a bloody album," 'cos I loved it. There was a load of stuff that, er…there were a couple of songs when Ian was ill, he came in from his deathbed and did an acoustic guitar bit and a rough vocal and then we put our bits to it, and then when he got better he came in and redid his bits, as it were. And I left great chunks of no playing on my part, because it was so beautiful. He really should do an album like that, and get together with David Palmer for just a few nice little things…

So, apart from the music, did you miss doing the mega-stadium gigs?
No, I got a really easy withdrawal from it, actually, 'cos I buggered off and didn't do a thing, until Chrysalis rang me up and said would I do Robin Trower.

That was with Jude?
Yeah, I did that for a little bit, which Chrysalis and Chris Wright – I said CHRIS WRIGHT! – screwed up. He wanted it to be a guitar mega-thing, which it wasn't. I mean, it was superb with Frankie [Miller] and Jimmy [Dewar] on vocals. In the end that fell to pieces and I did various session work in the big stadiums. All the time I'd been 'between', it was really good because I'd got a few businesses together while that was going off, and it had been a nice sort of withdrawal thing from it really. But, I dunno… You got used to it, you got used to doing it, but I never felt right really. I never felt like the sort of person who should be doing that job, y'know? 'Cos I mean the nearest person would be 20 feet away from me and it's a lot nicer…

But you used to have the massive drumkit which you couldn't get on smaller stages, presumably…
Right, yes. But it wasn't the kit y'know, it was just the distance from people. As I say, at the time it happened so quickly that by the time you got scared about it you were in too deep, as it were. But when I did play some smaller gigs, which I did in between some of the tours, with mates, I certainly got a completely different feeling off audiences. I suppose that's professionalism – you'd go on on a big stage and it's really like doing a rehearsal, only out there somewhere there's a lot of people.

What about Blodwyn Pig? You were back with them for a while - or rather, not back with them, but for the first time…
No, not really. I did, er… oh dear… [*searching memory*]… a couple of months of gigs with Mick, Jack Lancaster and Andy Pyle. It was one of them really where Mick sort of got it together for something to do really. It wasn't a rehearsed thing or anything. I mean, obviously we had a couple of rehearsals, but it wasn't that serious, it was just a good laugh really; mates, y'know.

I've got one old newsclipping, and then it seemed to peter out.
Yeah, but it was never serious – well, not on my part anyway!

How did Poor Mouth come about?
I did a tour thing with Jackie McAuley and an Italian guy called Bernardo Lambretti – we called him Gino Lambretta! He's quite a big bloke in Italy, and we did a tour over there which was hilarious – we did more restaurants than actual gigs. Jackie was one of the guitarists, and then… oh dear… quite a while later – I forget what year that was, but it was quite a few years ago – Jackie 'phoned me up, I'm not sure if it was last year or the year before, to say would I do a tour of Ireland. So I said yes, and I went over, and I really liked the band; and I just sort of stayed with them, doing the odd gigs.

So is it a full-time thing, or do you still work? [*Whoops, that sounds wrong, somehow… MW*]
No, I've got boarding kennels, and a factory, and stuff. No, this is a giggle, to get me out with people who are playing.

What about a record deal? Anything coming out?
No. We did some recording not long ago, but I don't know what's happening to it. It's like a part-time gig for me, as it were, this music. I'm getting old!

At least you don't have to stand on one leg!
No, right! He'll have to stick a salmon under the other one!

How did you take drumming up in the first place? What made to turn to drums?
Originally I wanted to be a guitarist. We were at school, and I learnt to play something pretty good, and we started this band. I think we had two acoustic guitars and there were four of us in the band. And then this other guy learnt something that was a lot better than me – I was going to be on the rhythm guitar and the other guy had learnt the guitar pretty well, so I used to just tap about on biscuit tins, and they said: "You be the drummer". And that's how it all started, it's as stupid as that.

What about when you got more professional – did you have any influences or drum heroes?

Not really, no. The drum heroes that everyone else had, I didn't. I mean, Ginger Baker wasn't a real hero at all. I loved the sound he had, and some of the stuff he did was quite impressive, but he didn't used to send shivers down my spine. People that got me were John Bonham, a guy called Corky Laing from Mountain – superb – and then stupid little drummers, actually, throughout America that were just doing things a bit different; I loved them. Then I got onto people like Buddy Rich, who was something else. It's strange really, I never classed myself as a drummer for years. I'm just starting to now, a bit!

What about modern technology? Do you use or explore that much?

Yes, I love it. To me it's an added percussive instrument. Not an instrument in its own right, it's just percussion to me; and if you think of it in those terms, it can't hurt it. It's brilliant. I love Simmons and stuff, because it's the same as anything really; say if you're a guitarist and they brought out a fuzz pedal or a wah-wah or something, and they say, What do you think of all this stuff?", you'll get the purist who'll say: "Oh, no." But to me, it's an extension that is there to be used in the right way. I mean, I can't ever envisage the day that I will play a Simmons kit and nothing else because to me that's like I'd given up drumming, but as a percussive thing it's great.

Are you self-taught?

Yeah.

No tuition, or anything?

The only, or the best tuition I ever got, as it were, was from Carmine Appice. We used to knock around a lot together. He's now started a load of clinic places in the States, and he writes books on it and so on. But when we used to knock about together he used to ask me about bits I'd do, and then he'd show me things. We had three days in Chicago once where it was Carmine, myself and John Bonham, and we were playing at the same gig. And we'd go down in the afternoon and just muck about with drums all afternoon for three days – it was brilliant. But the first ever guy that showed me how to do things properly – because I did everything single-stroke roll and made it sound like a paradiddle, and all that rubbish – was Martin Lamble from the original Fairport Convention, who got killed in that van crash. He was very very good at the time and he showed me the right way to do paradiddles and stuff like that. In fact, him and Gerry Conway, who later joined Tull for a couple of tours. I remember when we did one gig, there was a tent where you could set your drumkit up and have a tune-up, and Gerry and Martin were up the other end there and I was down here, like, 'cos I had a right duffo kit and they had brilliant stuff. I was sort of banging away, and they were playing all the proper way of doing rolls and stuff, and I said, "Blimey, what is all this?" And then as we went on stage, Gerry's missus came up to me and said, "That was a rotten thing to do," and just walked off; and they wouldn't speak to me, I couldn't work it out. But apparently they thought I was conning them before the gig. And it was ages before we were playing at a gig again, and I said, "What's wrong, why aren't you talking to me?" Gerry's missus said, "You know why." And I said: "Look, Gerry, I don't know." I didn't know then! After that we got really friendly.

Gerry's actually on the new Tull album [*Crest Of A Knave*]

On the new one??

Doane Perry – you know Doane Perry well, don't you?...

Yeah.

He had to go back to America suddenly...

Oh, so he didn't come back over?

He came back for about a week to do some of it, and Gerry stepped in to finish it off.

Oh brilliant, brilliant. I'm really chuffed actually, because I felt a bit terrible about that.

What, that you hadn't seen him?

No, that Gerry didn't continue with the band, with Tull, because I knew that he was really into it. I went to see him at Wembley or somewhere and I was chatting away to him, and he was really chuffed. And after that I heard that he wasn't with the band any more, and I thought, "Oh-oh".

I don't know quite what happened because he seemed to leave in the middle of a tour, or at the end of a leg of a tour, and Paul Burgess took over. Whether it was planned, I don't know.

I know something went on. I don't think it was planned, or he didn't know about it at the time, anyway. Because from being mates all those years ago, I said, "Phew, great stuff," and he was really chuffed. And then, as I say, it was only a week after that he wasn't in the band any more. And I thought, what's happening?

He also played on a single released last year – they did a remake of a TV theme [*Coronach*] and he played on that. So he's back, certainly in the studio – I don't know about the tour.

Well, that answers a lot of questions. I wondered why Doane didn't 'phone me up, 'cos I knew he should have been over, so that's probably what it was.

So you've been to see Jethro Tull since?

Oh yes, yes. I've got a lot with Doane Perry for a start – I gave him his first drum lesson when he was only 14 or something! The bugger brings it up all the time about "I was 14 when I came back to see you at Fillmore East" or somewhere like that! He's a superb drummer, Doane.

When was the last time you saw them live? Did you go to Milton Keynes?

Milton Keynes, yes, that's the last one I saw. That was a good day, it was great. That was really funny, because I didn't even go out the front to see the band. I got talking to Ian's missus and Martin's missus and everybody. It got to some points in the show, 'cos they did all the old ones, and it was like you'd get into that backstage thing, and I'd hear a bit and think, "Strewth, we're on!" I really had to smile to myself – it must have been 15 years, and I was thinking, "I'm on!"

Which brings me to something we've been suggesting to anyone who'll listen, that with Chrysalis looking for ways to celebrate the 20th Anniversary next year, Tull should have a reunion concert with all the old guys. Would you be interested in such a venture if it ever happens?

If it was done properly. I wouldn't do it as a laugh. I think the band owes it to the fans to do it seriously. Yes, I'd do it, if we could have a couple of blows to see if everybody's up to it, and then have a good set rehearsal, really get it together well, and then do it. I'd always thought about that anyway, when Ian felt like knocking it on the head; which I wouldn't have thought could have been much longer, with Tull anyway, although I could see him – he'd be an idiot if he didn't – carrying on music in some way, or it would be a great loss. But come the time for him to say Tull is going to finish as it is, I've always thought it would be a really good idea to do a little 'thank you' tour with almost the original line-up – without Mick Abrahams but with Martin – with half the gigs going to charity or whatever. It would just be a good thing to finish on.

I don't think he _is_ thinking of retiring yet!

He's one of those guys actually – he took a terrible knock on the last one, where he used the drum machine [*Under Wraps*]; and that's the sort of thing that would sustain him for about another four albums, 'cos he'd have to prove himself. But I hope he never stops. As I say, I can see him stopping Tull, but I hope he never stops writing, because he's got so much to offer, that guy. Brilliant!

Chapter 4

IAN ANDERSON

(Published in Issue #11, July 1987)

Although we had by now spoken to three of the Tull chaps, it hadn't really occurred to us that Ian Anderson himself would be aware of the magazine, let alone be interested in talking to us. However, we were in due course to learn that nothing gets past Ian Anderson. He had known about AND pretty well from the outset, and had been monitoring its progress. Although in retrospect some of those early issues now seem quite 'amateurish', he clearly recognised that there was a serious and sensible intent to our typed and photocopied efforts, and that we ourselves were not complete nutters. He therefore let it be known, through Tull's operations manager Kenny Wylie, that he was available for interview should we be interested.

Interested?? Does the Pope poop in the woods?? Thus it was that in April 1987 DR and MW found themselves sitting in the study of Ian's country house, chatting to the mastermind of the phenomenon that was, and is, Jethro Tull. We started by showing Ian the photo of The John Evan Smash which had been printed in AND #9.

Can you put names to those faces?
Ha ha! That's amazing! Oh dear, that's me in my Gene Vincent suit - incredible. Yes, I can name them alright. [*As we talked, he wrote down the names.*]

Do you have fond memories of those days?
No, I honestly don't. I was very unhappy as a child in the north of England and I didn't enjoy my formative years there one bit. I hated Blackpool. I imagine, at the back of it all, it was the single biggest reason for me wanting to be a musician, which I definitely perceived to be an itinerant lifestyle, or at least something that might lead me as far as the M6.

Is one of the people in the John Evan Smash photo Len Barnard, who co-wrote *Aeroplane*?
Yes, that's Glenn Cornick in fact. Barnard was his real name, but he took the name of his stepfather, Cornick, after that. Some of these other people though, I will remember them, it will come back to me in a minute.

Were any recordings made of The John Evan Smash, such as live recordings?
Oh no. There wasn't really any live recording equipment then, other than the ordinary domestic tape-recorder. Back then something called the Ferrograph was the professional recorder, and there was nothing in the price range of an ordinary musician. It wasn't like today where you can pick up any of these specialist mags and buy the kind of kit you can virtually make a record on. The only recordings we made were demos. We made one in London where we played that song we did on the Granada TV show you mention in your mag.

I bought a demo you made from Don Read a while back, *Aeroplane* and *Letting You Go*. Do you remember that session?
Vaguely. I remember doing *Aeroplane* but I don't recall another version of it.

It actually sounds like the same take but just a fraction longer. But it is recorded on a basic 2-track tape.
Mmmm... I mean, it's all such a long time ago. Going into a recording studio was actually very frightening. It may not have been the first time but very close to the first time we went into a studio was Studio 2 at EMI Abbey Road. We arrived there in the van at midnight or thereabouts so as not to be late for the session. We actually spent the night sleeping in the van which was parked outside the main door in front of the studios, and at the crack of dawn the

commissionaire sort of scuttled us in through the back door. I can't remember what it was for… it might have been for that Derek Lawrence fella. He kept telling us about this guitarist that he wanted us to get together with - you know, "a guitar wizard… he's really great," and so on. He kept on and on trying to get us to work with this guy and it felt like we were being promoted to be some sort of backing band to this whizz-kid guitarist. Anyway, we'd never heard of him - Blackboard or Blackmore or something! So we didn't take too much notice. So Ritchie and I nearly met up that way.

I have wondered why you have never worked with him, because he almost 'worships' you, I hear…
Well, I don't know about that, I think that it a bit overstated. I think he has some mild respect for me being able to do to some extent what he cannot do, which is to write music. I don't think he particularly likes me as a musician or as a singer; he certainly doesn't like Jethro Tull as a group. I think basically it's just that he is quite keen on the idea that somebody who is a front man and doing all that stuff can actually write songs and operate the 'band structure' to advantage, whereas he always has a problem getting on with people in bands. And although he is a good guitarist he doesn't have arranging or song-writing skills. So I think it is more a sort of admiration or respect rather than a real attraction to the music that I happen to write, although some of the 'Englishness' of the music might appeal to him. I did hear in fact that he has a life-size cardboard cut-out of me in his bedroom which he stole from a record store - one of those promotional things with me standing on one leg playing the flute.

Why has it been so long since the last Jethro Tull album?
It's for a lot of reasons really. I am sure you can appreciate that after doing nearly 20 years of playing under a certain identity it becomes very valuable to you not to throw that away - well, it is to me anyway - not to throw away something that in some ways represents a lot of time that I've not enjoyed, time that I might even think that I've wasted… some of it, here and there. Like going off on certain musical tacks that were not all that great. I think there is a feeling that if you keep on at the same pace with the same total commitment to something, sooner or later it will just run completely out of steam, in the way that John Francombe as a jockey could just one day decide to quit - you know, the fun has gone, so that's it. I've always felt that might possibly happen with music as well, which would be a terrible thing to happen. So around 1973 [*laughing*] rather than recently I decided I ought to try and slow down, not do everything with the same frequency as I had in the past. But with one thing and another it didn't happen in '73. I say '73 only because I decided then, after a brief jaunt with the rest of the group to Switzerland, that being tax exiles was not for us, and in '73 I decided I was going to live in Britain, and in that case I wanted to get away from hotels in London etc. I started to look further afield for something that would not be just a home, but something that one day I might get involved with. I have always been vaguely keen on 'the land' from a heritage point of view without really being able to define it at the time, but there was something luring me in that direction. I remember in '73 going to an estate agent in London just to see what they had on offer, and it took a long time, about four or five years, to develop into something tangible, which coincided with an interest in farming as opposed to just having a bit of land.

Anyway, to get back to your question… I was trying to break it down so that it wasn't going to be the same annual schedule, because that was what it was really like up to about 1978 or 79. The whole year seemed to be taken up with writing of music, recording of music, promotional activities, tour of the UK, tour of Europe, tour of America and so on, three days off and then start all over again. It was like that all the time. I was literally living in a suitcase, I had no base and no solid possessions for a long time. And imagine being in your mid-twenties and never actually been on holiday, never been to a football match, not played any sport at all since leaving school. I had absolutely no interests outside of music at all until the mid-'70s, and even then it was just interest born of reading something other than fictional work while sitting in a plane crossing the ocean. You can either just drink, or read the latest John le Carré book or you can actually read about something and acquire some knowledge. But it really got a bit much doing it on such a routine level, and I think if I'd carried on doing that the band would have folded anyway. But having finally gone on to a more spread-out schedule, and because Dave Pegg and Martin are the kind of guys who are able to look after themselves, I don't feel any longer that if I don't organise a tour or a record that I'm letting the guys down. It is such a relief. Before, there were, apart from the road crew, three of whom were permanently employed, five other people in the band. Eight people or so in all who could be saying, you know, "When he wakes up this morning will he decide to make another album or book another tour?" There was always this feeling that they were desperate because, well, it's their income. That is OK for a while, for a few years, but there comes a point where you feel it would be nice not to have to consider other people's needs quite as much as you've had to from the start.

Have your throat problems also contributed to the long wait?
Yes. That was a conscious deciding factor at the end of '84 that I was certainly going to take a year off. I had some kind of strain, an acquired muscular spasm, caused basically by singing. In fact, when I started the tour in '84 I was fine. It was OK until just after we got to America, then it started to get really tight and sore before the end of the show, and the only way to get the notes out was to sing even louder. It really was a problem and it got worse and worse to the point where after just a couple of songs on stage it was almost gone, and so that was incredibly depressing. So I decided when we came back from Australia that we would not do anything, I would not sing a note for a few months. And after about three months we were asked to do the Bach TV thing in Berlin, and it was pretty wretched. That was very worrying because it was obviously not something that was going to disappear after a couple of months rest. So quite a long time went by deliberately not doing anything, and that coincided with me wanting to spend more time up north. By then we had quite a few people on the payroll and 'commitment to bodies' if you like transferred itself from people in the group to people on the fish farms side of things. So I spent a year there, and during that year I learnt a lot about…plumbing! And the year turned into nearly two, so it has been a little longer than I had originally intended. I envisaged autumn, but it wouldn't have been any earlier than that anyway.
It would be nice to do music every second year, or perhaps I should say conspicuously every second year because you are always fiddling about doing things, writing songs or whatever in between. It is fabulous being a musician, after having grown up in a time when people had a 'hit' - I mean, all the people I can remember at the time, they would appear on *Top Of The Pops* or whatever it was at the time, and then you would never see them again. From the age of 14 or 15 I had this idea at the back of my mind that as soon as you had made it then that was it, it was all over; that was ingrained in me. I still thought that when we had our first degree of success, first here then in America and then again somewhere else. But after a couple of years had gone by and we were still doing well it was a staggering revelation that you could actually still be around, that it could possibly be a career. Even then I thought it could only be for five years, or ten at the outside. I thought it impossible to think that you might be 40 and still doing something - that would be outrageous!

What, even as a musician, aside from Jethro Tull?
Oh yes, absolutely. I was aware that there were one or two guys who were getting on a bit who still played, did sessions or whatever concealed at the back of the band. And we always knew that John Mayall was pretty ancient! But other than that the idea was staggering. I don't know why, because when I was 15 or 16 I thought Sonny Terry and Brownie McGhee were the business, and it must have dawned on me then that these weren't twenty-year olds, they were already in their fifties I guess. I don't know why it seemed so odd; I guess it's just the way you are brought up, the way you perceived pop music as being very much a product of young people, and as a fashionable thing.

How long do you think you could carry on playing live, given that people like B.B. King still do at a much greater age?
Well, I don't know… I think there is something a bit obscene about doing the sort of thing we do when you are old. It's the same thing for Mick Jagger and so on isn't it? As long as you can still jump into a tracksuit and run around the block, if you are slim and athletic and still got all your hair you might get away with it, but it is already getting a bit obscene for Mick Jagger because he is looking really scrawny now.

56

He says he is giving it up now though - with The Stones anyway.
He has said that before though, hasn't he!

It seems a bit sad if the music is as good as ever even if the stage image deteriorates. Can you ever imagine Ian Anderson, rather than Jethro Tull, going solo, just walking on stage with your guitar?
I can only imagine me doing it in the context of the group. And in that group there would at least have to be Martin - if he, for whatever reason, was no longer in the group then that would be the end of Jethro Tull. To use another guitarist after all this time would be like getting divorced and then marrying again the next day - no, Tull wouldn't carry on.

But look at Fairport - they don't have to jump around on stage etc...
No, they don't have to jump around, and they never did... until now! I don't know, I imagine it is possible to continue... I can see it for another ten years, yes, but beyond that it would seem more absurd than it did when I was twenty thinking I might be doing it at thirty. Then it wasn't something that I gave a great deal of thought to, but now you obviously tend to think, well, "how long?". It is actually a conscious thought now, it still seems a bit far-fetched to go beyond fifty. The trouble is we, like The Stones, don't have the luxury of being able to gradually quieten down and become a sort of cabaret or showbiz kind of group - there is no outlet. You have got to either go and play 'the gigs' you have always played or do nothing. It's like groups like... The Searchers or something, playing working men's clubs. Wouldn't it be awful? I couldn't do that. Imagine sailing forth on your long-awaited cruise on the QE2 in your retirement years and finding this bunch of old codgers called Jethro Tull were the cruise band. It just wouldn't be right, would it.

Have you been watching *Tutti Frutti* on TV?
Yes, very good. Very good for me, being a Scot and having an idea about that environment. Although I'm not from Glasgow to me it seems very rich and very authentic, very much the way it was. The guy smoking the cigar is a bit of a Don Read, but a bit sharper and more pushy. But Don Read was the same; unless he had a cigar - usually half a cigar butt in his pocket with the paper still on to make it look like a whole cigar - I mean, it WAS like that and I'm sure it still is. You can look back on that and think that they were all great times, but they weren't great at all, it was absolute misery. It's a miracle any of us survived bearing in mind we used to drive around in this little van; seven of us with all the equipment - and this was in the days of Leslie cabinets and Hammond organs - all that crammed into the back of a van. I can remember spending hours and hours on motorways and 'A' roads doing a fair old lick, sitting on the engine cover... no seat belts, not even in the seat, just sitting poised in the air three feet away from a flimsy piece of glass! We went off the road lots of times, we had quite a few bumps but fortunately nobody got hurt. That, plus existing on food that really was garbage, and always having no money - there weren't many laughs. And the reason there weren't many laughs was that we were never really close in the band; there was no great spirit of friendship really.

How did you get together? Through school?
Hmm... yes. Well mainly, that is how it all started. Jeffrey Hammond-Hammond and myself, and John Evans, who wasn't in my form but who was known to be... well, we'd heard he had a drumkit! John and I had in fact been in the same form early at school but we went our separate ways later on. We weren't friends or anything, but we heard he had a REAL drumkit. As you know he gave up drums later and went back to keyboards, which was his main instrument due to the fact that his mother was a piano player. I mean, the reason it was called The John Evan Band was that his mother lent us the money for the group van. It was a sop to John's mother: "You lend us the money and we'll be The John Evan Band".

Do you still see John or Jeffrey?
No, not really - well, I saw them a year or two ago at a meeting with accountants over royalties and things. But Jeffrey just decided he had got enough money in the bank, he'd worked it out that he didn't have to do it any more. I think he enjoyed doing it, but he was one

of those guys that when it stopped it stopped. I wouldn't want it to be like that, which is why I've tried to cultivate other interests in my life so as not to have to rely 24 hours a day on music. Jeffrey is a bit of a lesson to me in how not to do it, getting locked into it to such a point that when the cut off comes it has to be total. And John Evans doesn't do music at all as far as I know. He runs a building firm.

What does Jeffrey do?
Umm… he lives off his wife's earnings – which are perfectly proper, I can assure you! – and he paints. His first love was always painting and that is apparently all he does, or that's what he told me last time I saw him. It does seem strange to me that in over ten years he will not have earned a penny, he will not have earned any income whatsoever; I actually find that a bit obscene. One of the things I have a passion about is that if you are lucky enough to make it, as in a good income, you have some responsibility to turn that money back into the economy in some way rather than just stash it away. The idea of just living off the interest and so on makes me a bit mad. And Jeffrey has done just that, all he lives off are old royalties and whatever he may have saved whilst he was making a lot of money.

Does he sell his paintings?
Not that I am aware of. I don't think I would like to see Jeffrey's paintings – it would be really embarrassing if I didn't like them.

There have been rumours of a reunion concert. Judging from what you just said, it is not likely to happen. Or is it?
Funnily enough, Mick Abrahams of all people…

Err… we spoke to him about it actually…
Ah. Well, he 'phoned me up and mentioned something about a reunion concert. It is something that has been mentioned from time to time, but there are no definite plans as such. We will probably do an open air date in the UK next year, and it is a possibility that we wouldn't rule out if there were enough people available rather than just one or two, and if they were willing and sufficiently capable of getting up and doing something, then maybe it would be a good idea. And if we are going to do it then obviously I'll be happy to see Mick again, but it really hasn't got to anything yet. It is just the idea there, just because other people do it I suppose.

Tull fans would love to see it.
Well yes, exactly, There would be a small but definitive number of people to whom it would mean a lot just to see it, so it is a possibility. But as I say, there would have to be a few people from the past rather than just one or two, and I don't know if many people would be interested. The likes of John Evans and Jeffrey I don't think would want to do it; I can't see either of them doing it, and Jeffrey certainly wouldn't, He actually got re-auditioned for the job – not as a permanent thing, but we spent a long time trying to persuade him just to turn up. This was when John Glascock was too ill to do the tour, when we got Tony Williams to dep for a while. At that time we did eventually manage to drag Jeffrey out of the woodwork, persuaded him to come to a rehearsal, not with me but with Martin and Barrie. They sat down and loosened up a little just to see if he could do it, and apparently he couldn't. I wasn't there. I deliberately kept out of the way so that he could just get together with drums and guitar and sort of feel his way around, but just in that short space of time it had left him completely. According to Martin he couldn't even remember the names of the notes or anything, it had all gone. He had put down his guitar at the end of the last gig, burnt his stage clothes – which he did anyway at the end of every tour, which was just as well, remembering what they were like – and never picked it up again, and I'm sure he hasn't touched any instrument since. It's a shame. It's hard to imagine how anybody could do that, virtually every night, night after night, year after year, and then just stop and never touch it again. A funny kind of terminal state to be in to say definitely no more, and put it away forever. But he did. I can't imagine that Jeffrey would be capable of playing anything at all without six months dedicated effort. He wasn't really ever a musician, in as much as he played everything by… sequence really,

just remembering sequences of notes. Ha had a very good memory but he did not know what he was playing, he had no knowledge whatsoever of harmony, he couldn't see why he should be playing these notes but they were the notes he was told to play. But he was great on stage, he looked good and he was a lot of fun. He was also a slightly anarchic but creative force within the group during an important couple of years.

Maybe if you made a live album from the reunion concert and offered them royalties?
Well perhaps they would do it then, but it would be pinning an awful lot of faith on their ability, or the ability of all of us collectively, to turn in a respectable performance as a one-off. I mean, musically it is likely to be highly incompetent if we do anything like that, and also they would be incredibly nervous – I would be incredibly nervous as well because you are aware of all the things that could go wrong. I think that would be asking a bit much. It's not like you can just wheel out Eric Clapton, Jack Bruce and Ginger Baker and they could do it – they could do it if they wanted to. But they were, or rather they are, proper musicians. Dave Pegg is a proper musician and Martin could play along with virtually anything, anytime. But I'm not, I'm not that kind of guy, I can't play anything I haven't written, I've no idea about other people's music, certainly no idea about fitting in with other people's leads. I'm not that kind of guy, and Jeffrey certainly isn't either. John Evans, to a lesser extent... well, his only ability to play anything other than what he played with us would be playing some fairly basic Chopin or Beethoven or something. And Barrie Barlow is not really an all-round drummer, he's too fiddly, he can't really sit down and join in. I suppose Pink Floyd would be a good analogy; you can't imagine any of those guys, with the exception of Dave Gilmour, sitting down and playing with other people. It wouldn't surprise me if a couple of the members of Genesis were the same as well, but again probably to a lesser extent than us. But some of those groups, the magic of those groups is exactly because they can only be what they are with that particular gel of people, the identity of the music and the feeling of being in the group. The people, the individual bits which may have formed the group from time to time, most of them were not what you would call real musicians. Certainly not well versed in a background of rock music, an awareness of other people's songs, not being able to sit down and play *Hey Jude* and so on. None of us have really ever been like that – except of course Peter Vettese, that's what he is. He IS the guy who can sit down and play *Hey Jude* in any key, any Beatles song, any Elton John song, anything at all. He's heard it a couple of times and he's got it, complete with harmonies and everything. He is one of those. That's not really the kind of guy who has been in Jethro Tull in the past. The guys in the past have had something to offer but in a rather 'naïve' way – naïve in the sense of naïve painters. In other words, there is something there, something very expressive and bright and talented, but it only operates within that narrow confine of being 'felt', emotionally, it works but it is not... scholarly... It's not even stylised in the sense of fitting into the wider scope of rock or pop music.

Have you... "dispensed with the services" of Peter Vettese?
Not really, no. I don't think Peter would be right as a full-time member of Jethro Tull for a lot of reasons, not the least of which is that when he joined the group, for him anyway, it was a stepping stone towards making a living this end of the country – something that he could come in and out of as required.

He is not on the new album?
No, because I think we'd got to the stage with Peter where unless he had a great deal of influence in the way the music sounded, and to some extent involvement in writing... not usually basic themes but bridges, instrumental sections, intros and outros etc... unless he was able to put a lot into it he felt very frustrated. And the rest of us didn't feel like it was the direction that would be right to take; we didn't want to make another album that was going to be dominated by keyboards, and certainly not something that sounded like we were trying to update ourselves. Peter is very keen on fashion, both in music and dress.

You have asked Ric Sanders to play on the album.
Yes, he plays violin on a couple of tracks.

Was that after you saw Fairport this year or did you have him in mind anyway?

Well I had heard him before, in a band called 20/20 Vision or something like that, and I thought he was very good. And having seen him... the first time I saw Fairport was on the recent tour, and I was amazed, I thought they were fantastic.

They have a similar image to Tull – if you haven't actually heard them people just assume it is 'old-fashioned' stuff.

Well I've heard some of their recent albums, I've listened to them and thought they were a bit drab... but I remember Fairport when I was... small! They were a bit, er, wet even then. A bit of country, a bit of rock, whatever. They were OK, but this was in the late '60s and it was all very polite. And anything back then that was 'folky' was a sort of... you know, "they must have been or nearly been to University!" I wasn't at all interested in anything like that then, although Fairport were very eclectic, as we were also within a year or so, drawing on lots of different ideas. But Tull were more blues and rock'n'roll, a slightly darker musical form, whereas Fairport became a rather folky, English/American almost West Coast sort of sound. So they meant nothing at all to me until I had to listen to some of their records when Dave Pegg sent in some tapes when we were looking at him to replace John Glascock when John died. Listening to it then it sounded really turgid, but when Fairport surfaced again in the vaguely 'middle period', it was all sort of... 'falling down music', a lot of instrumental stuff, and such little as I heard I found amusing but very much traditional Fairport. Nice to listen to once in a while but not, to me, of any real interest. But I think they have now got back to being a creative little band again. And they do write some very nice tunes. But I was not prepared for the way they sound live. I was always led to believe by Dave that they were totally drunk onstage all the time, that they couldn't really play anything, everything falling apart at the seams in a total mish-mash. And so I was completely unprepared for what I saw which was, with the exception of Dave Pegg who might have had a couple of drinks, but the rest were stone cold sober and never missed a trick. They were absolutely dead on. It was a mini event, well produced, little bits and pieces and a lot of humour, and I thought it was absolutely terrific.

They do seem to be a lot more 'professional' lately. It seems the first tour with the new line-up went so well they have knuckled down and take it more seriously.

Well I like to think that they may, one way or another, have picked up something about what I've referred to as stage craft. Dave may have picked up something of the awareness of production themes that are involved in putting one of our shows together, There is obviously a lot of technical- and rehearsal-oriented effort that goes in, and I'm sure he must have learnt something about it from there, he and other members of the group who have come to see us. But it is very good, it's good for Dave because that sort of music is his real first love, and to be able to pick it up and put it down, for all those guys, do a little tour every year, is a good position to be in. And they obviously have a meaningful-sized audience globally, and it's a shame really that they can't get a major record deal, because with the right record they could do big numbers. If every potential person that might come to see them came on the same day or all went to the record shop that week to buy a record, if it was widely available, CD and cassette, etc, they could really do a lot of units. But of course it would have to be the right record. It is the same for us, to break through that barrier in numbers we would at least have to have a radio hit in order to actually get through to all those people at the same time, have them all buy a record over a short period and snowball into the rest of the people who might get into it from hearing it on the radio all the time.

Which brings us to Chrysalis Records. Are you happy with them?

Oh, no! No, certainly not. But the even more dreadful side to the story is that having looked at all the other record companies a few years ago, when Chrysalis was having 'the troubles' – it was in a terrible state, and the last couple of years suffered... I mean, they weren't GREAT records and they wouldn't have done that well anyway, but they certainly should have done better than they did, and Chrysalis did an absolutely rotten job. So we, Ultravox, Spandau Ballet and Pat Benatar, at least those four of us, were going to high-tail it out, try to get away from Chrysalis because we really felt that it was just not right. And I looked at all the other record companies, went to see a few and talked to them, but you suddenly realise that you are up against an institution. I don't honestly think we would be in any way better off, and in most ways we would be worse off, if we did actually leave Chrysalis. At least there are some people there who... although they are dressed in record company clothes, they go to record company lunches etc, they have got some loyalty to Jethro Tull, and you can get on with them to a point because you've known them for ten or twenty years. I don't think I could cope with a 25-year old A&R man from another record company who's a right little toady... nice to us while all the time thinking, "God, we are stuck with this lot!", you know. Chrysalis at the moment is definitely shaping up. They have now got a proper A&R man and they have also got themselves into a much more business-like frame of mind, both here and in America. I don't know many people on the US side of it but I'll be out there soon to sort out some dates and I'll be able to jolly things along a bit. But as I say, we would be up against another machine that we didn't know or understand and so 'better the devil you know' at this stage of the game. Right now at least Chrysalis are looking a lot better and I think they genuinely want to make a great effort on the next record.

Is it still set for September release?
Yes. Well we could... it's virtually finished apart from one vocal that I couldn't do as I had a cold, so there is an album almost ready to go. A couple of weeks to mix it and it could be out in a month or so. But it would be an absolute rat race to do it and we would be going with the first 40 minutes of music, and I think we owe it to our audience let alone ourselves to at least have a few extra things because, certainly by the time the mixing is done, I often think that some things could be improved. And I suspect that these days we ought to be thinking in terms of 50 minutes of music at least because of the CD and cassette sales compared to vinyl, and to be hampered with the old 19 minutes a side idea is silly. Records are expensive enough anyway so you ought to do a couple of extra tracks. Mind you, it was such an effort to persuade the record company to include the extra tracks on the cassette of *Under Wraps*. America just wouldn't do it, or I think they just put two of them on. To me it seems logical to make an extended version of the record for CD and cassette. Vinyl has been heading towards the grave for ten, twelve, fifteen years maybe. I can remember coming back in '74 and telling Chris Wright and Terry Ellis that they were in the ideal position to be prime movers in the beginning of a new era of replay media for popular music. A digital audio version of the videodisc seemed so obvious to me, but they just were not interested, they didn't give it a second thought. But it was with us, the system was there, and yet we've had to wait all this time. And you know WHY we've had to wait all this time – the vast investment in raw material vinyl, pressing plants etc, the whole industry was geared up to something it knew how to sell. Cassettes have only won the share of the market because punters have decided what they wanted. They have decided that Sony Walkmans are a better, more accurate way of listening to music rather than struggling with your wretched hi-fi system, setting it up in your room, only to find it doesn't sound right. Of COURSE it doesn't! I play things in this room and it sounds bloody awful. Oak panelling around the room, a flat ceiling – of course it sounds wretched. The only way to listen to music, unless you happen to have something better than the average living room, and rather better than the average equipment, the only way at the budget end of the market is to spend £30 on a cassette player and a set of headphones; and you will hear infinitely better music than if you had spent £500 on a hi-fi. I mean, I can live with a bit of tape hiss but I cannot live with inner groove distortion or clicks and turntable rumble. I cannot live with noisy vinyl. The most depressing thing about making records has been to have to sit and listen to test pressings – it is such a misery. A wretched piece of vinyl that has probably been recycled twenty times, with the sound of Mantovani still in the grooves! But... SPAIN!... and Israel, and Italy... my God, and the FRENCH! It's just terrible, and you think, "God, these things are going to be SOLD to people." It is just dreadful. Basically it is just very poor quality raw material. They do say old records used to sound better, and while I'm not sure if they did I am pretty sure the vinyl was better quality. The equipment today is better and so you try to do it, but if you try to stuff 24 minutes on to a side of a record the dynamics and phase problems of modern music will give you trouble. Particularly the inner groove problem. You can't finish an album with a big song because you can't get it on the record; you have to cut the whole bloody record 3dB quieter to get your

loud song at the end of a side, so you have to finish on a quieter song in order to keep the overall level up. All that is such a bore, but it doesn't arise with a cassette. The average quality now with Chrome, or even a decent ferrous tape, is pretty good.

The quality of tapes has certainly improved in recent years, but there is still a lack of packaging, information, photos etc compared to a vinyl album.
Well, I don't own a CD player, but I am very interested in what seems to be the ideal compromise in packaging terms. It's something big enough to have its own identity and you can contain all the information you might want to put there without needing a microscope to read it, as you do when we put the lyrics onto a cassette. But already we are facing the terrible confusion of audio digital tape – will it blow away the growing confidence in CD or will it become a companion medium to it? Certainly what it will offer will be the opportunity to preserve your vinyl records forever; play it once onto a digital tape and then just put it away. You could compile a vast library of music on just a small amount of tape. That's what I would do if I was actually interested in collecting records, but I'm not really. That's my entire record collection up there, which is made up of freebies which I never play.

I gather from your interest in the *Record Collector* discography that I did that you do not even keep Jethro Tull records.
No. There are actually one or two in there, but they are only in case somebody particularly wants a record, you know, if a kid comes round I give them a record with an autograph or something. Usually there are a few photos around here and once in a while it means a lot to somebody to have something autographed. But no, I don't have a collection of Jethro Tull records.

Have you got them on tape for when you want to play a certain song on stage?
What usually happens is that I send someone out to buy a copy and learn it! That always happens halfway through a tour, we'll say, "How about doing such and such a song?", so somebody will scurry off and come back with a tape and we sit and listen to it and say, "Oh, maybe it's not such a good idea after all…"

What does the new album sound like?
I don't know really. They always sound good at this stage. They all sound fabulous when you are getting near the end of it.

Is it a "typical" Jethro Tull record?
Again, I don't know. I'm the last person to ask what a typical Jethro Tull record is. It is certainly nothing like the last album, but having said that I don't think it sounds like any of the other records either, but it is more guitar-dominated music. I have made a deliberate attempt as far as the vocals are concerned not to invite a repeat problem when we tour again. I've deliberately tried to pitch the songs a tone lower than I would normally sing them. Although actually in the studio I've had no problems at all and I could be singing them a tone higher. But from past experience I know that if I do that I would be struggling halfway through a tour. So it doesn't sound as frenetic… the vocals would sound better, a bit more gutsy if they were pitched a bit higher, but it is better to be safe than sorry, better to be able to do those songs at the end of a six week tour than to have to ditch them half way through because I couldn't cope with it and have to go back to playing more instrumental music.

Will you be touring this year then?
Yes. I could almost give you the dates now although they are not actually confirmed yet. We are having problems with London, the Hammersmith Odeon not being available when we want it. We are a bit grey on Birmingham and London, but it starts in Edinburgh, then Newcastle and Manchester. We will do Birmingham and London but the venues are a problem. We don't like the NEC in Birmingham, there's just not the atmosphere. If it was Germany it would be fine, but an English audience in the NEC for us… well, not just for us because I remember seeing Genesis there and it was just awful, no atmosphere whatsoever. It is a weird place, the NEC, but it may be the only place to go.

Are you playing Italy? [*There was a reason for this question, but it's a long story...*]
No, we're not. Actually somebody told me that we were advertised as playing there last year, and apparently a whole load of people went there to see us. It was one of those Italian cons. The promoter announced we were topping the bill at a festival and when the punters were in he said, "I'm afraid the band can't come". But it was a total spoof, we had not even heard about it. They still do that in Italy after all these years - what a shower. But we will start off with ten or twelve dates in the UK and then off to Germany. It is not going to be a heavy tour schedule, it'll be three days on and one day off rather than seven on and one off; we are taking it a bit easier this time. Actually, the first time we ever had a really good time was when we did that little thing last summer. I mean apart from the first gig at Milton Keynes the others were great, it was really enjoyable, a good little outing.

Why did you play as support to Marillion?
Because we got offered a lot of money! The story behind that was that I got a 'phone call early on saying Marillion had booked the date and put tickets on sale and it wasn't particularly good, they had decided to make it a bigger bill and they were looking for a 'special guest' act, and they really wanted us to do it. And bearing in mind that I got their first demo tape sent to me... and although I thought some of it was pretty wretched there was a spark of something there trying to get out, there was something that was going to be a bit different for that time at least. Obviously the comparisons with Genesis or even us to some extent must be there, but at least at the time it was something. And I was aware that they were picking up a following at grass roots level in the clubs, so we decided to put them on the bill at the thing we did at the Nostell Priory. And it was amazing because we could see from the audience that people had come there to see them, and they were definitely going to make it if they kept plugging away. And the singer, the Fish fella, did have something going for him. So I felt in some small way at least vaguely involved with them... and it was nice to be asked to do it. They are very big in this country, and in Germany now I think, and it was nice to be asked. And when that offer came in it was for a substantial amount of money that allowed us then to put together a few more dates on the back of it knowing that we had all our pre-production costs covered. Because to do just three or four dates you would just lose money. It currently costs us, just for the two or three week period of getting crew together, rehearsals etc, not for a 'production' but just for a gig, the band on stage with no stage trappings, it is currently about £40,000 in pre-production costs. And we NEED seven days rehearsal, and that's assuming it's the same guys that played last time out.
Whatever we play there's a lot of work goes into remembering it. I mean, right now I can't remember any of it, I couldn't play any of the songs at all. I would have to work quite hard at it both privately and then in rehearsal. A lot of work goes into just the memory, although most of it does come flooding back after a couple of days. But just the number of notes, the sequence of notes, not to mention the lyrics you have to have in your head, there's an awful lot of stuff to memorise. And for Martin for example there's a lot of work involved in... not just playing 'a' solo but probably 'the' solo, or at least something, the general shape of which is going to be the same all the time, because that is what the punter hears. He's not just hearing a guitar solo but it's hopefully something that has this particular shape, that particular phrase in it. So your best solos you always have to learn... if not note for note then something very close to it if you believe as I do, and obviously Martin does, that they are not just improvisations, they are something more than that, halfway towards conceived music. When we are doing guitar solos in the studio now I usually leave Martin for an hour or so with two or three tracks to play around with and he puts down a whole bunch of bits – on his own, nobody else in the studio. The thing about Martin, Dave and myself is that we all have our own little studios at home and we all, now, understand how to engineer them so we don't need tape ops and producers and people hanging around, which is fabulous, because we can just get on and do it. If you can work completely on your own you very often do things that you might be a bit coy about doing with somebody standing over your shoulder, and that's a big help. Especially for me and Martin, anyway, because we've always been a bit... embarrassed if somebody is listening while we are doing it. But he puts his bits down and then I'll come back and we'll talk about various little pieces within maybe two or three tracks that work and we try to shape something together, and if we've got it, maybe out of three

different takes or phrases or pieces that will go together, then great, but we usually shorten a couple of bits or we will try to develop a short piece into something longer. We usually piece together something that started as an 'off the wall' thing, but it's never left that way, we always try it a few times and take the best bits and give it some form. But you have to strike while the iron is hot in terms of getting the feel of the thing – if you go back and do it another day it's just gone. You've got to keep it rolling, so we spend maybe four or five hours just doing a guitar overdub on a song.

You are producing the new album yourself?
Yes… do you think that's a good idea or a bad idea?

I think it's a good idea, but I got the impression that you enjoyed doing *Broadsword and the Beast* which was produced by Paul Samwell-Smith.
That's the name on the record…

Ah!
A hell of a nice chap. I did enjoy having the feeling that it was not down to me all the way through. I spent most of making that album reading brochures of studio equipment because I'd decided to move away from London and stop at home as the children were growing up etc, and travelling to London every day is awful… or staying there, you know, I might as well be on tour. So most of that album I sat at the back of the control room and I'd be reading a magazine while Paul was sitting at the desk. But I'd be saying, "Tell them to do that one again," or "Keep that one". But at least I wasn't having to sit there and be on the ball to everybody and having to play the role of PR man and 'our man in the control room' sort of thing. But nonetheless I certainly wasn't just leaving it up to him. Paul is a very personable guy and has some musical ability, a musical background, and he understands music, and he's an extra pair of hands on the mix. But I think he would be the first to admit that he wasn't the producer in the sense that he was terribly influential. He was instrumental in getting the final result maybe a little better than it might have been had he not been there, but he didn't really shape the feel of the music – the songs were all there before he came into it.

Would you work with a producer again?
It depends. I wouldn't want to pay somebody 4% who just comes along and feels they have to earn it. If somebody came along, and we do keep on the look out in the trade mags etc, somebody really special… But after all this time it would have to be somebody fairly flexible, as I would have to be suddenly very flexible working with somebody else – I would have to be met half way. It wouldn't be easy for me because I am very undisciplined in making records myself. I probably impose a bit of discipline on the proceedings, but as far as my own performance is concerned I'm very undisciplined. If I play guitar I have to do it in one or two takes, I just refuse to play it again and again, But I expect Martin to play it again and again! But when he's doing it it's very upfront, KAPOW!, you know, but what I do is always in the background and it's really just down to feel rather than 100% precision, so long as it is tuned up properly I'm not going to make a total balls up of it. Even playing electric guitar on this record – I play some serious rhythm - I don't hang around, I just get it done. Actually, I stand up and jump around, whereas Martin will sit down and be very studious. I enjoy doing it - when there is nobody else in the room I can jump around with the guitar and pretend I'm Martin! Although I'm just doing the chords it's good fun, and I like doing that. But I will spend a long time doing vocals; although I'm not going for precision or something that sounds beautiful, but for something that feels right at the end. Even if I have to do one line twenty times it has to feel like it links up with the rest, or the bit next to it which could have been the very first take. I might keep bits of it and ask myself, "What is good about that bit, the way I sang that?", and try and give the thing some shape. Now, a producer couldn't tell me what to do there because I know what it is I'm after. I wouldn't want somebody saying to me, "Do that piece again please," because I'd be saying, "No, no, that's the one, that's it," you know, and we would end up crossing swords over something. It would be useful and interesting to have somebody else for developing ideas for songs and arrangements for songs, because I'm bound to have set ways of doing that. I tend, well… we all do tend to take an idea

and start to do it a certain way, and it would be useful to have someone to say, "No, don't do that, play it with this instrument or change that around – let's not have any keyboards or any guitars," or whatever. You do tend to become a bit formulaic however hard you try not to.

Who plays drums and keyboards on the new album?
I play all the keyboards but, well, I'm not Peter Vettese. I can play a bit, I'm OK – it sounds alright, you know, but not great. I've got lots of toys like everybody else, multi-track sequencers and stuff like that for the bits I can't play but a good piano player could. But that only happens now and then, most of the time I play it straight. And again, with the keyboards I don't spend a lot of time at it, I try to stay within my ability to play it so that I don't have to do too many takes because it gets boring having to do so. And so there are no great flashy or dominating sounds, just simple piano-like sounds and textural things. I would say it is, although pianistically not on the same level as John Evans, the role of the keyboards is probably about the same as or a bit less than it was on *Aqualung*. You will get the feeling that it is really a guitar-dominated record. A bit of keyboard here and there but otherwise they play a supporting role.

Who will be playing on the tour?
I don't know yet. You see, drums on the LP are by both Doane Perry and Gerry Conway so I don't know who is going to end up playing on the tour, and I don't know about the keyboards. Peter might do it if he is free and wants to do it, but I doubt actually if he would. If you are doing sessions in London and you are flavour of the month, or year, and getting a lot of work, you can't afford to disappear for six months because you come back and the 'phone has stopped ringing. So I think he would actually be ill-advised to do it for that length of time, although I'm sure he'd like to if we were just doing a few dates in the summer again. In fact we were trying to find him a couple of weeks ago when a couple of festival dates in Germany came up which again were sufficiently big, money-wise, to cover our initial costs, but that has fallen through so we are no longer trying to find Peter. But I don't know who will be playing keyboards on the tour. It won't be Eddie Jobson and it won't be John Evans so it will have to be somebody else. We will have to start looking. But if Peter is available and wants to do it then he will be doing it.

Why did you use two drummers?
Well, Doane came over to do the album, but during rehearsals his mother died and so he had to go back to America. When he came back he only had about a week to do all the backing tracks, which is pushing it a bit - in 1987 you don't expect to do a whole album's worth of backing tracks in a week. Well, we DID do an album's worth of backing tracks in a week but they weren't all very good. Doane went back to Australia to play with a group called Dragon, and when we got the tapes back from Robin Black's studio I wasn't that keen on the sound or some of the performance. So some of them we redid completely and some of them we just replaced Doane with Gerry, because of course luckily these days the equipment allows you to chop and change each a little bit. And you don't have to do things all at the same tempo, you can programme them for choruses, then slowing down and speeding up and the little bits that will just keep things going. There's one long song on the album, a ten-minute song, which feels more or less like it is all the same tempo – it doubles up here and there but basically it has a certain feel to it, but in fact there are many tempo changes just by a fraction, all very carefully put in there so that just pushes it along. We did it originally in a flat tempo and it just sounded mechanical, but the very slight tempo changes we put into it makes all the difference. Where we use machines, I think we use them now in a way that makes them more… like one of us! I don't mind these things in the studio, but at the end of the day you have to go out and play it live, or substantially live. I don't think anybody minds the odd bit of backing tape; we've been using them since '72 so it's nothing new for us – I mean, not backing tapes with the band playing on them, but with whips cracking or sound effects or whatever, that has been with us literally since *Thick As A Brick*. The foot pedals that I use with lots of little bits on them, sometimes in the wrong order… I always remember [*prolonged laughter*] standing on stage somewhere in America, in some huge place with about 20,000 people there, and hitting 'the button'. And there was this new guy, or relatively

new that tour, who was in charge of the backing tapes and the sound effects and so on, and somehow he'd managed to get them in the wrong order. So when I pressed the button expecting some sound effect, what came blasting out was the tape of the singing intro to *Songs From The Wood*, in the middle of a completely different song! Normally I would have been absolutely furious, but I suddenly had this mental image of this poor guy, cringing in his pit, holding his head in his hands and thinking, "Oh, no, I'm going to lose my job tomorrow," and I absolutely cracked up. I was laughing so much I had to stop singing. And of course the other guys in the group, who hadn't heard anything wrong in their monitors, saw me doubled up and thought I'd had a heart attack or something, which struck me as being doubly funny, so I was literally on the floor laughing – I just couldn't continue.

Getting back to the new album, is there a theme, a concept, or are they completely separate songs?
I would have to say they are all separate songs. There are long songs and short songs, it's not all neat and tidy, and there's a fair amount of instrumental music. There is some really good guitar playing, Martin has done some excellent things on acoustic as well as electric guitar. I mean, I don't really know… it's sort of vaguely intelligent music, it's not rubbish, it's not throwaway, there's a lot of thought and effort gone into it, but at the same time it's… well, I write the lyrics in twenty minutes, or rather the first couple of verses in twenty minutes and then spend about three weeks trying to write the last verse! It's just a crazy mixture of unbelievable spontaneity and ruthless attempts to tidy up some of the things that have been done.

Do you write continuously over two or three years, or do you suddenly think: "Must do another LP, must write some songs"?
It tends to be "must write some songs". It's a wrench, because you put yourself on the spot by going into the studio. I usually start early in the morning, about 8am, which at least gives me a couple of hours before the 'phone starts ringing, and then again about six in the evening when the 'phone has stopped ringing. But I have to put myself on the spot by just going in and trying to do it, and something comes but it's not usually very good. And of course there is no point in saying, "I'll just sit here and wait for the muse to visit and come up with a wonderful song," because unless you put yourself in the environment surrounded by musical instruments and so on it's not going to happen. Having said that there are some songs that begin life while I'm not in the studio. I often get ideas, certainly some of the songs on the new album, when I'm just sitting in the car for example. They do not necessarily have anything to do with where I was or why I was sitting in the car, but it might start a little idea going round in my head which develops as I go along, and I'll get it down onto a cassette which I always have about me.

Do you find it hard?
I find it hard if I'm sitting in a 'plane somewhere and there is someone sitting next to me while I'm busily trying to sing into my little cassette recorder. I'm trying to sing into it quietly above the roar of the jets and they are probably thinking, "What's this guy doing??" And when I try to listen to it later, if I think, "Oh, where is that idea I had the other day?", and I play it back, all I can hear is the roar of the jets and a dreadful bleating noise in the background! But some of the songs have begun that way. *Too Old To Rock'n'Roll* was one in fact that began on a plane during a particularly violent flight somewhere. It was probably one of the band sitting next to me at the time, but even so you don't like to say: "LISTEN - I'VE GOT A GREAT IDEA FOR A SONG, LET'S PUT IT ON TAPE!", you try to do it discreetly, as if you are choking on a bit of airline chicken!

You said earlier that you like to record more than enough tracks for an album and then leave some off…
The trouble is that most of those never actually get finished; they don't usually get left off after they are finished, after they are mixed. There are some tapes but unfortunately, although it sounds like a lame excuse… and they are not BAD, but they are flawed songs. They've got a lot going for them, but there's something about them that's a pain in the arse and a real

major flaw, not just in musical terms but somewhere or other they are just not right. And there are half a dozen of those of which there are rough mixes, and in one or two cases they might even be finished mixes - BUT, somehow, a bunch of my tapes have disappeared. I keep them all under lock and key up in Scotland and I went through them when we were looking for some extra tracks a couple of years back, and I'm missing a whole bunch of stuff. There was a good final mix of *Jack Frost And The Hooded Crow*, but that wasn't around, all I could find was a 7½" copy. I went to get the multi-track but that was gone as well. So I started looking for a few other things that I knew we'd recorded but they weren't there. So I got on to Maison Rouge thinking maybe they were still there, but absolutely everything had gone. I can only imagine they've been nicked.

They can't have been stolen by a potential bootlegger because nothing of that nature has been released as a bootleg.
I don't know if they would be of any value. I mean, they MAY turn up yet, because as you can imagine we have so much tape, so many boxes etc, and sometimes tape ops are not very good at writing on the boxes what is actually in them. Things get lost, put into the wrong box or just not labelled at all. There is something in excess of a ton of recording tape spread over a big floor area, and to physically play it all, to go through it and look for it would be a mammoth task. But they may turn up one day. They are not bad, but they are flawed… they might be of interest to people… I've certainly no objection to people hearing them or having them, but it wouldn't be on to put those out on a record as a 'new' album. Those songs have, for one reason or another, been rejected, by me. And although some people might like to hear them anyway, the problem would be under what profile could you put it out so that you didn't risk people buying it and saying, "Hang on, this was recorded in '82 or whatever, and wasn't considered good enough then, so why should I be paying for it now?" It is a difficult one to work out.

You could do it through *A New Day*.
Well, I'm not averse to the idea of putting something out in a limited context but, again, it's a difficult one for any record company because obviously in a record contract relationship they have the rights to put things out. If I told them we'd like to put something out on some small label, a limited edition thing, they might then say they will put it out, rather than let somebody else do it. But then they would probably target it at the wrong people. In fact, I got a letter from Chrysalis in New York with a list of all these unreleased tracks that I was supposed to have recorded, some of which I've never heard of. Some of them were things we'd done on stage that were not recorded, and some instrumental things that had working titles, a few vocal things that perhaps we had thought about recording. But as I say, I just don't know where the tapes are - I certainly haven't got them. And I WOULD like to find the half dozen tracks I mentioned before, from the *Broadsword* sessions. All I have is a rough cassette, a live cassette of rehearsals, and a couple of things that actually sound quite good with just, literally, one mike and everybody thrashing away; they are quite interesting. All of those songs were recorded, taken up to the point of good mixes, just short of a few overdubs. The fact that I don't know where the masters are is a source of some annoyance to me, but I'm a bit of a fatalist about these things - if they have gone missing, it saves me the agony of having to decide if we should ever put them out. There is also another bunch of stuff missing from around 1973, a whole load of out-takes which should be there but they're not, and they could be in one of many recording studios. The trouble is there are so many tapes and most of it is just rubbish, stuff that would be scrapped and thrown out if you could identify it in the first place. I could spend a whole year going through it all, trying to identify things and log them properly, and if I did manage to find some material I probably wouldn't like it anyway. If I was going to spend all that time in the studio then arguably I would be better off devoting that time to writing a song that I could do now, which would be as good as the stuff we are talking about anyway. It is of dubious value. The fact that it has been done makes it of limited value except for someone whose mad passion is Jethro Tull music. You see, to most people it's about as boring as it is talking about salmon farming to you. You have to put it in that context, although I'm not trying to put down your obvious interest and doubtless that of your readers, but it is a narrow field. The appeal is because it is not to everybody's tastes, it's like being

really dead keen on a rather special little wine that you've found in a particular little vineyard, or you might live in London but you decide to support Forfar Athletic… I mean, WHY? Just because no other bugger does it, you know. I've got my narrow field of interest and I certainly know more about that than I know about making music, and to me it's incredibly interesting and I can, and do, sit down and talk about it, I like talking about it. And I am more important in that industry than I am in the music industry, in industry terms. But it is of NO interest whatsoever to the majority of folk and I don't want to ram it down their throats. But if you DO want to talk about if… if you insist…

[Time to change the subject - quick!]
The reason I asked about unreleased tracks was because *Original Masters*…
Well, the idea was the right idea. It was my fault, not the record company's; it was my fault because I let them do it, I just said, "Look, you guys do it, I'm busy doing something else at the moment", and I let them get on with it. If I had taken their original idea myself it would have come across in a different way; it would have been essentially the same, but there would have been no confusion. I would much rather have gone back and remixed those songs. A really keen purist might find now that there's a song which has been changed. I'm not sure what it is now, possibly *Locomotive Breath*… in fact, I'm not sure that I haven't re-sung a vocal line on *Aqualung*. There is a quad remix version of *Aqualung* where I redid something from the original version, just to sort out a dodgy bit from the original - I think it was a vocal line, and the remix was great, the whole song was just so much better and nicer. And although it was in quad it was mixed for stereo, it is a perfectly legit stereo mix and it's much better than the original, and I'd much rather go back and do that for the CD version, to try and improve upon it. The validity of the title *Original Masters* to me is the master 24-tracks, not the master mix. I'd like to take them all onto a digital master, giving the original music a new lease of life. By the way, I've never been keen on the idea of doing a *Best Of* album and sticking on one more song to try to entice people to buy it - that's not a good idea. And I think *Original Masters* was a complete waste of time anyway. It was just a *Best Of* album, not for people like you to buy, but for people who are aware of Jethro Tull and would be interested enough to buy one Tull LP that contained a certain bunch of songs - even though they have been on *Best Of* albums before. It would have been a good idea had we done it properly, but as I say it would have taken three months of my time and I was busy with other work.
Again, to put it into perspective, someone who has been lucky enough, as I have, to make a good living out of music for twenty years… well, I'm very keen on the idea that the profits don't just wind up in the bank, it should do something, work for a living. I employ currently about fifty people, and I think 50 to 1 is a good ratio; we should all be doing that. Imagine if everyone who has stashed away a pile of money created fifty jobs. I passionately believe in my responsibility to do that, creating not just employment but NEW employment. That is why fish farming to me is so exciting, because it is relatively new on the scene. There are new jobs in an area where there is no scope for other developments for the native population. The future for the kids at school now is being shaped by what's happening there now, and that is very important to me. Apart from the fact that I am a Scot, it is important because I have now been a part of that scene for nine years, a part of it in a much more tangible way than I could ever be part of the music business, because I've always been sort of on the edge of the music business, especially socially. I haven't many friends or acquaintances that are musicians, I don't mix with any of those people - not because I don't want to, it's just never really come up. But up there is something I'm a part of and it's something I can feel a bit more useful about, although the end product is another luxury, just the same as the music. I mean, salmon farming IS rock'n'roll. Every step of the way it is the same game. At the end of it you have something that people don't really need, they just think they want it. You go out and buy a side of salmon the same way you buy a CD, and it'll cost you about the same. So big deal, you could live without it - you could buy ten pints of beer or put it towards a holiday or something. It's all just spurious. In a lot of ways I would like to be doing something that people really needed rather than just wanted, I'd like to be doing something important. And unfortunately my second, parallel career is another one like that, but it is just something that is nice to do - it gives a lot of people a lot of pleasure, and it gives me a lot of pleasure to do it, but it is not essential or important.

I don't mean to be funny at all but in many ways I have a part of me that regrets not becoming a policeman. That would have been, by my standards now, an important job. And ironically I probably would have ended up in a nice little house, with regular holidays and weekends off, and a lot more time to spend with my family. It is only in the last couple of years that I have been able to think about holidays. In fact, that only dawned on me a couple of weeks ago when Robert Currie, the manager on the farming side in Scotland, said we ought to go onto the NFU rate on holidays, which he said was four weeks a year rather than the three we gave them. I didn't believe it could be four weeks but I asked Shona, who knows more about the NFU than I do, and she confirmed it, so now they are all on four weeks holiday. Four weeks with pay. And I suddenly thought, you know, "God, imagine if I had four weeks holiday…" I'd feel so guilty and wracked with feelings of… just goofing off and having a good time. But the idea of having four periods in the year where you can just take a week off… I've never done that, but that is what everybody does apparently. I've also heard, and I don't know if it's true, perhaps it's just a rumour, that people actually have their weekends off, they have a holiday every Saturday and Sunday! And so last week I didn't go to the studio at the weekend, the first time for a LONG time that I've not worked on a weekend.

But you are in a very privileged position of enjoying what you do. For most people work is just a basic necessity…
I'm beginning to learn, not just to enjoy it but to make use of it in a different way, which is perhaps what life is already about for a lot of people who have learnt to make use of a degree of leisure time and… enjoy it, yes, but also developing them in some way, be it playing sport or something; it is a very important thing. I am 40 this year and I have not actually got round to doing those things. I went skiing for the first time this year, with the children, and it was really good. The old knees aren't really up to it, but I thought it was great, and I also thought I should have done it when I was eight or ten, or twenty, you know. But of course when I was that age it was outrageous to go skiing, it was just for very rich people. But not now, it's a sort of £60 package deal, definitely the holiday for the masses. But I have only just done it, and there are all those sort of things that I don't think anybody would begrudge me doing but I've just always felt guilty about doing them, taking myself off to do something. I'm not a lying-on-the-beach type of person, I cannot just sit and do nothing, but there are things that I probably should do because I think they are good for the soul. I think this year we will take a second holiday, go away for the week. I'd quite like to go to Moscow, somewhere I haven't been before. And even the places I have been to, touring and so on, I've never really seen them. You just see the view from a taxi and the inside of a concert hall. To have been to all those places and to have done so very little, to have taken in so little about them is not good. I'd like to go back to those places and actually SEE them, if only to put into context the fact that 10,000 people actually bought tickets to see us here. And those people are probably still there; I'd like to go back and sneak a look at them. They do tend to be the pilots of the planes, you know, "Hey, I saw you back when I was 18" or something, those people tend to come back into your life later on, and that side of it is very interesting. You then realise that it did in fact actually mean something to them, it meant a lot to them. It was very difficult to appreciate it at the time, when it was just punters, tickets… and a lot of them threw things and shouted nasty things anyway. You didn't get the feeling that they were all people that loved us, we were just a curiosity – it wasn't always a heart-warming experience. But obviously most people were there because they did like us. And it is nice to meet people some years after, when they are more able to say to you, without being tongue-tied, what they would have found difficult to articulate ten or twenty years before. And you realise it was important to them, part of their growing up, in the same way that it was to me when I was starting out as a musician, going to see Steve Winwood or somebody. A moment of magic there… I wouldn't say it was THAT important, but it was important in that it was part of growing up, a part that you remember as being good.

Of course with Tull it's been a constant presence – we picked the right group to follow.
Well, terrific. I hope we don't let you down, at least not in the immediate future. It's an interesting thing. At this point in my life I'm very happy to… particularly when you take the trouble to do your magazine, and I take it it's read by…

Millions!

Well, more than just yourselves anyway! I've had your magazines in the past and thought, "I really ought to meet this fella and say what a good job he's doing and all the rest of it," you know, but I'm a bit shy about that sort of thing, coming forward, because… well, it might break the spell. The problem is you are gonna go away from here and sit in the car and the first thing you are going to say is, "Well, what did you think of him? God, what a bore!" you know, "Not at all what we expected," - but then of course you never are. You never are what you are expected to be.

[*MW*] I've met you before, actually, in 1984. I won a competition to meet you backstage.

Oh yes, that happens quite a lot, particularly in America. Was I nice to you?

Yes, under the circumstances. You were in a blind panic as you were late for the soundcheck, but you were very civil.

Oh good. I do try to be, but I can assure you in those circumstances… when we do it in America sometimes the other guys are involved in it and they have to stand around and talk to these people, and I'll walk into the room and somebody who has been talking to Martin suddenly cuts him dead and comes over to me for an autograph. You can imagine what that must feel like, a real downer. And for them it's embarrassing, sometimes humiliating being in that situation. But we are always more embarrassed, much more uncomfortable than the people who come to meet us, because they are usually very geared up anyway and so it does not matter what you say or do, they're happy – WOW!, you know. But we feel so uncomfortable, you feel a real sham just being there. So it is difficult meeting the punters as we affectionately term them… it is difficult to do. On the one hand we have this great feeling of warmth to all those people who have supported us, not necessarily over all the years – it may be someone who has just bought a Tull album for the first time ever – but you have this great feeling of warmth for them, but when you actually meet them in person there's this terrible awkwardness. Although, with the benefit of experience you try and set the ball rolling and say a few words, but you feel at least as uncomfortable as they do, and the spell is very easily broken, and I think very often people do go away thinking, "Huh, I don't like him much".

It happens to me, I've met lots of people and my illusions have been shattered, cruelly sometimes, by people's personalities. And on occasions I've met people that I really thought I wouldn't like but they've been terrific people, really nice guys - or girls for that matter. Like Debbie Harry, for example. Seeing her with Blondie on TV I thought, you know… wet, a stupid woman, a drip! But in fact she is a really nice girl, totally different to what you'd imagine she's be like, and that is a plus one. But there are others that I won't mention I'd thought were wonderful people but are actually awful people, dreadful people in person. I think, for everybody, what you do on stage looks, and is meant to look, larger than life. People always imagine I'm six inches taller than I am, and they have a stereotype visual reference. Even if they went to see us last year they won't remember that person on stage, they remember a fixed visual image of me a few years ago if they have followed us for a long time. If they bumped into me today they'd think, "Christ, isn't he old," you know, "The old hair's going, putting on a bit of weight," etc. But I haven't suddenly gone to seed in the last twelve months, but they won't remember it, they'll remember the one before. I always do it myself, watching TV or something. If I think of Cliff Richard I visualise him, but if I actually see him I think: "Christ, the old neck's getting a bit scrawny…" Whenever I think of my father, who is dead, I don't think of him in the last couple of years of his life, invalid in a wheelchair and hardly able to speak – I visualise him always in his late fifties or early sixties, when he could walk about and have a conversation, and I think we always do that with people… which is probably all to the good. 'Cos old Dave Pegg you know, he's not too good, He's been having… funny turns!

The male menopause?

I don't know what it is. I think it's imminent death, actually! He had a funny turn here when we had to carry a ewe that was giving birth. We were in the studio working when Shona came in to tell us that this supposedly barren ewe was suddenly having a lamb. So this lamb had its front two paws hanging out the back, and we didn't want it to be born in the middle of this field, we wanted her indoors. We managed to rope her but she refused to budge, so we actually had to pick her up and carry her the hundred yards or so to the house. I got the front end and Dave and Martin had half the back end each. Dave's back was going a bit you see, and he was staggering a bit – he was not long back from the pub in fact! – and he was a bit down on his side which meant he had more weight on him, and the head was out, not to mention various fluids and things. Dave Pegg was a bit... well, he's not exactly Mr Au-Fait-With-Nature, you know, and he found it all distinctly worrying, plus the fact that his back was about to break in the middle, he was struggling for breath, and so on. But we managed to get the ewe inside in time, whereupon Peggy just about passed out, he looked really ill. He recovered after about half an hour, but he has had a couple of funny turns since. Whether or not that's the toll of living his fairly high profile life in terms of drinking and late nights etc, I don't know. Hopefully it's something he can shrug off, but it is a worry nonetheless, because you can't go out and tour in that shape, having funny turns. And bear in mind that this is the guy for whom the door had to be broken down in a public lavatory in Budapest... or maybe Vienna. Some airport, anyway. We discovered Dave was missing from the departure lounge when the flight was called and so a couple of guys went looking for him. Eventually they heard this noise from inside the men's loo saying, "Please God, just take me now!" He was in a cubicle and they had to break the door down. He was actually standing in the toilet trying to flush himself down the loo! I mean, he had just gone, you know - he'd been out all the night before and got totally, paralytically drunk, surfaced later in apparently reasonable spirits, but the alcohol level evidently caught up with him and he was completely out of it. Anyway, to get back to what we were talking about, I'm pleased to hear that I was civil to you when we met!

Actually you talked about *A Classic Case* then, more or less saying, "Forget about it."
Well I was probably being a bit presumptuous, because I've still not heard it! I asked David Palmer to send me a copy but he still hasn't, and I suspect that he doesn't think I will like it either. I added my bits to it without reference to the orchestra, because I did actually hear a little bit of it and it sounded pretty awful to me, so I just... I'd made a commitment to David personally to do it and so I felt an obligation to do it, but I felt that David was under a lot of pressure when he took that deal with Ariola to do something that really was not adventurous. The original idea as I understood it was that he was going to orchestrate those songs in a creative and totally different context.

That is what we were hoping for really.
But all it turned out to be really was the same things, the same tempo with the wretched drumming and the orchestra just playing along honking the tune; I thought it was very uninspired. However, I have heard a bit of the subsequent one he has done with Genesis, on which I play a tiny little bit of flute - a wretched tiny bit of flute as well - and that one sounds a lot better. I'm not terribly familiar with the music of Genesis, particularly the early stuff, I didn't know what it was - something from the Peter Gabriel era I think. But it did sound more convincingly orchestral. Whether it was just the nature of the music or whether his arrangements were making more use of the orchestra I don't really know.

One track on *A Classic Case*, *Warchild*, came from the orchestral film score you were working on in 1974. Is there any more of that soundtrack in the vaults or was that all you did?
There was a six or eight minute, fairly grand orchestral version of that song, yes... he may indeed have used some of that. I think David did say something about using it.

That is the track that works best on the album.
That piece of music was OK. *Warchild* was one that David did pretty much on his own. There were some other things we did with an orchestra at the same time, and again they do probably exist in rough mixes; they were just interesting little snippets. They were basically just things we did on spec when we were thinking of putting a movie together and we compiled a sort of

musical portfolio as if to say: "Look, we can actually write this kind of music, a fairly stylised, grand orchestral version of these songs".

What about *The Water's Edge* ballet - was it ever recorded?
No. No, that was awful, hideous. Because with the Scottish Ballet Orchestra being, as all ballet orchestras are basically, lesser breeds if you like, couldn't make the second fiddle of the symphony orchestra sort of thing... they tend not to be very good. They are OK if they are playing *Swan Lake* or something they've been brought up with, but playing something a bit strange, they are not really equipped for it musically, and they did struggle very badly with it. It was embarrassing. There were bits in it, time signatures and things, that they just could not cope with at all. And given that rehearsal was no more than probably half a day for a live performance, you can't expect them to be able to play it properly. To go out and play *Swan Lake* for the thousandth time is fine, but something they have seen for the first time, they run through it once or twice and then have to go out and play it live, it is just a mess. And it was a mess, it was really embarrassing. The actual pieces themselves were OK, but if you were going to record them now you probably wouldn't try to do it with an orchestra, you'd do it with a lot of machinery and get something that actually sounds quite nice, where the music does work, and with perhaps an overall orchestral feel to it.

Were you asked, or did you offer, to play Live Aid?
No... I seem to recall that at the time they made the first single somebody 'phoned me to ask if I could come to London to sing on some charity record, but there was no great explanation given. Anyway, I couldn't do it for some reason, but I think that's what it was. I'm sure if I'd have gone I would just have been one of the many assembled voices in the background. You will have noticed this thing creeping up in the last four or five years, which I suppose is entirely predictable, there has been this little group of people, the Phil Collinses and the Midge Ures etc, who are kind of 'in' with royalty and so on.

But you did do the Prince's Trust Gala.
Well we did the first one, but that was only because David Bowie cancelled.

And you never got invited back?
Well it's not really a question of being invited back as we were just shoved onto the bill at the last minute. We weren't part of the rehearsed thing that the other people were doing, and we just did a couple of songs with Phil Collins playing the drums - and they were only rehearsed on the afternoon of the show. But we have never been asked back to any of those things and I can understand why, because we are not a high profile, mainstream pop act. It would be the same for someone like Gary Brooker, he wouldn't be asked back. He's still playing gigs and so on, but he is not in the vanguard of what's going on. I think my absence was only recorded by Prince Charles himself. I'm told that he actually asked where I was, as he apparently regards me as far and away the most interesting person in rock music that he has met. He came to open our factory in Inverness you see, and so I have met him a few times over a period - I don't mean to say that he is an acquaintance of mine, he is the future king and that's it, you know, but it is nice to be noticed for not being there. But as you are aware, these things are not decided by him, it's not a "Royal Command" to appear, it's the George Martins and the Chris Wrights and the people that are involved in putting these things together.

I hear Martin Barre is working with Paul McCartney.
Yes, he was a couple of weeks ago. I could tell you some fantastic off-the-record stories about that [*he didn't...*]. Obviously to work with someone like him is just awe inspiring... I mean, one of the top people in the universe when it comes to music. But it's the first time really that Martin has been asked to do anything like that. He got a 'phone call - Gerry Conway was up there, and put Martin's name forward, and so Martin was one of the many people auditioned by this Phil Ramone character who is producing it, and they sorted out a few line-ups from what sounds like hundreds of musicians. Apparently there were famous drummers going in meeting famous drummers coming out, one after the other going to the sessions and getting paid, like triple rates, just to turn up and play *Lucille* or *That'll Be The Day* or any standard

rock song. I'm surprised Martin got the job because he is not really that sort of player, he doesn't know any of the 'licks' you associate with that type of pop music. Martin only had to play one guitar solo on the Paul McCartney stuff, but apparently Paul didn't like it, thought it was too heavy, he wanted something a bit gentler, a bit safer, so I think his one guitar solo with Paul McCartney will end up with the out-takes!

Who wrote *To Be Sad Is A Mad Way To Be*, that you used to play in 1969? Is it an old blues? [*Since established to have been written by Brownie McGhee*]
You've got me there. The title sounds vaguely familiar, but I can't recall the song at all. Presumably it is nothing that was ever recorded?

Not on vinyl, but you did it on TV in Sweden in 1969.
'69? So Martin was with us then. It must have been one of the pieces we were getting together for the second album.

It is a straightforward blues song.
When Martin joined the band we had a bunch of stuff which was really Mick Abrahams kind of things, and some stuff from the first album which we carried on playing, but we obviously needed a lot of material in a hurry with a new guitarist, and we very quickly had to rustle up a whole bunch of things, and Martin was not really a blues guitarist. He is a particular sort of guitarist but he wasn't conversant with all of that stuff, so we struggled to get things together - so maybe it was just an attempt to come up with a song for Martin while having to do a TV show, perhaps it was something we were working on at the time. But many things from the *Stand Up* album were songs we were playing before on stage. In fact, I remember trying to get Tony Iommi to play *Nothing Is Easy*. We played a lot of those songs live before recording them because we didn't have much stage material when Mick left. We usually only played for 45 minutes anyway, with a lot of improvisations, not many songs at all.

On a TV show in Germany in 1983 you walked onstage to play flute with Fela Kuti. Was that planned or was it a spontaneous thing?
Ah yes, that was in a tent in Munich - we did a couple of things from the solo album. We did an amazing switch on the orchestra there. They were a terrible orchestra, and we had a run-through in the afternoon and it was just abysmal. They were trying to play *Fly By Night* and it was awful. Eberhard Schoener is a hell of a nice guy but he's away with the fairies, he's not with it! He's a lovely fella but he thinks he's really arty, into rock'n'roll and classics and avant garde type of things, but he is actually just mildly crazy. I knew the orchestra might be terrible because I'd seen a video of Ultravox the year before and that was awful, a total disaster. They were doing *Vienna* and it was a nightmare, the orchestra were in the wrong place, about half a bar out. I spoke to Midge Ure about it and he confirmed it. So I took out two tapes for the show, one with just the drums on it and one which had the orchestra sounds. David Palmer was out there to help with the score and so on, and he was in the control room for the live broadcast, and I got him to switch the tapes at the last minute, and so he played the tape with the orchestra on it as well. I told him to KILL the engineer if he had to, to make sure the orchestra faders were down on the live broadcast! And sure enough as the thing went out there was a count in, you know - one two, one two three four, go - and Eberhard missed the half, and he's like half a bar out, and I KNEW as soon as he started to conduct that he'd missed it. And so the orchestra were playing in the wrong places, and by the time they'd finished they were actually a whole bar out, they'd actually lost a bit more on the way, and I thought, "Thank God I switched the tapes!" And Eberhard didn't suss it, he didn't notice either then or since, and at the end of it he came rushing over to me and hugged and kissed me saying, "Wonderful! Marvellous!" and so on. And I couldn't say, "Eberhard you were bloody miles away, but it doesn't matter 'cos we switched tapes on you!" I couldn't bring myself to tell him. But it was wonderful...
Oh yes... Fela Kuti! Well I was in the bar afterwards talking to Jack Bruce, and he is one of my heroes, you know, and I'd never met him. I especially like some of his solo stuff after Cream, and before with Graham Bond, and so I'd always wanted to meet him, and here he was and I was busy bending his ear at the bar. And suddenly these people came rushing in and

said, "Quick, you have to go on stage!" I said, "No, no, I've done my bit, " but it was, "No, you must come and play with Fela Kuti, they are waiting for you!" And I could hear this kind of jungle rhythm going on onstage, and apparently they had actually announced that I was coming on to play, and once that commitment had been made for me without my knowledge I had no option but to leg it up there. My shoelace was undone and I didn't even have my flute, it was in its case backstage, so I had to run and get it and assemble it onstage! And there was this bunch of very untrained guys, all very rough and ready. And Fela Kuti, as you may know, is a total con man. He can't play at all, he does what Captain Beefheart does, just a lot of noises, and pretends he is an avant garde jazz man, but in fact he can't play at all, he knows nothing whatsoever about it. He is also a bit of a wizard... bites the heads off chickens and dabbles in black magic etc, a total con trick, complete bullshit. He is just trading on being a black African and a militant and so on. Some of the journalists, particularly in America, are taken in by him, they actually think this guy really is the business, a superb musician. A total con. And he didn't like me at all - to him I am a 'capitalist whitey', but I was up there promoting his career. Me and Jack Bruce and everybody else, we all got dragged up there, and it was chaos. I managed to ask somebody what key they were in and he said, "C!", as if to say, "Well, what could it be other than C?" And C is a rotten key for playing the flute anyway, it's a nasty cross-over between the octaves and it is not a good key for playing the blues. So it was just like 'tootle tootle' sort of thing but the music wasn't going anywhere, it was just this rambling sort of thing. Nothing was happening, it was just stupid, and it just went on until it ran out of steam.

Nobody seemed to know when it was going to finish - you stopped and had a cigarette at one point, didn't you.
I probably stopped and went off. I can't imagine that I hung around until the end, it was just one of those things where you grit your teeth and do it. But the people in the audience knew it was dead boring, a total waste of time, it wasn't impressing them. But that's the sort of thing they do on German TV, they get these 'arty' ideas. And the idea of people getting together and having a 'jam', that it will somehow give rise to this remarkable spark of something wonderful happening... nine times out of ten it doesn't happen, unless the people concerned all have some definite idea of what they are doing. Either you're working around the basic traditional framework of blues or jazz, and everybody knows the rules, or it is something that looks like a jam but in fact they have been rehearsing together for a week. But very rarely does anything great happen. I mean, if we were playing a conventional 12-bar blues we'd have had some musical format in which to work. And had they been good players it would have been OK - Jack Bruce would have done something, I could have done something, but this was just jungle music in the key of C. You know, terrific, but it just goes nowhere, a waste of time, but unfortunately it's one of those things I got dragged into.

Is there any chance we will see you at Fairport's festival this year?
Well I haven't been asked! Dave Pegg has asked me in the past, but unfortunately it has coincided with the time we go back to Scotland for a couple of weeks. But having seen Fairport play there are probably a couple of things I could do with them. I know a couple of their songs. *John Barleycorn*, I could sing along to that I suppose. Yes, having seen them, if they asked me to do something I would be quite pleased to do it, but they haven't actually asked me.

We are sure it is an open invitation!
Well. maybe it is, but, you know... I certainly wouldn't want to feel like I was putting myself forward and then they would have to cope with it. What I do doesn't fit in naturally anywhere, I'd have to be doing somebody else's bit, wouldn't I.

They have played *Jack Frost And The Hooded Crow* live.
Have they? I didn't know that. That was Dave, he did it on his solo album didn't he? Yes, I could sing a few things with them, but then is that really what people come to see? I don't reckon they'd be particularly impressed by me suddenly appearing on stage.

I wouldn't bet on that. There are a lot of Tull fans who have become Fairport fans as a result of Dave Pegg's involvement - us, for example. You check it out and discover you like it.

Dave Pegg does really well with that. He and his wife do everything, promote the whole thing and do the whole business. There's a lot of work goes into getting something like that together. Yes, I would actually quite like to do it. I mean, if Dave gets round to asking me or says anything about it we can talk about it, but I can't put myself forward, because I suppose Dave would say, "Oh, great, terrific!" etc, but I wouldn't want the other guys in Fairport thinking, "Christ, what are we having him for?"

They had Robert Plant last year and he's got absolutely nothing to do with them.

No, but Robert Plant can do a number of rock'n'roll classics and so on.

Dave didn't actually ask him either. He asked him if he would like to come along, but he doesn't like to ask people to join them onstage in case they feel obliged to do so. So perhaps he doesn't like to ask you and you don't like to offer until he asks?

Ah well, you see, the world may be denied this moment of musical hysteria just for the want of Dave and I actually sitting and saying, "How about it?" I'll make a point of not asking him tomorrow!

Have Strange Fruit Records been in touch with you about releasing some Tull BBC recordings?

Yes. Clive Selwood has sent me a tape of an *In Concert* we did in 1977, which I still have not listened to yet. He has also found some tracks we did for John Peel which he is currently sorting through. I'm sure something will come out. I did like one of the sessions we did, I enjoyed doing one of them, and I've asked him to send me a tape when he gets round to it.

Well, many thanks for talking to us, and for so long.

That's OK. Tell me, what do you two do the rest of the time?

[MW] I'm a civil servant. [DR] And I'm a printer.

A printer? In what context - your own business?

No, unfortunately!

Is that a help in producing *A New Day*?

It was at first, that's how it started, but I can't print it myself now.

How did your writing come about, journalistically speaking? What's the background to that?

There isn't one. I've never written anything else.

But that piece you had in *Record Collector* was a well written piece; I assumed you had some kind of journalistic background.

No, nothing else.

You mean I've sat here all morning talking to a bloody printer!! Well, when we get this record finished we'll make sure you get an early listen to it and maybe you'd like to write something about it. I'm certainly not suggesting you write nice things about it obviously, but if it would interest you to do it, write about it completely honestly, you might be able to get it into a couple of places with the privileged position of having heard it first. And if you don't like it… don't write anything!

I can't imagine that happening, to be honest. We do actually spend a lot of time writing to the TV and radio people asking them to play more, or even some, Jethro Tull music.

Well… they won't play this one! Actually, you probably will quite like this one. I'd imagine that most people who generally speaking like Jethro Tull will find that it contains some elements that they are familiar with. The songs don't sound like other songs. It's not like another version of something. It's got a fresh feel about it; and it's also nice to hear a lot more guitar from Martin. I'm pleased with it… It could go this way or that yet, depending on a few overdubs and mixes etc.

What about a single? Are you going to push for a hit single?
No, but… one of the reasons we don't want to rush to get the thing out straightaway is that it would be better, having got the album done, that we feel happy with it as an album, just to play around for two or three months because we are bound to come up with a few more songs which may be better than the songs we've already done. And it may well be that in the course of doing that we'll get some positive feedback or response from the record company or other people to give some indication whether or not this song or that song ought to be put out as a single. I would think something will go out – not necessarily in the UK but certainly in mainland Europe and America. I'm sure there will be a 'radio single', in the places where we can get radio play. In this country I feel they have to think it is something commercially viable before it's worth the cost involved in pressing enough records to be commercially on the market. And with the radio playlist, the small amount of records listed for play, some crazy amount…

I think it's about six from what I hear on the radio. I actually thought *Coronach* would be a hit single, I was surprised but… well, I had terrible trouble buying it, it was hopeless. There are people that still haven't got it, they write to me to ask where they might find it.
Well again that was one that was… it wasn't promoted!

Whose fault was that?
Ultimately the only way to promote it is to take it in and keep badgering them to play it. But if Radio One doesn't play it, it's finished. If something gets picked up on strongly by the regional stations, and by Capital, then it might just eventually get picked up by Radio One subsequently, but to an extent local radio tends to follow Radio One. So you are dealing with just half a dozen very influential radio producers, and they are working with a playlist of about 40 records, and only about four or five of those records are changed each week, and it is very difficult to be one of those four or five records out of the hundreds released every week. It doesn't really upset me because all the groups coming along now are, after all, 'the new groups'. I suppose they ought to be heard – it happened to us once upon a time and we got a few minor hits, arguably at a time when singles meant nothing and albums meant everything. And even these days the amount of singles you have to sell for a hit is absurd. 30,000 singles is a Top 20 hit, and yet it is still the criterion by which everything is measured. And really the success of an album, especially in America, will tend to be very strongly influenced by whether or not there is a hot single. And it is based on this rather artificial thing of 30,000 singles which is really nothing. People aren't going to rush out and buy a Jethro Tull single because they know it's going to be on the album, and the kind of people that follow Tull are not singles-buying people, for the most part. They're only going to buy the single if they are really ardent fans of the group and there is something about it that makes it different, like a 12" with a different mix and a couple of non-album tracks, or something that is basically another kind of con trick to get you to buy it. Otherwise you might as well wait for the album to come out.

But a single is useful in terms of opening up markets – there are so many people who simply are not aware that Jethro Tull still exist.
There are a few things happening this year that might help. We've been asked to do a special for *The Tube*, if *The Tube* is still on… they want to do a retrospective thing on Jethro Tull with old footage plus us playing live, which would be very helpful. And Tyne Tees are doing a thing which started as a *Farming Outlook* programme for the North of Britain, but has ended up being a longer programme with more music in it, which Channel 4 are taking. And just a couple of tellies could make a hell of a difference in the UK. The problem is trying to get them to come out at the right time. Channel 4 are talking about July but the LP won't be out until the last week of August, so people will have almost forgotten about it by then. It would be better for us and them if they show it a couple of weeks after the album is out, so

hopefully they will see the sense of waiting until September. But who knows... the next album could be a moderate seller or it could do well, it's impossible to tell. A lot depends on whether or not people decide that Jethro Tull is the thing to push at the time. In America for example we've not had a record out for a while; we may go there and find that everyone is waiting for it, everybody is really dead keen on it and it goes straight onto media rotation and conspicuous radio play, and it could do very well. It's whether or not the collective powers that be, a lot of DJs in America, decide they are quite keen on it. If they are it'll be a whole different ball game. But I was very surprised that *Broadsword* didn't do well in America. I still don't understand why it didn't because that was a much more deliberate attempt to make an album that sounded like a Jethro Tull album, it more or less embodied things about the group that we felt would give us a broad-based audience... plus using a producer, someone who might have been able to give an independent view, an objective mind about making it work on those terms. In Germany it was far and away our biggest album ever, almost doubled our traditional sales of albums there; and Germany has always been our second biggest market. And I was VERY surprised that it hardly did anything in America, very moderate sales. It didn't surprise me that *Under Wraps* did not do well because it was definitely off on a different sort of tack and I could see that could probably alienate a lot of people who thought they know what they wanted to hear from Jethro Tull. But *Broadsword* was strange... I guess it was just the wrong time – just another Tull album, just another tour, you know, and nobody got terribly excited.

[*We then took a couple of photos while Ian flicked through a previous issue of* A New Day]

Oh, this is Dave Pegg doing this interview then? How sober was he?

I wasn't there, but I don't think he was completely sober – he said a couple of things that I think he wishes he hadn't!
What sort of stuff do you two listen to, other than Jethro Tull?

[DR] Well I love the Australian band Mara!, who you won't have heard of – yet! And I particularly like The Smiths.
Yes, I think The Smiths are really very good. He is not quite as interesting lately, but their earlier stuff was excellent.

[MW] What about The Pogues?
Heard of them but never seen them. I know their manager.

[MW] Dave Pegg slagged them off too, but I think they are excellent.
[DR] I saw them once and they were easily the worst band I have even seen.
Well it's nice to hear you don't agree on everything!

Chapter 5

DON AIREY

(Published in Issue #12, October 1987)

With Tull due to tour the UK, Europe and America in late 1987, the apparently ubiquitous heavy rocker Don Airey was recruited on keyboards. DR and MW caught up with Don during a tea-break during rehearsals at Pinewood Studios – almost, in the process, exposing him to a bit of a wigging by making him late for the recording of some flute samples for the live show. He just made it back on cue, having gracefully given up his very limited time to have a quick chat with us.

In the press release from Chrysalis you are described as "an old friend of the band". But that is not true, is it?
No, I didn't know any of them, never even met them. I think I met Dave Pegg once, very briefly, but that was all. I got the gig with Tull after my roadie said I ought to get back on the road, because I had been doing a lot of session work. I asked around, and although I got a lot of offers from heavy metal bands I was not really interested, and eventually I got an audition for Tull. I told them I wasn't familiar with their music and asked them to send a tape, which they did, but I didn't have time to listen to it. So the evening before the audition I put the tape on and thought, "Oh shit!" So I had to write it all down and try to learn it and I was up early in the morning trying to do *Hunting Girl* and *Songs From The Wood*. But it was just great.

So up until then you had not heard a lot of Tull's music?
I'd heard a lot through hotel walls when I was in Rainbow because Ritchie Blackmore is such a big Tull fan. He 'phoned me once when we were in America and ORDERED me to go to see Tull at the Nassau Coliseum, and I was knocked out. I remember thinking it was the best out-front sound I had ever heard,

Why did you not want to join another metal band?
I just got fed up with it. It is great music, but the keyboards are too subdued, and I thought I couldn't go on like that forever. I moved into the studio session scene and I've been doing a lot of arranging and so on. I was working right up to the day I joined Tull trying to get it all finished.

Do you write songs?
Yes, I've just been working on my own material, and it looks like I've got a deal on it although nothing has been settled yet.

How have you found Ian to work with? You hear so many stories…
I am sure they are all true! No, it's been fine. I mean, I have worked with some difficult people, but I find that the more talented they are the more difficult they are to work with… it's par for the course. Ritchie Blackmore is exactly the same, but you've got to roll with the punches, you know. But Ian is great, and the band sounds really good.

What made you take up music initially, and keyboards in particular?
I've always played the piano, since I was about two years of age, and I can play a bit of clarinet. I was a classically trained musician at Manchester College.

They will probably have you playing clarinet in Tull!
Oh yeah, they've got me playing claves and tambourine, and they have threatened me with John Evans' accordion, but much to my relief they couldn't find it.

What were your musical influences?

I was very influenced by Jan Hammer from the Mahavishnu Orchestra, and Chick Corea. At the moment I listen to a lot of jazz… I like heavy rock, I am a heavy rocker, but I've kind of run out of guitarists to work with. One I really rate at the moment is John Sykes who was with Whitesnake – he is just great, a monster.

How would you rate Martin Barre?

There is nobody like him. Nobody else can do what he does. I really like his playing, it's very musical.

What sort of reaction have you had from your friends in the business since you joined? Tull are not a very fashionable band, are they.

Well, Gary Moore 'phoned me last week and he was amazed when I told him, but then he said, "Yeah, they are great," you know, because he played at the Milton Keynes gig last year and he got a big surprise. And when I first entertained the idea of joining Tull I'd heard from a lot of people that they blew everyone off stage, blew them away, because they were so much more professional. And I think maybe with this album people are beginning to think hang on, wait a minute… these guys are still going and they are GOOD, you know, and there is nobody else. There's not many bands out there who are not constrained by hit singles, marketing and image etc… maybe Genesis and Pink Floyd. But the fact is they can all still play, it all still works. They have not stood still and I could tell that as soon as I started playing with them. Ian floored me actually, because after we had played a few things he said, "Right, we will play something of yours now – make something up!" And I was stunned because people don't normally say things like that.

Have you got a solo spot in the set?

Yes, Doane and Peter Vettese used to do something together and Doane was very keen to keep that going, so I wrote a little piece yesterday for that. And Ian has asked me to write an intro, so we'll get that on tape tomorrow.

Any favourite Tull songs yet?

I love *Songs From The Wood* – I think that is a work of genius. And *Budapest*… all the deep ones.

Will you continue to tour with other bands?

I don't know. I've got a lot of work lined up for next year, and I don't know what Tull will be doing yet.

Do you see Jethro Tull as a full-time thing?

Well again, I don't know; you never know with groups. When Ian asked me if I would like to join I said I'd love to because just hearing them play altogether is… it's something you don't hear on sessions, it's a group. When they all start together it is just fantastic, magic really. And I would like to work with them in the studio as well. It's hard to break into a band that has been together for twenty years, but it is very enjoyable. And Ian has been great, he's given me a free hand, and I really couldn't wish for anything that would be more enjoyable, more of what I was looking for.

Chapter 6

MARTIN BARRE

(Published in Issue #13, January 1988)

AND's first interview with guitarist Martin Barre was conducted by DR and MW during a brief break in rehearsals for the September 1987 tour, shortly after the release of the album Crest Of A Knave.

Martin actually started the interview himself, in the best possible way... by praising A New Day...

I'm pleased to do this interview with you – I think you are doing a good job for the fans who would otherwise get very little information... and it's nice that Ian has given you that recognition too.

Maybe that is because he knows we are on his side. If we do criticise it is I hope constructive criticism.
Oh yes. The things I've read I've enjoyed... you were fairly straight down the line about Milton Keynes, and I thought you were right as well. It did us a lot of harm.

Being the support band?
In a lot of ways. It was light when we went on, it was the first show of the 'tour', and it wasn't... great. You don't do your most important show on the first date, you should do a warm-up or somewhere a bit less important. But it wasn't good. We were supposed to be second on the bill, but it looked like we were third, and I think a lot of Tull fans felt it was not good enough for them. It didn't look good, it wasn't us giving our best, and you shouldn't do that. But then we all agreed to do it so that is just the way it goes. But I thought your piece was good. I would rather hear honest opinions like "not a good single" or "shouldn't play that song" etc, and I think people who read your mag like it too. They do not want everything biased because it doesn't ring true. If it is backed up with reasoned criticism it creates interest. One thing that really annoys me is when people are condescending... if you talk to people who are just SO into Tull but it is not just a genuine support of the band, it is almost fanatical. I mean, nobody is that perfect. It is very nice, very flattering; but then again it's not, because it is not a very objective support because it is so over the top. There is black and white in all things – not everything is great.

If we could talk for a while about *Crest Of A Knave*. It features you much more than the last few Tull albums. Has that made it more enjoyable for you to make?
Yes, I did enjoy it. Since *Broadsword* I've come to enjoy making albums a lot more than I did. I used to hate them, partly due I think to being a bit in awe of recording studios, and of being afraid to fail. Failing in a recording studio means there is no let-off. Onstage you have got a bit of leeway, you can get away with things, make the odd mistake and things can still sound better than they are. But in a studio things probably sound worse than they are – you can't get away with anything. And I had the sort of studio attitude where I was relying too much on the guy in the control room. I was too neurotic about sounds, and it really only changed when I started setting up my own studio in Devon, and I found out that when you plugged in an amp and guitar, stuck it down a channel and switched out the eq you got exactly the guitar sound that you were playing. And I thought well hang on... these people get you playing a riff for an hour to get a certain sound, but really there is no problem. It was all wrong, and you realise that the right attitude to have in a studio is that all that gear is there to enhance what you are already achieving rather than fighting against it. And so it all really changed at that point. I knew I could get a good sound, so if the guy in there couldn't get it then I'd go and do it myself.

That was around 1982 then?
Yes, about then. And with Peter [Vettese] being in the band... his musical input to the band excited me more than anybody's – apart from Ian, of course, because Ian is like the core of everything. But the different input of other players that have been and gone that I have not always felt at one with... I mean, I have always enjoyed playing Jethro Tull music but I would not say that I have always been dedicated to everybody's ideas. I would go along with them and enjoy playing them, I'd do my best. But while Peter was with us I felt that he helped me a lot with my own playing. So the last few years have built up my confidence in my playing, and I enjoy playing more. I've worked harder at it, and I think it culminated with this new album, which was really me, Ian and Dave sitting in the studio with no outsiders. Water finds its own level and I think we found it with this album. A lot of nice ingredients, a lot of pleasant days in the studio when it all came very easily and knitted together well.

Were you involved with the writing of the songs?
Well... Ian writes the songs and we build the music around them, and it is rather pointless to say, you know, you wrote that little riff or that little solo.

Peter Vettese has been well credited in the past for writing contributions...
Yes, but Peter did have a strong writing influence, particularly with Ian's solo LP and *Under Wraps* – although on *Under Wraps* I virtually wrote most of one song... er...

Paparazzi?
Yes, that's right. And I kind of co-wrote another.

Paparazzi **was the best track on the album – it should have been a single.**
Yes, it's a bubbly song. I liked it because it seemed out of all of them to be a bit more of a group thing, a Jethro Tull identity. There are some great things on that album, but when I hear it I can tell it is wrong. Not the right thing for us to have done. But you just get so involved doing an album, when you are in the studio for a year or so you desperately believe in what you are doing. You get so involved in it that you can't step outside of it and judge it in a fair way.

I love the album actually, although I do find myself in the minority of Tull fans.
It is hard work to listen to, you've really got to concentrate, and I don't think people want that, they don't want to have to work at being entertained. I think that people want to sit back, eat a meal, have a drink...

A lot of Tull fans though are prepared to make the effort. *A Passion* **Play for example was enjoyable because it did take a lot of listening to. And a lot of people did come to appreciate** *Under Wraps* **eventually...**
Yes, I know what you are saying, but it was still probably not a good decision. It is very selfish to produce albums like that because you are catering for a minority rather than going for everybody, which is what music is all about. I don't think there should be any snobbery or elitism about it, I think music is... well, pop music, popular music for everybody.

So was it a conscious decision to make *Crest Of A Knave* **a more orthodox rock album?**
I don't think it was a conscious decision. It wasn't like sitting down and saying, "This is what we ought to do...", but I think coincidentally it was what Ian, Dave and myself wanted to play. We were of one accord as to the sort of album we wanted to do. It is very easy to think what you need to do and try to come up with riffs that sound like *Aqualung*, but inevitably they sound terrible, because if you are that consciously trying to do something there is no natural feel; whereas this album has a tremendous feel to it. There are lots of really gutsy pieces on it. You can listen to it and feel the emotion coming from it.

Have you felt frustrated between albums? Three years is a long time.
Very much so. Ian has a lot of outside interests, whereas I haven't really. I've never been a successful businessman or bought whatever other musicians buy etc. So I have always wanted

to do other things… there's not enough for me in the 'fallow years' if you like. I've had a few little things that I've done, odd sessions that I have really enjoyed. I've always enjoyed the challenge of being stuck in the deep end with something that would probably scare the pants off me, but I just have to think well, "Go for it", and usually something good comes out of it.

Who were they for?
Ah well, I'll have to think… The only one that really comes to mind was that Paul McCartney thing, but I don't really like talking about it. It was a very exciting week and I really enjoyed it, but I don't want to spout on about working with him unless the sessions appear on record. But other than odd sessions here and there, which don't come to mind at present, I just work in my studio at home. Of course I don't get paid for that, it is speculative work. And I suppose it was a bit unfortunate that I did one set of songs that were really fairly dismal and slung them round the record companies and… they slung them back at me! Last year I did some more of mine which I felt were a lot better, and probably closer to what I needed to do, but we got involved then with this album which took longer than I'd expected. And other, personal things - like babies - happened, and unfortunately your own projects always get put to the end of the queue. And also the studio in Devon was being hired out. I mean, really it is a load of excuses for not working round the clock. I don't like to work past eleven at night, whereas I should have done. So the solo album is "on the shelf" at the moment I'm afraid.

Do you think if you had the occasional 'Anderson/Barre' credit for some songs it would have given you more clout with the record companies?
I don't think so. I think they are very cold, calculating people. Your tape is put on the machine, if you are lucky, and within the first minute, on the merits of what they hear they are going to put their money on the line or move onto the next tape.

Regardless of your track record?
I think so, yes. I think there is too much at stake. And considering our age, our appeal, our image, I think it is a very… take it as they find it type of thing. But you know, it doesn't worry me, it's fine by me.

Are they all your own songs?
Yes. I would only do my own music. Mostly I end up with instrumental music – the songs were not that particularly successful. I'm not really a songwriter, more a music writer.

What style is it? Can you categorise it?
It's all styles. One thing will be very classical sounding, the next maybe rock – whatever comes to mind on the day I'm in the studio, so it is a sort of hotchpotch of different musical influences and tastes. I'm a weird sort of player really, I like a lot of different things, and I don't make a conscious effort to come up with something. I should do really, I'd be a lot more directional and probably come up with something that is a lot easier to come to terms with as a concept, but I don't seem to be able to do that.

Have you thought of going to a smaller, independent record company?
Yes. I'm sure I can get a deal, but I'm not worried about that. I'll know when I have the product that it the right thing, and I haven't yet. I will be aware of it before the record companies are, and the only thing that can happen is that I've got something that I really believe in, that I know is right and is the best work I can do, and at that point I'll start at the big record companies and work down, and if I can't get a deal I'll just release it independently myself.

So we will get to hear it eventually?
I would hate to promise you that… Yes - but it might take a few years. Or there is next year, which is not going to be very busy.

Isn't it though? There is talk of some sort of 20th Anniversary celebration.

Oh, I don't know anything about that. Really the things that are important to me are the things that happen with Jethro Tull. But it could be a hobby… I might release an album that sells a thousand copies, but that is not really work, until I become an entity and command a living in my own right. But that is just speculative and I can't rely on that in any form whatsoever. Right now the new Tull album is what is important to me. I mean I really feel that I'm very much a part of this album, much more than the others where I am sort of on the periphery of it all. I really feel I belong on this album, I have a very strong feeling that my neck is on the line as much as Ian's, whose neck is usually 90% on the line because his input to albums is a lot stronger than anybody else's. But I feel that it's my playing… there's a lot of me in there. I'm happy, I'm glad I'm in that situation, so all my energy and hopes lie within the success, hopefully, of this album and the tour.

Did you hear Tommy Vance play a track from the album last week? He singled you out for particular praise, saying you were one of the best guitarists in the world.
I didn't hear that, but that's nice. He has always liked us – he was a great friend of John Glascock. I've met him and he is a very nice chap, and it is very nice that he said that. And as I say, I feel that it is a great album. And while on the one hand I thought *Under Wraps* was great and, because you get so involved in it, it is very hard to believe that your own opinion is worth considering, I'm much too biased about it… but for what it's worth I feel stronger than ever about this album.

Have you ever made an album that you thought was… umm… duff?
Duff? No, I wouldn't say that. I mean, I'm always disappointed with my playing. I never do anything that I can listen to and think I couldn't do better, but I think that is true of most people. I think Ian is the same – we are very similar in the way we criticise our own music and our own playing, we are very much at one in that respect. But I have always felt some disappointment… more so when I am very disappointed in some tracks where there is not really much input from the guitar and I think there should be a lot more there. I am not an assertive person, my personality just does not have an assertive nature to it, whereas Ian has a very strong personality and I have to let that go into my music, into my playing, which is a terrible mistake. Other than when I'm on stage, where I always give it stick, but in the studio I tend to sit back, be a bit afraid and let things happen. It is a bad mistake to make.

Do you think Ian might have mellowed over the years and become more prepared to listen to your ideas?
I think Ian has always had an ear for ideas, but if there is somebody else with an idea you can't wait around forever for somebody to come up with a middle eight or something. Whoever comes up with one that works first then that is the one you use. And that is what it is down to – you are sitting in a room playing away and the first guy who says, "Hey, what about this?"… well, that is what it is all about really. Obviously it is easier for me when there's just me, Dave and Ian, but with somebody like Peter Vettese of Eddie Jobson, well they are lightning quick, there is music there immediately, they have a mental filing cabinet full of musical ideas, and so it is very hard to get in first. You are still thinking about it and they have already got the rest of the song while you're still trying to find a good key. So maybe that is why this album has been better for me. With just me and Ian it was easier to think it out around the guitar parts with no distractions.

Have you ever thought of leaving Jethro Tull? You did an interview a few years ago where you sounded very disillusioned...
Oh, I know the one, I remember the interview. I think I get depressed about myself, but I don't think I get angry or negative about Jethro Tull as such – always about myself. I mean, I never pass the buck – if I'm not playing well I never try to blame it on anyone else. Of course, it would be stupid to do so. It is just like everybody though. Everybody gets fed up of being on the road, or going to the office, travelling to London. I get fed up with travelling from Devon every week, living out of a suitcase. That hasn't happened for a while now of course. But I have my up and down periods, with Ian as well. We've had good years, and years that have been a little distant, but then that's OK, it doesn't matter, because the important thing is

that now, and over the last few years, we are closer than ever, and we have a real, sympathetic relationship with each other as far as music goes... well, in all aspects really.

Did you read the interview Ian did with us where he said he couldn't do it without you in the band?
Yes, that's a very nice thing to hear. I'm very pleased, it's a nice situation to arrive at. I always think that musicians are very replaceable. I've always thought it was a mistake to think you are irreplaceable, unique. Not just in Tull, but anybody. To think that nobody can challenge your job is a bad attitude to have because it means you might get a bit slack. I'm always working harder to play better, I won't sit back. I have done that in the past, but I won't now. I did maybe ten, fifteen years ago; but now, if only for my own satisfaction, I just need to improve as a player. I enjoy other people's playing too much for me to sit back and not work hard at what I do. I've always enjoyed playing with Jethro Tull, but as a guitarist I've got a very varied taste in music, and because of that I would enjoy playing a lot of different things. I hear other music and other players and I would really like to play with them, but I never really have. In the early years Jethro Tull were very solitary in their musical careers, never really mixed with other groups or did sessions and sat in jamming. We never did any of that at all, which never really bothered me, but now I'd enjoy it, I really would. I've always liked a lot of different types of music.

Anybody in particular?
No, anybody. I mean anybody good! I like any good music. There are a few musical styles that I don't go wild over, which I'd better not say again [*laughing*]. Every time I talk about folk music it always comes out sounding very derogatory about Dave, and it is very unfair to be that way – especially as he is standing on the other side of this door! But things like country music I just don't play well. Whether I like it or not I just don't play that music. In fact, folk... there's a lot of stuff that Fairport play that I could not play to save my life, I just could not play them technically. Very, very hard things. Maybe if I sat down and wanted to play them I could do so, but my mind doesn't seem to take me in that direction.

Did you enjoy yourself at Cropredy?
I did, yes, I had a great time. I really enjoyed some of the other acts as well. I think Fairport are a very good band, and some of the people they had up there with them I really enjoyed. I think Jerry Donahue is a great player.

Dave Pegg told me a story about that. The 'Hush Puppy' advert...
Oh yes. I heard it in the cinema, this lovely bit of guitar playing, and so the next time I went I took my tape-recorder with me. He is a great player. And I did enjoy the day at Cropredy, it was very relaxed and I enjoyed it a lot. I'm really looking forward to getting out and playing the next album. We'll do as much as possible from it and it is really strong stuff.

We've got to ask you this... One criticism of the album has been the 'Dire Straits' sound...
Well, yes... you see, it is a sound that has been made famous by Mark Knopfler. I mean, it doesn't bother me and so I'm not worried about it.

It wasn't deliberate then?
Well... it is a style of music. I can hear heavy metal players and, without mentioning names, they all sound the same. It is as relevant to me as saying one of those players sounds the same as whoever it was that started that style of playing. And I find that less forgivable, if you are going to criticise, because it is faceless playing really. It is all very good, there's a lot of great technical players and they play really well, but they just all sound the same and it could be anybody playing. And it lacks a lot of feeling. And there are a lot of people who play with the percussive strat sound that makes you immediately think of Mark Knopfler, but to me it is not particularly HIS style. It is a sound that he has made famous and probably he has 90% credit for. But I haven't suddenly started doing it, I started during the Broadsword album, or maybe even before that, I started playing a Strat. And that is the sound of a Strat, that's the best

sound you can get on a Strat, so really I did it as a way of getting a few different sounds on the album. I'm always looking for new ideas and sounds, as is every guitar player. So it has always been there really. The whole style of the song you are talking about lends itself towards Dire Straits.

Ian's vocals are a bit reminiscent of that too.
Well yes, I can't argue with it. I see what they are saying and it strikes me that way as much as anybody else, but I just take it on its own merit. It wouldn't worry me. Whatever is right for a song is right. It didn't need a guitar turned up to 10, it is very soft and held back, very melodic, and that is melodic playing. The blues played melodically. The pentatonic scale as everybody knows doesn't have many notes in it and there isn't a lot you can do with it; you are creating melody from it. I mean, they are all stock phrases, they are not particularly Mark Knopfler's phrases. They might be BB King's or Freddie King's originally, but because they use a slightly different sound you might not recognise it as such. That sort of stylised playing goes back a lot further than Mark Knopfler. They are all stock blues licks turned around.

I think it is just the initial impression, but of course that is what a reviewer makes his judgement on...
Yes, you are right. But, you know, I stand by it as much as I stand by anything that Tull do. There is nothing that I would disown and it would be very wrong of me to do so. If it goes onto the multi-track it is my decision as much as Ian's, and we all stand or fall by everything really, and I'm pleased to do so – particularly with this album.

Do you still enjoy playing live?
Yes, more than ever. I've rarely had problems playing live within the group. We've had hard times, personality-wise, with line-ups, a long time ago, but once they were sorted out Ian noticeably enjoyed playing live a lot more. I remember in the early days being in a limo with Ian... I wonder if he remembers it... when he dramatically said that he could cry some nights, it's so bad. And he really meant it...

The actual performance?
Yes, the playing. Ian is a tremendous perfectionist, his standards are impeccable. He asks more of himself than anybody could and he doesn't particularly impose that on other people. He is very sympathetic about what people can and cannot do, what their capabilities are. He has an amazing honesty with music and the quality of the stuff that he does; there is nothing thrown away. I can think of many bands who really do throw away tracks that sound like it took them a day to do, and you can tell they just leave it as it is just to get it done. He has never done that. He couldn't do it, it's just not in his make-up, and you have to admire that.

Does that ever drive you mad?
No. Not at all, because it drives you to and beyond your own limits of perfection, and while I wouldn't say that mine are as high as Ian's it has made me aim higher and higher. It is a great attitude. Whereas I go for feel more than performance - feel against performance more than Ian would - it has still helped me to look beyond my own capabilities. And as for playing live, it is all related to whether or not Ian is enjoying it. He is right at the centre of everything and if that guy is not having a great time and loving the music then whatever you feel you cannot enjoy it either. I've always loved and enjoyed playing the guitar, but you have to take that into consideration. But I feel Ian is happier now than ever and mainly because of that so am I. And apart from that I think that I, as a player, have improved more in the last few years than ever. I feel I can go out and give 'em their money's worth as a guitarist, whereas before I've always lacked the confidence and, to me, rightly so. I've always felt I wasn't really 100% and, as I said, Ian and I are our own greatest critics.

Has it helped being 'off the treadmill' now?
Well no, it hasn't helped me at all. That is why I am always looking for other things to do. It wasn't like a treadmill really because when we used to work that intensely we didn't have families and homes to worry about.

Since the *A* album Tull has had 'floating personnel'. Has that been a deliberate policy?

I don't think it is now. The nucleus of the band is me, Ian and Dave, and I think we would like to have a keyboard player that we used all the time; ideally it would be nice if he was part of the band. But it is dangerous to plan ahead. People like Don Airey and Peter have so many things they want to do. I mean, Peter literally did not want to tour.. He turned down Go West as well, so it wasn't anything personal. He just didn't want to go on the road, and really he doesn't want to be in the studio either... in fact, I don't know what he wants to do. He has an idea of what he wants to do and that's that. And I'm sure people like Don Airey are the same. They are very good players with limitless possibilities as musicians. I mean, he might want to go and do film scores next year, but as it happens he hasn't been on the road for a long time, he has been in the studio doing sessions for everybody and getting a bit fed up of it, so it is like a breath of fresh air for him. But I am optimistic. I know it always sounds good, but I'm optimistic that this line-up is going to be more than that. I've got a really good feeling about this one, and while we've always had really strong bands for tours I feel this will be even better.

Have you a favourite track on *Crest Of A Knave*?

No, not really. I think it is all really good stuff.

I thought Ric Sanders played on two tracks, but he is only credited on *Budapest*...

Um... he played on *The Waking Edge* too, which is on the cassette and CD. He was only involved in the later stages of the album so there wasn't a lot of time to experiment with the possibility of using more violin, but I think when the song was evolving we both thought we heard a violin in the part that he played as being a good idea right from the start. The whole album has got a lot of good elements of Jethro Tull in it. I think *Jump Start* is a bit evocative of *This Was* or *Stand Up*, or *Benefit*, the kind of bluesy feel to it. I love that album, *Benefit*. There are some great songs on that album. Of all the ones that I can play and enjoy I think that is probably the one I enjoy the most. And then again I think *Budapest* takes the best ideas of *Thick As A Brick*, a continuous piece of music that diversifies but has little themes in it. It brings back into Tull the *Brick/Passion Play* element, and I think it is the right sort of length. I don't think you can do any more than that nowadays. You couldn't go and do another *A Passion Play* because that is not what people want at all.

It's a shame.

Is it? I don't know... I could criticise those albums, the arranging of them etc, that would be very easy to do. Very meandering, I feel. When nobody else was doing it, when it was new, it worked very well, but I don't think it would work now. I don't think people would think they were getting their money's worth. I'm sure that Ian feels the same way. It was right at the time.

Can we expect a higher media profile with this album and tour? In fact, would you want that?

Well yes. We have never shied from the media. Ian works really hard at it. He's got so many interviews, a really frightening schedule. The unfortunate thing about Tull is that people go for Ian, and that has always upset me. That has always been a bit of a bee in my bonnet, and yet in a way I'm glad I don't have to do it. I would hate to do what Ian does, it is bloody hard work. And really everybody knows that Ian IS Jethro Tull, we all know that, but it does have its disappointing side, where perhaps Ian can't make an interview and so they say, "You can have Martin Barre instead", and the answer comes back, "No thanks"! You know, nobody would like that, and I don't like it. It is 20 years of my life as well and I find it a bit insulting. But everyone has their own chip on their shoulder and I suppose that is mine. It is fair in one way because Ian is the king-pin, but in another way it is a bit of an insult. But really the media profile is down to Chrysalis, and they handle it through Ian. Ian is their artist even though it is actually Jethro Tull.

But Chrysalis don't do much to promote Jethro Tull – people don't know that they still exist.

It is very easy to criticise Chrysalis. I won't do that now, but they have certainly let us down and given us a very low profile on the last couple of albums. But then they haven't done well and maybe they would argue that *Under Wraps* was not a commercial album; there was no single, no radio play. And radio would have played it in America if they liked it. So they could come back with that. They have probably got an answer. But I would certainly say that if they don't do a lot with this album then there is no forgiving that at all, no justification whatsoever. And if anybody wants to interview me I'll do it. Both me and Dave Pegg are really keen to do what we can to promote the album. There is no snobbery, we are not saying, "Look, this is the album, it is great - if you don't like it, up yours!" We have never been like that, never would be.

You need a couple of TV slots to let people know you are still about. Maybe the programme last night [*Fish'n'Sheep'n'Rock'n'Roll*] will help?
Yes, but that was just Ian's involvement with the TV people, nothing to do with promotion from Chrysalis. It was nice that the new LP was in it, but it is unfortunate that there was no half-minute advert from Chrysalis for the album. But it is a shame, because it was a band signed to Chrysalis, and now it's really just Ian signed to Chrysalis. There is no communication between me and Chrysalis, or anybody else in the band and Chrysalis, and all the promotion is done via Ian, so he has got a lot on his plate, and unfortunately that is just the way it is now. People look to Ian for interviews and they don't really know or care who else is in the band. You have to admit it has changed a lot so you can't really expect them to know who the keyboard player is THIS year. But it's a shame because it is a BAND – that's not a solo album, that's a band playing there. And I hope Chrysalis will try to accept that a bit more... I'm sure they won't, though. It is very easy to grouse, but I hope it doesn't come across that I'm the sort of person who begrudges not having more limelight. I mean, it doesn't bother me. I'd rather be at home with the kids than flying off to New York to do twenty interviews in a day, but there is the odd occasion where it does upset me.

Would you like Tull to get back to the No 1 album/hot single status, or do you feel that you have struck the perfect balance of success and personal privacy?
I would like everybody to buy the new album. I can't think of anybody who wouldn't want that, especially for us because there is no pampering to young fans – the kind of Duran Duran syndrome where you have got to manufacture that sort of product, present that image to kids 24 hours a day. But at our stage of the game you are totally in control of what you do. It would be wonderful, the best thing that could happen to us. There is no wish to be a minority music martyr. Not because we want to make more and more money, but because I want people to hear the music. Well alright, of course I want to make money as well... I'm not stupid. But when anybody buys the album it is a compliment, be it a granny or a six-year old kid. Music is for everybody. I hate music that is clever-clever and selfish; it annoys me. I don't admire music that doesn't get across to a lot of people, there is no credit in that. Bach, Beethoven and Mozart were the pop composers of their time, and it is wonderful stuff, and there is no reason why... I mean, there are big hit albums that are great music – Dire Straits, Phil Collins – there are a lot of good albums that reach No 1. Alright, there's a lot of rubbish, but there's a lot of good pop music around. I don't resent anybody getting to No 1. I don't hear people and think, "That's bloody awful – what a load of bastards for selling all those albums when they could have bought ours instead." You know... I buy it as well, and enjoy it.

Will we have to wait another three years for the next Tull album?
Oh God, I hope not. No, I'm sure, having spoken with Ian, that we are going to do something every year. Not necessarily an album... I'd hate to stick my neck out, but we will probably do another album, or start another album in autumn 1988. If this album does well that would be a good start towards doing another album, knowing that people do like what we are doing.

But surely that is where Chrysalis should get their act together? *Crest Of A Knave* **has just entered the UK chart at No 20, and that initial success should be followed up to ensure that other people at least get the chance to hear it.**

Yes, we always get a good chart placing when it comes out. All the Tull fans rush out to buy it, and then it disappears. The hardcore Tull fans are wonderful and you really could not wish for better fans; but you have to look beyond that, you have got to go for everybody. And I know a lot of people would enjoy it and I feel sad if they are not going to get the chance to hear it.

There is a possible hit single too if it gets a bit of airplay [*Steel Monkey*].
Well that is something that is out of my comprehension really. I don't know what is a hit single... well, I do know, but I've never heard a hit single where I've thought, "We could have done that". They seem to be the sort of songs that we just don't do.

I still think *Paparazzi* would have been a hit.
Yes, maybe. But anyway... I don't know them but I wouldn't trust the people at Chrysalis, in the UK at least, to judge what should be released as a single, mainly because they picked out *Broadsword* from that album. If I have ever heard a song that is NOT a single then *Broadsword* is the song. Everything was wrong about that for a single. Whoever thought THAT was a single??

We have thought for a long time it is always the least likely track that comes out. But doesn't the band have a say in what is chosen?
Well you know, they pay the money so they get the choice. But I mean... *Broadsword* s a single! Ever since then I've worried about Chrysalis.

So have we.
But they have changed around a lot in the last couple of years so maybe there's someone there with a bit more imagination. Someone with the guts and intelligence to pick the right music. Well, *Steel Monkey* is the single so obviously they have gone for the right one. Then the rest is down to us – and the radio stations.

Chapter 7

DOANE PERRY

(Published in Issues #13 & #14, January 1988)

After a period in which Jethro Tull used four different drummers in three years, Doane Perry joined the band in 1984, since when he has been the largely resident occupant of the percussion seat. Or, indeed, the large resident occupant. In the introduction to his 1988 interview in A New Day *we described him as a 33-year old nine feet tall New Yorker. Doane is actually "only" about six feet five inches, but inevitably we did get letters asking if he really was nine feet tall…*

DR and MW interviewed Doane over a curry in an Indian restaurant in Slough. Although tired after a long day in the studios rehearsing for the September UK tour, he covered a wide range of subjects at some length, pausing only to snatch mouthfuls of his soup and extra hot curry. In fact, such was his enthusiasm that the resultant interview had to be presented across two issues.

How did you come to join the band?

I don't want to bore your readers who may have read the story elsewhere, so I'll try and give you a condensed version, if it's at all possible.

I was actually quite a fan of the band, as you may or may not know, before I joined them. I'd seen the group and Clive Bunker play many times, and I really loved the music. And in fact when my friend Mark Craney got the gig for the *A* album and tour I was so excited for him. I told him, "Great, Mark, that is fantastic," and I almost felt like I had the gig, because he was my friend and he was doing it, it was wonderful. He's a wonderful player, that boy. Anyway, sometime in 1983 an advert appeared in *The Village Voice*, a slightly underground, slightly left American weekly publication. A friend called me up and said, "You're not going to believe this, but I was talking on the 'phone to a friend who happened to be reading the Wanted ads on the back of *The Village Voice*…" It was an amazing coincidence, because I don't generally read it, and my friend wouldn't necessarily. And he said, "Hey, check this out, 'Ian Anderson looking for a drummer'." It was a very funny tongue-in cheek Monty Python-type ad. This guy read it to my friend who said, "Wait a minute, I should call Doane and tell him about this, because Doane is a great fan of the band." So he told me - I was in California, so I certainly wouldn't have seen the ad - and I actually didn't do anything about it for a couple of days. At first I was a little confused because I thought maybe it was for a solo tour or something, as Ian's solo album had just come out. I figured a million people would be sending tapes in. But then I thought about it over the weekend, and mentioned it to somebody, and they said, "Doane, you're crazy, you're perfect for it. You've had lots of experience, you know the music, you're a working professional - you have a really good chance." At that point I was really more of a session player. I'd done quite a few records at that point, and quite a few major tours, so I wasn't like just a guy off the street or some guy in a basement looking for a big break. I had worked at a certain level for several years. So I thought well, if he's actually put an ad in an American newspaper he's probably tried people in England and hasn't got one, so he's now looking over here; so I suppose I have as good a chance as anybody.

Anyway, I called Chrysalis and said, "Is this for Ian Anderson's solo tour?" and they said, "No, it's for Jethro Tull," and I said, "Oh, my God!" But they said, "However, we've got so many tapes here that if you don't get one in by Friday that's the last bunch that's going out." So I thought OK, I'd better get on - it was like Tuesday at this point. So I put together a compilation tape of a lot of different things I'd played on from rock'n'roll to jazz to pop stuff, some of which had been hits to varying degrees. There was probably a large percentage of stuff on there that he wouldn't necessarily like, but I figured that if nothing else it would show that I can play different styles reasonably well. And I also sent an album that I'd done with my own band called Maxus that I was actually fairly proud of at the time, in that it represented something of some personal measure of accomplishment. We were on Warner

Brothers - it was kind of like a rock'n'roll Steely Dan, a really good band; it was a shame that dissolved. But unfortunately everybody in the band was like a session player and was always getting called to do everybody else's stuff, and made a lot of money doing it; so the commitment to the band as a unit was not as strong as, say, five guys who all they've got is their band.

Anyway, I mustn't get too sidetracked. So I sent this record and tape to Chrysalis in New York, and I also happened to call a friend of mine who was like a VP at Chrysalis and had produced some of the tracks I'd done with Pat Benatar some years before. He also knew that I was quite a Tull fan, and he said, "I was trying to get hold of you, I didn't know where you were or what you were doing, or if you were available or even interested, but I did think of you." Whether or not that was actually true, I don't really know, but I said I'd sent a tape, and he said, "OK, I'll be talking to Ian, and I'll tell him to be on the lookout for it." This was just before Christmas. And then sometime after Christmas I happened to be out at my great aunt and uncle's house on Long Island, on a Sunday afternoon, and I didn't think anybody actually knew I was out there. The 'phone rang, and they were dozing in the living room, so I picked up the 'phone expecting it to be Mrs Yehudi or someone from down the road. And this voice says [*affecting outrageous growling English accent*], "Hello, is Doane Perry there?" I recognised Ian's voice straight away, and I was really surprised that he had found me, and I was a little surprised that he had called, because it was one of those things where I thought, you know, I'll be really amazed if it happens. But he explained that they were still looking, and trying to narrow it down. They had a couple of people to see how they went on, but he asked me if I might possibly be free in two weeks or so to come over and audition, depending on how these other people worked out. We talked for about 45 minutes, and he was real nice, just basically told me what they were looking for, and asked me if I played double bass drum, and so on. Then after we got off the 'phone I had a kind of a strong feeling that I might get the gig; you know, if it's gotten to the point where he's rung me up now, I was confident enough in my ability to play the music, and hopefully convey that to them, to be able to think that I stood a reasonable chance of getting the gig. Anyway, they kept calling back and saying, "So-and-so hasn't worked out, and it's narrowing down." Obviously it would have been more economical for them to have a British person in the band, so I was thinking well, would have been a shame having gotten that close - I would rather not have got near at all, or not even heard from them, if it had gone that way. But as it was they called back one weekend and said, "Listen, could you come over on Monday, and here are the songs you're to learn."

So I went over, and I must say I was incredibly jet-lagged. I didn't sleep much the night before and had to play a really dreadful set of drums at the audition because my stuff was held up at Customs and didn't come until half way through the day. At the audition, to my mind, I didn't play very well. They seemed to think it was OK, but I was mentally not completely there. I think I played all the songs OK, but then they threw some new things at me that they were working on to see what I could do with that. The next weekend they were due to play with a famous name English drummer, and I thought, oh well, if he's in the running for it there's no chance I'm going to get it, because he's a really great drummer. But for one reason or another he wasn't really right for the band. If anything, I think this guy plays with more of an American feel, i.e. he plays more to the centre, to the front of the beat, while with all my musical influences, which were predominantly British, my drumming tends to be more from the centre of the beat to the back of the beat, which fits better with Jethro Tull. I don't know at the end of the day if that was the reason, or one of the reasons, but I think that maybe my feel being if anything more British than American possibly worked in my favour. But I was determined that I was going to get or lose the gig on my merit as… playing the music my own way, put it that way. Obviously Clive Bunker had been a great influence on my style, and Barrie Barlow to some extent too, but I really wanted to get the gig or lose the gig honestly; I didn't want to play too much like them, because I figured I'm not either of those players and they're going to have to deal with my style whatever they like or don't like about it. Trying to sound like one of the previous drummers would have really been the wrong thing to do. So at the end of the audition I knew I hadn't played as well as I could and I knew that I could actually play the music better, but fortunately they said they'd really like me to do the tour. So I came back four or five months later, and it worked out.

So that was kind of the *Reader's Digest* version…

That was the SHORT version??

[*Laughing*] That was the 45. Next time I'll give you the 12" long playing version!

On the back of the new album [*Crest Of A Knave*] it says, "Jethro Tull are Ian Anderson, Martin Barre and Dave Pegg," with a kind of a footnote, "Oh, by the way, Doane Perry played some drums." Did that upset you?

Good question. I must admit that when I saw that I was surprised, and I was very disappointed, because having done the record initially, the record went through a couple of changes. I definitely feel very much a part of the band, even though I'd not recorded with the band until this winter. But on a live level I contributed a lot to the live show; I felt that was something that I had the ability to… I wasn't just a sideman, y'know, it wasn't like, "Just sit back there and play what I tell you to play." There were certain things I learned the way they were supposed to be, but other things… I think I was hired for my ability to interpret the music as an individual and not to be a side man - I never really regarded myself as a sideman in this band, and that was disappointing and a little distressing when I saw that, because I thought, you know, what happened here? That's something that I obviously hope will change in the future.

Have you mentioned it to Ian?

No, but I intend bringing it up at some point - certainly I hope before this interview comes out! But it's something I couldn't just let go by, because I feel that I contribute a lot to the band in a live sense - and when we were recording we all had a lot of input, and there were certainly many ideas that I had when we were recording, even if those weren't the ideas that actually ended up on the record. As far as arrangement ideas, everybody's got used, and some of mine were used on there too, and I was glad of that. I feel that I have a lot more to offer the band than just being like a sideman who can pick up music quickly and keep his mouth shut. I've been through that, and I don't really relish being a sideman for the rest of my life. I enjoy being in a band, particularly this band. There are very few other bands that if I was given a choice I would join. This is what I want to be doing right now, I really enjoy this; and I don't take that for granted, and I hope I'm not taken for granted in the band. When we're playing live I think that the band is aware that I supply a lot of energy and a lot of drive - otherwise I wouldn't still be here, they wouldn't have asked me back.

I will say one thing - maybe I shouldn't! - but I reckon they're probably lucky to have someone like me in the band, who injects a pretty good amount of enthusiasm by virtue of the fact that I'd been a fan of the band, and I know the music very well. Some of it I can even do without the benefit of rehearsals or listening to tapes, because I know the songs. I think they're lucky to have someone who's not just like a hired gun who plays the stuff by rote, but who really enjoys playing it, and can play it with the enthusiasm and the excitement that a band like this needs to get the music across. I'm glad to be here doing that, and I think [*laughing*] that they're lucky to have me! I don't want that to be taken too seriously, but you know what I mean - when the other guys read it, they'll probably go, "Oh, piss off!"

But to answer your question, when we were rehearsing for the record my mother was getting very ill, so I went home to America, and unfortunately she died. This was a very important record, obviously, but the band were very nice, they waited; they told me to go home and take as long as I needed, and we'd do it when I came back. So I had to come back on the heels of that, and try to finish the album in a little over a week - we had to get the tracks done as we were breaking for Christmas, and Dave was doing his Fairport Convention stuff, and everybody was going away, and so on. So they were working on stuff at Dave's studio with the drum machine while I was away. I came back and did all the tracks, and I wasn't happy with all my tracks. I'm incredibly critical about my recorded performance - and in that way it is really nice to work with someone like Ian who's probably just as critical as I am. He doesn't mind if I say I can do something again and better, he just says, "Go ahead, do it until you're happy." Obviously you have to draw the line somewhere, you can't just go on endlessly - you need somebody to say, "Wait a minute, that was good, we can use that one." But he's willing to go a bit of a distance to get that, and I appreciate that. He doesn't hammer at you, but he'll make suggestions, and I don't mind that, because it'll take me a while before I'm really happy. Every now and then I'll get a take which is just exactly the take I wanted on the first one, but more often than not it's maybe the third, fourth or fifth take when I'm really warmed up to it, and I'm really inside the track. And I was aware that there wasn't a lot of time - we were having to do at least a track a day. And at that stage *Budapest* was the whole side of a record; unfortunately some of the best recorded playing that I've done is on some of those out-takes. On the other hand there's some things where the sound is not so good, because I was like Robin Black's guinea pig. I was the first drummer he recorded after the drum machines, so it was a little tiring at times, because every twenty minutes he would be saying, "Can you hit that snare drum again." I'd got my drums to sound beautiful, but it just wasn't translating from the room to tape, so I had to keep stopping. You can lose a lot of energy when you're just whacking a snare drum for twenty minutes, and then it would be, "OK, are you ready to do the take?", and you're like, "Uuuh, yeah, I guess so." You can lose the spirit pretty quick! And that happened quite a bit, it didn't really flow at all, although it wasn't Robin's fault, he was just doing his job. He's a really nice guy. But I wasn't thrilled with the sounds we were doing. They wanted a kind of middle ground which they could make either really big or really small or whatever, so they didn't want anything too extreme. There were some tracks where I felt I could have used a bigger sound.

Anyway, I worked really hard, and in a way the work was therapeutic because all the events at home were in the back of my mind, and it was a very depressing time - and the weather was just depressing beyond belief - so I was in a fairly unhappy state when we were actually doing it. But I was trying to transcend that and enjoy doing the record, and really concentrate on getting through it. But there were definitely tracks that when we were doing them I wasn't 'connecting', I wasn't happy with some of them. A lot of the songs on the eventual album are different to what I originally recorded. *Budapest* got chopped down to ten minutes from the whole side of a record - and there were some amazing parts on it. In terms of a piece of music there were some really interesting things, but I think as a whole this record actually holds together much better, the songs are better than the things we recorded. What ended up from those original sessions is *Farm On The Freeway*, which is the very first track we cut, and was only the second or third take, I think. *Steel Monkey* - I played on the original part of that. Strangely enough I played a pretty straight part on that, and I remember Ian asking me to embellish it a bit; it was getting more and more busy, and I remember thinking, and I even said it to him at one point, "Don't you think it should be more straight ahead?" At that point there were no lyrics. I have to say as a footnote to this that it is a little strange working very backwards making a record. I'm always very plugged into the lyrics of a song, and that usually determines a lot of what I actually play. And not only do you not have any lyrics, but I at least try to get him to hum me a melody line. Having now heard the album with the lyrics on it and the melody lines I would definitely have played certain things very differently had I heard them first. But I'd have to say, "Am I walking all over you here?", and he'd say, "I'll let you know if there's anything where you're walking on my vocal or anything like that." So I'd be working in the dark, hearing no melody or lyrics. Every now and then we'd be in the control room and he'd hum a melody, and I'd go, "What was that, what was that?!" I'm very song-orientated, and I think once I find some emotional thread in the music, the music tells me what to play, I don't really have to think about it. I mean, I think it did anyway, but it was harder. Ian's used to working that way though. Then he goes home and writes the lyrics and the melody. Well that's the strangest thing to me, because I'm not used to working that way round.

He claims to write the lyrics the night before a recording.
He does! It's a really oddball way for me to work, but it's something I had to get used to. Anyway, I played on *Steel Monkey*, and I was more inclined to play a pretty straight part, but he wanted a lot of other stuff on there. I had no idea what the song would be about, and nobody knew it would be a single. When I heard an advance copy of the album there were no credits, so I didn't know what I'd played on and what was machine and what Gerry Conway had played on, so when I actually heard *Steel Monkey* I thought oh, there's my part. As I listened to it, I thought good, it's got on there, but he's changed the EQ on my snare, he's got a good fat snare sound. And it was only after listening to *Steel Monkey* three times that it dawned on me, and I thought, "Wait a minute, I don't think that's me playing!" I think Ian took like the shape of my part and definitely used certain bits from it in terms of phrasing and

part of the bridge and certain fills. And it was disappointing, because had I been able to get that kind of sound in the studio I could certainly have played a part like that. In a way I feel like I did play on the song because there's certain elements of my playing that are definitely on there, though I'm not credited as such. Ian might take umbrage at that or take issue with me, but that's my feeling about it.

We asked Martin about credits, because it just says "Songs by Ian Anderson", and we got the impression that it's all built in the studio - Ian comes in with a song, but the music is a group effort...

Well, it certainly is in terms of the arrangement and in terms of form changes and so on. Ian might come in with the body of a song, and have the basic framework for it, and then we'll take that and adjust it, and change bars or chords here and there and shift things around. Ian definitely writes the lion's share of things, but Dave and Martin have a lot of input, and Peter did when he was there.

Anyway, to wrap up your question about the album, I played on an original version of *Jump Start* - that was a really good track. It was very simple, I didn't play a lot on it, but it was one of those things that I felt like I had really got the part nicely, and that I had done a good job on it, and I was pretty pleased with that. But it actually ended up getting rewritten with this whole acoustic thing at the front and in the middle, so they couldn't really use my part, because form-wise it's completely different now. So I feel bad about that abstractly, because my original part was really good; had that song gone on the record that way I hope they would have used my part as opposed to trying to redo it. I'm disappointed that some of my stuff didn't get on there from the point of view that people would go, "Wow, what was that?", because I took some chances and I really liked some of the stuff I played. Usually when I play on other people's records it's more like playing a pretty strict pop time-keeping role. We did a couple of other songs that didn't have titles or anything that weren't as good as the songs on the album, so those didn't even make it. The music for *Mountain Men* was originally part of the 20-minute version of *Budapest*. I played on the first half, and the second half on the record is actually drum machine. I actually remember doing the second half of it, but I remember that was one of the things that I wasn't happy with, and I don't know if that's why Ian didn't use it – I don't think Ian and I ever discussed that. But that was one thing on the recording that I didn't like my performance on very much, and it didn't go on the actual album, so I don't feel so bad. It actually sounds slightly disjointed to me in that the drum sounds change and it doesn't sound like the same person playing to me because of the tuning of the drums, and just the attack. If there's any complaint I have with the album in terms of drum tracks – and I think Ian wanted to get different sounds – it is that there's not a continuity, in that the drum sounds change a lot, and it definitely doesn't sound like the same person. I think had I been around when they'd done the rest of the tracks it would have given it a bit more of a thread of continuity. I like what Gerry Conway plays, he's a very fine drummer, but I would have definitely played things a lot differently from what he did. He took some of my things from *Budapest*, the original sections which they used, and he definitely was trying to play some of what I played; he sort of interpreted it in his own way, but he took the shape of my part and used it on there. And there are other things that were changed, on other tracks. *Dogs In The Midwinter* wasn't even around then, nor *Said She was A Dancer*, that was written later. As I said, *Budapest* was one side long, and what we're playing as the outro music at the end of the concert was the end of the record, a real boiling shuffle thing – it's a shame it didn't make it onto the record. Incidentally, *Budapest* was only called that because we were sitting there discussing it, and Dave said something like, "When we get to the bit that goes [*sings*] da da da da etc…" It had a Hungarian folk feel to it, and having just done this gig in Budapest, it was sort of fresh in our minds, and we thought, oh, that bit is sort of Eastern European sounding. So after that Dave, when we got to that part in rehearsals, would say, "Do the Budapest section." So that's how, to my recollection, it got called *Budapest*, and the song got written around it.

But I have to agree with Ian, I don't think the sounds were right considering the kind of record we were trying to make. By the same token I think that even some of the drums recorded at Ian's are a bit thin and flat sounding for my taste, and that partly maybe is the way they were recorded, partly just the way Gerry tunes his drums. I suppose it's a little difficult for me because I put a lot of time into that record, apart from anything Ian decided he desperately wanted to use a drum machine for. But having played a lot with machines I certainly feel I could have played anything as good as the machines. Now whether that's a matter of taste…!

It seems strange to use a drum machine on a record when you've got to have a drummer on tour. Why use a drum machine when, in this case, two drummers were available?
Well, that's why *Under Wraps* was done like that, because there wasn't really a drummer at the time. Actually I really love some of the drum programming that Ian did on *Under Wraps*, and his own record – beautiful drum programming. I mean, it wasn't stuff that a human being could actually play, because I've tried to play some of that live, and you'd have needed to have two drummers at least to accomplish that on stage; you'd have to have ridiculous independence, and you'd also have to have at least another two limbs to accomplish it! But it was really creative stuff. I use drum machines all the time. I like playing to them, I like writing to them, and there's definitely a place for them. And I think Ian uses them much better than the average person who gets a drum machine and just goes, "Bom bah, bom bom bah" – I mean, big deal, y'know? He's not hindered by a drummer's conception of independence. I mean, if I'm programming a part sometimes I'll be trying to get it to sound like I'm actually playing, so I won't try to do something that's obviously impossible, like this is going across the bar, meanwhile there's this ridiculous roll going while this hi-hat part's going, and so on. But Ian is thinking in terms of parts – he'll say, "Well this would sound good against this", he's not worried about the fact that it's an absurd thing for a human being to actually try to play. So in a way, being guided by a concept as opposed to being hindered by a technique gives him much freer rein. I think that's why he writes really well with the drum machine. However, he uses the drum machine on this album in certainly a simpler way to give it more of a live feel, and I think that some of that stuff might have benefited a bit from real drums. And of course that's a completely unbiased viewpoint!
Anyway, getting back to the original question, it was definitely very strange, and I'm kind of surprised that nothing was actually said to me about it before I actually saw the record jacket, because I went, "Whaaat??" I mean, apart from the obvious disappointment of not being able to be around to do the whole record… But as I say, I hope that's something that maybe on the next record will be different, and I do intend discussing it.

Do you write your own music?
Yes. I'm not a great keyboard player, but that's what I write on. Now at home I'm putting a studio in my house, and I'm really looking forward to that. I can see composing into my later years more than I can see playing the way I play. I play in a pretty physical way. I'm sure I'll be able to play when I'm sixty, but it's hard to imagine playing the way I do with Tull's music, which is very athletic music for a drummer to play. At the end of the show I've really had it. I have to have a lot of strength and stamina for that – whether I'll be able to play that way when I'm sixty I don't know! I could see writing music.

What, like a solo album, or film music, or…?
I've actually thought about doing my own record at some point. I don't know if I would sing on it, because calling it 'singing' would be very subjective! The band just laughs when I try and sing. I do sing on a couple of bits. On the last tour they played a really nasty trick on me, when they cranked my monitor up at the end of *Too Old To Rock'n'Roll*, and I've just been giving it, as you would say over here, heavy welly for over two hours; I'm practically hyperventilating, and I'm supposed to be doing background vocals, and I'm puffing away, when I hear this sound blasting out from all over the stage, and I'm going, "What the hell is… oh my God, that's ME!!" And the band were just in stitches on the floor, and they even taped the thing! But actually, if I'm alone in a room I can sing my parts and sing harmonies, and it's OK. It's just hard sometimes when Dave Pegg is laughing at me as I'm singing into his microphone! I do love to sing, but I certainly wouldn't do it if I ever did do my own album, except to teach a singer what I wanted. But I feel confident that I could actually write the music for it. I've actually done some producing back home, and I've recorded enough to feel that I know what goes into making a record sound good to my ears. That's something that I

think I could do easily, to move into producing music. I get on with musicians fine, I know how to get a performance out of people, and how to work with people, which is part of what a producer has to be – a coach, a psychologist, and so on. Whether or not I'd be a successful producer is another thing altogether!

One thing I wrote I thought would actually be really good for Tull, it would really sound good with the band playing it. I'm not sure whether or not I'd ever submit it – I might; because basically the stuff that gets recorded is Ian's music, and that's fair enough. I mean it's really his band in the sense that he's the one person who's been there through all the years, and he does the lion's share of the work. He comes up with all these ideas about the way the staging should be, and it's his masterminded project. But there is a lot of input from the band. The band would not be the same without Martin for sure…

Ian actually said that to us, that he couldn't do it without Martin.

I'm glad that he acknowledges that, because I've always felt that Martin is such a part of the sound. Martin is a brilliant rock guitar player, one of the best guitarists I have ever worked with. He's got a really unique, individual voice on his instrument. And I think he gets overlooked a little bit in the rock genre of music, because people look for the guys with hair down to their knees, and doing all that what Martin calls "twiddly stuff". Martin is a really thoughtful guitar player, he's a real compositional player – a lot of thought goes into his parts and his soloing. When I listen back to live tapes I really love the stuff he's playing night to night, because he really thinks about it. He's not a guitar player who lets his fingers do the walking like a lot of players who are, as I call them, "gobblers". Martin makes a real statement with his instrument. I think everybody in the band does, I think everybody has a very individual voice, but I sometimes wish Martin wasn't as overlooked. But actually, whenever I speak to other guitar players they always say, "Is Martin Barre still in the band? Man, he's great!" And he has a lot of respect from musicians and guitar players; but he's not the kind of guy who'll be on the front cover of *Circus* magazine, he's more of a quiet, retiring kind of person. But that's why he plays guitar the way he does, that's part of his nature, and that's great, because I don't think he could be playing the way he is and then be a completely different kind of person. So much of his person comes out on his instrument.

And Dave as well, Dave adds a lot to the band. Dave Pegg is definitely one of the best bass players I've ever worked with. He has a beautiful linear style, unlike a lot of American bass players who just do that thumb-popping thing – which I can quite appreciate, and I've worked with people who do that very well. But Dave has a very melodic approach to the instrument that probably comes out of his playing the mandolin, which he plays beautifully. And he has great time as well, his feel is beautiful. I love playing in the rhythm section with him, it's really effortless for me. He adds a lot to the band from the bottom end, and also harmonically speaking; just the way he plays lines, he's very nimble and he can get lines out very easily. Dave, having played the guitar and mandolin, has that ability to play things with Martin and with me and play very, very accurately. Sometimes I'm not sure that Dave is appreciated the way he should be. But as a drummer, playing with him is just a joy, and just effortless. The only time it was a pain in the ass playing with Dave was when he played sober one night! It was in America, and I vowed to make him never do that again – he made so many mistakes, and dropped his plectrum, his time was off and he messed up the phrasing and the changes, and missed cues, and everything you could think of. So at the encore we made him down half a bottle of wine before we let him back on stage! That's the only time Dave's ever let me down!

And Don Airey now, he's working out really well, his influences and his background style will add a lot to the band. I hope that it becomes more of a band as opposed to just picking up side-people along the way – we'll see. But I always look forward to playing with the band, because the band is a very consistent unit and everybody tries really hard every night. I really can't think of any times when we've gone on stage and it's been in any way blasé, like, "Let's get this over with". Everybody goes out there and tries their hardest to really play, and I really appreciate the level of consistency which that brings… I mean, if one guy is having an off-night, everybody tries a little bit harder. I know that on nights where I've felt I haven't really been connecting there'll be something that's going on around me that will inspire me, which will pull me out of that mental frame of mind. Sometimes you can make a mistake early on, and you think, "I'm just having a bad night," and you can resign yourself to that, which is not good, because I really believe that you can overcome that if you let it go. You have to have the attitude of OK, it's happened, and we'll just look at each other and smile, or laugh. I mean, it's not the sort of thing you want to bring the audience's attention to, if somebody drops a huge clanger and the whole band turns round and goes, "What the HELL was that??", because the audience goes, "What happened, what was that?" But everyone is a real character. Martin really cracks me up on stage. He's really funny. He'll come over and he'll make faces, or make out like he's trying to tell me something deathly important, and when he's got my attention I'll go and see what he's got to say, like, "OK, what is it Martin, what is it, did I miss my cue or something?", and it turns out to be some complete nonsense. Sometimes it's just chit-chat to try to make the other person laugh.

[MW] I've only ever seen one really obviously bad cock-up, and that was when John Glascock came in at totally the wrong place with a bass guitar run, and it took him several seconds to realise he was doing it. So Ian looked round and gave him an exaggerated look; and then when it came to the bit where he SHOULD have come in, Martin and Ian and David Palmer went over and they counted him in like conductors, and made a big joke of it. It was really funny, and the audience appreciated the joke too.
Yeah, we've had a couple of marvellous train-wrecks on stage, and I'm not sure if it's something the audience really noticed, but we certainly noticed them! And you can either just laugh, because it's so silly, or you can get completely and utterly depressed. It sometimes depends on what everybody's frame of mind is. You might go on stage feeling a little down, and think, "Aagh, they're sabotaging me, what are they doing to me?", or you might just laugh about it. And that's the only thing you can do, I think, because it's done, and that's it. But Tull is one of those bands which I think makes the most of those silly things that happen, because the band has a real sense of humour. Ian has certainly got a highly developed sense of humour, which is great, because that offsets the seriousness of the music in a way. And it is fairly serious music as far as I'm concerned – I mean it's not like playing in The Beach Boys or something like that. And I don't necessarily mean lyrically, although that's part of it – it's fairly serious music, but there's often an intent of humour behind a lot of it; there's a lot of humorous things in the music that even I might not get for a while, and maybe the audience doesn't get right away. But Ian's sense of humour I think gives the band a foil for... if you went out there and were real pompous and pedantic about the whole thing and real full of yourself, I think the people would just go, "Oh no, give me a break, eh?" I'm sure the band HAS been accused of that, but I don't see it from that perspective at all. I just think critics tend to dislike anything that remotely resembles something well played or well executed, well composed, well recorded and so on. It seems that critics so often want to hear or tout the next band that sounds like it was recorded in somebody's garage in 1966. There's some validity in that too, but I think critics really slag bands that have a degree of technical proficiency.

I think it's just that sometimes they're not prepared to make the effort to listen to something, or they literally haven't got time; they've got the next review to move on to, they've got deadlines...
Well yes, but I think it's also, maybe as in the case of Tull, that once a band becomes really popular it falls out of favour with the critics, because they look at that as 'selling out'. In fact they might have been playing that way all the time, it's just that it's come to the attention of a great many more people. And I really resent that as a musician. I spend a good deal of my life really working hard to try to understand my instrument and to understand how to play in a band, and PROPEL a band. That's the job of a drummer in a band – I'm the chief cook and bottle washer, or the traffic cop, y'know; I have to conduct a lot of things in terms of handling the dynamics and tempo changes and things like that. And I work really hard at the craft part of my instrument, and I really resent it when that is something that either a critic doesn't take the time to understand, or just thinks that it's 'slick'. I mean, would you say Yehudi Menuhin is 'slick'? No, he has great refined technique. I certainly fall short of that degree of technical proficiency, but I try to approach my instrument with the same seriousness as those people. And having studied classical music, maybe some of that has rubbed off on me, but I really do think that in rock music it's just as possible to bring the level of execution up higher than it is

on average with rock bands whose overall vocabulary is more limited than a jazz musician or a classical musician. I appreciate all kinds of music, and I want to bring all that into what I play. And in a lot of ways Jethro Tull is a very good platform for that, because the band combines a lot of classical music, jazz, rock'n'roll, R'n'B, folk music, fusion if you like – a lot of different things. It's very orchestral music. And that to me is wonderful, because it combines a lot of great music that I get to play every night. It's very exciting for me, that I get a chance to play so many different styles in one evening. Maybe the other guys in the band take that a bit for granted because they've been doing it for so long, but as a relative newcomer I really appreciate that. It's great because I get to call on a great deal of the music that I was brought up on, and studied.

You don't find switching from one style to another disruptive at all?
No, not at all. I would perhaps if I hadn't had some of the background in that music, to cope with all the funny time changes and odd bars in the music. I mean, the structures in Tull's music bear little resemblance to the typical A-A-B-A song format of 'pop' songs, either in America or in England. It's very idiosyncratic music – the form is like A-A-B-**X**, and then – **R**, say, and it's so off the wall. And that's great because it's real challenging, it's not just, "OK, now we do the chorus", it's very orchestrated music, and I love that. And I think that makes me think compositionally in the way that I approach my instrument. And we can't just say we're going to jam. Now, some people might say that that's really constricting, but I don't find it constricting because I like having parameters within which to work, and once I know what they are I have a lot of freedom in the band to play differently every night, so it's not constricting to me. You know, I don't even REMEMBER what your original question was! That was a MAJOR waffle!!

Do you get pestered by fans, and does it bother you?
Most of the time the fans are really nice. In fact, in the last three years I've gotten a couple of really nice letters from people, mostly musicians or drummers, who say that they really like the way I play, and a couple have even gone so far as to say that I'm the best drummer the band has ever had, or certainly in a long time. And that's very gratifying, because I feel that if I'm getting across to these kids, then I'm really doing my job. If when they come and hear the band they go, "Jeez, that sounds great, I really like what he's doing," as opposed to, "Oh, gosh, where's Barrie?" or "Where's Clive?" or whatever, then that's great. I feel good if I have imparted any of my enthusiasm to the audience. I feel that when I play I have an ability to get that across to people, and people often come up to me and say that. There was one guy on the last tour, who I think was trying to get an audition for the band and didn't, he was really pissed off that I got the job, so he sent some real threatening telex like, "That Doane Perry, he stinks, he doesn't deserve to be in the band." It was a terrible thing, right after I joined the band, when we did the Hammersmith show, and I was absolutely shocked, thinking, "How can anybody say this about me? This guy doesn't even know me, he probably had never even heard me play." Then I thought screw it, it's obviously just sour grapes. Occasionally there will be something like that, but most of the time people are really nice. Occasionally I get letters that are very annoying. There are people who sometimes don't leave you alone and don't know when to stop; they are real kind of pushy, and annoy the rest of the band, and pester the other fellas. I mean, it's their private life, and when the other guys in the band are being pestered about me, then that annoys me as it's an infringement on their private home life. Some people just push until you get really mad, and they go, "Oh, well, why didn't you say something?" and I say, "Well, I was trying to tell you without being rude about it." Sometimes it does take a more direct approach to achieve that.
Ian, of course, can get it worse than I do. The thing about Tull's music is that it tends to engender in people either great enthusiasm or real intense dislike! So some people do go to extremes, and it does make it hard for people like yourselves who have a genuine interest, and are sensible people – it takes a while for Ian to realise, "Wait a minute, these people are OK." You put together a really good magazine and it's obviously done very responsibly. It's nice that Ian has recognised and acknowledged that, which he certainly does.

This marked the end of Part One of the interview. Part Two appeared in the next issue, #14. The scene by now is that, between anecdotes, Doane has finally managed to finish his soup, the waitress has mopped up the table, and the main curry has just arrived. Meanwhile, Doane is still talking...

When did you first see Jethro Tull?

It would have been in 1969. The first time I heard them was at the end of 1968, because I remember hearing a radio advert for them appearing at the Fillmore East. They were playing *Cat's Squirrel*, and it was just an amazing piece of music at the time, really impressive, with a lot of fancy drumming and strong guitar, and I thought, "Wow!" When I saw them the first time I was utterly speechless, it was such an amazing experience. I think part of what attracted me not only to their music but also live was that I've always had a great love of the theatre. Living in New York I went to the theatre a lot – I actually used to play Broadway shows and stuff – and when I was a kid I did a little bit of acting. I was actually starting to get calls for commercials and stuff like that; they wanted a kid playing drums or something. Acting always seemed like a natural thing when I was a kid - I think it gets harder when you get older. But I always loved the theatre as a result, and always wanted to be on the stage. And seeing a band that combined music and theatre... Tull was really the first rock band that actually did that. This was long before they had big sets, but there was a theatrical element, they were like character actors, that was the sense I got from it. There would be little touches of things that would happen that would be more than guys just going out there in denims and playing guitars. I loved that about the band. Also, the music had a larger than life quality to it. It was very exciting, and excessive too – they all played kind of excessively, but as a kid you're thrilled by that. And of course it was the songs as well. So I ended up playing in a band that was very instrumental in my musical development in terms of rock music, and that's pretty unusual. Maybe that's why I ended up in it as well, maybe I was suited for that role having prepared for it unbeknownst to me for many years!

You were telling us the other night how much you really rated Clive Bunker as a drummer.

Oh, Clive was just a brilliant drummer. He was the best drummer I had ever seen at that point. He was like the person who bridged what Ginger Baker did with what Billy Cobham was to do later on with the Mahavishnu Orchestra. He was a guy with completely unstudied technique who played completely naturally by feel. I remember I'd written him a letter, and I took it to the Fillmore and gave it to an usher, and Clive came out to see me. I was like, wow, just speechless! But he was so gracious and nice to me – he brought me backstage, he got me passes to all the shows, and he showed me how to play all the stuff in the dressing room on his knees and so on. I remember saying to him something like, "Wow, that sure is a great six-stroke roll you have, " – a six-stroke roll, for readers who may not know or even care what the hell it is, is a very rudimentary term – and he said, "What is that?" He didn't even know what a six-stroke roll was! It turned out he was doing it in a different way, it just sounded the same, but he was doing it at this incredible velocity, and he just had this organic natural feel. Apart from that he tuned his drums beautifully. He really knew how to make his drums sing, and he played with a lot of finesse and great touch. I mean, he could play quite hard, but he also played lightly and very musically, and being a sort of frustrated keyboard player myself I've always tried to relate to music as much from harmonic and melodic aspects as from rhythmic. Now Clive definitely embodied that, I could feel it, he really related to things that were going on in the music other than just the rhythm. And he was beautiful to watch, which is something that people never mention. They talk about how great he was, there's a lot of drummers who will cite him as an influence, especially anyone who'd seen him live – on records he was very contained, he played more like Ringo, very simple, played the right stuff, and he was right there. But live he was a real character and he was very exciting. He looked like a dancer the way he played, he was really graceful. He had all these things going together, and of course it made a big impact on me. I thought, "I've got to find out how this guy does it," so I really analysed a lot of the way he played. So much of the way he played came out of the music of the band. He couldn't have played that way in some other group – it was very much that his style evolved out of the music, which is what made it unique as well. Clive is one of the greats in my book.

Is there anyone else who influenced you, or who you listen to?
Oh yeah, so many people. I could bore everybody to tears with a litany of people. Classical music was really the first music that affected me really deeply. I can remember being almost hypnotised, standing over the record player and listening to Mendelssohn's *Midsummer Night's Dream* and Schubert's *Unfinished Symphony*, just hypnotised by the sound and the power that this music had. Then I had classical piano lessons. I didn't know anything about pop music – I thought that The Beatles invented pop music! I had no interest outside classical music, although my parents did listen to jazz around the house, but that was more peripheral to my influences at the time. I hated my piano teacher, and she never let me play anything I wanted to – the usual story. Then when The Beatles came along I decided I wanted to play the drums - that was a fascinating instrument to me. So I taught myself for a couple of years, and I had a pretty good natural feel. But then when I saw Ginger Baker, Mitch Mitchell, Clive, Keith Moon and those kind of people I decided I wanted to study, and I went to music school where I had proper lessons, played in orchestras, and had to study theory and composition and all that. From classical I moved into rock, and then jazz – when I found jazz I wanted to be a jazz musician. But I was always getting called to do pop and rock gigs, and I could do those really well, and I really liked that music. Jazz musicians used to really look down on that. There was this attitude of, "Oh, you can play jazz, but you play that other stuff too??" But I thought, screw you, I'm not going to play with someone who's got that kind of closed mind way of looking at music. If music is well written and well played it doesn't much matter to me the origin of the music as such. I was also making a good living playing pop and rock. The fact that I can now combine my classical background and jazz and all those things with this band is really nice. So the answer to that question is that it's sort of a variety of music, and to cite individuals at great length would be very difficult and probably incredibly tedious for anybody who's reading this!

What about Barrie Barlow? Do you know Barrie?
I've met Barrie, but I don't know him. He came to the Hammersmith gigs we did last time. I like his playing a lot. I've got quite a few things off him too; he played some marvellous things with the band. He was a really idiosyncratic player – his playing was ideally suited for the band, but it was so quirky. I don't play everything the way Barrie played it. There's certain things he did that I really love which I definitely still do; other things I've edited out and play a bit more straightforwardly. If there's any influence I bring to the band it's – dare I say it – probably an American influence, in terms of being more R'n'B influenced. I probably play a little simpler; certainly simpler than Barrie Barlow. I have the ability to do things complexly, but I don't hear the music that way, especially in 1987. I mean, I'm not saying that Tull will ever be a big dance band, you're not going to hear *Living In The Past* in the discos, but probably I play the music more directly. Also probably an influence I bring to the band is a more levelling influence, there's a little more gravity now on the rhythm section than there used to be. And that's not taking anything away from Barrie or Clive or Mark or any of those guys, because they were all great. But that's maybe something that Ian was looking for, someone who COULD play the complex stuff, but I'm quite happy to play the simple stuff if that's what the music calls for. So maybe that helps, because there's a lot going on in the band as it is. If I was to play every single accent the band plays, and pick up every little nuance, my part would be so busy it would be pointless to try to tap your foot to it.

When you learn a new piece of music, either an old song or a new song, do you sit there and calculate, "Oh, this beat should be this, and that," or does it all come fairly naturally, and you just kind of fill it in?
Most of it comes fairly naturally. Obviously there are things which have to be analysed, and broken down into their component parts, and there are things which are pretty complicated that I can't just kind of cruise along with until we get to the chorus, because there's like road blocks everywhere; you've got to get over this, and get through this bar, and negotiate this turn and this dynamic! And I've got to be the one who has to control all that, who controls the

tempo and the dynamics, and all those things, so I have to know it almost better than anyone else. The drummer is like the conductor of the band. Ian's the front man, he's written the stuff, but at the end of it I probably have the most control of anyone on stage of the music I'm actually playing – if I screw it up, I can screw it up for everybody. If I turn the beat around, or lose it, the whole band just crashes. But if I'm really there, and I'm playing the part with conviction, then that also makes the band happen. So in that way, there is a very intellectual approach to what I do. I definitely listen to the stuff and I break it down, like that's a bar of 7, that's a bar of 9, then it goes to 3/8, then there's a retard there, and a little accelerando there, and I've got a feel change coming up here, going from triplets to whatever. I've got to think about all these things, so it's got to be something that intellectually and technically I can cope with and then translate into music.

A lot of times I've found working with this band has been really interesting and very different from working with American bands, in that if I was working with, say, an American jazz artist he might say, "This piece is in 9/8 or 9/16 or whatever, and the form is ABAC," or whatever, and it's written out like a road map. But Tull stuff is very organically conceived. I remember when I first joined the band asking them how they counted things; like in *Thick As A Brick* there's two separate times going on simultaneously all the time, and it may not be easy to hear but I'm actually playing both of the times, the 3 against the 2, or the 3 against the 4. And I had to understand that so that I would be able to cope with that and play the part with a good feel. You have to understand the structure, but once I get the song or piece of music inside me I don't have to count any more, and I find now I count less than I used to. Now, for example, in *Velvet Green* I'm aware of what time we're playing in, but I've never actually sat down and analysed it. I think of it in terms of the phrases, like the other guys do. They would say, "Oh, this phrase is this long, and then there's a little gap," and so on – they wouldn't say, "There's 3/16 notes, and then a rest, and then it picks up like a quarter note triplet after that." They don't think of it that way, they think in phrases. So it's very organically conceived, which is beautiful, and it's a real natural way to play music. And that's something that I've adopted to some degree. Not to say that there isn't an intellectual side that comes into play, because there very much is when I'm playing. I have to be thinking about a lot of things on a few different levels, from the energy, to the emotion, to holding the band together, thinking "Is somebody playing in front, is somebody playing behind?" So I've got to be in the centre, which is the comfortable place for everybody. If somebody's rushing I have to pull it back, if they're dragging I have to push it ahead. So I try to get the music internalised before I go out and perform it. I can remove that whole process, and then I can just play it as second nature. That's why we spend a lot of time in rehearsal, and I actually do a lot of homework on my own parts when the rest of the band isn't practising, mentally as well as actually sorting things out.

I noticed tonight at rehearsal that Ian was discussing something with you and saying, "This is 98 beats per minute," and I thought, "Blimey, that's pretty precise…"
Right. That was in *Budapest*, which is 98 beats per minute, but there's a little section that goes into the 'Hungarian' lick which is actually a little bit faster. So I have a little metronome on my snare drum. What can happen is that you get on stage and the adrenalin's really up, and so you play everything really fast; and you listen back to the tape and you think, "My God, we were just speeding through everything and it sounds terrible." So before the show I have my set list with all the songs and all the tempo markings, and I say OK, that's what we've agreed on. It's OK if we want to move it later on, but this is a point of reference that the band can have, and they have to trust in the fact that I'm playing accurately to the metronome. They might be going, "Christ, Doane is dragging like hell tonight," or "He's really rushing," depending whatever the frame of mind is, but I'm looking at the metronome, and that's the tempo which felt right. There might be times where you can pick it up a little bit, or bring it back, but that's a starting point. So that's why Ian said it's 98, because I had it written down as a beat faster – then it goes from 98 to 102 in the faster section, so when we get to that I just flip it up a little bit. So you can see there's a lot of preparation, we don't just go on there playing away like happy minstrels!

100

I really enjoy that about this band – it takes a lot of care and a lot of attention to detail, which a lot of other professional people don't. Everything from production, to lights, to arrangement, but I don't find it boring or overbearing that we have to work it all out; there's a perfectionist part of me that appreciates it. You know, when people come to see you, that's one of the things that attracts them – it's what turned me on about the band when I saw them when I was young, that it was really something, way above other bands, it was something really special. Now I KNOW why it's really special. People would think that Ian must be like a complete acidhead or something from the way he carries on, but he's not, he doesn't take any drugs, he's just very smart, and the whole band is really on the beam. They couldn't have lasted this long if they weren't, and that's why the band is successful, because of the attention to all of those things. It's not like, "Oh, it'll be good enough for the punters, we'll play *Aqualung* and it will be fine." That's not the attitude in the band at all. The attitude is that every time you go out there you try to give them something special, so they're going to walk away going, "That was great, I really saw and heard something there!" I try to as an individual when I play, and everybody in the band tries to do that.

I think that comes over as well.
I do too, and I think that's one of the things that makes this band really special, and why it has endured so long.

How do you find Ian, as a person? We were quite wary - if that's the right word - of him at first, and probably still are, to be honest; although he's never been less than pleasant and friendly towards us...
Well, I think like anybody he just takes a while to get to know. He has a very strong presence as an individual, and he certainly can be the centre of attention a lot of times, but once you get to know him he's fine. But he has a lot more weight on his shoulders, so he feels more responsible for what he says and what he does around people. People look at him, and if he says something in an offhand way that someone completely misinterprets, they'll go, "What a so-and-so that guy is," and he might not have meant it that way, whereas if you knew him you'd know it was just a joke, he wasn't being rude or anything like that. I actually enjoy being around him, he can be a lot of fun. I've noticed that in the last couple of years since I've got to know him a bit he's mellowed. Getting this tour together he's been really calm and happy and good to be around, and he seems to be happier. I don't claim to know him that well - Martin probably knows him better than any of us...

Martin did say the same thing to us, actually.
Yeah, he's easier to be around. He's a funny guy. He's certainly got his wits about him, and you sort of have to as well!

Well we came to that conclusion really, that being the figurehead he has to be more wary of people who approach him.
I have to say that he is a very fair man and a very honest man, and that's not always an easy attribute to pin on people who are really 'up there'. He's got a very good set of standards and ethics, and I really appreciate that, y'know, because I've worked with a lot of people who don't, who are very difficult to work with. Ian can be difficult from time to time, because he knows what he wants; but that doesn't scare me as a musician working with him because I am equally as confident in what I do as in what he does. I'm not a front person, but I'm very confident when I go out there and play, and the fact that he stands in front of me and looks at me doesn't scare me. The first couple of times when I played with the band it was surprising, because here was a band I used to watch from the front, and then all of a sudden I was on the other side, with Ian five feet in front of me, and his voice and his flute are coming out of my MONITOR, and there's Martin over there, and Dave over there, and I'm going, "Wow!" That was very strange for the first week or so for me. It took a little bit of adjusting to at first, but it wore off fairly quickly I think. But it's like any band, there's relationships that you have to deal with. This is a band that's been together for a LONG time, and you're walking in and dealing with people who've had relationships with each other for a long time – it's not just as simple as like, "Hello, how are you, let's get on with the music," there's a lot of other things

connected there. That's been sort of illuminating, having been a bit of a fan from before and now being in the band. Being in that situation is quite responsible. People who come to Jethro Tull gigs are very attentive, and I actually have a place where I can play things that I come up with that I could never use on sessions and on records for people; they just didn't want to know about that stuff. This band actually WANTS me to do this stuff, they want me to go wild and really give it stick, and to do all the things that I really enjoy doing. And that's great for me, I really enjoy that. And as I say, it's not something I take for granted. I get a lot of strength from that. When Ian comes right up to me when I'm playing and he's staring right at me, that doesn't scare me, I feel like it's like, "OK, I'll show him – just listen to THIS!" And it makes my level of consistency rise, because I'm playing with a band that really tries, and is really consistent, every time it goes out there and plays. That's been good for my playing too, and I hope that I've done something for the band in return. I have my shortcomings too, which I'm sure they'd tell you about [*laughing*], but you're never going to get everything, you just get as close as you can – half a loaf is better than none.

Tell us about Hunter. Is Hunter the same group as Dragon – was it just a change of name?
Yes, that's a little confusing! It is the same band, but the name was changed because the record label thought 'Dragon' had too many heavy metal connotations, which I completely agree with. I never liked that name, it just conjures up this whole... just a very gothic heavy metal image, which is not what the band is about. They are a really good band, very different to Tull.

Is it a full-time thing – would you say that they're your main band?
No. It's only in the last year that I've probably done that little bit more because Tull were less busy. I mean, I was in Tull before I was in Hunter. It actually came about as a result of them hearing me down in Australia when Tull finished the '84 tour. I was going to have a little holiday down there anyway, and they asked me if I'd like to do a one-off single and a festival tour. I said well, that sounds nice for a couple of weeks, and then I'll go home. And then there were more dates, and we ended up doing a whole album. Tull weren't that busy, so I was working with Hunter, and working back home doing session work and record projects and that kind of stuff, so that was keeping me pretty busy. We did the Summer Raid Tour last year, but we really didn't do a lot until the end of last year when we started to do the record.

Is it difficult being in both bands?
Well, one band is based in Sydney, Australia, one band is based in London, and I live in Los Angeles – there's a real ideal working situation! This year I had done the last record with Hunter, and we'd got the Tina Turner support slot, which was great. They're a huge band in Australia, but nobody knows them over here, so this was a great break. They needed a commitment from me, and I said yeah, this sounds fine, as it didn't clash with Tull. Being in two bands is a little bit difficult; but although a lot of people in Australia think that Hunter is my band, I do feel that my heart is more in Jethro Tull in a lot of ways. I'd hate ever to have to make a decision. I mean, Dave is in two bands, but he's in two bands in his own country. I'm lucky to be in one great band, let alone two really good bands. They are totally different from each other, worlds apart actually.
When I'm working with Tull I'm essentially living over here in England anyway. It's just when we're not working that I go back to live in my own country. Many times I've actually thought about living over here, even before the Jethro Tull thing came up, because I really enjoy the music scene over here. It's a very vibrant, live place to be in terms of music. I've always felt very at home in England, which is partially due to having gone to an English school in New York. But it's just one of those places in the world where you go sometimes and just feel at home in. The first time I came here I was about seventeen, and I immediately felt right at home. I love the British people, and the culture, the architecture, the music – it's a country that just fascinates me.

How come you went to an English school – was it the nearest, or something?

No. Actually I went to an American school in New York for a while, and I got very good grades. And my parents thought, "Wait a minute, this is a little too easy, let's yank him out and really put him in some place hard" – thus ruining my academic career! St Bernard's was considerably harder. I was an average student, maybe above average, but I definitely had to work harder, studying things like Latin and Advanced Maths. After I graduated from there I went back to an American high school in New York, and I was already a year ahead of the rest of my class, so the whole 9th Grade I didn't have to do any work. Which didn't exactly set any great precedent for the rest of the time I was there, because I thought, "This is easy," but when I got to the 10th Grade I had to work! I don't know if that necessarily reflects the academic system over here, but in terms of the teachers who were over there teaching, they were certainly well ahead of the Americans. Also, my father is a writer and historian, and he's always been interested in England. There's always been a lot of things about England around the house, so I think I always had an interest and a fascination about it. So living here wouldn't be a difficult adjustment for me; I have a lot of friends here. Apart from the weather, which gets me a little depressed sometimes, especially in the wintertime.

It does us too!
I mean, I'm from New York, which is not totally unlike England at times, with the four seasons. But I've recently moved to California, which is the other end of the spectrum where it's always sunny and nice, and you get used to that. I'm one of those people whose mood is definitely affected by the climate. When I wake up and I see the sun and the blue sky it's really nice. I would be close to suicidal living in Norway or some place like that!

A factual question – who else have you played with on record or live?
Oh dear! It's quite a variety of people. I did a world tour in 1978 with Bette Midler, which was great; we did a week in London, which was fantastic, the first time I'd really spent any time here. Then at the other end of the spectrum I did a couple of records and played live with Lou Reed – what a character! Pat Benatar, Laura Brannigan, Peter Allen – he's a very popular singer/songwriter in America -, Jim Messina, Dave Mason. I had a band with Dave in California for a while which we recorded with. It was a wonderful band called Bridges, with Peter Wolf on keyboards – not the one from the J. Geils Band, but Peter Wolf the producer. Then there's a lot of jazz people. I worked with this great jazz singer called Phyllis Hyman, as a drummer first and second time as her musical director – she's fantastic. But really there's too many people to mention.

Do you keep the albums you've played on?
Yes, I do. I like to have copies of the albums I've played on. I probably have about 30 or so albums that I've been on, and then there's some I don't have that probably aren't worth having anyway! At one point during the disco period I worked with lots if disco artists. I also played on lots of jingles and commercials. I made a good living from it, but it was pretty soulless music. Plus film dates, everything from *The Texas Chainsaw Massacre* to *The Twilight Zone*, a real sort of variety of things. I did a record last year with a group called Barnes and Barnes, it's like Captain Beefheart-type music, it's really wild stuff. And an Australian singer called Sharon O'Neill – I did a lot of work with Australian artists. I've never heard of Mara! before though. But that's probably a part of the music scene that I'm just not familiar with.

[DR] I don't think they're very popular... anywhere, really.
[*Laughing*] That was hard to say, wasn't it Dave! That was tough!

Do you like any 'modern' bands?
Oh, many modern bands. Because I play in Jethro Tull I suppose some people think I must be firmly entrenched in music of the sixties, and that I only listen to Traffic albums and so on. But of the current stuff, I'm a big fan of Nik Kershaw, his records sound great, his songs are great, his playing is impeccable. In modern drumming, Charlie Morgan is just the best, he is fantastic, and I'm a big fan of his. He's playing with Elton John at the moment. He lives here

in London, and someone I know knows him, but I'm too chicken to call him. I love Go West, Mister Mister, who I played with and recorded with when they were called Pages. People think of that as slick pop-rock, but I kind of like that stuff. I also like bands like U2 and Bruce Springsteen, raw kinds of bands, but I don't listen to them so much for musical influences; I just like the overall vibe of the music and the songs. I still listen to a lot of jazz. I take a lot of jazz and classical tapes with me on the road, I find a lot of inspiration there. Steely Dan, I love their stuff. Joni Mitchell, I'm a big fan of hers. There's so many people – people will probably think, "He's completely indiscriminate this guy, as to who he likes and listens to," because the fact is I really like a lot of people. However, I'm actually a very discriminating listener, but I'm the kind of person who before I see the bad in something I usually see the good things. I'm glad to say there are more things that I enjoy listening to than I don't. And it stretches beyond the kind of music I listen to – the kind of people that are my friends, the kind of places I like to go, the kind of food I like to eat, there's a lot of diversity; I'm not a creature of habit.

What about your favourite Tull songs?
There's a lot of songs that I haven't played with the band that I love, some of which we've toyed with the idea of playing, and rehearsed for about 15 seconds and everyone goes, "Oh no, forget it!" And then there's actually some songs that we've played that I thought would be fun to play but were really more fun to listen to. There's quite a few that I would love to get around to; but obviously in constructing a set for the band, you have to play a certain amount of material that you know the average fan is going to want to hear. If we didn't do *Aqualung* we would surely have rotten fruit thrown at us!

From a purely listening point of view, if you were on the proverbial desert island, which Jethro Tull things would you take?
At this point I'm too close to things to really be able to answer that, because obviously as much as I love the music… no, I will try to answer the question instead of squirming out of it! *Black Sunday* would really be right up there at the top of the list. There's certain things on *Black Sunday* which I'm really going to sorely miss this tour, because I think it's a great Tull song, and it goes down really well. The irony is that when we were discussing it with the band whether to do *Black Sunday* they said that they've done it every tour, and Martin and Dave said, "And all those funny bars threw everybody off." I said, "Are you kidding me? How many people do you see clapping along with *Songs From The Wood*??" I mean, talk about "funny bars" – they're all over the place!

Actually, in a poll we did in *A New Day*, *Black Sunday* was the third favourite Tull song after *Aqualung* and *Heavy Horses*, which was a bit of a surprise really.
I tell you, that's a great song live. It's good on the record, but it doesn't come across the way it does live – it's a great song to play. I love the words, I love the whole song, and I'm really disappointed we're not doing it, because I feel that's a song the band just boils on. Maybe it's because we've done it every tour, but I'm not at all sick of it. But I was taken aback when Martin and Dave talked about "all those funny bars" as if people are really tapping through some of those other songs. I DEFY anyone to tap through *Songs From The Wood* or *Velvet Green*!! *Thick As A Brick* is all over the place, there's a lot of crazy stuff going on in that. I thought what a weak excuse, but I'm sure we'll get around to it again, certainly if I have any influence on it!
Other than that, I always liked *Fylingdale Flyer* a lot. From the first album, I loved *My Sunday Feeling*, which was one Clive showed me how to play, and which we played on the last tour in America and Australia – I believe that was the first time the band had played it since Clive was in the band. I'd mentioned it to Ian, and he remembered it was a nice song and worth trying. *Dharma For One*, I like the revamped version of that best. From the second album I always loved *Nothing Is Easy*, and *We Used To Know* is a beautiful song. *For A Thousand Mothers* is a song I always liked a lot. From *Benefit* I liked *Nothing To Say*. Martin and I actually started practising that a few weeks ago. We thought that it would be a nice one to do, it's a beautiful song, but… there's so much that gets discarded in rehearsals, for one reason or another. We rehearsed *Teacher* once for about 20 minutes. *My God!* we got close to

doing this time round, but rehearsals didn't come to much really, and we do quite a bit from that album anyway, with *Wind Up* this time. *Hymn 43* and *Wond'ring Aloud* I liked. A lot of *Thick As A Brick* I loved. There's bit of *A Passion Play* and *Minstrel In The Gallery* that I really liked. From *Warchild*, *The Third Hurrah* was always my favourite, it's a beautifully orchestrated work. For some reason Don came in with the chart for that one, he thought he was supposed to play it. He'd got the orchestrations down, and I'd loved to have played it. Everyone's ears pricked up for a second, but then it got pushed aside in favour of something else. *Velvet Green* wasn't ever a song that was one of my favourites, but I've really enjoyed rehearsing it for this tour. I always liked *Orion*, and *Dun Ringill, Clasp, Watching Me Watching You, Pussy Willow*. There's always something on every album that you play over and over. Live, I really enjoy everything we play. I really have a good time. I don't ever find myself bored on a gig, thinking, "Did I pay the gardener before I left?" or "Did I feed the cat?"

Well, aside from feeding the cat, Doane eventually succeeded in feeding himself, managing to get most of his curry into his mouth when it wasn't actually engaged in talking. In his interview he mentioned his tendency towards being a perfectionist, and he proved the point by subsequently asking to see a transcript of the interview before we printed it, in case he could improve on some of the stories and phrases dredged up by his decidedly tired brain. He settled down to the task in the hotel bar after the Birmingham NEC show but, equally tired, and overwhelmed by the sheer volume of our notes, he gave up after a few pages, albeit reassured that it didn't read as badly as he had first feared. Nevertheless, it was a nice thought, prompted by his concern for the dedicated Tull fans who would be reading it, and hopefully at least some of the enthusiasm inherent in this amiable character imparted itself in the cold print above. On the odd occasion he waffled a bit, even the waffle was interesting. But take a tip from us – never enter a talking competition against him...

Chapter 8

JOHN EVANS

(Published in Issue #15, May 1988)

When we first started the magazine, by far the most frequently asked questions from readers were: "What has happened to John Evans? Why did he leave? Will he ever rejoin Tull?" etc. We spoke to John in December 1987, and originally intended including the results with the developing John Evan Band story [see Chapter 12]; but such was the interest in his whereabouts that in the event we went ahead separately with the 'Jethro Tull' section of his interview.

The circumstances surrounding our meeting were unusual to say the least... DR had spoken to David Palmer backstage at a Hammersmith Odeon gig. David had not only agreed to submit himself to an A New Day *grilling, but he had also hinted that John would also probably be willing to talk to us. A short time later we were told by Chris Riley, ex-John Evan Band,that John did indeed wish to speak to us. So in due course DR found himself standing by the 'phone about to call John, but worrying quite what sort of reception he would get – we had been warned that he could be "difficult" to talk to. Just as he went to pick up the 'phone it started ringing, and when DR answered it the caller said, "Hello. My name is John Evans. I'm a friend of Chris Riley." Uncanny...!*

DR and MW met John the following Sunday lunchtime in a Hampshire pub and, after a slightly awkward start, the interview itself went well.

Firstly, is it John 'Evan' or 'Evans'?
It is Evans. John Spencer Evans to be precise.

Having been together in The John Evan Band in 1966-67, Ian asked you back in 1970 to join Tull. Had you kept in touch in the meantime?
Well, we lived in the same house! While I was at University I had kept in touch with Jeffrey all the time, who was at the Central School of Art in London. I went down to London in September '68 to the Chelsea College of Science. He had already been in London for a year and got fixed up with a little bedsit in Tremlett Grove, and the people who owned that also owned a typically scruffy north London 4-storey terraced house in Kentish Town. Ian moved from Luton to be closer to central London – by this time I think there was the association with Terry Ellis and Chrysalis, and so they were gigging seven nights a week and earning money and so on – and he got one of the rooms in this Kentish Town house. When I decided to go to University in Chelsea I didn't want to live in Chelsea, for reasons of inverted snobbery which we were all prone to at the time. I thought right, I don't want anything to do with those jerks who go to pharmacy school and wear suits. I was going to be different... a James Dean character and wear jeans and a Levi jacket, and disappear every night and live somewhere a long way away – not socialise at all, and be a mysterious character. So I got the room which became vacant right next to Ian's. He wasn't there very much so I didn't see him very much; maybe once or twice a week he would turn up having been to Newcastle or Dundee or somewhere.
At University I was very keen to show the world that I was bloody good, intelligent and talented, and I used to work all the time. I was really keen on showing everyone that I could do all those exams and become a qualified pharmacist, and go on to become a research chemist where I could still wear Levi jackets and be even more mysterious and earn a pittance discovering cures for exotic diseases! But things turned out a bit differently...

Was that a wrench then joining Tull after you had been so dedicated to your studies?

Yes it was. I talked to several members of the staff at college about it, and I remember having a long chat with my tutor Metcalfe saying, "What can I do?" He said, "Look, it's pop music, there's a lot of money in it. It will only last for two years – go and do it for two years, get some money and invest it or buy a house or something, and come back." By this time I was in the Second Year, and I had actually come top in every single exam except The Law in Pharmacy, which I wasn't interested in anyway. I had won all the book prizes, more books than I could carry. It was embarrassing actually; every First Year prize it was the same name – I just kept going up to the stage all the time. After a bit I thought, "This is taking the mysterious thing a bit too far!" But I thought for once in my life I seemed to be doing something successfully on my own efforts.

Anyway, by this time Tull had done *This Was* which had been a success amongst the underground audience and got quite high in the charts after the Windsor Blues Festival, which had put them on the front pages of the newspapers. Then there was *Stand Up*, which was a good album and deservedly got to No 1 – you know all this of course! – and then they started doing *Benefit*. Ian said to me that they really wanted to alter the sound of the band a bit. He felt that he wanted to put some keyboards onto it, different things like organ, piano, mellotron – you know, those God-awful instruments that had tapes in that sounded like something from the 1920s. Disgusting instruments! So by this time I was getting a bit tired of working all the time and I thought about the good old days when I actually used to play a bit. So I thought I'd give it a crack, just go along and put a few overdubs on after college, and I did. Then they went away to Germany, and Ian called me up from Germany and said, "Look, we want to do these new numbers on stage, but we can't do it without the keyboards – will you do it?" I said I'd really have to think about it, and that is when I got into discussions with the people at college. They convinced me that I should do it, so I said OK, I'll do it. And that's all there is to it.

Did you ever complete your studies?
No.

Do you regret that?
Well, my life would have been different, and I am pretty happy now, so no. I wouldn't be where I am today if I hadn't done... It might have been better, but it might have been worse. I regret having left The John Evan Band and going back to Mum from Luton in 1967. My thinking at the time was that I could actually be at University and get qualifications and have a career, and so I opted for that. It was an easy way out, for which I suppose in a way I've felt a certain amount of regret because Ian has never forgotten that either. I think he felt let down by the fact that I'd gone – he felt a personal loss of loyalty, which I quite understand really. But I don't regret giving up college. It would be nice to have done three years... I could still be doing what I do now, but where it says "Director: J.S.Evans" it would say "Director: J.S.Evans B.Sc."!

You are remembered as an extrovert on stage with Tull, but you are actually quite a shy person, aren't you? I remember the first interview you did with the NME. They found you hiding under a piano because you didn't want to do it!
Probably! I went from one extreme to the other... Yes, that was with Nick Logan.

Did you find it hard joining a band that was world famous, as opposed to growing into success with them?
Well, it was certainly different! I did the Easter exams, so in March/April I was actually still a student. And by the end of April I was playing in the group in... Long Beach Coliseum was the first really big one. I'd never been to the States in my life, never been out of England, in fact – never been on a 'plane, and suddenly you land in Denver, Colorado! There it all is in real life – all those enormous cars. But the first time I went away was when we did two gigs in Germany, which was supposed to be a sort of a trial to see how I worked out. The first one was at Nuremberg – that was a bit of a trial... [*Groan! Eds*]. The second was in Hamburg. I'd never been on a 'plane, and it was magic looking at how everything worked. And there's all these things for free, like the air sick bag, and the safety card – "Yeah, I'll take that as a

souvenir!" and so on. Then you go to this real top quality hotel in Nuremberg with oak panelling everywhere. And I'm in this place, with a sitting room and a bathroom that was all tiled, with a marble floor, and I can't believe it. I never wanted to leave that room because it was the nicest room I'd been in in my life. I thought I'd never get another room like this, this must be something really special. I got outrageously drunk for the first time in my life – the first of many – because I was just so excited. I was just blowing my top; I was like it for weeks. I couldn't stop talking, I was doing and saying silly things all the time and drinking far too much. This was the life!

How much compositional or musical input did you have?
Oh, it was sod all really. I think that quite a lot of what I played came out of my own head within the structure of Ian's music, and I perhaps put in one or two small ideas. I can't really think of any examples... Ah, yes I can. You know the bit on *Thick As A Brick* which ends side one and opens side two? Thinking back on it, that was very derivative of one of my famous numbers in The John Evan Band, which was Graham Bond's *Wading The Water*. He was very influential on things we did at that time, in 1966 or '67. But I can't think of much else. Oh, there was the silly *Hare Who Lost His Spectacles* – I wrote the music to that. I was at a soundcheck one day and I just started plonking away at the piano, and Jeffrey said, "I could tell a story over that," so Ian said, "Well, let's do it on an album, as a novelty thing." And the things people remember! A good friend of mine is a bass player – he has played with people like Peter Noone, Edison Lighthouse and so on – and he says that Jeffrey was his hero. He had this black & white striped suit and his black & white double bass, which was all Jeffrey's idea. So there are things that go into the band which, as well as a few musical ideas, all made it what it was at the time and gave it personality. With me it was the white suit I suppose, and this sad clown image, the Charlie Chaplin or Harpo Marx character. I had to find myself a stage costume because I didn't have anything appropriate. I didn't have Ian's jockstrap, or the silly clothes Glenn used to wear like the sixties hippies – you know, velvet jackets and so on – and whatever Martin used to wear. All the time I was looking for ideas. And I went to see a Marx Brothers film one night and I was really impressed, not by Groucho or Harpo, but Chico – he was the one who appealed to me. He was the one who played the piano too.

Were you surprised that Jethro Tull got so big and went on for so long?
Well, it is something that you are in while it is happening, so you can't be surprised by it... you just keep going. I was a bit surprised when it all finished, but that's another story! But things changed over the years of course. I really kept myself to myself, certainly from 1976 to '80. I just thought, well, I have got a regime to live by, and I used that to stop having depressions.

What was depressing you? Life on the road?
It was the aftermath of this first exciting "life is just one big drunken orgy" and "everyone thinks I'm really clever because I'm up there" sort of thing... and you get a bit disillusioned because you realise that you're not. It is not you – not who you are, but what you are. It is not a personality thing, it is people looking to a "pop star". So I thought, "Well, what IS in there, what am I doing, what does it mean?" I used to spend a lot of my time just staring at the hotel bedroom wall, gradually hyperventilating and eventually losing the feeling in my fingers and my hands...

So did you decide to leave, or was it suggested that you leave? Or was it a mutual thing anyway?
[*Long pause*]... I got a letter. At the end of tours we used to go our own ways and people would get in touch with us when something was organised, like the next album or tour. So this was April 1980, we had just finished a long series of tours in '79 in the States and we'd had about two months off. Then there was a tour of England and Europe and so it was just the general opinion that we had had enough for a bit and instead of just having three or four weeks off we would go away and do our own things for a while, and then be in touch sort of thing. Fine. So I went away and tried to... I was in a sorry state financially at the time having had a divorce and bad business ventures, and been ripped off by accountants and so on, so I

was a bit low about the whole thing. I kept in touch with David Palmer, and I had always wanted to play a Mozart Concerto, which I reckoned was just about within my technical grasp. I was talking about this to David, and was going to get one of those music-minus-one records and play the piano part to it, just for my own satisfaction. David was tinkling around with synthesisers, trying to reproduce orchestral sounds for the purposes of making demos. He still had his own musical life of course, and he wanted to do demos of some his orchestral numbers, but without the expense of hiring an orchestra. So he suggested we do something together, get another couple of guys and give a little concert. I'd play a Yamaha piano, and he knew a good synthesist called Dave Bristow who was and still is a Yamaha demonstrator – I saw him at David's a few weeks ago. He is brilliant, but he wasn't interested in being a group player; he has one eye on the security of being a respected career person at Yamaha, which is fair enough. But anyway, we did this and practised it all through the summer.

And then around about July I got a letter through the post. I opened it and it was a second copy, a carbon copy from a typewriter, and it said something along the lines of, "Dear Barrie, David and John. I'm sorry this is so rushed, but basically Melody Maker is coming out tomorrow and the story in it – which I couldn't prevent, I didn't want it but Terry Ellis put it in without my knowledge – is that the group has split up. Really, I'm going to do something on my own, maybe called Jethro Tull, maybe not. But I am using different people and I thought I ought to let you know." I can't remember if Ian had signed it or whether that was a bloody carbon as well. I was stunned by this – you know, hurt. And after it had sunk in, I thought, "I'm broke, I have no career, no qualifications. I'm 32, and I get this letter which is totally impersonal, just typed out so that everyone has got the same, not even a personal thing." So it came as a bit of a shock. But we thought, blow it, we are doing this little concert as a one-off thing just for the reasons I explained, and we put on a show at Clamden Church Hall which is David's local church. For me it was an ego trip playing a Mozart Concerto and for David it was experimentation and learning about synthesisers. So we thought, "Now we are all out of a job, why don't we make a permanent thing of it and start a group, which Dave called Tallis after Thomas Tallis, who is his hero composer from a period of music which he is really interested in and knowledgeable about. [16th century Elizabethan church music.] We did a demo album which never got anywhere, and Dave Bristow didn't want to do it anyway, he wanted to get back to Yamaha. I was a bit disillusioned, and it just sort of fizzled out.

Was the demo album actually pressed up in demo form?
We did a master of it. But what I liked better was a tape we did at the church hall, which was live. I did have a copy of the album on cassette somewhere. Some of it was pretty dismal, I suppose. If we had gone on I expect we would have totally changed the direction of things and started doing more of David's songs, which are pretty good and might have had a limited appeal to a minority of people. Being a gregarious sort of person he knew everyone in Clamden. He wrote a very good song called *The Vicar And The Publican* which was about the local vicar and old Bert, the publican, who had both died of cancer. He also wrote one called *The Cathedral* which is also very good. But by this time I was feeling a bit disillusioned with things.

So at that stage you were still thinking in terms of being a rock musician?
Well, until Tallis fizzled out. But by then somebody had made a mistake in paying our royalties, and we were overpaid, which helped me get square again. We thought it represented a backlog of royalties, but in fact it was a mistake which eventually came to light, and there was a big dispute about who owed what to whom. I thought I'd had an understanding from when I was invited to join the group, but when we went to see a Q.C. he said, "Well, where is your contract?" We said, "What contract?" And of course he told us not to waste his time. So about 18 months ago we had a big meeting about it. Barrie was up in arms and didn't want to give an inch. Jeffrey was saying, "Let's forget the whole thing," and I suggested what I always suggest in such situations, split it equally. And that is what happened in the end. I haven't seen Ian since that meeting.

Did that disappoint you... from having been mates for so long it degenerated into squabbles about percentages and so on?

109

Yes, I suppose it did.

What do you do now?
I run a little company that does office refurbishment. It was a company that I took over from a friend who retired. When the Tallis thing folded I didn't know what the hell to do... I did a lot of things, actually. I had a boat that was a bloody disaster. I spent six months playing at being a farmer on a friend's farm, learning how to drive tractors and combine harvesters and things – that was great fun! I'd got this house which I couldn't afford to have anything done to, so I got the *Reader's Digest* book of Do-It-Yourself and I did it myself! I started tiling things and building walls and so on. I had never done anything like that in my life but I enjoyed it. And it happened that I was building a wall for the father of an ex-girlfriend of mine – he ran a company – when he got a 'phone call from his client, British Airways, who needed a kitchen put into the terminal at Heathrow. So he said to me, "Can you do tiling?", and that was it. I got out my *Reader's Digest* book again and did 250 metres of tiling in ten days! He was suitably impressed, so I had a few lessons from a professional and carried on with his firm. I did not know what else to do. I was earning £30 a day, which was a little less than I was earning with Tull, but what else could I do? I was fed up with sitting around at Auntie Joyce's because I was too frightened to go out and face the world. Anyway, my friend was due to retire soon, so he invited me to learn about actually running the business. I was worried about it, but he got me to do it, for which I am eternally grateful. He was a bit like a Dad. You see, all my life... My father was 58 when I was born, and people who are qualified to help me a bit reckon that has something to do with my adolescence lasting until [*laughing*] 35! He gave me the confidence to take over when he retired. I have been on my own for three years and the turnover has doubled, so I can't be doing too badly at it. I feel that once more I am doing something on my own two feet, that I don't owe to anyone else. I mean, I owe it to the old boy for giving me the chance, and I owe it to my wife who has kept me going at it when I would have turned round and walked away as I did from Luton, and as I did from college and so on.

Do you still play music?
The last time I played was Christmas 1986. I'm just so busy with the firm, and refurbishing and rebuilding the house, that I don't have much free time.

So is it fair to say that you have absolutely finished with the music business? You would never even think about getting a band together?
Yeah. I am quite happy. I just wish I had a bit more time to play. If you have fairly limited technique, which I have compared to people who can really play, you need to spend a lot of time practising to be able to play Beethoven Sonatas and the more complicated stuff. I do get pleasure from doing some of the smaller Chopin pieces, and Debussy, some Schubert... not the really heavy virtuoso kind of stuff. I got to about Grade 4 when I was younger, and then when I started really practising again in about 1976 I took Grade 8 and got a distinction, which I am quite proud of.

So presumably if there was ever any talk of a reunion concert you would not be interested?
No, no. I wouldn't have the time.

Do you ever see any of the other guys, apart from David Palmer?
I go over to see Barrie occasionally, but you know how it is. We inevitably end up talking about the old days, which isn't always a good thing. I haven't heard anything of Glenn since he turned up at one of the gigs at the Los Angeles Forum in around '78. He does keep in touch with some people in Blackpool. He was a really great bass player, apart from the fact that he just went potty! This rock star thing went to his head and he started playing up on stage and spent more time dancing around than concentrating on playing, and it got sloppy. Ian didn't like it, and it really was getting sloppy, so he got the chop. But he was a very naturally talented bass player.

Have you seen Tull since you left?
I watched the *Slipstream* video on TV the other night. I saw a tape of it and it really was fast-forward all the time – I thought it was embarrassing. That was from the tour just after I left, with Eddie Jobson – he didn't stay very long, did he! He didn't really look the part to me. I mean, I've got no sour grapes, I couldn't give a damn, but I just thought it was really quite embarrassing. Dave Pegg was playing around with a girl's bottom for some strange reason and I thought, "God Almighty, leave it out!" I got halfway through it and just fast-forwarded. And I missed the Channel 4 documentary because *Champions* was on the other side.

What do you think of the current music scene?
I have just started in the last year or so listening to Capital Radio [*pop music*] as opposed to Radio 3 or Radio 4 [*classical music and news programmes*], and for the first time since the sixties I am quite conversant with what is going on in the charts. And it seems so stagnant to me – it doesn't sound any different to the sixties. Plus the fact that everyone is doing stuff from the forties and fifties. I mean, when *When I Fall In Love* by Rick Astley came out the DJ John Sachs, without saying a word, played the Nat King Cole record, and if I was Rick Astley... well, he is making money, but if I was him I'd be bloody embarrassed! And as for The Pet Shop Boys and *You Were Always On My Mind*... that is diabolical. The piano is played by a 6-year old, and a pretty bad 6-year old at that! If you listen to the Ella Fitzgerald version it's one of the most beautiful records ever made. Superb! I mean, if you can't think of anything new to do, alright, do things that sound like the sixties, but don't slaughter things that were good thirty or forty years ago. No, it all seems a pretty bad state of affairs to me. I think I'll stay in building!

Well, thanks very much for talking to us John.
It is a true account as I remember it. Everybody has their own viewpoint, but that is my unbiased, honest view. Well, it might be biased - but it is honest!

[*Turn to Chapter 12 for John's pre-Tull reminiscences.*]

Chapter 9

MICK ABRAHAMS

(Published in Issue #18, March 1989)

In the late 1980s Mick Abrahams started gigging again under the name of Blodwyn Pig, with a line-up that included original bassist Andy Pyle, long-time buddy and ex-Tull and ex-Pig Clive Bunker, keyboard player Bruce Boardman, and sax players Bernie Hetherington and the utterly legendary Dick Heckstall-Smith. DR and MW caught up with Mick before a gig in Milton Keynes.

Why have you decided to bring back Blodwyn Pig?
A very good question! A number of reasons really... A good friend of mine has been on at me for ages, telling me off for not playing enough, and last year he mentioned that a friend of his was having a complete refit at that club you came to, and they wanted me to put a band together for the opening. And so I said, "Sure. Do you want McGregor's Engine – which was me, Andy Pyle and Clive Bunker – or the Mick Abrahams Band, or even... EVEN yer actual Blodwyn Pig??" I was only joking actually, but they said, "Yes, great!" I booked Bernie, who had played with the Mick Abrahams Band, and I booked Clive and Andy, and then we were looking for a keyboard player. Some friends took me to the Pizza Express in Bedford, and lo and behold Bruce, who I'd not met before but had seen play a couple of times, and Dick were on. So I just walked into the dressing room for a chat and Dick was freaked out. "Wow, Mick Abrahams – and he's still alive!!" And while we were talking I mentioned that Pig had a gig on the 3rd and he said, "What? You've got it back together?!" So I asked Dick and Bruce if they would like to join and they jumped at it.

You knew Dick before then?
Oh yes. I've played with him a couple of times. I played with him when I was with John Mayall, and I sat in with Colosseum after I left Tull, although I had the Blodwyn Pig thing firmly set in my mind already. It's funny, because Dick Heckstall-Smith would have been the ideal man for the original Blodwyn Pig because I liked the Graham Bond Organisation and Alexis Korner's Blues Inc so much, and so I'm really pleased to have him now. And it doesn't deter from what he is doing, because he has this magic jazz band called DHSS – Dick Heckstall-Smith Septet – which is going really well. And as you know, Poor Mouth have split up leaving Clive Bunker free to join us, so it's all looking really good. We all have very clear ideas of how the band should sound and it's shaping up well... which is really why we are doing it. We can take this band into the '90s with a more modern Pig – yeah, Modwyn Pig! – but we don't want to stray too far from the roots.

What about your job?
Well, that's OK. It is my own business and I have people who can take care of things while I'm not there, so I am free to commit myself to Pig or whatever. I have made the conscious decision now that I am going to spend more time playing music, because that is what I do well, and I want to do a lot more. I'm also doing a lot more gigs now with Bruce as a duo, and sometimes as a trio. It's really fun.

Did you think of asking Jack Lancaster to rejoin?
No, not really. I don't mean that as a snub to Jack, but he has gone to the States and I haven't seen him for years. I believe he is still playing and he'd be completely welcome to come back any time he wanted – and I'm sure he would really like to play alongside Dick. But the thing is, Dick is here. And Dick, strangely enough as I said, is the guy that I originally envisaged for Pig. I've always idolised him from the time he was with Graham Bond. I remember standing there absolutely numb thinking, "Yeah! This is what music is all about!" And they didn't have a guitar player! I always wanted to say, y'know, "Please Mr Bond, sir – can I play...?"

Any plans for a new LP?
The plan at the moment is to hire or borrow or steal the equipment to make an album very soon - 16-track, because I can't see a band like Pig needing more than 16-track. And then we will be able to go to the record companies, tell 'em who we are and say, "Look, this is our album," and hopefully persuade them to bung us some money. We are not looking for an enormous advance because we are never going to get a deal like that, but I like to think we will get enough to promote the record and set up a tour on the college circuit, which is where I think our strength will lie. But if we can't get a record deal then we can always do it ourselves.

Are you planning any sort of tour yet?
We will. We are playing places like this right now because we want to warm up and play. It doesn't matter where. We want to move on to places like The Marquee, Dingwalls, The 100 Club etc, and we will do – assuming they book us! But we are in a situation now where they say, "Well, fine – have you got any tapes we can listen to?" And at the moment we haven't. And none of us wants to just do a tape of four or five Blodwyn songs, we want something representative of what we are now. We do play some of the old songs, but that's not all we are about.
Oh, by the way, I'd just like to drop something in here on a personal note. Just to say thanks to you guys for bringing me out of myself a little bit – you have been instrumental in getting things going through your encouragement and the things you've written, and you actually saved a great friendship. Andy Pyle and I have sorted out the problems of the past and I'd like to say publicly now that we are really the best of friends. And that is largely due to you two guys. [*Blushes all round. Eds.*]

Martin Barre told me you 'phoned him recently. What was that all about?
Nothing, really. I just 'phoned or a chat, to get some general feedback on what's happening, y'know. I've always been friendly with Martin, there's never been any animosity between us about the job. I actually like his playing a lot better now than I ever did... oh no, that sounds awful... I said that wrong. I've never thought him a bad guitarist, he has always been a good guitarist - but I never saw him originally as suited to Tull, because I had this, I suppose, blinkered view of Tull as it was when I was with them. But strangely enough, what Tull are doing NOW is how I would have envisaged Tull evolving within six or seven years from the start, and for me it is magic. What they are doing now is great. There was a lot of stuff in-between that I didn't take a lot of notice of. Ian's songs are good, they always have been, and they only ever made one bad album for me which was *Thick As A Brick*. I thought that was awful – but all the other stuff I thought well, yeah, great, and just left it at that. But Tull have never been the sort of band that I thought it was originally. But now, all of a sudden, I've heard their new stuff and it is fucking magic! I'm really impressed, and I'm very pleased that it has gone that way because it is nice to like the band now. I've always worried about not liking it in case it was just me being a c***!

Martin Barre told me last week that he still regards you as Jethro Tull's guitarist and sees himself still as your replacement, because you impressed him so much the first time he saw Tull.
Really? That's weird... amazing! I'm well chuffed!

When you make the new album are you going to ask Ian Anderson to play flute on it?
Well, why not? I am sure he would do it actually. He is really quite friendly now, much more so than he has been in a long time. And I would like to see him again... have a beer and a bit of grub with him. As I said to him a few weeks back on the 'phone, you know... there's a lot of water under the bridge, and we do go back a long way...

Chapter 10

BARRIEMORE BARLOW

(Published in Issue #19, June 1989)

After many months of letters and 'phone calls DR and MW got to meet Barrie Barlow at his delightful home in Henley-on-Thames. Barrie spoke very openly and at length about his time with Jethro Tull and before that with The John Evan Band, and would surely have gone on much longer had he not had to dash off that evening to a party to launch the 'new' Yes. In fact he did speak to us for much longer than he should have done really, and so Issue 19 recorded our thanks to Barrie – and our apologies to his wife, Dee!

As with John Evans [Chapter 8], we split the interview into two, and included the pre-Tull reminiscences in the John Evan Band feature [Chapter 12]. Before the tapes were rolling, Barrie flicked through the previous issue of AND. He was very interested to learn of the reformed Blodwyn Pig, and mentioned that Mick had asked him to join the original Blodwyn Pig after Mick had left Tull. And he recalled how it was that an album by The Graham Bond Organisation (with Dick Heckstall-Smith) had really been the catalyst which had spurred on the youngsters who were to become Jethro Tull to start playing that style of music which eventually brought them fame and fortune. The conversation then turned to the 20 Years Of Jethro Tull box-set, and we were shocked to learn that Barrie had not been given a copy by Chrysalis, but had had to fork out £26 in W.H.Smith for it! He continues...

I bought it because there were tracks on there that said I was playing, but they meant nothing to me because we didn't have any titles for them. So I was interested to see how they had come out. And it was like listening to somebody else, because I had forgotten all the songs anyway. I remembered a couple of little riff things... It sounded alright, though. Well, some of it did, but I can see why some of it was scrapped.

Anyway, let's get on with this – ask away. I must admit I don't feel very comfortable doing this – it's a bit like being in the doctor's!

An easy one to start with – what is your real name?
Barrie Barlow.

Where did 'Barriemore' come from?
Ian, really. Just to make it a bit more interesting, I suppose. But I wasn't christened Barriemore.

OK. Now, to go back to the transition from The John Evan Band to Jethro Tull... How did you feel after you left the band in London and then they went on to enormous success?
Well, I went back to Birmingham and had probably the worst six months of my life ever, because I had to try to pick up the pieces, pick up the threads. I didn't know anybody from school at all, and I didn't know anybody musically because all of my music playing had been in Blackpool. My Auntie Nora, God bless her, got me the WORST job in the world... And I was really low, really low. And John Evans came down for the weekend, and Jethro Tull were playing at Mothers in Birmingham. They turned up in this blue van to take us to the gig, and Ian came walking down the path. My Uncle Albert was in the front room and he looked out of the window and said, "What the BLOODY HELL is that??" Because Ian at the time looked totally outrageous, because he was away from home and could do whatever he liked without any aggro from his Dad, y'know. And he did look... stunning. Because he was SO outrageous. So anyway, we went to Mothers with them – it was Mick, Clive, Ian and Glenn – and they were fabulous. They were ace, really, really ace. And I felt nothing but pleasure for them because they were so good; I enjoyed it so much. Each one of them was really strong in their own areas, as individual musicians and collectively. Ian playing harmonica, and Mick playing harmonica, and they were doing these blues things... They were doing some Sonny Terry and

Brownie McGhee type things and it had, like, come full circle. It was included in their style then. And it was really exciting. And it was just a matter of time before it became a national success. And it HAD to be, because it was that good. It was unique. And of course the flute had never appeared with The John Evan Band or Smash because Ian then just played the guitar.

I bought the first album *This Was*, but I didn't really hear much about them then – I think they went to America. But obviously... a situation that you have been in and left of your own accord... when it becomes famous and successful there is a part of you that thinks, "Bloody hell! I wish I was doing that instead of turning this bloody lathe", you know. But I was very pleased for them, obviously. And then John joined, who I'd kept in touch with anyway – we are like brothers really, John and I.

So I was just gigging around with loads of people. I did my apprenticeship and all that number. I met Dee and we got married. I was back in Blackpool by then, and I had two gigs – I was working through the day from 8am till 6.30pm and then I used to go and play in The Gaiety Bar with a keyboard player called Ronnie Ogden – "Mumblin' Ronnie Ogden" That finished at 11pm, and then I'd go and play at a night club with Tony Williams and Mike Proctor in a band called Requiem. I'd finish that at about 2.30 in the morning. So I used to finish day work and go to sleep for an hour or two, wake up and do the first gig and then straight to the second gig, go to sleep and then back to work again. And in the middle of all that our little car packed up and was off the road for two months, so I was doing all that on a bloody bicycle! I mean, I really worked my arse off, you know. But we managed to save up enough, Dee and me, got a mortgage etc. And all the aspirations about being a professional musician were pretty much finished. We'd had Katie, our first daughter, we got our house, and we were just sort of floating along really. I was playing music as well, and playing football – I mean, it was all the things I like, a good balance of everything apart from my day job, which I really hated. I remember driving home one evening and stopping the car before I got home. I just sat there thinking to myself, "Well, this is your lot. You've tried, you've given it a good crack, but this is your lot. Accept it."

And about two weeks after that it was the FA Cup Final. I was at my mate's house who had the colour telly, and so were all the other footballers. We'd got some cans in, like you do for the Cup Final, drawn the curtains, got rid of the women, you know. And suddenly Evans comes screaming up the road, drives over two people's gardens, completely pissed out of his head! He'd just finished the American tour and he had come back as brown as a berry with hair down to his back-side. And he just walked into this mate Ziggy Shaw's house, stormed in and he said, "What the fuck are you doing with this bunch of c***s?? Come on, you don't want to associate with this bunch of c***s!" Because he was drunk, you know – he was getting a bit arsey! So I had to usher him out of the door, you know, like, "See you in a minute, chaps..." So I said, "Look, John, I want to watch the Cup Final. It's great to see you, but I really want to watch the match." So he said, "Come and watch it at my mother's! Come on, come on!" So he dragged me, still in my slippers, round to his mother's house a few doors away, and I had to leave this big colour telly and watch the game on a tiny 15" black and white thing. So I'm sat there right in front of the telly, not talking to him because I'm trying to concentrate on the match, you know, and he's talking away and I'm just going, "Yes, very nice, but look John, I'm trying to watch the Cup Final!" And then he said, "Clive is leaving Tull. Do you want the gig?" And it was like a double-take, you know – "Yeah, yeah, hang on a minute, I think it's a free kick or... WHAAAT???!"

Anyway, I'd only got the *This Was* album, and when he said they would come up to give me an audition I had to nip out and get the albums because I didn't know any of the material. John ringed the ones that I would have to play on. Requiem were rehearsing at that time in a children's home in St Annes and the equipment was all set up there, so Ian and John came up. Ian and I just had a jam together to start with, and it was great, because Ian is a great rhythm player, really good to play with. And then we did *To Cry You A Song* and stuff like that. And the rest, as they say, is history.

How did it feel to walk into such a massively popular band?

Peculiar. Very peculiar. Because Clive was a great player. A well-known player, and an integral part of the first Jethro Tull. So I felt obliged to try and do my best to play the songs like Clive played the songs.

But I had been to see Tull about six months before that, at The Opera House in Blackpool, and I actually couldn't understand it. With all deference to all concerned, I couldn't understand what was going on then because they weren't playing together. It was like five different people playing in five different bands, and it wasn't as good as lots of bands I'd seen. The tightness had gone – it wasn't that band I'd seen a couple of years ago at Mothers, that tight unit. There were some good songs there, but... I don't think they liked playing in Blackpool anyway. Ian has an aversion to Blackpool, I think.

I think that was the last time Tull played Blackpool.
Yes, it probably was. They didn't enjoy it. Anyway, one of the first things Ian said to me when I joined Tull was, "Don't worry – nobody can keep time in this band"! So that was... really encouraging, you know!

So it was like absolute madness for me from then on. I handed in my notice at work and headed off to the big city. We did *Life Is A Long Song*, that little EP thing, in a couple of days, and then it was rehearsals for the tour. It was insane, crazy for me, because I had been in this routine of work, work, work, and then it was... well, it was heaven! Because now all I had to do was play, you know? Having said that, I'd got to work really hard just to cut it in the band because I know there were lots of players around then that could have taken the gig over. And if I had been them I might have looked elsewhere. Michael Giles from King Crimson was doing nothing then, and he had been THE guy for years – he would have been great with Tull. Well, I left this gig playing at The Gaiety Bar with Ronnie Ogden and three weeks later I was doing The Salt Palace, Salt Lake City, a 10,000-seater! I was scared to death. I went down to the soundcheck on my own, and it was like standing in Wembley Stadium – obviously it wasn't that big, but that sort of perspective – and it was totally intimidating. I can't really remember much at all about the first gig because I was so nervous. But the second gig was at Red Rocks in Phoenix, a natural amphitheatre with seating for ten or twelve thousand, and fifteen to twenty thousand showed up...

Ah... the riots!
Yeah, riots... and that was my second gig! They were dropping tear gas and all that stuff, and there were babies younger than Katie strapped to girls' backs, those hippy girls, all smoking dope. A great cloud of dope, tear gas everywhere, people turning over police cars and setting fire to them.... it was a bit heavy! I did this drum solo, and I was so nervous I got off the kit and started to do a tap dance, just to make it a bit different! Afterwards Terry Ellis gave me a bollocking because I couldn't play a drum solo like Ginger Baker, so I said, "Well why didn't you get Ginger Baker then?"

What about your style of playing? What did you think of Ian's comments in *A New Day* that your style was a bit "fussy" – well suited to Jethro Tull, but he couldn't see you sitting in with a rock'n'roll band?
Well, perhaps you should ask Jimmy Page or Robert Plant that...

Well, yes, we were a bit taken aback. We were surprised he said that, but do you think it is fair? Do you think you have a fussy style?
I think maybe I had with Tull; I think I played far too much with Tull. I was too busy, got in the way of things. But having said that, for the majority of songs we didn't know what the top line was going to be. When we did *Warchild* there were massive spaces in the backing track, and I'm thinking, "What is happening here? Better fill this bit, it's boring," you know. But then we hear it, and there's vocals on it and all manner of things and I would NEVER have played those things had I known. And it is hard to work like that, without the whole song in mind. It was the same in Martin's case. If he is given a guitar solo to do he will sweat blood to make it the best possible guitar solo he can do, regardless of the song around it. But music was like that in those days, you know. Whereas now... people send me tapes, or I'm helping

someone write in the studio, and I'm thinking about the song totally. So I cringe when I hear some of the things I used to play because it is exactly what I am telling people not to do. But that aside... well, Ian has often had a go at me. He always did.

When you were in the band?

Oh yeah. But, really, that is something that I don't want to talk about, because I have got immense respect for Ian as a musician. But I disagreed with a lot of personal things that he did. It's much too personal for me to talk about.

When I first joined Tull it was really happy. It was like being in The John Evan Band – John was there, Ian was there, Jeffrey... And it still had that sort of schoolboy humour. Just being together – it was like a family. And we were earning! It was great. If all you have ever wanted to do is earn a living playing music, and you are doing it with your friends... It was heaven, you know... But it changed...

Do you think that was largely due to the pressure on Ian, as the frontman?

Oh, I think every frontman... The very nature of that role sets them apart from everybody else in the world really, because they are the people who communicate with the audience directly. I always saw my role as marshalling the rest of the band, keeping them together. I have to keep the beat together through different time changes so the band can play to it. Ian is a great time-keeper, a great rhythm player, but he was playing acoustic guitar and a lot of the time it got lost. And on reflection, that was the reason it was so bad when I saw them at The Opera House. Clive couldn't hear him, and the whole thing was falling to bits.

But... this is really why I've been keeping off talking to you guys, because I don't want to make any big waves, you know. I don't want to give people the impression that Ian and I spend all our time having a go at each other. I had a happy time with Tull, and I'm very grateful for it, thank you very much. I miss John Glascock. I miss him dearly.

You have said before that you were like brothers. What was he like?

Well, I'll tell you what he was like. He couldn't do anything other than play the bass and guitar. He didn't want to do anything other than play the bass and guitar. He lived a fairly rock'n'roll life before joining Tull. And he was like a shot in the arm for Tull, a marvellous player.

Because Jeffrey... Jeffrey wasn't really a bass player, but he was a friend of Ian's you know. And I think because Glenn Cornick was very "rock'n'roll"... Ian didn't like that, and I think ended up not liking Glenn because of that. And Jeffrey used to play bass in the old days, and Ian was living next door and hanging out with him. Ian bought Jeffrey a bass guitar one Christmas and taught him all the bass parts, and then brought him into the band. Jeffrey's input was very sort of "off the wall", artistically, and was really exciting, but his execution of the bass parts took a very long time. So we all became quite proficient badminton players! We would turn up at rehearsals with our little cassette recorders – because nobody reads music, it is so much easier just to put it on tape – our cassette recorders, our badminton racquets and shuttlecocks, and somebody would have the net. And the other four of us would have these quite involved and serious badminton matches while Jeffrey learned the bass parts. And WE all knew the bass parts, we could all sing them before Jeffrey could play them. We would invent little sayings and phrases to help Jeffrey as well. You know... "rum-ti-tum, riddle me di-do" was actually the percussive part of one of the bass lines!

So there was clearly a very close friendship between Ian and Jeffrey, and Ian put a hell of a lot of effort in on Jeffrey's behalf. And Jeffrey really didn't know how lucky he was to have stepped into the position he was in, and when it suited him he just stepped out. He wanted to step out when we had been working in America a lot, trying to take advantage of the double taxation treaty between the IRS and the Inland Revenue, but we got clobbered and had to do two tours to pay off the IRS. But Jeffrey didn't want to go, and he just said, "I'm leaving." And Ian went APESHIT! - as you would. He was furious. And when it became clear to him that the rest of us had known how Jeffrey had felt I think he realised then that he had drifted away from us; it had become him and us. On the one hand, Ian had sort of stepped away from us, but on the other hand we hadn't done anything to try to rectify that, so it was six of one and half-a-dozen of the other I suppose. But everybody else was OK with each other. Well, Terry Ellis did some... amazing things - but that's a whole other story...

So, Jeffrey left after we had been touring with Carmen, the flamenco-rock band. John Glascock had been at the side of the stage watching every show, loving every minute, and he was elated when he was offered the gig. And he found it really exciting and adventurous to play with Tull and, like I said, he was really a shot in the arm. With all deference... I mean, I love Jeffrey, but with all deference to him, having a PROPER bass player, for me, was fantastic. And at the soundchecks and so on we would play all the time together. At the soundcheck after everybody had gone off the stage John and I would always be there. In the hotel rooms after the gigs John and I would be together, making things up on his guitar. And the band improved, without a doubt the band improved. But although he was a great player, Ian didn't really like him, and I think he got a really bad deal all round. And I used to get really angry on John's behalf, to see the way he was treated. And you know, he was the best bass player Tull ever had, in my opinion. He would work really hard – at the end of the gig Ian and I would literally wring out our clothes, and John was the third person to do that when he joined Tull. He'd put everything into it.

We used to share the same dressing room, and he sat down one night with his hand on his chest complaining of heart-burn. I put it down to him not eating, or something. Anyway, we finished the tour and went back home, and after a couple of days to recover I called Jackie, John's girlfriend, and she said, "This lazy sod's been in bed for two days." And John was renowned normally for staying up all night – some hotels in America, he wouldn't be there in the morning because he was still rockin' and rollin', you know. So she got the doctor out and they rushed him to hospital, and he had to have open heart surgery. I was shattered.

But... we had another tour to do, and we needed a bass player. Ian asked me if I knew any bass players, and I said. "I now a geezer who can," as they say. So I shot off up to Blackpool, got hold of Tony Williams and taught him all the bass parts – because I knew them all, from the badminton! So he came down for the audition pretending not to know any of them, and of course 'picked them up' straight away! It was like, "Hey, isn't he quick!" So he did that tour. John came back after that, but his circulation had been affected and the feeling in his fingers wasn't right, so he had to bow out. But he could still play acoustic, and we started to write some things together.

Anyway, we needed another bass player. Ian wanted to get this guy who had been at Harvard Music Academy or something in Boston, a sort of pseudo-funk player. He was a very good player but he wasn't the right guy for Tull, and I was quite surprised that Ian wanted him. So I said, "Look, Richard Thompson is playing at The Hexagon, I'm gonna go and check Dave Pegg out." So I went down there and I thought Peggy would be absolutely ideal. So I got Peggy down here and he got the gig. And he was great, you know, learned it all quickly and so on. But Peggy brought the sort of folky element into it which was... well, it wasn't the closest thing to my heart, you know. But, a very nice man, a great player, and added something as well, as anybody does when an individual joins. But I missed John. I couldn't help it, I missed him. So we did an American tour, and towards the end of that tour we were in L.A. and I called John and I said, "Look, do you fancy getting together with me and David Allen (from Carmen) and forming a band?" And he was absolutely elated. So I called David Allen and he was up for it. I met him, we had lunch – he had booked his flight that very day. And the next day John died. And I just... we had one more gig to do, and I didn't want to do it, but the management bludgeoned me into doing it... and I cried all the way through the gig. I was like a zombie. I must have been like a zombie for months and months. It hurt, it really did. And the hurt was multiplied by the way I felt he'd been treated. He had not been properly looked after financially – to the extent that I had to pay for the funeral.

A lot of people see the credits on *Stormwatch* as in pretty poor taste. Did that annoy you?
Check the mixes on that album too – on the tracks where Ian plays bass you can hear every bass line. But then, it's balancing that... er... well, if Ian didn't have a big ego there wouldn't be anything to talk about, would there? You know what I mean? You have to balance that. There is a certain genius in that guy, and where people excel in some areas it is natural to have faults, if you like, in other areas. And nobody is perfect; we all make mistakes, we all rub each other up the wrong way, from families to towns to nations. We have wars – global

wars, and domestic wars. And like I say, I've had a lot of personal differences with Ian, but at the end of the day he does have this genius. He is a superb musician and a very, very clever man. He is very shrewd and always has the perfect answer for anything. Anything that might crop up at a meeting for instance – which is great when he is on your side!

Anyway... So John died, and David Allen had booked his flight over, and there was this guitarist called Robin Hill who was an excellent player. It was supposed to be John, Robin, David Allen and myself. So now David and Robin came down and we started auditioning a series of bass players, and Chris Glen got it. We had to do another Tull tour, which Ian announced would be the last for some time, because he wanted to carry on with his fish farm. So we were rehearsing at Shepperton, and Tull rehearsals would be from 10am to 6pm, and then, with everyone's permission, David, Robin, Chris, myself and Tommy Ayres on keyboards would rehearse 'til midnight or 1am. So I was getting this band together before I left Tull, to make it smooth, you know, so everybody could be friends.

We did the Tull tour, my last Tull tour, came back, and I had a meeting with Ian and we agreed to go our separate ways, shook hands and everything. Everything was fine. I called Terry Ellis within a couple of weeks to see if he was interested in the new band because it was really going well, it sounded great. And he said, "I haven't heard you sounding this happy for years. I've never heard you so into something." So I said, "Please come down and see us.".... "Promise I will. Promise I'll be there." Then the next issue of Melody Maker came out. It said, "SACKED! SACKED! SACKED!" And I went fucking mental, as you can imagine. Ian had sent a note of apology before it came out, and I thought, "Hell, it can't be that bad." But of course it was. And David Palmer... his daughter was at school, and the kids were taking the micky out of her in the playground – that's how David found out he'd been sacked from the band! And John Evans was really shattered, you know. He just didn't know what to do. When you are on the road with a major band everything is done for you, and suddenly to take that away from him – he didn't know where to start. He came to live here for about six months. Took his piano with him and he used to practice all day long – nearly drove us crazy!

I carried on working with David Allen and Robin Hill, rehearsing in our cottage near Blackpool, but then I had to go away to do an album with somebody. And when I came back David Allen had gone and tried to get a deal for himself. Everybody wanted to kill him! So then I got together with Zal Cleminson and formed Tandoori Cassette. If you come over again I'll show you the video of our last Marquee gig. It Bites saw it the other day and they were knocked out by it. Tandoori Cassette was something that really absorbed me. It took all of my mental energy. I used to work really hard in Tull, but I worked three or four times harder with Tandoori Cassette because I had to play Ian's role, organising everything. But the audiences were always full of musicians armed with tape-recorders and nicking all our licks! And the record companies just did not know what to make of us at all. The rules were, if you've heard it before don't play it. And Zal was a great fella to play with.

Why did it break up?

Because we couldn't get a deal good enough to keep us going. I was putting all the money in and eventually I had to turn the tap off; and we all went our separate ways. Zal has packed up music completely now. Zal was like... he's got the rhythm of Ian, the artistic "off-the-wallness" of Jeffrey and the awareness of what was then today's music. In fact, it was tomorrow's music – dare I say it was just that bit ahead of its time. It sounds... it sounds like the Peter Gabriel album two years hence. And that is annoying. Really annoying.

What or who is The Storm?

The Storm? Ah, well, somebody really caught me off guard there. I was working with a keyboard player, who is now working with Trevor Horn. We wrote some songs together, but we couldn't get a deal on them and he then went to work with Stock, Aitken and Waterman for a year. And it drove him absolutely crazy, and now he is working with Trevor Horn. But we didn't have a name, and when this guy asked us what we were called George, the keyboard player, just said, "The Storm" – so that was it. But it was something that was finished just a couple of months after that.

Are you playing in a band now?

Not really, no. But watching those guys in there, It Bites, that is the first live thing I've seen for ages that I think is really good, and it is inspiring me now to start going for it again. But of course it is who you play with as well. I played with Robert Plant for a while and... well, it wasn't anywhere near as good as Tandoori Cassette.

What about Jimmy Page? Was there any chance of you getting the live gig?
No, not really. I just did a couple of sessions because he had heard this track I had done with John Miles where I turned the beat around. Jimmy wanted that style of playing on a couple of tracks, so Jason (Bonham) told him to call me.
The last gig I played was a good 'un. Jon Lord on piano, Roger Glover on bass, Joe Brown on vocals, Sam Brown on vocals, me on the drums and George Harrison on guitar. That was great, and we played for about two and a half hours.

Where was that?
At Ian Paice's house. Because there are a lot of rock'n'rollers living round here, and we all get together from time to time.

When did you last see Ian Anderson?
About 18 months ago, at a meeting of accountants. Oh, and he came to see John Miles when I was touring with him. And I do get the impression that he has mellowed very much; he is a lot more approachable now. That's down to having kids, I think. It is sad really that there is this thing between us. I suppose I became a sort of spokesperson for the group whenever we were unhappy about something. They would all come to me to moan about this and that, and I always ended up having to confront Ian. And it has left a scar between Ian and myself... but I still think he is a great musician, I really do. And I thought his solo album was really good – apart from the production. He really should have got somebody in to produce it, because there are some really good songs there, but it is flat all the way through. No dynamics at all. And it's spoilt because of that.

What did you think of _Crest Of A Knave_?
I've only heard a couple of tracks, but I honestly thought it was Mark Knopfler from Dire Straits, I really did.

You've heard it won a Grammy as best Hard Rock LP?
Well all the musician people I know have been taking the piss out of it.

But that goes back really to what category could you put Tull in?
Well, I think they are in their own. And good luck to them for that. Because you can't copy that, you know. And that goes hand-in-hand with longevity. And it will go through highs and lows, peaks and troughs. It did go through a time when everybody thought they had broken up, but well, you know, they are back!
I did go to see them at The Royal Albert Hall in 1981 when they had Mark Craney and Eddie Jobson in the band, and I thought it was dreadful. I walked out, I really did. But it wasn't... I mean, they were great at Mothers, you know, and they were not as good at the Albert Hall. OK, there were some really ropey nights when I was part of the band, but I tried my hardest all the time. I think we all did. But it seemed like Eddie Jobson was 'doing them a favour' by being in the band, you know?

Do you have any particular favourite Tull songs or albums?
I only ever liked particular songs from albums really. Well, I really like _Stand Up_, I think that is a great album. And I love _Sossity_, that is a wonderful song.
I don't know how relevant Tull's music is these days, or indeed how relevant it has ever been. What is relevant in this business really? It is a luxury business, you are peddling luxury goods, and if you can make a living and really enjoy what you are doing – well, really, you can't ask for more than that, can you?

[Turn to Chapter 12 for Barrie's pre-Tull reminiscences.]

Chapter 11

MARK CRANEY

Interviewed by DOANE PERRY

(Published in Issue #20, September 1989)

In issue #20 DR wrote of his amazement at finding an exclusive interview with Doane Perry in the May 1989 edition of The People's Democratic Republic of Yemen Angling Times. *Doane's reply to the question of whether he had any unfulfilled ambitions was as follows:*

> *"Well you know, people seem to think that I have just about everything a guy could want. I have made dozens of records with people like Bette Midler and Lou Reed. I'm with Jethro Tull, the greatest rock group in the world, and I'm tall and good-looking and desired by women the world over. But all I've ever really wanted to do is write something for* A New Day, *which is undoubtedly the finest publication I have ever seen. I would love to have something printed in an edition of that. My greatest wish would be to change places with David Rees, the editor, just for a day."*

Readers still unsure of the veracity of the above finally fell in when DR went on to say that he would be drumming for Tull in Inverness on 18 September…

The real story was that Tull's erstwhile drummer Mark Craney had recently suffered a serious illness. Sadly, despite the optimism expressed below, Mark never really fully recovered, and he passed away in November 2005 at the untimely age of 53. However, in mid-1989 he was enjoying a spell of better health, and was keen to talk to A New Day. *We had no plans (a.k.a. funds) for a trip to Mark's home in America, so Doane, who had been close friends with Mark for many years, volunteered to undertake interviewing duties while, at the same time, DR completely failed to learn how to play drums.*
As it was, although it was supposed to be Doane interviewing Mark, it didn't really work out that way as inevitably Doane had one or two things to say himself. So in effect we had the privilege of eavesdropping on two great mates chatting…

Mark, you have been away for a long time now, and a lot of Tull fans want to know how you're doing. They know you were sick and they'd like to know what happened to you. You had a lot of mail from Great Britain and Europe, so there's a lot of people thinking about you.
Yeah, I suddenly started getting a lot of mail, I guess from what was said in that edition of *A New Day*. It was a little after the fact because I was well on my way to recovery, sitting on my front porch in sunny California, when the letters started coming in. And it was really great to hear their support and hopes that I was coming back – and that is what I intend to do. I guess if I can put the last two and a half years of HELL into words… It started in '86 when I had kidney failure. I was touring with The Tower Of Power, and we were in a small 'plane which lost altitude very quickly, and I think my kidneys went into shock. I've also been a diabetic for some time, so that played a part I'm sure. So I went for dialysis for about a year, and then I got a lot of complications and infections from doing the dialysis, and I had a three month stay in hospital through that, went through therapy, and ended up in a wheelchair. A lot of things deteriorated. I lost a lot of muscle. And then in March '88 they called me to say that they had a kidney for me from a car accident victim. So I had no time to think, "Well should I or shouldn't I?", I just went in and it was in me the next day. At first I rejected it very intensely, so they gave me a serious drug called OKT3 for about three weeks. I hallucinated – Doane was usually on the ceiling when he came to visit me! It was quite an experience! That was a little over a year ago, and since then it's just been steady. About two months after it was

installed the kidney kicked in and started working perfectly. It's been a steady climb back to health.

I think a lot of people didn't realise how seriously ill you were at one point, and how close you came to dying – at least twice that I can think of. That having happened must have dramatically changed your outlook on life in general, and music in particular. Obviously it affected your physical well-being and ability to play the drums. Can you look back on that and put that into some kind of perspective?
Yeah. The perspective is that death really isn't very frightening any more. I think what would be frightening is any kind of relapse that would lead to any deterioration. That would frighten me, but I don't expect it and I don't intend for it to happen.

You do seem to be on an upward climb. I mean, the other night I went to see you play with Greg Bissonette from Dave Lee Roth's band, and it was the first time you had played in two and a half years, which was pretty amazing. I think I'd have been petrified, well or not, to not play for two and a half years and then go and do a gig. That alone must have been very difficult, but you played incredibly well, and so much of your style, your finesse and fluidity was still there – it really was remarkable. And you played three sets on top of it, which must have been good for you to do. And it must have surprised you as much as it did us who watched.
Well, I've read many times about out-of-body experiences, and I think that was my first one, that I can identify anyway! It was very thrilling and very frightening at first. Greg, bless his heart, pretty much forced me to do it. Borrowed a truck, hauled my drums down to the club, and…

[*Laughing*] And I hauled them back!
That's right! There I was, styling at the bar talking to babes, while the drummer of Jethro Tull and the drummer from Dave Lee Roth are schlepping my gear! That was kind of a thrill. But honestly, just to play again after two and a half years… I hadn't played more than ten minutes at a time during that period, and not at all for about eighteen months of that. And so at this gig I was hoping maybe to do a tune or two, and we steamed through the first set and I couldn't believe it. Then we did the second set, and just had one more to do, so I had to go for it. And there I was outside of myself looking at my legs and seeing they were still moving and my hands and arms were still moving. And it was a real hurdle to get over because I was very fearful of it. But now I'm starting to imagine doing other gigs and even trying to imagine doing tours again, and recording. The recording is very accessible thanks to all the gadgets that we've all got.

You have done a bit recently with Gino Vinelli haven't you?
Yes. I did a track with Gino and Joe, which took about six days and was very painstaking. But it really came out well, and it felt good. They did it because they wanted me to have something out now – that's the kind of people they are. So I'm getting all these little footholds that come along – that track, that gig, some practice. It's like what we have always been told – you get back what you put into it. And you CAN do anything you set your mind to. I really have to work at playing now to try to get it back, whereas before it always came very naturally… but, well, that's OK, you know…

But having watched you play I can see that it is only the physical aspect of playing that has deteriorated, some muscular deterioration, but mentally the same things are going on. It is just a matter of getting back into shape – but I think as long as you have the mental attitude that you seem to have then you can bring the muscles back around again.
Yeah, everything is still in my feeble little mind, that's for sure. I can't execute the different ideas or statements that I want to throw out, but I went for a few the other night and it was OK.

You did incredibly well. It was inspiring to see - to play like that with guys you hadn't played with before, who maybe didn't even know your story and thought you were just another guy in the band. And you held your own. I guess maybe it's good when that kind of thing happens suddenly and you don't get a lot of time to think about it. Perhaps if you'd had weeks to prepare for the gig and think about it it's easier to get psyched out about it...

Oh, I'd have gone nuts. Having to do it instantly was the best way. Just confront the fear. Face the lion and it disappears. As much as I wanted to think of a reason not to do it, there was never any doubt that I would do it, and I guess that comes from some of those life-threatening things that have happened. You always have a choice, and you can go either way. You can give up or you can keep going. I can look back now at a time when... like if I was a 100 watt bulb I maybe had 5 watts left, and all I used those 5 watts for was to put together a programme of getting healthy again. If I was too weak to get out of bed then I'd maybe roll over a couple of times or something as simple as that. It even got to be such a way of life that after I was out of the woods and getting healthy again I was still clenched fists and gritting my teeth waiting for the next one – only it wasn't coming. And as wonderful as that was, it was a real adjustment just to kinda back off from myself.

There was a time there, around April '87, when they wanted to take your foot off, and you wouldn't let them do it. I know they took your big toe, but you held fast to that. Whether it was just the fear of losing that, or maybe knowing that it wasn't necessary... because it wasn't, you still have your foot and it is operating fine.

I've even come to learn that the surgeon wanted to take it off at the shin just to be safe. But there's no way I'd sign that, no matter what medication I was on. And it has enabled me to slip in a good joke that maybe a Scotsman would appreciate, where I can get 10% off a pedicure!

Tell us about the benefit they did for you in L.A.. I know they tried to organise something similar in England but it didn't work out, but it was really amazing. I wasn't in town when it happened but I've seen the video, and it was a wonderful thing to witness all those people getting together to pull for you.

Yes, it was amazing. It started with Gregg Bissonette, who was my room-mate at the time, and he was talking with Myron Grombacher at a time when I was pretty down and out in hospital with no insurance, and they were thinking what to do to help me, to raise some money. And they mentioned it to Steve Smith, and he wanted to play, and suddenly everybody... Vinnie Colaiuta, Terry Bozzio and so on.

And I witnessed all of this while I was in hospital, and it just got bigger and bigger. They had it at the Guitar Center in Hollywood and sent out flyers and put up posters. Luckily it was so overwhelming that I was able to break down in the hospital rather than on stage at the benefit, because by then I was under control! But it was very, very touching to see these guys, and they worked so hard. All my friends were putting flyers on car windscreens and parking lots. Everybody pitched in. We got a stage from Journey, a sound system from Yamaha, and all the different drum companies donated kits and cymbals and snares etc. And it was a fabulous day. The drummers were Terry Bozzio, Vinnie Colaiuta, Steve Smith, Vinnie Appice, Carmine Appice, Randy Richmond from Lone Justice, Gregg Bissonette, Mike Fisher, Ricky Lawson and Myron Grombacher. They all played singularly and then all together at the end.

That must have been a hell of a racket!

Yes, it was! But it was a wonderful day, and they raised the money that has enabled me to take enough time to really get back on my feet – before I go out and fall flat on my face. Not that that can't happen to any of us – remember that Doane! So it has really helped. It's made my life a hell of a lot easier, and we are thinking now about doing more – maybe setting up a fund to help other people who might need the same sort of help. It was great, a real thrill. And everybody worked together. Everybody, roadies included, donated their time and effort.

Let's go back now and talk about your background – who you played with before Tull.

OK. I grew up in Sioux Falls, South Dakota. At the age of seventeen I went on the road, touring the south. You English readers would get a real kick out of the south – there is some amazing culture there! I bounced around and lived in most of the major cities – Kansas, Denver, Boulder – and ended up in L.A. at the end of 1975 to play with a guy I'd met in Kansas. Barely a month later I was auditioning with Jean-Luc Ponty.

A gig that I nearly got but that you beat me out for in fact! And that was actually how I met you, because I came down to see who this guy was from South Dakota who I figured couldn't possibly be any good if he's from there! I was from NEW YORK CITY so I came down with guns blazing to The Bottom Line to check this guy out, and sat there... astonished! Then went up sheepishly and made friends with you.
Yes, that's right. I remember that well.

You were a killer on that tour.
That was fun. It was kind of the tail-end of the fusion era and I was really into Billy Cobham back then so I was able to expel six trillion notes per tour! Which I think is necessary at one point in any drummer's life... because they all wonder. And doggone it, all these guys that say, "Well, I don't wanna be Dave Weckl, I just wanna play a groove," – I know what they're saying, but I can't help but think they would be thrilled to sit back there and do some of the stuff that Dave Weckl does. So I played with Jean-Luc Ponty and did a record...

You did two records with him didn't you?
Yeah. Well, actually the second one *Civilised Evil* I snuck in between doing the Tull *A* album, then coming home to do the Ponty album, then going back to London to take pictures for the Tull album.

How did the Tull thing come about, because I know you were working with Eddie Jobson before that?
Well, that was a good lesson for me. A friend told me Eddie Jobson had an ad in *Village Voice* in New York for a drummer, so I sent him a demo. He liked it so he flew me out there, low budget. I took the subway carrying my cymbals and suitcases and groaning all the way. In fact I stayed in your apartment in New York while you were out of town. And we did a demo and then I grumbled my way back to L.A.. And I was out mowing my lawn one day and Kenny Wylie, Tull's mainman, called and the next day I was on my way over to England. It was going to be an Ian Anderson solo album, and the record company liked it so they wanted us to be Jethro Tull. So Ian called and said, "Do you fancy joining the band – can you tour?" And that was it, off we went.

Working with Tull, learning the arrangements, is different to how it's done in the States. I know I found it very different, and I guess you did too, because you are learning music which, as you put it, is very organically conceived. Did you find that difficult, because there was some very tricky stuff on that record?
To be honest, that was right up my alley because most of the reading stuff I've done has just been kind of faking my way through. I learned reading on the job. I did rehearsals with the Fowler Brothers when I first moved out here. They used to be with Zappa and they had these Zappa-type charts, so once I could see what they sounded like I'd try to mentally file it away. But with Tull it was perfect. I just played it as I wandered around the hotel room, or in the car, and I just absorbed it.

Did you come up with all the parts pretty much yourself, or did you get direction from Ian and the band?
I never got any direction, especially rehearsing the old stuff. The new stuff I just came up with according to how it fitted into the time signatures, the bars, and whatever Eddie Jobson was coming up with.

Like, in *Black Sunday* – now there's a song that is still one of my favourites to play. It's a very exciting song in itself, and it is also an exciting song for a drummer to play. I had to

transcribe that recently, and in doing so I realised that there are so many twists and turns. I mean, I'd never really counted it before, although I was aware of certain changes and bars etc. But when you were learning something like that, which is a very involved song, how was it presented to you? Was it Ian or Eddie just playing it to you and saying, "It's this long," etc, or did they actually break it down?

There wasn't much breakdown. Keep in mind there was no vocal at that point, so it was just the rhythm. I don't know if any of the guys really knew what the time signature was [*laughs*], so I just kind of left it at that, you know. Some of the things I was counting, but...

The Pine Marten's Jig – that, I remember, we attempted one time at the end of my first tour in 1984, in Sydney. I remember thinking that that was something where it was almost better not to count because there were so many twists and turns in it. I just tried to listen to the part and tried to hear the phrases, rather than take it apart in an analytical way, because I thought that would ruin the whole feel of it.

That's funny, because that is the one that I probably do know how it goes, what the count is! I did follow that. But there was some very interesting stuff. In fact, when I listen to *A* now it seems like that was a really creative period for me, coming up with stuff and just being involved in the record and being really into it. It was such a difference from here in the States. When I got there we were doing it at Ian's estate, and then we'd hop on these moto-cross bikes for a break, and me and Dave Pegg would go down to the rifle range and shoot some clay pigeons. I couldn't believe it! I mean, you know how it is here, the clock is running and everybody is stressing...

...and the most you can hope for is maybe a break to go to the deli to grab a sandwich. But life is different over there. And they still do it that way. I think that is maybe why some of that music really works so well. I think the thing that makes a band like that unique is that they have always gone their own way. And we still do that, you know – the band just goes its own way and I think that's probably the best way to play and write music, because you can't chase the carrot anyway.

Yeah. And there is nothing worse than following the trends, trying to predict what should be out in the market right now, and what's gonna go. That is a completely useless exercise.

Did you find playing with Tull to be particularly different to playing with Jean-Luc Ponty for example, in terms of the way you played in the rhythm section? Given that Dave Pegg is what I think of as a very linear bass player, and very un-American, which is what I really dig about his playing. Apart from the fact that he has great time, he plays in a way that is very melodic. But I don't relate to him in the typical bass/drummer relationship like you do if you play with Marcus Miller or someone like that, because he plays in a very different way. So I always felt the rhythm section was constructed very differently.

Yes, you're right. I too think of Dave as having fabulous time, but I don't think of him as really playing WITH you, like, making a groove together. But you know that he's gonna be right there – when you've finished, he's finished with you.

Do you have any favourite songs that you enjoyed playing with Tull?

Well, probably my favourite story in a song is *Heavy Horses*. For some reason I can almost see the horses, veins bulging and sweating, working away. It's a great song. And I can really appreciate what a special person Ian is, or entertainer... I don't like to say that – it sounds like Sammy Davis! But when I saw you guys at the end of '87 here at the Amphitheatre... he is just a classic stage persona I guess... I really liked it. And it felt great to have someone in a band that sweated as much as I did!

Yeah, me too. Like, you get to the second song and you look at his back, and he is drenched in sweat.

Yeah, he's there, he's there.

And I don't understand how he does it, because he never exercises or anything. I'd probably have a coronary if I didn't warm up and stretch and so on. Because, as you know, playing a gig is so incredibly athletic and you really have to be in good physical condition.

I remember the first gig I did with him here in the States. I was so excited I had blisters on the top of my toes after the first gig! I took my shoes off and went, "Bloody hell! Look at this!" [*Laughs*] Well, other songs... We had a version of *Locomotive Breath* that was kind of a shuffle, a sort of Eddie Jobson type shuffle, and that was neat. And I always liked *Hunting Girl* just for good "riff-rock". And I liked *Skating Away* because I got to come out and play bass guitar.

Oh, that's right. They didn't let me have a bass guitar – instead I had some weird percussion instrument that I had to play, and I spent half of it playing brushes on Dave Mattacks' shoulders while he played tablas! Because Fairport used to come out, and everybody from Fairport played on that song. At the end of it I had to go back and play drums, but I had more fun playing on Dave's shoulders.

Well, you'll be able to do that on the next tour if you have Poison or somebody like that to open for you! I'm sure they'd come out with tablas and bouzoukis!

OK. Have you got any good "on the road" stories that the readers might find interesting?

Well... There was a time we were going through customs in Stuttgart in Germany. I had just been to my favourite homeopathic chiropractor and he had loaded me up with these herbal mixtures, so my suitcase was full of them. And one of them was something grass – chicory grass, or something. And the German customs guy saw the word "grass" and a light bulb went on over his head, you know, so they pulled me over...

Oh yeah, like you'd be carrying marijuana around in a jar labelled "Grass"!!

Yeah, like, "Here it is guys! It's good stuff!" But I gotta say here, I've never smoked grass in my life, thank you very much. Anyway, they pulled me over, brought the sniffer dogs in and they wagged their tails, so they took the stuff upstairs for tests. Meanwhile the rest of the band had gone off to the gig! Like, "OK, you take care now. Bye bye!" So Gerd Burkhardt, who is now Tull's tour manager, stayed with me. They went through all these tests, and he talked and talked, but I didn't catch too much of it. And then they gave me all the herbs back and said I could go. So I'm walking though the door and saying, "Well thanks guys, I know you're only doing your job," you know. And when we got out Gerd said to me, "Yes, they were doing their job, but for some reason they let you go – they could have locked you up because all the tests were positive!"

It shows you how accurate those tests are then!

Yeah, and the funny thing is I've been a diabetic for some years, and so about an inch from where they looked in my suitcase there were about twenty or thirty hypodermic syringes! I'm sure that would have been easy to explain to the German border officials...

We have been behind the Iron Curtain a couple of times, and as you know I am an inveterate vitamin-taker, and I'm always concerned about that because they don't see that. All they see is pills of some sort. But it keeps me healthy, and I don't expect to be able to go out in the middle of Budapest or somewhere like that and find vitamin B etc.

Hey, listen – leave 'em at home. You can last!

I'll have to if... they are talking now about going to Russia next year, and if they do that I'm not even taking aspirin with me!

Apart from that, it was pretty tame stuff on the road. Our security was too tight for any of that stuff. We really should have Greg Bissonette here if you want road stories.

The thing I enjoyed most about being with Tull was their hospitality, each individually. Ian and Shona would have me out for a nice meal, and Dave took me up to his place in Banbury. Dave and Chris took me out, to Stratford-upon-Avon... Stonehenge...

Stonehenge... where the demons dwell...
Yeah, if that was the real Stonehenge. It wasn't very big, y'know! We've got BIG things over here in America – like Mount Rushmore in South Dakota! But their hospitality was great. And we went down to Martin and Julie in Devon and shot some more clay pigeons and drove around in Jeeps. I really enjoyed it, and all the London stuff.

Life moves at a different pace over there. When I get there I'm always edgy for the first couple of days, after coming off hyper-speed over here. Although I go over there to work, and I always work a lot harder in a physical sense than I do here, going to England always feels like a vacation. Oh, no – I shouldn't say that 'cos if they read this they'll cut my free time! But maybe it's because you're working in the country and you have nice surroundings. And you are also doing just one thing, whereas at home you have all the other daily responsibilities to deal with at the same time. Being on the road can be like a vacation, when all you are responsible for really is the two hours a day on stage. OK, the rest of the time you have to prepare for it, and so on, but you are away from the fifty other things you have to do every day at home. I always find that to be a nice situation.
Yeah, it's productive. I've always found it easier to keep things together on the road rather than at home. Of course, our preparation when I was in the band was intense table-tennis, right up 'til we had to walk up the steps and hit.

You never practiced before gigs, which amazed me. I remember seeing you with Gino, and while I'd be busy with the practice pad trying to play single stroke rolls at 97 mph, you were lying on your back on a bench looking like you were about to go to sleep, or probably WERE asleep! And they would come over and say, "Mark, it's time to go on stage," and you would go on and BURN! And I just don't know how you managed to do that. But table-tennis – those guys! It's still an ongoing backstage sport. I don't participate in it, as Martin Barre will tell you, because I told Martin – and fortunately he believed me [*laughing*] – that I played Jimmy Connors when I was a kid. In fact, this will be where he finds out that I didn't! So we went and played real tennis in Scotland and I actually beat Dave and Martin, but only because they were laughing so much on the other side of the court that they couldn't return my serve! So I never really got invited to play table-tennis, because I didn't meet the required standard.
I played tennis with Martin too, during rehearsals one time, and he was pretty victorious. I used to play a lot of tennis when I was a kid. I played tournament tennis until I decided that drums might be a little more exciting.

Martin is the band's athletic director. He gets all the band's tennis, table-tennis, golf. I haven't seen him golf yet, but... So we look to him for athletic inspiration because there is very little about anywhere else. But it has done a lot for him. He has lost a lot of weight, so I'm trying to follow suit, being the Michelin poster man for 1989! I've got to work on that before I go on the road!
Yeah... I kinda noticed that!

Ow!! OK, what are your plans for the future? I know you are getting back into playing, and are you going to do some programming and get involved in electronics?
Ah... I'm not really excited about programming. I'm starting to like Octopod and triggering and things like that into computers. Programming still hasn't appealed to me. I went through a period where I was very fearful of not being able to get back to playing drums, and now that seems to be a definite possibility I don't have to kid myself anymore and pretend like I don't really want to. That is really what I want to do, and my zest for health isn't just to be healthy and alive, it is to be able to play again, more importantly.

A lot of people are waiting for it. When I'm on the road people are always asking about you, because they know we are friends. You have made a great impression on many people, drummers and other musicians, who saw you play with Tull.

That kind of support has been really helpful, and it's kept me going. Hearing that stuff when I was sitting in a wheelchair... you can't imagine what it meant to me then. And this recent influx of letters after the *A New Day* issue that mentioned it has been really inspiring. In fact the first few letters that came honestly came on a day when I was starting to think again that maybe I'd better look at something else, some other occupation, so it was very timely and I really appreciate it. Everything... the benefit and all the people. I mean, everywhere I go, I have never heard anyone say, "Well too bad. I think you'll make a good car salesman," or something. So I am going back into it. I'm talking with different drum companies. Drum Workshop have been really helpful, sending me new inventions, a new trigger pedal. And I wanna get back into it full blast. I'm tired of sitting round a table with ten other drummers and listening to what they are doing and what they think – I wanna be back in there again, and I've got to do it myself. All your support has been priceless, but the fact is I've had to do it myself, like anybody else. And I've started collaborating with a singer-songwriter-guitarist and I'm finding I've got a lot of ideas in my head. A lot of melodies and lyrics. And it is good working with somebody I don't know, because I'm not inhibited. Even to sing the tritest lyric, you know...

I know you've written in the past, because Night Flight have recorded some of your stuff.
Yes, that is just another thing I've got to do. And now I've done that, with this gig and a little writing, I've got a lot of motivation again and it really feels good. I even find myself having a hard time falling asleep, just through energy and wanting to do things. I even scrubbed my shower yesterday!

That's always a sure sign of mental health!
Well, it is another sign, something more to cling on to on the way back. And I don't want this to sound like "poor me" because it certainly never has been that. Either I was too out of it to know what was going on, or as I became more aware then I just had this focus of getting back, being able to walk again, to drive again, and so on.

I know that what you have been through has had a deep and profound effect on many of your friends, myself included. You have fought your problems so courageously, and did not let it overwhelm you, when it could have at any point. It would have been so easy just to succumb and just give up. And seeing that helps others to put into perspective life's little problems that previously would have bothered them. You re-evaluate your own lifestyle and what you consider to be important. When you get that close to the edge you see that some of these other things you get worked up about really aren't important. You really gave your friends a lot of strength to deal with their own lives, and hopefully we will remember it.
It is probably easier for me to keep that fresh in my mind. I too have watched and seen other people not well, or even pass away, and yes, it stays with you for a while and then you get back into your normal shallowness and every little thing starts to bother you again. But I'm discovering that this is staying with me now because things just don't rile me anymore. Like my beloved dog Sandy... when she doesn't obey me I don't totally fly off the handle and scream at her. I'm learning a lot from that damn dog. Just that I don't have to have control over her, and control over my own world, because really there is no such thing. Just as long as I am 100% responsible for my own actions with nobody to blame for anything but myself, and that comes from having some big problems in the past. And now, scrubbing the shower is great! Doing the laundry is great! All those little things. It's like most of these serious experiences – now that it is over, I really wouldn't want to have missed it! Just for the perspective that I got out of it.

It's funny, because it didn't just happen to you in a vacuum, it happened to all of us, and ultimately it had a very good effect on everybody around you because of the way you dealt with it.

Yeah, well, the way you guys rallied round... I'll never forget it. If you were in town for just a few hours you'd come and see me in hospital, wheel me round the neighbourhood, you and Gregg.

Hey, remember that hat, the leopard-skin turban that I wore and you thought you were hallucinating?! I've got that and I'm taking it to England. In fact it might turn up in some Tull promo shots. It's like the Edith Beale Memorial Turban, but you can wear it like a beret.
Yeah, I remember that. My God! It kinda looked real, but I wasn't too sure!

I have one last question for you, Mark. What size sticks do you use?
Ha! The cheapest size! I don't know what size, but they're the cheapest.

That's for all you drummers out there who needed me to ask at least one question like that!
Well, Mark, thanks for taking the time out to do this. I know a lot of the readers will be delighted to know you're doing so well.
Hey, I'm glad to do it. I really wanted to get some of these messages out as I have not been able to write back to everyone. It's getting a bit better now, but I've had to write with my left hand 'til recently, and it looked like the handwriting of Freddy from *Friday the 13th* - like I was writing with a dagger dipped in blood or something! So I couldn't write back, but I want people to know how much I appreciated their letters of support. Young drummers wrote to me to say that some of the recordings I've done inspired them. I mean, that is the pay-off for what we do, for what I've been doing for 23 years. And that's why I wanted to do this, although I usually make it a habit not to tell hospital stories. The most important thing is living in the present. The only time I dig these stories out is if I'm at a party or something, and the conversation gets round to, "Oh, I slammed a car door on my finger," or, "I once pulled a nose hair," or something. I sneak up on the group and wait to hear the best pain story, and then I go IN and go for it like Mike Tyson! But it is important to live in the present, and I'm happy that I'm doing a good job of that right now.

Lots of us are looking forward to seeing you play again soon
Well if they come they might have to help me pack up like you did the other night!

Oh yeah – I'll probably be leaving a little bit earlier at the gigs you play from now on...
No, no, no. We'll be dedicating the last song to you, Doane!

Mark's optimism expressed during that 1989 interview was fully justified, and he successfully resurrected his music career by touring with Randy Myers (The Eagles) in 1993 and with Eric Burdon from 1994 to 1996, as well as playing on albums by Dweezil Zappa, Maestro Alex Gregory, and Doug Jackson. DR and MW finally got to meet Mark in person at the 1993 Jethro Tull 25th Anniversary video-shoot in London, and what a thoroughly nice chap he was.

Sadly, Mark's transplanted kidney eventually failed, and he underwent a second transplant in 2004. Despite his health problems he continued to play and record, but in August 2005 he suffered a brain stem stroke. He contracted pneumonia while in hospital, and passed away on 26 November 2005. Doane Perry penned a long and moving tribute to his old friend which can be found on the official Jethro Tull website

Chapter 12

THE JOHN EVAN BAND

*(Published in Issue #21, September 1989, Issue #27, February 1991
and Issue #95, July 2008)*

*As every dedicated fan knows, Jethro Tull evolved from the Blackpool (later Luton) based
group The John Evan Band. Five members of that band eventually joined Jethro Tull, namely
John Evans, Glenn Cornick, Jeffrey Hammond-Hammond, Barriemore Barlow and of course
Ian Anderson. Indeed, of the 1971-75 line-up only guitarist Martin Barre had not previously
been in The John Evan Band. But despite Jethro Tull's fame, very little was known about their
precursor, largely due to Ian Anderson's apparent reluctance to talk about the early days.
Whether that was because he felt they had no relevance to the Jethro Tull story or whether it
was because he simply couldn't remember an awful lot about them was not clear. But there
was never any reason to disbelieve him when he said (in the 1977 UK tour programme) that:
"We were not the worst group in the country, but probably close".*

*We were therefore absolutely amazed when Don Read, former manager of The John Evan
Band, sent DR some souvenirs he'd kept of the band which revealed that they had once
appeared on television. Now, despite some of the ropey acts which have appeared on* Top Of
The Pops *and the like, back in the sixties a group was not going to appear on TV if it was
(nearly) the worst in the world. MW therefore decided that matters required investigating,
and as an opening gambit wrote to the* Blackpool Evening Gazette *in the hope that they could
dig something out of their archives. They couldn't, but Entertainments Editor Robin Duke
kindly ran a short piece in his weekly column with the plea for information.*
*For a while it remained all quiet on the Blackpool front. But some months later MW was
contacted out of the blue by a chap called Chris Riley, who had somewhat belatedly had the*
Evening Gazette *story pointed out to him. Chris broke the news that he was the original John
Evan Band guitarist, and had a couple of items and a store of memories which might be of
interest to us. Might be??? Once again the* AND *world exclusive interview machine sprang
into action, and in September 1987 Chris made a special journey down from Blackpool to
London, which helped to kick off a series of interviews which provided us with more
information than we could ever have hoped for. So it was that, twenty-two years later but for
the first time ever, we were able to present the full story of The John Evan Band (and its
predecessor The Blades), as told by five people who were actually there.*

CHRIS RILEY

*Chris Riley settled on a career as a professional musician, teaching amongst other things
flute and guitar at a Blackpool school, and playing guitar and saxophone in a rock group
several nights a week. He is a quiet, fairly serious man, but very genial with it, and fond of a
pint or three. The twelve hours or so we spent with him in London flew by as he told
wonderful tales about not just The John Evan Band but also the innumerable famous and
nearly-famous bands and musicians he had worked with over the previous twenty-five years,
which all helped to set the mid-sixties music scene and give some perspective to what being in
a band then was like and, indeed, how thin the line can be between fame, fortune and
anonymity.*

*"What I'm proud of," he told us, "is the fact that I'm still playing, even though there was
many a time when I thought, 'What am I doing this for?' Because I'm not ever going to make
it big now – although at one stage in my youth I never had any doubts at all. There must be
thousands of us who came out of that era who are still tooling along; really, we are the
backbone and unsung heroes of the business, I think. I'm teaching kids now, and it's
surprising what they come to me with and say they want to learn. And it all goes back to the
same thing – the blues, always, without fail. They have these high-faluting ideas that they*

want to sound like Bon Jovi and so on, great bands that they are, but they want to run before they can walk. So I get a lot of pleasure out of passing on the basic knowledge and keeping the roots alive. Because, let's face it, for all these famous bands that's where it all started. Rock'n'roll stems from all that, jazz stems from all that, and all the others too are just different avenues off the same street. Roots are very important."

And here is the story of Jethro Tull's early roots. Chris had come well prepared, and so we simply presented him in full flow rather than in the usual Q&A format.

THE ATLANTICS : THE BLADES : THE HOBOS

I read an interview with Ian in *Melody Maker* sometime after they'd had a couple of hit singles, and one of the banal questions they asked was, "What made you think of joining a group?" He said, "We went to see this group at our youth club in Blackpool and I thought 'What a great way to pull the birds'." And that was us! The band was called The Atlantics, and there was me, Michael Stephens, Frank Blackburn and Ronnie Brambells on drums – he played on that LP Roy Harper did recently with Jimmy Page. He used to call himself Ronnie Lee as a stage name – poser! After we'd named ourselves, a singer joined whose name, his real name unbelievably, was Johnny Breeze, so it became Johnny Breeze and the Atlantics. He's still going strong, singing in the clubs. This was all about 1961 or 1962 when I was fifteen or so. We used to do all the local hops, Tech hops and youth clubs, gradually moving on to the clubs and so on. We eventually worked with some big names like The Animals, Gene Vincent, Billy Fury, Manfred Mann, and others. In fact I remember running down Blackpool pier on a couple of occasions with Paul Jones to escape hordes of screaming fans. It may sound unbelievable, but they used to come at you with scissors for your hair, or buttons, or part of your jacket – a bit dangerous!

Anyway, in the early days we used to play at this particular youth club called The Holy Family, a church-run thing, and Ian Anderson and John Evans used to come and watch. That would be my first recollection of Ian – it would have been somewhere around 1962 or 1963. We started getting into R'n'B and blues and stuff, and they became very interested in it. There was a bit of rivalry and kidology between us, because with all due respect we were better players than they were at the time. But it never came to any fisticuffs or anything, we were just kids. And the next thing I knew, they'd formed a band called The Blades. Michael Stephens had started palling out with them, and he decided he wanted to join another band, so he tiddled off and we got another bass player, Brian Hood. I kept in contact with Michael because he'd been my friend through school, and we went to see The Blades when they got a gig playing at a coffee bar in Blackpool where they and other students used to hang out. There was Ian – just singing, I don't think he played guitar – Michael, John Evans on a little drumkit, and Jeffrey Hammond on bass. Jeffrey was kind of like Stu Sutcliffe from The Beatles. He really had to concentrate on pointing his fingers in the right direction, and I'm sure he won't mind me saying that. Actually Jeff was sort of on the fringes of it all at that time, from what I can remember. I don't think he played very much. In fact, Ian wasn't up to much as a player then, as a guitarist. They used to do a lot of Pretty Things songs; they copied virtually everything off an early album the first time I saw them. Early on in their existence there was also a fella called Hartley there, just to play harmonica. Whether that was his surname or first name I don't know, but I still see him now – he's a bus conductor in Blackpool. He was Bob Dylan before Bob Dylan, I think; he used to write poetry, weird stanzas and stuff. Jeffrey used to write obscure poetry too – I don't know whether it was done for effect or whether it was genuine.

We used to see The Blades playing in different places whenever we could, 'cos we were the big band in the area, working six or seven nights a week. In fact I was probably earning more than my Dad was, strange to say. But the next step for me was that I got very disgruntled with The Atlantics. We had a management, and we did a couple of records which got nowhere, and looking back I can see why. [*Amazing but true trivia fact: in October 1988 John Peel played one of them on BBC Radio One!*] Everything was changing then, The Beatles and The Rolling Stones changed, and there was a growing awareness of black music. I wanted to play more of a blues and R'n'B thing, but this management still insisted in putting us in suits and so on the play venues like Blackpool North Pier, and they were giving us garbage songs to play. In retrospect they possibly had the right idea, if you're talking about money and 'getting on'. But I didn't want any truck with it, so Ronnie Bramballs and I left in 1964, and we formed a band called The Hobos, with Chris Wooton – stage name Kriss Manton – on organ and Glenn Cornick on bass. He was Glenn Barnard in those days, and actually called himself Glenn Douglas, because that was his middle name – Glenn Douglas Barnard. He didn't like Barnard – we used to call him Barnyard. We formed more of a Georgie Fame type band. I had a soft spot for Glenn really, even though we never really hit it off. I think we were a bit too alike. He was very fiery, and I think I was too at the time, moody and so on – you learn as you get older! – and we used to have some ding-dongs, me and Glenn. I remember kicking him up the backside on stage once because he was pratting about. But he was a very good bass player, in a different class to Jeffrey. He came from Barrow. I think that's where we first met; he used to come and see our gigs up there. He eventually ended up in The John Evan Band too. The Hobos used to get good work, playing with people like The Walker Brothers, The Hollies, and The Yardbirds, with Eric Clapton. In fact, I worked with Eric Clapton in several of his different guises. The John Evan Band supported him at Nottingham when he was with John Mayall. I've still got a pair of cuff-links he gave me.

We battled on with The Hobos for two years from about 1964 to 1966, and we just ground to a halt really. We were doing the same places, playing the same tunes, working a lot but with no recording contract, and it just kind of fell apart. Then in March 1966 I got a message saying would I be interested in joining The John Evan Band? I don't think I'd actually heard them play, but we'd heard through the grapevine that they were a pretty good band. They'd started to get better as players, and the stuff they were doing was more up my street. They'd gone from The Blades being a four-piece – two guitars, drums and bass – to having a rhythm section with a sax and trumpet man. They said are you interested in joining, and I said yes.

THE JOHN EVAN BAND

We used to go round to Mrs Evans's house and used to practice in her garage. I pass it twice a week and never fail to think about those practice sessions. I was quite impressed by the sound they were making. John had wanted to get off drums and play keyboards, so Barrie Barlow had appeared on the scene. Barrie was an apprentice toolmaker. In fact there was only me and Barrie working – I was in the Civil Service – so we were the only ones with any money; needless to say we bought all the beer and fags. Ian was forever tapping fags off people – he'll probably own up to that! Not being snidey about it, but he was as tight as a duck's arse, he would never put his hand in his pocket! Anyway, I decided to join the band. They'd started getting a few gigs around locally, and they had a bit of agency management, a lad called Johnny Taylor. He was an electrician, and he suddenly got this impresario hat on and decided he was going to run a band. And we were the one he decided to go for. We didn't make a lot of money then; in fact we probably made less money at that time than we had done with the other bands.

They'd had a studio photograph taken before I'd joined, an expensive venture in those days. So when I joined, rather than do another they sent me to the studio on my own, took a photo of me, and added it on to the picture. It was known as the seven-heads-twelve-legs photograph! So then I was a fully-fledged member of The John Evan Band, which was called that because it sounded better, even though John's surname is Evans with an 's'. The photo was captioned 'John Evans Band' but there should have been an apostrophe. And while we're at it, I should point out that Jeffrey was born with only one 'Hammond' in his surname, and Barrie wasn't christened 'Barriemore', that was a made up name! The other two people were Jim Doolin and Martin Skyrme. Jim Doolin was a trumpet player. He was a nice guy, from the brass band school of trumpet players, but he used to play riffs and what have you. Martin Skyrme was a sax player, and is now a very fine flute player. The instruments in the photo were Ian's Strat guitar, an alto sax which I think was there just for effect, because although Ian used to blow it he didn't make a lot of sense out of it, Martin's tenor sax, and the red Farfisa organ, which was the nearest sound we could get to a Hammond. A friend of mine called Ernie Robinson – who's since played with John Martyn amongst others, and was one of the first people from Blackpool to write his own songs; another unsung hero really – was a big blues fanatic, and he was also asked to join The John Evan Band. I was talking to him the other day, and he said, "I came out with the classic blunder of all time – I said: 'I'm sorry Ian, I can't see myself making any money with you'!"

We had an old Commer van, for which Mrs Evans stumped up the money, and which John always used to drive, and we set off doing gigs. The first one I can remember playing was a competition in a place called The Elizabethan Club in Kirkham, just outside Blackpool. And we won it hands down. With all our rehearsals we were so tight it was untrue. Ian was becoming quite a good singer, although he was still no great shakes as a guitarist. But in my eyes John Evans was originally the musical force behind the band. John and I used to sit down and work things out. We got to do some quite complicated stuff at that time; we'd discovered the 4th chord just about then! We used to make quite a good noise, quite impressive really.

INFLUENCES AND GIGS

Regarding influences, there were many, although at the time we didn't always really know what we were listening to. John and I used to listen to this album regularly, and I've only just recently found out what it was, 'cos I bought it just by chance. It's an Oscar Peterson jazz LP with Sonny Stitt on sax, and we were mesmerised by one particular track in a blues style. John used to try to emulate that sound of the piano playing, at home that is, not at gigs. Sonny Terry and Brownie McGhee were big favourites; John Lee Hooker, who I've actually worked with a few times; Mose Allison – we used to do *Parchman Farm*. We did a lot of Graham Bond type tunes, and a heck of a lot of Georgie Fame tunes. James Brown was a very big influence around that time, we did quite a few of his songs. Charlie Parker came into the picture somewhere as an influence – although it wasn't really fashionable to own up to following modern jazz, trad jazz was still the thing – and of course Roland Kirk, although Ian hadn't started playing the flute when I was in the band.

We always used to open with *Sock It To 'Em J.B.*, an instrumental with a sax riff and a nice little organ bit. I'm not sure if 'J.B.' was James Brown or James Bond. We were so smooth we didn't always stop between each tune, we'd segue into the next one; and we used to go straight into *Get On The Right Track, Baby* by Joe Turner – Georgie Fame and many others did it – a real good raunchy swinging one to do. *Green Onions* of course, by Booker T.; that was the first thing we learnt. Everybody did it, but we used to play it right. John had the left hand riff right, which nobody else did; he was the first person that I can remember who actually played it correctly. *In The Meantime* was Georgie Fame again, and I remember doing Marvin Gaye's *Pride And Joy*. *Pink Champagne* was almost a standard, like something Frank Sinatra might do; it wasn't really a pop tune or a jazz tune, but somewhere in-between. We did some real obscure stuff. At the time when we were doing things like all-nighters at Manchester's Twisted Wheel we used to have to do long spots, so we needed a hell of a lot of tunes, and we prided ourselves on being able to do enough not to have to repeat any. *Point Of No Return* was a good 'un, written by Carole King but nothing like you'd expect a Carole King song to be; again, not a pop song, but in this no man's land. *My Girl* was by Smokey Robinson, everyone did that one. The classic one which I used to love playing because it was my one chance to have a bit of a wail on the guitar was *Every Day I Have The Blues,* by Joe Turner I think.

The presentation of the music in The John Evan Band was down to Ian. He'd have some sort of spiel which was generally always the same thing; it was like a rehearsed speech, it wasn't spontaneous. He didn't have the funny ad-libs like he does now. He had a bit of a black humour side to him, but he was quite serious really. But when he did let himself go… he was a bit of a schizophrenic character, Ian – or perhaps that's not the right word, but he was various different people really, chameleon-like with whoever he was involved with. But it was always a show, and an exciting show, not just a string of tunes.

Our audiences were I suppose art-school type people; a lot of them were a hangover from the trad jazz scene. We never really had a following as such, as we played all over the place at the sort of venues that people went to every night as a 'local'. I don't think they quite knew how to take us – we were a bit different. I don't think we ever played anywhere where it wasn't full. And some of the venues were prestigious places, like The Golden Torch at Stoke, The Twisted Wheel in Manchester, The Cavern in Liverpool, and so on. We worked a couple of times at The Twisted Wheel with Georgie Fame and John Mayall; and Eric Clapton was with John Mayall when we did The Britannia Boat Club in Nottingham, and also The Aztec Club in Sunderland. We did that one for the same agency as another occasion, when there wasn't a lot of people in and John Mayall refused to go on, so we ended up doing the whole night. I think they paid us extra for that.

I remember we did a gig in Carlisle once, though. Carlisle was, and still is, a military base, and this place we played was always full of soldiers. Ian looked a bit, y'know, effete on stage, and these squaddies took exception to this and we had to beat a hasty retreat! A big punch-up ensued, but we were long gone by then!

Another memorable gig was at Bolton Palais, backing a fella called Brian Rossi from Belfast, who died fairly recently. He was quite a big cabaret singer. He'd been with a band called The Wheels, who were big mates of Them and Van Morrison, but he'd gone solo and wanted a decent backing band. So the agency we were with decided to use us. The place was absolutely packed – old-fashioned ballroom, revolving stage, big balcony upstairs, etc. Anyway, we're on stage for a little set of our own, and then it's, "Ladies and gentlemen, introducing Brian Rossi," and the kids all rush to the front screaming, and we start off with *Green Onions*. And it goes on and on for ten minutes, and there's no sign of him anywhere. Then all of a sudden this figure appears on a balcony above the stage, completely decked out in white; white leather jacket, white PVC trousers, shaved head which was his trademark, big black shades and a gold medallion – and all these girls are screaming for him. So the first thing he does is he leaps off this balcony, which is about fifteen feet up, over the top of Barrie, and lands on the plugboard and completely smashes it, so that everything stops dead! So while that was mended they had to build up the excitement again, and we went all through the *Green Onions* thing again. They ripped him apart.

We'd got the Brian Rossi gig through a chap called Peter Yates, who represented us. I was at work in the Civil Service one day and I got a message saying, "'Phone your mother urgently." So I did, and she said that a geezer called Peter Yates had been on the 'phone for me, and also a telegram had arrived from him. I thought I'd won the pools or something! So I got in touch, and it turned out that he wanted to represent us full-time with the agency run by Don Read. So we went down to see them, and decided to join up. Every so often they used to send us a gig sheet including what we'd be paid. £10 sometimes, between seven of us! It's interesting to see how far we used to travel for gigs – you can see that we weren't making much money! The Commer van eventually became not big enough, so we bought a brand new Transit on the drip, so obviously any money was going towards this new van. We'd only had it about six months when we were motoring down to some place or other on the motorway, and the piston broke and blew a hole in the front of the van. That cost us an arm and a leg.

CHARACTERS

We were a motley crew, really. Tony Wilkinson, who later joined on baritone sax, was a giant of a fella. Barrie was a little shrimp. Martin Skyrme was a very serious sort of guy. I was sort of laid back. Ian, John and Jeffery suffered from varying forms of eccentricity. I had a soft spot for Jeff. I thought he was a nice guy. The more I think about it, the more I like the Stu Sutcliffe comparison. He was painfully shy, and Ian used to rib him unmercifully. I mean, really badly, y'know. The chap used to get quite upset about it. Perhaps Ian didn't realise he was doing it. Ian was later always described as eccentric, but in my view the eccentric was Jeff – a true eccentric. I think Ian nurtured his and worked on it a bit, it was an image thing, whereas Jeff was genuine. In tiers of eccentricity I would have put it Jeffrey, John and Ian.

Jeffery was into Charles Mingus. Not particularly because he was a bass player, but he was a bit arty, and Jeffrey cottoned on to that; so maybe his eccentricity is second-hand too! No, he's more genuine than that, but that was definitely an influence. His mother and father had a boarding house in Blackpool. I can remember Ian or John telling me that Jeffrey didn't get on with his mother and father; he was like a mummy's boy, and he hated it. When he did talk he was very articulate, very nicely spoken. But he used to get so cross with his mother that instead of actually shouting at her he apparently, according to Ian or John, used to go and sit in the toilet and smash the hotel's plates, How true that is I don't know, but I can believe it actually. I'd like to see Jeff again, although I don't know if he'd care to be reminded of the past. The last time I saw him was the last Jethro Tull tour he was on, *War Child* I think. How on earth he came to play that black and white striped double bass, I've no idea! Jeffrey is not the best bass player in the world, and he'd be struggling even more with an upright bass. Mind, that's Charlie Mingus again, it goes back to that. I've spoken to John, and John's never been forthcoming about Jeffrey, he just says he doesn't see him much nowadays.

John was a madman. He wasn't extrovert, he was just extremely strange – still is! – which used to come across on stage. Again, he's shy, even today. A very intelligent man, perhaps verging on the genius. He's far easier now to talk to, but I still struggle a bit, and he won't mind me saying that because he knows it. It's funny that we've stayed in touch over the years – out of the whole band we'd be the last two people you'd have expected to. I still see his mother quite often, and I see John reasonably regularly. He's working at Heathrow at the moment doing joinery, a manual job, although he did study for a degree in pharmacy. [*We later discovered from John himself that he actually runs the building firm, but that he admits to playing himself down. "My mother thinks I paint aeroplanes," he said!*] He strikes me as being the sort of guy really who would now just like to forget all about those days. I don't think it ever gave him a great deal of pleasure. His mother taught him to play piano, and he was very good even then. John could have been, if he'd been a different sort of fella, on a par with Keith Emerson or Rick Wakeman on the organ, he's that good a player I think. He could play anything, given time to learn it. To be quite honest, I thought Ian in your interview [Chapter 4] was rather scathing and unfair about John's ability, and of Barrie's, and about Jeffrey too. It was rather personal really, I thought. In my eyes that stemmed back to a little bit of jealousy, reading between the lines, because as I said Jeff was the true eccentric and Ian – who was quite a good artist from what I remember, he used to be quite a good painter – I think Ian was a little bit… not in awe of him, but as I say he used to rib him terribly, so perhaps it was a bit of jealousy. Well, maybe then, if not now.

In my view, without John Evans there wouldn't have been a Jethro Tull, not in the form it's taken. He may not be aware of it, because looking back it's taken all this time for me to see it, but Ian used to clock things that were going on. He used to take influences from different people. Which reminds me – when we used to play the smaller venues I always used to wear an overcoat on stage, and I'm sure that's where Ian got the idea! But seriously, John was definitely a big influence in his life. They were close, and I think John really pushed him, without possibly realising it, in the right direction. John was without doubt the musical inspiration at the beginning, and it is unfair and misleading for Ian to say that the band was called after him just because his mother paid for the van. He used to work everything out. John and I used to sit down with piano and guitar, because I'd had all the experience of all those other bands and working stuff out was second nature. Ian really, with all due respect to him, was no musician then, he struggled a bit, and he hadn't quite yet got the blues thing. And in that interview he said that Barrie is a fiddly drummer, and wouldn't be able to join in a rock'n'roll jam. The only reason Barrie is a quirky drummer is because of the stuff they did with Tull. Barrie respects immensely Ronnie Brambells from The Atlantics – every time I see him, Barrie says: "What's Brambells doing?", and he always goes to see him. And in fact abut ten years ago we did a reunion gig of that first band and all the old R'n'B songs, and Barrie did exactly that, he got up and joined in a couple of numbers.

[*We later had the privilege of watching at Chris's house a home video of that reunion gig of The Atlantics – at least MW did. No point in asking DR about it; sad to relate that the combination of too much northern beer and the strain of having just put together another issue of* AND *caused him to fall fast asleep during the third number, thereby missing a musical treat, including guest appearances from Barrie Barlow and Tony Williams.*]

Ian and Jeffrey were considered the arty type. They both ended up going to the local Tech College School of Art. But from what I can remember, I don't think Ian was very happy – he left before the end of the pre-diploma course. At art school he always used to dress a bit oddly. I remember seeing him in town in Blackpool in a pub called The Blue Room, which was a student hangout, and I hadn't seen him for ages. At the time it was reasonably fashionable to have long hair, and he turned up to this pub with it all shaved, really close to his head, and tight black trousers and these winkle-picker boots. Unfortunately I haven't got a photo of him like that! But I do think that he worked on his eccentricity. He had one job in his life after he left school; he worked for Lewis's clothes store as a sales assistant. I had to go and see him once about some gig that we were doing, and he was wearing very tight greeny-browny checked trousers off a suit, a jacket from another green checked suit which didn't match the trousers, a blue and white striped shirt and a big red tie, horrible pointed suede shoes, and a stubbly beard. Trainee manager in Lewis's! It would be interesting to remind Ian of that. He may not own up to it, but it's a fact – I can still picture him now! I think it was the one and only proper job he ever had. Mind you, we all used to wear some weird stuff. I think it was probably a deliberate attempt to be different and present some sort of a new image on stage.

Back in those days Ian wasn't even a front-man. Ian took a long time getting off the ground personality- or character-wise. He was a bit unsure of himself, and it came out in an aggressive way, in the way he'd have a go at Jeffrey – he used to give John Evans some stick too. We'd be travelling to some place, and there'd be constant bickering and things like that. In fact it got a bit annoying to a certain degree, because I was an outsider, they having all been at school together – I was on the fringe of their friendships. Barrie was too, really, at the start. And the other point is that, as I said, Barrie and I were the only ones with any money, so if we stopped anywhere we bought the fish and chips and teas and so on, and Ian was always cadging a fag off whoever was handy. In fact I had a row with him one night in Stockport. I had a girlfriend who used to come regularly to see us. And because the van was always full of gear I used to go back with her in her car, and sometimes one or other of the band would come along too to make things easier for travelling. We were coming back from this gig, and Ian had been bumming fags off her all night. She was quite wealthy, this girl, and she was so nice she'd have given him her left arm if he'd asked for it, and it really got on my nerves that particular night. He took a fag off her, and I whacked it out of his mouth. Really, looking back, I don't think we got on too well; possibly because we were all young and a bit fiery. But we were all individual characters; the band did have a bit of character, no question. And to his credit Ian's stuck with the whole business right from the beginning, and I admire him. He's very talented, and you see he's got something that really is the vital ingredient, which is to be able to write his own stuff. The stuff that he is writing and has written is different from anyone else's, which I admire. He's never been a run-of-the-mill rock act. After Tull's first album, which had stuff like *Cat's Squirrel* which everyone and his dog was doing, he got his own quirky way of doing it. And he's come on thunderously as a flute player!

Eventually I got a bit disheartened with life on the road with nothing to show for it, and I opted out – round about the same time as the van blew up and all our money went on repairing it. As I say, I was working in the Civil Service, and they were pouring me out of the van into work in the morning, having slept in it and so on. If I hadn't had a job I'm sure I'd have stuck it longer, but I didn't have the same dedication or 'killer instinct' as Ian. I mean, you've got to live; I think Ian's mum and dad were still helping to support him then.

Barrie decided he was leaving round about the same time as I was. We put an advert in *Melody Maker* for a new drummer and got various replies, one of which was from an Indian guy from Leicester called Ritchie Dharma, who later played with the Mick Abrahams Band, amongst others. We played a gig in Manchester and met him at a pub called The Rising Sun. And Ian was like, "You talk to him, you go and talk to him," – didn't want to know! So I got the onerous job of interviewing this guy. Lovely fella, and a good drummer. He'd brought his kit and ended up getting up and doing a tune with us, and he was very good. So he joined the band as Barrie's replacement. I'd like to meet Ritchie again, actually, 'cos I had quite a long conversation with him on that particular night, and we became friends. He played with us on odd gigs while he got back into the business. I can't work it out, actually, because somehow or other I was still playing with the band when Barrie had left, and yet Barrie did the Granada TV thing. So he must have rejoined when Ritchie Dharma left.

The South Bank Jazz Club in Grimsby is where it started to change. We were on with this band, can't remember their name, who had a very good guitar player. Some time later we played there again. I'd decided to leave, and they liked this guitarist, so they asked him to join. His name was Neil, but they called him 'Chic Murray' because he spoke just like the comedian. So Barrie left first, and then I left. Just before that though we did the only original song I can remember us doing, called *How Can You Work With Mama?* which Ian wrote, and which we actually recorded in Mrs Evans's garage. I think they were thinking of doing that song for the Granada TV show, but chose *Take The Easy Way* instead. I can remember watching the show, and seeing Ian in his lurex-type suit. That TV programme I think was a big turning point for Ian in his efforts to get away from Blackpool, which he hated. I'd already left the group by then, of course.

AFTER THE JOHN EVAN BAND

After I left The John Evan Band, Barrie and I formed a group called The All Jump Kangaroo Band, 'cos in those days everything was a 'jump band' – think about it! Jeff Hammond came up with the name for that one. It was Barrie on drums, me on guitar, a guy called Paul Hargreaves on bass, and Andy Truman on keyboards – and Andy later became Jethro Tull's tour manager. It was a pretty good band too; we did a lot of soul and Tamla Motown stuff.

I also came across Glenn Cornick again. After The Hobos split, Glenn disappeared and went back to Barrow. When he came back we were in another band together called The Executives. Tony Williams was the guitar player – you can see how things were all interconnected in those days. Tony left, and I had to audition for the job, which I hate doing, but I got it. We did two or three records which all sank without trace. And it's worth mentioning that Barrie also had a group, with Johnny Breeze, Frank Blackburn and Brian Hood from The Atlantics, and Chris Wooton, who was one of Glenn Cornick's friends from The Hobos in Barrow, called McGregor's Engine, under which name Mick Abrahams and Clive Bunker had played. As I said, things all the way through this story were all amazingly interconnected. [*Actually, Barrie has admitted to us that he nicked the name off Mick and Clive because he couldn't think of a good one himself!*]

JETHRO TULL

For my money Jethro Tull have never been given enough credit for what they were, or are. Ian is very talented, and I'd never take that away from him. In fact I'd go so far as to say that Ian's contribution to English music is on a par, in its own way, with Vaughn Williams and Elgar, and it's a disgrace that it hasn't been widely recognised as such. I'm sure it rankles with Ian that he doesn't get the kudos that the Phil Collinses and so on of this world get. He'll have to die I think before it's recognised what a great English-Scottish-British talent he is. And I think there is the potential for Tull to have a whole new audience, it they want to do anything about it.

The first time I saw Jethro Tull was at The Marquee, when they'd just started to 'make it'. The dad of a mate of mine called Chris, who used to drum with me, paid for us to come down to London for our 21st birthdays to see Buddy Rich at Ronnie Scott's, and we saw Tull at The Marquee too. I was introduced to Mick Abrahams that night, and we had a long chat, although he won't remember me. I bought *This Was* and I loved it. In my view Mick Abrahams was equally important in the band as Ian, and I don't think that would have gone down too well with Ian! I think it was touch and go who was going to be the main man in Jethro Tull, and I'm sure there's some truth in the story that Ian tells about the record company wanting him to stand at the back and play piano, strange as it might sound now. But Ian was very single-minded; he knew what he wanted right from the beginning and wouldn't be side-tracked.

The one and only time Tull ever went back to Blackpool was in 1971 on the *Aqualung* tour, at the Opera House which is a big 3,500-seater. It was full, and I think Ian was expecting an absolutely rapturous homecoming. He popped his head round the wings and the spotlight went on him, and all he got was polite applause. And you could see that he was annoyed. All the way through the concert he was annoyed that he wasn't getting the reception he'd expected. And they've never been back, even though The Opera House is still there and available. Although to be fair, no-one plays there. It's the kiss of death to play in Blackpool, unless you're Freddie Starr or Cannon & Ball. Genesis, ELP, Paul Young – they've all died deaths there.

The next time I saw Tull was in Manchester, when Andy Truman was the tour manager. He used to work for Mars, he was a real salesman. I went backstage with Mrs Evans, and he was there in a smart white suit with big lapels, and a big sticker with 'Tour Manager' on it. "Oh,

Mrs Evans, Chris, lovely to see you!" he said, and stuck these big 'Jethro Tull Backstage Pass' stickers on us. And Ian was stood at the back of The Apollo stage, again in tight black trousers and black T-shirt, leaning against a wall, and he looked absolutely ill, he looked as if he was dying; very thin, and white, and so on. And that stuck in my mind. It must take its toll, all that travelling and touring and being responsible for such a lot, not just his own livelihood. In 1978 Tony Williams and I had a band. Tony is an excellent guitarist and a lovely singer. His forte is his voice, very rich. He's got an uncanny knack of being able to sound like whoever he is covering, like Billy Joel, Neil Diamond, Chris Rea. He's a very talented musician, and still working as The Tony Williams Band. Tony's claim to fame prior to 1978 was being the bass player on Stealer's Wheel's first LP with Gerry Rafferty; he's got a gold disc at home for it. Incidentally, John Evans told me that he once played one of his gold discs and it was a Harry Secombe record or something! Anyway, when John Glascock was ill, Tull were in need of a bass player. So having kept in touch with Barrie after being in groups together before Barrie joined Tull, Tony got the call. On the day that they did that satellite TV show from Madison Square Gardens we all watched the TV in some club manager's office – because we were still playing as The Tony Williams Band – and, wait for it, he's playing my bass! That's one thing I could never understand – all the power and glory and money that Tull have got and he had to borrow my bloody bass! He took my Fender half-way across the world and it came back with different pick-ups on; I must ask Tony about that. Tony's not really a bass player, but he took his chance, and did the tour. I mean, if they could teach Jeff Hammond to do it, they could teach anyone to do it. Sorry Jeff!! Tony came back looking more like Jethro Tull than Jethro Tull, leather knee boots and all the rest of it

People ask me if I have any regrets or am ever envious that so many of my old colleagues ended up with Jethro Tull, but that I didn't. If there are any regrets it's that I haven't been able to develop a style of my own, really, 'cos I'm always playing someone else's stuff. It is frustrating sometimes, but we get the work, and I've got to pay the mortgage. But there was only one time really that I was a bit envious. I was always, and still am, a big Ray Charles fan, and soon after Tull had made it they went to America and played the Newport Jazz Festival. Ray Charles was on that bill, and that's the only time really I'd have liked to have had the privilege of being there.

POSTSCRIPT

We were truly grateful to Chris, who had made a special trip down from Blackpool to London to talk to us, having undertaken a good deal of prior preparation and research, including talking to other characters involved in the story with whom he is still in touch. Later that evening, sitting in the bowels of Oxford Street's 100 Club, Chris emphasised that, in spite of anything he'd said about personality differences, we should ensure that the story sounded a positive one. And it is to be hoped that nothing he said looks like sour grapes in cold print, because it certainly wasn't the way he told it. He is merely a little irked that the achievements of Jethro Tull have obscured the fact that for two years The John Evan Band was a fine, working group. "Y'know, I often have a dream," he said, "In which I'm about to go on stage with Ian and John and the others, and just as I step up something goes wrong, like my guitar goes all floppy, and I can't go on. Perhaps deep down it's a sense of frustration in never having been able to set down on record the story of the early years of The John Evan Band – maybe thanks to your magazine I'll be exorcised now!"

JOHN EVANS

As related in Chapter 8, it was as a result of our meeting with Chris Riley that John Evans then got in touch. His musings on his time with Jethro Tull are set out in that chapter – but he also spoke at some length about The John Evan Band.

You've told us that your proper name is Evans. Where did 'John Evan' without the 's' come from?

We were looking for a name for the band. We used to be The Blades, but that seemed a little passé, and Jeffrey thought that The John Evan Band sounded good and that The John Evans Band didn't. So that's all there is to it.

Why was it named after you anyway? Ian tells this story about your mother putting up the money for the van...
That's got nothing to do with it. I mean, it's true that she paid for the van - and not only the van, but quite a lot of the early equipment.

So it wasn't a sop to you, or her...?
No. No, it was Jeffrey's idea, I distinctly remember that. I'm positive about it, or I wouldn't say so.

Chris Riley put it down to you being very much the musical influence in terms of direction and the type of music you played.
Well, I was undoubtedly the one who knew most about music in a formal kind of way - keys and harmonies and things like that. I did 'O' Level music; I'd been taught to play the piano since about the age of four by my mother. And the headquarters of the band was centred at our house, the practice room was our garage. Surprisingly enough we didn't get that many complaints from neighbours. In fact, some folks nearby now say that they used to take their little girl - who's now about thirty or so! - for a walk and used to stand there for quite some time and listen to it. It was a bit different in those days - these days you've only got to make the slightest noise and you get the Noise Abatement Society on you. In those days you couldn't walk down the street, particularly in Blackpool, without having guitars and drums coming out of somebody's house - it was every other house!

And it's amazing how all the groups seemed to be interrelated, starting with The Atlantics...
The Atlantics were the first of the professional-type groups, really good. Frank Blackburn was literally one of the best guitarists around. He sold his guitar about ten years ago and now he's a panel beater. Going back to about 1963 I can remember one night working out that their equipment was worth about a thousand pounds, when a Vox AC 30 was about £120; they had a drumkit costing £200 when mine cost about £90. I was about fifteen or sixteen at the time and, to me, listening to them was exactly the same as listening to the records. They used to do Cliff Richard, The Shadows, The Ventures, The Tornadoes, and so on - Frank was then a Hank Marvin copyist, note perfect on everything he did. So that's where Chris came from. He left and went to The Hobos with Glenn Cornick, and by this time we were starting up, mainly due to Jeffrey's guidance. I was quite keen on doing the pop Cliff Richard stuff, but neither Jeffrey not Ian liked that side of it. Everyone was getting into the blues. If you were an art student your idols were John Mayall's Bluesbreakers, Alexis Korner, and later Graham Bond. And from that we had a look at who THEY got it from, which was the black bluesmen. Anyway, we started off doing the Liverpool stuff, with me playing drums, and we'd mix in with it numbers by Muddy Waters, Willie Dixon, Sonny Terry and Brownie McGhee, Howling Wolf, Little Walter, and so on.
Then after a bit I got fed up playing the drums, simply because I didn't know how to, really. It used to hurt my hands, and I felt frustrated because I could play the piano so much better. At this time The Animals and Georgie Fame had just started off, and I used to watch the progressive groups who'd bought an organ and see some idiot playing with two fingers and think, huh, I can play with ten! Well - at least five and a bit of help from the left hand if Ian thinks that ten is exaggerating a bit! But I could get round Jimmy Smith licks, which no-one else could, simply because I'd done Grade 4 or 5 on the piano. So we interviewed for drummers, and for a while we had a lad who was very keen, a bit older than us, called Paul Jackman, another art student who was a real blues fanatic. He had a bed-sitter in his landlady's house and every single one of his records was that of a real blues buff. He wanted to play this all the time, but he wasn't very good - he was more enthusiasm than ability - so we advertised in a local paper. One or two people turned up who'd been in the more semi-pro groups and asked about money. Of course we hadn't got any, and weren't earning any - we'd

be just about covering petrol and expenses - so we'd have to say, "Er, there isn't any money"; and of course they'd turn round and walk off again! But then Barrie turned up. He was fourteen, with the thickest Birmingham accent I'd ever heard. He'd just left school and come up to live with his dad, who lived in Blackpool, and he got the job.

Why did you play drums in the first place?
What else could I do? I couldn't play the guitar. I did try to learn, like everybody else did, on some battered old Spanish guitar. But I could play piano so well that I didn't want to start fiddling around realising it would be months or years before I could actually do something on it. Whereas you can pick up drumsticks and it seems a lot quicker route to actually getting on stage and doing what The Big Three and The Beatles were doing. Let's face it, if Ringo could do it, anyone could. Then shortly after there was Charlie Watts, who I thought was great – I really thought that's the way a drummer should be. He still is, really.

Were you playing gigs at this stage, when Barrie joined?
Oh yes. I'd already been the drummer, and we were doing gigs. The very first gig we did was this little Youth Club at a Roman Catholic church just round the corner from me called The Holy Family. We used to go up there to rehearse a bit, to try out somewhere with a bit more room than a 1930s garage that was built for an Austin 10 or something. And they said, "We had The Atlantics on and paid then £15. We can't do that for you, but if you want to come and do a Friday night we'll give you £2", or something. So we worked up from there.

It must have become a fairly hectic life. The John Evan Band gig lists show you playing in places that wouldn't start until midnight, all-nighters and so on...
Yes, The Twisted Wheel, Stax Club, all those places. Sometimes we'd do an evening gig and pack up and set up somewhere else for an all-nighter. I was the only member of the band with a driving licence. I remember once, it was the middle of December, our Blackpool agent Johnny Taylor rang us up and said, "I've got a gig for you tomorrow night – in Scotland, in a place called Strathpeffer." We looked on the map, and it was about thirty miles north of Inverness. He said, "They want an Irish showband, but when you start playing they'll like it. Just talk with an Irish accent." We said, "You've got to be joking – how much is it?" It was £35, so we said, "OK, we'll do it." "And don't forget, you've got Nottingham Boat Club the night after," he said. So, we set off at four o'clock on the Friday afternoon – I was the only driver – and we got to Edinburgh about six o'clock on the Saturday morning. It took us all bloody day to get from Edinburgh through the worst blizzards they'd ever had. We were following snow ploughs, and the only way you could tell where the roads were was by the tops of the telegraph poles sticking up through the snow. It took us about fourteen hours to get there, crawling all the way. We got there about eight o'clock thinking we were going to be too late, and dashed in, started to unload the gear and set it up on stage. And the Scotsman who owned this caravan park came over and said, "Hey, you're not Irish!" I mean, there was no way we were going up there and start talking like a load of Micks, so we said, "Well, no, but we're a band, we've got saxes and so on..." "Oh no, no, sorry," he said, "This is a Scottish and Irish type thing, and we must have a showband or we can't put you on. What sort of numbers do you do?" The most commercial of our numbers were like Stax label things, Wilson Pickett, Otis Redding and so on. What he wanted was *Green, Green Grass Of Home* and bloody ceilidh stuff. So he said, "Terribly sorry – can't give you any money, but we'll give you a meal." It had taken twenty-eight hours to get there, and we'd got a gig the next night at Nottingham Boat Club. So we had a quick meal, and I just drove straight back again. The weather wasn't so bad coming back, straight through Scotland at night – which I can't remember a thing about – and then down the A1 throughout the next day. I do remember driving down the A1 past Durham as the sun was coming up and all the fields were white; and everyone was fast asleep, the van just echoing to snores. We just made it, getting there at six o'clock Sunday afternoon, played the gig, put the gear back in the van, and went back to Blackpool, arriving about four o'clock Monday morning. I'd been driving almost non-stop since the Friday afternoon. That is fact! There was only Tony Wilkinson, who was one of the sax players, who could drive, and he just wouldn't for some reason.

When Chris Riley left, you recruited Neil Smith. What was he like?
Neil was a talented guitarist. We called him 'Chic Murray'. He was totally individual, and would only do his own sort of thing, which was like a light jazzy style. Self-taught. He used to play a number on his own, not on stage, to amuse us called *Make It Straight, No Chaser* - an old jazzy song. Superb, individual style. One day we said to him, "Listen to this Eric Clapton record" - it was just about the time that Clapton was becoming 'God' - "Why can't you learn to play like that?" On stage we'd do things like *Every Day I Have The Blues*, just 12-bar blues, and he'd play these really thoughtful, clever, tasty jazz solos, but not that impressive. And all of a sudden that night he came out with this Eric Clapton sound, and played note for note a Clapton solo, exactly the style! He could do anything, but he just didn't want to. He didn't have any ambition for public acclaim, and didn't want to compromise his style. He eventually went back to the Civil Service in Bolton.

Did it surprise you that Ian became as famous as he did with Tull when you think back to what he was like with The John Evan Band? Was there any spark there to suggest that he might become a success?
Oh yes, I think so. I mean, Chris Riley will tell you that the whole band was me and Jeffrey, and that Ian was really in the back seat. But he wasn't, that much... He was a front man and the singer. He was like Paul Jones was to Manfred Mann. We started off doing the Liverpool stuff, and then the bluesy kind of underground stuff; and then we wanted to become more popular and earn more money, so we started doing the Stax, and Georgie Fame, Rolling Stones and some of the black stuff - at The Twisted Wheel in those days you had to play Otis Redding stuff, that's all they wanted to hear. So Ian was only "just" the singer until he started writing his own songs.

Do you remember much about the Granada TV show?
I remember I stopped the whole of Granada TV when I plugged in my Hammond organ! A technician saw me doing it and everybody walked off. I was just doing what I do every night; you know, if a plug comes off you strip the wires with your teeth – I've got a cap off a tooth missing through doing that – and fiddle around with a screwdriver and plug it in. So the technician said, "Right, everybody out! An electrician should do that, along with a mate, and a guy to make the tea." So they all stopped for half-an-hour, went to wash their bottoms so that somebody could lick them, and then came back. Our appearance had been arranged by an agent we had at the time in Bolton called Don Read – I think it was him; either that or Johnny Taylor from Blackpool. Somebody who purported to be our manager at the time, anyway. The *Firstimers* TV programme was like a primitive *Opportunity Knocks*.

How many songs did you do?
Just the one, *Take The Easy Way*.

Did it do the band much good?
No good at all! We didn't win it. We were in the competition in the same period as Amen Corner who were just being pushed. They had a record called *Gin House* which was just going into the charts, and were fated to win it, so it pushed the record along. Andy Fairweather-Low used to go down on one knee at the end. He reputedly did it one night on stage right onto a drawing pin.

I was a bit surprised more wasn't made of it – the subsequent gig adverts in the local papers didn't say anything like "As seen on TV".
No, well it wouldn't. We played down things like that.

Deliberately?
Yeah – just inverted snobbery, I suppose. We didn't want to appear the same as everyone else who made these spurious claims to fame. I mean, there used to be a group who played at The Beachcomber Club in Luton called The Warriors who had some personnel, including Jon Anderson, who went on to become Yes; they used to be billed as "Straight from the Ed Sullivan Show in New York". People used to believe it. WE used to believe it!

What about your various trips into the studio?
There was the session which produced *How Can You Work With Mama?*, *Take The Easy Way* and *I Got You*, which I've got a tape of. We did some more demos, including *Aeroplane*, at Abbey Road studios in the summer of 1967 before we went down to Luton. But I can't remember *Letting You Go*, which you mentioned [*We got the title wrong – it was actually* Blues For The 18th, *since released on a Derek Lawrence compilation*] , except that at the time Traffic were pretty big, and we all thought that was the way to go; those songs did have a Trafficy feel to them. But I've never heard them since, apart from *Aeroplane*, and I just can't remember the first thing about them. We did some other recordings as well, at CBS Studios in Bond Street; so that was three lots altogether, but I don't know what happened to them. We did a big-band type number called *The Man*. It just wasn't us at all - at the time I thought it sounded more like Bobby Goldsborough before he did things like *Honey*. That came about through Don Read again.

Nobody ever tried to do a live recording, then, with a portable tape-recorder?
Well, this was before the days of cassette players. Jeffrey had a big reel-to-reel thing, and he did a few tapes of rehearsals just to see what it sounded like. But no live shows.

So what about the end – did you go down to Luton?
Yes, I went down to Luton.

Why did you eventually jack it in?
I didn't like it. Not so much Luton, but I couldn't see, in the foreseeable future, that I'd ever be (a) financially self-sufficient or (b) doing anything other than living in bed-sits. When we went down to Luton, Glenn was living at home with his parents who had a big pub at Thornton Heath, but Barrie, Ian and I were shacked up together. The reason we were in Luton was because of Mick Abrahams, who was living at home. And when Barrie left we got Clive Bunker, who was Mick's mate from his old group McGregor's Engine, so he was living at home. So it was just me and Ian. And Ian by this time, I think, was becoming quite single-minded in his purpose of making it in the rock business. I wasn't so committed. Plus, I have to say, I wasn't at all happy with the direction the music was going in. I was disenchanted with playing the type of blues which resulted from Mick's involvement. I mean, I loved the original black artists, but it's the old "can the white man play the blues?" thing. So I took the coward's way out and went back home to live with my mum, and went back to college to make up for the fact that I'd failed all my 'O' Levels because we were out driving all over the country every night.

TONY WILKINSON

MW was speaking to Ian Anderson after a 1987 Hammersmith Odeon show and happened to mention our plans for a John Evan Band retrospective. Ian failed in his attempt to feign complete disinterest, although his reaction was somewhere between amusement and pity for these two "obviously completely crazy fans" (as he described us in the 1988 box set booklet). MW started to explain that we had met Chris Riley. "Chris Riley?" Ian interrupted, "Y'know, people like him really annoy me." "Er, why?" MW asked warily, inwardly mortified that Chris might be persona non grata in the Jethro Tull camp. "Because every time I see him he never looks any older!" laughed Ian. Phew, what a relief!
Anyway, Ian still wasn't at all forthcoming about any of his own memories of the band, but he did casually say, "Tony Wilkinson would be a good chap to talk to if you want some good stories about the old days." So, with such a recommendation from the highest level, we did just that. Although he had not seen Tony for many years, the indefatigable Chris Riley tracked down his whereabouts, on the outskirts of Blackpool, and MW spoke to Tony by 'phone. He agreed to meet us and, although it took a while to organise, we went up to Blackpool in March 1988 and, accompanied by Chris, we motored over to a nearby village to see him.
The interview with Tony was printed in Issue 27. But our pleasure in finally getting round to Part 2 of the John Evan Band story was completely overshadowed by the news in late 1990

that Tony had been killed in a motorcycle accident. Although we met him only once, we had been greatly impressed by this larger-than-life, jovial character who spoke to us with great humour and genuine warmth. With the blessing of his family we went ahead with printing the interview as a tribute.

Although Tony's association with the music business ended on the day he left The John Evan Band, he willingly dredged his memory to speak amusingly and affectionately of his times with the band. When MW had made contact by 'phone with Tony, he had referred several times to Ian Anderson as "Elvo". So we began by asking him why…

"ELVO"

We all did at that time. We played a gig at Warrington Co-op Hall, which was as salubrious a sort of place as it sounds! We died, as it happens, as we did in most places. We played there with a band who were much more appreciative of our music than the audience we were playing to. After we'd done our bit we went downstairs to get changed, and some fellow burst in through the door and said to Ian, "Man, you sound just like Elvo!" We said, "Who? What's he on about?" And he said, "Elvo! The King – Elvis!" Ian was pretty upset about that, as you can imagine, but we were all highly amused. So "Elvo" was something that stuck for an awful long time – it was just a silly little nickname. And I've never thought of him in any other way but that. When I write to him I still call him by the same name. To call him "Ian" now sounds a bit pretentious somehow – odd, really.

THE BAND

Anyway, to start at the beginning, when I joined the band Chris Riley was playing guitar, Jeff Hammond was playing bass, and there was Martin 'Marvo' Skyrme, John, Barrie and Elvo. What happened was that I had heard that there was an opening for a sax player. I was playing drums at the time, but I wanted to play saxophone. There weren't any bands around who were playing saxophone men, because you have to remember that at that time it was all 4-man guitar-dominated groups in the charts. The only way to get in a band playing saxophone was to create a band of your own and play your own material. I wasn't a good player, but I was very dedicated, and that's often as important as ability.

So Elvo and I had a meeting in my car. At the time I had a 1955 Chevrolet Bel-Air, which was an absolutely wizard car. In fact, apart from getting the gear there, we could all go to gigs in this one car, four across the front seat and four across the back seat! It was the most revolting colour – cream and sky-blue with leopard-skin seats. It would be worth a fortune now; I'm very sad I never kept it. I paid £50 for it, but it was a bloody magic car. Anyway, we met somewhere and had this meeting in the car. I was a bit nervous because I was being taught in a very formal way and I found it very difficult to play without written music. But Elvo said that it would be no problem, as John could write it all down. And that's what happened – anything I had any difficulty with, John would write it down and I'd learn it so that I could play it live. The improvisational aspect was always very weak, so it was never a problem. And baritone sax wasn't a good solo instrument anyway – it's always been regarded as a bit of a back-up type of instrument rather than a front line, apart from great exponents of the instrument. And you must remember that at that time Georgie Fame was the only person, apart from maybe Zoot Money, who was using anything like that line-up. It was very low-key on commercially released records, but very prominent on live performances. So we modelled ourselves on him quite a lot in that respect. Regarding my own influences, Gerry Mulligan was a big hero, but the people who really made me want to play were the tenor players on the early Little Richard and Duane Eddy records, rather than any jazz giants – you know, simple stuff, but brilliant.

The John Evan Band was the only band I was in. I didn't play in a band because I wanted to "play in a band", I played in The John Evan Band because it played the music I wanted to play, and I didn't want to do anything else other than that. I hadn't done it to become a star; we were all doing it then because we were all frustrated blues/jazz musicians and wanted to play that music. That's all we were bothered about, and if we got paid along the way, so much the better.

REHEARSALS

We used to rehearse sometimes at John's house, and also at my mother's house which had a very big kitchen. We used to rehearse in the kitchen, which she used to get furious about, because the pegs on the front of the drumkit used to dig into the floor. My mother would arrive home at tea-time and the kitchen would be totally occupied, stacked up to the ceiling with amplifiers and gear and so on. She was a very fierce woman, my mother; she's a direct descendant of Boudicea, and we were absolutely terrified of her. She'd come through the back door like hellfire and damnation and the music would just die instantly. And the kit would be packed up and wham, out of the door in seconds flat.

Later on we used to play the Stax Club in Manchester and we negotiated a deal with the guy who operated it – he was a bit shady, I think – to rehearse there, so we'd have the place to ourselves. Also, there used to be an enormous convalescent home across the road from my mother's house, and it had a massive hall to it. I knew the nuns quite well, and we used to rehearse in there. It had a stage and everything – just what we needed.

GIGS

I remember doing a lot of Tamla Motown stuff on stage like *Knock On Wood*, which we thought was crap. But the problem was, before we graduated on to doing the Universities and so on, we'd go to a gig such as the Bolton Palais where Mavis Scruggins just wanted to gyrate about with her boyfriend, and the band were totally insignificant, just a noise. So you had to do current material.

I remember us doing a gig at the Banqueting Rooms at the Tower Ballroom in Blackpool, which was a crap gig - it was full of piss-arsed Scotsmen who just wanted to get drunk and stab each other. And at that time we had the Hammond organ, not to mention a Leslie cabinet, which was a bastard to hike up and down stairs – any gig we ever played always seemed to be upstairs! We got set up and had a blow to get ourselves going, and we played *Every Day I Have The Blues*, which was a number we used to open with. We played that sort of material really well, and the reason we played it well wasn't because we were accurate, competent musicians, it was because the soul of it was within us, so we played it with a passion, and it really did swing. And two or three of Charlie Barlow's Band, who were in the Tower Ballroom next to us, drifted in to watch us. They thought it was bloody great, and they were telling their mates to come in and see these lads, because they could really swing. And they made us do something else, like *Let The Good Times Roll*, which was probably one of my favourites, or maybe *Pink Champagne*, and in the end we had half the Tower Ballroom Band jamming with us! They were really into it, and were saying, "God, do you get much work playing this sort of material? I'd love to get out of the crappy band we're in." And we said, "Yeah, but you've got to do it for three bob a week!"

There were four good gigs we used to particularly enjoy doing. One was Grimsby Jazz Club, because we got such a receptive audience. They also had a good resident band there, and we used to have a good jam with them. And there were the three Boat Clubs in Nottingham, The Britannia, The Trent and The Union, where we actually performed on the same stage as Graham Bond. That was at a time when Graham Bond, John Mayall, Jack Bruce, Dick Heckstall-Smith, Manfred Mann, Eric Clapton and all of that bunch were playing together. They were heady days those, when I think back on the mega-talent that we were onstage with at the time. And they were big news for us because they were doing the material that we really admired.

CHARACTERS

John was never an easy character – in fact he was hard work. He perfected the art of being rude – he always played gormless. But he was very placid. He'd just go along with things. At the time we had a red Thames van, which used to break down all the time. We were forever diving into 'phone boxes to ring up the gig to say we'd broken down and we'd be there in an hour. It's no wonder they never paid us! Anyway, nobody was allowed to drive this bloody van except John. We'd be going along the motorway and he'd be starting to snore! And we'd say, "For Christ's sake, let somebody else drive," but no – he was obsessed with it. And he was absolutely like a man possessed when driving that van. The only things he reacted to were traffic lights and policemen, and then there was some response.

I remember another obsession John had. He had a Ronson cigarette lighter which, like any other lighter, turns the gas off when you put the top down; and it had a wheel to adjust the flame. He perfected the technique of lighting his lighter, and putting the top down, and then he'd turn the wheel right off, so that when he put the top up again he'd have to turn the wheel on before he could light the lighter. It's funny how you notice these stupid little things, but those were the sort of obsessions he had. He was quite unbalanced in that respect, but very docile in lots of other respects. And very, very intelligent – grossly underestimated and dismissed by the majority of people, us included. Because it was just too much horsework to actually get through to him, too difficult.

What John had the ability to do was to grasp hold of what everyone else was doing and take, for instance, the melody line out of it and set it so that it became the first permanent fixture of whatever it was that we were trying to do, and the arrangement would come from that. I mean, Elvo became quite a competent musician, but later rather than sooner. Elvo was just messing about with a guitar then. He was always a good vocalist though, and he had lots and lots of basic raw talent which I recognised, funnily enough, even then - in other words, it was so obvious even to me at that age that he was going to become very successful at some point because he was just too talented to remain anonymous. But John, because of the formal training which his mother had given him, had the ability to take all that quite naturally and set it out in a legible and workable form, so that we could then progress it. And had he not done that we would all have circled around with lots of little bits of ideas, and nothing would have actually crystallised and materialised. So John was the key person in that respect.

Neil Smith became our guitarist when Chris left, and he was a bloody good guitarist too, that kid. He was very tall and very, very thin, and had absolutely no presence about him at all. He was just like the wallpaper, and we couldn't do anything with him to make him more prominent. If it was a very deep stage he would settle somewhere at the back where nobody could see him, and where no-one in the band could see him for that matter. His nickname was 'Chic Murray' after the Scottish comedian who made obvious statements, but in a very amusing way, and that's exactly what Neil Smith used to do. He was a very responsible person, and very serious. He was still trying to hold a job down at the Inland Revenue in Manchester, and I think he must have slept all day at his desk. We're talking about the days before motorways covered the country. So we'd finish a gig at midnight or one o'clock, and then take an hour or so to get packed up and get paid – which was a major part of the operation – and then load all the stuff into the van, set off, find some transport café that was still open, get something to eat, and then everyone used to crash out in the back of the van in a heap, and by the time we'd arrive home we'd be coming in with the milkman. We used to drop Neil off at his office in Manchester, and he used to go straight in and try to do a day's work. Some poor bastards in Manchester must have got a real pasting on their tax bills if Neil was involved!

Jeff Hammond was a bit odd, I thought. Again, as with John, I found it hard work because he wasn't very forthcoming, and again I would have said that a lot of his eccentricities were in fact simple bad manners and inability to communicate – as it is with most eccentrics, in some way, unless they're very outgoing. I found him a bit like the wallpaper too. He's not a person who stands out in my mind particularly, because he never had anything to say. He never did anything particularly constructive or useful or profound in any way. He just arrived, played, moped about very moodily, and we dropped him off at home and that was it. Or he wouldn't come for some reason, like his mother had said 'no' or something. He was the butt of all Elvo's jokes, and he used to let himself be ordered around terribly. He used to slope off on errands for Elvo – he was a bit like a primate the way he walked, with his knuckles dragging along the ground. But not a fool, don't misunderstand me.

Martin 'Marvo' Skyrme was a bloody good tenor player. I remember we all got our hair cut once, trying to look cool. Marvo was sat in the chair and the barber asked him what style he wanted, and he said, "Just give me a jazz player's haircut, man!" He ended up with a real short back and sides, silly sod.

We used to call Neil Valentine 'The Forest Ranger', from the Yogi Bear cartoons. He had a really strong beard and had to shave twice a day, and he had this constant black line as if it had been pencilled on. He had a very smooth face and carefully coiffured hair, and looked just like a cartoon character. He used to work for British Rail coach-building division. Ranger was heavily into straightforward mainstream jazz, and was a damned good tenor player. He used to get a remarkably full sound and a good tone – whereas I could never get that tone. At the time my big hero was Mulligan, so my playing was very much along his lines, and I got a very similar sound which would tend to be softer and a bit in the background. I was never as good a player as Ranger, he was really good.

Barrie Barlow and I never really got on – in fact we used to hate each other with a passion. Perhaps we were just too young at the time. I haven't seen him since those days, but it wouldn't be like that now, of course. He was like a little terrier, wouldn't let go. We had some real stinking rows. He was quite a handy little lad, actually. I remember one night driving to the Club A-Go-Go in Newcastle; I was in the front of the van and he was behind. We were passing remarks as usual, and we eventually ended up having a fist fight across the two seats while John was trying to drive the bloody van. Barrie was a confused little bugger really. He had family problems at the time and lacked security, which manifested itself in basic aggression. And I didn't understand what that was about, so I was aggressive back to him, a real base reaction. And also, because I was the biggest at the time, I was always the one who went to whoever was paying us to actually get paid. The big ballsache with being a little band is that no bastard ever pays you – you know, "The cheque's in the post," or "We'll send it to your agent," and all that bloody nonsense! And I'm sure Barrie thought that I was working the cash, and that John and Elvo and myself were doing a three-way split and giving the rest of them the change. [*Laughing*] Now, we're talking in the first instance of, at the most, £20, and there were seven or eight of us – a bloody farce! And there was the van to pay for, and more gear to buy…

But Barrie was a knockout drummer – even though he could never play with his eyes open! He was never afraid to try anything new, he was very inventive. And he used to practice really hard, which is something I didn't, and which was really my downfall. In fact, none of us did really – we were always too knackered! I think he's a very talented drummer, and I'm sorry that he's not very prominent at the moment because he's capable of being a very major part of a very major band.

We picked Derek Ward up in Grimsby Jazz Club when Jeffrey left. He called himself Bo because he was a Bo Diddley freak. He was really smelly, and had one of those Zapata moustaches. We said that our bass player was leaving, so he said that he played bass and asked if he could join. We said OK, so he went home, got his guitar, just got in the van and came back with us! And he lived in the van. I used to take it home, and he'd be asleep outside in the van in a sleeping bag. My mother used to go out and drag him out and forcibly wash him. I remember once she took his vest out of his guitar case with a pair of tongs and threw it on the fire. Mind you, we all kipped in the van at times, or if it was summer we kipped underneath it. God, it was a smelly hole, that van!

In fact, I remember playing a gig in Newcastle once, and we were so knackered because we'd been at it for so long we said we'd splash out and have proper digs where we could sleep in a bed. We got hold of the address of some theatrical digs, which was a mistake – we'd have done better going to Mrs Scruggins's B&B down the road. We arrived very late, in fact early morning really, and we pulled up and asked could we stay, and they said, "Sure, come on in." And I actually got into a bed that another guy who was going out to do a day show had just got out of – the bed was still warm. Disgusting when you think about it, but that's what it was like. Terrible!

Andy Truman was a very amusing character. He used to roadie for us – for a long time in fact. I can remember paying him for a week that he roadied for us – one ten bob note. I'm glad to hear he's doing well; he's the sort of person who would do. He wouldn't have anyone putting him down, and was certainly a very dominant and loud sort of person. Elvo said that when Andy was the road manager for Tull, on one American tour he hired so much bloody labour at top rates that by the time they were half-way through the tour they were already on a loser. Andy did everything with this terrific extravagance. When Tull were in America Andy did more radio interviews than Elvo! I remember him in The All Jump Kangaroo Band with Barrie Barlow and Chris Riley. I'd like to see Andy again sometime.

RECORDINGS

We did quite a few studio sessions. There was one at Regent Sound in London at which we recorded *Take The Easy Way, How Can You Work With Mama?* and *You Got Me*. I've still got the acetates, if only I could find them. We also did a lot of messing about with MGM at a studio in Bond Street in London. We did an awful lot of material in there; quite a few songs of our own, and one or two of theirs, one of which was a Ray Charles song *The Man*. The intention was that it was going to be put out as a single and as part of an album. I don't know what happened to any of that material, whether in fact anything was ever done with it. I remember another piece which had a very complicated passage in it for baritone and tenor sax which we had a lot of trouble with. We spent yonks rehearsing it, and it was bloody hard to get right. It was modelled on an instrumental that James Brown had out at the time.

And then there was the thing for Granada TV, which John Hamp produced. That came about through Don Read, who was a bandit of an agent. He was a slimy toad – a bald, porky opportunist. This was the sixties of course, and he was very trendy. He worked as a booker for the Ian Hamilton organisation in Manchester. He had a little shit that worked for him called Peter Yates, and the bastard nicked our dough one day. We were all absolutely gobsmacked, because he pissed off with all our cash. We all swore that we'd have his bloody legs broken, and do God knows what else to him. [*Pauses... Thinks... Laughs...*] In actual truth, he didn't piss off with our cash – he pissed off with the commission we never paid him! He used to come to quite a few gigs. I remember being sat in the back of the van with Peter Yates and Elvo, and he was talking all sorts of mega-business. Yeah, he was a real toad as well.

Anyway, there's a great story about the TV show. It was broadcast at tea-time, and on the day it was shown we were on the way back from London in the van. For some reason we weren't all together – there was just John, Elvo, Barrie and myself I think. So we were flying up the M6 trying to be home in time to see the show on the box. We'd already gone past a service station when the bloody van ran out of petrol. Shit! It was about half-an-hour before the programme was due on, and it was a good half-an-hour from there to get home in time anyway. Everyone was going absolutely wild, and as I was driving they were all going mental at me for running out of juice. So we thought shit, we'll have to do something, it's just too important. We all piled out of the van and we just literally flagged the traffic down on the motorway. We stopped this guy who by chance had some petrol, and we got a gallon off him and set off again. Of course by now we were very late and had no chance of getting home in time. So we went straight into Preston and looked around for a TV rental shop. And luckily we found one, pulled up outside, piled out of the van and ran into the shop. Of course all the TVs were on, so we were shouting, "Put it on Granada!" – we were just in time, it was almost like something out of a film! Sure enough it came up on the screen, and we were all watching it; and this shop assistant looked at the TV, looked at us, and suddenly realised, "Hey, bloody hell, that's you on the TV!" He was absolutely flabbergasted. Of course, by then we were all really cool about it, you know, [*laid-back voice*] "Oh… yeah… of course".

I wrote to John Hamp, actually, to ask if the film had survived, and he wrote a very nice personal letter back saying, "I'm really sorry. I'd been looking myself and I'm afraid the tapes were all wiped some time ago." So it's gone for ever. I remember Andy Fairweather-Lowe and Amen Corner won it, and we were really pissed off because they were the only other band who had a similar line-up to us. Out of that show we got a string of gigs on the South Coast, which we really thought was a big deal – like a tour. It was OK for us because, although we would do some work for my father between gigs when we were skint – he must have been insane! – we were really only playing in the band; but Neil Smith and Neil Valentine had to arrange time off work.

You know, it was very silly and a great sadness really that we never took any 16mm movie film of the band live. [*Thinks...*] Although, we didn't actually have a 16mm camera, so it's hardly surprising really! [*Temporary halt in the proceedings while all present suffer varying degrees of hysterics!*]

By 1967 I'd had however many years it was of kipping underneath the van, or not eating, or not getting paid, and being skint and almost like a down-and-out, and so on, and I'd had a basin-full of that. There comes a time when you start to yearn a bit for the home comforts, like having a bath and a clean shirt when you want to, and eating at a table at a set time. Although in fact I'd done my best to organise my life like that even when I was in the band. One of the ways I did that was… when we first moved south we went as far as Dunstable, because Mick Abrahams lived there. Mick used to come and see us at Caesar's Palace in Luton. We were doing a lot of our own material by then, lots of bluesy material, and he was really into it. Mick was a brilliant guitarist, better than anyone we'd ever previously experienced or seen. Neil Smith had had to make the choice between the band and working for the Inland Revenue, and had chosen the Revenue, so Mick was the perfect replacement. But he couldn't come up to Blackpool for whatever reason, so we moved down there, because it was time for a move anyway. At this stage everyone was really into, "We'll have a flat of our own, a bedsit, we can all be really cool and trendy", and I thought, "Bollocks to that, it'll be a sack of shit, I know it will!" Mick Abrahams' mother had a friend who took in lodgers and by chance her husband was the manager of all the Dewhurst Butchers branches in the area. So of course I paid thruppence a week for lodgings – or rather, my mother did, actually – and I ate like a bloody king all the time! There was so much food in the house it was unbelievable; and I had clean laundry, and slept in a proper bed – it was magic! Of course, the others who were being hip and trendy were all opening cans of beans and eating them cold, and they were all dirty, and they couldn't pay the rent, and it was bad news. Oh God, it was bloody funny.

In Luton we were finding it very hard to get work, but Don Read got us a gig at The Marquee. I remember we had a pair of those candy-striped hipster trousers with a big deep belt. There was only the one pair between myself, John and Elvo, and the three of us used to wear them in rotation. It was a fight as to who could get these trendy pants on before we actually went on stage, and I got to wear them that night at The Marquee. We were called The John Evan Smash by then, which was because of Don Read. He didn't think 'The John Evan Band' sounded exciting enough. We objected, and refused to change the name, but then when we got to some gig there would be posters advertising 'The John Evan Smash', with 'Smash' written in a kind of broken glass effect. Absolute crap.

The romantic story of the eventual split is that we all decided that the band couldn't get enough work to support seven or eight of us, therefore we had to cut it down; and it was going to change direction anyway, so those who weren't all that fussed packed it up and the rest carried on. But I suppose in truth that wasn't really correct. The two Neils were working, so they left, and Mick Abrahams had stepped in. Barrie got pissed off and packed up, and Clive Bunker took over. And then John left. I stayed with the band a little longer because, as I've explained, I was very happy until I decided to turn it in. I'll tell you, quite seriously, why I never became a part of Tull. My oldest friend, who used to come along to gigs with us, said to me when we were getting very serious about things, "How far do you intend to go with this band?" And I said, not knowing what the hell we were doing, "I don't know really - as far as we can ever get. As long as we can get gigs and people will listen to us, then I will play." And I remember very clearly thinking even then - and I was only seventeen, and I was pretty thick at seventeen - that one way or another Elvo was going to make it, because it was impossible for that much talent to remain undetected for any length of time, unless he completely buried himself, which he wasn't doing. I thought that we as a band might have some success; although I suppose I never really believed that Elvo would be quite as successful as he has been. But I never thought that I would be that successful either, and the reason I eventually left the band - or one of the reasons, anyway - was because I just wasn't good enough to be in a band of that standing. It takes more than just musical ability, it takes a great deal of basic acumen and durability and determination and dedication to achieve any level of success, certainly in the music business. And I wasn't the creative influence in the band; Elvo was the creative person in the band, and I think that was obvious to all of us. He was always the person who wrote the material and came up with what was effectively the melody line, which is what record companies base royalties on, and so on. He would draw on the variability and the creative ability of the rest of the members of the band, but in truth he could have drawn on another half a dozen people in some other band and still achieved the same level of success. So it wasn't to do with us, it was to do with him in its entirety; the band was purely peripheral to his abilities. Not only from a composing point of view, but I think also from a consistency of performance point of view. Because that's the other thing - you've got to be consistent, because you have to turn out immaculate performances on every occasion, as every time you do it someone's paid to go and watch it. Elvo was able to do that, and I wasn't. And I think I knew it then. Other members of the band too were able to turn out consistent performances - John Evans was, Barrie Barlow certainly was, and Neil Smith too. But had I stayed with what was then the transition band from The John Evan Band to Jethro Tull, it would not have been much after that that either Elvo or the residual members of the band would have made the decision that Tony Wilkinson was no longer an asset to the band, or some management team or recording manager or whatever would have said, "You don't need the baritone sax player - get rid of him."

And oddly enough I don't regret leaving the band, because I left for the right reasons. Although I am not a part of that band now, I was a part, and I helped it in whatever nebulous way to become what it is, and was a contributory factor to it. And although the time for me to leave was right for the band, above all else I remember thinking at the time how important it was that the band for its own sake continued, and that Elvo continued, because it was important that all of that talent was made to work. And of course, that's what happened. Having said that, with hindsight, it wouldn't have been hard to put odds on that; it was obvious that it was going to happen. But I'm glad it worked, and it pleases me a lot when I see them on TV or they have any success with records - it's good, because it is a talent which should be recognised.

IAN ANDERSON AND JETHRO TULL

Some people find it strange that after a background like The John Evan Band, and indeed the first LP, Jethro Tull moved right away from the blues - but I don't, and I'll tell you why. If ever anything was orchestrated and manufactured it was the blues aspect. What you witnessed with Tull proper was Elvo's creative talent completely unfettered. That was very clear at the time because the material was so peculiar compared to anything else around. On the other hand, although *Take The Easy Way* and *You Got Me* are very jazzy music, you can hear certainly in those songs an element of Tull starting to come out already. I think Elvo's voice with Tull is very contrived. When he sings without... how can I put it... making it come from his throat, as it were, his voice is extremely good, when he's not contriving it to sound how he thinks it ought to sound; when it's much more bass and natural, I think he sounds very much better. And although Tull's music was very different to what The John Evan Band played, nevertheless I could see that the construction of it was similar. I mean, I don't think he'll admit to that, because that would tend to make it sound as if he'd been influenced by what had gone on before. But the truth is, everything is, we all are, nothing is truly original, everything is to a certain extent reflective. But if there were bits of Tull that originated in The John Evan Band, that's largely because Elvo was so powerful in the band. I mean, it wouldn't have made any difference, as indeed it doesn't make any difference in Tull, whether he had John, or anyone else, with him, the band would sound exactly the same, because the band IS Ian Anderson.

Although I think that there was obviously an element of Elvo's showmanship manifesting itself with The John Evan Band, what accelerated it to a point where he became recognised for it was the confidence that a little bit of success gave him. What often happens - which is a bad thing, and you see it now with a lot of modern or struggling bands - is that they become very aggressive and short-tempered with the audience when the audience doesn't respond to the material which the band thinks it should. In other words, "We're here, and you've all paid your money, but we're going to play what we want to play, not what you want to hear." It's a very common failing, and we were very guilty of that, because we were all terribly frustrated with the material which was around. So Elvo was a bit aggressive with them when they didn't react to the material we wanted them to react to. Now, the showman aspect of it was obviously there at the time, because no-one else in the band had any anyway; we were all so obsessed with being cool and laid-back and sophisticated that leaping about the place was far too mundane and plebeian for us even to consider. As a vocalist, as with all vocalists, Elvo had the opportunity to leap around a bit more, but there was certainly nothing there in those days as you now know him on stage. And when I see him do it with Tull I still see it as being slightly alien to him; I see it as something he considers a necessity to occupy the audience as well as to play to them. I don't like to see him doing it actually, because I think that he should spend his time delivering his music. But I can understand why it's hard for him to do that in a large concert setting where today's kids want to see lots of action, and would think it brainless to just stand on stage and play. And on the other hand, I'm sure that when he is in an environment where he feels the show is going well, and he is performing well and the sound is good, I imagine that excites him and it does come quite naturally to him.

Elvo is a damned good blues singer, and it's a pity that he doesn't do that type of material any more because he does it so well. We ought to have a reunion, you know! Most people are still playing in some capacity, and with some solid rehearsals it could be good. And I reckon personality problems could be overcome, especially after all these years. Without it sounding wrong, as difficult as you may consider Elvo, John and Barrie to be, someone like me could catalyse them into doing it. And the only reason I could do that is because I am not a pale personality; those three people need getting hold of by the neck and being made to do it. I had to do that many times in the past, as you do in a band. I mean, you can't put seven or eight people together with them eating, sleeping, breathing and living together 24 hours a day without there being personality problems. In truth, I don't know if Elvo ever realised that he was as talented as he now knows he is - if indeed he does know it - but he was always conscious of how he should appear. I think he still is, and I think that's a great shame, because he is "alright", in inverted commas. He may feel that he's now in a position where he can't just let his hair down. I mean, he must work very, very hard all the time and live under very different circumstances from the rest of us. But I'll tell you what, it would be a hell of a band! I'd love to do that old material again. Even if he did it privately, it would be very exciting.

Sadly, Tony's untimely death meant that he never got the chance to catalyse that unlikely reunion, but we were grateful that we'd managed to capture his entertaining reminiscences and some views on Jethro Tull that younger readers especially found a touch controversial. That said, it was interesting to note that some of the previously unreleased Flawed Gems *on the 1988* 20 Years Of Jethro Tull *box-set demonstrated that "Elvo" and the boys were not averse to still playing the blues in the privacy of their own studio…*

BARRIE BARLOW

It was in the course of our working on that 1988 box-set project that MW liaised a couple of times with Pete Frame, compiler of those extraordinary rock family trees. Pete mentioned that while preparing the Jethro Tull tree for the box-set booklet he had spoken to Barrie Barlow, who had demonstrated a sharp memory of the pre-Tull years in Blackpool. Which led us to think that we really ought to try to speak to Barrie ourselves, to allow a redressing of balances - firstly between the number of interviewees who did and didn't end up in Jethro Tull, and secondly in the views expressed about Barrie by Tony Wilkinson!

Part of Barrie's interview is at Chapter 10 but as well as talking at length about Jethro Tull, Barrie also added his own recollections of The John Evan Band story.

You're originally from Birmingham. How did you come to meet up with Ian, John and Jeffrey in Blackpool?
When I left school I went up to Blackpool, because my Dad had a job up there. I'd already started playing drums with a school band. Oh, and I played football for Aston Villa schoolboys - you must mention that! I answered an advert in the *Blackpool Evening Gazette*, and I got through an audition and seemed to cut it. That was with John, Jeffrey and Ian, in The Blades, around 1963 or 1964. But at that stage that only meant playing in youth clubs and so on. In fact, at that time John was still at school. John used to have the group van to drive to

school. We all daubed lipstick on it, saying, "I love so-and-so" - there were never any birds chasing after us, 'cos we were all so ugly, so we had to do it ourselves! As for me, I was just a punk really - I was like the original punk!

There are a lot of characters I still remember from those early days. I never actually played with Mike Stephens. He was on the periphery, socially. I think he knew a few chords and so on, but he was never part of the playing line-up, not in my time anyway. And Harry Hartley again was just a friend from John's school who'd go to gigs but never really got involved in any playing. He had a photographic memory that guy - he was top of the class in everything. There was a guy called Tom McAllister as well who was a friend of Ian's. And Geoff the Cake! He was a friend of Jeffrey's. I think Jeffrey modelled himself a bit in his mid-teens on Geoff the Cake, who was the ultimate beatnick. He used to walk through Blackpool with a carrier bag. And for no reason at all he would start running at full pace, and then stop and carry on walking. People witnessed it! Jeffrey used to meet him at the station, and they'd be there going, "Hey, yeah, man," and having strange conversations. And so did Ian as well. They thought it was really groovy to be seen hanging around with Geoff the Cake. I think he was a few years older. He was a real character; I'm surprised Ian's never mentioned him.

The Blades used to play *Bright Lights, Big City* and all that sort of thing. The reason I'd started playing was because of The Beatles, it was a sort of fashionable thing. And when I met those guys it was bluesy sort of Sonny Terry and Brownie McGhee stuff. Then along came this album, with Ginger Baker, Jack Bruce and Dick Heckstall-Smith on it, called *Sound Of '65* by Graham Bond. We learned that entire album, and used to play three-quarters of it in the set. That was when I became really serious about playing.

Did you have any idea then of becoming a professional drummer as a career?
Well, when I first started working with The Blades I had an apprenticeship as a plastic moulding toolmaker, which is what all my friends in Birmingham seemed to be doing. I didn't really know any different or better. My father was a toolmaker, so he'd always be saying, "Get a trade behind you," and so on. But because I was always gigging I'd always be late for work. And it got to the point where they said I'd got to make a choice, and they'd give me a day to think about it. I said, "I don't need a day, I'll make my decision here and now." So I turned professional. I think we were on the princely sum of around £2 per week then, and I became a full-time part of the various versions of The Blades, The John Evan Band, The John Evan Big Sound, The John Evan Smash, and so on.

Was there a definite point at which The Blades became The John Evan Band, or was it a gradual metamorphosis?
It just really slid into it. Around that time there were a lot of organ-oriented bands - Wynder K Frog, Georgie Fame, Graham Bond, Brian Auger - and it just seemed that all the bands were named after the keyboard player. So we got a Hammond organ and called ourselves The John Evan Band. Simple as that really.

The first line-up of the John Evan Band included trumpet player Jim Doolin, a tenor sax player Martin Skyrme, and Chris Riley on guitar. A smashing bloke, Chris. I saw him the last time I was up in Blackpool. I've just started looking after a band called Fantasia, and Chris came down to one of their gigs. We downed a few jars, talked about the old days, and concluded that nostalgia is not what it used to be...

Jim, the trumpet player, used to go mad at me because he could only play from music, and he had a music stand which he put right next to my hi-hat. And every time I closed the hi-hat it would blow his music off, and he thought I'd got a personal vendetta against him! I remember one day when I'd taken a day off work and Ian was playing the wag from college, and the two of us went up to Jim's house, and we all dyed our hair green, like teenagers do. I've got teenagers myself now, so I'm reliving it all! As you know, we went to do a gig as the backing band to Brian Rossi - no rehearsals with him, incidentally. I remember waiting outside Jim's house that afternoon, and he didn't turn up. Eventually we had to go - and we never saw him again!

After a while Jeffrey left to go to Art College, and we got a bass player from Grimsby Jazz Club called Bo. He used to iron his girlfriend's hair! She used to have long black curly hair, and she'd say, "Iron me, iron me!" The sax player, Ranger [*Neil Valentine*], used to live in

Manchester, Chic Murray [*Neil Smith*] the guitarist lived in Bolton, and Bo lived just outside Bolton. So whenever we'd do a gig we'd have to do this round trip picking everybody up, even if it was to play in Preston. We'd have to go out and bring everybody back, because they'd got day jobs. And then Bo just didn't turn up for a gig. So I knew Glenn and got him in as a replacement. Glenn was living on his own in a flat in Blackpool. His family background was a bit of a mystery. He was a civil servant, and gigging with a band called The Executives, with Roy Carr, who went on to write for NME. John and I both played with The Executives for a time - in fact, everybody played with The Executives when things weren't happening with their own particular group, because they used to get the best gigs; although nobody could really stand working with them 'cos they were so bad. Roy Carr was not too affectionately known as Easter Egg, because he actually looked like a bloody Easter Egg! His father was Tony Carr, whose claim to fame was having written *March Of The Mods*, and The Executives did that on stage. It got some award. Roy used to take you to one side and give you money, and say furtively, "Don't tell the others how much you're getting," and so on. It was really awful, but it was a gig, y'know. I mean, you can't really afford to pick and choose when you're working to save up for mortgages and things like that, which is what I was doing at the time.

Are you recording all this? What's the matter, can't you sleep?? Anyway, I hope all this accords with your own researches.

So far! Now, Chris Riley reckons John was the musical leader of The John Evan Band...
No. I mean, we were doing other people's stuff. So it was down to every musician to learn their parts and then play it together. The decision on what music we played was a collective one. John would be the last one to say it was his band, I'm sure. Chris was there for a particular chapter in the story, but it was an early chapter, one which - with all deference to Chris, and no fault of his at all - was fairly uneventful relative to later on, when Ian's talents really emerged. But I have to say that at any time in its life it WAS a pretty good band...

The Beatles once had an audience of 19 at Aldershot; U2 pulled in 9 at The Hope and Anchor... Did you ever have such an all-time low audience anywhere?
Not as such. Although, I think the lowest of the low was when Johnny Taylor, our agent at the time, booked us into Preston Co-op Club for six quid - and there were seven of us in the band! I remember I went mental at him. But I think one of the worst gigs was the British Cellophane Club in Barrow-in-Furness. We used to have this old Thames van and we'd be completely loaded up with equipment, the seven of us in the band, plus Andy Truman. Andy was the equipment blagger. People used to blag equipment from the local music store for the weekend's gigs, and take it back on the Monday and say, "Sorry, we didn't really like it". The equipment would be strategically placed in the van to provide a seat all the way along, and our knees would be THAT close to the edge of the van and we'd be staring at the side of the van like this [*hand in front of face*]. And if you were really knackered you could slide up and lie on top of one of the Glebe home-made cabinets. But that's no different a story from any other band - except that in our case, going through the Lake District to this gig, because the van's engine was so knackered we had to push it up the hills! Anyway, we did the British Cellophane Club and the 99 Club supporting Herman's Hermits - who we blew off the stage - but we'd nowhere to stay. So we decided to sleep in the van. I think it was Ian and Jim, the trumpet player, who drew the short straws and had to sleep in an open rowing boat on Lake Coniston. And of course it poured with rain! So we let them hammer on the van for a good five minutes or so before letting them in, just for the craic, y'know...

You left The John Evan Band for a while. What's the story behind that?
When Tony Wilkinson joined, it seemed like he took over everything, and was calling all the shots. Which, quite honestly, I remember I didn't like, because he didn't do anything to prove to me that he was worthy of calling the shots, i.e. he wasn't very good. Whereas Ian certainly was. And John was. And if there's nothing to be earned, the criterion for calling the shots has to be musical prowess. Having said that, we got on really well sometimes, and then we couldn't stand the sight of one another at other times. I haven't seen Tony since about 1967. But I realised later why there was such a conflict - Tony had the hots for the girl I was going

out with, and who eventually ended up as his missus. So I can understand that now, you know. But it's basically true to say that I left the band because of Tony.

When I left The John Evan Band I formed The All Jump Kangaroo Band with Chris Riley, Andy Truman and a guy called Paul Hargreaves. We used to do things like *Ain't Too Proud To Beg*, and all the birds used to dance in the middle of the dancefloor around their handbags with their long leather coats with splits up the back. I had a Rogers drumkit which sounded like a piece of shit and took me four years to pay for. When I joined Tull I traded it in and got a pair of bloody bongos for it! Paul Hargreaves could be a difficult character. Andy Truman, who went on to be Tull's road manager, was managing Yngwie Malmsteem not so long ago. While I was with The All Jump Kangaroo Band, The John Evan Band got in Ritchie Dharma on drums. They were really good with Ritchie; he was a really neat player. Ranger had joined by then. And Ranger was a fab player, a great sound, really melodic solos, really commercial sax player. They sounded really good. Anyway, I saw them playing in Blackpool one time, and they asked me if I wanted to rejoin. And they sounded so good that I did. The reason was always the music. It was all sort of big-roll swinging stuff then. I'm sure the only reason we ever got re-booked was because the bar-takings went up because people wouldn't dance to it!

Do you remember doing The Marquee?

I certainly do. Supporting The Herd. That was really exciting, coming down to the big city - we felt like Dick Whittington. We went down a storm, as well. We always had a very mild, polite response from the Northern audiences who just wanted to watch Geno Washington or dance to Wilson Pickett, whereas we were playing this sort of swingy stuff and a few of our own things - or things which Ian had written, like *Take The Easy Way*. The London audience was so responsive, it was really encouraging. And The Herd were really good as well.

Did you think that might have been a breakthrough, coupled with the Granada TV thing?

Well, nobody ever sort of took hold of anything like that. I don't know who got us the Marquee gig - it may have been Don Read - but I don't think Don Read had anything to do with the Granada thing. But there was never really any concerted push towards 'making it'. We were really just trying to make a living out of playing, which was possible because there were so many places to play in those days. We played loads of places scattered all round the country, like the three Nottingham Boat Clubs where you could earn £40, and if you did five of those per week you could pay for the van and have £5 or £6 each to live off. And there must have been thousands of musicians who were living like that, of whom just a handful made it, y'know?

But eventually we all decided to make the break from Blackpool, because we realised that you'd got to be near London to have contacts with the best agents, and possibly record companies. I mean, we really didn't know anything like the kids of today know. People come into my little 16-track studio to make demos, and they know all about publishing deals, they know all about this, that and the other, they've got all the business side of it sussed, and then they can't play. But it was the other way round for us. We'd already been down from Blackpool to do a gig at Dunstable, which was stretching it for Chic Murray. It became obvious that he'd either got to leave work and come down with us, or something had to happen; it wasn't practical. And Mick Abrahams was playing there too - I think he was playing there on his own, I don't think Clive was in the band then. Mick was really good, very distinctive. So after we'd got together with Mick and he'd agreed to give it a go, Tony Wilkinson came down on reconnaissance to get people's accommodation sorted out, which he did. He got himself living with a family where all his meals were cooked, he'd got his own room, and it was all hunky-dory. Ian and John were staying in this big house that had flats in it - it was pretty depressing. And then Tony dropped me off at the place he'd got for me. Well, it was like a Hammer Horror production - I'm not exaggerating! There was this house on the top of a small hill, and as you opened the gate - which had chains on the bottom of it - it creaked. Tony did come in with me to the door. We rang the bell, and this woman opened the door; she'd got a white uniform on like a psychiatric nurse, and one eye! So Tony just said, "Right, there you go," and left me. I was seventeen and naïve, and bloody terrified, quite frankly. I was taken into a sort of little living room, and there was this chap in there who had been seriously burned, he had burn scars all over him. It was damp, and it stank. They took me up to my room, which had no lock on the door. I could see my breath, it was so cold. I lay on top of the bed and didn't sleep at all. Then at about five o'clock in the morning there must have been at least a dozen huge Irish guys queuing up to get into one bathroom - there were huge roadworks going on all round Dunstable and Luton, and all the Paddies filled everywhere. I went down to breakfast, and one of these guys had his foot on the table, bursting a blister while we were being served raw ham for breakfast. I'm not kidding you! When Tony came to pick me up I said, "That's me out of here. No way in the world will I stay - I'll sleep in the van, it's ten times better." So I moved into the house that Ian was in, which was marginally better. But I felt totally intimidated and alienated. In some ways I may have been older than my years, but in other ways... I just felt like I shouldn't be here, I felt awful.

Anyway, we started rehearsing with Mick in a school classroom, and we got a few things together. But it was all shuffly 12-bars. Great for the guitar of course, and it was the thing that was going down, with John Mayall and all the others, when the audience used to crowd round the guitarist. We'd go and do gigs, and true to form all the audience would form a circle round Mick. I think Ian's nose was a bit out of joint too. But from my point of view, I just didn't like the music. I think the best blues is played by poor black people. I can't play it, I've no interest in playing it. So I said, "It's not for me guys, this, but I'll stay with you until you get a replacement." So Mick then got in Clive, and taught Clive the set. We'd go to gigs, and I'd do half the set, and he'd do half the set, so that there'd be a smooth transition and no gigs lost. And John didn't want to know either, for the same reason, so we left Luton together. As for Tony, he stayed on. But where the baritone sax fitted in round *Cat's Squirrel* I'll never know! I mean, he used to just take his sax out, polish it, go "Heeee Haaaw" a few times, put it away, and go home for his dinner and watch the telly. Just slightly feathered his own nest there!

To be fair, he did own up to that...
Did he? [*Laughs*] Good!

[*Jokingly*] You don't miss those days then?
[*Seriously*] Umm... I miss the good times. I mean, there's nothing quite like having a bunch of blokes together, whether they're schoolmates, or sportsmen, or musicians, or whoever, with a common interest, and having that sort of friendship. You will have had that yourselves, in some way. But music does make you a bit closer, I think, because even if you can't speak the same language you can still play music together. [*Laughs*] Yep, the good old days!

NEIL "CHIC MURRAY" SMITH

That should have been the end of The John Evan Band Story as far as A New Day *was concerned. However a backstage guest at Jethro Tull's 1989 show in Inverness was Neil Smith, who had already featured large in the above interviews as the guitarist after Chris Riley and before Mick Abrahams. Someone gave Neil a copy of* A New Day #21, *with the Chris Riley and John Evans interviews, and he was sufficiently impressed - and astonished - to contact DR with a view to imparting his memories of the band. And so it was that in late 1989 Neil Smith made the long journey south to the rock'n'roll wastelands of Hampshire to surrender himself to an* AND *grilling from DR and MW.*

Shortly after leaving The John Evan Band and his job with the Inland Revenue, Neil went to seek his fortune in America. Having failed to find it he returned to Scotland where he tried his hand at milk-recording on farms and psychiatric nursing. He was currently working as a social worker in Inverness, and he was still playing guitar and writing music, although he hadn't played live for some years. Over a couple of evenings, which also took in a trip to Milton Keynes to see Mick Abrahams play live, Neil expounded in his soft Scottish burr his own memories of The John Evan Band.

How did you acquire the nickname 'Chic Murray'?

I'm not the person to answer that really. Tony Wilkinson decided that I sounded like Chic Murray, the Scottish comedian, but I don't know why really; there's no similarity. But the band wanted nicknames for me and the other Neil to save confusion, and Neil Valentine, the sax player, was called The Ranger, because they thought he looked like the Park Ranger in Yogi Bear! I do prefer to be known by my proper name, but even my royalties statement for the track I played on on the box set [*Aeroplane*] was addressed to Chic Murray. Fortunately the cheque was made out to Neil Smith!

What's your background? You're not from Blackpool obviously...

No. I was born in Aberdeen, moving to Bolton when I was thirteen, and worked there in the tax office when I left school. I'd been in a band at school, and my father promised me a guitar if I passed my O-Levels, so I worked really hard and got them. He bought me a cheap electric guitar and I took it from there. The first music I got into was the blues, and I played with the school group called The Diords – I'm afraid I have no idea what the name means. Then I formed my own band, The Neil Smith Soul Band, doing Tamla Motown and James Brown stuff. And I remember two of the group felt the drummer wasn't keeping in time and that he should be sacked, so they came to me because I was the leader of the group. I didn't like having to sack someone, of having that responsibility in the group, so I think the band just split up anyway. It was about that time that The John Evan Band was advertising for a sax player and a guitarist. That's where Chris Riley got it wrong. He reckoned they had seen a guitarist playing in Grimsby. He maybe thinks that guitarist was me, but it wasn't, because I actually answered an ad in the *Manchester Evening News* for a guitarist to play with The John Evan Band. I think they had been without a guitarist for a while, and that Ian Anderson had been playing guitar as well as singing. I'd never heard of them, but I phoned up and spoke to Tony Wilkinson. He said they were playing the Bolton Beachcomber the next night, so I went along. Ian lent me his guitar and showed me the chord sequence of a Jimmy Smith song called *The Cat*, and I just played along and improvised.

They were playing the kind of music I really liked and it felt good playing with them, so I was in the band. Neil Valentine had seen the same ad and had joined a couple of weeks before me, around October 1966, when the group also included Ian Anderson, John Evans, Tony Wilkinson, Bo Ward and Ritchie Dharma. I never actually met Chris Riley or Jeffrey Hammond, by the way. Bo and Ritchie left shortly after I joined, and they approached me with a view to forming a new group with a different singer – they thought Ian wasn't commercial enough! I thought they were crazy, but they went ahead and left. Barrie Barlow was quickly recruited again – I liked Barrie, he was a great drummer – and then Glenn Cornick. I can't remember the official reason for Bo and Ritchie leaving. Bo was a good bass player – a bit crazy. It was his job onstage to get people going at the beginning of one of the numbers called *Twine Time* by shouting a lot. Funnily enough, I didn't think Glenn fitted in as well as Bo, in a way, with the sort of stuff we were doing at the time. But we didn't have much in common so I didn't get to know him very well. I preferred playing alongside Bo, but he and Ritchie wanted to be commercial and play whatever was popular at the time.

Neil Valentine was a Jehovah's Witness, though he didn't bother trying to convert us. He had a superb Jensen car, which he was very proud of. Neil was a jazz man really, and I don't think he would have lasted long playing the blues down in London. I did meet up with him later and he was telling me of his experiences in Luton, and how Ian really did miracles coping at the time with what sounded like a pretty miserable life for them all. I liked John Evans, but like everyone else I didn't find him easy to talk to. Very quiet and introverted, but at the same time he could be quite manic. It used to be my job to sit in the front of the van and talk to John to keep him awake, but being rather a quiet person myself I wouldn't say much – Ian would then have to keep talking to me to make me talk to John!

John said he did all the driving because nobody else would, but Tony reckoned John wouldn't let him drive...

No, I think he would, but John always got lumbered with the driving. Tony was... well... not very subtle, shall we say. He was a very direct person. He was put in charge of the money side of things because he would shout louder than anyone else. If we were in danger of not getting paid Tony would go and make a fuss about it. I remember one night in Birmingham where we had booked into two clubs on the one night, the second starting around midnight. That was apparently not the thing to do because the clubs felt they wouldn't get so much money if one group was playing two different venues. We almost didn't get paid at one of the clubs, and it was good to have Tony around at times like that. And from what I remember he was a pretty good sax player too. The sax arrangements were just in the background, but he did the occasional solo. It wouldn't have fitted in with the way Jethro Tull developed, but he got a pretty tight sound with us. I do vaguely recall Tony's feud with Barrie. In fact, Ian reminded me in Inverness of the incident on the road up to Carlisle when we had to stop the van because Barrie had said something to Tony and they had started fighting. Ian was normally quite a calming influence, but I don't think he could do much on that occasion. I really admired Ian for his ability to persevere under considerable hardship and to get people to do what he wanted them to do. I think he liked to have people around him who he could control, and who weren't too individual. But like any good leader he would give praise as well as criticism when warranted.

Ian was clearly the boss then?
Oh, I think so. He was certainly the front man, and there was no-one else who could have been regarded as the boss. Tony was the administrator, with the money and so on, but not musically. John, I suppose, was the one who was regarded as the one who worked things out musically. I wasn't involved in that myself, I just did my bit after John had worked out the arrangements with Ian.

Who decided, for example, which songs to play?
Ian, I think. And I don't remember anyone objecting to doing the things he started to write. [*Laughs*] I think Ian is a difficult person to make objections to anyway... He was quite clearly the leader. He was the most confident, and he knew what he wanted. Of course, we had a manager, Don Read, who also made decisions for us. He was obviously a businessman trying to make as much money as possible out of pop music. But Ian was pretty predominant at that time in the decision-making. Although having said that I remember that in Blackpool I'd sing a kind of gospel song called *It's Alright*... I think the group liked the idea of me singing a song just for a change, and I think Ian always liked the idea – which he clearly still does now – of getting each group member involved in some little thing from time to time. But Don Read saw us do it one night and thought it was OK as a novelty but not really what we should be doing, and we never did it again. Ian did some pretty weird things from time to time, and had a pretty weird sense of humour. He was playing to a lot of audiences who didn't appreciate him, and on a typical Palais dance type night he'd be really sarcastic to the audience. He'd say, "We're going to do a number now called *Everything's Gonna Be Alright*... which it obviously isn't..."! You could tell he was not happy at not being appreciated.
I enjoyed talking to him when I got the chance to speak to him alone. We had something in common having both come down from Scotland, and our parents were against us getting into the rock world, mine to the extent that I ran away from home. In a way, Ian was the most sober of the lot, he had a good business head. I'd agree with Chris that he wasn't as odd as, say, John. I always felt he was in control of things. He knew what he was doing and he had a plan to create a more English sound rather than just do American covers, and he eventually did it. And I admire him for that. I always knew that Ian Anderson was going to make a success of something, though I wasn't actually sure it was going to be in music. I wasn't even sure that he would carry on with music although I probably should have known it. But I knew he would be a success.

At what stage did Ian start writing his own songs? Was there anything more than the four songs listed in #21 of *AND*?
No. I remember *Take The Easy Way*, which we did on television, and *How Can You Work With Mama?* which I sang harmony on. *The Man* was a recording aimed specifically at the American market, but Don Read said it couldn't go ahead because of the connotations of 'The Man' in America being the Head of Police, for some strange reason it couldn't be released in America. But that wasn't one of Ian's songs, it was presented to us by Don Read. It wasn't bad – has a copy survived?

Not that we know of.

I'm sure we did *Mama* at the CBS studio, but *The Man* was somewhere else, but I can't remember where. And to be honest, I can't remember doing *Aeroplane* at all!

Ian knew I'd written a few bits of music, and before he really started writing himself he actually borrowed a reel-to-reel tape that I had and listened to what I'd done. Some of it was really awful, and he would laugh at it... unfortunately there was nothing on it that we could do as a band. But I do remember that when he started writing himself he always said he wanted to create an English sound rather than an American sound.

Do you think The John Evan Band played soul because they had to, or was there a genuine interest there?

Hmm... I don't think they'd have played things they didn't like. I certainly liked the music. But it's probably true that Ian didn't perform that music as well as other people could; I don't think he, or we, were at our best doing that. He sounded really good on some jazzy things, he had a really good voice for jazz songs, and pretty good for blues, certainly better than for soul. But having two saxes and an organ in the group lent itself more to that music rather than straight blues. Ian himself certainly did have some leaning towards jazz, and I remember him being tremendously proud in 1969 that Roland Kirk had mentioned onstage at a gig at The Marquee that Ian Anderson was the only other good flautist around.

Do you have any memories of a best and worst gig?

Well, like John Evans, my memory of the worst gig would be Strathpeffer in Scotland. In fact, they really had to do a big persuasive job to get me to go on that gig because I should have been at work that day. As it was we travelled overnight from Blackpool to Edinburgh, where we stopped off at Princes Street. Ian's brother worked at Boots The Chemist there, so while he went to see him I phoned the office to say I was sick and wouldn't be in. And then it was as John described, driving all the way up through the snow. I think I was the first one Tony blamed for the gig being blown... I must have opened my mouth first. The owner of the club directed a question at me – like, "Are you Irish?" or something! – and I really wasn't going to say, "Yes, I'm Irish and we are a showband," so Tony blamed me for giving the game away. He could be a bit unrealistic, Tony! The way I remember it we got a bed for the night rather than go straight back down, and set off for Nottingham really early in the morning. Yeah, that was the worst gig!

The best one...? It would be really hard to think of a very good one! My favourite venue though would probably be the same as everyone else's, the Nottingham Boat Club, where the atmosphere was really nice. I played at Grimsby Jazz Club only once, but that was good too. The audiences at both places were really enthusiastic about the band. One memorable gig was at a University – can't remember which – with The Pink Floyd when they were doing their psychedelic light show. I really enjoyed that one. Another good one was at Matlock Bath in Derbyshire with The Crazy World Of Arthur Brown.

What was doing the Granada TV show like? Nerve-wracking? Fun?

It was very easy really. We didn't stay very long, just went through it twice. [*Long pause...*] No, I can't remember very much about it at all, really. We just went there and the cameras pointed at us. It wasn't any big thrill or anything...

You're being very cool about it...

I dunno... Maybe it's just so long ago. It was just some *Opportunity Knocks* type thing, and lots of people go on that and are never heard of again. I suppose if we'd won we'd have been more excited about it, and entitled to think it would get us further. Perhaps if I had written the song I'd have been pleased at reaching a wider audience. As it was I'd only heard *Take The Easy Way* a week or so before we did it on TV, and I wasn't even that keen on it. I just played a strumming guitar, which is what Ian wanted, so it didn't mean that much to me.

Tony Wilkinson told us that as a result of the TV thing, through Don Read, you got a 'tour' on the south coast. Do you remember that?

Oh yes. It was like a week's holiday, walks along the cliff tops and so on. We played in Swanage with Simon Dupree And The Big Sound. I don't remember it being as a result of the TV show though. We were getting bookings all over the place anyway, everywhere from The Marquee in London to Newcastle Club-A-Go-Go. Ian reminded me, up in Inverness, of something about the Newcastle scene. The only place where you could get something to eat at three or four in the morning was the railway station buffet. All the cutlery there was actually tied by chains to the tables and they used to come around now and then and wipe the knives and forks with a cloth. Dreadful!

Did the quality of life on the road get you down, or was it a kind of 'minstrels on the road' romantic sort of thing?
I suppose it was a mixture of the two – one offset the other. It was great playing onstage, but it was counteracted by the slog.

Whose idea was the identical made-to-measure stage clothes?
Probably Don Read's. It was done for the TV, but we carried on wearing those outfits for a while afterwards. The shirts were grey and the trousers were blue, while Ian's suit was black. I also used to wear a white jacket with thin black stripes, which Ian actually asked if he could have off me when I left, so I gave it to him. I played Ian's guitar for quite a while after I joined the band. I had a guitar of course, but I preferred his until I bought a Fender Jazzmaster, which I later swapped, much to my regret.

What about your own image? In our interview with Tony Wilkinson he said you just used to stand at the back of the stage and remain as anonymous as possible. Is that fair?
Yes, in a way. I remember, just before I left, Ian saying he was happy for me to stay in the band but that I'd have to change my image. I didn't like that much – I didn't think much of "image" at the time. But perhaps I was too much in the background... I don't know. Ian used to have a little chuckle about me, because he noticed that when I was playing something I was really getting into I unconsciously stood on one leg. Makes you wonder... But I think that what John Evans said about me was a bit unfair, in that he mentioned that I could play in an Eric Clapton style, but that I did it only once. Actually that one time was when Mick Abrahams was joining the band, and we got up together after a gig in Luton just so that he could play with the band. We both played a blues thing, although we never really played blues as a band. We were doing things that had been worked out for sax and organ, Otis Redding and Georgie Fame type things, which was all sax solos, and there was no place for guitar solos anyway. When I joined they really just wanted the guitar as a rhythm instrument. But after that thing in Luton I remember Tony being really annoyed at me for playing so well! "Why don't you play like that all the time?!" he said, but we just didn't do that type of thing. At the end I shook hands with Mick Abrahams and said, "Well played," and he said, "Yeah, but you blew me off the stage, man!" I don't know if he would remember – or admit to that!
I have to say that I feel better when I'm doing something different. I get inspired by new situations, and if I play the same stuff over and over I get in a rut. And I suppose that's partly why I left the group, because I felt we were in a bit of a rut in the things we were doing. I mean, if you're playing *Hold On I'm Coming* there's not much you can do with it, other than play the same thing every time, no improvising or soloing. I did ask Martin Barre if he played the same thing every night. He said he didn't, he does change things a bit. But Ian himself has said to me that people think that things are being improvised, but that really they are well worked out. That's one thing he said to me in 1969 or thereabouts, that he did miss the small club atmosphere and the improvising of the early Jethro Tull. But I wasn't that keen on the stuff that Ian had started doing with The John Evan Band, such as *Take The Easy Way* and so on. Plus, there was a move planned down to London to where the more appreciative audiences and the record business contacts were, which would have meant me giving up my job. It had been a pretty hard slog, and I'd got fed up with sleeping in the back of the van, which I'd been doing for quite a while.

So you never actually made it as far as Luton?

No. It was crunch time – either I gave up my job and went down, or I left, and I left. After I left I felt a real sense of freedom after being ground down, playing the same stuff over and over again and trying to work five days a week. Part of the problem was that I was based in Bolton while most of the band were based in Blackpool, with Neil Valentine in Manchester, so we never got time to get together to practice. In fact, I remember rehearsing with them only once – we just played together at gigs. I'd really liked to have been around in Blackpool when Ian Anderson was fifteen or so, and been at school with him and John. I think then it might have worked out differently if I'd developed with them, and we'd hit it off better. I did feel that Ian was good musically, and I admired him as a singer and for his musical taste.

Did you join another band after The John Evan Band?
I had a break for a while. Then just after Jethro Tull had made their first album a guy called Derek Hodgson who lived round the corner from me had heard that I used to play with Ian Anderson, and he came and knocked on my door. He was a real Jethro Tull fan – he played organ and flute, probably because Ian did. Ian had just started to teach himself the flute when I left The John Evan Band, although he didn't play it on stage then. So Derek asked me to join his group, which I can't even remember the name of. We actually played *Living In The Past*, but I did wonder if I should be playing Jethro Tull covers; I felt a bit bad about it. Good song though! Funnily enough, I probably enjoyed playing with them more than with The John Evan Band because we were improvising a lot more, with ten-minute solos etc. And I wasn't on the road sleeping in the back of a van...!

When was the last time you saw Ian before Inverness?
It would be about twenty years ago. After I left the group obviously I got to hear of Jethro Tull, and it eventually clicked with me who they were. I phoned Tony and got Ian's address in London, and popped down to see him. They were just going off to some gig, so I slept in his bed while he was away! That was the last time I saw him, which would be... Martin was in the group, so about 1969 I suppose. After that I kept in touch with Ian on an irregular basis over the years. By coincidence I spent my honeymoon on Skye and stayed in a cottage on Ian's estate, without even knowing he'd bought the estate. I thought I'd see him when I was later working in the Western Isles, as I passed through Skye very often, but no...

Was it strange meeting him again after twenty years?
Yeah. [*Pause...*] Yeah, it was a bit strange meeting him after all that time, although I had spoken to him on the phone a few times. But I feel I know him quite well through seeing him on TV and so on, so it wasn't that strange me seeing him after all that time - it was probably stranger for him seeing me after twenty years.

When did you learn that you were on the Tull 20th Anniversary box set?
When I phoned Ian earlier this summer. He just mentioned it in passing. He said there was a photo of me in the booklet, and he gave me an office number to ring because apparently people were trying to find out who this Chic Murray was, to pay him royalties...

MARTIN SKYRME

As it turned out, having belatedly added Neil Smith to our collection of members of The John Evan Band who didn't end up in Jethro Tull, nearly 20 years later there was a second postscript to the story. Whilst the JEB's ever-changing line-up meant that there were other non-Tull members who had escaped our clutches, to be honest we hadn't tried very hard (well, OK, at all) to track them down. I guess we thought that nothing much more could be added to the story already told.

Wrong!

One of the special guests at Tull's Blackburn King George's Hall show on 15 May 2008 was Martin Skyrme, who played flute on Griminelli's Lament, Bourée *and* Locomotive Breath.

Martin had been the sax player in the first incarnation of the John Evan Band back in 1966 and, having been introduced to us by Ian Anderson, willingly agreed to dredge his memory banks and chat about those formative days. It would have been unfair to have collared him there and then so, having sent him the previous JEB interviews as an aide memoir, *MW spoke to him by 'phone a couple of weeks later. We started with some biographical background.*

Were you born in Blackpool?
No, I was born in Bath. I lived in Bristol until about the age of nine, and then we moved up to St Anne's. My Dad was a civil servant, and had got a new job in the area. My Mum has always been a keen amateur musician. In fact she still teaches piano and singing, even though she's in her mid-eighties.

So was it your mother who inspired you to play music?
I think yes, really. My grandfather on my mother's side played the violin, so it came from that side of the family. I did piano lessons for a year, and I absolutely hated them. I had the wrong teacher. She was a very good teacher, but she was very academic, and incorporated singing into the lessons. I used to be very shy of singing, and in fact I still don't like singing. So I only did a year on piano, although I did start to learn how to read music. I then took up the guitar, although that was more of a rebellious thing. Blackpool isn't that far from Liverpool, so we used to get the Merseybeat bands playing locally – or 'groups' as we called them then. It was quite exciting and inspiring to hear this new sound, and we copied it really. I formed a little four-piece band at school which we called The Bandits, as it sounded rebellious. We did OK, we were getting paid, but eventually we went our own ways. But out of that I started to get interested in blues and jazz, which is how I came to link up with the John Evan Band.

Were you playing saxophone by that time?
No. I was only about 14 or 15. I've been thinking about this for the last couple of weeks, but I can't really remember how the saxophone came into it, although it may have been through a teacher called Charlie Adams at Blackpool Tech. Once a week we had a Liberal Studies afternoon, and I sat in with his music studies group. The poor guy was trying to teach us to read music. That's where I met Ian Anderson and Jeffrey Hammond – I can't remember whether John Evans was there or not. But it may have been then that the idea of taking up the saxophone arose. I honestly can't remember, although I do remember selling all my guitar gear to get a saxophone. We used to just jam together, but I did also have proper saxophone lessons.
Incidentally, that Liberal Studies class was quite interesting. I remember that Ian was quite bolshie at that class. The way the teacher was presenting it was quite formal, and Ian was questioning it. If I'd have been the teacher I'd have found him quite difficult. Ian would be asking why we needed to learn to read music, and posing some quite fundamental questions, like if you are playing blues-type music, why do you need to read music? And I think after a number of sessions Ian decided it was a waste of time and stopped going.
They were art students, but at that time I was destined to become a hotel manager. I was doing a catering course, decked out a morning suit uniform kind of thing with grey pin-striped trousers, black blazer, white shirt and silver tie. The catering college in Blackpool was quite well known – still is - but it was very unfashionable in those days, and people weren't interested in cheffing and restaurants like they are now.

So how did the John Evan Band thing happen? Ian, Jeffery, John and Barrie were The Blades at that time – was your joining kind of the start of The John Evan Band?
Absolutely, yes, I'm sure it was. They invited me to come along to rehearsals. I remember Sunday afternoon rehearsals at Mrs Evans' house, in the garage, along with a trumpet player called Jim Doolin. We both started right from scratch. I was an absolute beginner on saxophone, and Jim didn't play by ear, he really wasn't a jazz player, although he had some rudimentary ability on the trumpet. So we just started to put it all together, working on parts with John – John would tell us where to come in. I remember working out some of the harmonies. I was 16 by then, and it really was quite an exciting thing. So as I remember it,

that was the start of The John Evan Band, although I guess it may have been going for a little bit before that. Perhaps you know?

Well, it's always been a bit vague as to when the transition from The Blades to The John Evan Band did take place. I guess it's like you say, they just picked up a few extra people along the way and changed the name.
That would be my take on it. I got the feeling that they were saying, we're The Blades, but we're changing the direction of the band – or group, I should say. The word 'band' wasn't much used in those days, although there was the Georgie Fame Band. Maybe you were a 'band' if you had a brass section...

Can you remember the first gig you did with them?
I've tried to, but I have struggled with that to be honest. I can't guarantee it, but I remember playing at a place in Kirkham called The Elizabethan, and that was certainly one of the first.
As to other gigs, we played at a dreadful working men's club in Fleetwood, which was a busy fishing port in those days, and a rough place. And I remember a lot of the other places that the other guys mentioned in their interviews, like The Twisted Wheel, the Torch in Stoke, The Aztec Club, and the Whisky-A-Go-Go in Newcastle. I remember very well in the early days playing several times at Brian London's 007 Club in Blackpool. Brian London was a famous heavyweight boxer in the 1960s. He was a formidable man, and [*laughing*] he'd be his own security! He'd stand at the front door and shepherd people in and out – so everybody used to behave themselves... But that was fun, playing at his club.

What about The Cavern [*in Liverpool*] – did you play there?
I do remember doing The Cavern. There were a lot of bands on in one evening. Getting away, we had all these fans chasing us, literally running down the street doing the screaming thing. [*Laughing*] It was quite scary really - and quite thrilling.
One venue which wasn't mentioned by the other guys was The Belle Vue in Manchester. Jimmy Saville was the DJ there. He kind of created what we now know as a DJ. That was a big place. And another I remember was a very curious gig at The Silver Blades ice rink in Birmingham. It was an afternoon session, and we were on this big stage while people were skating as we were playing! That was very, very strange.

So were they just ignoring you, or were they attempting some sort of dance moves to it??
No, they were just skating round and round in circles while we were doing our stuff on stage!

And what about the Brian Rossi gig that a couple of the guys mentioned – do you remember that one?
D'you know, I don't. That was at The Bolton Palais. I remember Brian Rossi very well, but I don't recall the gig.

Perhaps a difficult one, but do you remember the biggest and smallest audiences you played to?
That is difficult... I think we did have one or two disappointing gigs, but I can't remember where they were – probably Preston or somewhere like that. The largest was probably somewhere like The Whisky-A-Go-Go, which was pretty big, or possibly the Bolton Palais gig.

And how receptive were the audiences to the music?
I always felt we were quite a lot different to the usual run-of-the-mill bands. I think in general we had good audiences and went down well. I don't remember being disappointed by audiences. In fact, I have a clear recollection of the Empress Ballroom at the Blackpool Winter Gardens - that would have been a huge gig, that would take a lot of beating. That was for the annual Blackpool Tech do. The reason I remember the audience reaction at that one was because I knew some of the audience. They used to take the mickey out of me playing all these one night stands with this band, they couldn't really understand it. I did feel aggrieved at them making fun of the band, and of John Evans in particular. When he played he seemed as

if he wasn't there sometimes, almost like he was in a trance, in his own world. But I remember a number of the guys coming up afterwards and saying it was brilliant, and they stopped taking the mickey after that. I think we were pretty professional really, compared to a lot of the stuff that was going on at the time.

That was going to be one of my questions, about how ambitious you and the band were. Was there any thought at that time of becoming professional musicians, or were you just so young it was a gig at a time?
Well, it was more a case of dropping out from your college or your job. I could see that Ian was always very focussed. He was always making notes, and formulating things, and organising things, he and John in particular. But the big problem was that there was no money. I don't remember ever getting paid at all – or if I did, it must have been some very small amounts. In fact, jumping forward to the time I left, when I did come to leave that was one of the reasons, there being no money. I thought, I can't carry on like this.
What also happened was that Ian had bought a flute, and we were both playing the same flute – he had it for so many days, and then I'd have it for the other days. I started having lessons on it, and taking it seriously, and I started playing one number on it with the band, which was *The Cat* by Jimmy Smith. So when I left, Ian said that they hadn't got any money to give me, so he gave me the flute. So I had this Selmer Gold Seal flute, which was a pretty crap basic instrument, but it did start me off on my career as a flautist.

Well, that's really interesting, because the way Ian tells it, he didn't buy a flute until Mick Abrahams had joined the band and he realised that if he wasn't going to be the guitarist he needed to find another instrument. But it sounds to me as if he was playing the flute at the time of the John Evan Band...
I mentioned it to him when we met in Blackburn, and he'd forgotten it completely. I mean, he wasn't very serious about it, and I more or less commandeered this flute, but it was definitely his flute. So when I acquired it when I left the band he must have had to go out and buy another one a year or so later.

You might have just solved a mystery, actually! Ian always tells the story that he traded in his guitar in a shop, looked around, saw a flute, and thought, well that will fit in my pocket, I'll have that. But Glenn Cornick said that he clearly remembered that somebody owed Ian some money, so he went with Ian to this chap's house; the chap hadn't got any money, so he gave Ian a flute instead. There was always this discrepancy between the two stories of how Ian got his flute – but maybe there were two flutes involved!
Could well be...

Did Ian ever play the flute on stage with the John Evan Band?
I don't think so. I was playing the wind instruments, and I don't remember him playing flute on stage. He also used to mess around with a battered old alto sax, which is in the photo of The John Evan Band. [*Laughing*] I remember him chucking it on the floor because he could hardly get any notes out of it. But he was never serious about it.

Was there any indication then of how good a musician Ian would become?
I don't think there was, really – because they were early days, you know. He played guitar on stage once or twice, and I was surprised because I didn't even know he could play guitar; but I remember thinking oh, he's pretty good. But he was the singer. And I thought he was more of an ideas man, just trying to put things together. He was always planning, and listening, and asking questions He was definitely the front man of the group, being the singer, but to be honest I did also feel that Ian was driving the band, particularly as time went on.

And what about John? How did you get on with him, because some people seemed to find him a bit difficult to talk to...?
I liked John very much. He was very quiet, and very intelligent, but I related well to him. And I respected the fact that he could play the piano 'properly'; he'd had a bit of classical training

as well as being able to play the blues. I think musically the germs, or the seeds, were there even in the early days of what came later, in that there was always an element of cross-over, which as we know is what Ian does with Jethro Tull. John had that cross-over of classical, and blues, and jazz. I suppose Ian was searching for his musical identity, but they were very much formative years. But I did get on well with John.

And Jeffrey?
I was probably closest to Jeffrey out of all of them. We used to meet at lunchtimes when we were both at college and go round to his boarding house and listen to records. He introduced me to the music of Roland Kirk, with some of those musical techniques of singing while playing and various other things which Ian developed. Roland Kirk also played more than one saxophone at a time, and I actually tried that with The John Evan Band, using Tony Wilkinson's tenor sax as well! The only thing I was any good at in school was art – I took art O-Level a year early - and really I should have been at art college not catering college. So Jeffrey and I had that art thing in common. He also had a lot of Charles Mingus records, and The Graham Bond Organisation – they were a big influence on us. Yeah, he's a fascinating character, Jeffrey.

And is it fair to say that he struggled as a bass player? I sometimes wonder if people weren't a little unfair on him...
Umm... Well, what I felt about Jeffrey was that he was different. He wasn't a technical player, he wasn't technically advanced, but he did his own thing, and that was fine by me. He had this streak of originality, definitely, and he had his head in modern jazz and stuff like that. If it had held the band back it might have been more noticeable, but I don't think it did. Like a lot of bass players, he did his job, and it worked. Nowadays I work with all sorts of bass players, and there are people who can play a million notes a minute, and play the bass like a banjo, and that can be equally as big a problem. But at that time I didn't think Jeffrey was anything less than adequate. He was such an original character, and a real part of the band.

And what about Barrie Barlow?
Oh, a fantastic drummer, a whizz-kid. He taught me a few things, actually. I used to tap my foot, and he pulled me up once because I was tapping my foot to the rhythm instead of to the beat. I think because of his young age he was a little feisty sometimes. I almost fell out with him once... but he was a very likeable chap. We all got along fairly well, really, considering our ages, although Barrie and Tony Wilkinson didn't get on.
I liked Tony very much, a very genial and generous person. He called me "Marvo". I don't know why... just fun, I guess, "Elvo" and "Marvo". We used to travel together in his huge American powder blue Chevy car, with the white wings at the back and big bench seats. I remember coming back with him one night, I'm fairly sure it was from Liverpool, very late – in fact it was getting light – and I looked across and realised that he had his eyes closed and was falling asleep! So I grabbed the wheel to try and wake him up – we used to have these long journeys back, and we'd be talking him home. When he joined the band it was on tenor sax, same as me. His family were quite well off, and he went out and bought this absolutely top-of-the-range baritone sax which had a special low-A extra note, which is very important when you're doing the funky-jazz kind of thing on a baritone sax. He learnt the baritone sax very quickly, and we became quite a good horn section. He had a lot of go in him.

Tony told the story in his interview about you going to the hairdresser and asking for a "jazz-player's haircut". Do you remember that?
I do, actually, yeah. [*Laughing*] I got a real short-back-and-sides...
Something I remembered that the other guys didn't mention was when our management decided to kit us out in stage clothes. In those days you couldn't get flared trousers very easily, but we all went to this boutique in Blackpool, where we all had to take it in turns to be measured up for these flared trousers. What we didn't realise was that the tailor there was a notorious gay, and he spent rather too much time measuring up your inside leg. We were saying, it's your turn next, watch it...! I ended up with these skin-tight trousers with big black-and-white squares, so with the flares I looked like a walking chess-board! I had a feeling we

had a photo taken in our stage gear, but if we did I certainly haven't got it. In fact, I haven't got any photos from those days, I'm afraid, apart from the one where Chris Riley was pasted in afterwards.

Chris Riley was a very good guitarist. He had a Gibson electric guitar of the kind jazz players used, and he had a nice style of playing. I think he was a civil servant – we used to drop him off outside his office at all hours. He was a quiet kind of guy, but I got on well with him. When Chris left, he and I and Glenn Cornick thought about trying to form an actual jazz group, but we'd only got two tunes really, *Summertime* and *My Favourite Things* which we nicked from John Coltrane.

You mentioned Glenn. Was Glenn in The John Evan Band while you were there, or did you just know him from around Blackpool?

No, he wasn't in the band with me. When Jeffrey left we got Bo Ward in, the guy who we met at Grimsby Jazz Club and who lived in the van. But I got to know Glenn when he was with The Hobos. When I saw Jethro Tull play in Manchester in 1968 he and Mick Abrahams were in the band, and I had a good chat with him then.

I remember Ritchie Dharma well. I'm sure he first did a few numbers with us at The Oasis club in Manchester. I was very impressed with him, a tremendous drummer. I loved going to his family's place, and sitting round with this Asian household, eating those sweetmeat things – that was really different. He was a really good guy. He didn't last too long though, because Barrie came back.

Ranger [*Neil Valentine*] took over from me. What happened was that these one-night stands were getting further and further away, and I not surprisingly failed my first year at college. So I was effectively given the choice of giving the band up if I was to continue studying. But by that time I was wanting to learn the classical flute properly, and I was frustrated by not being able to play it all that well, because when you're a beginner it's all air and not much note. And the guy who was teaching me helped with that decision. I'd done my Grade 5 theory, and was due to do my Grade 8 less than a year after I'd left the band, which is actually too fast a learning timescale. But I'd got this challenge, and through all that I got an audition to go to music college, and I got in. It was a complete change of direction. When I went to music college the first thing the flute professor said to me was, you've got to sell your saxophone, promise me you won't play your saxophone. Well, I didn't sell it, I just kept it under the bed. So I was at music college for the next four years.

And did you get your Grade 8?

D'you know, I didn't even take it. Things were different in those days. Because I'd passed the college audition, they said I didn't need it. From then on I did the college exams, which were above Grade 8 anyway. I mean, it was the sixties. Nowadays I have to get my students up to Grade 8 distinction before they can get any sort of performing job.

How much influence did you have on the choice and arrangements of the music with the John Evan Band, or was it mainly a case of Ian and John deciding what should be played?

[*Long pause*] Well, I had another mate who also had a very good collection of jazz and blues records. I used to go round to his place once a week , and he introduced me to a lot of music, which are all well-known names now. I was very keen to introduce the flute into the band, so as I say I managed to get Jimmy Smith's *The Cat* into the set. But I can't really remember how we used to come up with set-llsts, to be honest.

My own influence at that point was jazz, and I was always trying to talk them into playing at Blackpool Jazz Club. I did play the occasional gig there myself – we played for beer, actually, although I was under-age then; but if you played a piece or two you'd get a free pint of beer! So I knew the people at the Jazz Club, and I told them about The John Evan Band, and they said yeah, you must come and play. So I kept on at the band, but they never did. I think perhaps they thought they weren't ready in some ways, because they were quite professional jazz players at the Club. But that's probably where my influence was, as that was the sort of music I wanted to play.

164

Did you feature on any of the unreleased studio recordings?
No, I didn't. But after I'd left the band and been through music college, I was freelancing. And I met Ian in a music shop, where we were both trying out flutes. We went for a coffee, and he invited me to play on *A Passion Play*, which I did...

[Strange, strangulated gargling sound from AND interviewer...] **Really???**
Yes, I played with the chamber orchestra as a session musician.

Are you credited on the album??
As far as I remember they said they'd credit me, but I didn't buy the album, so I'm not sure. [*I've checked, and they didn't – not even on the remastered version. MW*] I played a few notes on piccolo. I remember the recording session well, at Morgan Studios in London. David Palmer did the arrangements and conducted the orchestra. The band weren't there, these were overdubs or underdubs or whatever, but I did meet up with them again, or some of them – Ian, and John, and Barrie were certainly there.
Personally, I came full circle. I did the classical freelancing thing for a number of years. I was desperate to play rather than teach, so I joined the band of The Scots Guards, based in London. They were advertising in Melody Maker for a first flute player, and they needed somebody trained. My Dad saw this, and he knew somebody in the army, and he said, you've got to do this Martin – 'cos I'd been on the dole for six months. I just couldn't break into the orchestral scene. I remember going for one audition and being very miffed when some unknown called James Galway got it! So I did the Scots Guards for three years. But now I'm back playing jazz again.

Did you follow Jethro Tull's career in the early days?
Only from a distance. I did turn off from 'pop' music for a while to concentrate on classical and jazz. But I've been catching up recently, I've been listening to Ian's solo albums, and the flute playing is wonderful.

When did you last see Ian before Blackburn?
That was at the Blackpool Opera House show about two years ago.

Was it strange meeting him again after all those years?
It was, yes. I didn't know how he'd be, but he was very warm, and friendly, and chatty. I suspect that twenty-odd years ago you wouldn't have been able to get near him for managers and chaperones or whatever, but he seems very relaxed nowadays, and very down-to-earth, like travelling everywhere by train. I also met up with Jeffery again at that Blackpool show, and we see each other regularly now, for a chat over coffee, usually about art and stuff.

And how did you actually enjoy the Blackburn concert?
It was amazing! I mean, don't get the idea that I'm a 'jazz' or 'classical' musician, I'm a lot more flexible than that, and capable of improvisation, so I enjoyed getting into the music. And I loved the band. I thought they were a lot more accomplished and at ease than the Blackpool show a couple of years ago. Ian had e-mailed me the music to learn a couple of weeks in advance, but really we just had the one run through at the sound-check. I was disappointed really that I had to use the music stand and sheet music, but it was tricky stuff to remember. I'd love to do some more stuff with Ian sometime.

And what about yourself nowadays? You obviously teach – but do you still play?
I do, yes. I have a trio or quartet, which goes under my name, The Martin Skyrme Trio – or Quartet – in which I play the tenor sax and all the family of flutes, playing jazz and Latin standards. So yes, I'm very much a musician; and like most musicians I'd like to play more. I still get the odd bit of freelance session work coming in, and I'm teaching five days a week.

And no regrets about leaving The John Evan Band?

Lots of regrets! After I'd left the army I played in several jazz-rock and jazz-funk bands, so looking back I sometimes wish I'd stuck at it. Although I'm not sure that my music and instruments would have fitted in with Jethro Tull...

Well, the flute would have, but there wouldn't have been room for two, would there...!
Well, the nice thing is that I didn't fall out with The John Evan Band. And it was great to play with Ian again, and we've said we must get together again and have a meal or whatever, so that's great.

So there you have it - even more pieces of the John Evan Band jigsaw, including the forgotten fact that Ian Anderson had owned a flute pre-Jethro Tull... and the startling revelation that the Jethro Tull A Passion Play *ensemble contained even more ex-JEB members than we'd realised!*

Twenty years previously MW had set the ball rolling by getting the Blackpool Gazette *to run a short piece appealing for information about The John Evan Band. It hadn't even occurred to us since to check the new-fangled internet for information about any of the other chaps. We were therefore somewhat taken aback and chastened upon our return home from the Blackburn gig to discover that Martin has his own website - www.martinskyrme.co.uk – through which he was contactable all the time. Doh!*

What Martin's website does reveal, which he modestly made no reference to in the interview, is that he has played with the likes of household names such as Lulu, Matt Monroe, Bruce Forsyth, Vera Lynne and Larry Adler, and has co-written and created a series of educational music CDs, including for the flute and saxophone. As well as playing jazz clubs, his band is also available for the traditional weddings, bar mitzvahs and funerals should any Northern England readers be planning to get married, come of age or pass away – contact details via the website

Chapter 13

IAN ANDERSON

(Published in Issue #24, April 1990)

In February 1990 DR and MW visited Ian Anderson's home armed with a wad of questions about (then) unreleased tracks, promotional strategies, future plans, and matters which had been bothering all Tull fans for years, such as, "Who is Barry Diamond?" We got the answers to those and many more probing questions, and managed to avoid completely – almost – the subject of salmon farming, which was high on Ian's own agenda at the time. Ian was in sparkling form, and we ended up talking for over three hours. So much so that we had to edit the interview to squeeze it into almost an entire issue of A New Day, *and the world at large never got to enjoy his ruminations on Prince Charles, Mikhail Gorbachov – who appeared to be the nearest thing Ian had to a 'hero' figure – and "nutters" who are so obsessed with Jethro Tull, and in particular Ian Anderson, that it becomes "quite damaging to their well-being". And that's the way it remains, as looking for the tape under 22 years' worth of accumulated, er, 'filing' in DR's office was a veritable reconstruction of the old needle/haystack scenario. Sorry.*

Tull were about to embark upon a 19-date tour of the UK, having toured extensively in 1989 in support of the album Rock Island.

Did you enjoy the last tour? I gather there were some difficulties – problems with the sound, noisy crowds etc. Did you have a good time?
Well, that is very subjective. In reference to the "noisy crowds" – I mean, your quotes, not mine – it's a subjective thing because of what may impose itself on me, in the context of someone sitting three rows in front of me screaming, "Whoooah-Yeah!!!" when I'm playing or singing some quiet piece, and I'm trying to listen to what I'm doing and what everybody else is doing, as well as trying to actually enjoy what I'm doing. Some clown is there just inanely screaming – the quieter the music, the louder he, she or they will be. And it's not the whole audience, it may be just a few people, but it really ruins the mood. And when it happens night after night, as it does to some extent – usually in America – it gets you down a bit. And there were a couple of places in America where they were particularly noisy – "they" being that element in the crowd that messes it up for everybody else, as well as for me. But there were other nights when it didn't bother me, because of particular acoustics, or maybe they weren't right in front of me; perhaps over to the left a bit they were screaming and shouting a lot, but it didn't affect me quite as directly... but [*laughing*] it REALLY pissed off Martin, you know! So there were a couple of nights when some of the other members of the group got really upset about... shall we say "interference" from people shouting out or walking about in front of them and so on. It's variable. But it wasn't like it was a major problem. It's been like that... FOREVER! And in America it is much less of a problem than it was ten or fifteen years ago. At the end of the 1972 tours I'd reached a point where I said, "I quit! I've had it!" That is the only time I've ever come back really seriously saying, "I just don't want to do this any more. I'm just not prepared to go out there and to try to play acoustic or sensitive pieces, and have people screaming at me. It's a complete waste of time." It did really upset me then. But of course, as always, you decide to give it another go, and gradually people seem to have got used to the idea. Either they know that it upsets me so the majority of them are quieter, or I suspect the reality is that people are just a little bit more sensitive and a little less "rock'n'roll" in the sense of it being a football match as opposed to a music concert. People are generally more tolerant and better behaved.

What about the other extreme, in London last year, when they just didn't react at all?
That's right. That was very strange, and I just don't know why, because from what I was doing, and the way it felt onstage, it was fine. We just felt it was a very staid audience.

London has always been a bit like that, but that was certainly noticeable to the band. We were worried that there was some horrendous problem with the sound or lights or something, of which we were unaware on stage. But… I just can't explain it. People in crowds behave with a sort of corporate mentality – that's what being in a crowd is all about really, isn't it. You respond because your neighbour is responding, and so it sort of just picks up. For one reason or another in London it just didn't happen. The last night was OK, but the first night was very quiet – and yet you would imagine the first night, if it was the one that went on sale first, would be the one with the keenest fans as it were… but maybe it's not. Maybe the ones that get out first and buy the tickets are the…

The touts?! We think half the problem was the first rows being bought by touts and then sold to latecomers.
But surely the mechanism to prevent mass ticket sales to one person should prevent that happening? You see, there is a bit of a problem here, because it would be easy enough for me to pull out the first ten or fifteen rows and then put them back on the box office later on when the touts are less likely to buy tickets, with the specific arrangement that no more than two tickets are sold to one person, and hope that would discourage the touts from trying to buy them. But then I'm sure they would find a way round that, if they were dedicated to doing it. We already have it in our contracts that in the first fifteen rows there are to be no comps at all – not for the record company, the hall, the band or crew. They are ALL on sale to the public. But, as you say, that may lead to the touts having access to those perceived prime rows, and therefore they do go on sale to the people with the most money, and they may turn out to be the sort of people who could afford… well [*laughing*] afford to go and see Eric Clapton! And maybe that affects the audience as a whole, if the front rows aren't buzzing. That's very possible, but I don't know how to get round it.
Of course, there are those people who argue that the tout system is not wrong or immoral, and that it caters for a demand. I don't go along with that, but there are people who do. The touts will say, "If people WANT to leave it 'til the last minute, if they WANT to pay two or three times the ticket price in order to get that privileged ticket, we are only catering to a demand – it must therefore represent value for money to some people." The time to be worrying is if you see lots of unsold seats at the front, if the touts are responsible for buying them and then being unable to sell them. That would be a bad situation.

That did happen to a certain extent last year.
It happens with comps. I now insist that I see – or if not me personally, then Kenny or Gerd – the complete comp list, and they have to justify names, who they are, where they are from. Because if you give out, say, thirty comps to the record company in America, they end up being passed around. Somebody gives them to a friend, who gives them to someone else, and in the end nobody comes at all and the seats are empty. The tickets are out and there's nobody there, so what can you do? It's embarrassing, and it shows an abuse of the comps system. So we do limit the number of comps. A lot of gigs that are… well, a gig at the Hammersmith Odeon would be a case in point. There are a lot of groups who play the Hammersmith Odeon for whom probably half the house has been given away. Playing the Odeon is a show-place gig, and there will be many hundreds, maybe a thousand or fifteen hundred complimentary tickets just given away, to make it look good. And just given away to anybody, you know. Obviously if the group aren't popular enough to sell out the Hammersmith Odeon then they are unlikely to be able to give them out to attendant members of the press and media! So they end up being handed out to anybody – passed around, like offering somebody a drink in the pub, you know. So who knows who gets then in the end? And very often, in the end, nobody at all turns up. But if WE get unused comps, we put them back on the box office. And if there are empty seats we often try to get somebody down there to discreetly move people from the back, if they are stuck somewhere where we know they can't see that well - if they have bought tickets and they find themselves stuck in front of the PA or something. It's like that every night, trying to make the best of a bad job. I mean, some gigs in America, I've had to stop the soundcheck and I personally was down there moving chairs, because I refuse to accept that people, as was the case sometimes… there would be seats, laid out and sold by the hall, where they could see the stage but they would be sitting closer than I am to you in front

of multi-range speakers. Not just the bass bins thumping them in the chest, but full modular system with damaging mid-range frequencies at a level that would seriously impair their hearing! No doubt whatsoever. I've called house managers and said, "What do you think you are doing here?" you know. "Don't expect ME to be responsible for this!"

[We were then briefly interrupted when Ian's wife Shona came in with the news that if we didn't leave soon we looked like being snowed in! She departed rapidly and Ian told us, with some degree of incredulity, that she was off picking snowdrops. "Snowdrop Sunday" is a traditional charity event locally, and that year involved picking them in a mixture of torrential rain and snow storms – in Ian's own words, "Unbelievable! I mean, you couldn't possibly pay people to do it, but every year everybody mucks in and gets out there. Well, I don't... I draw the line at helping with the car parking and counting the money at the end"!]

During the last tour you mentioned on stage "the very expensive box-set". Do you think it IS expensive, for what it is?
Umm... No, it isn't expensive for what it is. If you relate to the full price of CDs or records or whatever, it's five albums' worth for the price of three, so it is in the mid-price, budget sort of category. But, bear in mind it's a low-cost starting point because a lot of the material was lying there anyway, so it was only about two months' work to put it all together. It is expensive, because it is expensive to lay out that kind of money in one go.

Obviously I agree with you. But I wondered if perhaps you were having a dig at Chrysalis about it.
No, not at all, any more than I would have a dig at Chrysalis or any record company, if what one reads in the papers about the true manufacturing costs of CDs is in fact the case. Because it does seem iniquitous that record companies, if this IS the case, and I don't have the full facts... I'm sure that if Dave Pegg were here he would say yes, it is the case, because he manufactures CDs for Fairport Convention and for other people on Woodworm, and he says it's dead easy. And it can't be that expensive, because these days if I do an interview for a radio station it gets made into CD copies, so it must be relatively cheap and easy to do it. One suspects the price has come down a lot, and it hasn't been recognised – it's a way of beefing up the margins for record companies. But they are facing higher costs through having to manufacture in three formats. I should think a lot of record companies are losing money on still pressing vinyl records, because the quantities are relatively small, and they still have to be distributed in the same very wide pattern; and the volume going out would probably suggest that it's not a cost effective way of distributing the whole catalogue of all artists, with all new albums in the now relatively small selling category. So I suspect that their margins are now much higher on CDs, but they don't want to pass it on to the wholesaler or the retailer or the public... or to the artist either. We actually make slightly less on a CD sale than we do on a vinyl sale.

Don't you think that more of the Jethro Tull back catalogue should be out as mid-price CDs?
Some of it, yes. But I'm concerned about the... You see, when you drop down into that so called mid-price catalogue, it actually produces 51% of the royalty – we take a real chop. And, you know, the record company might want to do that to a new album after a year or so. So I can't really say I'd like to see it too widespread. The mid-price thing is a thorny issue. In the UK most of our catalogue, nearly all of it, is at full price, but in America and Germany most of the catalogue is at mid-price, and that is a policy decision taken by Chrysalis without reference to me, except in a few cases where I have agreed to mid-price albums when I thought it was appropriate. But I am concerned at this because I only make half as much on a mid-price album as I do on a full price album, whereas I suspect that the record company make... rather more than half their normal margin. The things are stacked against us, but that is a problem we are looking into. But I have no disagreement with certain records being in the mid-price level, such as certain compilations and several others, but I would still argue that there are certain records that I wouldn't like to see, in a sense, devalued by being in a mid-price bracket, because a lot of people buying them now are first time buyers. *Aqualung* and

Thick As A Brick etc are being bought mainly by first time buyers. I can't understand though why the record company has a policy of mid-price in America but not in the UK. Why don't they do it here? Presumably it's a bit like the ticket touts – the demand is there and people are buying them, so why reduce the price?

To get back to the box set...
No, wait a minute. First let's talk about the price of CDs – and the price of going down to the curry shop for a meal! You see, I've always had this rather simplistic and probably irritating analogy to make here, in that a night out – whether it's a rock'n'roll concert ticket or buying a new album – should be about the equivalent of what it costs to go out for a pint of beer and a good curry! Without going over the top you'll be looking at a bill of around a tenner, and that seems to me a reasonable sort of parallel. It is a luxury anyway. No-one NEEDS our, or anyone else's music, and no-one NEEDS to go out to treat themselves to a curry – you can eat a lot cheaper. You could make it yourself for a quarter of the price. So no-one needs to do it, but if you choose to do it that seems to be a reasonable guideline as to what things are worth. But what is annoying is when somebody is cleaning up on it, making real big bucks, you know. And it is clearly the concern, in the case of CDs, that if the actual manufacturing costs have been radically reduced then that ought to be passed on to the consumer. End of story. And the assumption would therefore be that it would increase the number of albums sold overall if they were a bit cheaper. In that case, we are saying that the cost of a CD should be about £7 of £8 instead of £10 or £11. That would seem appropriate. But as I say, my belief is that they are losing money on vinyl and making up the losses on CDs, but I don't have the necessary figures to prove it. It would perhaps be better if instead of still having to distribute vinyl over the whole range of shops, there was just one specialist store in town stocking vinyl – but the vast majority of shops still stock all three formats, even in the USA where you hear these stories of stores stocking CD and cassettes only. They are only a tiny minority, and with talk of DAT coming in... well, with four formats it's going to be very expensive. So record companies are looking to make their bucks somewhere and preserve their margins, or increase them if possible, and it would seem they do so at the expense of the CD buyer. Obviously they will deny it and claim to have much higher costs than have been reported... but I suspect they are lying! Not just our record company – all of them. But let's face it... well, Chrysalis lost 20 million dollars in America last year, with overall losses of 16 million dollars – or was it sixteen million pounds? So... maybe they need to charge double for CDs!

Right... the box set! You weren't too keen on some of the old tracks, the "Flawed Gems", at the start of the project. But after playing them a few times you liked them, to the extent that I gather you felt they would have made a good album on their own...
Well, yeah, they would have made an OK album. The songs that are on there, with the exception of... there are two or three that I think are pretty... rubbishy! *Aeroplane, Sunshine Day, 17* – is that on there?

Yes. You cut it in half!
Oh well, it just went ENDLESSLY on and on and on! It's just...

Hypnotic?
Yeah, exactly! [*Laughs*]. But yes, I thought they were pretty ropey, but I suppose the spirit of the thing was to try to give people some of that sort of stuff, and it would have been missing the point not to include it, as most of the other rare stuff was. But the rest of it I thought was OK. And I have listened to it a lot – I've listened to it since, and it is quite good. But I don't think it would have stood up as "a new album", in quality terms, to put it out as a single album of unreleased stuff. People would have had the feeling of getting a sweeping up of the rejects, whereas in the context of the box set it was part of the whole which represents an overall look at a long period of time, but wasn't just the obvious thing of... well, like the Eric Clapton one is the fairly predictable sort of stuff. There wasn't a lot of unusual or rare or unreleased stuff on there, just the hits really plus well-known stuff from The Cream and John Mayall.

But would you consider releasing some more of those songs, or have you now put the lid on it?
Umm... how do you mean, any more? Unreleased songs, you mean? I don't remember there being anything that was actually complete, or nearly finished... I don't know, you'd have to tell me.

Oh yeah, there were quite a few more. Some would need work still, as you did with some of the others, by adding the flute parts and so on, but that's not what I'm saying... you weren't keen on the others originally until you had listened to them again properly and realised they were actually very good, so maybe if you went back to them again you would find some more?
Well, if I knew what songs they were, but off hand I can't remember what was not used. And some of the things you heard were from a rough mix tape, and we could not find the masters for them, so that was another factor in what could and could not be used. So I don't think there is too much there that we could use.

Why didn't you play *Part Of the Machine* in Britain?
I don't know, I can't tell you why. I play that myself quite often, sitting in the dressing room, because I really like that song, but I don't know why it just doesn't work on stage. We played it on most of the American tour in '88, but it never really settled down and felt comfortable. I thought about doing an acoustic version of it on my own, but I didn't in the end. But I don't know why it doesn't work – I wish it did.

What about *Undressed To Kill*, which was dropped after a few UK shows?
Oh, just cutting down the set - and it wasn't a very good song to play live, it didn't feel like it came alive. We always start with a song or two too many, just in case we want to change the set, and that was one of the ones we decided to drop. And particularly in America, where *Rock Island* wasn't getting much reaction at the radio, the audiences were very unfamiliar with the record, relatively speaking. So it was a struggle, doing the new material was not that easy in America. It is very much a sort of nostalgia trip in America compared to here and in Europe where people are much more open to us playing new songs. But then obviously the record did much better here, and in Germany where it was number five in the national charts and number four in the CD charts, which make up most of their sales, so it was a very successful album in Germany, by anybody's standards. So the punters knew the songs. They'd got the album and then gone to the shows. By that I mean 30% or 40% of the audience were familiar with the songs, whereas in America it might be 5% or 10% of the audiences had the album. So it was a struggle, with the new songs dotted throughout the set, and there were times when it fell a bit flat from the audiences' point of view, because they were hoping to hear one well-known song after another. We found the same even with *Crest Of A Knave*. *Steel Monkey* got a good reaction, but the others didn't get that great a reaction. I don't know what it is about the Americans at all. It's much more about nostalgia, that plays a much bigger part in the American attitude, and there seems to be a greater prevailing feeling that we should be playing all the best-known songs. Things like *Jack-A-Lynn* they just didn't know at all. It went down OK, but [*laughing*] you sometimes get the feeling it's just the relief that it has ended that gets a good reaction!

That was the high spot for me, because it was so unexpected.
Hmm... it was unexpected for the rest of the group as well, because at the end of rehearsals I started humming it to myself and said, "Hey, what about trying this one?!" [*Laughs.*]

On the subject of finished tracks, what happened to *Hardliner*, which was left off *Rock Island* at the last minute?
Hardliner just languishes on a piece of digital master tape here. It doesn't sound really very "Jethro Tull" – it sounds a bit contrived somehow. We all felt it was quite a nice song – we all liked it, but it sounded a bit... not really us. We felt detached from it in a way

But you wouldn't rule it out as a B-side or something at some time?

171

I wouldn't rule it out, but I wouldn't want to force it on people, as if we have to use it just because it is there. Just because we have done it doesn't mean it is good or appropriate. It's all very well putting it out, but if people didn't like it, what is the point?

It's just the thought that *A New Day* readers know that it exists, and it becomes one of those eternal questions...
It sounds a bit like a... M.O.R. American rock group track. Like one of those fat balding American rock bands, as opposed to a fat balding English rock band!

An American hit single perhaps?
I doubt it, somehow. But, out of the people who heard it, a couple liked it but a lot of people seemed to indicate it was OK but nothing special. And at the end of the day I was determined that we should adopt a policy of making the vinyl, cassette and CD the same in terms of tracks, and we cut to the absolute limits on vinyl. We had to do test cuts on vinyl before we could confirm the running order and the songs that would be on the tape and CD. It was a long record to cut, but surprisingly it is one of the better cuts, in spite of its length. These days vinyl can be quite good. Despite its standing as a dwindling format, people are better at cutting it now.

OK... *Jack-A-Lynn* – widely regarded as "Classic Tull", and you have played it live now so I guess you must quite like it yourself – how could you have dropped it from the *Broadsword* album in the first place??
Well... it was probably a close contender for the album, but I would guess it was the response of the people – in the band and the record company – and it somehow got pushed out. We had a lot of songs, about twenty songs to pick for *Broadsword*.

Do you not feel that, even now, it would make a good single?
Well, I don't know. What is a good single? I have not... I'm just... I am utterly and completely confused by... I listen to the radio quite a lot. I bought myself a new radio just the other day, because I am interested in listening to the radio and being able to pick up a lot of FM stations to see what everyone is playing, and it just seems to be the same thing. I swear, one afternoon, I tried three different stations – Capital, GLR and FOX FM – and I thought my preset programme buttons had gone on the blink! I thought I was getting the same station on all three, because as I flicked through them they were all playing the same record, which was New Kids On The Block, and they must have started playing it within seconds of each other because it was the same part of the song on each station, just fractions out of synch! I actually found myself counting the bars and then switching the stations, and they were just fractionally out of time with each other. It just shows how much programming uniformity seems to exist within radio stations, and I don't understand why they should be so attracted to singles anyway, because I don't believe they sell that large a quantity. It is a fiction created by the media and record companies because it is easier to focus on one song, an artist and the image that goes with it – but it is basically a means, in most cases, of selling albums. The volumes of singles being sold are, with rare exceptions, far below the volume of albums being sold by the same artists in the same week. Somebody at the record company told me that in the first week of sales of *Rock Island* in the UK, if it had been a single it would certainly have been Top 20, and maybe Top 10 that week.

[*Enter Shona once more, to point out to Ian that he had not yet performed his duties regarding the removal of certain cat deposits in places where they didn't oughta be! But he made us promise not to tell anybody so... Mum's the word, eh?*]

Were you disappointed with the reaction, or lack of it, to *Another Christmas Song*?
Yes, I was disappointed. I mean, I didn't think for a minute it was going to be "a big hit", but the reaction to the song, particularly in Europe, was very strong. It really did sort of click. Not so much in America, although there were places where it did go well – halfway through the song people would strike matches and lighters and so on. It was a bit like a Rod Stewart gig! I thought, "Strange – why have they picked up on this song particularly?" It was one of the

songs I enjoyed singing and doing on stage. I liked it, but I was surprised. And I thought maybe it's something that might just scrape into the lower end of the charts. So it was disappointing, because it didn't do anything at all.

Do you think maybe if you had made a video for it...?
I don't think it would have made any difference at all.

They just did not play it on the radio.
Well, it had a few plays here and there from some of the DJs who do play our things – a few of them do, when they have the freedom to do so. But what they did with the Christmas releases this year, so I'm told, differed from the usual system. In the past they have elected certain songs to be on the playlist, and so get emphatic airplay, several times a day. This year they decided not to have an official Christmas playlist at the BBC, whose policies also affect all the commercial and independent radio stations, because they tend to compete with the BBC for the same perceived listener, the same demographic, and they basically adopt the same programme. And so, not having a Christmas playlist... I mean, if we hadn't been on it then we wouldn't have had any plays or sold any records, but if we had been on it then we would have been guaranteed a certain number of plays and it might then have crossed the threshold of enough people hearing it, and it clicks, you know. But with no official playlist it was up to the DJs to play what they wanted to play, broadly speaking, and therefore the number of plays was split very thinly over the vast amount of Christmas releases, and only the one or two really obvious ones that everyone was playing made it with any success. But again, you can't argue with that. That is a free system, and if we didn't come to the fore within that free programming system then it can't have been, in "single" terms, a very good song, and so we didn't make it. So we can't blame the BBC for not putting it on the playlist thereby making it a flop, because there wasn't a list! Well, that it what I am told, anyway.

It seems like the kind of song that would be played on the radio. Had it been by anybody else I think it would have been played.
Well, I do think Chrysalis made quite an effort here to try to do their best with it…

But do you think it's the name "Jethro Tull"? The DJ sees "Tull" on the label and therefore ignores it?
Yes, of course it is. Absolutely. Absolutely. We are, to a lot of people, packaged in there along with memories of Mike Oldfield or something of that sort. Some quaint, hippy sort of thing. The average Radio 1 DJ would probably say, "Yeah, I think they are still about – they occasionally make a record and play some gigs." They probably know we exist, but would not be aware that we do actually go out and play the same places as lots of other people they hear about every day.

Is it worth your while aiming for a higher media profile, or are you not worried about it?
I am personally not worried, because I quite like it the way it is, and I think our audience probably do as well – and if they're happy, I'm happy. A lot of times it's nice if what you are into, in terms of what you are interested in and follow and associate yourself with, is not a mass appeal thing. It gives you a feeling of belonging to a slightly exclusive club, and that small exclusive club is one that has somewhere between half a million and a million paid-up, subscribing members! And that's probably part of the fun of it for them. I'm sure it is, and that's fine. I'm quite happy with that as long as [*laughing*] I don't get the impression they are ALL driving around in Citroen 2CVs and NECESSARILY going to Fairport Convention concerts! I'd be a bit worried if it were such a cosy little family scene, like a bunch of rather decadent, middle-aged ex-hippies. Thankfully it's a bit broader than that!

You have said often, and lately, that you don't want to put out another live album, but...
Well, I don't have a burning ambition to do so, but I'm not... I think it's very likely that sometime along the way we will do something that is...I would think it would not be like a single concert, we would do something culled from a lot of live performances. We wouldn't

aim it in the same bracket as a new studio album, but probably something more like the box-set. A sort of mid-price album relative to the content of it – maybe a 3-CD set for half the price or two thirds of the price of three single CDs, that sort of thing. But we wouldn't do it as long as we were out there playing – it would be more of a fill-in thing if there were to be a long gap between studio albums.

So there is nothing coming out to tie in with this tour?
Nothing at all.

No single... No video...?
No, nothing at all. This tour must be seen in the true perspective. From our point of view it is just going out purely on a very low key level. One coach, one truck, a slightly reduced crew and obviously slightly reduced lighting and PA systems because the venues are a lot smaller – the average size is about 1,700 capacity. And even on that reduced scale we have to just about sell out all the dates to cover the cost of doing it. It is a very, very tight operation. We need to sell nearly all the tickets, otherwise [*laughs*] it will be a goodwill mission that will cost us to do! A bit like our proposed trip to Russia, where they wanted us to go and play five nights in Moscow and five nights in Leningrad. They offered to pay us twenty thousand dollars for what would have amounted to two weeks work, assuming it was tacked onto something else so there was no extra rehearsal as well. And we would be losing about thirty thousand pounds at least, because we have to pay the crew, you know. The crew don't particularly want to go sight-seeing in Moscow, they wanna get paid the same as they get paid wherever we are playing. So we would lose a lot of money – I'd rather go and do two shows for the appropriate fraction and lose a little money. But we've been on at them now for two years to let us go and do two shows in Moscow and two shows in Leningrad, and no promoter – or, effectively, the state – will allow it because they insist on under-selling the concerts. They will not risk the demand for tickets being greater than the number of seats available – and they say the demand for tickets would be such that we would have to do five nights. I don't believe that. I don't think for a minute Jethro Tull is that popular in Russia, and I think that the access they have now to their own music is such that there would be... well, a lot of people playing to half houses. And I am not prepared to go and spend a lot of money, personally pay to go and play under those circumstances. I'd like to go and play a couple of sold out shows, and lose a little money; I think that's fair enough. But not two weeks in Russia playing to half houses. No way! They MIGHT be right and maybe I'm wrong, because I don't really know if people there know about us or not. I imagine that some do, and there would be curiosity because we'd be one of those bands that are "part of rock'n'roll history", but...

I think Tull are or were one of only three Western bands with a record released on the Russian state label. Two or three years ago I believe only Tull, The Beatles and The Moody Blues were on the state label.
Really? I didn't know that! Not heard that at all... I know we don't get any royalties, but presumably they would have done that with the record company.

I imagine so. It is *Original Masters* – same cover and so on...
Well - that's the first I've heard of it! Anyway, we're still battling with the Russians to try to get them to let us do just two shows. We were talking about going this Spring to do some dates in Czechoslovakia, Poland, East Germany and Russia, but nobody really wants to do anything under the current circumstances, because the situation is so unstable now that everyone is really nervous. I mean, people feel very buoyant that in the future there's going to be a lot more bands going to these places, but right now things are very volatile. Under the old regime at least you knew what the rules were, but right now everybody is nervous about public gatherings and people using it as a political platform and so on, so it's kind of on freeze. But we are still pursuing, even now... if something comes up in East Germany we might go and do it, but it just looks very dodgy at the moment. But these options are continually being explored – you know, the right time, the right place. But to avoid losing a lot of money we would have to do it on the back of an existing tour. But it is unlikely just now.

174

We are also talking at the moment about doing a big show in the UK. It is very early days yet, but we are trying to put something together for July or August, but we are still trying to get information on the other things that might be going on. Springsteen, the Stones, Tina Turner and others are all doing something, and we don't want to be in a situation where we put a show together on the same Saturday that The Stones decide to play somewhere – because we'll get a caning! And it would be silly to assume that a lot of people who might want to come and see Jethro Tull but who also really don't want to miss seeing The Stones, you know... I mean, I couldn't possibly blame them for saying, "Shit! Let's go and see The Stones!", you know! So it doesn't help anybody to pick the wrong time, and we are trying to get that info and find a time in the holiday period where we can do a show, maybe in a football ground or the stately home type show. Nostell Priory had been discussed amongst us as a possible venue again, but we haven't approached them as yet, and we have had an offer from a football ground which might be possible. It is still a question of where and when. We know we can't do it at Dave Pegg's Cropredy venue because the infrastructure there is stretched to capacity, and while the local people are happy to have Dave's festival there for a couple of days, to have another weekend would be putting the pressure on them in terms of roads and shops and the intrusion into the local community, and they wouldn't be happy about that.

But, anyway... no new album, nothing at all. This is just going out and doing it. We are trying to play the places we haven't played for years, and where we expect people would be quite pleased to see us play. Like Bradford... Nottingham... you know... we haven't been there for fifteen or twenty years, but they are all towns that we played once upon a time, maybe at a blues club or a small theatre. We have been saying for a long time, "We will go out and do a PROPER British tour," – but even so, we're leaving out loads and loads of places. We've had real problems. We started looking for venues in October, and it's just UNVBELIEVABLE the demand there is for the places. The places we just could not get! It's taken a long, long time to actually get the tour sorted in terms of availability of halls and in the right order. It was an absolute pig to get together.

Is that why you are not playing London?
Well, no. That is because we did three shows in London last year, so we are playing around London – Oxford, Reading, Brighton... they are areas in the London catchment. If we were only playing London people would come to Hammersmith from those areas, so we are only... "taking our music to the people" as it were, rather than expecting them to have to drive through the night to come and see us. But I don't know. Maybe it will be really disappointing, the demand for tickets...

I don't think so, somehow.
Well, who knows...?

Do you think there is a danger of some critics seeing the small-scale tour as a sign that Tull can't play venues like the Hammersmith Odeon anymore? "Can't fill large venues"? Or don't you care how the critics see it?
I don't particularly care what they think. There are lots of people who are going to say that, but I mean we did play three nights at the Hammersmith Odeon. That is 15,000 people, or a Wembley-and-a-half.

But you have made no provision for playing larger venues as well?
No. And we have already played London within this period, within that 12-month period, shall we say.

Yes, I'm just thinking of the people who are not aware of that, who will suddenly see Jethro Tull playing small venues. Although the tour will probably pass them by anyway, because people don't seem to be aware of when Tull are touring.
All we are doing initially is just an ad in the local papers. We are studiously avoiding doing any national publicity for the tour until the local demand is satisfied, because the whole point of doing it is to give people who live in those towns the chance to see us play there. Let us

just assume, in the unlikely event that there is more demand for tickets than there are seats, we want to make sure people who live in those towns get to go there. Not people from London saying, "Yeah, let's go up to Birmingham and see them at Birmingham Town Hall!", because that could easily happen. If we advertise a Birmingham show in London at this stage maybe Birmingham would sell out, leaving a lot of people in Birmingham saying, "Shit, this is our town, and we can't get in!"

You are playing Birmingham then?

We are actually doing Birmingham, only because it's... shall we say the NEC is one of the least satisfying gigs from an audience's point of view, and to play it is a very sterile environment, and so Birmingham was the exception where we said we would go and play to 1,400 people, which is the capacity of the hall. We are doing it I suppose because it's a slight feeling of guilt that the NEC is not a great gig to be playing. It is not one that we would choose to play, although it's bigger and obviously we can play to more people. And so we think maybe Birmingham has been a bit short-changed, and one assumes that the majority of people who come to see us at the Town Hall will be the people who saw us at the NEC, and it may also give some people the chance to see us in Birmingham who would not go to the NEC simply because they don't like the venue. So Birmingham is the exception. There is a slight exception also because we couldn't get a date in Glasgow, which we haven't played for quite a few years, and the nearest we could find that was a smaller-scale place was Livingston, which is between Edinburgh and Glasgow.

I thought that was a fairly big venue...

No, no, it's only a small place. You must be thinking of Ingleston... where the fish-farming conference is! I'm there in a couple of weeks – that is the next gig!

Some of the dates are at standing venues. Any thoughts on that?

Yes, I have. Again it is a question of trying to maximise capacity. In some of the venues there are seats upstairs, so we've kept them in, but made it standing downstairs to try to make it up, as far as possible, to around 1,700 average. But I myself wouldn't want to go and see a show and have to stand up. I really wouldn't, but we have done it a number of times recently, against my original better judgement, and it has in fact been quite good, and the audience has been OK. In the Zurich Sportshalle, we always used to play that to an entirely seated audience, but the demand for tickets grew to the point where we decided to make it standing the last two times we have been there, and it's been OK. The audience seemingly are used to standing up there if the demand is there, and they don't mind it. But I'm not too sure how that'll be perceived in the UK. There may be some adverse comments about it, and I wouldn't be at all surprised, but the argument would be that if the demand for tickets is there then it is the only way of fulfilling it, as far as possible.

But some people prefer to stand anyway.

Yeah, some do.

You wouldn't want to stand to listen to a folk singer all evening, but for a rock band it's OK.

Well, that again is part of the problem, because I think there will be more emphasis on... a slightly more eclectic performance on this tour. We will be playing a lot of the songs we did on the last tour, but we will play some different things too, and they will tend to be... not necessarily acoustic, but a bit more eclectic in the sense that they won't be as straight ahead rock'n'roll as we sometimes play. So there is that worry – a standing audience, if it's not hearing Status Quo type stuff, may start shuffling their feet, you know. But, I just don't know. It's a difficult decision to make, and I don't think there is an ideal answer to it. I prefer to play to people sitting down... I mean, I prefer they were sitting down and I was sitting down some of the time! But if, at these particular gigs, the audience are aware of the venue and expect to stand at gigs there, then I feel more comfortable about doing it, even though of course we may be talking about entirely different people. Maybe the average gig that's on there is some little chart group or something that plays to teeny-boppers, who do stand. But the hope is that people won't be expecting plush seats and so won't be disappointed when there aren't any. But anyway, the majority of the gigs are seated, with just a few standing venues.

Have you any plans to play anywhere else this year?
Well, we did consider going to do Spain, Portugal, France, Belgium, Holland, Sweden, Norway and Denmark...

Oh, just a few then!
Well no, we knew we couldn't do them all, but we were looking at dates in the UK, dates in Europe and Eastern Block dates, and we thought we will do a month, or we will do two months – a goodwill mission. The East Europe dates fell down, on our terms - or Russia anyway - and the European stuff didn't make sense financially, because if we were ever going to do Europe we had to gear up for a bigger level of tour – more crew, two coaches, two trucks and so on – and then we would have been really over-gunned for the UK; or if we scaled it down for the UK we'd have the problem of having to do a switch of gear, a stage up for the larger venues we would have to do in Europe. So, economically, it was a non-starter. So we decided doing the UK was more important, because the main reason for doing anything this year was to play the provincial dates in the UK. It was then whatever else we could fit around it, but in the end we decided we couldn't, and decided to hang on for a bit to see if anything came up in the summer in Europe. There's talk of a couple of things in Germany, but I don't know what they are yet, or who else is on the bill, or how much they are going to pay us, and so on. But we are interested, in principle. It will be sorted out within the next couple of months, as to whether or not it's happening. So there is the possibility of two or more open-air dates in Europe... a strong intention on our part to do a British date, whatever happens, just as a one-off. Really, just to try not to go too long without playing some gigs, basically.
It would be nice to play some dates, but obviously we don't want to go and tackle something that's too big a commitment. We have had offers to go back to Brazil, and things like that, but... not this year I think. I think we'll just do the things that really will be fun. Going to Brazil once was fun, but it wouldn't be so much fun the second time, it would just be 'a tour', and that is not a good economic prospect either – it's another goodwill mission. Goodwill missions are great because you just go out to play and to have some fun, you're not trying to play to huge amounts of people and make vast amounts of money. It is fun for a month, but it's not fun if it goes on for too long, because there is no pay-off, and possibly if you are not playing to that many people you feel it is sort of below the scale you usually work at. So, we are doing a month in the UK and then just keeping out options open for July and August, bearing in mind that the latter part of August is out because Dave has his festival then.

You asked some ex-Tull members to guest on stage last year. Are you going to ask them again this time?
I haven't really thought about it. I'm meeting with Dave and Martin in a couple of days to go through the tour details – the hotels, travel arrangements, talk about the songs we are going to play and so on. So we will discuss that then.

Did the responses you got last time put you off or disappoint you at all?
The responses to what exactly...?

You asked John Evans, for example.
Oh, the responses from the people themselves, the ex-members of the group? Yeah, I mean... John Evans won't do it. He was very clear, he just did not want to do it. It would have been good if John had just come to play the piano at the beginning of *Locomotive Breath* or *Wond'ring Aloud* or something, but he just wouldn't do it. He would not be too worried about it technically or whatever, but he just does not want to go back to doing that, which is... well, that is what he says, and that's that. If I could persuade him differently, or if I thought there was a chance he might change his mind, I'd certainly have another go at asking him, but he sounded so emphatic, and I don't want to keep badgering him about it if it makes him feel uncomfortable, and that did seem to be the case.

Umm... Jeffrey won't do anything. Barrie might or might not, but it's a problem with a drummer because they'll only ever play their own drums, you know, and we can't set up two drum kits. They can't really play each other's drum kits, because everything is in a different place – things just ain't there when you try to hit them. And... who else...

Peter Vettese?
Yeah, that's a point. Yes, if Peter's around... that's a good idea, yes. And Clive Bunker, he's a good guy. If he's around maybe he'd come and play a bit of percussion, you know. That would be quite a presentable thing to do. And Mick Abrahams... although the problem is there's nothing we play or have played that he played on. That would be a tricky one. There was one we played, in '82 or '84... what was it? It had a riff that went [*sings something akin to "daah-dah daah, dah-dah daah ..."*]

My Sunday Feeling...
Ah! *My Sunday Feeling*, that's right. We have played that, I suppose. I've spoken to Mick a few times on the 'phone over the years, and he's always very friendly, you know – "Hey mate, we must get together for a drink," and so on.

Have you heard Blodwyn Pig since they reformed?
No, I haven't. What are they like?

Very good. Excellent. Mick is still a tremendous guitar player. They are playing near here next week, actually...
The problem is, people always seem to expect this glorious reunion type thing if I were to go to their gig. That would be possibly embarrassing for Blodwyn Pig and certainly embarrassing for me because I can't even remember the names of the songs we used to play when Mick was with Tull, as you have just amply discovered! What do they play? Blodwyn Pig material plus bits and pieces?

Just two old Pig sings plus some songs written for the new album, but it is basically very much back to the blues.
Well, I'd be happy to get up with them if, as you say, it is a blues band, and play some flute on a couple of standard blues numbers. Just get a feel for the arrangement, what key we are in and where we are going. I wouldn't mind playing along with that – that would be fun. But if it was a complicated arrangement that involved actually rehearsing together it would be difficult. It's a bit like the Fairports. If they asked me to come and play a couple of songs at Oxford, say, I'd say, "Yes, great, OK." I'd get the record or a tape and learn it. But for them it's a real hassle, just as it's a hassle for us, when you're doing shows night after night and then suddenly there is a change because someone is coming that night and they are gonna get up and play in such and such a song and so somebody has not to play in that song, or change the arrangement or something. And whereas it seems such a good idea at the time, it causes lots of aggro. And Fairport's annual thing at Cropredy - well, the whole evening consists of that, and I know last year that they were just... the complexity of all the songs, and all the changing, arranging who's playing what and what key it's going to be in and so on... it just gets immensely confusing for them because they are playing different arrangements of the same songs they play every night on their own and suddenly they have to change it to accommodate an ex-guitarist or singer or whatever. I think of late they have decided to minimise the number of guest appearances because, whereas for the guest it's just a couple of songs as a one-off, for Fairport it is happening all the time. People turning up and expecting to play something. It is a problem, because you owe it to your guest to rehearse, and allow him the scope to be doing more than just standing at the back strumming a guitar. To justify the presence of a guest he has to be somewhere a bit prominent, to be featured in a meaningful role and not just a token thing. So you owe it to your guest to make him look good, and there isn't that time at the average soundcheck. Fairport, right now, will be battling through the snow or floods or whatever, and may not arrive at their gig until six. No soundcheck at all, so what happens if a guest is coming tonight and there is no chance of any rehearsal whatsoever? It's not good for the guest and it's not good for the group or the crew. So it's not as free and

easy at it appears to the audience. You just assume, "Well, they know the songs. He just stepped up there with his guitar and joined in!"

Will you be going to Cropredy this year?
No, we will actually be on holiday that week, so we won't be going.

To get back to Tull, will the 1978 Madison Square Garden video ever be released?
I think that it probably will be. I've looked at it, although I haven't actually watched the whole thing. I think the problem I had with it was that though most of it was OK, there were a couple of dodgy moments. When we were doing that we actually thought the whole thing was a complete balls-up because just as we were walking onstage there was a major problem with the transmission link, and the last thing I knew as I walked on the stage to do the show was that the whole thing had gone horribly wrong, live in front of millions of people! And I knew nothing to the contrary basically until half-way through the show, when somebody told me, "Yes, it's on again - there was a problem, but it's OK." But, imagine from my point of view as well as the other guys in the group. I mean, there's just the humiliation really, as we understood there was a major problem but we HAD to do it! The total embarrassment of it stayed with us for half the show, so it wasn't an easy concert to play. We just had to try to blot it out and say, "Look, it's the audience HERE we have to worry about," - which in itself was difficult because it was in the middle of the bloody afternoon, in Madison Square Gardens, and it's just not the same atmosphere, you know? People are used to going to rock'n'roll shows at night, and indoors in the afternoon at the MSG just felt wrong to us, and wrong to the audience.
It was a very strange sort of thing because we'd already played a few songs before, went off and then came back on to do the live televised bit, so the songs were all being played in the wrong order from the rest of the tour, and everything seemed weird. PLUS, it was supposedly a total balls-up! I'm not trying to make excuses for a bad performance, but just explaining why, from my point of view, it was not a great show. It wasn't a disaster, but it wasn't very good, and there are a couple of things in it where clearly we are not all entirely happy, and we are definitely sort of... struggling, you know. So my feeling was that quite a lot of the televised bit was OK, but there wasn't a full-length video's worth of material there. It's not fair to sell people a video with only 30 minutes of music on it, because if you buy or rent a video you expect an hour's entertainment at least. So I don't know what we would do to beef it up because we don't have much other stuff, and any meaningful stuff has already been utilised, presumably, in the *20 years Of Jethro Tull* video, which I still haven't seen.

No, it hasn't actually. There is a whole load of stuff available that they just didn't look for. Concerts as far back as 1969 that clearly still exist because various, very brief clips are shown from time to time in different countries.
Oh well, maybe that's the answer then. I'll speak to Chrysalis about it, to see what we can do about that stuff. Last time I spoke to them about it I told them that most of it was OK, but we needed more material. Also, there is somebody touting me at the moment - although they haven't spoken to me yet - but I'm told somebody from a UK TV company is trying to get hold of me to do a documentary with us on the road during the May tour, which would feature some live performance but would be more about "being on the road", and there'd be more interviews and so on, and not just an attempt to film a concert. We were asked last year by Central TV to let them film Birmingham, just to be shown as a whole concert broadcast, and I said we didn't want to do it, because personally I find live televised concerts very boring, because it is very difficult to capture on TV whatever, on a good night, is in there in the audience – you're somehow remote from it. And I said to them, "If you want to make a programme that's more than just a concert, if you want to travel around with the band and so on, or combine it with other old footage or something, OK. But it's got to be something that is more than just a live gig." And he said at the time, "I know what you want to do, but my brief is to try to get live concerts from the NEC," and so that one was put on the side. But if this other documentary thing happens then that would put some stuff "in the can" which might be available later to combine with the MSG and other footage for a video – which would at least bring it more up to date. The only other stuff I have access to is a concert filmed in Brazil last

year, which didn't really look or sound very good to me, so we've got nothing really up to date.

When do you anticipate the next Jethro Tull album?
March or April next year. We'll be trying, basically, to record the album this autumn, and it has to be finished by Christmas with a view to releasing an album in March, April or May, and as far as I know the availability of the guys in the group is geared around that fact. But I don't like to be in a situation of saying we ARE going to have an album out then – that is assuming we are all excited about whatever it is we are playing, and we all feel good about it. But I would like to think the likelihood is we will have it wrapped up by Christmas, but if it goes into February or March we would miss the pre-summer slot so it would be the end of August again.

Why is your name on the back of the 'Rock Aid Armenia' *Smoke On The Water* **single?**
Is it? I have absolutely no idea! All I can tell you is I sat here by the telephone for two days waiting for my instructions as to where I had to be at what time, and they never called me back – having called Kenny Wylie several times previously to ask me to do it. I'd gone and bought a copy of *Smoke On The Water* so I knew how it went – obviously I knew the riff, but I couldn't remember the arrangement of the song. But Shona was away for two days and the children were off school, and I didn't want to go to London and just hang around waiting, so I said to them, "I'll have to bring my children with me, but give me an hour or two warning and I'll get there when you're ready for me to do something." I asked them to call me back, but nothing happened. So I tried to call the studio, but there was nobody there who was actually in charge – lots of people who were in some way involved, but nobody who could say when I should come. They said, "Just come down and we'll sort it out when you get here," but I said, "I don't live in London, I have no means of transport so I'll have to hire a car, and I've got my children with me who don't want to be up half the night," you know. I wasn't trying to be awkward, just realistic. So I sat here waiting, for the whole weekend, and by Sunday afternoon I was in a really bad mood because I literally had to stay in the house in case they 'phoned to tell me to come down. So I was really annoyed about it – I thought it was extremely bad form and very inconsiderate. Maybe they felt they I was being awkward by saying, "'Phone me when you need me," and maybe they were offended by that, I don't know. But I was perfectly willing and happy to do it, but they didn't call me back. So it must have been such an amateurish affair that they didn't realise I wasn't there at all. Maybe they thought I slipped in with the chorus or something and that's why they put my name on the record?

No, they have a list of the artists and a list with "Special thanks to...", and your name is in that.
I see. Well anyway, I'm very sceptical about these things. I'm not going to do any more unless it really is something incredibly meaningful and well organised, because I did the same thing in Germany with this wretched rain forest thing...

Ah! That was the next question...
I had my arm twisted to do it, and I made a considerable effort to do it at very unsociable hours, and - I suppose everybody's complaint - on actually hearing the record I can hear a hint of flute right at the beginning of it, never to be heard of again and sort of smothered up with a load of lush voices and whatever else.

On the instrumental version on the CD the flute is slightly clearer.
When I played on it it was just me, Herbie Hancock and Chris Thompson plus a drum machine and bits of synthesiser or something. It was a nice keyboard part, and I played flute that just fitted around that, and in fact I was pleased with it when I heard it because it actually sounded pretty good. But I said to the guy, "If you come to the end of it, don't feel embarrassed if you leave the flute off, or leave my name off. I'm really very pleased to help out, but don't feel you have to flatter me just because I have done it... because I know if you've asked me to do something you'll feel terrible if you sort of hide it in the mix, or you

180

don't think it belongs, or there is something better that somebody else has done that you feel is actually more useful and therefore you can't use my bit. So don't be embarrassed, just leave me off – I won't mind." So they did... and [*laughing*] I'M PISSED OFF!! But it wasn't a great song. I must say actually that I went in and I'd rewritten the lyrics [*laughs*] because they sent me the lyrics and I thought, "This is just garbage, awful!" – because it didn't say anything about the rain forest at all in it anywhere, it was just awful, really banal lyrics. Terrible title too. It sounded a bit like a Pepsi Cola commercial type song. And although Chris Thompson is a very good singer, he is just "one of those guys", you know. He is not in Lou Gramm-land, he's somewhere else... a very, very good singer, but not a "special" singer, if you know what I mean. And I tried to persuade them... I actually rewrote the lyrics and I had them on my lyric sheet, but talking to the guy who was doing it I realised it had actually got to the point where it was not my place to start suggesting major changes to it, so I hid them! But I did suggest very strongly to them that they get Joe Cocker to sing the whole song, because the thing where people sing a line here and a chorus there has been done a million times. I said, "It's been done a lot, so why not place your faith in one person?" And at the time in Germany Joe Cocker was big again, with a hot single and an album, and it was the sort of song... not a great song, but he could have breathed that passion and fire into it to make it good. So they got Joe singing on it, but they only gave him a verse. They told me they had an alternative version with him singing the whole song, so I suggested they put their version on one side of the record and put the version with Joe doing the lot on the other side, and then let radio decide which one they liked, feeling fairly confident myself that they would go for Joe, because he'd add that bit of guts to it. But I don't know what they did – the version I have has Joe singing a bit of it with lots of other people singing bits of it.

There are four versions of it, but not the Joe Cocker version.
Oh well, there you go. Maybe we should do a single for the NSPCC this year? We could call it *Snowdrop Sunday*! I could get Barry Diamond to sing on the choruses!

Er... who is Barry Diamond?
Ah, so you haven't heard about our new pet comedian Barry Diamond...? I think we should bootleg a Barry Diamond tape to all *A New Day* readers! He is an American stand-up comic. He plays the comedy store in L.A. and so on, and was in a movie called *Bachelor Party*. A very funny man, a very clever comedian. I have only once ever been to see a comedian perform live, which was when we were on the way back from a restaurant where the Fairports, Richard Thompson, Gerd Burkhardt and I had gone to eat in L.A., on a night off. And having eaten a meal we were off for a drink, or back to the hotel or something, but the Fairports decided to go for another meal! They didn't like the first one, so they were going to go straight on for another meal, and I could see it heading for one of their legendary eating and drinking things, you know, so Gerd and I set off for the hotel. On the way back we saw the Comedy Store and thought we'd give it a try. We waited about twenty minutes to get in and then sat through some pretty turgid and aggressive four-letter-word sort of stuff from various American comics, and it was really embarrassing. They weren't very good, and the audience were really loud and challenging to them. But then this unassuming guy came on and straight away you could tell this was a different class of person. He looks like a thug, but alternates between a very effete character and a deep southern Texas cowboy macho sort of thing, in mid-sentence. Great! Very funny. Very American, but a clever comedian who uses four-letter words and lots of fairly explicit scenarios, but there is a point to it, and most of the other guys just use that sort of thing without a point to it at all, just for maximum shock effect, just for the sake of it. On the last tour I managed to get a tape he'd released, and everybody I played it to thought it was incredibly funny, and somewhere along the tour we were going to L.A., and we called him up. He said he was a big Tull fan and he turned up at the show and was a very amusing, funny guy. A nice guy. We saw him three times in all on the tour, and so we struck up an accord – so I am an unashamed promoter of Barry Diamond's humour.

To change the subject completely, what was your relationship with Captain Beefheart in the '70s?

Just that he rang up one day, because I'd mentioned to somebody at Warner Brothers that we – that is, Jeffrey Hammond and I – particularly liked Captain Beefheart and Frank Zappa, but not much else about American music at the time. Somebody at WB must have mentioned this to Captain Beefheart and one day, out of the blue, he rang me and said he would like to be on our next tour as the support band. I was a bit nervous about it because, although I thought they were a very interesting band and I enjoyed the things they did and could see that he was obviously a real character, I worried that the American audience might not like him, because he was really unknown in the USA, although through the efforts of John Peel he'd become very much a sort of cult hero in the UK. So I was nervous about how he would go down with the Americans, but we agreed to have him for at least part of the tour. And they did die a death pretty well all the time, the audience really didn't like them at all. But they were travelling around with us, and we were all fairly chummy and matey with all the guys in the band – but Beefheart was a tyrant and a bully with his own boys, and a very insecure man. Very charismatic, and used to total domination, but that was covering up for a very deep-seated insecurity. If he didn't feel he had manipulated and totally controlled you he was desperate to try to do so; desperate, and terrified if he hadn't gained the power, which he seemed to have over lots of people that he met, as well as the guys in his band. He was a very strange guy – very intense. He used to ring me in the middle of the night and say, "Hey man, can we rap?" and I'd say, "Don, look, it's three in the morning, I've got a show tomorrow, can we talk in the morning?" you know. "Hey man, I need to talk to you..." "Sorry Don, I can't talk right now, I'm going back to sleep. Goodnight!", and stuff like that.

So he had a strange relationship with me where he was trying desperately to make me one of his "followers", and I was singularly unimpressed by it. He was a nice guy, he was OK, but he was just one of those incredibly intense and domineering people who just had to control, and was very insecure. He would cover his insecurity by forcing himself on people, and be bolstered by having a constant entourage around him, and if you didn't want to be part of that he wouldn't just ignore it, he became even more determined that he had to be your pal, on his terms. So it wasn't exactly that easy a relationship with Don himself, but the rest of the guys were really nice fellas. But he was a bit hard with them. I've seen him reduce at least two of the band to tears, by publicly humiliating them as to their performance onstage – by "publicly" I mean offstage, but in front of several people – and actually not quitting until they were both crying. He was a real bully boy.

I saw him a couple of times after that tour. I went to see the show back in England, and he came to my house for dinner, but we gradually... well, the band split up and he got another Magic Band. So I got the old one together and said, "Right, come on guys, why don't you have a go?", you know. And I said, "You should call yourselves The Magic Band – you WERE The Magic Band!" It brewed up into some nasty stuff, and they chickened out. We researched it legally and we felt they would have been quite justified in calling themselves The Magic Band, but they chickened out and decided to call themselves Mallard. And I insisted they should not try to replace Captain Beefheart with another, less charismatic frontman, but try to do it themselves – but that's exactly what they did, they got a friend in to sing the songs. And it wasn't a great album. We paid for them to come over to England, put them up for a couple of months and paid for all the studio time and so on.

Were you involved in the recording?
No, no. I kept out of it. In fact, I think I wasn't about at the time, I think we were on the road. I just basically said, "I'll give you the studio time. If you get a deal and make some money, pay me back." But, although the record did come out, nobody made any money so I didn't get paid back. I've seen Rocket Morton a couple of times since then, but... I don't know... Captain Beefheart went back to his trailer in the desert with his wife Jan, made a few more records...

He's painting now, isn't he?
Well he always was, and that's what he went back to, to carry on with his art. But he was a... one of life's characters, who... I mean, music is much, much the richer for Captain Don Beefheart, but like a lot of people of that peculiar sort of naive talent, he was not an easy man. He was doomed by his own personality to destroy everything around him – relationships with his musicians, other people, and particularly his relationships with record companies. He had

this giant chip on his shoulder – everybody was out to get him all the time – and it became insufferable really, because his attitude was constantly that everybody was against him and he was a true artist, and you know... we all KNEW that. He was a talented, special guy. A crazy man, but he had a special something, and he didn't need to keep telling everybody about it all the time. It got really boring, and it pissed off record companies. He would get advances and then go and spend all the money, and he had no concept at all of running the group and the business side of it. He would get money from the record company and then go and spend it all on himself, and the other guys had no food, nothing... I mean, it was just awful, the stories they told. They lived this life, they all wanted to play with Beefheart, they'd all gone into the desert and become his camp followers, but they were actually pretty straightforward guys, all of them... well, apart from one chap, who I think went off the rails a bit, but otherwise they were all fairly regular guys, and they deserved better than they got in terms of both the financial side and the personal relationship that Don insisted on maintaining, which was not too far away from that... was it Rev'd Jones or somebody, who killed all his followers in their hide-out? He was one of those guys, Don. He was a Fuehrer sort of personality, and everything was done by this power and charisma. And people fall for it. Whether it's in Romania, South America... Charlie Manson, Adolf Hitler... there are people out there who are able to somehow carry this off, to dominate people and persuade them against their better judgement. And Don, in a very minor way... I mean, I'm not painting him as an evil figure - well, I am, but I don't mean it to really sound that way - but he had that degree of power should he have wished to have applied it in a particularly unsavoury fashion. As it was he was just a bit of a bully boy, and the guys just cracked up under the strain of it eventually, and it was all very sad.

But he was a great and very talented fella. Maybe he still is – I don't know if he still plays music. The album *The Spotlight Kid* is, for me, the peak point. *Trout Mask Replica* had some great ideas and some fun things on it, but it was kind of hard work. He couldn't play any instruments – he just could not play anything at all, but he used to sit at the piano and just play anything, just a random series of notes, and record it on a cassette and then say to Bill [*Zoot Horn Rollo*] and Mark [*Rocket Morton*], "Right, learn that!" And they'd go off and sit there and learn it note for note. I mean, they could have had a monkey running up and down the keyboard, but that was how the songs were done. And Rocket Morton had the job of always having a notebook with him, and they'd be sitting in a restaurant or something and Don might say something and then say, "I like that. Write it down!", and Rocket Morton would write it in his notebook, and that became part of the lyrics. It was ridiculous, and there was a degree of self-parody in the way that Don did it, because when he was in a good mood and was being fun and cheerful and we were all having a laugh about it he did appreciate... he did parody, in a sense, his own thing, and he could laugh at it – but he used to get very black moods when it wasn't fun, you know. He was a complicated chap.

OK – a quick one before we go. Have you played on any records that we might not know about?
No, I've only played on a few. The Maddy Prior *Woman In The Wings* album. Roy Harper... I played flute on a song called *Home*, in the middle of the night! He was another one who called me in the middle of the night – people must think I stay up all night. Honeymoon Suite... Brian Protheroe... Men Without Hats. I think that's it, apart from the rain forest thing.

Anybody you would like to record with?
Umm... Actually, somebody has asked me to make a record at the moment. There's this flute player in America, Dave Valentin, who wants me to do something. He is very good, an excellent player, a proper jazz flute player. I told him I didn't really want to fly to New York, and I can't play jazz. I said, "I've only got a very limited technique. You may not recognise it because I write my own music, and I only play what I can play. You'd be asking me to play what I can't play." But he got back to me and said he'd really like me to do something on his record. He sent me one of his records, and it is slightly new age, Windham Hill type stuff... the sort of stuff I do, but a bit arty, you know. So I told him to send me a tape, and if I can do anything to it if he sends me the multi-track I'll add something to it – but I've not heard from him since then, so I don't know if anything will come of it.

OH! I HAVE played on another album!! Shit, yes, you've just reminded me! Oh yes!! [*The exclamation marks reflect Ian's genuine excitement as he leapt to his feet to search for the tape.*] It's a group called The Six and Violence, who are a sort of trash/metal/punk/crazy band. I've played on two of their songs, *Bursting Bladder* and *Theological Guns*. You've probably seen this guy Kurt? He's been to gigs here. He is the lead singer. And they are UNBELIEVABLE! They are... I mean, they do make a racket, it's crazy stuff, but it's... it is just on from Captain Beefheart. It's Captain Beefheart meets... the Zorg people! It's a punk... sort of Batman, Gotham City scenario kind of weird punk group, and they scream and shout, and they hurt each other on stage – they come off bleeding! And the drummer has no bass drums, he just plays tom-toms and snare drums, incredibly well, at unbelievable speed, and his feet never touch the ground. I swear his feet are up in the air, and he's still playing. This guy levitates! Apparently he used to keep cutting himself on the cymbals through leaping about so much, so now they have a separate set-up with another guy just playing the cymbals. He tried using bass drums once, but couldn't leap around so much, and you couldn't hear them anyway, so he plays the bass drum parts included in the tom-tom beats. This is a new kind of drumming – kamikaze stuff! Everything is incredibly fast, the songs are never more than about two minutes long, but they are about REAL things. These are out of work, young kids in New York, garage music played with total abandon. They know they are never going to make it, but they do it because they HAVE TO – they have to have a go. And they have a little following around Long Island, New York, and they are actually very good. I went to see them play this club in New York – basically they got a gig there because I said I would come and see them play – and they were surprisingly really good. They really are. John Peel would love them! Well, he wouldn't if I said, "Hey John, listen to this," but if he discovered them himself he would. There is just unbelievable energy there, and some intelligent, if simple, songwriting. The rest of Tull don't like it at all and they don't believe that I really like it, because they do make a total racket and it is quite mind-boggling, but it clearly is all well arranged, and I really do like it. And they are really nice guys as well, a good bunch of kids. Totally dedicated to it, and they have got a lot better in the last couple of years, and they are really quite tight now. BUT... Jethro Tull fans wouldn't like it. The fact that I'm playing... I just played loosely within the context... I just tried to say, "OK, I'm not like them, I don't come from their background and I don't really understand what they are doing," but I treated it in the spirit in which I think they were intending it, and I just tried to play along with it. I just played in that rather "over the top" style, just going for it, you know. One of the songs I played on is really fast, the other is a quirky thing called *Bursting Bladder*.

Ian was spot on with his description of The Six and Violence – magnificent mayhem. And interestingly, given his comments about the three songs on the 1988 box set that he felt were pretty "rubbishy", The Six and Violence's finest recorded moment is indisputably a thrash punk version of Sunshine Day, *littered with hilarious Tull musical references. A masterpiece.*

Chapter 14

MARTIN "MAART" ALLCOCK

(Published in Issue #25, August 1990)

In the summer of 1990 the news reached A New Day Towers that Martin Allcock had recorded a solo album, the eponymously-titled "Maart", due to be released on Woodworm Records that August. DR therefore enticed Maart out for a few drinks (not the hardest task in the world, to be honest...) in his home village near Banbury, Oxfordshire. Poised ready to leap in with a mention of his current fave band Mara! at the earliest opportunity, DR kicked off the interview by asking Maart how he had found the time to record a solo album.

I recorded quite a lot of it on tour, with my midi set up, and polished it up at home. I had in mind before I went into the studio exactly what I was going to do – analogue, if you get my drift, with real guitars and real instruments, and so it only took four days in the studio and two hours to remix the tracks.

Is it all instrumental?
No, there are vocals on three tracks – I had a go at warbling! I play all the instruments as well, apart from a sample of my daughter talking at the end of *The Eight Points Of Guinness*. She had been warbling away while I was using the sampler, trying to get some rain from outside, and every time I switched it on it stopped raining. But she was nattering on and suddenly came out with this one bit that sounded like, "Yeah Daddy!", so I stuck it on the end of that tune. She is 21 months old, so this is her recording debut!

Did you write all the material?
No, there is some of my stuff and some traditional stuff. One of mine, *The Eight Points Of Guinness,* was supposed to be coupled with a tune that I'd heard called *The Seven Points Of Roguery*, but I couldn't find it anywhere in any of my songbooks. I discovered later that it was actually called *The Nine Points Of Roguery*, which explained why I couldn't find it! There are a lot of keys on the album and acoustic guitars, acoustic bass guitar, electric guitar, mandolin, bouzouki – I even borrowed one of Ric Sanders' fiddles and had a go at that. And a bit of singing.

Is there anything you CAN'T play?
Anything that you have to blow or hit. The drums on the album are programmed by me.

Have you ever tried to play a wind instrument?
I've tried the flute. I can play *Bourée.*

Well, you can play the flute then!
I get giddy! I've tried the oboe – I love the sound it makes, and I'd love to play it, but then you are forced into symphony orchestras and so on. Name me one oboe player in rock. No, name me one other flute player in rock...

Thijs Van Leer... the bloke from Horslips... Ray Thomas in the Moody Blues... Men At Work...
Yeah yeah, alright. When I first heard Men At Work I honestly thought it was Ian playing.

Did you take the album round the record companies or did you want to put it out on Woodworm anyway? Did you approach Chrysalis, for example?
I was going to put it out myself, but when Peggy heard it he said he would do it through Woodworm. I don't think Chrysalis would be interested...

Probably not, but maybe one of the bigger companies would be.

There is more chance of getting some airplay with Woodworm I think, and it is a very small-scale venture anyway. We've only done 500 cassettes and 500 CDs, and if it doesn't sell then it means I haven't lost too much money, whereas if it does sell we can easily get some more made.

You have pressed it on vinyl as well?
No, because vinyl is getting too expensive, and so much can go wrong at each stage of production. I've heard a rumour that EMI are phasing out vinyl, although they are denying it at the moment.

But surely 1,000 copies will go just at Cropredy?
Well, that would be great, but I won't be too disappointed if they don't. But there is no new Fairport material in time for Cropredy, so... I'm in with a chance!

Were you always going to play everything yourself, of did you think about getting other people in to work with?
Well, Ralph McTell gave me the idea. I had most of these bits done already, and I was showing him round my midi set up, just showing him what it could do, and he said, "You should put some of this out." It is funny, because I'd been toying with the idea of doing a solo album for ten years and I had all these high-falutin' plans of who I would have on it. But when it came to it I didn't have the time or the availability of musicians, so I just did it myself in the end. I was only going to do 500 tapes originally, but Peggy said, "Let's do CD as well so that we can get airplay." I've got enough material for four or five albums, and I do see myself making another with a full band, but I've talked it over with Peggy and he reckons this one stands up by itself.

Was it all recorded this year, or have you got bits and pieces from various years on it?
It was all recorded this year. I've been playing some of the tunes for hundreds of years, and I've had arrangements of some of them worked out for years.

I'm surprised to see there are no Kieran Halpin songs on there.
A lot of them are untouchable in terms of copyright. He has a lot of problems himself with a lot of his songs, with the politics of the record industry. And the new ones he's doing, he's doing them so well himself it would be a poor imitation if I had a go at them.

You say you've been thinking about doing a solo album for ten years. What were you doing ten years ago then?
Umm... making a solo album! There's a guy called Bill Leader who basically started up the Irish folk revival in terms of recording them and getting them onto vinyl, and in 1977 - when I was with Mike Harding – he gave me unlimited time in his 8-track studio to do whatever I wanted, and so I had a go and did it. And then I couldn't get a deal because I was completely unknown. And a couple of years later when I had the chance to put it out, when I was with the Bully Wee Band, in retrospect the material all seemed too varied and rather obsolete.

What was it? Just folk songs, guitar and vocals?
No, it was... everything. Backward guitar solos and the lot. There was one track that had seven bass guitars and trouserleg! I had these corduroy trousers and put the mike up really close and played them like brushes on a drum. That was before technology!

So nowadays you would sample the trouserleg, obviously!
No, I'd always play it live!

Will you be playing any solo dates to promote the album? Folk clubs and so on?
No. Some of it has been done with Fairport, and maybe one or two others will creep in, but I won't be doing solo gigs. To get that sound in a folk club you'd have to take all the midi and everything, and the few folk clubs that are left are completely against all that sort of thing. Like, how many folkies does it take to change a light bulb? One to change the bulb and 19 to

complain that it's electric! Or one to change the bulb and 19 to sing about the passing of the old one. But this album has got an overall folky feel, and my own tunes are in the traditional style. I like to think that my tunes can be played by anybody who writes folk music, and I've even heard one of my tunes played in a bar in San Francisco by some old guys on their fiddles, and it was a great thrill. It is all stuff that would fit in well with Fairport, but Fairport is a song-based group and there isn't the room for too many instrumentals with the group. I'm doing a few gigs later in the year with my wife Gill, who is a great singer – we'll be playing folk clubs in Bodmin, Truro and Exeter, and it should be a good laugh.

Why didn't you ask Gill to sing on your album?
I just wanted to have a go at doing everything myself really.

You don't want to be the new Richard and Linda Thompson then?
No way. For a start, Richard can write songs, I can't. I write instrumentals, but I can't write songs to save my life. Gill doesn't try to write either, but she sings other people's brilliantly. Every time I try to write lyrics I realise that somebody else said it much better years ago! In fact, nobody in Fairport writes songs.

Is there none of your "The Edge" type guitar soloing on the album?
No, not really. *Lowlands Of Holland* has got a bit of a hairy guitar solo on it, because I bought a Les Paul and I had to use it! A lot of it is very rocky, but still with this traditional theme behind it. A bit more rocky than Fairport might be sometimes.

Have you played it to Ian?
Not yet, no. I gave him a tape of some rough demos at the end of the tour, but he hasn't told me what he thought of it yet. I did one tune that he liked, on the *Master Craftsman* album last year. He really liked my tune and so I said he could have it if he wanted. And a singer called Vicky Clayton liked the tune and wrote some words for it, and is recording it for her new album. She sounds so much like Sandy Denny it is unbelievable.

Ah! Is that the singer whose tape was being played at Fairport's gig in Cullompton when you said to me, "I think that's me on the bass, but I don't know for sure if they kept me on the album"?
No, that was Beverley Craven. There is a review of that album in *Q* this month. It WAS me, by the way – they kept me on three or four songs. There was this note that only my bass makes, and I thought, "Yes, that's me!"

Really? You could tell like that?
Yeah. With it being fretless it's such a personal sound, and there's this one note where there's like… I've played that note so many times that it has worn the wood away underneath and it's got a little growl to it, and I realised it was my bass. I was in a shop a few miles away buying a bottle of wine, and they always have Radio One on, and I heard this intro and I thought, "I recognise that." It was one of the tracks I played on for Beverley Craven and it was all I could do to stop myself from shouting, "I played on that record!" And one other time I arrived home just as they played a Sally Barker track that I played slide guitar on. I rushed into the house to listen to it but I couldn't find Radio One on the tranny, so the wife and I went and sat in the car and listened to it!

You've said previously that your favourite instrument is whatever you are playing at the time. What are you doing at the moment?
I'm really into the bouzouki at the moment. I've ordered a new one which is a cross between a bouzouki and a guitar… it's called a bouzaar. I'll be one of the few bouzaarists in the world! It's got a monster sound. Put a microphone on it and it's like metal. Acoustic metal! I should have that in time for the Tull album, if Ian wants me involved in it.

When will that be?
It is rumoured to be October/November, but it is only a rumour at the moment.

Is the new Fairport album finished?
No. There's another two or three weeks recording to do yet, and then mixing.

Have you asked Ian to play on this one?
No, there are no guests. If you get one guest in then you have to get lots of guests in.

Er... why?
Because there are so many other people that we owe as much to, if you get my drift. I'd love to have David Bromberg play on the album because he is great, and we'd love to have Beryl Marriott play the piano, but then, where do you stop?

Yes, but with Ian playing on the album that would be a bonus for Fairport wouldn't it?
Oh yeah, it would definitely boost sales, but how many people would be buying it because Ian is on it and not because it was Fairport Convention?

Lots, I imagine – but then those people would get to hear Fairport, and I think most would like what they heard. There is already a great deal of crossover of fans of Tull and Fairport, and I only discovered Fairport when I had to meet somebody in London and suggested a Fairport gig as a meeting point. I'd heard some earlier albums and had not really been impressed, but when I saw you live I was utterly amazed. But it is a question of forcing yourself to listen in the first place.
That's right. There's a lot of bands about that if people only listened to them they would be knocked out by them. There's too much to listen to, that's the problem. Too many bands.

When did you join your first band?
When I was at school, when I was about twelve. We used to play Tull and Yes and Gentle Giant, that kind of stuff. I first went to see Tull on the *Thick As A Brick* tour when I was fifteen, and the first album I ever bought was an Island sampler which had *A Song For Jeffrey* on it. I thought, "Yes, great – I'll have some of that!"

Yeah – "In twenty years I'll be playing in that band!"
Ha! Never thought that at all. With Fairport I actually actively did everything I possibly could to join that band, but Tull just came completely out of the blue. In the backroom of this pub on New Year's Day '88, Peggy said, "Ian wants you in the band, playing keyboards." And I said, "Well, you know Peggy that I haven't got any keyboards and I can't play them...!" Apart from that it was no problem! But I rang him and he said he only wanted somebody to play the simple parts and could play the guitar as well, so the advantage of the lack of technique I suppose got me in!

So you actually managed to join your two favourite bands.
Well, amongst some others. I'd always loved Hatfield And The North... Jimi Hendrix... The Beatles...

Not much chance of joining them, I guess! How do you mean, you actively tried to join Fairport?
I used to go and get their autographs – a lot – so they would recognise me, and in '75 Fairport came to Leeds where I was at college and I followed them the next night to Lancaster and helped them load up the gear and so on. I was going to sleep rough that night, but Peggy said there was a spare bed in his room, so we just talked until eight in the morning and he realised that I wasn't just a duffer, you know. So then I would send him tapes of stuff I was doing and we stayed in touch. I sent him tapes of everything, and I was there at important gigs and so on. He got me the odd session here and there, and the day after Live Aid he asked me to join the band.

You said to me a while ago that you decided to devote your life to music when Manchester United started playing badly...
Yeah, that's right! We won the European Cup, and then after that they did nothing, and I needed something else. I wanted a telescope, so my Dad bought me a bass guitar! Just think, I could have been the Royal Astronomer by now... could have had a proper job!

Have you a telescope now?
No. I've got lots of guitars though.

It's been mentioned to me that your collection of instruments pictured in the recent tour programme was pretty small, and did not include any keyboards...
Yeah. When Kenny rang to tell me to get my instruments together for the photo I thought he meant the instruments that I'd be playing onstage. And I didn't bother with the keyboards because they look much the same as any other. But Peggy decided to get everything he owned out, things with an inch-thick layer of dust on them! When I saw the programme I wished I'd got all mine out, because I've got some really nice instruments. I was mizzled!

What jobs did you have prior to becoming a professional musician?
None. I've always been a musician since leaving school. I knew that was the only thing I wanted to do. So prior to Fairport I was scraping round in folk clubs, Mecca ballrooms, Pontins holiday camps, a symphony orchestra, a reggae band, a Teddy Boy band called Route 66 – we had to wear all the Ted gear and groom your hair forward with Brylcreem and all that. We played all these working men's clubs in Yorkshire to these ageing Teds, and if we played one note wrong, one note that was different from the record, they threw things! I was on second guitar, so I was safe, I just stuck to the chords. I played with Mike Harding, the Eric Delaney Band, Edmund Hockridge who was big in the '50s, Hinge and Brackett...!

Really?! You weren't in drag were you?
No, they were. They were in drag, and it was a radio show! The things you have to do to earn a crust... And I worked in theatre as well., in pit bands. I worked for a while with the band that came between The Albion Band and Home Service. That was great, giving it real welly!

You give it some welly with Tull at times, don't you. Do you want to play lead guitar?
No. Too much responsibility, especially with Tull, because you have to follow the flute, you know. In Fairport it is a bit easier because there is a lot of room to do what you want in all the arrangements. Even though the arrangements are fairly set you can still play more or less what you want, whereas with Tull it is much more like playing in a symphony orchestra because you are playing almost, but not actually, written parts.

Have you had any part in the arrangements with Tull in the studio?
On *Rock Island* there are a few ideas I came up with which were kept, but I'm not sure that they weren't things that Ian had subliminally suggested to me in the first place! A few times I thought, "I like that. Yeah, I'll do that," and he didn't complain - then later I thought maybe that's what he wanted me to do all the time, so I wouldn't want to take any credit for that. It's really interesting working with Ian in the studio because you go in for a few weeks and do the backing tracks, then he takes it all home and writes the songs. And with middle-eights and things he'll say, "Right, we'll go to this chord now, then I think we'll go to this one, then we'll go back to that one," and you think, "Oh yeah," and you're writing it all down; and Doane says, "What do you want me to play there?" and Ian taps out the drum part on his knees and Doane has a go at that... And there was one song – I can't remember what it was now – and the middle-eight, he was shouting all these chords out and I thought, "This is really weird, where is he going? How is he going to get back in?" He was going further and further away from the original key, and I thought, "Jesus! How is he going to get back in??" And all of a sudden there were these two little phrases that brought it all back, and then I realised that it was a rhythmic figure, but not a figure that you'd recognise over two bars but over something like sixteen bars, and it just blew me away. It was just brilliant.

Do you have an idea in your mind of what the finished result will be?
No. Even when you're doing your own stuff you can't tell. It is often hard to capture the feel of the original demo once you start doing it seriously, and you think, "Now, what did I have to drink that night to make me play like that?"

Tull never sit in the studio and just jam, to see what happens?

189

Onstage yes, but mainly for a laugh. Not in the studio.

Has Ian always got everything worked out in advance then?
I don't think so… He often comes in and seems to make it up as he goes along. He'll lead us in one direction and listen to us playing it, and maybe decide he doesn't like it, so we take a different direction – but each route we take COULD be fab, and I don't know where his self-editing comes from, how he knows which way is best. But it's all great stuff, and in spite of how complex it can be it's always got that steady rock beat that Americans get off on. Even if it's got alternating bars of seven and nine you can still play four across it.

Er, yeah… I'm sure that means something!
Well, it's mathematical. A bar of seven followed by a bar of nine, then repeated but with different chords, it still adds up to sixteen, which is divisible by four, which most rock'n'roll is in.

Do you ever find that frustrating… when you are in a groove and Ian says, "Let's change it here"?
No, because I love odd time-signatures.

Ah! You MUST like Mara! then…?
Oh, well done! Actually, I saw them in Brittany and they were pretty fab, yes. I was impressed. Danny Thompson was with them then, and he is my hero – one of them… Especially my hero on the stringed pig!

Who are your other heroes?
Lots of people. Kate Bush – I think she walks on water. And especially her recent stuff with the Irish music from guys like Davy Spillane and Donal Lunny. Irish music really moves me, and Kate Bush really moves me, and to put those two together is a luxury I wasn't really expecting. I like Richard Thompson, although he has moved away lately from the style that appealed to me originally. Thomas Dolby is great, has a good sense of humour. Keith Richards… I'm hoping to see The Stones next week, sceptic finger permitting!

It's a pity Tull weren't asked to support them! How do you feel about supporting Fleetwood Mac?
Great. They're a good band – sold lots more records than Tull ever did.

Yes – but so has Max Bygraves I think!
Ha, yeah. But there are quite a few Fleetwood Mac records that I do actually like, and I'm not talking about the old days, which was before my time. I like *Rumours* and that sort of stuff. They have done some good tunes.

How about supporting Peter Maffay? [*at the Hockenheim Festival, August 1990*]
…Well… he's big in Germany…

But so are Tull aren't they? I know Chris de Burgh has always been massive in Europe, but it seems strange that Tull should be third on the bill.
Well, we can't headline every year. Anyway, Chris de Bore headlining gives people with taste a chance to get out of the car-park!

There is Cropredy before all that of course. Doane told me he hopes to guest with Fairport this year.
Yes, we hope he will. The itinerary I've just got from Kenny has Doane arriving a few days after Cropredy, but he is trying to organise it so he can get here earlier. He was great playing with Fairport on the American tour a couple of years ago, and it would be nice to get him onstage with us again.

OK – that's enough of that! How about we start on THESE questions now…?

Chapter 15

DAVID REES

Interviewed by MARTIN ALLCOCK

(Published in Issue #25, August 1990)

At the conclusion of Dave's interview with Maart he turned the tables and interviewed DR…!

As DR wrote at the time, A New Day *was therefore… embarrassed to present the interview that even* Q *magazine couldn't get (unless they wanted to).*

How can I possibly print it? I can't print an interview with me can I??

Yeah! Everybody I've talked to about this thinks it is a great idea, and long overdue. Especially in the band. Ian's dying to read it. Ian and Doane have given me some questions to ask you as well.
Right – when did you first hear Jethro Tull?
1972. I was heavily into Slade and T.Rex at the time, but I stayed at a friend's house for a week and we waded through his older brother's record collection, which included *Led Zeppelin II, Sticky Fingers* and *Stand Up*… and I was knocked out by Tull. It was like nothing I'd ever heard before, although I confess I remember thinking originally the singer wasn't up to much! Then I bought *Living In The Past* on cassette, then *Thick As A Brick*, and then everything else they had done.

When did you first see Tull live?
1974, on the *Warchild* tour. I hadn't been to a concert before, being more concerned at the time with following West Ham, but I remember feeling shattered when I read the "Now Tull Quit" thing in Melody Maker, realising that I would never see them live. So naturally there was no way I was going to miss them when the next opportunity came around. I'm still distraught at missing the *A Passion Play* tour though – especially as Martin Webb did see it!

How many times have you seen them now?
I really couldn't say. I've never counted.

Did you start *A New Day*?
Yes.

What drove you to organise a magazine about Jethro Tull?
It was in 1985, and Tull had disappeared. There was no news anywhere and I didn't know if they were even still in existence. At the time I was working permanent nightshift in a printer's that really had no work at all for ten months of the year. So I started taking my Tull bootleg tapes to work and listening to them all – not that I would dream of owning such things now of course – and I read all the music papers, getting more and more frustrated at not being able to find out what had happened to the band that had become really important to me. And in the adverts in the music papers I noticed all these "fanzines" about groups that I'd never heard of, and I thought, "Why doesn't somebody do one on Tull?" And it did eventually occur to me that I was "somebody", I could read and write, and I had sod all to do for three nights a week. I thought if I put one or two out, maybe somebody would be inspired by it to do it properly.

Did you check to see if there was one already?
I would have known about it if there had been one. So I wrote to Chrysalis to seek their permission, and I wrote to Ian via Chrysalis. I got no reply, so I just did it. And it was crap really. But I made 50 copies of the first issue, and I remember my wife thinking I'd gone mad when I came home with them. She was aware that I'd been doing something, but she thought

I was compiling a scrapbook or something! She didn't believe there could be another 49 people with the same fascination for Tull! But I sent a couple to people who I used to swap tapes with, and put an advert in *Sounds* and they went immediately. So I did another 50, and then another 50, and I think it was about 180 in the end... or the beginning, I suppose.

Is the mag more, or less, successful than you imagined it would be?
More successful, because I never imagined at all that Ian would one day agree to print details of it on the cover of a Tull album!

How big is the circulation now? And is it stable, growing or declining?
About 3,000. It is stable at 3,000, but with many different people all the time. I guess about 6,000 people have had it, and some don't continue or maybe drop it for a year, but about the same amount of new readers join as leave each time. But I must have had about 15,000 enquiries, because people in America think it is free, an official Tull publication.

Did you have any previous journalistic experience? Did you realise what was involved?
No, I've never been a "writer". And I didn't really think about what was involved, because it didn't matter at the time – I didn't really have anything else to do!

On reflection now, would you have started the magazine?
[*Pause*] I don't know. Yes, most of the time it is really enjoyable.

How do you see the mag? Is it an information/history/news/reviews kind of thing, or is it more of a contact thing for the fans.
I see it really as just something to read about Jethro Tull. But when Ian was talking about putting it on the back of *Crest Of A Knave* he said, "What shall we call it?" I said, "Fan Magazine", and he said, "Information Magazine"... which is awkward, because I try to get the information, but - as you know – you can never depend on it! Everything is always changing, and anything can happen between me writing it and the day it actually arrives in the post, and it does concern me that people might be reading everything I've written as gospel, when it might not be by then.

How do you get your facts and/or rumours, and how do you check them out?
In the beginning I used to get them from all over, and they were always rumours – and they were always wrong! Now I hear rumours and I 'phone Kenny Wylie to see if they are true or not, and he says, "Might be...!" No, I always try to leave it until the last minute to check with Kenny, and then just hope it is still the case when people are reading it.

How long did it take you to get through to Kenny?
He got through to me. I remember getting a letter from him saying he would like to meet me. He wrote, "It's OK. We are not going to sue you or anything, but I'm hoping you might be able to tell me what Tull are up to!" I guess John Belville or Dave Pegg must have shown him the mag, and he quite liked it, and he has been really helpful ever since, and so has Peggy.

How much of your time does it take up?
Far too much.

How do you balance running the magazine and following the band against running your own personal life and career?
Not very well apparently... so my wife tells me.

How do you know when to stop working on the mag?
When it gets to two in the morning usually.

But you follow football too, so...
Not really. I follow England, but as a West Ham and Aldershot supporter I have no real interest in League football!

Do you welcome input for the mag, like photos and articles etc? Does that take some of the load off you?
I do welcome input, yes. It doesn't exactly take the load off, because it is not really writing the mag which is a pain, but the mechanical aspects of mailing them out, recording subscribers, opening letters etc. But even that is something I feel I ought to do myself. Many people offer to come round and help me, which is very good of them – but for some reason I've never felt comfortable about people doing things for me which I can do myself, even when I hate doing it. You could call it stupidity, I guess!

Where does you humour come from, especially in the written word?
That must be Doane's question. I don't know... I'm a miserable git really...

Well, that's what comes across! Er, no... The way Doane put it was when he meets you, you keep yourself to yourself, but in the written word there is this sense of humour which comes across.
Well, I don't know. I get letters, twenty or thirty a day, and many of them are really humorous, friendly letters, and when I'm writing the mag I'm really just writing a long letter, which 3,000 people will read. I suppose I am naturally humorous – but deeply miserable with it! Well, cynical, I suppose.

How many of the subscribers have you actually met?
Hundreds now, because people recognise me from the *20 Years Of Jethro Tull* video and come and say hello at gigs.

What's the most bizarre thing that's ever happened in connection with *AND*?
This is! Definitely.

Before that then?
Probably when a girl asked to have her photo taken with me at Cropredy because "it is the next best thing to Ian Anderson"! Or maybe the guy who kept 'phoning me from America at 3am demanding to speak to Ian Anderson. Like we live together! That was partly why we had to change the number and go unlisted, which is a shame because it means genuine people have no way of contacting me in a hurry if needs be. Ian told me that would happen, but I really didn't think people could be so stupid.

Do you see some fans' fanaticism for the band as being almost unhealthy?
Yes. I don't think anybody that I've actually met has been so afflicted - with maybe one or two exceptions – but I get really weird letters sometimes from people who are really in serious trouble regarding their attitude to Ian. In fact Ian told me that would happen too, come to think of it. But people send pages and pages of quotations from the Bible, threats and all sorts of things...

How do you mean, threats?
Not to me, to Ian. If he doesn't "find The Lord" he will be forever damned, you know. Some think he is God, some think he is the Devil.

What do you do with those?
I bin them. I have to read the letters I get for Ian, because I am not going to be in the position of passing on crank mail and death threats – but of course most of the stuff is from normal, sensible people.

How do you, and other people, get so caught up in a band that you become a "fan"? Is it like the music speaking to you?
It's hard to say. I can't speak for others, because some are more fanatical... I don't mean in the "unhealthy" way we were just discussing, but many people tell me that Tull is all they listen to, nothing else at all, which is something I just cannot relate to. I've always bought lots of records, and still do, and many bands have been special to me. But Tull have always been that

bit more, and I really can't say why. I could say, "Because they have always been there", but so were lots of others for years like Floyd and Zeppelin and Deep Purple, whose records I bought religiously until a certain point when I found I didn't NEED the new one. I may have bought it, but it didn't matter so much. Whereas a new Tull album has always been a major event.

How do you feel Tull have changed since you first saw them?
I think they have... aged well! They are still brilliant.

Back in the '70s it was like a very eccentric, mad band. Do you still see that now?
I suppose they had more "characters" then, with Jeffrey and his zebra and John in his ice-cream suit, but maybe it is more of a musicians' band now – but still with lots of humour. Less Pythonesque, more laid back. The humour now is far more natural. On the last tour Ian was really, genuinely funny, almost like a good stand-up comic, and your antics on the side of the stage were like a little side-show of its own. It was great.

What about the music? Do you think Ian still has some clout in terms of what he is doing now?
Oh yes. Songs like *Rock Island, Ears Of Tin, Jump Start* etc are in the same league, in my opinion, as some of the very best from any Tull era, and even Tull fans who would not agree with that still see recent Tull as being head and shoulders above 99% of anything else happening now. It is true that Ian doesn't sing as well as he did before his throat problems, but he has overcome that largely by writing things that he can sing well, and it all feels like a natural progression.

Do you play an instrument, or are you a frustrated musician?
I am definitely a frustrated musician. I'd love to be able to play the guitar, or the sax... or anything, come to think of it!

Have you ever tried?
Yes. I was inspired by Sid Vicious, of all people, because I thought, "If he can play an instrument, anybody can play one!" I bought a guitar, but I never really had the time or patience to practice, and it seemed very difficult – one of those things you can either do or you can't, and I got the impression that I would never be able to play.

Do you own a flute?
No. Maybe I'll win one in the next competition!

When you're at the gig, and you're... [*laughs*]... grooving, do you imagine you are part of the band, taking an active part in it?
No, never. It's not something I could imagine myself doing at all.

What is your secret dream or ambition?
[*Pause*] I don't think I have one. I'd like to see the *20 Years Of Jethro Tull* box set go silver or gold, because me and Martin Webb would qualify for a disc apparently... and a million quid pools win would be fairly useful!

How much longer can you see Tull lasting for?
Well, Ian seems really keen right now and, as I said, I thought this last tour was one of the best, ever. I see no reason why they shouldn't go on for many years, albeit at a slightly less frenetic pace now. The new material would seem to allow for a more laid-back, but still hard-edged live performance. Well, Ian seems keen to me – do you think he is?

Yes, definitely. I get the impression that it is more of a hobby now, in the sense that he is doing it because he enjoys it.
If you had never heard of Tull, would there be any other band you would be driven to write a mag about? Umm – apart from Mara!

I don't think so. I like lots of bands, but I wouldn't want to write about them.

Have you seen any other fanzines?
Yes, I do exchange mags with a few other people.

How do you think *A New Day* compares with the others?
It's the best, obviously! A lot of them are very good – *TAP, Rock & Reel...*

Have you seen *Dirty Linen* recently?
Oh yeah, that's amazing. They have done really well in such a short time. It's better than *Folk Roots* now, and that is very good in itself, despite the anti-Tull and anti-Fairport slant.

[*Laughs*] It's not as good as Andrex! Do you think *A New Day* is good value for money?
Yes. You definitely get "more Tull per pound"! If I paid a quid for it I would be well pleased.

Do you want to expand it, go full colour, etc? Is that possible?
If I do win the pools, yes! I would like to, and it might be possible to do that now and again, but not on a regular basis. [*All issues are now substantially in colour. Eds.*]

You must get a lot of artwork sent in. How do you select each cover?
I just take the best one – assuming I can find it when I need it! I do have many good pieces which I intend to use, but often something comes in which is really excellent. The next one [*#25*] is brilliant, although I imagine it might offend some people...

Do you ever get feedback from the artists if they send it in colour and are disappointed with the result in black and white?
The artwork is nearly always in black and white anyway, but I have many colour photos that are really stunning, but would not translate at all to monochrome, which is a bit frustrating at times.

Would you like more people to send in photos?
Oh yeah. Everything is useful, even if it is not used at the time – you never know when you will need it in the future. And the more photos people send obviously the more chance there is of getting something a bit special.

If Chrysalis were more conducive, in the sense that they took you on full-time as press agent for Tull, how would that go?
I'd love to do it full-time – but then if I did, Sod's Law dictates that Tull would suddenly knock it on the head and I'd be out of work!

Is it at a point where it's almost full-time anyway, like having two jobs?
Yes, it is almost another full-time job – but most of the time I love doing it. I can't actually do it as a job, because I wouldn't get any money!

But if Chrysalis paid you?
What a job that would be! It would be like being the bouzouki player with Jethro Tull, wouldn't it?!

If Tull does pack it in, do you have any aspirations to do something else, using your experience of doing *AND*? Writing things freelance for magazines, for instance?
It would be a nice job, but I wouldn't be able to do it well. To be a good music journalist would be a very difficult thing to do, which is why there aren't many of them.

You do a better job than most.
Well, I would agree actually, but so would most people who read *AND* do a better job. I'm not trendy enough to write for what is now the gutter music press, and I'm not good enough to write for *Q*.

A technical question – is the mag organised on computer or just typed?
It is done on a word-processor now, which is a bit of both I suppose, but I've not yet ventured into the computer side of things. The instruction leaflet has 600 pages in it, so I went to about page 250 for the word processing and called it quits! But I got it mainly to compile a mailing list, which will save me weeks of work in the future... I hope!

What do you think about Tull using computers onstage?
The keyboard parts, you mean? I think it's OK, it's just for the "mood" stuff, isn't it? I don't regard that as cheating, although I know some people do. I thought Don Airey was a bit off when he pretended to actually play it, like the *Steel Monkey* track, but it's fun watching you conducting the keyboard and "playing" the part on the wooden box surround. It is valid when used only for things like that. It's not as if Ian is miming the flute parts or something.

But in the past Jethro Tull have maybe gone a bit far with computers?
In what sense?

Well, that's what a lot of fans have told me.
Oh, *Under Wraps*... well, I thought that was brilliant. But I am in a minority there I guess. Do you like it?

Er... I don't know it! I've never had to learn anything from it. It is a problem joining a band that's been going for twenty years, there's too much music to catch up on. I don't know all of Fairport's stuff either. But I really like Peter Vettese, he is a brilliant musician. I'm very envious of him because he is so good. Do you go to see other bands that have ex-Tull members in them, like Simple Minds?
Oh no. I wouldn't go to see them just to see Peter Vettese. I like Peter and I would go to see HIS band, because I think he would have a good band, but not Simple Minds. I go to see Blodwyn Pig, but that's because they are a great band.

Chapter 16

JEFFREY HAMMOND-HAMMOND

(Published in Issue #28, April 1991)

One of the most memorable characters in Jethro Tull's history was bass-player Jeffrey-Hammond-Hammond. His name was legendary to Tull fans even before he joined the group, having appeared in the song titles A Song For Jeffrey, For Michael Collins, Jeffrey and Me *and* Jeffrey Goes To Leicester Square. *He had even been mentioned in the sleeve-notes to Tull's first album* This Was *– "He is one of us but doesn't really play anything. Makes bombs and things."*

As someone who had been at school with Ian Anderson and John Evans, and had been with them in the pre-Tull bands The Blades and The John Evan Band, Jeffrey would obviously have an interesting tale or two to tell, not least because no interview with him had ever previously been published. Indeed, just tracking him down was a challenge in itself – but, like the Mounties, A New Day *always gets their man, and one afternoon in 1991 DR and MW motored to his house buried deep in the English countryside to nail our world exclusive. Jeffrey had earlier warned that there were certain things he would rather not discuss, which was a bit worrying; but thankfully that was just a desire not to talk about his current life and his paintings, and he spoke with great frankness, humour and charm about his time with Tull and the pre-Tull bands.*

We started by talking about the 1990 Jethro Tull Fan Convention, which Jeffrey had attended unannounced. It seemed that he was pleased with the way it went...

Yes, I enjoyed the Convention very much. I was a bit dubious about it at first, to be honest, because obviously I had no idea of what it would be like or what sort of people would be there. But I thought there was a very nice atmosphere there, and I was quite touched in a way that people should actually remember me and recognise me from what was really quite a long time ago. It was a bit of a humbling experience in a way to realise that it was and is important for many people. And I do remember somebody saying as I was leaving, "Thanks for giving up your Saturday to come here." That was nice, and really that was one of the things that convinced me I should do this interview, because obviously people are still interested, and it is the least I can do.

You told me on the 'phone this week that this interview would be a new experience for you. Is this actually the very first interview you've ever done?
No, I did one before, shortly after I left Jethro Tull, and I was not particularly organised in myself to do it. I did it because I was asked to do so, and I rather regretted it afterwards because I said quite a lot of silly things which had more to do with my state of mind at the time than with things I really wanted to say. That is the only other interview I've ever done.

Was that for a music paper? We've never seen it...
No, it was for an Australian chap who I think was writing a biography. He came here and we got snowed in, and we got to talking probably rather too much, and as I say maybe I got rather carried away and said things I regretted. But fortunately nothing came of it... [*laughs*]... presumably because of what was said! I think Barrie and John talked to him as well, but the book never appeared.

Was it that Ian didn't allow you to speak to the press, or you didn't want to, or were you never approached?
I think it was a mixture of reasons. I think Ian, being so articulate, took the lead in the matter, and he was terribly good at it. Maybe nobody else felt the need to speak to the press unless one was asked – and I don't think one was asked very often. So this is quite a big occasion!

It's surprising to hear you weren't asked, because when you were with Tull they were at the very top of the league, weren't they?
I was very fortunate in that I joined them when they had become really very successful beyond England...

It's surprising then that the whole group, rather than just Ian, were not pursued by the music press...
Well, I don't recall it, you know. I've always been quite secretive about where I live [*laughs*] so possibly it was quite difficult to get hold of me. But I honestly can't remember me or any of the others being approached, and as I say Ian took the lead in the matter anyway, as he had done before I joined, and obviously he spoke for everybody.

We always seem to start our interviews with, "What is your real name?"...
Hmm... my real name is Jeffrey Hammond. When I joined Jethro Tull Ian suggested Hammond-Hammond, and I must admit I liked the idea. It is actually not too much of an affectation because my mother was called Hammond before she married my father. People had the habit, especially Americans, of calling me Hammond-Hammond rather than Jeffrey, which I rather liked. Of course I gave it up when I left Tull and reverted to a singular Hammond.

Were you born in Blackpool?
Yes, I was.

When did you first meet Ian?
We were both at Blackpool Grammar School and we met in the 6th Form there. That's how I met Ian and, shortly afterwards, John.

Did you become friends initially because of your interest in music, or was it friendship first which led to the musical partnership?
Well, Ian and I had been in the same class for some time without speaking to one another, but I do remember him coming up to me in the Geography room and saying something like, "You look like a musician, " or "You look like a bass player," or something that indicated I might be interested in music. Obviously I said "No" because I didn't play an instrument. But I'd always loved music, and that was how we became friends, just through wanting to play an instrument, which Ian managed in a strange way to be able to teach me... something about it, anyway. So that was how The Blades began. It wasn't what you would call "the school band", but that was the catalyst for starting it up, the school friendship. We were at that age when you look for interests beyond school life and it seemed quite a natural thing to do. I don't know how far Ian and John had got in terms of thinking about a group. As you know, John had a drumkit and had learnt piano formally, and Ian had started messing around with the guitar. Ian did have a friend called Hardman - which was something of a misnomer because he was a bit of a wet fish - but he seemed to quickly drop out of it. So the three of us spent quite a lot of time together learning music, listening to music, and generally becoming great friends. The process of it becoming a group was I suppose actually quite a long-winded one, because after all I couldn't play a note when I first became friends with them. It took some time to even get to the stage where we could thrash out one tune.

Ian has said he was inspired to form a group after seeing The Atlantics. It seemed like "a good way to pull the birds"...
Yes, I remember reading that. I think that was partly true. John and Ian had been to a youth club close to John's house, and I remember them enjoying that band and liking the idea of being in a group, and it was impressive – but as an idea rather than the actual music they played or anything specific about them as a group. They were very clever at copying other people's tunes, and very professional. They had obviously been going some while I should think. I would though take you to task on that family tree (*AND #21*) which appeared to show that The Blades sort of grew out of The Atlantics. That was not strictly true at all. As much of your original information came from Chris Riley who was also in The Atlantics at some point

I can understand that he would see things from that perspective, with The Blades being a continuation of the story – but The Blades started as a separate entity and didn't grow out of The Atlantics in any way whatsoever. Michael Stephens came from them and joined us at some point later.

So The Blades actually started as a three-piece?
Well, yes, in a way I suppose it did, although it wasn't actually thought of as a three-piece because it didn't actually do anything as such, and yet it existed simply as people learning about music and what a group should be. We didn't have anywhere near the sort of equipment needed for performing and it did take quite a while from the initiation of the idea of there being a group to its fruition in terms of its first performance. So many months went by when at weekends and holidays the three of us congregated in John's mother's front room. Certainly when Michael Stephens came to us from The Atlantics it became a more sensible outfit in terms of having a guitarist, which I think then allowed Ian to concentrate on singing. We began to rehearse in The Holy Family youth club, and I still remember the first time somebody came into the room while we were rehearsing – what an odd feeling it was the very first time I knew that somebody else had heard what we were playing. A very strange feeling, but quite pleasant in a way.
But, to get back to The Atlantics, that was where we saw them play, and I think Ian and John were perhaps more impressed than I was, probably by their musicianship, because as you know I've never thought of myself as a musician. One had a lot of respect for their ability to be able to play so well other people's songs, and I suppose you have to do that to a certain extent when you begin, and it is good to be able to do that; but my interests were slightly different, in that I think I was looking for other things rather than simply the willingness to slavishly copy other people's material, however well it might be done. I don't mean to be... well, obviously I am being over-critical. I don't mean it to sound too derogatory or in any way pompous. It just wasn't the sort of thing that appealed to me.

What made you choose bass as your instrument?
I think because it seemed to be the simplest. Only four strings, no chords... Ian sang and played the guitar, John played the drums, so the only opening for me was to be the bass player. You see all of this must sound quite strange, but it seems quite natural to me, in a way, in that the music, although a very very important part of it, was ONLY a part of it. To me – and other people might disagree with this now – at the time friendships were a really important part in one's growing up, and there was a sense of togetherness. Whilst other people might not agree with that now, I think it would be rather sad to forget that one went through a period of time when... well, we were very close friends.

What about your very first gig?
It must have been... I don't remember, really...

You don't remember?? It wasn't a nerve-wracking or eventful night?
Well, I suppose it must have been, but I really can't remember it. As I think I indicated before, the most memorable moment was the first time somebody actually heard us rehearsing. I remember that as my most nerve-wracking moment, and funnily enough I can't remember the first actual gig. I know we used to do a rather wide range of music, never one particular thing, and that was interesting. One might have had a period when one was engrossed in a certain kind of music and two months later it would change. It wasn't a case, as with The Atlantics for instance, where they would do whatever was in the hit-parade at the time. But of course they were professional, or semi-professional, and they had to do that sort of thing, but I don't think we ever got involved in doing that.

That was one of the reasons Chris Riley left The Atlantics, because they had a management that pushed them into doing that.
Yes, so I believe. They actually had a management. I mean, that was quite serious! In many ways we were... well, it wasn't amateurish, because we really were quite sincere about it - but

it was before it became really serious that I enjoyed it the most, in terms of just enjoying what you do for its own sake.

Was there ever a thought when you started that this would be 'your profession'?
Not with me, I don't think so. It just grew out of friendship and it was just another thing to do, another... 'hobby' is perhaps not the right word. It became in a way an all-consuming interest in time because it did become more serious, but for me personally it wasn't something that I thought I would do for the rest of my life. It was a natural thing to do that people did at that time. Being in a group was the thing to do, and I was fortunate to be involved with people who were musically talented as well as having something to say. Because it was about that... having something to say, having a direction and a purpose about it rather than just copying tunes. There was a real sense of direction about it, a real sense of spirit. That's how I remember it.

Does the name Harry Hartley ring a bell?
Oh yes, he was in the same class. He was mostly interested in folk music, but he was an amusing sort of character and so I think I sort of dragged him along occasionally and he did perform with us a few times, playing harmonica. But he often used to sit on the stage and read a newspaper or something... just to look the part, you know. But he wasn't actually a full member of the group.

Apparently Ian was impressed with your huge record collection?
I don't remember that Ian had many records – I don't think he did. I think John had some. John's taste was... [*laughs*]... slightly odd. When I say odd, I mean just different from mine, but he had a classical training and he had a good knowledge of the classical side of music. I was interested in a broad range of music, and I suppose I did spend money on records. Music was always an important part of my life before I even got involved in The Blades, and we did all often sit around and listen to records. The trouble with me is that I tend to get highly obsessed with one performer or type of music and want to listen to that all the time, find out as much as I can about it and buy every album by that person, and then absorb and discard it and move onto something else. A terrible habit, and I still do it sometimes. And it means of course that I don't listen to some music from years and years ago when, you know, there is nothing wrong with that music, but you feel in a way that you've grown out of it. That might be a good thing but... well, it was certainly a good thing then because it did allow me to hear a wide range of different music, and when one begins any kind of creative carer it's probably not a good thing to have just one or two heroes - particularly if they are idiosyncratic, when one can end up being a poor imitation of whatever that is. It is important to have a wide taste in music.
In fact, another of the things that convinced me that I should do this interview was reading the interview that Martin Allcock did with you in issue #25 [*Chapter 15*] You said that Jethro Tull, as much as you like them, isn't the only thing that you listen to or are interested in, and I thought that was rather pleasing, because I was slightly... well, I didn't know anything about you, and I was slightly concerned about the thing being fanatical in that kind of bizarre way that one finds in America, and it was reassuring to know that you have a range of interests beyond the group... [*laughs*]... as interesting as they might be!

Do you still buy a lot of records?
Not really, no. I have a small collection of CDs, mostly Haydn, Handel and Mozart. I do listen to classical music on the radio, but I'm slightly out of touch with rock music, although I'm aware of the more popular aspects of it. But I suspect I miss the better quality music which probably needs seeking out. I don't really have time to do that. It's probably laziness on my part.

When did The Blades become The John Evan Band?
Well, again I'm hopeless on dates. I did try to think about it when I knew we were actually going to talk about it, and quite seriously I seemed to discover years missing from my life that I couldn't account for at all. It was a real struggle to look back and try and work out what

happened. But I'm sure there was that period when we were in the 6th Form together, when we were The Blades. Ian left school at some point. He realised he didn't want to carry on studying, so he got a job at John Lewis's as a trainee shop manager. When Barrie joined we were still called The Blades, so it must have been some considerable time... about two years I suppose, as The Blades. I don't mean two years as a working group, but from the very start of getting together to become a group, as it were.

It was a lot of fun, very enjoyable, because although it was serious in a way, we didn't have to worry about what other people thought of us. We didn't worry about whether or not we got re-booked to the various sweaty youth clubs we played. But as to the actual transition from The Blades to the John Evan Band... I'm afraid I can't help you. It was clearly a gradual change. When we first started there was a Polish chap called Henry who was a friend of John's mother, and he used to drive us to gigs in his builders van. That was very helpful, as was John's mother in terms of helping us buy equipment and so on. And John was exceptionally good at building speaker cabinets, and my very small contribution was to paint names on the side of the cases and the van! Later on John passed his driving test and so became the permanent driver, and also he decided that he wanted to play the organ rather than the drums, so we had to get a new drummer. Barrie came along, and of course he was eminently suitable – extremely young, but very capable and enthusiastic.

What is your recollection of the reason behind calling yourselves The John Evan Band? We've heard theories ranging from John being the musical force behind the band to John's mum having paid for the group van...
I seem to recall it was just a nice sounding name, and other groups named their band after the organist. I'm sure that's all there was to it. I wouldn't say John was the major musical influence in the band, but because he had the formal training he did organise and clarify things perhaps, so that we did things correctly. And obviously it was a great help to have somebody with some classical training. Somebody who knew what he was talking about, in fact.

What about any of the other characters in the band? Presumably you've heard about Tony Wilkinson...?
Yes. Very sad... I liked him a lot. He was, as you described, a larger than life character. The only disagreements I remember in the band were when he and Barrie [*laughing*] didn't get on very well. But it is inevitable really that things like that will happen. I don't know what sort of a musical impact he had. It was changing from the four-piece to a six- or seven-piece band, and the music changed too, to a sort of popular soul music. I liked that music, but I didn't particularly enjoy playing it. The group was changing, and growing from a thing that one did largely for reasons other than just the music into something more serious, where one had to take account of what other people wanted to hear. There was a certain amount of pressure to perform a certain type of music which required trumpets and saxophones – the type of music that is on that tape of yours. And though that was... well, quite good, it became almost exclusively that sort of thing, inevitably so because of course you had to make use of the extra musicians. Yes, it was interesting, it was growing, but growing into something that I didn't enjoy as much as what had gone before. But they were entertaining people... Tony was a nice chap. And Martin Skyrme and Jim Doolin, I liked them too.

Is that why you left, because the music changed?
It was partly that, but partly it was a loss of... well, a crisis of faith in a sense. It seemed to me that it was becoming one-dimensional, and obviously a lot more serious. There was by then a management involved. That was good for a while, it was exciting with all these new people coming onto the scene, and we did all these gigs that you've heard about, going up and down the country with John driving all the time. But it started to become repetitive – the same kind of clubs, the same kind of music, and there seemed to be a lack of direction in terms of a creative side to it. I'm talking here almost beyond the music, if you know what I mean, because as you know musically I was somewhat inept. It was more the feeling rather than the actual music which caused me to leave. I also had a certain amount of parental pressure to actually do something with my life, which was fair enough, you know. I was at that age when

parents do tend to [*laughs*] make a nuisance of themselves. Just the kind of thing that everybody goes through. So it was partly that, combined with this lack of direction. I suppose if I had been stronger musically, had I been capable and 100% committed to it, I'd have stayed and tried to do something about it, to change things and make my own feelings felt. But probably the case is that I knew I wasn't like that, and I knew that my interests in the long-term lay elsewhere, so I left to go to art school. It was rather sad, mainly because of leaving the friendships and people that I'd know for such a long time. It wasn't an easy thing to do, but then changing direction isn't an easy thing to do. It was just something that I felt I had to do.

Did you completely lose contact with the band?
Yes, I did, for a couple of years. Of course they carried on in a more serious and committed way, doing all these gigs and trying to get on. I think Ian didn't start writing songs for some time after I'd gone. If he had been writing when I was in the band maybe that would have put a different light on things for me.

You mentioned earlier pressure to play certain things – was that pressure from audiences, management, or elsewhere?
Well, perhaps pressure is the wrong word. It was just that if one wanted to do well it was expected that one would do certain things. I even remember dressing in those bizarre hipsters and throwing talcum powder over my hair in The Twisted Wheel in Manchester, just for the sake of having to do that, to get on, as it were. But again it goes back to that lack of direction. Had Ian been writing songs there would have been a much more creative spirit to it, and more of a reason for carrying on. In a sense, although it's easy to say this with hindsight, perhaps one was looking for that kind of thing then. One wanted - well, I know I did anyway – to play that kind of music that he later wrote. Obviously I was incapable of articulating that to him then, just as he wasn't ready to write that music then.

To what extent was Ian "the frontman" at that time?
Oh, totally. He was the singer, and he was significantly the frontman. Obviously everybody within the group had their own ideas and they would throw in their ten-pennyworth, and in a sense that led to the lack of direction because there were so many people all pulling in different directions. Again, perhaps if Ian had been strong enough at the time, which he obviously later became, to be not just the frontman but also writing the material which then meant that it became his group as it were, with him fully in charge... I do think that groups tend to work better with somebody firmly in control, with a clear sense of purpose. But they were still doing this soul music, and I just couldn't see any chance of the group being successful in any way, shape or form because of this lack of creativity. And of course in a way it was only when Ian began writing that they started to become successful.

Were you surprised at the subsequent success of Jethro Tull?
Well, in one way yes, of course I was, because it is a difficult thing to do - to create something, and for it to be wanted, to be liked. So in a way I was surprised, but in another way of course one had always admired and respected Ian's talent, even though I'm talking about the years I knew him as a friend, even when he wasn't writing music. One could tell there was something there, as other people may have said, that he had this ability, musically or otherwise. Again, not just musically, but this sense of purpose about himself and the tenacity to see it through. And that showed too when the others started dropping out, when John and Barrie left, for example. It wasn't very long after that that Jethro Tull had such enormous success, largely through Ian writing songs. To me, that is what it is, and always has been, about.

Did you go to see Tull in those early days?
Oh yes.

You'd obviously got back in touch then?

Well, I'd gone to art school in Blackpool for a year. They carried on as they were, and you know the story from there, with people leaving and Mick Abrahams and Clive Bunker joining, and they were planning the move to London. By then I was in my first year at art school in London, and Ian was looking for somewhere to live. Somehow or other he got in touch with me and I was able to get him a room in a house owned by my landlord, although not in the same place as me. Later John came to London to go to University and he too took a room with the same landlord, so I saw a good deal of him then, listening to music together etc. It was the early days of the band though when they had just decided on the name Jethro Tull, and I used to go to gigs with them at weekends, and we all travelled in a van, so they had obviously not become too successful yet. They used to play University gigs, pubs, small halls and so on, and I would go along and enjoy their performances.

Were you impressed?
Oh yes, very much, because of course it had changed dramatically from the band that I had left. It was a totally different thing. Ian was writing interesting songs and they were giving quite serious performances. It was really enjoyable to see him being rewarded for all the previous hard work. I suppose that would have been just before they recorded *This Was*.

You are credited with "making bombs and things" in the sleeve-notes to *This Was*. What exactly is that all about?
I don't know. I haven't a clue... nothing to do with me!

How did it feel having songs written for you, like *A Song For Jeffrey* and *Jeffrey Goes To Leicester Square*?
Quite flattering, I suppose. I must admit to a certain amount of vicarious pride and pleasure at being associated with the group, however tenuously. I'm not sure whether these songs were for me as it were, it was probably just a name, you know. But it was just nice to be back in touch really, because after all I had left and been out of it, and I'd made no attempt whatsoever to keep in touch, which is what I'm rather famous for doing, and just got on with my life. It was really rather nice to know this friendship was to be renewed. And yes, I enjoyed those songs a lot, and it seemed that was what they should have been doing three years before. It was great to see them doing that sort of stuff, and doing it tremendously well.

You were 15 years ahead of *A New Day* with your newsletter *Jeffrey's Journal...*
What was that? I don't know anything about that.

Really? It was an attempt at an official Tull fan club, purportedly run by you. Your signature was on it.
I've never even heard of it! I'd be interested to see it. I honestly don't know anything about that at all. I supposed they just used my name.

Another oddity – when you joined Tull Ian told the press that you had previously been engaged in making owls...
No, that was a friend of ours called Frank. He used to make owls from rabbit skins – which won't of course be of interest to anybody reading this, but it does illustrate an instance where [*laughing*] embellishments were used by Ian to make an amusing story. It was an odd little story. But I don't mind that sort of thing at all.

You say you don't mind, but I think it was Chris Riley who said you tended to be the butt of Ian's humour, and he thought sometimes it was a bit cruel. Is that fair?
Well, you know, I think friendships are a two-way thing, and in public it might have seemed like that, but in a way it was almost like a Laurel and Hardy type thing. Perhaps it seemed odd to outsiders, but it wasn't to those who were closer to us. And even today he ribs Martin terribly onstage, but everybody knows it is a bit of an act, and they are actually very good friends.

How did you get the call to join Jethro Tull?

I was just leaving art school. I was in this dead-end situation where I wanted to carry on painting but it was going to be very difficult to do as a profession. I'd kept in touch with Jethro Tull, and John Evans had just joined them to do *Benefit*. In fact I remember going to the studio to hear them record that *Witch's Promise* single. Glenn Cornick left the group "by mutual agreement" as they say, after an American tour. I was living in Ian's house – in fact I was decorating it for him – and so Ian said, "How about joining Tull?" So I was very fortunate to be in the right place at the right time, and to have the old boy network working in my favour. It was a really tremendous opportunity and exceptionally exciting. So as soon as they came back from the tour we started recording the album *Aqualung*, and getting ready to tour again. I remember going around buying some unusual stage gear, flying goggles and so on. I very clearly remember the first concert I played in Odense in Denmark. It was a long time since I'd been onstage anywhere and I hadn't realised how hot it was - and I was wearing these goggles which just steamed up half way through the first song. I couldn't see a thing! It was very much a case of "in at the deep end".

Ian had this "ostrich theory", in that the more clothes you wore, the less people could see you...
[*Laughing*] Yes, I think that's probably true. The goggles, long black cloaks, the trilby and so on, trying to keep out of it as much as possible... which wasn't really the ideal thing to do in a group which was hugely popular. But I think it was just the shock of being in a group, and a very successful one at that. It wasn't as though I had served a great apprenticeship, except in the very early days. It was a shock and it took some time to get used to it.

How would you put your creative input into Jethro Tull?
In percentage terms, you mean? About minus 100...

Ian described you as a very creative, anarchic force in the band.
Probably not directly musically. Obviously not in the terms of actually writing music or anything like that. Maybe in other ways though, which would be hard to define. I wouldn't be the ideal person to talk about that anyway.

***Thick As A Brick*, for example. The concept and the concerts involved more than simply music. Plenty of Monty Python type humour...**

Well... yes, I can see the Monty Python comparison, although I wouldn't actually agree with that. Yes, there were lots of other things going on aside from the music but, as I said at the beginning, to me the group was always more than just the music. Obviously the music was great and very exciting, and a very very important part of it, but nobody just stands on stage and plays music. Of course things like that, stage performances, have gone totally over the top in years since then, but at the time I suppose it was fairly innovative and different, although it seemed to me to be completely natural. It wasn't forced or contrived, except of course that we had to work out what we were going to do. It all seemed completely natural and went well with the music. It was quite a creative period, and I suppose you are right to say that some of that came from me, but to categorise it would be impossible to do. Talking of *Thick As A Brick,* it does remind me of people in America constantly talking about the crossword puzzle on the sleeve. That, to me, was taking things to an absurd level of fascination because, OK, it was interesting, but it wasn't what it was all about. It wasn't the essence of the thing.

***The Hare Who Lost His Spectacles*, slap in the middle of *A Passion Play*, was anything but natural. It was extraordinary really, wasn't it?**
I think it was rather, yes! You see, *Thick As A Brick* had been quite a departure from what had gone before, and it is always difficult to follow something like that. I know a lot of people thought what came after that, namely *A Passion Play*, struggled to keep up with it. I did not see that myself, but I think maybe things did get out of line where one felt one had to do more and more of it, and it became almost manic in a way. In fact when one thinks about it, I probably wasn't a very good influence after that, in the sense that perhaps those kind of things got too important in relation to the music. Eventually of course they dropped away quite naturally, but it did take time.

Well what about *The Hare*... Are you a natural storyteller/writer?
Well, you can tell I'm not a natural storyteller by the way that I'm talking to you. It was described, probably correctly, as a bit of whimsy, which is OK – but I suppose it is very difficult to measure how much of that kind of material one should allow to creep in. Perhaps that was rather too much...

When we were listening to unreleased tracks for inclusion on the *20 Years Of Jethro Tull* box set, we heard the version of *Sea Lion* with you on lead vocals. Was there more of that stuff recorded?
Ah yes... *Cecil Was A Sea Lion*. What I do remember liking is - and this is getting away from what Jethro Tull, or rather Ian, is all about – was that at that time we were recording at the Chateau studios we had a lot of free time when the equipment was set up, and we could go and mess about and do stupid things, which I think can be quite a rewarding thing to do, although maybe from Ian's point of view [*laughing*] that wasn't the case. It was that kind of thing that really excited me, and it probably wasn't good for Jethro Tull - it was getting away from what the group is, and what Ian wanted to do. And generally Ian does what he wants to do, which is fair enough because he is in charge of the whole show. I think there was quite a bit of music recorded for *A Passion Play* which wasn't used. A lot was recorded in the Chateau studios which was quite good...

Surely Chrysalis have sent you a copy of the box set?
No, I haven't had one.

That's unbelievable! Well, they found about twenty minutes of the Chateau recording, of which about twelve minutes or so were included on the box set.
I think there was quite a bit more than that recorded. Barrie has heard some of it since and he said it was very good. He was quite proud of it I think.

It is tremendous stuff. Most people seem to regard it as the highlight of the whole collection. Do you recall why it was not used at the time? Was it purely Ian's decision?
I imagine so. I can't honestly remember now. I just remember it being enjoyable to do. But I don't think that what replaced it was any worse or any better. I personally liked and enjoyed playing the *A Passion Play* music, although I know many people are perhaps not as enthusiastic as I am about it.

One of the few things that we both agree on is that *A Passion Play* is possibly Tull's finest album.
Oh really? I very much enjoyed doing it, and I know that when it came to live performances it was difficult, technically, to get the show off the ground, and it didn't go terribly well. But I do think it was a fine piece of music, and followed on from *Thick As A Brick* very well, which was quite a difficult thing to follow. What I like about both of those albums is the move away from the idea of music being just three-minute songs. I know there were at that time a lot of so-called "concept albums", but I think in many cases people did them purely for the sake of doing them. But I think in the case of both those Jethro Tull albums there was nothing of that idiom about them at all, but rather it was the kind of music that the group, really as a group rather than just Ian taking too firm a hand, produced quite genuinely and naturally. I don't mean to say that each member wrote some of the music, but the band as a whole developed the music in a genuine sense of togetherness which wasn't always evident at other times. It was good, and I am pleased to hear that you feel the same way.

Do you think with hindsight that it was a mistake to premiere it live rather than to release the record before the concerts?
Probably. I seem to remember [*laughs*] it was not critically acclaimed at the time, and I think it was Terry Ellis, the manager, who announced that the group was offended by what the press was saying and so they were to quit playing live. That was the most catastrophic thing he could say, and I just did not understand it. It was completely beyond me. Because I didn't read the reviews, and I don't think any of the others did. You know, who gives a shit what

anybody else thinks anyway? But there was no truth in the "Tull Quit" story, and for whatever reason it was put out it certainly back-fired and it did the group no good at all. I remember people in the band being furious about it.

What did you think of *Warchild*, which started as a very ambitious project, with the planned feature film and accompanying orchestral soundtrack?
Ian did talk to me about it, but I was not really involved in the film side of it, so I can't really tell you much about it. I know it was a serious project, and it did seem that it was going to happen, but I don't know what became of it. I liked *Warchild*. I thought they were good, short songs, and again it was something different to what had gone before. I particularly liked the string section we used, and they were a nice complement to the live shows as well. I don't think they enjoyed it quite so much though because they were generally seated next to my bass speakers and were continually asking for the volume to be turned down – it used to make them bounce up and down on their seats, and I think they were probably stone deaf by the end of the tour!

That was the time of your striped suit and striped bass...
Was it? I remember quite some time before that trying to find some material that had stripes on it, but I couldn't get any. So I bought some white jeans and a white T-shirt and Ian and I taped some stripes on. But that didn't work too well, so we actually sprayed stripes on with paint. That didn't work too well either because [*laughs*] we found you could actually stand the trousers up on their own! But when we got back to England I managed to find some material and had a suit made. So I had a striped suit and a striped bass, so the zebra went well with those, and seemed to fit in with the gorilla suits and rabbit suits that the band used anyway at the time!

Everybody seems to regard you as being eccentric. Is that fair?
[*Laughing*] Well, you've met me. What do you think?

You would seem to be absolutely normal!
Exactly. Somebody you spoke to described me, quite remarkably, as being both "eccentric" and "like wallpaper", all in the same sentence. I know of some people who would regard that as a compliment, but I think most people that know me would put me somewhere between those two extremes. Exactly where, I wouldn't like to say...

Do you suppose that reputation comes from the outrageous stage clothes you used to wear?
Maybe. But again it was quite a natural thing to me, it wasn't forced or false in any way. Everybody used to wear odd things, you know. It was probably bound up with the way that people wanted to express themselves. There was no great reason behind wearing those clothes, but again it was simply me doing something because I wanted to do it. Obviously I didn't wear those clothes when I wasn't onstage. In fact, my clothes offstage were far more outrageous! Stage clothes were an important part of the presentation of the individual characters in the band. And certainly when I was in the band they were all very distinct characters... Having said that, I'm not meaning to be derogatory about those who were in the band either before or after me, I don't mean that at all. In fact I very much enjoyed listening to them after I'd left. It is very difficult when you're involved to appreciate it as much as when one can stand back objectively and see it. In one sense I enjoyed the music more when I wasn't in the band. I really enjoyed them before I joined, when I could stand back and admire the performance, and musically they were considerably better after I'd left.

Have you seen the band often since you left?
I went to see them in Bristol a few years afterwards, and I enjoyed it very much indeed. That was when David Palmer was in the band. And it is good to see them carrying on and writing the same standard of songs throughout all that length of time. It's excellent to have that longevity when lots of other people have simply fallen by the wayside, as it were. And Ian has done that in a way that I very much admire, doing what he wanted to do for himself, and not

caring too much about this business of fashion and trends. One takes account of that to a degree, but it goes back to this business of having a single-minded, clear idea of what one wants to do.

Do you ever miss being in the band?
Umm... I miss the people. I can't really say I miss being in the band. It was something that I did, it was a part of my life, and I thoroughly enjoyed it, but there were other things that I wanted to do for myself. I think if I'd been a good musician [*laughs*] then maybe I'd have formed another group, because whilst I was perfectly happy with nearly everything that Ian wanted to do, I have a personal drive that I have to express in my own way, which is something I can't do musically.

Is that true though? Would you really say that you are not a good musician?
I would, yes. Fortunately I'm able to say that now. Having read what other people have said about me, I don't feel at all embarrassed or disloyal about saying it. I think in the past one of the reasons I was paranoid about doing interviews was how on earth I could pretend otherwise when it came down to actually talking about being a serious musician. But it seems that other people have said it enough times now...

What Ian said exactly was that you weren't a natural musician, but you could play anything once you'd learnt it...
I was capable of doing what was required, that's the truth of the matter, and in a funny way maybe they had to come down to my level, because they were all very fine musicians. And I do think one can go too far the other way. It may sound odd, but virtuosity in itself is something I've never particularly admired... [*laughs*]... not just because I'm incapable of it. Some groups have in the past tended to want to show their virtuosity, at the expense of having something to say, and I never cared for that. That was never the case with Jethro Tull, because the songs were so strong that the virtuosity never got in the way of the music.

Why did you leave Jethro Tull?
Well, as I say, I wanted to be able to express myself, and I couldn't do it musically. I've always known that I've had things to say, and it's important to me to carry on my journey, as it were. There were several times... Ian is a very persuasive character, and there were times when I felt I couldn't contribute as much creatively as I wanted to, because I wasn't capable of doing so within that sphere, and it became very frustrating. Over a period of time it became more and more frustrating, and I realised that to do what I wanted to do I would have to leave the band. I had to make a decision, and it was an awful business because I had to do it in rather a blunt way, because as I say Ian is a very persuasive person and I suppose I was rather concerned that I might be persuaded to carry on longer than I wanted to. I could have carried on for a year, or two years, or three years etc, but there had to come a time when I had to stop. And anyway, they were much better musically when I left.

What was Ian's reaction when you left?
Well, the sad thing was that it was blurted out at a meeting, so it wasn't terribly well done. It's probably difficult for Ian to understand, even now, my reasons for doing it, and what I'm about in that sense. Clearly, after being involved for five years, it wasn't a very pleasant thing to have to do, but they benefitted by my leaving, as I say, so something good came of it.

Ian tried to get you to rejoin in 1979...
That's right. Sadly John Glascock died, and they were looking for someone to go on the tour, and I got a call. In a way I wanted to do it, to be of some use, to help. I went along and they very sensitively arranged for me to go through some old songs and so on. That was difficult in itself because I hadn't played at all since I'd left, but more than that I think I'd just got to the point where I felt I'd left it all behind and found my new direction, and I think I was a bit concerned at finding myself back at square one. Having left something behind I didn't fancy going through the whole process again and taking another two years to get myself sorted out once more. In a crazy way, despite all the pleasure one gets from playing in a band, it is a very

strenuous existence - and to return to your earlier point I would certainly admit to becoming eccentric after five years of doing it. I was becoming somebody I didn't want to be in a way, and it wasn't really what I wanted to do.

Ian said you ceremoniously burnt your stage clothes when you left...
Well, that sounds like a nice story! It was a final thing, you know. I know that he has spoken about me cutting off from music completely, not wanting to be involved in any way, shape or form, but it's not... as you know, I'm not a natural musician, so it's not a case of just picking up a guitar and joining in and jamming along, as much as I would like to. But it is more than that anyway. As important as it was in my life, to be part of that group, to know Ian, John, Barrie and Martin, to have close friendships and enjoyable times, it was only a part of my life. I was only in Jethro Tull for five years, so that is less than one quarter of the group's life span so far, and as a part of my life it is only a small part, in terms of time anyway. One isn't tied to something for the rest of one's life, and I've got to do what I've got to do, and if people don't like that, well that's unfortunate.
Without being too sycophantic, I still admire the group and enjoy its music. I certainly feel a great deal of affection for the various times I was associated with the group, particularly those years with The Blades, getting it started, and in the three or four years when I became part of Jethro Tull. I feel very strongly about that. But, nevertheless, even though one might share the same path for part of one's journey, inevitably people's lives lead off in different directions. And I have my own sense of purpose, my own direction, which I suppose conflicts with that of Jethro Tull.

So what have you done since? What is your sense of direction?
I keep talking about that, don't I? It is personal, and I'd really rather not talk about it. But I don't mind saying that I paint. That's what I do.

Commercially?
No, no. I'm rather uncompromising in that sense. I paint what I want and have to paint, partly for my own pleasure but for other reasons as well. I don't take commissions and I don't exhibit my work, except for what you see here in my home. Music is still terribly important to me, and as I've said I listen to a good deal, but my life is bound up with painting. The quiet contemplative life that I lead now, which probably seems to be a complete contrast to my hectic time in the band, is the life that I want to lead now. But that, as the saying goes, is another story.

Fair enough. Many thanks for talking to us. It's been very interesting.
It's been interesting for me too actually, to sit here and remember those things, to talk about them. I've never actually sat and analysed things in that way before, and I have enjoyed it.

Chapter 17

IAN ANDERSON & MARTIN BARRE

(Published in #29, July 1991 & #30, September 1991)

DR and MW's visit to the rehearsal studios in June 1991 brought an entirely unexpected bonus in the shape of an interview with Ian Anderson and Martin Barre. The idea was to base it around the new album and tour, but inevitably other points were raised, most notably the reasons behind Ian and Martin changing the make of guitars that they had used for many years – hence our needing to split the interview across two issues.
Although Martin was there for half the interview he studiously avoided saying too much, and took the first opportunity to scarper when it arose, so we were unable to question him about his long, long awaited solo project and his collaboration with John Carter which we'd referred to some time back in A New Day. *Naturally we got our man in the end, as set out in a later chapter.*

Ian Anderson opened the interview himself...

OK, let's start with your questions. In fact, I know what they are going to be!

Er... go on then, what's the first question?
You are going to ask us why it is, after many many years... twenty in my case... of allegiance to particular manufacturers' guitars, we have both changed on this tour. After all that time of playing Martin single 0-16 New Yorkers, why have I suddenly changed to playing a modern Guild... and I don't know the answer! [*Laughs*]. No, it has to do actually with the fact, unfortunately, that it's just total noise, because the Martins... well, they have a great sound, and a great sound when you put on the adhesive transducer pick up that is actually attached to the surface of the top of the guitar. It picks up the whole sound of the guitar, not just the sound at the bridge. It is a great noise but unfortunately it's not very loud, and it's prone to feeding back. The guitar acts as a big microphone and feeds all that noise back again and so it becomes a bit unwieldy. I'm always a bit short of volume on the acoustic guitar on certain songs.

[MB] Somebody told me they are traditionally made to be student guitars. That size Martin was never meant to be a concert guitar.

[IA] Well that size of guitar derives from the parlour guitar of the late 1800s. The single Os and the Ones and Twos, the different prefix Martins. However, all these modern "electro/acoustic", guitars as they are termed, which have transducers under the saddle - you know, the little white ivory or plastic bit by which the strings pass over the bridge - sound absolutely awful. The ones you buy in the shops, whether you spend £150 or £1,000, all sound, to a man, total crap! Because they have this unbelievably artificial 'plinky-plunky' little sound and the volume is hardly ever equal from string to string, so they are just a complete disaster. I've been trying them all for years, since the beginning when Ovation started doing them, but they really don't sound good at all, to my ears. They do not sound natural, very artificial. However, finally, when I went to the Frankfurt show specifically to see if I could find a state-of-the-art modern guitar I came across a company called Fishman America, who I had heard of before. They were very helpful. They make the pick-ups, and they actually supply the pick-ups to the latest generation of Martin guitars that come equipped with pick-ups, and a number of other guitar manufacturers, including Guild. Guild actually currently produce a small bodied electro/acoustic with a Fishman pick-up fitted... because I like the ones with little bodies.

Guitars?

Well, it actually has to do with women as well. I mean these big jumbos, these big dreadnought guitars that country & western singers play... I think a man's guitar is very like a man's women... Oops!.. I mean woman!

[MB] That's a give-away!

[IA] Hey, whose side are you on?! No, but I really like the small and curvy guitars. I wouldn't want one of those big and boxy kind of things... kind of traffic warden guitars! [*Laughs*]. I like the petite dancer type of guitars. Whoops! That's another give-away! Anyway, Guild happened to make a nice small bodied little chap, a pretty little guitar, and they were kind enough to send me one, as indeed Fishman were kind enough to send me some pick-ups and pre amps, and many hours later [*laughing*], having rebuilt the Guild which like all the others didn't quite balance up and wasn't really right, I finally managed to get it sounding great. I used it on all of the album... when I wasn't playing mandolin, which I was most of the time. So I've switched to playing those, and I have three of them now. I think they have the best compromise of a loud and clear electric sound with something that still sounds as if it has it's origins in a tree. And that's a really hard thing to do. It is certainly the best I've found yet, and Fishman as a company seem very willing to talk about ideas. They seem to be quite a go ahead bunch. Well, that's why I've changed. Martin, why have you changed away from Hamers after all this time?

[MB] Hmmm... I think it's just that they seem to be so motivated by making profit that quality control suffers. It came to a head with Hamer over what is more of a personal thing, where I think they had lost interest in me as an endorsee. I had a big problem with a guitar in Chicago. It was actually just falling to pieces and they wouldn't send anybody down to fix it for me, even though I'd arranged to meet them in Chicago so they could have the guitar for a day. The end result was they sent me a package to the hotel with all the parts in. Like, "Here are the parts. Do it yourself!" So I thought, forget it, you know. If they don't think it's important enough to send anybody from the factory to sort out the guitar then obviously I don't owe them anything.

[IA] It should be said that Paul Hamer was by this stage no longer with the company. He was bought out by his fellow directors and basically got kicked out of his own company, and that was really when things started going downhill. Paul is still a personal friend of all of us, a great guy.

[MB] Yes, unfortunately Hamer guitars now have got nothing to do with Paul Hamer, they just have the name.

[IA] Paul will have to change his name now! Paul Fender or something?

[MB] He's going to build guitars still. He can make a guitar called a "Paul Hamer" guitar, but not a Hamer guitar, due to copyright. But anyway, the Ibanez people who Dave Pegg was dealing with were very helpful and lent an ear whenever I saw them. Their guitars are not perfect by any means, but they go to a lot of trouble to help you get exactly what you want.

[IA] Ibanez are amongst really the best of the Japanese... and I mean Japanese as opposed to Korean or Taiwanese guitars. They really are very good mass-produced factory guitars. I have an Ibanez mandolin which is a copy of a Gibson F5, which I bought in Chappells in Bond Street in about 1974. It has been a really good mandolin. Very good and very cheap. It is made probably as well as any of the Gibson F5s. I've another mandolin, a Kentucky, also made in Japan. Japanese-made instruments, be they acoustic or electric guitars, for factory produced instruments, really are very good, but the fine tolerances, the fine quality control aspect is rather lacking. It is cheaper for them to deal with the complaints, write off the odd guitar here and there, than it is to introduce fine quality control. Because quality control of musical instruments means employing fairly expert musicians who can play them and say whether it feels right and sounds right. That can't be done just by chaps with rulers measuring things. If you have hundreds if not thousands of guitars rolling off the production line every week you can't possibly hire expert musicians at the fee that they would command. You'd need several people and they all have to be incredibly good, and it would cost a fortune. Much cheaper then just to write off the guitars that aren't up to scratch, accept the refunds etc. Like the mass produced computers and so on that you buy in Dixons or wherever, if one comes back they just smash it up and replace it with another. Whereas in the FOOD INDUSTRY - he says having to get a word in here! – [*groan*] quality control comes first because you can't risk a customer complaint, you just daren't do that. Some things have to be just perfect when they leave a factory and there is no room for any below par product, whereas in other areas you can say, "Why bother? The odd one or two will be really crappy but if somebody complains we'll just give them their money back." But that makes me very sad when it's musical instruments because when you think of all the kids who are going to save up their three, four, five hundred pounds or whatever and go to their local music store to buy a guitar, perhaps a fairly prestigious Japanese- or American-made guitar, and find that it really is lacking, but perhaps as novices they don't know why. They just know it buzzes or it doesn't sound right, but they can't really pin-point the problem. I think it is very sad for people starting to play music that seemingly there are really not reliable sources to buy a decent instrument. It's not just guitars either, the same thing happens with flutes. I've had kids come to me with flutes that they've just bought for three or four hundred pounds and they don't play. They've come out of the factory and they're not set up properly. It's scary.

[MB] I think they're passing the buck to the retailer, where they can't afford to have quality control at the factory so they expect the retailer to set up the instruments. But of course all the retailers are cutting each other and because of that they are buying in huge quantities and turning it round literally out of the box. You buy a guitar in a cardboard box.

[IA] That's right. As it came out of the factory it is in that cardboard box. No-one has looked at it, no-one has set it up, and when you think it's come from Japan, how many thousand miles away? When we nervously open our guitar cases when we travel from one place to another… knowing the temperature and humidity changes, the bangs and crashes and bumps and all the rest of it, even though they are in triple protective containers. These things come from Japan in a cardboard box and they really do need a lot of time spent on them to get the best out of them. I bought my son an electric guitar and I must have spent the best part of three hours setting it up for him. Putting the right gauge of strings on, setting up the octaves, getting the tremolo arm balanced... the whole thing was just completely out to lunch, and that was one that was supposedly set up for me by the importer, specially because it was me dealing directly with the importer. That is really sad because I know how to do it, but what about some 15 year old for whom this is like a dream come true to have a guitar. It's gonna be shitty forever if he doesn't know how to do it, and he probably won't know how to do it. All of which has little to do with what the average *A New Day* reader wants to hear but he's just heard it anyway!

Not as such...but it will do!
But some of those people reading this will have their own guitars. Somebody out there is going to buy a flute and they should be on their guard that the chances are they are going to buy something that really I would not play. I would not be **able** to play! I'd be going [*a series of strange but artistically meaningful coughs and splutters ensued, all captured on a trusty Walkman for the next official* AND *bootleg!*] and it would sound even worse than I usually do! It can be dodgy, and you really need to take with you someone who is already a player. Someone who can say, "This one is no good," or "This might be OK but it needs working on. Fix it before I give you the money". That is the issue really.

Are you on commission for mentioning these trade names in *AND*?
No, I don't get anything… well no, I've had very few things for nothing in my life, I always offer to pay. The only things I've ever had free are Shure microphones, which I used for years before they ever gave me some. I use them onstage and in the studio, they are excellent microphones, but I used them for about 15 years before I had any for nothing. La Bella

strings have been very helpful, and I've hardly ever had any problem with their products. But I'm not really into endorsements, except that I mention on the album the things that I play, when I think they are good.

[*Good to hear that Ian is not into this endorsing caper eh? This interview was recorded onto TDK SA cassette via a Sony Walkman Pro. Played back on a Denon deck from Farnborough Hi-Fi and transcribed onto a PCW 9512 and subsequently a Packard Bell PC, under the influence of Theakston's Old Peculier.*]

On GLR radio two or three weeks ago you played a new Tull track called *Truck Stop Runner* that sounded decidedly "country & western" in style, and you said it was going to be on the album...
[*Smiling*]....I lied! Well, I didn't lie, it was just that I was mixing songs at the time and I took along the two that I'd finished, but afterwards I decided that it was a bit wet, so I chucked it out. Gone!

Good!
[*Laughs*] It was OK, but it didn't quite click. It was actually quite fun when it was just me singing and playing guitar, but we had real problems trying to make it into a credible band piece. Martin and I did a demo of it which was alright and sounded quite promising, but when it came to it it didn't quite gel as a Jethro Tull song. So that one went by the board. You'll never hear that again.

[MB] Unless somebody taped the show.

I've a feeling one or two people might well have taped it! Has the album got a title yet?
Yes, as of today. Title is *Catfish Rising*. We didn't know whether to go for a track on the album or a completely separate album title, like *Crest Of A Knave* for instance... or indeed *Stand Up*, *Benefit* and so on. In the end we decided it was better to go for a ... slightly enigmatic sort of title that could be well illustrated with a simple image. We played around with various ideas, came up with several different titles - but I'm not going to tell you what THEY were! - and the one that everybody went for was *Catfish Rising*. The album cover is based on the techniques of exotic acoustic instrument decoration, i.e. it is an ebony surface inlaid with a motif, and a monogram on the back of the cover. It's basically inlaid like the kind of inlays in guitars and mandolins, a sort of multi coloured shell. All the colours of the rainbow sort of thing, so it looks something like a stained glass window effect. The trouble is that nearly everybody is buying in, at best, the CD format, or cassette, and you don't have the luxury of working to a large size album cover now, but you are working to tiny areas. The irony is that you still have to come up with an image that's going to look good on a T-shirt, or in Germany on a 6 foot high poster. So you need something that works on a cassette box and a giant poster as well. It really is restricting, because it means things like the *Broadsword* album cover, which was great on a 12" square album cover and a big poster, are no longer viable because there is too much detail when you come down to cassette size. These days you have to start off being a lot simpler in your approach, and it needs a great deal of rethinking. I started off by saying, "Let's do something that has something to do with music, or instruments. A pretty picture that still makes a good T shirt."

Is that how it usually comes together? You have an idea of what you want and then ask John Pasche [*Chrysalis Records art designer*] or somebody to create something along those lines?
In this case it was having the idea of the sort of medium we wanted to work in, the kind of image, but we didn't know what that was going to be exactly. So far we haven't seen it. I've seen various bits and pieces, rough design layouts, and I think it's going to be really nice. It will have the simplicity and graphic nature of *Crest Of A Knave*, nice but not too complicated. Album covers are always enormously taxing, because there is so much work involved. You can imagine my lyric book, my note book, where I scribble out my lyrics when I'm working on a song. They get modified when I'm working in the studio, and

perhaps even totally rewritten so they are scribbled over, and I put marks and chord symbols all over the place, little notes to myself, and it looks a complete mess. And then when you actually come to copying out the lyrics after you've finished singing it you realise that in fact you didn't sing what was on the page anyway! You sang a line slightly differently, used a different word or something. So you have to go back and listen to the entire album again to write out what's really on there. It more or less corresponds to the original notes, but not quite - I have to write it all out with all the correct punctuation and line lengths, then I get it typed out, then it goes onto computer to the desk-top publisher for typefaces and so on, then it finally goes out to the printers for separation and setting and so on. And every step of the way somebody fucks it up yet again! [*Tell me about it! DR*]. Another mistake creeps in, or ten mistakes, and I have to proof read the bloody thing about ten times, which drives me crazy. No-one ever gets the lyrics written out or typeset yet again without making mistakes. Even I may well miss some when I go through it, so there will probably be a mistake somewhere amongst the 13 songs on this album.

So... how many mistakes will there be in the lyric book, which will be out... when??
Oh... thousands! [*Laughs*] Really, it will be out... I've done about half of it, but it really is such an enormous job, it's hard to find the time to do it. We definitely will do it, it will happen, and we will just publish it ourselves to be sold at cost, basically. A few thousand copies to be sold mail order or through specialist music shops. Lyrics to all the Jethro Tull songs, with a few nice illustrations.

OK. To get back to the song *Truck Stop Runner*, you said on the radio it was "inspired by" a song that Steve Cropper had sent you...
Yes, because it was fun guitar playing, but it wasn't the right song for us. I found it was inspiring because Steve Cropper is the guy who played guitar on *Green Onions*, which was one of the first things a lot of us who grew up in that era heard and really liked. Really spunky and exciting guitar playing, raw and intriguing.

[MB] He also played guitar on *Sitting On The Dock Of The Bay*, which is a classic guitar sound. To me he was, in his day, way out front.

I just wondered why he sent you a song. Has he done that before?
No, it came through Chrysalis. You see, I don't have a problem with other people's songs. I would quite like to sing some other people's songs, and for many years I've said to Chrysalis "If you get any great songs send me one, I'll try it". They hardly ever come up with anything, but on this occasion someone in the L.A office said, "I've got this song from Steve Cropper and Billy Burnett which you might be interested in". I listened to it, and it was OK. Not a great song, but a good country & western album track I suppose, but not worth doing in the sense that it would be a great song for us. Lyrically I just couldn't live with it, but there was something about the style of guitar playing that appealed to me. I tried to sing it, but I couldn't really do it, but I did learn the guitar part. I've never played that kind of thing before, and it was quite fun. So I employed that finger- picking technique subsequently on two or three songs on the album. It's the first time I've ever done that, I've always played with a plectrum before. Oh, not quite, I think actually the original *Christmas Song* was played with my fingers... that's the only time I think I've ever done that. But it was one of those things where in learning somebody else's song I had to learn to play that way, and it sparked off other things on the album. If I hadn't had that song from Steve Cropper I wouldn't have played *Rocks On The Road* in the same way; I would have played the song, but it would have had a different feel to it. So it was useful to me in that respect, playing somebody else's song, because although I listen to a lot of other music I don't ever sit down and try to play it, which perhaps I should do from time to time... or perhaps not!?

The album has more of a "live" feel to it than most, as though it was recorded in one go with all of you together.
Well some of it was actually. *Sleeping With The Dog* mostly is one straight take. The vocals weren't done at the same time, but everything else was. But some of the songs were

quite the opposite in the sense that it was just me doing mandolins and vocals etc. to a click track, and the guys didn't hear them at all until they came in to record their parts. And sometimes after that I had to re-record my parts onto theirs to make it fit finally with the rest. I often re-do my guitar part, although I do try to keep the vocals. If a vocal feels right at the time I like to stay with it, because if you do it again you never get the same feel. I've always been a great believer in just singing them the one day. Trying it first time and developing it and then just whacking it down, and you'll get something that's maybe 80% right. You go back and you spend a lot of time just refining the odd line or word, just trying a line a different way. I suppose that's how actors work, try to change the nuance, the way you say something, Most of the song comes fairly quickly, after a couple of hours of working on it from never having sung it at all to getting the master, but then you might spend another two hours on one or two little lines that really hang you up; you just can't get them to sound the way you want. The delivery is so important, regardless of the kind of song it is, but particularly with songs like *Budapest* or *Rocks On The Road* or *White Innocence* on the new album. You want them to have a... dare I say a poignancy about them, without making them too laboured. There's always a couple of lines in there that you want to have the same feel as the rest of it but you just can't get it, and the more self conscious you are about it the harder it gets. You have to go away, go for a walk or something and come back and start again, or suddenly do it and catch yourself out! But I do quite enjoy singing in the studio, after I get going. It's horrendous starting, it's a very nervous feeling when you haven't sung for some months, to go in to record your voice for a record. It's very scary, as indeed it must be for Martin playing guitar after a long break. When you get to the difficult intricate pieces, and you haven't done it for two years.

Who plays keyboards on the album?
There are three keyboard players, or four if you count me. I played a few little bits and pieces, but you'll have to try to guess what tracks I played on! I started off wanting to do songs that were a bit more bluesy, not so organised and arranged as before, a bit rougher sounding. So I really wanted to get back to it being piano and organ rather than synthesisers. I really wanted someone who is a good pianist and Hammond organ player. As you know, John Evans is just not interested otherwise he would have been a choice. Pete Vettese is another, but a lot of these guys just aren't available much of the time.

Did you ask John Evans or just assume he wouldn't do it?
I didn't ask him this time, but I asked him last time around and he just didn't want to do it. It would have been nice if he could have done it, but he didn't want to know. He's selling his equipment anyway. So, we got a fella called Rabbit, John "Rabbit" Bundrick, who played with Free and The Who and people like that. He's a good player and he slipped right into the music and very quickly got the right feel, and I didn't have to tell him anything, he got straight in there and it was good stuff. But, Rabbit is a fighting man, and gets a bit crazy. A nice chap, but gets a drink inside him and gets pretty crazy, and one way and another I don't think it was going to work out, so that relationship was severed after he'd done quite a few tracks - but only one of which actually ended up on the album, which is *Sleeping With The Dog*. Then a chap recommended by Peter Vettese called Foss Patterson came down and played on *White Innocence*. And during the course of recording the album I'd advertised in local papers looking for some guys to work with some time, next year probably, to play some low key gigs. Some local musicians who would be available at short notice to play small halls or pubs and so on. People I could phone up and say, "What are you doing Wednesday? Can you play a gig in the pub?" or something. Martin [*Barre*] and I are quite keen to do that, because as you know Dave Pegg and Martin Allcock play in Fairport and they are often off doing things with them, and Martin does occasionally play with other people down in Devon, but I've never played with anybody else so it would be quite nice in these menopausal years not to lose it altogether and just be able to go out and... just stay in contact with the idea of playing to people and to keep playing live music. Not necessarily Jethro Tull music, but something... although I suspect we would have to play some Jethro Tull music because of people's expectations if they came to see us. But anyway, it never really came to anything. We listened to masses of tapes from people, and we auditioned a few

people, but there was nothing really that convincing. But one of the chaps we heard was a pretty good keyboard player, and I did three songs for the album very late on when nobody was around. Dave and Martin were away with Fairport, and this Martin was on holiday. I managed to get Doane back here for a week and we went into the studio with Matthew Pegg on bass and Andy Giddings on keyboards, and Martin played guitar when he came back. So there are actually three tracks with the son of Pegg on bass.

Have you now abandoned the idea of playing with a second, low profile band, or will you still go ahead?
I would really like to do that next year. It's just a question of finding people who are available and not committed, either amateurs or lightweight professionals who are only playing local areas from time to time. It's just trying to avoid having people who live in other countries or who are away doing major tours all the time.

You could be joining Blodwyn Pig then.
[*Laughs*] Well, yes, on a good night! I mean a good night for me, you know. The problem is I'm not really too up on other people's music, and joining in with other people. I've never done it and so I don't find it very easy, because I've really only ever played my own songs. It is difficult to know what it would be like having to do other people's stuff. I don't know if I would enjoy it or not. There's only one way to find out and that is to do it, so... we'll see.

Did you start thinking about this after playing the Tull Convention last year? Is that where the idea came from?
I wouldn't say it gave me the idea, but it reminded me that playing a small room in an informal way could actually be quite fun. I haven't played to a small audience like that since the Marquee days. I enjoyed playing the Convention, and we will I hope be doing more of that sort of thing this year in America. Martin, Dave and I will be doing some promo for the press and radio, and we will hopefully play some live acoustic sets for the radio stations, and maybe do some little gatherings where competition winners on local radio can come and hear the album and meet the band, and maybe we could play them a few things live. There is a programme over there called *Rockline*, and it's a good atmosphere and it's exciting, because it is actually live across America. Maybe there's a million people listening in and you are actually playing to them live. If you stopped and thought about it it would probably scare you shitless!, but the fact that it is such a good atmosphere, and people are ringing in and talking to you, I really do enjoy doing that. I love doing acoustic music that's got an attack to it and that's what I've tried to do on this album, to make really acoustic songs but slightly more pushy and aggressive. Three quarters of the album was written on open tuning mandolins, so therefore the songs have a kind of bluesy feel about them even though they are not 'the blues' as such, in much the same way as *Farm On The Freeway* and *Budapest* have that feel about them. I've taken those ideas and those feelings but tried to go somewhere else with it both musically and lyrically and make it a bit more... you know... a bit more "Surrey". [*Laughs*] A bit less Louisiana and a bit more Surrey.

Any chance of you playing *Unplugged* on MTV?
Yes, we're trying to get an *Unplugged*. We're doing *Rockline*. And we hope to do David Letterman's show this time, because we couldn't do it last time out because it came too late, just after the tour when we were headed home. But we hope to do a few things like that in America, and here too in September.

You mentioned last year the possibility of playing a small gig for an invited audience for TV. Any more thoughts on that?
It won't be this year unfortunately, but I would like to do it, probably next year. But I don't really want to do just a straight gig for television, because that can be so boring. I really think it should be something different, in a different environment. Perhaps we should do a gig in the fisherman's mission in Mallaig? Or then again perhaps we shouldn't!

[MB] We've already done that. We did Exmouth Pavilion down in Devon. We played to 1,000 people and raised £4,000. "We" being the group we have in Devon. The charity I ran for in the marathon... basically the more you get involved with the people [*laughs*] the more they ask you to do, but they are such nice people so it's great to be involved anyway, not least because you're doing something that you enjoy doing anyway. I got to know the guy who runs the charity through last year's marathon, and he actually takes charge of the group as well as working with the handicapped people directly. He told me about this guy who has MS and really is desperately ill now, who used to play in a band in Devon. His old group reformed to play the Exmouth Pavilion to raise money to send him to Disney World, and in his record collection they found some Jethro Tull tapes. He wrote to me and told me what had happened, and asked if I would just go to meet this guy and talk to him because he liked the music. So I said I'd get a group together and play at his benefit gig, which was the start of the group in Devon. We are going to play three or four more gigs in September.

Is that "Big Blue"?
Oh you know about "Big Blue" do you? No, it's nothing to do with them, although one of the guys in the band is from Big Blue, on congas and flute.

[IA] Flute? Is it me? Are you inviting me to play Martin??

[MB] I was going to yes. Not in front of somebody else, but I was going to...

[IA] [*Laughing*] Only three times in my life has anybody asked me to play. The 6 and Violence, Roy Harper and that Canadian group whose name I can't remember now [*Honeymoon Suite*]. Oh, and Brian Protheroe.

And Nixon? A group called Nixon.
What? Who? That means nothing to me I'm afraid....Ah, I've just thought of something else I did, I never heard any more from them, and I'm sure I played on their bloody record. They never even sent me a letter. A group called "Blue Mercedes" I think. I actually played on this record for these guys, I sent them their multi-track back, and I don't think they even sent a letter to say thank you. That was sometime last year, they sent me their multi-track, and it wasn't a bad song. I can't remember what it was called, but it sounded like a Marc Bolan type thing from the sixties.

There was a, 12" disco type single released last year by a group called Nixon. The *Aqualung* remix of *Crazy Love*...
CRAZY LOVE! Oh wait a minute, *Crazy Love* is the name of the single I played on for this group called Blue Mercedes!

The Nixon single is purely instrumental, a jazzy/disco type thing.
It had lyrics when I did it, and as I say it sounded like Marc Bolan. Well that really sounds like a very dodgy crew, because if you ask somebody to do something in good faith... I did it because I thought they were some struggling band trying to get a record deal and maybe I could help them out, you know. But I didn't even get a courtesy reply, and then whatever happens to it isn't even that, they do something else with it...

Maybe it's down to the producer? Pop music is all about producers doing remixes now rather than bands playing songs.
There's somebody else been sampling things as well, taking bits of *Cross Eyed Mary* or something like that. They said, "Either you give us permission to use it and we'll pay you a couple of cents per million records, or we just steal it anyway"! I gather there's some semi famous outfit that just make disco records using samples of whatever, usually James Brown and so on. They sent us a tape of the record, and it wasn't even well done, it wasn't in the right tempo and it just didn't fit together. There's no excuse for that, because the equipment exists to time compress it or stretch it to fit. So not only was it not original but it was not well done. Dreadful stuff.

To get back to your group in Devon Martin, what is it called?
[MB] It hasn't got a name yet. It's made up from people who have been in my studio over the last couple of years. Obviously you get the odd duff band, but I've kept my ear open for any good players and there is now a drummer, a singer and a second guitar player...

[IA] Matthew Pegg's band is called "Blinder"... there's a group called "Stryper"... so why don't you call yours "Jogger"?!

[MB] [*amidst much laughter from everyone else*]... I'll bear that one in mind. But I was going to ask you to come down and play with us some time. We just do old songs that we all like, which is really enjoyable. As you were saying earlier in some ways it is quite interesting doing that, learning to play other types of music.

[IA] The trouble for me is there isn't much music for a flute player within rock'n'roll. A couple of things from the Moody Blues perhaps, but there's not many songs where you can easily fit in a flute player. You end up with the prospect of playing guitar riffs on the flute, which I could do but it might not be most people's idea of a good time!

What about playing harmonica? That fits into every blues song.
Yes, but that's one of those things that you really do have to work on. I found it really difficult trying to learn to play that again after such a long time. It was awkward learning to play it when I said I'd do that thing at the Convention with Mick [*Abrahams*]. Some of it came back but I was flailing about a bit.

It sounded great to us!
Well, it didn't have the fluidity. I've heard people play subsequently and I couldn't play like those guys. I suppose what I would enjoy doing most would be some of my own songs, perhaps in a different way, and some other people's songs again in a different way, in a smallish group context, in a small environment. And without having to play for two hours! It would be nice to get up and play for half an hour and then go to the bar and have a drink. Play another half hour and then bugger off home, and still get to the curry house before it closes, like other people do. I suppose it would be nice to find a couple of other guys, like Gary Brooker for instance, so we could do something together but they would carry some of the weight of doing some of their songs, so you are not on the spot all the time. It could be fun but still be sufficiently serious and professional to be reasonable entertainment. That would be a fun thing to do as a second group project, without the touring syndrome which is a big effort.

At the other end of the scale, did you enjoy playing Wembley Stadium last year with Fleetwood Mac?
No, I think we all hated that, because it was a very uncomfortable thing. We felt very strange about it because the atmosphere was not good. As far as Fleetwood Mac were concerned it was their gig, and they all arrived in separate... not even separate limos, but separate buses with their entourage. I wasn't allowed to use certain parts of the stage; they cordoned them off so I couldn't use them! I couldn't believe how petty it was. I mean **they asked us** to do the gig, it wasn't something that we'd asked for. We were asked to help out because it was selling so badly to begin with. I'm not saying that we made that much of a difference but we were certainly responsible for some of the ticket sales anyway. The thing that totally threw me, and I didn't know about it until 20 minutes before we went onstage... I had assumed they had a star vision screen, so that you would be able to see the video screens in daylight, but in fact they only had the old fashioned kind that only works at night, so only Fleetwood Mac could be seen because there was literally no point in switching it on when we were playing, you simply would not have seen anything at all because it was still daylight. Had I known that before I would not have played the gig. OK, the things we're doing in the summer, in East Germany and Czechoslovakia and so on, I would think there are not going to be any screens, but you accept that when you know ahead of time that's what it's going to be, but there it's different anyway because they don't expect all that. The fact

that there's a gig and you've turned up counts for a lot, and the songs we're playing are not very different to the set we did two or three years ago, a sort of "Best Of Jethro Tull" set, which is what you've got to play when you're playing in almost every case to people who have never seen us before. We have to do the mostly up tempo type of songs for festivals. We are only doing one new song, *Doctor To My Disease*, but even that is only in the longer set, the two hour set for a few of the gigs. We also have a 75 minute set and a 90 minute set for the various festivals... we aren't headlining all of them. INXS are headlining Leysin... we were sort of co-headlining Aalborg with Status Quo, but they've pulled out and Chuck Berry is now ending the show. I suppose we are headlining, and we were given the choice of ending the show, but we couldn't play it at all unless we play an afternoon slot because we have to get into East Germany for a show the next night. It really doesn't worry me when we play. It's nice to play at night because it's dark and you can use the lights which makes it a bit more special, but it can make it tight time-wise. As it is we need two lots of equipment for these shows where everything is doubled up, because the trucks just couldn't make it from one show to the next, so it's horrendously involved getting everything organised. It's an awful lot of work for Kenny [*Wylie*] and the crew. The pressure is added to at a lot of these festivals because you don't get the chance of a proper sound check, you just have to get on and go for it. In fact I'm taking a roadie outfit with me so I can go onstage and soundcheck my own gear in front of the audience in between acts. So I'm going on in shorts and a T shirt, and my hair tied back in a pony tail..... shit, I'm giving it all away! [*Laughs*]

Why are you not playing any dates in Scotland or Newcastle on this tour?
It's not because we didn't try. We did try to get the S.E.C. I was there for a fish farming conference, I went round all the halls and so on, but it just isn't available at the right time. It is just impossible to get some places. Booking in the UK you're talking about nearly a year in advance now to try to put a tour together. In all seriousness you just can't pick up the dates. You can get places in the Norwichs and Harrogates of this world, but the key places like Glasgow, Manchester, Newcastle, Edinburgh, London and Birmingham in particular, the major cities that you want to build it round, in many cases you are looking at 9-12 months in advance. God knows how other people do it. It's not that easy either in Europe and America, but Britain seems to be the most difficult. But, Brazil, you're not quite sure where you're gonna play until the day before! They'll just say, "We'll play this town on Saturday," you know!

I gather David Palmer has been working with you recently.
Yes, he came to put an orchestra on a track on the album. He wrote a string arrangement for it and recorded it with an orchestra, but when I listened to it it wasn't really what I wanted. It was OK, but a bit too elaborate for the track, so I ended up doing it again on keyboards.

Did Gerry Conway and Charlie Morgan actually play on the album?
Gerry and Charlie came to demo some of the songs before Doane came in, when we started recording before Christmas, but we haven't used their stuff on the album. I mean, there was nothing wrong with what they did, but we either didn't use the song at all or re-recorded it when Doane was with us.

Martin Allcock isn't on the album at all?
No. He might well have been, but for the fact it ended up being much more of a guitar/mandolin acoustic instrument oriented album, and keyboards, such as went on, tended to be the traditional Hammond organ and piano, and I'm sure Martin would be the first to say that's not really how he came into it. He's really a guitar player, bass player, whatever, and he's into the high tech keyboard stuff, much more technology oriented stuff, which is what he's very good at doing. He's very able and adept in the technology end, using his musical training in the context of the high tech stuff. But it's just not the sort of thing that I'm interested in right now, I'm fed up with all the synthesiser noises. Maybe another time I'll get into it again, but now I quite like things that are made of wood.

It sounds like that actually. There is a lot of energy in the record. Do you like it?

I enjoyed all the tracks that are on the album. I really enjoyed them at the time of doing them, but you have to remember I've heard those things now probably two or three hundred times, so whereas, yes, I expect I still like it, but at the moment I'm at saturation point. You'd have to ask me again in a year or so, and I'm sure there will be some I think are really awful and some, I hope, that I think are really good. I have actually been playing through some of the new songs on my own while the others have been at lunch this week, and I feel good about playing them. I think I'm going to enjoy doing them because they feel... to me they are convincing pieces, I enjoy the lyrics and the way the songs are played, but I'm not sure how successful they are going to be as group songs because they are that delicate mixture of acoustic and rock and roll, which is the hardest thing to do. As soon as you start playing drums over the mandolin it gets a bit tricky, so it requires a delicate approach to get the energy there without it becoming a noisy mish-mash. So I'll have to work on them. But I really am very happy about the songs at the moment.

The only slightly disappointing thing about the album is once again no songs with just you and an acoustic guitar...
Hmmm... well, you have to understand that I feel really guilty if I do that, because I mean most of the songs started off that way. I really like it, but it is a group after all so I can't say, "Oh, I'll just leave myself on this one guys, don't bother coming into work." I'd feel pretty wretched doing that, obviously!

Dave Pegg would like you to. He's always wanted you to make a solo album of acoustic songs.
Well, if I do it would be next year. I would like to do that, but then I wouldn't want it to be a solo album that ends up being with the guys from Jethro Tull playing on it in their spare time, but at the same time I don't really want to record with other people, so if I made another solo album it would probably be just me playing everything, and I'd like to keep it fairly simple but at the same time pretty 'up'. But you never know... maybe next year.

Chapter 18

TONY WILLIAMS

(Published in #31, January 1992)

Tony Williams, an old Blackpool mate of the John Evan Band, played bass with Jethro Tull on the 1978 North American tour, standing in for the unwell John Glascock - including the famous live TV broadcast via satellite from New York's Madison Square Garden. DR and MW spoke to Tony way back in 1988 while we were in Blackpool researching the story of The John Evan Band – even by A New Day's *standards, four years from interview to publication was stretching it a bit... Sorry Tony!*

Tony has had his own band for many years, playing mainly in the pubs and clubs around Blackpool, and we were fortunate enough to catch his band playing live while we were there. Although the set consisted largely of cover versions it was excellent entertainment, illuminated on the night by the guest appearance on saxophone of the brilliant Ian Kirkham, just back from filming a video in Brazil with Simply Red.

How did you get the call to help Jethro Tull out?
From Barrie Barlow. Barrie and I had been in a band together years ago in Blackpool, and we'd kept in touch. And we'd done a few little gigs together in the meantime, for fun. I was working for a company - who I still work for - and I was actually in a shop serving when the 'phone went. He said, "I've been waiting five years to give you this call - do you want the Tull gig?" I said *[laughing]*, "No, I can't handle it! Not playing bass, there's no way I can do that". He just said, "Yes, of course you can," and that was it. He had a cottage near Blackpool and we spent every available moment going through, literally, the show. He'd worked out what we'd be doing on stage, and Martin remixed some of the tracks and brought the bass track right up. In fact over the top, so that all you could hear was the bass track - with no association with the tunes at all. So I literally learned everything parrot fashion. As you know, with Tull there's no element of improvisation through any of the set.

How much rehearsal time did you have with the band?
It must have been a couple of months. We had to keep it fairly quiet, no-one was supposed to know in advance. We rehearsed at Pinewood Studios. I remember one time, Ian called a halt and said, "Let's get some grub in". And Barrie started nudging me and whispering "Watch, watch - seafood!" And sure enough Ian asks for some mussels and cockles and so on. Barrie just said, "Wait!" The thing is, Ian loves the stuff, but he goes green. And when he'd eaten it he had to go and lie down on some packing cases! But he can't stop eating the stuff. We went to a Japanese restaurant in San Francisco, and I was sliding my sushi across to him, and he was really digging into it - but he's actually allergic to it. That's why I thought it was so ironic that he went out and bought a salmon farm! *[Collapses laughing!]*

Did you do the whole tour?
Yes, I did the whole North American tour.

How many gigs was that?
Oh, I can't remember. It was a lot! About 40 shows, I suppose, in the space of three months, coast to coast, starting off in New York and finishing off in L.A. It was a plane every day, sometimes two, and we used to get two days off a week.

Were you hoping to get the job full-time? Did you feel as if you were in the band then?
No. It was John Glascock's gig, without a shadow of doubt. All the bass parts I'd learnt were John's bass parts - which were good; he was a good player. I suppose I

always thought that if John wasn't ever well enough to do it I might be permanent reserve, as it were. But I think it was obvious that I wasn't into that kind of music anyway - I've never been a Tull fan, although having played with the band I did get into it. And funnily enough, I had auditioned for them when Mick Abrahams left and before Martin joined. But John did actually come back to do another tour, the very next American tour, although it was the last one he did, of course. And I think by then the seeds had been sown in the band, in as much as Barrie wasn't very happy with the way things were going; and even though of course it was not known what was going to happen, it was clear that there were going to be changes anyway. And I think John dying just finished things off for Barrie.

So you're a guitarist, not a bass player really?
That's right. Although, I was in Stealer's Wheel before I joined Tull, and that was playing the bass.

What was Ian like to work with?
He was very helpful. I only had this one association with him, so that's as I know him. I mean, I could see that it was a case of the band and him. And Barrie, for example, can be scathing about things. But I can only say that for the time I was there, in my situation, Ian was fine. He had his odd moments, but because I wasn't really in the band he was OK with me. In fact, Ian and I got on very well - he's got a good sense of humour. We are exactly the same age, born in exactly the same week. So if you believe in star signs there should have been some natural friction, and indeed there'd be a bit of sarcasm flying around. But he was particularly helpful at a couple of rehearsals, and on the whole he was quite tolerant, I suppose.

Did you know him from years back?
Yes - not very well, but I knew him. I met him for the first time through Glenn Cornick. Glenn and I were very good friends. Glenn left the band I was with to join The John Evan Band. I remember meeting Ian sat in a transit van outside a chip shop in Blackpool, dressed all in black. They called him "Elvo" in those days. And then briefly, later, through Barrie.

Did you record anything, demos or whatever, with Tull?
Only the live TV thing, nothing in the studio.

What was that like, doing Madison Square Garden before an audience of millions?
I didn't know about it until a couple of days before, which was planned obviously! But really it didn't worry me at all. Madison Square Garden is a strange place. It looks smaller than it actually is. For my mind, we'd already done bigger gigs, in Rochester, so actually going out there on the night wasn't too horrific. And in fact, the Rochester gigs were much better, I thought. Ian is liked in New York, they like his music, and it's weird when you look down in Madison Square Garden and there's five or six guys who look exactly like him, even down to the boots.

Did you at any stage think about them all watching it live back in Blackpool?
Well, I was going to come out with a big placard "Good Evening Cleveleys", but I thought it might not go down too well!

What was it like playing the first big show with Tull, after playing the clubs of Blackpool, and so on?
It wasn't as bad as I thought it would be. I'd always fronted a band, but of course Ian was the front man, so it wasn't me 'out there' - I was just part of a jigsaw puzzle, so I knew that if I made a mistake no-one was going to fall about going "Nah na na nah nah!". There was tension, but I saw tension with old hands too. *[Laughing]* Kenny Wylie, the stage manager was a bag of nerves...

221

He's like that at <u>any</u> gig...!

Right! So he sort of made me feel calmer, 'cos I thought if he's like that, I'll be alright. And I was. But that's not to say that things went smoothly every night. You know where everyone leaps up in the air at the end of Aqualung, and lands on their feet nearly doing the splits? I had these riding boots which were made of rubber, and the whole stage was rubber as well. I was well known for drinking wine on stage, about three or four bottles a night, and I must have spilled some. So I leapt up in the air, skidded, and my pants were so tight they just went 'pzzztt' and split. Martin couldn't play for laughing! Barrie was doubled up behind the drums, and even Ian allowed himself a smile, while I was just crawling round the floor!

And John frightened the shit out of me one night. You know how he used to loon around in his white suit. And I'm trucking away at the front, and John's gone on his wander. And you get isolated, you're in your own space, you know where everything is around you - behind you is your amp, your roadie's over there, and everything's fine. And I happened to turn round and John was like 'that' [hand a foot in front of his face, manic expression]!

If you speak to Barrie, tell him I haven't forgotten about my cap, either. [We forgot.] I bought a cap in Greenwich Village, one of those big Bronx bonnets with the button on the top. And everyone started taking the piss out of me - mainly David Palmer, actually. But it went missing after a show one night - I couldn't find it anywhere, so I was sulking away. It turned up on the very last show on a hook, very creased and very crumpled. They'd been hiding it from me of course.

Talking of David Palmer, I remember we were about 200 miles north of New York somewhere, just before we did the Madison Square Garden thing, waiting for a 'plane. The flight was called, and off we went downstairs. The 'plane was absolutely tiny; we could only just squeeze in. I swear there was a Mexican woman with a chicken in the front. David Palmer was stuck at the back, really cramped up, in his big fedora. We started to taxi down the runway, and he totally went flippo. "Let me out!" he screamed, "I'm going to hire a car!" Martin was saying, "You can't hire a car with cash, David, you need a credit card." Dave was insisting, though; and the pilot was looking round thinking, "What the hell's going on here?" He couldn't believe it. Barrie as usual was asleep as soon as he'd got in the 'plane. And David's up and getting his bags and saying, "Stop the 'plane, pilot, stop the 'plane!". So Martin said he'd come with him, and I said I would as well, because I didn't fancy this thing much either, really. So the three of us walked back to the airport with our bags, and we said, "Right Martin, go and hire us a car". And there were no cars available. "Right, get a limousine," said David. But there was nothing. Shit! We've got a gig tomorrow - what'll we do? I was actually quite enjoying it all. There was a taxi rank just outside, and we collared this old guy, about sixty years old - lovely guy - and said, "Will you take us to New York?" And he looked at these three strange Englishmen and just said "Woah, woah". He phoned in and checked it out with his wife, and drove us there - came to the gig, got rip-roaring drunk, and spent the night on Martin's floor!

Had you seen Tull live, after Barrie joined?

No, I'd never seen the show, but Barrie used to tell me about it over the 'phone. He used to ring me up and say, "We've tried this thing out today, what do you think of this, Tony?" And he'd tell me about the white coats and the tent, and how he had a little 3-piece kit at the front to do a swing-jazz thing. And those would be Barrie's ideas. Barrie was great at coming up with things like that - that whole circus element would have been down to Barrie, and indeed Jeffrey. It's a shame that that was lost, because that was such a part of the eccentricity that Tull were famous for. But the reason for that was... You remember the grandiose tours they used to do with ballet dancers and the orchestra? Well, everyone knows that you lose money on tours like that, but you sell albums. I think that at the end of the day the band was looking at the balance sheet, and looking at the cost of the tours, the album sales and the royalties, and so on, and realised there was a big fat nothing happening. So a meeting was held - it was probably Barrie who called it, he was like the shop steward - and it was decided that this was ridiculous, they couldn't carry on like that. Ian actually turned round and said, "OK, how about if I just pay you a salary, and I take care of the tour expenses, win or lose?" They all thought he was a mug, 'cos he was bound to be on a loser, so they all said OK. A figure was agreed, and they were still on salary when I joined.

How come you were never in The John Evan Band?
I nearly was... [laughs] , but I couldn't afford to pay for the organ! I was in a band called The Executives, which was a hard working pop band. We played some place - Bolton, I think - where I saw John loading his Hammond organ into the transit. They actually owned a transit van, we had to hire ours. And it was a great band, by all accounts. John said to me that they were looking for a guitar player, and I was really fed up with what I was doing, so I said, "Yeah, I'm interested". But then I heard stories from other people that you didn't get paid because all the money was allocated to the organ and the van. I thought, "That's no good, you can't get drunk on that!" But Glenn left The Executives to join The John Evan Band because he was very impressed with their musical ability. Glenn was only with The Executives because it paid the rent, really - summer seasons at Morecombe Pier, and that sort of thing. Glenn is still in Los Angeles. When I did the Tull gig, I called Glenn, and took him backstage. That was the first Tull gig he'd seen since he left the band. Glenn used to respray his guitars - he was always a bit strange-thinking like that. I was in his apartment in L.A., and he'd got his wardrobe door open with a guitar hanging in there. He'd got a spray can to do the whole thing red, including the neck and machine heads and everything. He was working then with a sort of glam-punk band, a sort of Gary Numan type nouveau punk outfit... can't remember the name of the band. But that was eight or nine years ago. He's probably with a Country and Western band now.

Have you seen Jethro Tull since you played with them?
I went to the Apollo in Manchester in 1987. It wasn't a good gig. It was a strange gig. It was a sell-out, and I stood at the back, and all the way through I thought, "There's something wrong," but I couldn't put my finger on it, until I realised that everybody was sitting down. And I think that the band itself had mellowed and softened up, even on the older material.

It did seem on that tour that they weren't as tight as they used to be.
That was one of the amazing things about Tull at the time I was there, the tightness of the band. It was unbelievably tight. And that was down to one guy, who was driving the engine, and that was Barrie with his sense of timing and the way he held things together, and the way he worked everyone in the band. He didn't just work himself, he worked everyone in the band, all the cues came from him. Barrie used to shout at me on stage and give me a bollocking. We'd worked together for a long time and were mates, with a kind of mutual respect. So it worked well.

Finally, what do you do for a living now?
I still work for the same company, doing promotions and training. It's the day job, although I'm always on the lookout for opportunities in music.

Tony is now a well-respected local politician, and at one time was Cabinet Member for Culture and Leisure at Blackpool Council, His brief stint in the Jethro Tull spotlight is not forgotten, however, and (unlike some of the other Tull deputies) he featured on the commemorative Year Planner available from the merch stand on the 40th Anniversary tour. And DR and MW had previously both been delighted to renew acquaintances with Tony at the 25th Anniversary 'reunion' video shoot.

Chapter 19

ANDREW GIDDINGS

(Published in #33, June 1992)

It's a dirty old job, but someone's gotta do it...

You people, you don't know yer born! We didn't wanna go. We didn't wanna go swanning off yet again following Tull into Europe when we could have been printing in Farnborough and civil servanting in London. It would be wasting time - we could be painting the roof. But somebody had to interview new keyboardsman Andy Giddings, so selflessly we sallied forth to Utrecht and Brussels, Walkman in hand, accompanied by Frank "The Snowman" Smith, to get the griff from Andy.

The interview begins in the time honoured A New Day *cliché-ridden fashion...*

How did you get the gig with Jethro Tull?
Ian got a tape from somebody who I assume he knew, while they were finishing off the *Catfish Rising* album, of a pub gig of a band that I was in at the time, and he expressed an interest in the keyboard player. A guy I knew in London told me they were looking for a keyboard player to finish the album, so I got in touch... and here I am.

You didn't actually send Ian the tape then?
No, I think it was the drummer who sent in the tape. It was a local scratch band, musicians just thrown together now and then, called The Chase.

You weren't a Tull fan then, actively trying to join the band?
Well I've always been aware of Jethro Tull obviously. I knew the songs but I couldn't say I had the whole album collection... although I have now! But it's not possible not to know about Jethro Tull, unless you're living in a cave somewhere. Everybody knows Jethro Tull, so I knew of their existence and I knew the sort of thing they were playing, but it never occurred to me that I would be playing it with them.

You've just finished touring with Sniff 'n' The Tears...
Yes, it was really just down to their hit, *Driver's Seat*, from 1975 or something, being used for a Pioneer TV ad in Europe. That gave them a number 1 hit all over Europe, so they decided to put together a tour on the back of it. They reformed the band after a break of ten years or so. Right after this Tull tour they are making another album which I'll be working on, and then a couple of weeks touring Holland. I guess they'll still be playing all the old stuff, the old favourites. *Driver's Seat* is the one thing that everybody knows, but Paul Roberts, who IS really Sniff 'n' The Tears, has made two solo albums as well as the five band albums, so there is a lot of material there and they have quite an "underground" following.

Were you an original member of the band?
No, I only joined for the tour. That came about because I'd done a tour with Leo Sayer, with a guitarist called Les Davidson, who was an original member, and he got in touch when the gig came up. I was really pleased; I like the band, and I bought the record when I was at school, you know.

How are you getting on with the Jethro Tull material?
It was a challenge. I spent a solid week, every day from nine in the morning 'til one the next morning, with all the stuff set up at home, and went through all the tapes and made myself learn it. There is nothing predictable about any of the material, so it's not the sort of thing you can just jump in and busk. There is a lot of home-work to be done before you can even attempt to play it.

224

Is it fun to play?
It's excellent to play! It's probably the most taxing stuff I've ever had to play, both mentally and physically. Keyboards are a bit different to most instruments because it's not only learning the tune, but it's programming the various noises. A tune on a piano is one thing, but you have the piano down here, bells and flute over there, string parts etc up there and so on. So it's not just a matter of writing the chords down, you have to go through each song one by one and think, "How many noises do I need? Where do I get them?" Etc etc. It is quite involved, so I had to do a lot of work on my own before we actually went into rehearsals proper.

Are all the keyboard parts actually live now, or do you use sequencers?
Nothing on sequencer at all. They are all played live.

That's been a bone of contention for some fans over the last five years or so.
Yes... I do use sequencers, I know how to use them, they are very valuable tools, but I hate to see them on stage, or tapes of any kind. As a keyboard player - and this is all very boring unless you're a keyboard player - it's always a real wind up for me to go to a gig and see two, sometimes even more than two, keyboard players doing a job that one man should be able to do if he really put his mind to it and forced himself to do it. It's really frustrating to see two people doing not very much when one man can actually do it with technology now, and without the aid of sequencers. You can play lots of different parts; it's a matter of recreating the sound even if you are not emulating totally all the different parts. You create the image that you are playing those parts, where they come up. You mix and match, if it's organ here, piano there, the crucial bits work in and you can overlap them, so it sounds like you're doing the whole thing even if you're not. Obviously it's impossible to play more than two things live, but you can create the impression of playing much more.

How did you feel on the first night in Plymouth.
I wasn't nervous on the first night, but it caught up with me by about the third gig. Had I thought about it too much I would have been very nervous, because it's not the sort of stuff you can bluff. If you lose concentration for a second it is very dangerous. Two or three gigs in I started to get nervous. I realised the magnitude of it all; the capacities, the type of gigs, the professionalism of the whole organisation, and then I started to think about what I had to do, whereas I hadn't really thought about it before. I mean anybody who says they don't get nervous must be telling an untruth. You must get nervous before you walk out in front of an audience to play.

I'm sure it helps to be nervous doesn't it?
Yes, it does, but obviously if you're too nervous it has an adverse effect, you could end up all over the place. There is a thin line between being nervous and confident enough to carry it off, and it's like that all the way through the gig. There might be a part that has given you problems in rehearsal, and as it approaches in the set it can be a worry. It's nice to get that out of the way and get on with the rest of the set!

Is there anything in this set that still worries you? A piece coming up that you're not looking forward to?
There's nothing that I don't look forward to. There is one piece in *White Innocence*, the 'orchestral' piece in the middle, that was on sequencer, but I made myself play it. There are not a lot of notes, but there is a big gap between each one, and it is a bit difficult to play. It doesn't worry me, it excites me, it's a bit like going down a ski jump. You can either land safely or you can land on your head. I've certainly got my wits about me at that point. It is difficult, but it can be played. A keyboard player that's playing with a band like Jethro Tull really ought to try and play it. If it's an impossibility then fine, but you should try. And if you keep trying and you keep ruining it then you can say, well, OK, it's too hard, it's a physical impossibility, which is no reflection on the man, it could be any number of reasons why it can't be played. But you must try and then be defeated gracefully if you can't, rather than just say, "That seems like a lot of notes; I'll bung it in the sequencer!"

Have you had a bad night yet? Come a cropper somewhere?
Well, yes. But it's not the sort of thing that people notice. It's bad for me particularly. Midi is my big hang up, because Midi, for all its pretences, still decides now and then to do something when you don't want it to, and won't do something when you really want it to. I've had a few technicalities, but no big problems. No elbows on keyboards or anything like that.

Did something happen at the end of *Serenade To A Cuckoo* tonight?
Yes, that was the midi. It's a note off. Again, dull stuff, but it tells things to play notes and to stop playing them, and very often if you play lots in very rapid succession it just gets confused and the Midi buffer, which is the brain if you like, just says "FULL", it just can't deal with any more, and instead of just going off it tends to leave one note on indefinitely. But that's the only thing I've fallen foul of really.

Talking about nerves and so on, you must have played some big gigs with Leo Sayer before...
Fairly big. They weren't as big as any of these. Well the biggest was 16,000 in Moscow, but it was so big that you couldn't see many of the audience anyway, so it was difficult to think there were 16,000 people out there. You couldn't see or hear them, so it didn't really bother me. But the size of the crowd isn't everything, but it does make you think when you walk out and you can see all these people, it runs through your mind that there are a lot of people you could embarrass yourself in front of! On the other hand they are obviously focusing on Ian anyway, he is the person they are looking at, so it might well be that you'll make a mistake which really worries you, only to find out that nobody noticed anyway, they were all concentrating on something else... the master with the flute! Which is kind of what it's all about.

You've played with Eric Burdon as well; was that before Leo Sayer?
Yes, that was first. In my "apprenticeship" I was playing up and down the Old Kent Road in London, in the pubs. My first job was as a commercial artist, doing paste-up. It was OK but I wasn't really interested in it, and I was doing all these gigs every night after work, blowing myself out for work the next day. I used to gig with a bass player, Steve Stroud, who was at the time playing with Eric Burdon, and a couple of times he called me and asked if I was interested in doing a tour with Eric Burdon. I had to turn it down because it would be difficult with my job, but one day I realised that very soon they would stop asking me. I wasn't enjoying what I was doing, so I thought, "I'll say yes and see what happens". In those days when you were offered a gig there was always an element of doubt - "Why did they ask me? Is it because they think I'm good, or can't they find anybody else?", you know. But it was fine. I did the tour, then another, then an album in America followed by more touring for about three years.

What is he like? Is he a hell-raiser as often portrayed?
Well, obviously as years catch up with him he's going to mellow, but he's still the same Eric Burdon. He's still touring now, and he still whips them up into a frenzy. The gigs were always busy, to say the least, never a dull moment in his set. Arrangements of songs going into another one, or he might decide to change one half way through; I had to be on my toes all the time. Great gigs though, really good rock & roll gigs.

Have you played with anybody else we might know? Any horrendous punk rock skeletons in your cupboard?
No, nothing like that. I spent a lot of time doing sessions for European bands, French and German bands. A lot of albums that never got released!

How did you first take up the keyboards? Piano lessons at school?
Yes, obligatory piano lessons - which I hated! I started when I was six, and my mum put me in for all these festivals in Brighton and Eastbourne. I'd be playing *Fire Engines* on a grand piano! I gave up when I was twelve. At school I really liked Gary Numan, I

226

decided I wanted to be him, so we got a little band together and played some of his songs; not seriously, but from then on I was always in a band, and it built from there.

Do you write music?
Not physically, as in 'dot', but I do come up with a few things. The little instrumental thing in this set, after *Tall Thin Girl*, is just a doodle... well, a refined doodle now... of something I had knocking around. There was an opportunity to create a mood before the next song so that is one of my "compositions", if you like. I think every musician has hundreds and hundreds of little tunes that they are either bored with or embarrassed about playing to other people, just in case! But everybody who plays an instrument is going to come up with a tune they think is nice.

You don't actually write songs as such?
I have done. I have a studio set up at home, and I do demos and programming and jingles for anybody and everybody, and I've got stacks of tapes that I've given to singers. I'll give them the bare bones of a song, the intro, verse, chorus, and ask them to write some words for it.... which is kind of the wrong way round really! [*Laughs*]. It is obviously hard to do that; I guess you should really come up with the song, the words, and provide the music to complement that. So consequently of course none of them have ever been turned into hits!

What about arrangements of the songs onstage? You said you learnt all the songs, but how much free reign did Ian offer you?
Well, with a gig like this when you're playing well known songs... I think it's important to be sympathetic to what you're trying to play. If anybody goes to their favourite gig, I think the worst thing is for someone to be looking forward to their favourite song all night long and then finding out that it's been updated or changed because of a new member in the band. Institutions like *Locomotive Breath* or *Thick As A Brick* or *Aqualung*, you daren't really change. There might be a subtle difference in sound somewhere, but I think basically people want to hear the record they bought. Well I do, if I go to a gig. Crowded House is my favourite band, and they play all their songs like the records. I bought the records and I love 'em, and I want to hear those songs, not a version of them. I like to hear what I bought. So for me, as a newcomer to the band anyway, I'm happy, and I'm good at copying the original arrangement, or maybe a combination of the original and the last keyboard player. The arrangements then have nothing to do with me; I'm too new! I'm just happy to play it. Anybody can come up with an arrangement, anybody can stick another two bars of 7/4 on the end of something, but that doesn't necessarily make it a new improved arrangement, it's just another two bars of 7/4! You have to go for what's right, and that is obviously what's gone before, it's been tried and tested. Why change it if it's good?

Who else do you listen to other than Crowded House?
Pink Floyd. Sting. Ozric Tentacles. Thomas Dolby. Steve Hillage..

Ah! The Orb? [*Editor's Note: as I was once again lumbered with the job of driving on this escapade, I made my passengers suffer with some choice cuts from my CD collection en route. The The, Talk Talk and even Mungo Jerry were tolerated, but The Orb made the buggers squirm a bit! DR*]
Is that a band, The Orb? I keep hearing this name, but I don't know what or who it is.

Well Steve Hillage is in it, in a way, but I don't know that it could be called a band as such.
Steve Hillage is into a lot of projects these days, everything from dance to psycho-Indian! But, what else do I listen to...? Prefab Sprout, they're good. *Catfish Rising*, that's good!.

What do you think of Tull's back catalogue?
I've only just got it all, and I'm still working my way through them. I haven't really had a chance to listen to them, other than the ones that we do. I listen to those in case there is

anything that I'm really missing. After a few weeks of thinking I've got it right, I go back and listen to them again and sort of re-programme myself if I can improve on what I'm doing. It's a bit of a pretentious thing to say, but it's good to do. I think you should keep yourself in check because there is nothing worse than getting complacent, and then you shock yourself, you listen to the original and think, "Christ, I don't play anything like that!"

Do you fancy having a bash at the rest of *Thick As A Brick* one night then? The full 45 minute version...
By all means! I'd like to think I could learn it all. If it presents itself I'll set up my gear at home again and learn it. I learnt *Heavy Horses*, which is itself fairly complex, but we don't play it, because it is a very involved song, and the set doesn't allow for it.

It's unlikely to present itself! Have you a favourite Tull track?
Lots of them. I really like lots of them. *Heavy Horses* is a favourite, and I was really looking forward to playing that, so I was disappointed when it was dropped.

What's the future for you as regards Jethro Tull? Are you just contracted for this tour, or do you hope to do more with the band?
I hope to do as much as they want to give me. I enjoy the gig. It's the most enjoyable gig I've had, it's the most taxing, and I come off stage every night knowing that I've worked hard, which is great. Obviously Jethro Tull are getting offers all the time, and there are offers through the rest of the year, which I'm in the picture for, so I hope that I'm asked repeatedly to do them, because I like doing them. I get on very well with the band, we seem to share the same sense of humour, which is obviously very important. It's not like we are together all the time, we don't walk round the town as a band, we all do different things. Martin goes running in the morning, I have a cup of coffee and a cigarette. I might stagger downstairs at about eleven in the morning and he's already run 50 miles! So everybody does their own thing, but we get on when we are together. The older you get you begin to treat life on the road as something other than a holiday, which is how it might seem. I remember I did a three month tour in Australia and everybody said, "Wow, you lucky bugger!", you know, but for those three months you're getting on a plane every bloody morning, getting to yet another gig, another soundcheck etc. I know it sounds all very bloody blasé, but it does get to you. It's not "hard work"; anybody that says touring is hard work is not really speaking the truth. You get tired, you get fed up, but the way I always check myself is when I walk into a gig feeling knackered I think about what the crew has been doing. They've driven through the night, set all the gear up in the morning. The hardest thing I've had to deal with is having to find a smoking section in an international airport! That really is the biggest task of the day!

What's Ian like to work with in the studio and rehearsals?
Well he is the boss. The way I look at it, again as a newcomer, is that he has struck on a formula that has worked for 24 years, he knows what he wants in the studio and live, and if he wants me to do something then I ought to be able to do it. He has definite ideas of what he wants. He won't suggest a certain thing, but he'll say, "I'm looking for...." this thing, which is good, it works, and has done for 24 years. He knows what he wants, he knows the sound he wants to create, he knows what he requires of all the musicians. I like to retain a certain distance... I mean, he is my employer, you know. Familiarity breeds contempt and all that. People don't command respect, I think they earn it, and there is a big difference between commanding respect and earning it. He has earned respect, because of his past, and if he wants me to play one note all the way through a song, then I have to do it, and I won't bat an eyelid. You have to be able to be told what to do... and if you're gonna make a suggestion you've got to hope that it's a ginormously popular one! Gotta be, otherwise for evermore you're gonna be thought of as the person who made THAT suggestion... which was probably crap anyway! So don't make suggestions if you're working for someone who knows what they want - just do it! Obviously I've not done much with Jethro Tull so I can't say if he invites suggestions when recording, but every thinking musician will always have ideas of their own, and if you want to try something you can't be afraid to say so, but if you make lots of useless

suggestions you won't be asked again. You've got to know it's good before you suggest it. But as I said, they are his songs, he knows what he wants, and he's not going to look to me to make him a hit record. Jethro Tull are living proof that what he does works.

Well it's been great talking to you Andy. Just enough tape left to talk about The Mechanics... what a great band they were! [*Editors Note: The Mechanics, the second greatest band of all time. An unbelievably powerful trio from Cornwall who made but four singles in the early '80s and then disbanded to become Leo Sayer's backing group. Andy joined up with Leo Sayer just after The Mechanics left, so I just had to find out if he knew them. As it turned out subsequently, Martin Barre is also familiar with the band; small world innit? DR*]

Yes, what a great band they were. In fact, still are.

What?! Still are??
Yeah, The Mechanics in Cornwall. Yes, they're still doing it. Steve Jackson, Dave Quinn, Al Hodge. The drummer is a good friend of mine. Fantastic musicians all of them, a good band.

With this news DR lapsed into a fit of apoplexy, trying to figure out how to get from Utrecht to Cornwall urgently. The Mechanics had reformed! Little did he realise then the effect that this would have on the next fourteen years of his life...

Chapter 20

MARTIN BARRE
(and MAGGIE REEDAY)

(Published in #34, September 1992)

On 11 July 1992 The Summer Band, featuring Martin Barre, played a charity gig in the garden of Martin and Julie's Devon home. It was the first in a set of just four gigs which culminated in their tremendous performance at the 1992 Jethro Tull Convention the following Saturday. The 250 or so people lucky enough to be in attendance were, for the most part, residents of the village and friends of the hosts, but in the midst of the well heeled and respectable citizens there lurked a small but gruesome selection of motley reprobates and ne'er-do-wells known collectively as "that lot from A New Day". *Our mission was two-fold. Primarily, to have a bloody good time eating and drinking... well, just drinking, really... to excess and listening to a truly excellent band. Our second mission was to take some photos for the Convention programme and to get some information on The Summer Band. We'd heard of Martin Barre somewhere before, and Matthew Pegg rang a bell, but the rest of the band were largely unknown to us. The first part of the plan went smoothly, but when it came to actually finding out anything about the band it got difficult. We did, however, finally manage to pin down Martin Barre, figuratively speaking, for a few minutes after the gig and we got in a question or two before he made his escape. So it was that once more* A New Day *was bemused to present an interview... well, more of an interviewette... OK, OK, a bit of a chat with Martin Barre (ably assisted by singer Maggie Reeday).*

If we can talk first about The Summer Band... is this just a one off thing or do you see it continuing in some way?
It's a sort of "putting your toe in the water" type of thing. I love the music, the old standards and the blues things. It's the sort of stuff that Ian [Anderson] and Dave [Pegg] would love to play... and they could if they did what I did! I'm testing the water and if it's good, if we get on well together and we make some good music and it sounds great, then I would like to do more with them. But it's a very easy going relationship where we might finish this week and never play again. They might not want to do it again, or I might not. There is no pressure. But if at the end of the week we've all had a good time then maybe we'll carry on.

Are there any song writers in The Summer Band
Craig, the keyboard player is a jazzy sort of song writer, but I don't think anybody else writes music. That's good in a way because it might give me a bit of an opening!

Have any of the band been in any other bands that we might know... other than Matt Pegg of course?
No, that's the good thing about it. I've never really been excited by the thought of using people that have done the rounds, because it dilutes their talent in a way. To me it's exciting to find people... well I mean, you look at those two girl singers tonight...

They are amazing! I can't believe they have not been part of successful group before...
Well, they have been in groups, but all local groups. They are just people who desperately love music and they put everything into a performance. But if you have people who have done the rounds and played with everybody it's just another gig to them. I really enjoyed tonight. That music is great fun and there is a great feel to it. We have been rehearsing every day this week, and very often you go in first thing in the morning and you think, "Christ! I don't know if I can do this". You can trudge through the first couple of hours and then something happens, it sort of comes alive with emotion. That's the wonderful thing about music, when emotion is introduced to it, it takes off. It's like "ingredient X", you can't learn it or plan to do it, it just happens. And it was great tonight.

Wasn't John Carter fantastic tonight!? [*John was the singer in Martin's first band The Moonrakers back in 1928, and made a guest appearance with The Summer Band at this first gig. He did so in 1991 also when Martin put a band together then, when DR described him as being like Screaming Lord Sutch, but not so laid back! He was even more dynamic this year!*]

He was great! I loved it. He is another guy who puts so much into what he does.

Are you still going to make an album with him?
I don't know now. It's on the shelf at the moment.

This solo album that you are making... possibly... maybe... this year perhaps... Will that be blues music?
I dunno. I like playing the blues, so maybe it will.

Do you sit in the studio and come up with bluesy things?
Not particularly, because I find it very hard to write simple music, in the same way that Ian... not that I would compare my song writing to Ian's!... but Ian finds it hard to write simplistic music. But I couldn't write a 12-bar blues, because whenever I write I'm automatically into chord changes and little intricacies. I find it very hard to be a very basic sort of player. And I don't mean basic as a derogatory thing; it is a very hard thing to be a simplistic player, to play the bare essentials and play them well. I wish I could. I've tried to learn to do it. But I don't know what the album will be; I can't plan what I'm going to do. I'm just gonna do it!

Are you going to do it? A Martin Barre solo album??
I've got August to work. I might end up with nothing, who knows.

Will it be just you, or will it be with The Summer Band?
I'll be working with Mark Tucker in the studio, and I'll just get in whoever I need as I go on. I don't want to say to anybody, "I want you in the studio for a week", I'd rather just do something and decide what it needs, what sort of playing, and who should do it. I'll just take it as it comes.

What about all these superstars who rate Martin Barre as a guitarist? Would you get them in the studio?
Err... like who?

Joe Satriani. Iron Maiden…
They are not fans of mine, they are fans of Jethro Tull.

Largely because of you.
I wouldn't have thought so.

Oh yes. Did you not know that Joe Satriani thinks you are one of the greatest guitarists in the world?
Really? That's peculiar. I can't personally understand it. It's very flattering though! He is a very different sort of player to me. He is on a different plane to me, a great player.

Are you not a great player?
No, I'm learning. I find the learning process exciting, everything I learn is exciting. I think there is a lot more to learn, there is a lot more that I could do, and that's great. But somebody like Joe Satriani is way beyond me technique-wise. He is an amazing player. And Gary Moore is another player who I think is absolutely wonderful, and he has a great voice. He has so much emotion in his playing, and I'm really pleased to see him having such success, because he's been around for a long time, worked so hard at what he does, and as a guitar player I just can't praise him highly enough.

[*With that Maggie Reeday, one of the singers with The Summer Band was press ganged by Martin into taking his place at the table to continue the interview whilst Mr Barre informed us that he was "going to get pissed'. We were not personally familiar with the exact meaning of the phrase, but it must be a musician's term because we've heard Dave Pegg and Martin Allcock use it often...]*

Well, how does Maggie see the future for the Summer Band?
I'd like to think we could play some more gigs, but I have a feeling that we may just be together for this week. I'd love it to carry on because it is so enjoyable. I'd love to do some recording with the band too. This is a really good band. We've done so much work and it would be a shame to finish after just a few gigs. But who knows? What I would really like is for Martin to make a solo album… so that I could do some vocals on it!

That's what we would like him to do too!
I've heard whispers that he might be doing something....

He needs a kick up the back-side to get him to do it!
Really? Well, I'm just the person to do it! [*Laughs*]. I think he's a bit scared of me! But he is so brilliant, such a brilliant guitarist. He makes me want to weep when I hear him play.

I think he under values his playing
Yes he does, he does. I keep telling him that. He played something the other day in the studio, and when he finished we all just stood there and applauded, it was so great, but he just kind of shrugged it off. He is really inspiring, a superb guitarist. Trouble is when I tell him that he thinks I'm just taking the piss! But I'd love to do more work with him… I wish he'd make that album! But maybe you're right, maybe he does need a kick up the back-side.

Whether Maggie did in fact subsequently juxtapose her proverbial boot with Martin's virtual backside is lost in the mists of time, but history does record that two CDs eventually saw the light of day – 1993's limited edition live recording of The Summer Band, imaginatively titled A Summer Band, *which is now **impossible** to find, and Martin's first solo album* A Trick Of Memory, *which was released in 1994. Of which, more later...*

Chapter 21

GLENN CORNICK

(Published in #37, March 1993 & #38, April 1993)

In February 1993 a large number of current and past Jethro Tull members gathered at the Westmorland Arms pub in London to film the 'reunion' segment of the 25th *Anniversary video. Our own involvement in the project meant that we were lucky enough to be invited along to this extraordinary event, where we met some of the old boys for the first time ever. One of those was Tull's original bass player Glenn Cornick, who had flown over especially from California where he now lived. We both failed to recognise Glenn when we arrived, and we were somewhat taken aback when introduced to him. Short hair, no headband, clean shaven, no glasses - hard to believe meeting the 1993 model that in his Tull years from 1968 to 1970 Glenn Cornick had looked like the archetypal hippy.*

Despite some initial wriggling, the poor chap didn't stand a chance in the face of the full persuasive might of the A New Day *interview team, and towards the end of the proceedings he was gently guided to a corner of the bar and manacled to a Sony Walkman. As well as being a founder member of Jethro Tull, Glenn had been in The John Evan Band, and he gallantly ignored the heckling of erstwhile Tull colleagues to talk to us in a strong Lancashire accent which only occasionally betrayed his American residency.*

Our first question was the traditional one...

In the early days you were known variously as Glenn Barnard, Glenn Douglas and then Glenn Cornick. What is your real name?
Glenn Barnard is my birth certificate name. My mother remarried in the mid-sixties and I adopted my step-father's name. So Glenn Cornick is my real name - not the name I was born with, but it's not a stage name. Douglas is my middle name.

And is it Glenn or Glen?
Glenn. There was a misprint on *Stand Up* - *This Was* and *Benefit* got it right.

What we propose doing is working from square one up to the present day...
Hang on - I've got to leave on Friday! OK!...

Was The Hobos your first group?
The Hobos were my first Blackpool band. I'm from Barrow originally, and my first ever group were Joey and The Jailbreakers, so called because the other two guys were jailbreakers. Seriously! They were about fifteen years older than me, in their thirties. It depended who was out of nick at the time as to who was in the band. I'd never played bass before then. I played guitar, but the job came up for a bass player, so I nipped out and bought a bass. I was with them for about two months. Then I played with a band called The Vikings. Seems like a long time now, but it was probably for about a year or so. Then I was with a band called Formula One, again in Barrow. From that, I moved to Blackpool to put together The Hobos with Ronnie Brambells, Chris Riley and Chris Wootton - all of whom I've seen within the last three days. Ronnie Brambells I hadn't seen since that band broke up, which is a long time ago. I'd been out of touch with Chris Riley too, but I was with him two days ago; while Chris Wootton has been a long time friend of mine. I can't remember how long The Hobos lasted, but it must have been at least a year and a half. From there I went to The Executives, with Roy Carr, who I've arranged to see, and Tony Williams, who's here today of course. And then it was The John Evan Band.

How did you come to join The John Evan Band?
I probably needed a job!

But was it a newspaper advert, or what?

Oh no, it was just the local scene. I think the bass player before me, Bo Ward, lived in Scunthorpe or Grimsby or somewhere, which made things a little difficult for a Blackpool-based band. Although, as I recall, Chic Murray [*Neil Smith*] lived in Manchester. We were a bit scattered about for a 'local' band. I just heard they needed a bass player and went round and saw them.

When I joined the band it consisted of John Evans, of course, Ian, Barrie Barlow on drums, Tony Wilkinson, and the two Neils [*Valentine and Smith*] on sax and guitar. I got on well with most of them. I remember Murray was a really nice guy, but a bit of a strange character. He used to play a Fender Jazzmaster with all those knobs and buttons on, but he never knew what any of the controls did. He was a great player, but one night he'd sound great and the next night he'd sound terrible, because his guitar would get knocked around in the van and all the knobs would get changed. He only knew what the volume control did, so we'd have to run over and try to readjust him. An oddball character, but I enjoyed working with him. Ranger [*Neil Valentine*] was another strange person to have in a band. He was a Jehovah's Witness, and shouldn't really have been mixing with people like us, out playing rock'n'roll in pubs. Wilkinson was very pushy. Barrie - I never really got close to Barrie in those days, but I get along well with him now. At that time I guess I was getting on with Ian fairly well. John Evans I always really liked. John was playing the same game then as he does now, making people think he's not half as intelligent as he really is. I got very close to John because we'd play a lot of gigs way out of Blackpool, two or three hundred miles away sometimes, and John would always drive the van home at night because he could stay up all night. I could stay up all night too, so John and I used to talk a lot. If I had to pick out one person I was closest to, I think it would have to be John.

Did you keep in touch?
No, I lost touch with John around 1974, same as with Clive and Jeffrey. Last time I saw those guys before today was at the photo session for the *M.U.* album. I was living in West Berlin, and they flew me out to Los Angeles, which is indirectly why I ended up living there.

Do you have any memories of best or worst gigs?
We didn't have any good gigs.

Oh, come on, now...
No, there weren't any. We were playing in the soul scene at the time... [*sings*] "Call me Mr Pitiful…" and we were all bloody sick of playing that stuff. We wanted to do more kind of swing-jazz stuff. We thought we were hot shit, although we probably weren't. We wanted to do Jimmy Smith organ music and so on, but because of the club scene we were working in we had to do *Knock On Wood* and *Hold On I'm Coming* and all those things. So I really don't have any good memories of gigs.

A New Day put out a CD which Neil Smith had of The John Evan Band live in 1966, when Bo Ward and Ritchie Dharma were in the band, with the same sort of stuff on it...
In 1966? Sure it was 1966? I seem to remember that by 1966 I was well into that band, because by 1967 it was the start of what turned into Tull. I may be wrong, but I reckon that would be earlier than 1966.

What about The Marquee, which you played as The John Evan Smash?
That's right, supporting The Herd. I've got a flyer for that somewhere.

That must have been a good gig, come on!
Er... I don't remember that we went down that well; I guess we did OK. I don't have a lot of memories of that gig, although I remember being very impressed by Peter Frampton at that time, although I didn't stay impressed by him. I can't remember how the gig came about, but I'm sure it was before we'd moved to London - we went down from Blackpool. Yeah, when I said there were no good gigs, that's not quite true; basically, we weren't doing what we really wanted to do. And the audiences were bloody tough, and miserable. It was all soul, dancing stuff. If you didn't make 'em dance, you were shit.

So it was a question of having to play what the audience wanted to hear?
Absolutely. A lot of the clubs would send you a list of songs - Wilson Pickett, Otis Redding, Sam & Dave and so on - and you'd more or less have to agree to play those songs before you got the gig. I'm talking about gigs like The Twisted Wheel in Manchester - out and out soul dance clubs, and there wasn't much else in the North of England apart from that.

Do you remember doing *Firstimers* on Granada TV?
Yes, I do. We did *Take The Easy Way*. My best mate Jan, who I saw a couple of days ago, has promised me a copy of his tape of the acetates of the John Evan Band studio sessions, which Tony Wilkinson had.

Yeah, we've heard it. It's not good quality, the tape is damaged. I think Barrie has a good copy, and possibly John. Perhaps we should pursue that for the second box set...
Has anyone got a tape of us as Candy Coloured Rain doing *My Green Tambourine*??

It's disappeared, apparently. Have you got a tape?
No! But somewhere in this world there is such a tape. Wouldn't it be hilarious to have a copy?!

Have you got a tape of *anything* from The John Evan Band days?
No, you have more than I do.

Do you remember doing *The Man*?
Yeah, that was with Derek Lawrence, who we did *Green Tambourine* with, and *Aeroplane* of course. There were some other cuts we did with him, although I couldn't give you titles.

Didn't you ask for tapes of stuff before you left the studio?
Well, you're talking about the days before everyone had cassette machines. Technology has changed. I wouldn't walk out of a studio now without a tape of what I'd done. It's unfortunate - I wish I did still have some of the early stuff.

Did you think that something more should have been made of the *Firstimers* thing on TV - that perhaps it should have been a springboard to some sort of success?
Looking back on it - no. I don't think the band was that good at the time. It was better that it had the couple of years more to turn it into something that was really good. If we'd started having success at that point we might not have made the later adaptations.

Was there any indication at that stage that Ian had the talent to go on to become a big success?
I don't recall it at the time, no.

Was Ian the boss at that stage?
Tony Wilkinson was the loudest one. I wasn't aware of Ian taking any control, although he did write those three or four original songs.

Was there an actual point of change where you thought, "We'll play what we want to now"?
Yes, there was; there was a definite change. If you were living in Blackpool, or even Manchester, you'd never make it, you had to be in London. The big thing in London was the blues, with groups like Boilerhouse, Peter Green's Fleetwood Mac and Black Cat Bones. So when we moved down to London it was to be a hot shit blues band which was going to make some money - that was the prime motivation. You could say that oh yeah, we wanted to do our own thing, but there would only be a small element of truth in that. There was a definite motive behind playing the blues; it wasn't pure chance.
What happened was that we did a gig in London and met Mick Abrahams. He could play all the blues licks which nobody else could, so it was at that point that we decided to make the big move down south to London and become a blues band. So Mick joined, although we kept the full-sized band at first. This is also the point where Terry Ellis and Chris Wright come

in. They had been University Social Secretaries, booking bands, including us, for their Universities up north. They had moved to London and got an agency together in a little office, with one secretary. By that time they'd discovered Ten Years After, and they decided that they wanted us to come down too. So they were influential in pulling us out of Blackpool down to the London scene. So we moved to Luton, and Mick joined. Clive Bunker then came in because Barrie went home after a couple of weeks. We played around as a full-sized band for what must have been only a few weeks, when we figured out that economically we couldn't do it. So we cut it down to a four-piece, because basically that was all we could afford to have. Ranger was happy to go home. Tony Wilkinson didn't want to go home, and John I'm not sure. It was 80% a financial decision. It was tough getting by then; £15 for a gig between seven people is not easy.

What made you stick it out?
They needed a bass player! I'm not saying that was the only reason - I mean, I was really keen on doing it - but fortunately I didn't play saxophone, or I'd have been sent home!
At that point we didn't really know where we were going; we were playing the blues because everyone was playing the blues. The John Evan Band had in the past, before my time, played blues stuff, so Ian was familiar with it. It was round about then that Ian got his flute. Someone in St Anne's, just outside Blackpool, owed Ian some money. I went with Ian in the van to get the money, but the bloke couldn't pay up. But he had a flute, so Ian got the flute off him instead of the money. Forget any stories about a music shop - I was there!

And you became Navy Blue, Bag O'Blues and then Jethro Tull.
And I'm sure there were more names, though I can't remember them. Candy Coloured Rain was just for the recording sessions and was never used on stage.

So was 'Jethro Toe' a mistake?
No. That was that silly producer Derek Lawrence. He didn't like the name Jethro Tull. He knew what it was supposed to be, but he didn't think it was cool enough. It wasn't a misprint.

Clive Bunker has always said that, too.
Yeah. Yet 'Jethro Toe' sounds even less cool. I can remember fighting with him about the name.

***Aeroplane* was co-written by you...**
Yeah, it was something Ian and I banged out. We were up in Barrow, and we banged out some chords on a piano, and Ian put the vocals to it. But 'Len Barnard' was a misprint!

Was that your only collaboration with Ian?
Yes.

In a wider sense, then - what would you see as your creative input into Jethro Tull?
The bass player! I think that on those first albums I was a big part of it. I wrote all my own bass parts; Ian had nothing to do with things that I played. I played a lot of things that put hooks into the songs, but it's not standard to get writing credits for that. My own personal feeling is that there might be a point sometimes when you deserve it - but legally, no. It's a shame! But Ian would come in with a song, he'd sing it and play it on guitar, so the words, the melody and the chorus were already there. We arranged it, and sometimes added bits that made a big difference, but the song was already written by the time we got it. Much as I would like to say otherwise, I guess it's fair enough the way it is.

What ambitions did the band have in 1968?
Well, before the Sunbury Jazz and Blues Festival we'd played... it must have been 300 or more gigs that year. The most we ever made was £20 a night, all over the bloody country, playing all those little blues clubs that were around then. Some wouldn't hold more than about thirty people. We played every one that there was in Britain! We got to play face to face to everyone who was interested in that type of music, and we became very popular on that scene. At the same time we

got a residency at The Marquee in London, Tuesdays or Wednesdays, playing with Taste, Rory Gallagher's band. John Gee from The Marquee told us that he wanted us to play at the jazz-blues festival at Sunbury, and that was absolutely the turning point of the band. I'm sure everyone else says that too. No-one in the audience knew who was going on in what order. Before we were even announced, John Gee walked on stage with Ian's carrier bag full of flutes and claghorns and things, and the whole audience stood up and cheered. It was one of the best moments of my life. Everyone in the audience had recognised this old ratty carrier bag. The thing was, we'd played to all these people in little 30-seat places, and every one of them was there. Before then, we were a small band. From that point on we were a big band. There was no question in any of our minds after that that we were going to make it. [*Laughing*] I'd like to have another moment like that one of these days!

At the time, did you see *This Was* as the achievement of a goal or a step on the way to something else?
I think honestly speaking that *This Was* was just the next step we had to take. We didn't analyse it. Before Sunbury, nobody had ever written a bloody word about us. After Sunbury, every music paper was tearing the doors down to get to us, and every record company in Britain gave us an offer. Up until that point we'd already talked to Island Records, but to nobody else. Spooky Tooth had recommended Island to come and see us, and through that we ended up signing to Island because they were closest to what we were trying to do. It was the only label that really knew what was happening at the time. What can I say about *This Was*? I don't know that we knew exactly what we were doing. We just had to make a record, I suppose.

Presumably it was based on your stage performance at the time?
Yes, some of the songs were stage songs, some of the stuff was written for the album. But it was fairly representative of what we were doing on stage, with a mix between Ian's stuff and Mick's stuff.

How did the split with Mick come about?
We drove him home, parked the van outside his house, threw all his equipment in the street and said, "You're fired". In the three months or so before that happened, Ian was living in North London, I was living in South London, and Mick and Clive were living in Luton. Mick had the van most of the time. We'd go up and play a gig in, say, Newcastle-upon-Tyne, get home about three in the morning - or rather, get back to Mick's home at three in the morning - and Mick would drive Ian and me to Luton station for us to wait in the freezing cold for the seven o'clock train back to London. We really appreciated that! And there were a couple of other occasions which triggered things off. Ian and I would take the train up from London to Luton, take the bus up to Mick's house, and Mick would say, "I called up the AA and all the roads up to the North are blocked." Ian and I were both on the telephone in London, but he'd wait until we got up there. So we'd go back to our flats in London, and then get a call from the Chrysalis Agency the next morning demanding to know why we hadn't shown up at the gig. We'd say the roads were blocked, and they'd say, "Well, Clouds went up further than you were supposed to." So it would turn out that Mick had been bullshitting us. There was loads of stuff like that. I built up a grudge against Mick, and really didn't have any time for him. A great, easy going bloke - a great acquaintance, which was why we got him in the band in the first place, but I couldn't work with him. If you're in a band, you're in it together, and he wasn't in it together with us. Sorry I couldn't say anything nice about that bit.

How did you get on with Ian, Martin and Clive?
Well, you probably saw that I got on magically with Clive and Martin today - and actually, I got on well with Ian today. Ian and I had some fairly close times at one point, living in Luton. It was like the old sob story with violins. We had two... we'll call them 'flats', in the same building, although they don't deserve to be called flats - they were two hovels in the same shack. If you listen to the words of *We Used To Know* on the second side of *Stand Up*, it's all true. "*Remembering mornings, shilling spent...*" - we'd be bloody looking for shillings to put in the gas meter; we'd be sharing one can of Irish stew. Ian and I went through that together. But we definitely grew apart, no question about it.

Why?

I've always felt it was because of his upbringing. Ian's parents didn't approve of the way he looked and behaved after he got famous, and his father would not walk down the street with him because he looked so weird. Ian didn't want his parents ever to come to see him play, but my mother used to sneak Ian's mother into the back of gigs to see him. And even though Ian claimed to be an atheist or agnostic, he retained that streak of Scottish presbyterian puritanism in him. He was very offended when we toured the States when I was off chasing girls. I mean, I was twenty-one years old, and there was more available than anyone could handle in a hundred years, so I took advantage. But Ian never liked that. If you ever did a psychological profile of Ian, his family and his religious upbringing would be a very important part of it.

That does seem to be reflected in some of the songs...

The whole of *Stand Up* is about Ian's relationship with his parents.

When Mick left, and Ian took the helm, were you actually pleased to move away from the blues?

You know, we weren't even really aware that we were moving away from it. It wasn't a case of, "OK, now we can stop playing that effing blues stuff." I don't think that bands change that way. I think that what happens is that if you've got twenty songs and fifteen of them are blues, then you're a blues band. You get a couple of new songs which are not quite as bluesy, so slowly you turn into something which is less of a blues band. But when *Stand Up* came out I think we still thought we were a blues band.

But it was quite different...

Yes it was - because we'd never played the blues properly anyway! We were really never a good blues band. If you listen to, say, the first Fleetwood Mac album, they knew how to play the blues much better than we did - although I'd still rather listen to us, anyway, because I guess I wasn't that committed to real down-home blues. So it all happened step by step. And we got very bad press when we put out the *Stand Up* album, very badly criticised by the music papers.

I don't recall that.

I have copies of the reviews. We were criticised by a lot of people because it wasn't a straightforward blues album. As I say, we didn't realise how things had changed, because we'd been playing most of the stuff on stage. But the blues purists didn't like it because we didn't sound black - even though I don't think we sounded black on the first album, which is why I say that I don't think we were a good blues band. *This Was* was different to anything else around, and if you're a good blues band you don't play it different.

Do you have a favourite Tull song, or album?

My favourite album is *Benefit*, without question. There's some great songs on there, and a much greater variety than on *Stand Up*. A lot of it is about Jenny, of course, rather than Ian's family.

What was it like to tour America for the first time?

The first tour was tough. We ended up being there for three months, which was much longer than we'd expected. The trouble with that tour was that we played primarily at weekends, doing the Thursday, Friday and Saturday at one place and then having four days farting around, not knowing where we were, what we were doing, what the scene there was. There were good and bad things about the tour; it wasn't a whole lot of fun.

It was on the first tour that we recorded *Living In The Past*, in the Vantone studio in New Jersey owned by one of the guys from The Four Seasons. Martin could not get the chords right, all the way through the song. So on the released version there's actually still one wrong chord in it. Martin will tell you which one! It was really funny, 'cos we brought in people from the New York Symphony Orchestra to do all the 'da da da da' stuff, and these blokes, supposedly the best players around, couldn't read in 5/4 time. I mean, Stravinsky is in the weirdest time signatures and they could have played that, but 5/4 time, no way! So if you listen closely to *Living In The Past*, all the strings are in time, but they don't play with any rhythm; there's very little accent in it. But it sounds great on the record, because we all played it with the accents.

I hear there is a new, remixed version which takes the old tape and turns it into a 4/4 disco beat. How you can turn that song into a 4/4 beat is beyond me.

The bass line is one of the few things on the 12" remix which has been kept from the original.
How can they turn that bass line into 4/4 time? It's such an off the wall bass line...

Technology.
[*Groan*] So I have to learn it again...? I also remember Ian firing a bunch of guys who came in from the London Symphony Orchestra to do strings on *Sweet Dream*. They were deliberately out of tune because they thought we were a bunch of rock'n'roll wankers. Ian was dead right to run them out of the studio; he and David Palmer rustled up some good musicians instead. Talking of David, I was sorry he wasn't here today. I liked him a lot. He was there from the very start; he did some arranging on the first album. He was a wonderful arranger - certainly the best I've ever worked with. He called me up some years ago when he was at a loose end and suggested we got a band together with John Evans, Clive Bunker and Mick Abrahams, but I didn't fancy it.

Were you playing small gigs in America, or big venues in support of name bands?
It varied. Our first gigs were at The Fillmore East playing with Blood, Sweat & Tears. We went from that to playing some clubs and some ballrooms, mostly supporting other people, like Led Zeppelin, Vanilla Fudge. We headlined a few small clubs. We built up a following everywhere we played, so we achieved something with all the gigs. The Newport Jazz Festival was a good one. I remember playing on the same bill as Roland Kirk, who Ian was always accused of copying. Roland Kirk was really thrilled to meet us, and pleased that Ian was doing all that stuff because it had made Roland Kirk famous! We had a good time with him. The Newport Jazz Festival was interesting because it was the first year they'd had any sort of rock'n'roll on, so we were breaking new ground there.
The way America worked in those days, you established yourself on the coast, New York, Boston, San Francisco and Los Angeles, and then worked inwards from there. Hence we played a small club in Boston called The Tea Party, but it was a very important gig. Once you had those first four places covered then you could spread into the other markets and get a little bit of a word going round about you. But it was tough at first. Touring if you're not working every day is shitty, depressing, you're lost. There was no momentum at all to that tour. I guarantee we lost money. We certainly didn't come home rich and famous; but it broke us in certain markets so that we could go back the next time and do better. Later tours were a lot more fun.
Mind you, it was even tougher for the roadies. Ever hear of Roy Bailey? He could tell you a few stories! He was Tull's roadie right from the Luton days in 1967 until around 1975. In the very early days he was living out in Welwyn Garden City. He would come and pick the band up, he'd set up all the equipment on his own, we'd do the gig, then he'd drive us home, finally get home himself about five o'clock in the morning, and then be picking us up again at ten o'clock in the morning. He'd be doing an eighteen hour day seven days a week, and all for £10 a week. A really good fellow, he worked harder than anyone I ever saw. Another stalwart roadie was a fierce Scotsman, Fraser Aitken, who everyone called Fraser Gnash. He got his nickname on a tour of Scandinavia in the middle of December. We'd played in Sweden, and the band flew to Finland. The road crew had to drive over a hundred miles to the ferry in a creaking Mercedes van, the sort that has the massive front window, with a car full of roadies following. It was snowing, and about minus two zillion degrees - and the windscreen broke! So they had to drive for about two miles at a time, lift out the driver who'd be frozen solid, put him in the car, and replace him with another roadie. They finally reached the ferry, all completely frozen and completely pissed off. So Fraser got legless drunk on the ferry, leant over the side to throw up into the Baltic, and threw up his top set of false teeth straight into the sea! He turned up the next day at the TV studio toothless, and immediately became Fraser Gnash for ever more.
I remember another tour of the States, later on in 1969, when two thirds of the gigs we did were rock festivals. A bloody depressing tour if ever there was one. We did some good gigs; but we'd show up at these rock festivals, supposed to be on at seven o'clock at night, and they'd be running eight hours late, so we'd be told to go and take a rest and come back in the middle of the

night. I remember playing outside Toronto and going on at four o'clock in the morning. It was bloody cold at night, and my fingers were dropping off as I tried to play. We were in New York when the Woodstock Festival was going on, and we were invited to play at Woodstock. Ten Years After were up there, so we called them up and said, "What's it like up there?", and they said "It's pissing down with rain, it's out of control, it's one of the worst effing gigs you've ever seen!". So we decided not to go. Probably not one of the better moves we ever made…

Well, I dunno. It saved you being pigeon-holed, for example.
It would have been nice to have been there - but yeah, looking back on it from this perspective I can see that it did us no harm. But that was the year of the festivals, and they were all a disaster, certainly from the performing and logistics aspect.

Was it at all frightening a year later when you were THE band?
Hell, no! It was great. We'd worked our way up to it and each success was just one more step up the stairway. There's nothing tough about being famous, believe me. I know some of the other guys in the band said they hated touring, but I don't think they would have traded the experience for anything.
On one 1970 tour we were touring with Mountain, who were our best friends out there on the road. We had a deal going with Mountain that we'd joint headline and take turns on who'd close the show. We played Red Rocks in Denver, which was wonderful, except for being out of breath on stage because its a mile and a half above sea level. It's a magical place to play, a natural sandstone amphitheatre. That was where there were riots at a Tull show, although that was after I'd left the band.

So how did you come to leave Tull?
Ian kicked me out. We finished a tour at the end of December 1970 in Buffalo, New York. We got out to Kennedy Airport the next day to fly back to England. We were just about to check in at the gates and gave all the tickets to our manager, Terry Ellis, and Terry said to me, "Come and have a coffee with me." He took me into the coffee shop, and said, "Ian doesn't want you to play in the band any more". Then he said, "I've cancelled your reservation; you have to fly home tomorrow." They got on the plane, and they didn't let me on, because they didn't want to have to talk to me. That's short and sweet!
I think the main problem, seriously, was that Ian didn't respect my morals at the time, chasing girls and socialising. I was never out of it on stage; I did my job great. In fact, it couldn't have been my playing because they replaced me with Jeffrey! I mean, Jeffrey's a great bloke, I always liked Jeffrey from the days before Tull; but he's not a bass player - and Jeffrey would tell you that. Ian just didn't like my general mode of behaviour. But I've never forgiven him for not having the guts to speak to me direct. Imagine that at the airport, with people waiting for me at the other end...

And what were your feelings about Terry Ellis?
Well, I know a lot of people don't like him, but Terry Ellis was bloody marvellous when I was with the band. There would not have been a successful Jethro Tull without Terry. He was the bloke who got us to move from Blackpool and being a soul band to London and being a blues band. In 1968, before we did the *This Was* album, Terry sat down with a piece of paper and wrote out a timetable for the band, including dates for the first Top Ten album, first Top Ten single, first American tour, and so on. He planned every move we'd make down to the last month, and he was absolutely right on everything. That takes some doing. And for the next three or four years he directed every move that the band made. It seems he rather went off the rails later, but that was after my time.

What happened after you'd left Tull?
I put Wild Turkey together because I didn't know what the hell else I should do with myself, and nobody came up with a great offer to do anything else. It was a fun band - I got a bunch of people together who I really enjoyed working with... but I don't know that I was smart enough or grown up enough to know what to do with the band.

Was it your band?

Yes, it was my band. We did two albums and two American tours, had some of the best times I've ever had on the road, and some of the best times in the studio. But looking back on it, we didn't really know what we were trying to do.

Are you in touch with any of those guys?
I'll be seeing probably three of them next week in Swansea; Gary Pickford I'll be seeing in a couple of days, plus Tweke Lewis and maybe some others. I keep in touch with most of the people I've worked with.

What happened when Wild Turkey broke up? I remember Paris...
When Wild Turkey broke up, Gary went off to work with Rick Wakeman on the *Journey To The Centre Of The Earth* album, and I went to live in Berlin. I was getting a bit sick of working in England at the time. I called everybody that I knew all over the world, and said to myself that the first offer I got out of England I'd go. I got a call from someone I knew in West Berlin, so I went there to play with a German band for about nine months. It was a good break - no great musical value to it, but it was fun to be away. Then I got a call from Chrysalis. They wanted me to fly out to Los Angeles for a week to do the photo session for the *M.U.* album, all expenses paid - unlike today! I met up in L.A. with my first wife Judy [*featured in several 1969/70 group photos*]; she was friends with Fleetwood Mac, so I met up again with Bob Welch, who I'd known for a while. Bob had left Fleetwood Mac, so he said, "Why not come out here, and we'll put a band together?" It was certainly a bit warmer than West Berlin, and with really not a lot more thought than that I went out to L.A. - not thinking that it would be for the next eighteen years! Paris did two albums, but basically it just didn't work in the end. We had a lot of fun on the road, but I guess we made a few bad moves. We didn't exactly split up... we just didn't go any further! That was around 1977. From there it was kind of downhill for a while. I did session work, and worked with a couple of bands which were pretty pointless - can't even put names to them, and certainly couldn't give you reasons why I did it other than I had nothing else to do. Then there's a whole blank period when I got so depressed with the music scene that I spent a few years not playing.

Ian has often mentioned that you became a cat food salesman...
Oh, give me a break! I'm a sales manager for a food company, not an effing pet food salesman. It's not what I want to do for the rest of my life, but it keeps me going. But that's like me calling Ian a fishmonger!

When did you last see Ian before today?
Six years ago at the Universal Amphitheater in Los Angeles. I went with a colleague from work, and we got drunk before the show as I wasn't thrilled about going to see them. I really hadn't followed their career - the last album I bought was *War Child*. But it was actually nice seeing Ian today.

So what is the position at the present day?
Well, a few years ago someone called me up and invited me to play on some Irish music sessions. I explained that I hadn't played for five years, but he persuaded me to do it, and I ended up head over heels in the Irish scene, and have been there ever since. The latest venture is with Blended Spirits. We've done a tape in the studio live to master, the first time I'd ever done that. We could have spent longer in the studio and done a better production, but it only took three hours, and was great fun. The tapes aren't available commercially, but perhaps we could work something out through your magazine.
Beyond that, I'm fed up of Los Angeles. It's become a depressing bloody city, and I've been here longer than I've ever been anywhere in my life, including Barrow where I grew up. So the plans are that within the next two years I'll be either in London or in Galway in Ireland, working in the Irish scene.

Our thanks went to Glenn for allowing us to drag him away from the bar to speak to us - without, it must be said, any prior warning. Pardon? What's that I hear you say? We forgot the most important question of all? Of course we didn't...

Finally - whatever happened to the headband?
With the red and white Indian pattern? I've still got it at home!

Chapter 22

IAN ANDERSON

(Published in #41, November 1993)

The A New *Day interview squad of DR and MW (with subdued back up from Frank The Snowman) spoke to Ian Anderson on the morning before the second show in Manchester in October 1993. As always Ian was in fine form, witty and articulate and, above all, completely frank. We were constrained by time and could not touch on all the topics we would have wished, but the following pages offer a fascinating insight into the side of Ian Anderson that is often overlooked, even by us - that of the totally dedicated and passionately creative musical innovator. As we talked it became increasingly obvious that despite his incredible achievements of the previous 25 years, he was still possessed of the same fire and enthusiasm for his art that must have burned within him at the very beginnings of Jethro Tull. You will read that he "speaks from the heart" when he wishes that he had ignored the back-tracking congratulatory emphasis of recent Tull releases and had concentrated instead on making a __new__ Jethro Tull album, and believe us, he **really** meant it. A welcome and heartening statement at the time, and one that reassured readers aghast at wild rumours that the 1993 tour was Tull's "Farewell" tour.*

Our conversation was hampered by the "background" music in the hotel foyer, an enjoyable but highly intrusive helping of trad jazz. Ian battled bravely to be heard until he could stand it no longer and ordered the reception desk to turn it off - so apologies if the singing voice was not so good that night as a result! Read on…

Firstly, congratulations on the success of the American tour which I hear went really well. Were you at all surprised by that? Or did you __know__ it would be a great success?
Well you have to qualify what "really well" is. We did OK business, a reasonable amount of people turned up. Compared to a lot of other bands on the road I think we got more than our fair share of the interest and attendance. But the concerts themselves, from my point of view, were very taxing, as I have always found in America when you're playing outdoors. It always seems to be temperature extremes, and I can only think of three or four shows where it was comfortable on stage, where it was in the normal range of between 20 and 30 degrees; otherwise we were looking at crazy temperatures. In Texas it was 102 before the stage lights came on, you know. That is so far above body temperature that you just can't lose that heat. You can sweat as much as you like, but you cannot get below your blood temperature and you are literally running out of steam, and apart from anything else it gets dangerous doing that sort of stuff for two hours, so it's not a lot of fun in the physical sense. And then there were a few gigs when it was very, very cold. We flew into a snow storm in Denver, the first snow of the year, and I'm told it had been 92 the day before so obviously it was a great surprise! It was above freezing during the gig, but still very cold. It's probably harder in those circumstances for Martin than it is for me and Doane, because we make our own heat, we have our own built-in boiler house, whereas Martin doesn't, it's hard to keep warm and his fingers must suffer.

Have you seen any of the reviews? They were really quite positive.
I've seen a few of them, yes. I read them if I can get them. They were on balance OK reviews. The shows toward the latter part of the tour I think were probably better performances, and the second half of all the shows was probably better than the first half, because it was cooler! So I didn't have the physical burden of trying to work in unfriendly temperatures.

And the tour continues till... when? March? April?
Well, from here on in we go to South America, then we have fixed, as of last night, another six shows in the USA. We thought we were going to South Africa after South America, but that seems to have simply evaporated. From having actually had dates, venues and a deal it

just suddenly evaporated and the promoter didn't seem to be there anymore, so that has gone by the board. We are now talking to another promoter about doing something there next year, but that's likely to be after the elections, and after the elections I personally feel very, very worried that South Africa will very possibly become unplayable again for another ten years, for a totally different set of reasons to the last ten years. All of which is very sad because it's one of those places that I've always wanted to go, not because I understand what's going on there, not because I have any great moral or ethical need to get to grips with it, but just because it fascinates me how things got to where they were, and the dilemma of how to proceed from here on in. I would just be grateful for a few days to be in it and meet people and talk to people and look at people just to try and get some understanding of what is ultimately a very confusing situation. But I think that's somehow going to slip by us altogether, which is a shame. But anyway, South Africa not happening means that rather than call it a day after the South American section, when everybody, all the crew, was expecting another week's work [*laughs*], I thought we might as well hop up to do at least one of the two broad areas of the USA which we didn't play on this tour, which would be the south and south east. Then we are off for December and January, and of course Dave has his Fairport tour January/February. I can't remember the exact starting date but we should be touring India sometime in February. We have the dates but we have a question mark over Delhi which is difficult logistically, so to compensate for having to accommodate Delhi I thought we might as well slip in a few extra dates to make it worthwhile. So although we haven't fixed those dates yet we will be trying to play in the North West of the USA on the way back, Honolulu and Alaska and so on. Those are alternative ways of coming back from Australia and New Zealand where we finish up. We'll try to do Seattle, Portland, Vancouver... Calgary this time I hope, possibly Montreal and other places, primarily in Canada that we haven't played before. But it will finish somewhere around the end of March, in the North East of North America.

What's the story behind Japan? It seems a long way to go just to play one very small gig...
Well, it's just that Japan is one of those places which has always been somehow denied to us as a place where we really achieved anything back in those days when we should have done. We went into Japan twice, once just for a couple of shows and then we went back and played six or seven shows in '74, but we did encounter some stern advice from the promoter back then which was don't leave the Japanese market for a year; you have to come back within a year otherwise they will forget you and move onto something else. We didn't really believe him, and with other things that came up we just didn't get back to Japan, and a couple of years later we said, "Well, how about Japan?", and [*laughs*] they just put the phone down, forget it, you know, dead and gone. I went there around '76 I think, with Terry Ellis when he was doing some record company promo trip and I just went along for the ride, and it was pretty obvious that Jethro Tull had no profile at all there... and we don't sell any records. Well obviously there are a few dedicated fans, but we are talking about a very small number of people. But at the end of last year I contacted all the EMI offices around the world and told them I was going to do a dedicated promo trip in advance of the world tour, and if they wanted me to do anything to let me know. To my surprise Japan were interested, so I added it to the list of places to visit. Part of the reason for doing those promo trips in those sort of places was to check out and meet the promoters and record company people to see if there was interest in the band going to do some dates. In Japan we eventually decided to go in there and do one showcase gig to see if there was any interest from the press and the media, and if the reaction was good we would try to come back to play a few more dates.

What was the reaction?
I actually don't know first-hand. I didn't meet the promoter afterwards as he was off partying while we all sloped off to bed suffering from jet lag, and he turned up at the hotel too late for us to talk to him. But he called a couple of days ago, I assume as a result of... the er...
[*Ian's train of thought was derailed as the already rather loud background music became a crescendo of noise. He left us temporarily to get the music stopped...*]

Where was I?... Yes, Japan. I think he wants us to do a few dates in Japan next year, but it wouldn't be around the time that we could easily fit them in, so we'll have to just bear it in mind for the future.

Have you plans after March, or is it too early to even think about?
It's hard to tell. We are actually only half way through the tour, and it really is very difficult to predict how we are going to feel at the end of that number of dates. When you get off the plane at Heathrow Airport at some bleary hour of the morning... I mean we don't even speak, you just get your luggage and people disappear. The most you're ever going to get is, "I'll give you a call next week". People just disappear and no-one ever knows how we will be feeling then. Martin is talking about doing another solo album. I'm sure Dave Pegg will want to be doing a Fairport record. I think I can confidently predict, just for practical reasons, that we are not going to be jumping into the studio a week later and starting work on a Jethro Tull album. Everybody's gonna need some time, a few weeks off, sorting out their unpaid bills, personal life, children, Easter holidays and so on. I think around May we'll be weighing things up and if in December/January I have managed to write enough material I guess we will then be talking about doing some studio work. But it will be very touch and go even then, bearing in mind that for a realistic October deadline for an album release, practically speaking the album would have to finished by mid June. That only really gives six weeks to make an album which is difficult. The old days when we were all living in bed-sits and hotel rooms, all in the same place all the time, and all you had in your life was wake up in the morning, go to the studio and work until you drop every day it was OK, we could make an album in two or three weeks, but that isn't the way it is anymore, we can't do that now. Not with the geographical dispersal and family and friends and all the rest of it, the reality of domestic and social obligations. So it really would be a tight squeeze to make an album. I have been approached by Chrysalis and EMI on other things as well, so I'm not quite sure what I might do in parallel or separately to Jethro Tull.

I heard that you were thinking about doing a "classical" album...
Well I was approached by EMI to discuss with them the idea of making an album for the EMI Classical division, but I stress that that doesn't mean what most people are going to think of as being a classical album or a piece of classical music - because there is no earthly point in me getting up and trying to play Vivaldi's *Four Seasons*, or do anything that's in the regime of the James Galway area of performance, because I can't play that well. So it certainly wouldn't be me playing the classics. The only way that would work is if you took some classical themes and did something different with them, but then it wouldn't really belong on EMI's classical label, it would belong on the jazz side of things or the pop or disco or the funk side, you would be taking it away from that kind of performance level. I think the interest they have in me is to write something and perform something that doesn't sound like Beethoven or Mozart, but is within the scope of a more esoteric kind of piece of music for those people who like classical music who might like to hear some predominantly instrumental music that would involve me as a writer, as a flute player, but not regurgitating the pop classics. So in terms of what that might be, I've had a meeting and further discussion, and I will present to EMI a proposal for a... if you like a slightly thematic or conceptual piece of music that might or might not work, and if they like the idea I'll do a couple of demos in December/January period, and if they like those I'll go on and do a couple of finished pieces, and then maybe the whole thing.
But at the end of it it will have cost a lot of money to make, and it's not something I'm going to embark upon lightly. The way I work is I deliver finished product at my own expense, I'm really not interested in scoring big advances or ending up with somebody else losing money on something that is as whimsical as a musical project that really doesn't have a defined point of contact with an existing audience. Obviously... I mean, you know me, I'm not going to do something that's a David Palmer type orchestral album, and I certainly wouldn't want to make a record where anybody was thinking that the audience or the buyer for it was going to be the people who would otherwise rush out and buy a Jethro Tull album, because that would inevitably be, for most of them, disappointing. So it would have to be marketed and promoted and thought of really as being an album for those people who are likely to be reached

through the type of promotion and advertising that would be applicable to a classical work. It will be something that is definitely out of the realms of Jethro Tull-ish sounding music. But it certainly won't be for a big orchestra, and nor will it sound like your or my idea of classical music in the sense of it being music by people who died a long time ago, which is what most of it is. Outside the hotel there's a huge list of concerts going on, and every single one of them is Beethoven this, Mozart that, the same old bunch of dead people! Of course there are new people, new composers, but hardly ever do they get through into any kind of commercial acceptance. Usually because it tends to be modernistic, it tends to be dissonant, not to have the relatively catchy nature of those favourite classical pieces that for three or four hundred years have had plenty of time to impress themselves upon people's minds and memories. But then again I'm not going to do an Andrew Lloyd Webber, writing really catchy themes and doing them in an orchestral or semi operatic fashion - that would just be obscene beyond belief. I am kind of wed to the idea of trying to bring some vocal music into it, as that immediately becomes something intrinsically more attractive. At the moment I do have some fairly defined ideas about where I'm going with this, but I don't really think there's much point in going into detail because... things change. Suffice it to say there would be a degree of multi-lingual and multi-national nature to this recording, partly because I've got to be realistic about it that in order to try to sell enough records to cover everybody's costs we've got to aim at not just one market but a bunch of them.

Are you also doing some film music? You had a meeting with Disney...
Hmmm, yes. They haven't sent me anything yet. I saw the guy again briefly in Los Angeles but I haven't heard anything from them, but that's not... well really quite honestly it's not something that I would anticipate, and I probably said that in the meeting. I probably came across as being very lukewarm about it, which I've always been, because whenever I've been asked to do anything like that I've been put off a bit by the realities of working within the framework of making movies. As a writer you tend to get dragged in pretty late in the day, and the director still has total control over the music; if he doesn't like a bar he'll chop it out or change things. Also, how many movies completely stiff? They could have a great soundtrack but still completely die at the box office. So nobody hears the music, there's no soundtrack album, or if there is it gets no additional publicity to sell it, and at the end of the day your music gets heard by very few people and is tied up conspicuously with somebody else's failure. So the idea of spending two or three months working on something like that only to find that it dies a death perhaps regardless of how good or bad the music might be is not a very rewarding area in which to be working. Obviously a successful movie soundtrack is very rewarding financially, and you can certainly make yourself a lot of money doing it if you become in demand doing that sort of thing, but I don't think it's really what I want to do. I would do it only if there was a movie that interested me, subject material that interested me, and if I thought I could do an acceptable job, because the worst of all things for me would be to enter into something and really not do it very well, or let somebody else down because you might have a great movie with some rotten music. I would have to be sure that I could do it well enough. Another thing that bothers me about it is that there is no obvious performance follow up. That's what I find difficult about those things in isolation. I mean Eddie Jobson spends all his time writing music for ads, and he's now working on a pilot for a TV series, but all you ever do is patch the thing together with computer driven technology; you never actually get to play the thing, you never get up on stage and play it to real audiences which would certainly disturb me and I know it must disturb Eddie. I can only think about music as... well, when you finish making an album it is the first part of a much greater whole that embodies taking that music on into months or even years beyond that into a performance level that might be exactly the same or become different from the original recording. That seems to give the music some credibility when you go onstage and play at least some of it.
And that's one of the aspects of doing that "classical" album for EMI, it would have to be something that I felt could be performed. That's where it gets really difficult, because whereas you can go and rent a bunch of LSO guys and put them in a studio and do an orchestral album, and you can pay them all triple time to double track and do everything else you have to do and patch it together that way, when it comes to doing it live onstage you are talking about something that's going to lose tens of thousands of dollars every time you perform it. So the only way to do it is through the auspices of local orchestras in various cities of the world who basically include it in their programme, and it becomes part of their millions of dollars or hundreds of thousands of pounds budget that they get from Arts Councils, local

authorities, charity donations etc to operate at a loss, and I am intrinsically opposed to music that has to be subsidised. I don't like the idea that it must be preserved in aspic at the tax payer's expense. I think that music should live and survive because it has a vitality of its own that means it operates in the market place and at the going rate. It's very hard to make that work with operas and ballets and classical concerts because of the numbers of people traditionally involved, and also because union rates and union scales mean that everybody's getting paid just for sitting there reading the newspaper. Rehearsals become more or less out of the question because it costs an absolute fortune to stage. On the other hand anybody in the first violin section is familiar with most of the classical repertoire by the time they've left college because they have played it so many times in practice and learning their instrument. They have probably been playing those same things for 15 years of their life. To run through that sort of thing you are talking about a day's rehearsal before a series of concerts with a guest conductor. You're really just talking about interpretation, those guys know all that music backwards anyway. But if you write them a new piece of music, especially if it embodies anything **to them** weird, like strange time signatures or any rhythmic involvement with which usually they are never at ease, let alone the conductor, then you're in deep problems. So my approach would be to work with a very small ensemble, probably four dot readers and... probably two other people. The only thing that would define what I would write as being classical music would be that it would not and could not contain the modern jazz kit drums, i.e. the rock 'n' roll drum kit, but technically it's the kit that evolved out of jazz music. As soon as you do that, start to play "time" in that sense, you end up with something that's going to sound like the LSO play Deep Purple or what have you, and it goes horribly wrong, it just becomes a pastiche. So you take away the drums and you take away the rock'n'roll element, you take out the jazz, and you have to build rhythmic sense back into the music through different devices. That's the job of work to try to create something that has... something that's gonna make your foot **almost** tap! Without having to have Doane Perry sitting there - not necessarily that that would make your foot tap either! It might cause you to break out in a rash or rush to the nearest launderette. I did my laundry last night after the show. I bet Doane didn't, I bet he's sitting up there in a room that you wouldn't be able to go into without serious breathing apparatus!

Did you play with David Palmer in the Hollywood Bowl last month?
No, he called me about that a while ago, but he never called back. He asked me what I was doing, and I had a free date. I said I could do it if it could be done with minimum rehearsal. "Keep it easy for me and if you want me to do it then I'll do it", you know, but I tried to make it clear I would do it as a personal favour to him, and asked him to let me know. But David does that, he'll be on the phone and then you don't hear from him again, he blows hot and cold. Sometimes he's very charming, sometimes he's very distant. I mean he's had tremendous problems in his domestic life with his wife being very, very seriously ill for so many years, and I'm sympathetic with his need to earn a living and do the things he does, but nothing else came of that. And [*laughs*] I wasn't going to call him up and remind him. He did go out and do some stuff, I heard he was doing concerts with various orchestras around America.

Did you ask David to play at the Hammersmith concerts?
[*This interview was conducted a week before the two "25th Anniversary" concerts at Hammersmith Apollo. In the event Mick Abrahams, Clive Bunker and Gerry Conway joined Tull onstage. We had known for some time that it was on the cards but did not directly mention it in A New Day for reasons outlined by Ian himself here.*]
No, he's still out in America I believe, so I didn't contact him. I spoke to Barrie Barlow, John Evans, Jeffrey Hammond, Clive Bunker and Mick Abrahams. Barrie, John and Jeffrey... I mean I suggested to them if they didn't want to play then just come up on the stage and say "Hi", there would be some people who would really appreciate just seeing you. Or if you want to come up and play something, whatever you would like to do, just for a bit of fun. Some people in the audience would really appreciate seeing it, it would be a nice gesture for you to be there, and whatever you want to do we will fit in with you, at any level. But I said, "Don't say yes or no now, think about it and I'll call you back next Tuesday". So that's what I did, and Barrie Barlow said, "I've given it some thought and I think I'd rather bow out of this one". He didn't really give any reason why but it was obviously a decision he had made so,

fair enough. John Evans asked for money, very pointedly, a sum of money with several zeros on the end, and I said, "The thing is, John, this is really not about that, this is just about a bit of fun. No-one else would be getting paid, it's either a bit of fun or it isn't". He said, "Well in that case, it wouldn't be". End of conversation. I don't know how you take that one. Martin, as I was, was deeply pissed off by that, and I'm telling you this because I know you'll write it, and I hope you do, and I think John Evans is conveniently forgetting the fact that twice every year he gets paid a royalty cheque, and that if nothing else he might just stop to think that maybe he just owes it to a few people who still buy records that he played on, just maybe that it might be a nice and polite and respectful thing to do to say, "Hey, thanks for paying for my holiday," or something, which he has acknowledged in the past. It just seems to me a very predatory attitude to take to say I'll do it for X amount of money. I thought he was kidding me, I thought "he has to be joking", but the conversation revealed that was clearly not the case, it was take it or leave it - this is how much I want.

Perhaps he was just throwing the onus back onto you having to say no? Maybe he didn't have the bottle just to say no?
Maybe, maybe. But I'm sure there are other ways of doing it. There's always the old "I've got to wash the car", or change the baby or my wife's got flu, lots of easy ways of getting out of it. Anyway, Jeffrey gave it some thought and we discussed things that he might possibly do, but at the end of it he said he would be too terrified to get up on stage, he would be so nervous and embarrassed and he really couldn't do it. That leaves us with Clive and Mick, both of whom said, "Sure, no problem we'll be there". So they will be there for the first London show.

Not the second show?
Well we haven't really discussed it. The point is, what I'm trying to avoid for their sake as well as ours is that... we don't want to publicise these things with a view to putting bums on seats. For me, and for the people who have bought their tickets, it's something extra. You can't try to sell them the idea on the basis that this is gonna happen because you don't know how it's going to work out. I had no idea until a few days ago whether we were going to have five ex Jethro Tull members on stage with us or whether it would be none. To try to present that at the time when people are buying tickets is a bad idea, because it's something that you can't guarantee. But if it's good on the first night, and they are free and willing to do it again then we might just do it.
But there comes a point where doing something like that once is a bit of fun, but then... well put it this way, the guys in the band are not going to be interested in paying some other guys to play there who happened to be in the band before. As a bit of fun, a one off, it's great, but if you start advertising it then it becomes a different thing altogether, you are using them to try to sell more tickets, or increase the ticket price or whatever, in order to pay those guys for doing what they do. But if somebody asked me to play on their album, or get up onstage with them, I would never dream of sending them an invoice for money, I just wouldn't do it. If somebody asked me to play on their record, if they're unknown, it's their first album and I like the artist, I like the song - they can't afford to pay me, so I'll do it for nothing. If on the other hand it's someone who's music I respect, or an opportunity to play with someone I would really enjoy to be with for a little while, then again that is the pay off, not money. I've never charged for anything that I've done, and I never would, at least not in that way of making that relatively impromptu contribution.

Moving on to the forthcoming *Nightcap* set, was it your decision to forget the 4CD format and reduce it to a double CD?
It was the only way to make it a viable proposition. Number one thing was that it had to come out at a reasonable price retail-wise, and with a 2CD set we could put it in one of the new slim-line packs which is much cheaper packaging, keep the whole thing to minimal artwork, minimal content, no lyrics, no fold out, no nothing, and keep the price at what I've always felt could be done, which is a little over the retail price of a single CD. But as soon as we stretch to including additional live material it gets really expensive. And all there was was a bunch of live stuff that you've all heard before, i.e. the stuff from Madison Square Garden. When I actually

sat and listened to that I thought, "What's the point? This is just the *Bursting Out* album again". Just a different performance of the same arrangement, made within weeks of those *Bursting Out* recordings. It doesn't seem to me to be worthwhile doing that, except in the context of it being the stereo soundtrack of a video of that particular thing. That has been suggested to Chrysalis/EMI, but I don't know if they want to do it or not. There are lots of other live recordings, I have oodles and oodles of live tapes recorded everywhere in the last few years, but I have the feeling that for people who want that there are like a hundred different bootlegs on the market that might be grossly inferior in terms of sound quality, but they are there for people who want that stuff. But if we put that stuff out as part of another 4CD set then it's going to work out as a very expensive CD.

But this double CD will include the complete "Chateau Tapes". We've included the section that was on the first box set as well. It would have been the easiest thing in the world to leave it off and say well you've heard that already, but there will be people who didn't buy the *20 Years Of* set who will buy this because it is so much cheaper, and they'd be annoyed if they didn't have the whole thing. So I thought we'd better fold it back in because... well, it's a bonus, it's not like it's replacing something else. Putting it in is just giving people all of the recorded material, or at least everything that is sufficiently complete, sufficiently meaningful to be considered as a worthy bit of music.

There were another few minutes...
Of pure and utter crap! [*Laughs*] I'm sorry, you're never gonna hear that, along with hours of other tapes that I have found. Because we're talking real shit, we're talking rubbish, either lyrical or musical crap. There comes a point where my decision really is final on that, there is nothing else left, believe me. We have got tapes in from places that I never believed we would find them, and I've spent what must be weeks of my life listening to these tapes that come in boxes and you haven't got a clue what's in there. To begin with it's like Christmas, you know, "Ooh, I wonder what's in here!", but you put it on the machine, you lace it up, you are having to clean the heads every 5 seconds because of oxide shedding... it's a real pain in the arse. You spend maybe an hour to find that what's in there is absolutely utterly worthless, it's just the backing track to a song that got re-recorded another ten times or what have you, something that's just meaningless, just nonsense. To begin with it's fun, it's like Christmas Day, after two or three days it's becoming a real chore, and after a couple of weeks of going through these wretched boxes then it starts to become **extremely** boring and extremely irritating because there is so little that is genuinely complete pieces of music that were not utilised. So much of it is doodling in the studio that never evolved into anything complete. There are bad notes and dodgy bits in it, and although something like that is sort of amusing, it really is scraping the barrel. There has to be some kind of criteria laid out in this kind of a project, and that is that it's really got to be stuff that could legitimately have found its way onto any Jethro Tull album in the past, and that's what I have said.

Well, I would say there is one exception and that is *A Small Cigar* which I personally loath and detest and really don't like, but it's only because I've heard from, well, you guys and some other people who say, "Yes, it's quirky and a bit silly, but we kind of like it". So I had my arm slightly twisted on that one, but the rest of it is all stuff that I feel really belongs somewhere, pieces that definitely would have been happy sitting on *Warchild* for instance if we hadn't been constrained back then by vinyl releases on which you could only legitimately fit say 42 minutes of music. A lot of that earlier stuff is still sitting out there because we were still releasing vinyl up until fairly recently. In 1984 we put some extra stuff on the CD and cassette, and we have done it once or twice since, but it causes a lot of bad feeling. A lot of people complain about it because the vinyl enthusiasts feel they are being cheated. But right now the sales of vinyl are so low it's just not worth bothering with. Maybe it's time to give serious consideration to giving people traditional LPs that have nothing in them, just give them a chance to have the album cover and have the artwork at a size where you can read the lyrics and see the picture. I've actually got a few copies of the vinyl version of *A Little Light Music* because that is something that one day somebody will be pleased to have, even if they never play it, even it remains in the shrink wrap, because it is probably one of the last purpose-made vinyl records, from us anyway. These days it's down to thinking CD and then cassette, at least as far as *Nightcap* goes. Chrysalis think they don't want cassette versions, but when they stop and make some enquiries they are gonna get requests from various places for a cassette version as well. I got onto Chrysalis International and insisted they ring around, and yesterday I got a fax requesting approval for running order for a cassette format. So they will be releasing it on cassette in some countries and there is even discussion underway now regarding a possible cassette release in the UK. So hopefully, and I personally think they should, they'll go for a cassette version as well as CD. Some people don't own a CD player but most own a cassette player.

Why didn't the box set come out on cassette? The packaging would have been the same.
It has, or it is, in India. They were the only territory who came back with a tangible request. In fact I actually called them first and said, "Look guys, rather than moan about it later, if you want to release any of this stuff you're gonna have to reconfigure it for cassette", because there is no CD market, so they had to come up with a revised selection. It had to come down to two cassettes, containing more than half the material but of course not all of it. Obviously without the booklet and all the rest of it it had to have a special, condensed little amount of bumph with it for which I wrote a little message specifically for the Indian folks. Those are the ways I think you have to treat it, you've really got to look at it country by country, market by market, to try to do the right thing for each particular place, in order to keep the price at a realistic level. And in this case I was able to, and if this doesn't end up happening I can certainly tell you who you can take to task over it, but I've finally been given a retail price commitment from Our Price and others to keep the price at £1 more than the price of a single CD. I've always said you should be able to do that if everybody takes a drop in their margin and you reduce the royalty rates. Everything is scaled down to a level where everybody can still see some element of profit in it, and that's the way it should be. But I'm also giving the royalties from the song writing on these two CDs to two charities, because I don't really feel that in a case like this where you've held onto something for a long time and then you finally put it out... there has got to be an element of goodwill about it, which is keeping the price down, not being seen to profit unduly by it, and basically just trying to see that it's done in a good spirit and for the right reasons.

It's certainly not "rejected material", although I suppose you could argue that the Chateau Tapes are rejected in the sense that we abandoned that project before it was finished, but looking back on that as I have in some depth, trying to remember what was going on at the time... I mean a lot of it was salvageable stuff, you can clean up a lot of the things that were wrong with it. Back then we couldn't, but these days there are all sorts of gadgets for making things sound better, de-clicking etc, doing all the things that were wrong with it technically, you can make it sound OK. But it was the emotional side of all of that period, it was turning into a real nightmare out there, with people being ill and very unhappy, getting to that point of being away for nearly a year, and for those with families or even girlfriends it was proving to be a very difficult time emotionally, and it was really taking its toll on the band as a playing ensemble but, more pertinently, as individuals. I don't know if you know the story, but at least two guys in the band said, "Look, sorry, but we can't do this. We have to go, we must leave. We don't want to break up the group but we just can't remain away from our homes, the places we were brought up in. The money isn't important, we just have to go home". And so it was a question of either we all went back or the band would have literally broken in half at that time. So I threw in my towel with the 'go homes' and everybody agreed that's what we should do. And that all took place within 24 hours after getting a phone call to say that our papers had come through to become residents of Switzerland, which of course meant we reduced our tax liability to about 20% instead of 83%, and we had worked for a year to get those residency papers. The day they came through we took the decision to go home! So we just abandoned the whole thing and went straight home, and to pick up the pieces again after that would have been very difficult. Of course nobody had anywhere to live, we just had our suit cases and nothing else, and we thought, hey, by the time we try to pick up this album again, sort out the things that aren't working, we might as well just start again, and we did. But some of the feeling... in fact I think I've described it in the notes on the *Nightcap* CD... we then went and started work on the more down-beat *A Passion Play*, because it **was** in relation to the music we had been working on, all of which was quite bright and cheerful and silly, although it had its darker, negative side. That contrast was echoed all the way through it, whereas Passion Play was altogether a much more... not a dark thing in the sense of it being brooding or negative, just that it was a lot more sombre and a lot more serious, and it obviously lacked as an album what *Thick As A Brick* before it did have, which was the elements of warmth and humour and brightness and major keys and things which made *Thick As A Brick* ultimately much more acceptable than *A Passion Play* to the casual listener. So I think that this missing album in between, in some ways had it turned out to have been completed, and technically as proficient and audio-wise sonically as acceptable as *Thick As A Brick* then it might have been a more fitting successor to *Thick As A Brick* than *A Passion Play* turned out to be. But I should think 30% of the material would have had to have been re-recorded, substantially changed in terms of writing and arrangement because we were getting closeted in a strange way in that studio and some of the writing was getting a little... desperate, shall we say. And certainly some of the members of the band were having such a bad time they just weren't enjoying what they were doing at all. It was just a real negative few weeks of our lives. We probably just chose the wrong place to be, you know. We could have gone to one of many studios to make the record but we happened to choose one that didn't suit us. The food was awful, technically it was a **rotten** studio - I can't believe that Cat Stevens and Elton John actually made records there. I mean I've never ever seen such a place that was so awful, so disorganized, so dreadful place to be, but doubtless some people in their haze of continuous party time might have found it a great place to be, and if somehow all the equipment worked on the day they might have made a good record, but we certainly couldn't. We made some interesting snippets, and that's what is on the album.

Do you think you will be performing any of this material live?
Well that's a good point. It would obviously not be now. I think we'll check it out, it might be amusing to do it, but I think we'd have to bear in mind that most of the places we'll be playing after it's released will be places we haven't been to before or for many years, so it would have to be weighed up as to how vital any of that material might be in relation to whatever has to be ejected to make room for it. I think it would depend on how the album was doing, whether anybody was listening to it in those countries we will be visiting. We'll have to wait and see really if it looks like being something the band would enjoy playing. Obviously some of the recent stuff on *Nightcap* was recorded by the current band, but the stuff from '72 might be a little harder for them to get into. But what I did on a lot of that stuff that had no vocals on was... well either it was left as meaningless nothingness or I either had to write lyrics and sing them now to something that was recorded 20 years ago, or do what I did, which was to take the melodies - I was pretty sure what the melody was in most cases, or what I would have been doing if I'd been playing the flute - and in most cases I played 'the tune' if you like as a flute piece, which seemed to me the correct half way house to take, to give the music a sense of completion rather than to do what I think would have been impossible, which is to write lyrics 20 years later which would have been in keeping with the rest of an album that was so far back in time. It really would have sounded like something which had been grafted on whereas the flute seemed the better option to take to give it it's final "voice", be it instrumental or human vocal. There are some funny things in it. I have to say I quite enjoy it. I didn't think I was going to but I did, and I really speeded through and worked intensely on it because I didn't want it to run out of steam. I worked long and hard while the interest was there, and I found to my amazement at the end that I hadn't got sick of it, I even quite enjoyed listening again to the production masters. It sounds OK, it has a feel about it, a buoyancy which is quite engaging, especially because it represents a period of the band's history which is definitely <u>history,</u> and it is an authentic 1970's album. It's like discovering a pair of your dad's flares in the attic. It's not like something you just bought from Marks & Spencer's, flares MK 2 or the revival, this is the real thing, these were actually from some boutique in Chelsea or the Kings Road circa 1970. The real thing, and that to me is certainly worth something. So it's quite amusing, and I'm quite pleased with it, but again there is this terrible thing of the amount of time I've spent on it. I've spent a huge amount of time in the studio doing all this stuff, from the *Light Music* album on through to this thing, it's been an enormous amount of time and an enormous amount of concerts as well doing things that

are historical and retrospective. It's a trade off, because what you don't have is a new Jethro Tull album, and now at the end of this tour there is a reasonable finite amount of time before we can do anything else. It is impossible to do all the things that you would like to do.

Entirely from the heart, without meaning to sound unduly negative, but if I could go back say 12 or 18 months and weigh up again whether or not I was going to do all this effort in terms of touring and studio work for all this *25 Years* stuff, I would say... "No!", [*laughs*]. I'd say, "Let's go and make a new album". I think it would have been much better for the band to have done that and got on with something new and just left everything exactly where it was, which was lying in a bunch of recording studios scattered around the world and in cardboard boxes down at the warehouse. The feeling I have right now is that everybody of sane and proper thinking ought to be so heartily sick of people's compilation albums and their box sets and so on. In the past couple of years it's just become obscene. Everybody's done it, everybody's doing it, there's a good few more to come as people reach these milestones and have this build up of material that people are wanting to trade on in terms of being able to repackage and resell things that a lot of folk have from before. I think we've made two mistakes: 1) that we did it at all and 2) we've tried to make it something more than just a repackaging, we've tried to give it some credibility by making it a little bit different, but it's still fundamentally, material wise, something historical, something from the past. If all that could be done without it taking a minute of my time, and could be put into the market place at really low prices, then I would go along with it - but unfortunately I feel committed to spend that time myself doing it, I just can't let it go to somebody else. At the end of the day they're gonna come to me anyway to see what I want them to do, how I want it to sound.

A lot of the recent stuff on the album had no flute or vocals so they have been finished this year. It's been a lot of work for me and it could not have been done without me, and ethically speaking I had to do it. For me it's really important that if it's going to be of any merit at all then it has to demand from me at least almost the same effort that I would put into making a new record. That's what I've done, and [*laughing*] that's what I regret! Because my time could have been better employed doing something new. At the moment I feel really frustrated because I don't have something new to play. And I also know that if I sit down and write some songs now... in fact I already have written some new material, but nothing will happen to it for another few months, and when I go back to it I'll be seeing it as something that is already in the past, it's not like NOW, you know. That's one of the scary things about making records or doing any writing thing, you suddenly find this thing, this new idea... a few lyrics or a bit of a tune... and you really want to go with it, you don't want to have to stop in mid-field and put the barbecue on. You want to run all the way down to the other goal with it while you've got the ball in your hands. [*This would not of course be permitted during a game of what is correctly termed* proper *football!*]. It's a real compulsion, a real drive to get something and really go with it, and that is totally disrupted obviously by playing live concerts. But at the same time I have this horror, next year, of not being able to go and play shows every week, because for me it is murder now to try not to keep doing it, both physically and mentally. I have this horrible feeling that if I stop doing shows... for a week... I mean I'm really nervous about playing the next one! Not in the sense of going in front of the audience, but physically and mentally it gets harder and harder to pick up the pieces again every time. And after **months** off without concerts it terrifies me that it's gonna be harder and harder to start up again. Ironically if I do a lot of dates I don't actually end up singing worse as a result; if anything I start to learn my limitations, I start to become a little bit more balanced. The first week is always the worst for me, and the first two or three dates are absolutely the worst because of the whole tension of dealing with that problem. But when I'm relaxed and comfortable, getting used to humidity and temperature changes and sound checks... and usually the longer the tour goes on the less promo I do which is also a big factor. Before the tour and at the beginning of it I'm on the phone and talking to people all day, so I go into every tour already tensed up around here [*gestures to his throat*] and for me playing the shows is the best way of staying alive. And I don't know how I can do that when we stop these things that are coming up.

Last year I was trying to put together some low-key little band, ideally involving some local musicians with whom I could go and do the odd pub or club, just so that once or twice a week I could just go and do something. Just to keep that live performance thing going. But it's very hard to find people anywhere, let alone locally, who are available and whose musical standard and interest are compatible with that sort of thing where I might say, "Hey, next Friday at so and so pub". But it has to be on that level, because as soon as you get back to "The Band" playing big clubs or small theatres a few times a month or once a week, you're talking about road crew, equipment, hotels, wages, and the whole thing is back to... well, you're talking "A Tour" again! But you can't tour and play once or twice a week. In the UK for example you've got to play four shows to cover your costs and on the fifth show you might make some profit. Basically you have to play three on, one off to be making a profit, based on what you have to pay people and what it costs to do "the circuit". You might expect me to do it for nothing, you might expect Martin to do it for nothing, but the other guys might not feel that way about it. They might say, "Hey, I could be sitting on a beach somewhere. I don't need to do this," you know. You have to accept and respect that decision. People like to be rewarded for what they do. So I can't say, "Well come on guys, let's all do this for nothing," because it wouldn't be fair on them. So if I do something like that it's gonna have to be with a bunch of other people, and it'll have to be on such a low-key level that... even you will never hear about it! It will be something that's just a bit of fun. But what I don't think I could do is go out and join some local R&B band as an occasional guest performer because I think I would find difficulty in really enjoying that. It's got to be a little more dangerous than that. It's got to be original material and a bit more scary than doing a few dates with Mick Abrahams and singing the blues. I don't mind the odd 12-bar thing, but if I had to play three in a row I'd be yawning. It is wonderful music, but beyond a little flirtation with it is not, for me, a satisfying format in which to work, because harmonically and with the progressions it is the same every time. One or two of those is great, but I couldn't do an evening full of them. I couldn't do what Martin does with his band, because they play a lot of covers of other people's songs. That's OK at a wedding or a birthday party or something where the familiarity is a good thing; we all know the songs and we can bop along to them and drink as much as we like and fall over and vomit and it really doesn't matter because everybody's having a good time. That's OK, but I wouldn't want to do that.

I don't know what I could do. Maybe I should call Simon Nicol who is the only Fairport guy I haven't played with? Maybe I should ask him and somebody else and go and do some dates. That would be interesting.

You said to me a while ago that you'd like to work with Gary Brooker. Did you talk to him about that on the tour?

It's very difficult to talk to Gary about anything really! He's a really nice chap but he has a habit of somehow disengaging himself from conversation and... the solar system, at the drop of a hat. You can be chatting to him and somehow suddenly he's just kind of not there anymore. He physically just drifts away as well. I thought it was maybe that he didn't like me, but other people said the same thing. A very nice guy, but very vague and non-committal, very hard to pin down on anything. I mean he's very good at what he does, and Procol Harum as an opening band in America worked out really well. I can safely and seriously say that as a support band they were, from our point of view and I think from the audiences as well, the most satisfying balance that we have ever found. Well since perhaps the few concerts that Yes supported us on. Procol were really good. But I don't know if Gary has that hunger to do things, he's an easy going guy. He's not impassioned. He's always in a pleasant mood. People who are always in pleasant moods are not the Van Morrisons, the Bob Dylans, the Jimi Hendrix's or the Jimmy Pages. The great people. The great people are the guys who will walk past you in the corridor and just grunt, if anything. The great people are the ones who just get out of bed one morning and hate the world [*Hey, I must be GRRREAT! DR*] and the next minute they are laughing and being cheerful with people, [*oh well, maybe not... DR*] The guys who are Mr Cheerful all the time are the guys to sit and have a drink with, but not necessarily the guys you want to work with. Things should be more volatile somehow. It brings its ups and downs, but the great moments come out of that element of danger and personality clashes. It is probably a strange irony that the guy who would want to get up and play with Jethro Tull would be Mick Abrahams. I mean, without going into any history, he and I obviously have a fairly healthy kind of... wariness of each other. There is a part of his character that has a heart of gold, really nice guy and all the rest of it, but there is an element of danger in that which is appealing in itself. So it is kind of nice to engage with that slightly more nervous moment rather than just have somebody who... I mean Mick can look after himself onstage, whereas if we got poor old Jeffrey up there and what he did just didn't click, it would be just so awful to have him die a death or mess it up. It's better to have Mick up there; he will do the stuff, he will deliver the goods. He will succeed with whatever it is he does. If you get together with a guy like that then it is going to work, and it will work because there is that sort of tension, that element of danger applied to a good end that means it will turn into something worthwhile. But with other people who might just be nice guys, it could be awful. Anyway, we will never know! We will never know if John Evans would still be able to play the introduction to *Locomotive Breath*!

On that reflective note Ian had to leave us, but we were left with plenty to ponder on. At the time DR wrote: "The thought of a classical-type album sounds wonderful don't you think? Ian is obviously aware that several major turkeys have been produced in the past when rock musicians have dabbled with 'classical' projects, but I reckon if anybody could pull it off successfully it's Ian Anderson. Let's hope something comes of it."

What became of it, two years later, was Divinities: 12 Dances With God - *which was exactly as he'd described it above. Wonderful!*

And as a footnote, Mick Abrahams did indeed produce a storming performance on both nights at the Hammersmith Apollo, playing So Much Trouble *and* I Wonder Who - *the first time Tull had played them live since 1968.*

Chapter 23

TONY IOMMI

(Published in Issue #43, June 1994)

It might come as something of a surprise to some readers to learn that Martin Barre was not Mick Abrahams' replacement in Jethro Tull when Mick left at the tail end of 1968. In fact, Tony Iommi, founder and ever-present member of Black Sabbath, was originally recruited as lead guitarist, but he stayed with the band only a matter of days.

This blip in Tull's history might have gone unrecorded had it not been for Tony's appearance with Ian Anderson, Glenn Cornick and Clive Bunker in the The Rolling Stones' television extravaganza Rock'n'Roll Circus. *Directed by Michael Lindsay-Hogg and intended as a BBC Christmas show, it was filmed in a circus big-top and featured clowns, jugglers, fire-eaters and lion-tamers as well as live performances from The Rolling Stones, The Who, John Lennon and Yoko Ono, Eric Clapton, Marianne Faithfull, Taj Mahal and, of course, Jethro Tull. Tull played one song,* A Song For Jeffrey. *At the time, the Stones' own performance was considered by Mick Jagger to be too erratic, even by their own standards, and the film was shelved until 1995 when, thankfully, it did get released on video.*

Jethro Tull fans had never quite been sure whether Tony Iommi played that gig as a full member of the band or as a favour because Tull hadn't found a full-time guitarist yet. It seemed to MW that as good a way as any of finding out was to ask the man himself. And so it was that he found himself in a London hotel in the middle of Black Sabbath's 1994 European tour, listening to Tony Iommi's soft Brummie voice explain his cameo role in the Tull story.

Starting at the point at which Mick Abrahams has left Jethro Tull – did you actually audition to be his replacement?
Well, what happened was that Earth [*who became Black Sabbath*] did a show together with Tull the night Mick Abrahams left. They were passing each other notes on stage – Mick was giving Ian notes saying, "I'm leaving," and so on! They asked me that night if I'd be interested in the job. I told the rest of our lads that Tull had offered me a job, and that I didn't know what to say. They said it was up to me and that I should take it, and not think about them. The next thing I got a 'phone call saying that Tull were holding auditions in London and would I come down, just as a formality. I got there, and there were so many people there I thought, "I can't stand this," and I actually went out to go back home. One of the group came running out and said, "No, don't go, just hang on, we'll get to you in a minute." So I did the audition, went back to Birmingham, and got the call to say I'd got the job.

Can you remember who else was at the auditions?
Hmm, it's all so long ago. But I remember Martin Barre being there, and the chap from The Nice, Davy O'List.

Ah, I was going to ask you about him. There was actually a press report at the end of 1968 that he had joined Tull, but it obviously fell through. Would that have been before or after you?
After me. Nah, I don't know anything about that one.

Do you remember much about the audition itself, and what piece you played?
I can't remember now, to be quite honest. It was really just a jam with Clive, Glenn and Ian.

So as far as you were concerned, you'd got the job in the band, rather than just a one-off for the *Rock'n'Roll Circus*?
Oh yes, absolutely.

So was the *Rock'n'Roll Circus* the only thing you did with Tull?
It was really, yeah. What happened was, we started rehearsing and they were writing some stuff. Geezer [*Butler*] came down with me to the rehearsals and sat in on them. I felt really

bad about leaving Earth, very uncomfortable. I mean, I liked the other lads in Jethro Tull, but it just felt a funny situation to be in after being with a load of people I knew so well. I told Geezer that I really didn't feel comfortable with it all. He said to give it a bit of time, but I said I didn't know if I could. We had a few more days rehearsal, and then I spoke to Ian and told him that I didn't feel right about it.

Was it the music, or the people, or what?
No... I think I just felt uncomfortable within myself, being in such a new situation. It just felt so different. I was so used to hanging around with everyone, but the Tull lads seemed to be separate in some ways. Like, Clive and Glenn would be together, but Ian would be sitting at another table, and it seemed alien to me. The first time we went to eat, I went and sat at a table with Ian, thinking we were all together, but [*laughing*] apparently not! I don't like situations like that. If it's going to be a band, it's got to be a band together.

Did you actually play live on the *Rock'n'Roll Circus* or was it mimed?
As far as I remember, one track we played live and the other we mimed to a backing track and Ian sang the vocals live.

Two tracks???
Yeah, *A Song For Jeffrey* and one I can't remember – but they only used *A Song For Jeffrey*. And I've never even seen the film, actually.

I've seen a dodgy bootleg copy. There's always rumours that The Stones will be releasing it on video, but nothing ever seems to happen. Were you disappointed at the time that it wasn't shown?
Yes, I was. Someone did tell me they'd seen it in the States a long time ago. Bill Wyman keeps promising me a copy, but I've never received one.

So did you play on the backing track, or was it an old one with Mick?
A Song For Jeffrey would have been Mick, I think. It's all a bit vague actually, although it was a really great thing to be involved in, with a lot of jamming going on in the afternoon with lots of different people. It was the first time I'd met The Rolling Stones. I really enjoyed it. I got to talk to different people, and to see different music – it was great.

And you can't remember what the second song was?
No... Mind you, I can't remember our own bloody songs that I'VE written!

You wore a large white hat and kept your head down most of the time. Was that a conscious effort to hide?
[*Laughing*] No – I always have my head down when I play, and it was Ian who came up with the idea of wearing a hat. We were mooching through some stores backstage which had all different costumes and whatnot. Ian found the hat and got me to try it on. I didn't really have any stage clothes anyway, so they stuck a jacket and hat on me, and that was it.

How did you get on with Ian?
I thought he was OK. I thought he was very polite to me – no problems at all. I do know there was a vibe with him and the rest of the guys at the time. We'd all be talking away together – and then Ian would walk in, and they'd all shut up. And Sabbath did a gig with Tull once in the States and the same thing happened. It was strange – it just didn't seem right to me that that was going on.

So how did you come to leave Jethro Tull?
I asked Ian if I could have a word with him, and talked to him outside. I can't remember the exact words I used, but I said I wanted to leave. He suggested I give it a bit more time, but I explained that I just didn't feel comfortable, and that I didn't think things were going to work with me. So he said OK. But he asked me to stay on to do The Stones film, because they couldn't replace me that quickly. Which of course I did.

Even today, magazine features about Black Sabbath mention your stint with Jethro Tull. Does that annoy you, amuse you...?

I'm actually grateful to Tull in a lot of ways, because it taught me a lot of things about the way our band worked. We had always been a bit half-hearted about rehearsals and stuff. Tull were so strict about rehearsals – be there at nine o'clock in the morning or else – and I'd never heard of that! But it was a good attitude really, and I went back to our band with that same attitude, saying we've got to start rehearsals on time and not just roll in sometime in the afternoon when we feel like it. So it taught me a sense of responsibility and authority which I was able to pass on to the rest of our lads to get ourselves on the way. Yeah, it did help a lot.

Did you keep in touch with anyone afterwards?
I saw Glenn a few times. In fact, Glenn supported us on an American tour with his own band Wild Turkey. The last time I saw him was at his house in Los Angeles, but that was a long time ago. I haven't seen Clive at all. In fact, I've often thought of Clive – he was a really nice bloke. I saw Mick several times when he was with Blodwyn Pig, but again not for a long time. I kept running into Martin at various studios and airports. I must admit, I didn't think Martin would stay with Tull for very long, but he did, he stuck it out. I last met Ian in Iceland in September 1992, when Sabbath were playing the same place the next day. As I say, I never had a problem with Ian. I never had a problem with any of the band.

[*At this point MW produced issue #37 of* A New Day *with the photos of the 1993 reunion for the* 25 years Of Jethro Tull *video shoot. Tony was stunned!*]

Bloody hell! Is that Glenn Cornick? I wouldn't have recognised him. Woah, look at Mick! And is that Clive?? Bloody hell! I wouldn't have recognised him either. Oh dear. Say hello to him from me. Ian looks well there. Ha ha – Dave Pegg. He's always got a drink in his hand, has Dave. I know Dave from old. The music scene in Birmingham was so small that everyone knew everyone else. I used to go and see him many years ago when he was playing with people like Plant and Bonham. He seemed to be in a different group every week. So they all get on alright with each other now, including Mick?

Ian, Mick and Clive have played together live recently, actually. [*MW then explained about the 1993 Hammersmith and Camden gigs and the 1994 Altenkirchen Convention.*] There seem to have been a few hatchets buried.
Oh good, that's how it should be. These things get silly, don't they. Sabbath are a prime example of that, with Ozzy and so on. I don't know why it happens – probably the lives we lead, on the road and so on.

Did you follow Tull's career over the years? Did you ever think, "That could have been me," or "That was a lucky escape"...?
I bought the album which I would have been on had I stayed – *Stand Up* – and I heard a few albums after that, but I never really followed them closely. But I think I did go through a period early on when I wondered if I should have stuck it out.

You'd probably have felt worse if Black Sabbath hadn't been so successful...
Ah, but we hadn't made it at that time, and Jethro Tull had! But then I thought, no, Black Sabbath is where my heart is, this is what I want to do.

Are you surprised that you're still doing it after 25 years – or surprised that you're doing it with Black Sabbath after 25 years?
You don't really think about it – it just goes on and on and on. It's such a part of your life, you don't think about stopping it. And even though we've had line-up changes, me and Geezer will stay in touch for ever, and I talk to Bill [*Ward*] on a regular basis, and I was in touch with Ozzy a couple of months ago. Despite all the slagging off that goes on, we're almost like a family really.

So what are Black Sabbath up to nowadays? Obviously you're in the middle of a tour at the moment...
The new album [*Cross Purposes*] came out a couple of months ago. We did an American tour with it, which went really well, then Japan, and now we're doing Europe for a couple of months. After that, I dunno. We'll either go back and do some more dates in the States, or do another album.

256

Chapter 24

MATT PEGG

(Published in issue #44, August 1994)

With Dave Pegg constantly trying to balance his duties with both Fairport Convention and Jethro Tull, something had to give some day. Peggy found the ideal solution by putting forward his son Matt to dep for him in Tull when he was committed to Fairport; not only was he a very fine bass player, but he would never try to pinch the gig on a permanent basis!
We cornered young Matt backstage at Tutbury Castle before the Tull set, and somehow managed to get sensible answers from him despite the constant barracking from a nearby Andy Giddings....

We normally start by asking "what's your real name?" .... but it is Matthew Pegg isn't it?
Well, yes.... but it depends who you ask!

Ah! Well moving right along..... can you tell us a bit about your musical beginnings?
Well my dad (Dave Pegg) taught me to play mandolin when I was about three years old....

Was that by force, or did you want to?
(Laughing) Well, sort of, maybe. I was slightly more naive than I am now. I just kind of slipped into it..... and of course it was the only thing I could get my hands round because I was very small! So I learnt the three tunes that I still know now on the mandolin, and annoyed everyone with it until I was about seven or eight, and then I was in a heavy metal band playing guitar.

When you were eight?!
Yeah, it was called "Aggressive Hardware", with a couple of friends from the village. Mum though of the name, and it was just a bit of fun. We used to go and play in village halls and at fetes and things. And when I got to "proper" school they asked me if I could play bass. I said "yeah, no problem" – it was a crappy jazz band who all read music, and I can't read music at all, so I just had to bluff my way through it. So that's how I started playing bass, when I was eleven.

Did you ever have any formal lessons on any instrument?
No. Dad never really taught me scales or anything, he just told me to learn it with my ears. It's the best way, for sure.

Were you always aware as a child that your dad was a bit of a pop/rock "star"?
Well, he's not really is he? *(laughs, and barracking from an adjacent Mr Giddings)* Well really all the people I knew were just the same as other kids' dads' mates *[editor's pause for contemplation over (a) the meaning and (b) the positioning of the apostrophes]* They were round the house all the time or down the pub just like everybody else. I was always surrounded by it as a normal thing.... and I guess that's why I'm doing it now.

A lot of things you are doing are in some way Tull connected; was that simply a question of being in the right place at the right time, or did you actually set out deliberately looking for the gigs?
The only major gig I've got for myself is Procol Harum... though I guess that is also slightly Tull connected because we supported Tull on the tour. But I got that on my own merit, having done an audition.

Oh sure, I don't mean to suggest that you didn't get the other gigs on merit, or that you just dropped into them purely because you are Dave Pegg's son....

Yeah sure, but I mean I have to a certain extent I must admit. I mean particularly this gig with Tull, obviously. And Martin Barre asked me to play in his band after I'd done the first Tull stuff.

Did you go to many gigs as a child?
All the time. I remember when Richard Thompson was there, Trevor Lucas and so on.

Did you like the music? Most kids react against their parents music don't they?
Well up until I was about eleven I didn't know there was any other music, I just thought it was the people who came round the house, you know, and that's what music was. I didn't really realise you could buy records and all of that. I never bought records. I thought Fairport were great, and Traffic.

Do you buy records now?
No, I can't afford them.

Do you buy your own cigarettes?
Yes I do. [*No, you don't! Andy Giddings*] [*a chip off the old block! DR*]

So was *Blinder* your first professional band?
Yeah. I went to college to try to get something to fall back on. My parents were insistent that I do something else, just in case music didn't work out.

Were you always going to be a musician then?
Yeah, I thought I was, but my parents kept on that I should have something to fall back on, but it was a really hard course, and there's no way you can do it unless you really want to do it. It's the same with music, you know. So I only did six months and then dropped out, left home and moved to London, and joined Blinder. I stayed with them for a few years. They've got a deal now, they are like a thrash metal band. They are called Headswim now.

Ah, I've heard of them; I didn't realise the connection.
Yeah, same band, different bass player. But they've gone really heavy. I heard it the other day and it's pretty good. Not my thing really, but not bad at all.

How did you get that gig? Were you all friends originally?
No, I answered an ad in the NME or something. It said "Bass player wanted – influences IT BITES etc". At that age I was totally into that stuff, and so were they. Now they are completely different, and so am I, you know. I hate that stuff now, and I'm not gonna be playing it.

But you are working with Francis Dunnery now aren't you?
Well.....I don't know about that..... I can't get hold of him at the moment. But his album came out just now.

Yes, I finally got hold of it last week.
Ah, have you heard it? I'm quite proud of that one, there's some good stuff on it. But we did that.... well, I've lived in Australia for a year since we did it, so it was a while ago.

Is that the album that was a Japanese only issue? I tried to get it ages ago....
No, that was the one he did to get out of his deal. This new one is called *Fearless*. It has only just come out, but it must be 18 months to two years since we started work on it. But I didn't do much, I just did my guides. I was there for three days just doing the guides, and then he said "you might as well go home"! Because he has his computer and so on, and he can do what he wants then. I heard it and thought "is that me? It sounds pretty good!"

Is he the egomaniac that he is reputed to be?

(laughs) Well I really like him because he has helped me out since I was about 13, he took me under his wing and taught me loads of things. I would have gone on a lot longer path to get where I am now if he hadn't got hold of me and said "Look, don't play like that, you're not gonna get any work, basically. You're gonna dig yourself into a hole". Like It Bites did really.

But they were such a great band. They seemed to be right on the verge of great success when they split.
It was really muso stuff though wasn't it? Right over most peoples' heads. That's why the new album is just "pop", just songs, you know. And he is really good at it. But I'm quite happy – at least my name is on the album, it has done me some good.

It's very small though, printed in pink, difficult to read....
I haven't seen it, he didn't send me one. I've been trying to get it for three weeks! But since then I've done the Procol Harum thing, and that's been great fun.

Is that an ongoing thing or was it a one-off tour?
Well Geoff, the guitarist, is off to America for four months with Roger Daltrey, so there is no band anymore for this year really.

But it's not like they have split up though?
Well we've done our year's work. We did three nights in Portugal - that is Procol Harum's total output this year as a band! And Gary (Brooker) is off doing his own thing at the moment.

We saw them on the Tull tour in Europe, just before you joined, and they are still a great little band aren't they?
Oh yeah, fantastic. I love it, and I love all the songs. They are great people to be with too, nothing matters really. Have a good time doing it, that's the most important thing, which suits me down to the ground.

Just like Fairport really!
But worse; they drink more! We trashed Peggy a few times! But it's all good experience, I'm happy doing anything. I'm certainly happy doing this with Jethro Tull.

What was it like for you when you first recorded with Tull on *Catfish Rising*?
Well I'd been in the studio already for a week, in the same room, with Blinder, and we had really been going for it, we were all trashed. The next morning Ian was in, and it was all very civilised. Ian wrote it all, told me what to play, "just keep it simple", you know. I'm not very happy with what I played, I wish it wasn't just a session, because you have to come up with it all on the day. I was only there for one day, no tapes beforehand. It's always a shame because you listen to it a few months later and think "Oh no! Why didn't I play that bit differently?" It's always the way.

How did you get on with his way of doing the backing tracks first, without knowing the melody? Doane (Perry) is always saying "I wish I'd known what the melody was because then I would have done that differently...."

Yeah, that's why you end up three months later thinking maybe you could have done it better. But I don't know, I just do the job, keep my head down – I don't want to get involved in anything that is not my business.

Are you into Jethro Tull musically?
Oh yeah, I love it. I don't really listen to it at home though, unless I'm learning it. All I ever listen to at home is Joni Mitchell, George Harrison, The Beatles..... a bit of Procol Harum maybe. My wife plays Joni Mitchell's *Blue* every day.... it's on all day long. You play it, and then you can't play anything else, you just have to play it again! I love that album.

Do you remember much about the 1991 TV appearance with Tull in Italy? That was a long way to go to......
To mime! In puddles! Oh I enjoyed that, it was great fun. I don't know if anybody else did, but I loved it, being on the telly and all that. The Jay Leno show was the most fun though. We actually played live to a huge audience. (laughing) I got recognised in America through being on that show – that felt weird. We were supposed to play *Thick As A Brick* on the show as well, but one of the guests, a football coach who is like bigger than God over there, just wouldn't stop talking and we ran out of time. We did the Lonestar gig that year too, and that was brilliant. It was really small, more like what I'm used to, and it was really rocking. A proper old-fashioned pub gig, but with Jethro Tull! It was really happening, brilliant stuff. There were a few mistakes but everybody had a good time. We only had a day to rehearse; I'd flown from Sydney to L.A. to New York, my bag went elsewhere, all that shit. And then we had to rehearse when we got there for the show that night.

But surely Tull's music is a bit too complex to be thrown into unrehearsed? It's not like stepping into a blues band is it?
But I've heard it so many times, that's the thing. I've heard him learning it, I've been to so many shows..... it was easier this time around because on the Procol tour I saw it every night. So I knew how the show went, it is implanted in my brain.... then I just had to work out where my fingers have to go, and try to do it at the right time in the right order!

Did you feel particularly nervous about stepping into your dad's shoes?
No, I don't really get that. I don't know why, people say I should be nervous..... I remember being nervous at school, playing in front of my mates, but.... I don't know. I like it, I enjoy it too much to get nervous I guess. I'd be nervous if I didn't know the songs so well. The only thing I really can't get the hang of at all is all that dancing around, especially the silly bit that Andy came up with where we have to shuffle across the stage behind Ian during *So Much Trouble.* My feet get tangled up, and the people in the front can see it!

But were you ever worried about comparisons with your dad?
No, I play completely differently to him anyway. Not deliberately, but that's just the way my style developed. I used to be all over everything like a rash when I was a teenager, like all kids, young guitarists, who are playing all the time. But then I went back to a fretted bass and learned how to play properly if you like, sensibly. The best gig that taught me how to calm down a bit was Procol Harum, because you just play the part and it sounds great anyway. With Tull I try and play what dad plays, but it's difficult sometimes because he plays with a plectrum and I prefer to play with my fingers. Some things are easier with a plectrum but others are easier with fingers, so if there is anything that's too hard I simplify it or play something that I feel comfortable with.

You don't feel tempted to stick an extra fiddly bit in here and there?
Ha! Well you might hear a few! No, I don't know.... I don't know what Ian thinks of my playing, so I just try to get it as close as I can and play as well as I can.... and any bits I don't know, I play what I think sounds right. That's why I got the gig with Procol, because they had a guy who learnt all the songs, but learnt them all note for note, and didn't really understand what was going on. I only had the plane journey from Sydney to England to learn all the songs, so I didn't know them. I knew how they went, but I couldn't try playing them on my bass on the plane. So the next morning I drove to Gary's house and said "well, I've heard the songs", you know. Like "I'm sorry, I'm too young, I missed Procol Harum!" It was really embarrassing saying "I only know *Whiter Shade Of Pale"*..... and I fucked that up too! But he liked what I played, even though it was probably completely different to what he'd heard before. So he didn't want someone who knew the songs backwards, he wanted someone with a feel for the music.

Which led of course to hundreds of people being disappointed because Martin Barre had to cancel the gig at Putney Half Moon. DON'T YOU FEEL BAD ABOUT THAT?!!

(laughing) Ah, yes..... but we'll probably be doing that in October won't we? *[Possibly not actually, but let's hope so DR]*

Do you see that as an ongoing thing for you?
I don't know, it's up to Martin really. I enjoy playing with the band, though I do get fed up rehearsing the covers over and over. I don't think there's any need to rehearse those standards, they only get worse the more you rehearse them! But you know, I like playing; I like playing with anybody, it's what I do. I'm no good at anything else.

Do you write music?
I'm just starting to get that together. I really want to do it because I've never done it before. I've always spent all my time trying to be good at playing the bass, but now I feel am, I can play what I want to play. Now I've got a load more instruments, acoustic guitars and things, that I just can't play, and I sit at home and annoy my wife with them.

No thoughts of putting your own band together?
No. Too much hassle!

Why did you leave Blinder?
They kicked me out.

BASTARDS!
Ha! No, it was the best thing that could have happened. They wanted to go this way, I wanted to go another, you know. I wanted to stay a bit musical, with proper songs and stuff, because we actually got quite musical at one point. But I just got really fed up with it, I'd turn up late for rehearsal and so on. It was obvious that I didn't really want to do it, but I didn't have anything else so I just went through the motions. They obviously needed somebody who was really into it, and I wasn't, but I didn't want to tell them I was leaving.... so they booted me out! I've been much better off on my own, I've done more things, I'm married and we've got a house and so on. If I'd stayed I would still be playing the same pub gigs and not have learnt so much, which is the main thing. I've learnt heaps in the last couple of years. And made a bit of money too, for the first time!

Who else have you played with?
Well I went to Australia for a year because my wife is Australian and I had to meet her family. **[long meeting! DR]** I spent a year playing in all sorts of bands – cha-cha-cha, cabaret bands, then got the gig with Procol. The rest you know. I've been very busy with this stuff, moving house and all of it. My diary for next year is all relying on what people have said might be happening. Gary Brooker said he might do another album and tour. He didn't say he was going to use me, but I'll keep my fingers crossed.

What reaction have you been getting from Tull fans? This will be the first time we've seen you with them...
It's hard to tell. I can't really see or hear anybody shouting "where's Dave?"! I feel a bit sorry for the people I see wearing Fairport shirts. That's obviously the connection.... well, they must be Tull fans as well I guess.... but clearly they are Fairport fans who got into Tull because of the connection, and they've paid all that money expecting to see Dave Pegg, not some young punk on bass.

How do you get on working with Ian?
It's good. He's never been nasty to me.... in fact he never says anything to me really. He tells me off if I'm being a pain in the arse, and that's fair enough; I probably am most of the time. He's very business-like, and I've got a lot of respect for him. He's still doing it, and doing it really well. I guess I can't be doing too much wrong if he hasn't said anything to me – and of course he knows and I know that I'm not after the gig, it's not ever gonna be my gig. I'm just depping for the old chap.

Would you like it to be?
Oh yeah, I'd do it! I'd love to do it. I need the work apart from anything else...

Do you know Mark Parnell? Is he a mate from the past?
No, I met him when we were doing the Francis Dunnery album. He lost his flat and needed somewhere to live, so I let him stay at our place in Mile End. We were a newly married couple in a tiny flat so obviously it wasn't comfortable and.... what with one thing and another.... we kind of fell out. So no, we are not exactly friends.

He only did five gigs with Tull and now Doane is back; what's the story there?
I don't really know. Maybe Doane was busy; these gigs were kind of thrown together late on, which is why dad couldn't do it because he is working with Fairport. I suppose Doane had booked himself other things to do.

We were under the impression that Mark was supposed to do the whole summer tour.
Yes he was, but he didn't learn the music properly; it was a bit of a mess....

Were the gigs bad?
They were a nightmare for me. There were lots of songs I'd never played, and I'd learnt the tape with Doane playing, and suddenly you are playing live with someone playing *Locomotive Breath* like a thrash song! It was so fast, all up and down, nothing at the right speed....

Nobody has sent us a tape of any of the gigs
No, you won't get one! If you do I'd love to hear it. But it was terrible, and Doane was back in a flash. I mean, they were big gigs, 15-20,000 people, with no soundcheck and only two days rehearsal, so it is not easy for a drummer to step into that, but he really should have made a bigger effort to learn the stuff.

We are really pleased to see Doane back
Oh yeah, he is the only drummer for this gig, for me. He is excellent, really happening.

OK then, on to the important questions; can you really drink more than your dad?
Ha! If I'm in the right company. If he is there! I saw him off a couple of times on the American tour, because the way they tour.... they are always flying, up really early, and they are often really tired, whereas we just get on the bus and either sleep or party all the way to the next gig!

We have found that often ourselves. We say goodnight to them in the bar because they need to get an early night for an early call in the morning, and yet we are off to the same place the next day all crammed into a car!
Yes, it's funny how it works. With Procol we are on the bus overnight, we might have been asleep for 15 hours or something, and we feel great when we get to the gig. But with Tull you are flying all the time, maybe three flights in a day, and you are knackered by the time you get there. That's half the reason we had such a great time on the Procol tour. Nobody wanted it to finish.

Do Procol have any plans to tour the UK?
No. I don't think many people would be interested would they? I think America is where people still know them.

Surely a band like that could still play reasonably big gigs in the UK? One or two thousand seaters?
Maybe. I'm sure it would be worth a go. My dad's always pestering Gary to do a Fairport type tour. Fairport book the halls, sort out the PA, and it doesn't cost too much to put on a gig. That is how Fairport make their money, booking inexpensive halls, reasonable ticket prices,

and people go to see them. No massive production costs, no need to stay in the best hotels, you can just drive home from most of them.

We thoroughly enjoyed the Procol shows we saw with Tull. I think they would do OK.
Well yeah, they do a great show, and we all really enjoy it. It's still good even when we are all completely drunk. Oh, that was the question wasn't it? Drinking. Yeah, we trashed the old man a few times, but I wouldn't want to try it on a regular basis! Because I'm not really a drinker, you know, but I had no choice with that lot. We rehearsed in New Mexico, so we were eating raw chillies all day and drinking bottles of Tequila and Mexican beer. By the end of the tour I could drink a bottle of that and go on-stage and be perfectly alright.

You've got a sad future ahead of you!
I couldn't do it now, not in this band. I'd freak out if I went onstage drunk with Jethro Tull. The music is too hard. And we have to get up too early! We have to be at Heathrow tomorrow at 6am to fly to Switzerland.

Have you got any good Peggy stories for us?
Ooh! I don't really know any. I know all the Dave Swarbrick stories but I never get to hear the Peggy stories. I bet Giddings knows a few though..... **[all eyes turn to Andy Giddings awaiting delivery of the dirt on Dave Pegg....]**
AG: Well, I don't really know any because he is so well behaved at all times.

Do you have a favourite Tull album or song?
Err....*Thick As A Brick.*

A smartarse eh, answering both questions with one answer!
I like *Minstrel In The Gallery, Living In The Past...* I like the obvious ones really.

Do you prefer the 'progressive' stuff or the more folky things?
Oh no, I'm crap at all that folky, jiggy stuff. That's what my dad does really, it's what he has always done. I've seen videos of him at Glastonbury in 1971, with all his hair, really going for it. It is all twice as fast as it is now, you know, WOW! On that horrible Fender bass that he used to play.

Doesn't that worry you, to see your dad with hair like that? A bit like yours is now....
Ah, I remember when he shaved it, and it never grew back! Yeah, mine's receding, it's going fast!

Chapter 25

DAVID PALMER

(Published in #46, October 1994)

They said it would never happen... and we were beginning to believe them! We had been trying to get David Palmer to speak to us for ages, but he had remained elusive, modestly refuting the idea that we were keen to hear what he had to say. But finally the A New Day Interrogation Squad *of DR & MW were granted an audience with the man who was an integral part of the Jethro Tull set-up, in one way or another, from 1968 to 1980. David left Tull, along with John Evans and Barrie Barlow, after* Stormwatch *in 1980. He had been a full member of the band for only three years, but his orchestrations and arrangements on earlier albums were at least complementary but more often pivotal to the classic quality of '70s Jethro Tull music. As they do say, sometimes you don't know what you've got until it's gone.*

Let's be frank. David Palmer has done it all. He has written and orchestrated for everybody, he was a part of one of the biggest and greatest rock bands in the world, and now he works with the world's greatest symphony orchestras. So, what else could we do? What else could be our opening question to the man who rubs shoulders everyday with the greatest musical figures in the world? It had to be...

Well... what we really want to talk about... the reason we are here... is Singalongamax!
Ah yes, you bet! In that case I'd better roll up something stronger! [*As he spoke he replaced the Dunhill in the packet and reached for one of the bloody 'orrible French fags that are made from cow-pats. Yes people, our hero David Palmer was responsible for the resurgence of Max Bygraves in the '70s, and we were going to get to the bottom of it!*] Are you joking, or do you really want to know?

Well, we would like to know how that happened...
It came about because a producer at Pye Records had heard some of the singles I had done for Jethro Tull, and he called Terry [*Ellis*] at Chrysalis. So we met for lunch, and the producer told me he had several artists that he would like me to work with, but asked also what kind of thing I liked to do. I explained that I like to write music for acoustic forces, and I like making records, because it's all very exciting. I'm involved with Jethro Tull as an arranger, and that's the kind of thing that appeals to me most. So we went back to his office and he played me a motley selection of artists. Well they weren't all bad, there was a Scots folk group who I thought were very good, with whom I actually made an album later, and a girl named Maxine Nightingale who I did some singles for, and she eventually had a big hit, which was good. But as we got to the end of the meeting he spent a great deal of time talking about the final artist, and then played me the first cut from an album. When the band started up I first thought it was Billy May or Les Brown or any of those great American 1950s bands, and then this voice came in and... well, my heart dropped! I said to the producer, "Shouldn't this singer be singing 'Pink tooth brush and a yellow tooth brush'?". He took the album off and said, "Yes, he did. It is Max Bygraves". His last album had sold about 14 copies, you know, and he asked me if I could help. So I said, "Well what do you expect me to do here? You've heard music that I'm involved in, passionately involved in; it is the underground rock movement, which is changing the face of popular music. What on earth do you expect me to bring, with my experience of that musical genre, to Max Bygraves?" He said, "I thought you would have a fresh approach". And so I recounted a story to him of an experience I had several years before. When I was at the Royal Academy I used to play in strip clubs and pubs all over London, and one night I found myself in some pub in Penge. I played Bill Evans, Thelonius Monk etc., agonising music I suppose for those people who are not aficionados of it, and then moved on to *On Green Dolphin Street* and *Body & Soul* and all the great jazz standards. But I could hear the comments from the locals in the audience, like, "He can't play the fuckin' piana", so I lashed into some wild Oscar Peterson type jazz chorus to try to drum up some

interest, but it only elicited more put-downs. After about 45 minutes of this I decided to take a break. I walked to the bar to get a drink, but before I got there the landlord stopped me. He was holding a pound note, which was half the gig fee, and he stuck it in my hand and said "It's not working out, is it? Let's call it a night". The landlord was in fact Max Bygraves' brother, and I told the Pye producer that Max Bygraves should not be singing the songs that he had on his record, because they are songs that can only be sung by great singers. The arrangements were brilliant, but the choice of songs was wrong. Max Bygraves must sing the songs that I didn't play in his brother's pub! *Red Sails In The Sunset, Show Me The Way To Go Home, Roll Out The Barrel* etc. The things I had heard as a child coming from the pub opposite our home. He thought it was a great idea, and asked me to orchestrate them. So I said I would, in as much as those songs can be orchestrated, I told him which musicians and backing singers to hire, and I orchestrated about fifty of those songs in medley form. It took about a day to write, and we recorded the whole album *tout ensemble* in two sessions. Of course I hadn't discussed a fee, as I very rarely did. To digress slightly, when I did the very first Tull album, I had been recommended to Terry Ellis, and the very first thing he said to me is, "What's this going to cost?", but I hadn't learned, from the knee of Terry Ellis even then, to nail down a fee. So I was paid about £60 for the first Singalongamax! But that was OK, it was 1971 or something, Tull had broken, and I was writing music for every man and his dog, driving around the West End in a sports car from one studio to another. So I accepted the £60, it was OK. But it was unfortunate that my mother's next door neighbour asked her to pick up a record that was currently at No 1 in the charts. Returning home on the bus she opened the carrier bag, and there was Singalongamax, and on the back she read "Orchestrated and conducted by David Palmer" whereupon she promptly got out of her seat and walked around the bus saying, "My boy did this!" So that was the bitterest pill, being paid such a pitiful sum for a record that was No 1 in the chart. But I went on to do four more in the series, and I thought I would be asked to be the musical director for his TV series, but I wasn't. That's when I came face to face with the machinations of power and politics in the music business. We had a couple of hit singles also. *Deck Of Cards* was one of them, which I believe featured in Kenny Everett's chart of the world's worst records. So, having created a kind of musical albatross... a very close friend of mine is a guy named Chris Gunning, who currently writes the music for Poirot. He wrote the music for the Martini adverts some twenty-five years ago. We discussed this recently, in that his musical albatross, which is still used, brings him a million pounds every five years or so, whereas my musical albatross is that the very first question you ask me, in a magazine that is to do wholly, solely and totally with Jethro Tull, is about Max Bygraves!

OK then, onto more musical themes! What were your early musical influences? Classical? Jazz?...
No, Bill Haley. And traditional jazz, the clarinet, trumpet and trombone playing... that counterpoint with an infectious beat. And I love reggae music. I mean I really do love reggae music. It hasn't replaced trad jazz, but it's got that happiness, and it asks you to join in, it invites you to be a part of it. My instrument at the Royal Academy was the clarinet, and I'd go miles to play in a little trad jazz band. Later I got to learn of the great American bands, Les Brown and Billy May as I mentioned earlier, and I started to pursue that kind of thing, until the sixties when the whole face of music changed completely. I didn't completely lose interest in the mainstream, or what is now termed MOR, but I first became involved or accepted into the "new pop music" when I was invited to orchestrate Roy Orbison's music for a tour in 1967 I think, just before Tull. We did a whole tour, with Roy Orbison topping the bill followed by The Walker Brothers and Lulu. I was doing the charts, playing keyboards and conducting the orchestra. All those influences add up, and by then I'd got a music degree, so I had the complete catholic background to music. And then I heard Jethro Tull. It was Ian, Glenn, Clive and Mick, and I thought, "Christ, there's something that's really unique". If ever there was a band that was going to do something, it was Jethro Tull. I was currently working as a ghost music writer for a famous English film music maker, and I was in and out of the studio, Sound Techniques in Chelsea, all the time. I'd been in that studio for a month, and Terry and Ian went there to suss out the studio. They asked the engineer to recommend a music writer to help them with their album, and it came my way. Terry called me and said I'd been recommended to him. "Can you work with musicians who can't read music?" I said, "Yes."

"Can you write orchestrations for any combination of instruments we require?" "Yes I can." "Would you like to do some work for us?" Again, "Yes of course I would, that's what I do for a living..."

So he said he wanted me to write some parts for horns. Now horns, to me, meant French horns - the generic term "horns" as it is now accepted, was coined long after Jethro Tull started, it was a musicians' term in Los Angeles and New York but it certainly hadn't reached England then. So I thought immediately that he wanted French horns, so I'm thinking Strauss and Mahler and so on, and I said, "What's the name of the group, by the way?" He said, "Jethro Tull" - if my house had had a suspended floor I would have gone straight through it! So I met Ian and Terry outside the Mitre Hotel in Hampton Court. I played Ian some French horns, and then I played him trumpets and trombones and horns together, from a Quincy Jones album, and Ian said, "Ah, that's the sound I want". Hence Mick's song, *Move On Alone*, was recorded. We did the first take and went upstairs into the control room. There was a wrong note somewhere, the guy had misread the key signature, and Ian said, "Stop the tape!" I had heard what he was going to go for, and he rewound the tape and said, "There it is - a mistake." I thought then, "Yeah, he's alright, I'll work with him." So we finished that, and a few weeks later I was in the studio recording an album with an orchestra, and the producer handed me a tape which had just arrived with a despatch rider. So I listened to it during the break. Ian had sent the tape with a note asking me to call him at Morgan Studios. I called him and said I liked it, it was interesting, and Ian said, "Can you write me a string riff for it?" By now I had become accustomed to Ian's terminology, and I thought it's probably something rhythmic that he wants for a string orchestra. He said, "Something tight and chamber-like". I said, "OK, no problem," but then he said, "Now the bad news - we want to do it tonight!" So I finished the session, sat down and transcribed the tape, wrote the orchestration, got the copiers to copy the parts, I ordered some string players, and went over to the studio. We recorded it, and then Ian junked the backing track and kept the strings, and then re-recorded everything to the strings. That was *A Christmas Song*. I didn't meet Mick [*Abrahams*] at that time, and he didn't even know that horns had been added to his song until the album came out. He left the band of course soon after.

But that album was like... not a mish-mash, that's quite the wrong word, it was a mixture of styles, but it had an underlying identity. All of those songs were linked, they were all pointing towards that one identity, which as everybody knows was a far cry from the next album that came along. It had moved on quite diametrically from what the blues roots were. They were there, in songs like *A New Day Yesterday*, but they were not worn on the sleeve, they were far more subtly written into the structure. It was a remarkable transition, a moving forward in a young man's musical development, in Ian's musical development. It was a very important, urgent kind of thing, which was what I have always admired about Ian, that raw, unequivocal evidence of a real gift, a real creative gift.

How did you work with Tull then? Did they tend to finish a song and then send it to you for your further input?

No, later on my input came in the early stages of songs, when I became a much more integral part of it all, until I actually became a full member of the band, flying off to Belgium for my first gig with the band. As Ian's development as a writer went apace, and I was able to stand on the side and... watch it... and I look back now and can see that things were going off meteorically then, so my involvement with Ian as a friend and a musician went the same way. I suppose it was probably predictable from day one that I would eventually get a black leather jacket and a suitcase and be a member of Jethro Tull. I would have liked to have joined earlier than I did, but then of course had I done so then perhaps John Evans would not have gone into the band. And we are talking about things that have happened, they cannot be changed, you can't rewrite history. Things may have taken a slightly different course. My input to the band, as a writer and as a creative person... it certainly didn't rank alongside Ian's, I complemented Ian's work. I mean Ian IS Jethro Tull. Anybody who thinks any differently to that must come and see me to receive six strikes with a cricket bat. Ian and I had a great rapport, as talkers - as you've already guessed - and as musicians. I certainly was very closely involved with, for instance, *Too Old To Rock'n'Roll* and *Minstrel In The Gallery*, you know. We worked long hours together as a team, where we had the ideal ingredients. To make an omelette you need eggs and heat, it's as simple as that. We had Ian's unending flow of creative outpouring, and I was able to add those dimensions that Ian perhaps wasn't interested in, but assumed that I would be able to supply. We had an ideal working relationship. A good example is *Velvet Green*, or *Pibroch*. We rehearsed the song, and looked at it in its "Lego" form, with that piece there and this piece here, and Ian would say "Can you come up with something for that? What do you think should go there?" So I would go home and write something, and the next morning teach the chaps what I'd written, and Ian would come in and listen to it, and either go with it or not. It was a happy musical relationship, and they are few and far between. Even Simon and Garfunkel didn't have that, although their names are inextricably linked. Art Garfunkel was the singer, Paul Simon was the brains. I'm not saying that Ian and I were comparable to Simon and Garfunkel as a partnership. Ian was the truly creative music writer, and I was the guy with all the tricks up his sleeve to put the final touches to things, and add chunks that were necessary. Well, necessary but not necessarily germane to the success of the song. But I've always felt that my contribution to the band's music was... I felt it was important. It was useful... and possibly important! [*Laughs.*]

Indeed it was. In fact some time ago I found Aqualung on cassette in a store, and the legend on the spine read *Aqualung, Jethro Tull, Orchestrated by David Palmer*. You had almost equal billing with Tull - was that your doing, or Ian's?
Really? Goodness me, I've not seen that at all. I was not aware of that. It certainly would not have been instigated by me, or any record company that I've ever worked with.

It must have been Ian, or Chrysalis, although I can't see why Chrysalis would do it.
Speaking of Chrysalis, that reminds me of a story I heard, though I wasn't there, of one of their conventions which was held in a hotel in Runnymede. There were about 150 people there, and Terry Ellis walked into the room, and before they sat down he said, "I want you all to pick up your chairs, turn them upside down, and read what it says." Underneath every chair was written "JETHRO TULL". He said, "That band has given you your job. Now put your chair down, have a good lunch and enjoy yourselves, but don't you ever forget it!" He was then a very pushy guy, quite the pushiest guy I've ever met. People used to sweat at the prospect of having a meeting with him. Heads of major record companies were scared of him.

Bob Dylan wasn't scared of him, was he? [*ref. the famous interview in the film* Don't Look Back *in which Terry Ellis was made to look like a complete prat!*]
Ah, but he was learning then. In that movie you can see who Terry Ellis is - he's trying to get out. He actually says, "I may do something that will make me some money," or something similar. You can see Terry's embryonic character in there.

Can you tell us anything about the *Warchild* film and the accompanying orchestral soundtrack? We have heard bits of it, but how much was recorded?
We recorded quite a lot of music. Martin [*Barre*] wrote a piece, a little acoustic guitar piece which we developed into something much longer, but there was one particular piece that Ian wrote which was very good. I think it was called *Waltz Of The Angels*. He played it on the guitar, and it was almost like Benjamin Britten; it reminded me of Tchaikovsky and Britten, it was a very, very good piece of music. Ask him about it, because I haven't got a copy. We sent off the only copy we had of that to London Weekend Television, because they wanted some music for a series they were planning of orchestrated versions of rock music from the Albert Hall. I felt very sad about that film, because we worked very hard on that, Ian and I. We had a meeting with Sir Frederick Ashton at his home in Chelsea, and it was like going into Mrs Tiggywinkle's cottage, you know. We invited him to do the choreography, and after he heard the music he was up for it. John Cleese, who is a friend of mine, was to be the humour advisor. But then the big mistake was made when Bryan Forbes was invited to be the director, because then it was, "Hurry-hurry-wait, hurry-hurry-wait," until eventually within the time frame of a major touring band like Tull it had to be shelved. Ian might say for the better, because we were all young and eager to become involved in a movie. But Ian wanted to do it, and he had it in himself to pull it off, that's for sure. When I say pull it off I mean make a movie, start at A and end at Z, then offer it up for people's approval or disapproval. But Ian

certainly could have supervised the whole bloody thing himself. It may well have elicited less than glowing critiques from those people who hold themselves up as film experts, but he could have done it. It's all part of the development of a musician's life. I can remember starting to write an opera when I was at the Royal Academy. I mean, I was still studying, I hadn't got far past Mozart's operas, let alone Wagner, Verdi and all the other lot! I was a mile out, but I still wanted desperately to do it because it was all move-move-move on, you know? And I'm sure that was the motivation behind Ian wanting to write that film.

Was *The Water's Edge*, the ballet from 1979/80, ever recorded?
It was recorded with a hand held tape recorder, but never properly recorded. But I have sad memories about *The Water's Edge*. It was commissioned, and Ian wrote some themes, Martin wrote a couple of pieces. Martin wasn't entirely aware, I think, of the structure of astrophic song, or the more complex structures of developed balletic sequences. They have to be conceived as what they are, not as a little piece of music and "see if that will do". It has to be constructed, not contrived. And that is not to speak disparagingly of Martin's aspirations as a music writer - I mean he has proven with his album that he can write songs - but we are talking about *The Water's Edge* which was 1978. Ian wrote one particularly good theme, and lots of very interesting pieces that I took and developed into balletic sequences with Robert North, who incidentally is now one of the most celebrated choreographers in western ballet. I gave that all I had, and that was at the time we were recording *Heavy Horses*. I think Ian thought it was taking me a long time, because I write so quickly, but I was actually giving it the complete works. In fact as a kind of endorsement, or a seal of approval of what we ended up with, I was having drinks in a hotel in Montreal last November with the musical director who conducted the piece in Scotland. He is now the musical director of the Winnipeg Symphony orchestra. He sang to me whole chunks of the ballet, and asked me, made me promise, to do an orchestral suite of the ballet for him to perform and broadcast, and probably record with the Winnipeg Symphony Orchestra. But going back to what I was saying, I was distressed because I had given it my all... it is a bloody enormous score, it's as thick as that speaker over there! It's BIG, nearly an hour long, for a full symphony orchestra. And I went to the press conference in London, and walked into the room which was full of the leading London ballet critics etc., and I chanced upon a bunch of hand-bills on the table. I picked one up and it said "*The Water's Edge*, a ballet written by Ian Anderson" and I walked out. I think that was the only petulant... well no, it wasn't petulant, it was merited... I walked out of the place, caught a cab home and thought, "Well fuck that!" We had a rehearsal the next day, and Ian said to me, "You didn't stay long," and I said, "No. And surely it is evident why I left?" He said, "Yes, I know why," and picked up the phone and sacked the person responsible for that. But it should never have happened. I mean, I'm not washing my dirty linen in public, but you asked me about it and it was tainted with that. It was a great shame. But within that ballet is a piece that begins...

[*David walked over to the grand piano behind him and played a piece from* Elegy. *We asked for an encore but sadly he declined!*]

When we came back from the first performance in Glasgow Martin Barre said, "That's a pretty tasty piece of music." Of course you have heard it since the words were added.

You said a few years back that you were hoping to release that new version as a single.
Yes, I will. All in good time; it exists now as a song, with words, and I play it at every gig I do, and make alterations until... until it's right. A song that I have no respect for at all, I think it's a dreadful piece of music writing, is *Vienna*, but that song started its life ten years before it emerged as a recorded piece. Midge Ure is that kind of guy, he beavers away and beats things until they come into shape. So it will appear eventually, but the lyric which you heard at Basingstoke IS the lyric. It's allegorical, and it's for anyone to make whatever they want of it. But that song came out of *The Water's Edge* which in some way makes up for the blow to my pride that I suffered, and I only have to play four notes of it in America and the approbation is immediate. It's very gratifying. And I hope, I really hope, that I can find time to pursue the request to write a score for the Winnipeg Symphony Orchestra. I would like to do it, but when

I spoke to Ian last December there were obviously... issues more important in his life at the time than worrying about where the copyright lay for *The Water's Edge*. But I've just finished *Sgt Pepper* for EMI, and when that's out and up and running there will be an opportunity for me to talk to EMI who hold the catalogue. We will get a lot of plays around the world, that much I know.

One thing that I became aware of, around about 1984, was that demographically, what I was then setting out to do would be absolutely correct at a time to be determined only by people's awareness of what I was doing - namely writing music for symphony orchestra and rock group that was integrated, really integrated as opposed to muzak or Radio 2. All the people that Jethro Tull were playing to in 1968 are now 40 to 50 years of age, they've got the house, wife and two kids, two cars, a mortgage, they've been skiing, they've got the classical collection from Vivaldi to Verdi through to the contemporary figures like Górecki, and now they are looking for something else. And they feel very happy to go to my gigs in their thousands; it may be twenty years on, but I'm still honking it out - it's just dressed in different clothing. They enjoy it, and the life that an orchestral suite from *The Water's Edge* could have in the repertoire of orchestras large and small, celebrated and not so celebrated, around the world is just incalculable. There are some very good pieces in there. I don't imagine Chrysalis will be busting to do anything with it, but I feel we ought to do something. I know Ian has just done a classical album, so perhaps he will remember our conversation and get back to me. It's just that there are so many things I've got to do. I have to live in today rather than yesterday, much as I would like to do *The Water's Edge*. We should do it, but unfortunately I am probably the only person that could do it, having written a great part of that ballet. I can't remember it all but I've got sufficient sketches out in one of the stables over there. You might be pleased to know that two years ago we were going to sell this place, and I emptied out one of the barns which I had designated as my library, [*laughs*]. There was music piled to the ceiling - there might even have been some Max Bygraves scores in there - tied in plastic bags. We had a great bonfire, it took all day to burn that music, but I kept every piece of Jethro Tull music, every sketch, right from *Move On Alone*. So one day I will be able to bequeath to the Jethro Tull Foundation all that stuff. And it's all on yellow paper, which used to be a big joke, The Yellow Pages. And I've got my score of *Baker Street Muse*, on which I've written Baker Street 'Mews', because how could I know of the typically English play on words? But I've got my original yellow pages score where Ian has crossed through "Mews" and written "Muse" above it.

Moving on to Coronach in 1984 - you told me once that you wanted Roy Harper to sing that originally.

Yes, I called Roy, and he was kind of half available. And of course that's not good enough in time frames that you operate in with commissioned music. I remember once Ian producing a letter from Roy - we were in the library in Ian's house, all six of us - and Ian asked me to read it out. It was a plaintive missive from Roy about the way he had been treated by Chrysalis while he was on the road in America. I think Roy always wanted to be a 'Rockstar', but he was up there, you know. He and Richard Thompson are two of the great unsung heroes of the revolution in English music. Richard Thompson has the recognition, but it is not expressed in Rolls Royces, country houses, Swiss bank accounts etc. But that's irrelevant, it really is. I have none of those things because they really aren't important. But I wish I could write like Richard Thompson, and sing like Roy Harper. So yes, I did ask Roy, but it seemed it would not be possible, so I asked Ian. Since I left the band Ian and I have maintained a relationship where I feel I can call him and ask him to come and play flute for me, and if he wants me to write something for him I'll write it. So I called Ian, I did the backing track and he put the vocals on and some really tasty little guitar parts. And we were a whisker away from having a hit with that song.

It wasn't in the shops. It was so hard to find.

Hmmm. There is a further anecdote on that. I called Chrysalis and told them I had been invited to write the title song and under-score for a prime time programme on Channel 4 that will attract quite a lot of viewers. We need to get a record out. I said this to Chris Wright. Ian and myself, Chris Wright and Terry Ellis are four guys who know the colour of each other eyes, you know. I know exactly who they all are, and they know who I am. So I said this to Chris and he said, "Well you'll have to come in and see me, David." But I said, "Look, this can be done on the phone - we just need a record out. We can record it tomorrow and get it out." The continuity announcer, two weeks running, had said, "I do like that music," and Channel 4 were, if not inundated, were certainly slightly besieged with phone calls asking where they could buy the music. But Chris said it was too late to do anything, so the next day I burst into his office and said, "Look, we have got a song that people like, they want to buy the record. I wrote it, Jethro Tull recorded it, Ian sings it - it is a Jethro Tull single. What are you gonna do?" But they wouldn't do anything until the series was repeated. Eventually it came out, but it had no major marketing effort, and I think we missed slightly in the arrangement. I think we should have gone for something like Clannad, and multi-tracked Ian's voice. If we'd done that we would have had a hit; it would have been just a fag paper away from Enya. It would have been good for the band, good for me, good for everybody. But it was one of those things, you know. But I'm sure there will be others. I will one day write something that will suit Ian, I'll write a song that Ian's voice fits round nowadays, rather than when you could write anything and he could sing it. That was a great shame - but it happens to everyone. But you rise above those disappointments. It would be nice one day to re-approach that song, but it's tough trying to find the time for everything. You have to move on with what you are doing today. I don't know if Dave [*Pegg*] remembers, but when we were recording it Dave was walking round saying, "This is gonna be a hit!" You should never say that, it's like mentioning "The Scottish Play" by its name, you know. You should never say something is going to be a hit, because it's not up to us. It's up to us simply to enjoy what we do. One thing about my life is that I am doing what I like, and I'm liking what I do, and I actually can't think of any time that I was ever doing anything else. And that's worth a big lot in the pay packet. I know it doesn't put milk in the fridge, but as long as you have a pint of milk in the fridge and you are happy doing what you do, then you are rich. As Ian always has been, because come the hour, come the song, Ian will knock them out.

Adding to that, we were involved in the making of the box set in 1988. Ian played us an instrumental piece that we really liked, and we said it ought to go on the album, but Ian said, "Well, it's not finished, it's only half a song." The next day he finished it, with flute and vocals and really complex lyrics, and it was christened *Mayhem Maybe*. It was amazing!

Oh well, it's that about Ian, that's one of the things that I've always admired about Ian. We were in the studio in Monte Carlo recording *Too Old To Rock'n'Roll*, and we were going up a one way street with *Pied Piper*. We were stuck, and we couldn't get out of it. I think part of the problem was down to me, changing the key structures of things. But Ian went back that night, came in the next day with "If you think Ray blew it, there was nothing to it," etc. He played it to me on his guitar, and it was brilliant. He is formidable, a formidable talent. Another thing about Ian, which is certainly worth recording, was when we were working on that same album, which had started out as a musical...in fact, it was to have starred Adam Faith, who was going to appear on a motor bike going down the centre aisle of a West End theatre and arriving onstage on a plank going over the orchestra! I mean, such are the things you think, but obviously he couldn't have had the engine running, he would have to have been towed by a glider or something! But, we were in a hotel in Montreux, and Ian and I were working on material for the album, and I was sitting in my room writing out a song that never went on the album. A lot of things were written and binned. But I could hear a steady knocking sound, about three in the morning, which went on for about five minutes, in perfect time. I thought it was a valve in the pipes or something. It stopped and started, stopped and started, all through the night. I lay awake trying to figure out what would cause such a steady beat. The next morning we had arranged to meet for breakfast, so I went up to his room and he ushered me into his bathroom and said, "Listen to this, see what you think." As you know, all musical instruments sound good in the bathroom! And he started playing his guitar, tapping out the tempo with his boot on the pipes - just as he had been doing through the night - in perfect time. He has a metronome in his head. Drummers in Jethro Tull have to die, or commit suicide, because of his sense of rhythm and placing. I have a great sense of pitch, it's there and it's been developed, because I need it. If somebody is there farting around, playing the wrong notes, I have to hear it straightaway, name it and put it right, That's part of the job that I do. But Ian's sense of rhythm... if I had to engage a rhythm guitar player, and I could choose from everybody in the world, I would call Ian Anderson first.

We were at a rehearsal once and he stopped playing and said, "Doane, you're playing it at 100 beats per minute - it needs 96".
Oh yeah, it is that acute. It is a great gift. All great musicians have a gift, and they weld to that gift skills. If you don't have the gift, don't give up your day job, because the gift is IT. The gift is put there at the moment of conception, you add the skill later, and it's usually called experience. Ian's most obvious gift is the creative talent, but the sense of rhythm is profound. I remember watching Ian recording *Moths*, he sat down, played the guitar and sang, and that was remarkable to see; it's not a simple piece. When you work closely with someone like that you learn a lot. One of the great assets I have is that in a rehearsal with any of the great symphony orchestras, I only have to hear one hair of a bow out of tune or out of place and I'm on it. And I won't have it. It ain't what I wrote, and it isn't what I want. And sometimes I smile inwardly and think... it's not Ian sitting on my shoulder, but it's Ian sitting by my side. I value that experience, without being sycophantic, highly. Whereas there are other people who might look at Ian and think, "Shit! He's a termagant, a devil," but it isn't that, he is in pursuit of what is right. It is right or wrong, there are no degrees of nothing, so if there is a right way to do it, let's have it, you know. One of the strangest personal experiences I had was when we were in San Diego, and the band had played like the Mexican Tramways Orchestra. It was appalling, a dreadful gig. And afterwards we were called into the food room and I thought, "Ah, good. We are going to get a bollocking! We are going to be told to get a grip," and I thought it was late in coming, I thought it should have happened a couple of weeks before. And Ian came in and said, "Is everybody here?" and I thought, "Oh, it's gonna be a major bollocking!" I honestly thought he was going to say we were playing like crap, and if we didn't sort it out he was off - because he didn't have to say we were fired, if he went the band was finished. But Ian said "John Glascock died tonight."
And that was such a strange experience, having expected him to say something else, and then he said something that actually really did completely demolish us. I know that's life, something like that happens once to all of us at some point, but that was salutary, for sure.

What can you tell us about "The Big Split" in 1980?
Oh, it was time. It was time for me to move on, that's for sure. What I'm doing now is what I'd planned, other than Tallis, which happened soon after leaving Tull. With all artists there is a need to involve one's self with other artists. Tull was... not incestuous, but very familial, if that is the right word. It was time for that to stop, and new horizons to be looked at. The fact that the result of having a new Jethro Tull was an album called *A*, which fell far short of what I had been certainly striving for and wanting to see preserved, is incidental. There is clear evidence of artists going off tangentially, in pursuit of rainbows' ends, and not finding them, but eventually coming back to a position where they can see them... even if they can't find them. It was certainly time for me to move on but - I would say this - I think the best Jethro Tull was the band that existed in the mid to late '70s. That band produced live performances together with recordings that were pretty damn good! I'm certainly very proud to have been a part of that. But I think I have always known the direction in which I was headed, though only time would tell if I would ever achieve those objectives. You can't predict success; it's like doing the pools. But to have a pencil in your hand, and to be one of the quickest writers in the west, with an understanding of orchestral and rock music was something that I had to move on with. And I suppose, looking at what I do now, my credentials are impeccable. I am conducting major symphony orchestras around the world, performing rock music of the '70s and David Palmer music of the '90s, and I have a credibility factor on two counts. I am the product of a celebrated music establishment, taught by some of the finest brains in western music, in so far as they were available to teach at the Royal Academy in the '60s, and I've been a member of one of the biggest and best rock'n'roll bands in the world. They are credentials which should get me into the White House! I am certainly a very proud ex-member of Jethro Tull.

Was the Tallis project a big thing, or was it just a case of a few weeks?
No, it was more than just a few weeks. That was an interesting exercise where I tried to go as far as I could with synthesised sound. I started getting into synthesisers when I was with Tull though I did find it difficult at first. One of the worst things I found was in the days of analogue synthesisers, playing them on-stage trying to emulate orchestral sounds. It's no good trying to emulate orchestral sounds if you are playing like an organ, because it is no longer an illusion - it's an organ. If you are playing something that is alluding to a string ensemble, the timbre is wrong; strings don't come in with a bang, you hear the ictus, the drawing of the bow, unless it's drawn really quickly. But in slow music, any *adagio, lento* or even *allegro moderate*, there will be an attack, but it will be preceded by the ictus. And I had difficulty in putting across to the rhythm section that I wasn't setting the pulse with the keyboards, I was playing with it as a string orchestra. In *Heavy Horses* for instance, there is detailed orchestration that I was recreating with synthesisers, so I was playing slightly behind the beat, because that is the way strings sound. So when I started work with Tallis I was able to do what I wanted to do, without having to adhere to the beat. Sure, the drums and bass and lead guitar play on the beat, but the vocal doesn't, it floats above it all, and the string texture weaves in and out. Listen to *Heavy Horses* or *Moths* and you'll see what I mean. So with Tallis I was able to take it as far as I could at the time, it was interesting to do, and it had great possibilities as a live performing band.

As far as the time-scale of Tallis went, it was regulated by my need to find something for the band to do. I need a deadline, we all need deadlines, and mine was that I was asked to do something to raise money for a local church. I thought, OK, I'll put a band together to play a concert. So I orchestrated a Mozart piano concerto for three synthesiser players and solo piano, and that went well so I did some more pieces, including some original songs. Then John Evans, Bill Worrall, David Bristow, myself, another keyboard player and a drummer got together for intense rehearsals, got the stuff really cooking and did the gig, which was a great success. We then went into the studio and recorded an album, and because I had not long left Tull it was very easy for me to go into any record company and play the tape to the A&R man, not some minion who would play ten seconds of it and move on. And there was uniform appraisal - "It's very good David, it's new, it's forward looking, but where can we sell it?" I said, "We will go out and play it to people". They said, "Yes, go and play it live, get some fans, then we'll go with it." But then I was in the position where five guys, myself included, were depending on the success of my band for their livelihood. They needed guarantees before they could commit themselves, and of course there are no guarantees. So sadly, it never happened. Maybe someday I'll get another band together and do something similar, but then why should I do it with synthesisers when I can do it with the L.A. Philharmonic or the London Symphony Orchestra? Over the last three months I've written a lot of songs, personal songs, and I have enough music now for probably three albums. I have just started putting down backing tracks. When I say they are personal songs I don't mean "I Love You Babe" songs... it's like Ian's songs, he writes what he thinks, and mine are the same. So I've moved on from the Tallis thing, relying purely on synthesised orchestral sounds, to me singing and playing keyboards backed by bass, guitar and drums. I've reduced everything back to its basic form, because if I need an orchestra all I have to do is ring up and engage one of the world's major orchestras to record for me. But I'm not into doing that, because I want to express myself in the old rock'n'roll terms. It's the song, it always was the song, that wins the day. It's not the lights or the effects... mind you, Pink Floyd are getting away with it!

I know I've asked you this before, but I have to ask you again "on record" so to speak... is there absolutely no possibility of you releasing any of the Tallis album, even through the "limited edition" back-door of *A New Day*?
No, because... [*l-o-n-g pause*] ... what we could do, probably... there are a couple of pieces which you could use for a collector's edition CD, if Dave Pegg gave you a couple of tracks, and Martin threw something in, and maybe Ian would come up with something. That would be a nice idea. [*It certainly would!*] I'll play you a couple of tracks before you go - but you can't take a tape with you! [*Curses!*] Do you know the hymn *All People That On Earth Do Dwell*? It was written by Thomas Tallis. I took the theme from that and made it into a piece which is not a million miles away from Jethro Tull, the quirky flavour of it. And there is the

Mozart piano concerto which I orchestrated in a way that would show Mozart in a completely different light. And further on from that, I orchestrated three Mozart piano sonatas that I'd discovered when I was a student, that I thought he had probably conceived as orchestral pieces rather than piano pieces. Because often he would be invited to compose a sonata for one of his pupils by an over-zealous parent. They'd give him 20 Crowns or whatever, and before he had his cornflakes he would write a sonata. The reason I orchestrated those pieces was because when he wrote them he had just returned from Mannheim, which was where the first celebrated orchestra was in residence. They could play loud and soft, quick and slow, with one or two other desirable inflections that other orchestras couldn't do. He was mightily impressed with this orchestra, so I think he had written these piano sonatas but was thinking in orchestral texture. So I orchestrated them and recorded them electronically. They are worth an ear, because this was my synthesis in 1986, and if you could go back then and look at the state of the art of synthesis then, it is out in front. When RCA heard of what I was doing they wanted to release it, but they thought it was going to be something like *Switched On Bach* with dreadful moog sounds, but what I'd actually created was orchestral sounds without any pre-programmed sounds, we contrived them all. It was a document for myself, a frame of reference as to where I was with synthesis.

During my time with Tull I was playing instruments which everybody in the world was still learning how to play, it was exciting and challenging. Needless to say, since then I have fallen out of love with them; synthesisers now to me are useful instruments for playing on-stage, but because I am so heavily involved with what synthesisers sought to emulate it seems unnecessary to pursue it any further. Not only that, since digital synthesis was introduced and developed, I have no more idea of how to get into one of those synths than I have of getting into Fort Knox. And, quite candidly, synthesised music now is a very unruly dog, it's out of its kennel and it's biting everybody on the arse. I don't see any longevity, it's absolutely of the moment. There is very little that's come out of the techno-rock movement that has any enduring quality about it. I do interviews every day when I'm on the road, and people always ask me what I think of today's music. I say, "When they can write songs like *Aqualung* then they will be able to fill this auditorium in twenty years' time". My son has been doing some work-experience with a record company and out there on the table there's about 500 CDs. I've tried to play through them but my ears can't take it. Last night I watched some of the Mercury Awards thing - we are back to The Jam and The Clash, you know, what's new? When I heard *London's Burning* I thought that was the greatest thing, raw music that wasn't gonna last but, my God, it was energetic! But Blur, Oasis, there is nothing new there, nothing has moved forward. Two albums I listened to a lot last autumn were *Ten Summoner's Tales* by Sting, and *The* by the Pet Shop Boys. Two very different pieces of work, both first class. Let them follow that. The Pet Shop Boys' lyrics and music is just great, great pop music, and Sting's is sophisticated music to suit the audience that wants it. But you go round the world and those songs are everywhere. They are enduring; they've got shape and form, they've got design, they are orchestrated and produced well, and performed well. That's what music is, not that lot I saw on TV last night. Journalists will say, "Oh, that old fart David Palmer," or "That old fart Ian Anderson," but was it not ever so? People have always been quick to point the finger and say, "What you do is passé mate, this is what's happening now," but those people are playing at being musicians. Today's music is being supplied by people who are approximating to being musicians, and I'm afraid people who approximate cause awful disasters. People who are precise and purposeful about what they are doing will cause nothing more than a raised eyebrow because of the significance of their efforts, but people that mess about with music the way they are doing now will destroy it.

Do you think that's because they don't have to 'pay their dues' like they used to?
Yes, exactly, they've never been in the back of a transit van! I used to go up and down the country, playing in places that my mother would have died had she seen me in! The English rock movement, the flowering of that movement in the '70s, was nurtured in the back of transit vans by groups of four or five chaps who can't see out because there's no bloody windows, you can't breathe because it's full of smoke, driving from here to Galashiels and down to Land's End to earn 30 bob, doing what they like and liking what they do. Because that is the income, that is the choice. The money is for beer and fags. [*Well, obviously! DR*]

And if you are visited with eventual wealth as a result of your endeavours, fine - there is a limit to how much money you can actually ever need. I've never been anything but a smoked salmon socialist! And look at Ian, a very wealthy man, but he doesn't drive around in a Rolls Royce displaying his wealth, because it is incidental. The song is the thing, and I'm afraid with today's music there ain't going to be any songs in ten years' time, the way they are going, they will find something else. Pop and rock music now is in dire straits because of the amount of interest that's been generated by computer games. Where it stretches to I don't know, because I am not computer literate at all, but those games are eroding the interest in music, and it will die if we're not careful. We ought to examine the remit the record companies have, and what lies within it. Maybe we'll do that in interview #2! They are just looking for the next buck, but there was a time when you could play something to an A&R department and they would say, "That's good. Let's put it out." Now there is no A&R man, there is a snotty nosed 18-year old being controlled by a suit, with clearly identifiable puppet strings coming through the ceiling from the office upstairs, who says, "Will this make any money?". That's the difference. All the real greats - Ian Anderson, Dave Gilmour, Roy Harper - all of them, if they had to present themselves now to record companies with today's mentality and attitude, would not stand a chance, they wouldn't get a sniff. And neither would I. I would be a music teacher in Bangor-on-Dee secondary modern school. Heaven forbid!

Well, interview #2 did eventually take place, in 2003 – but we could not possibly have guessed in 1994 the circumstances which would lead up to it.

Meanwhile, 1994's David was as good as his word, and he did give A New Day *a wonderful Tallis track for inclusion on the 2001 CD* It's For You, *which came free with Issue #75 and featured exclusive tracks from the likes of Fairport Convention (with Dave Pegg), Blodwyn Pig (with Mick Abrahams and, for one night only, Glenn Cornick), John Carter (with Martin Barre). Maart Allcock, Solstice (with Clive Bunker) and, yes, Jethro Tull themselves. Still dreaming of the full Tallis album release, though...*

Chapter 26

DAVE PEGG

(Published in #47, January 1995)

The second half of 1994 saw Honest Dave Pegg on a leave of absence from Jethro Tull to attend to his commitments with the other legendary outfit with which he plays, Ian Anderson's favourite band, Fairport Convention. With a wonderful album due in January 1995, and another gruelling winter tour (nights off? Pah!), it seemed like a good time to catch up with him before he disappeared into the snowbound wastelands of Olde England. The venue was his favourite boozer, The Half Moon in Putney, just before Fairport Acoustic Convention took to the stage. DR was joined for the interview by Terry "The Innocent" Coates, and MW who arrived half way through to take photos.
We got the beers in, set the Walkman, and DR checked that he had enough cigarettes to last for an hour with Peggy.

This year [*1994*] was the first time that Jethro Tull's schedule has clashed significantly with Fairport's, due to Tull's commitments rolling on incessantly. Did you find that irritating?
Well, sort of, but you can't be in two places at the same time. The Tull tour kept getting extended, and we had already made some commitments with Fairport because we were desperate to make a new album. It is hard because there are so many people involved and it's a case of getting the time when everybody's around to make an album. So we had to do it really, we had to make the album then. Traditionally we tour every January and February, and we have Cropredy in the summer, which also clashed with Tull commitments. I felt bad about not being able to do them, but luckily Matthew [Pegg] had already done some dates with Tull and he knew most of the material, and Ian was very happy for him to stand in. That was great for me because then I didn't feel bad about it. And Matt loves playing that music, and it's good for him as well because he gets to play with some really great musicians which kind of expands his philosophy about bass playing. He really enjoys it, and I don't think the band suffers as a result of me not being there. In fact it's probably more advantageous having a thin person with long hair on-stage... with all due respect to Ian and Martin!

Did you get to any of the gigs that Matt played?
Unfortunately not. I really wanted to come to Clapham, but the problem was Cropredy was the day after. It's absolute hell trying to put that festival together, and the week before Cropredy is just insane. We had been to America with Fairport as well, doing the Newport Folk Festival, the weekend before. So it was actually impossible for me to get to the gig. I would love to have gone, I'd love to see the band with Matt playing. He amazes me actually, he just gets better and better on bass. I know I'm probably biased, but he really is a great bass player - better than me! I don't know how the chaps feel about having somebody so much younger in the band. Because Tull isn't really a sociable band, it's not like Fairport. It's like the pub lunch every day on tour. Our tour is built around the good pub guide; if you can get to a certain boozer in time to have lunch you can do a show there that evening. That's the way it works. It's very much a bunch of mates, it's a sociable thing. It's not like that with Tull, everybody keeps themselves to themselves. But don't get me wrong, it's a very friendly band. We all get on really well and we enjoy each other's company - which is amazing considering the years.
So yes, I was a bit upset at not being able to do all the dates, but we had done an awful lot of dates doing the same show. I mean there are an awful lot of places to play, and I think Tull played everywhere there is to play, so I don't think it was too much of a problem for them to cope without me. I'm sure the chaps would verify that. So it worked out fine in many respects. We would never have finished the Fairport album in time - in fact we only finished it last week so it has taken from June till last week to get it together. We are just in the nick of time to get it released on January 9th, because the whole world closes down in the music business for Christmas and the New Year. It's been a real race to get it ready for January.

It comes out a couple of weeks before the tour; is that because you would rather people bought in the shops as opposed to buying it directly from you at gigs?
We would prefer people to buy it in the shops, yes. We are sending our newsletter out now, which goes out to 16,000 people, so our house now smells throughout of freshly printed paper. [*Tell me about it! DR*]. We have asked our fans... [*laughs*]... well, you can't force people to buy a record, but for us it's very important because it's the first studio album we have done for four years. There is over an hour of music, and there are no "filler" tracks, you know? Usually with Fairport we have two or three good songs, and we are desperately looking for more. This time it's been the other way round, we've rejected half a dozen great songs and we've still got fifteen titles which we all really like. As an album we think it's probably the best thing the band has ever done. I know people often say that, but we are quite cynical, The Fairports. We don't often go around shouting about ourselves, unless we have just come out of the pub at the end of an evening

Err... that's every evening isn't it?
Umm... yeah! But we are really happy with it, we're really proud of it. It sounds really good, and we think our audience will really enjoy it. So we are hoping they will all rush out to the record shops on January 9th and buy it, or if it's not there, order it, because it is really hard to get your stuff in the shops nowadays. Well as you know from Martin Barre's experience with his album, or the stuff you are doing yourself. What we do is like minority music, and it is very difficult to get the chains to take it, for example, to get into HMV or Virgin.

But with a mailing list of 16,000, is it not better for you to sell it direct, rather than through a shop with the distributors and retailers both taking a big cut?
Well, in a way. It would be nice if 10,000 people sent us £11 each! Some of them will, some prefer to buy it mail order from us because maybe they don't live near a record shop. We will be selling it mail order and at gigs, along with the other stuff, the T-shirts, the back catalogue etc. Financially it is not as good if people buy the new album from the shops, but we need the credibility in order to get our stuff into the shops. Obviously, if a Virgin shop will take two or three Fairport CDs, if they are sold the first week it gives them the incentive to re-order which means you are probably going to be on the shelf for two or three months. I mean, hopefully not sitting there with nobody buying it, but it will have a longer shelf life if people buy the record from the stores. It is VERY difficult to get your stuff in the shops. The last time I tried to do this, which was many years ago, it was quite scary then, the things you had to go through. It would be a lot easier if we were an all girl band! But all these chains want you to spend money with them advertising your product, and their advertising rates are like twice what I would normally pay, myself. Being a real cheap-skate I always get really good deals with people like The Guardian. Because we are not a big label, we only put records out sporadically, and there's only so much you can spend on advertising a folky type record which is only going to sell two or three thousand CDs, in the case of like a Fairport solo project. So the reason we are going through the normal channels, as opposed to trying to sell them all ourselves, is to try to get the band's credibility up a bit more with the shop-keeper.

With that in mind, Fairport have always shown admirable restraint in not calling in all your megastar musician friends to guest on your albums. I mean, you know *everybody* in the rock business don't you?
Well, quite a few - we could have asked some people, but it's a Fairport album and we don't want to do that kind of thing. That doesn't appeal to us at all. I mean, we enjoy playing with other people, and we love playing other people's music. Like at Cropredy, it becomes something very special to us... well, not this year, where it was more or less four hours of Fairport... but the year before, when we had Planty and Roy Wood and Everything But The Girl and so on - we played 46 songs, only 11 of which were Fairport songs. So it's a fine line. We would rather play other people's material at Cropredy, because it's a different thing, it's a festival, there's a lot of people out there, and much as we love playing our own stuff, to play it for three or four hours... it's got so many ups and downs, the long ballads, the gentle instrumentals, the element of rock 'n' roll - which is a very necessary part of a festival appearance, because people really just wanna boogie most of the time; it's a long weekend, it's like an endurance test really, and you have to be very careful what you play. People want good time music, and we can't do that for three hours, so it's great for us at Cropredy to be able to bring on people that we admire and respect and play their music for a while. So I think

276

definitely next year at Cropredy we will have a few more surprise guests. The reason we didn't do it this year is because we had a small percentage of people write in and say "What's the matter with you lot? This is your gig, and you've only done 11 songs out of 46". You can't win really, because everybody likes different things. Fairport are so eclectic, and the fans come from different backgrounds, they have different musical preferences.

Do you think they would have been happier if you had played a straight Fairport set on the Friday, with the usual guest appearances on Saturday?
Yes, that is another alternative, and we have done that in the past - the 25th Anniversary for instance. We did a two hour set on Friday, and played for four and a half hours on Saturday. But then we were bringing back lots of ex-members of Fairport, and covering 25 years of the band's history, which took six hours, and we still left out a lot of really important songs. It's maybe 20 albums' worth of material, and if you only pick two or three songs from each album you go on and on forever. Another time we did it, one night we played *Babbacombe Lee*, which was great fun, when we got Swarb back.. *Babbacombe Lee* is an album which you can only perform in its entirety, and that was a great discipline. It was really hard to do because... well, once you've started it you can't get off the boat, you've got to carry on to the end. Another problem has been that it's four years since the last album, four years since we had new material to play. We now have fifteen songs, probably about ten of which we could do live, so the new tour set will be completely different to the last one, and hopefully we will keep a lot of it in the set for Cropredy. But to get back to your question about guests on the album, it has never been a temptation, just to sell more albums. You try to do certain things with a band, and with Fairport we have always done exactly what we wanted to do, we have never compromised. You could pick any album from the group's career and compare it with the last one and you would never imagine it was the same band. There has never been any conscious attempt to sell more records or to get on *Top Of The Pops*. We realised many years ago that was an impossibility, and we have always gone along the route that if the majority of the band really like something, we will have a go at it. It may not be all five of us in agreement but it's usually three of the five. It's a democratic process.

Is that always the case? Do you ever record songs that four of you aren't keen on but one of you *really* wants to do?
Well, we'll have a go. Like for this album there were 20 or 25 songs that we considered. We listen to them - usually other people's versions of a song, or a traditional song that Maart has found in a book and he'll sit there and play it to us - and from those 25 songs you are looking for an hour's worth of material. It's the songs that get the vote, it's still a democratic decision. I might not like some of them, but I'll go along with them because the majority of the band likes them, and vice versa. You just get a feeling that something's gonna work. Like the Leonard Cohen song *Closing Time,* which is my favourite track I think. It is just right up our street, it's like a gift from above for Fairport really because it's got all the connections with our pub activities [*laughs*], and it's quite a cheerful song. Well actually it probably isn't a cheerful song, but the way I read it it's like, the end of an album, "let's go down the pub!" That's the way it was recorded and it's basically what we did! And I love the Steve Tilston songs *Slip Jigs and Reels* and *The Naked Highwayman*, which is gonna be unbelievably difficult to perform live. We did actually do it at the soundcheck tonight and Simon managed to get through it. It's almost impossible to sing. It's like trying to sing thirty tongue-twisters in three minutes. I mean I can't do it at all, but Simon actually managed it tonight... before he'd had a drink. I don't think we'll risk it during the performance! [*They did of course, and it was great. It came early in the set though*].
We have a great set of songs on the album, with Ric's and Maart's instrumentals. There is quite a lot of involvement from the band on the writing level. There's a Ralph McTell song which Maart was heavily involved with, as he was with another song by Ben Bennion from Freeway Jam. He was the guy who played with us when Robert Plant did his set at Cropredy. So there is more than the usual writing input from the Fairport band themselves.

When you start to prepare an album do you call your friends and ask for songs, or do they come to you?
We are always on the look-out for material It's something that you do just as a matter of course, because none of us write songs. You are always looking for something that might be suitable for the

band. And we get so many tapes sent through the post from people who think they've got material that's suitable. Sometimes it is, we have recorded a couple of things that have dropped through the door on a cassette by unknown song writers. I must get 500 tapes a year now, it's unbelievable. I've still got a large box of tapes, usually from bands who want to play at Cropredy, and I just haven't got the time to play them. I write back now and tell people to send a video, because that's the only way to tell, if you haven't got time to see them live, if they are good enough for the festival. A band might sound great on a CD or tape but live they could have zero personality. We won't book just anyone, I can't abide anything if the stuff is not played well, but in addition to that they must be good live. We want all the bands to go down well, it would be terrible to see somebody die a death. Luckily we haven't really come unstuck too much in that respect. We haven't had any great disasters.

It was a bit shaky with Roy Harper this year....
Yeah well, he had a bad gig, you know. It's one of those things.

It wasn't so much a bad gig, it was a bad moment, wasn't it? [*A ten minute delay early in the set for Roy to tune his guitar.*]
He is notorious unfortunately for… he is one of those guys who is paranoid about being out of tune, and from what I'm told he lost the audience completely. I can see that because a lot of people aren't into Roy Harper at all, but then there's thousands that are. I was never a big Roy Harper fan myself; people have been trying to get him onto Cropredy for years, and I've always said, "I don't think it will happen". But I kept getting these CDs through the post, and I played them and they are just **brilliant.** I love Roy Harper now, I play all his CDs often. He was here at the Half Moon a few months before Cropredy, and it was absolutely terrific. He had the people in the palm of his hands, and it was like going to church! His audience was that reverent, and he really did have complete command over the people. I thought he was sensational. That's why we booked him, and for a lot of people it was a great success, but with so many people there are always gonna be a lot who are not into it. They can't take the time to listen to a long lyric, all they wanna do is boogie. It's that element who you really have to cater for. I felt bad that Roy had had a bad night, because he was very upset about it, I think.

It was the same at the Tull gig in Clapham. That was the one section when people got restless. We [*DR, Terry the Innocent and the just arrived Mr & Mrs MW*] **all think he's great, but there's a lot who can't get into him.**
[*Terry*] Basically he held up Cropredy for 10 minutes, and you just can't do that can you?
Well it is scary being on the stage at Cropredy. It's hard for Fairport, we get lulls, and you can detect that the audience is getting restless. All you need to do is get two or three songs in the wrong order and you lose everybody. Then you have to try to pick them up again. That's the trouble with Fairport's material, because there are so many things that we want to do but a lot of them are quite subtle, and unless you are really into the band you may not want to hear things like *Red and Gold* or *The Hiring Fair.* If you're a fan you know all the words, and people like that association, they like to know what they are listening to. I'm the same myself when I go to gigs. Your brain really doesn't want to struggle with trying to find out what the guy is singing, because often you can't decipher the words anyway. If you know the song it's fine, it doesn't really matter, but you're there to have a good time and you don't want to take the trouble to get into the song. Some people do but 90% of the people don't.

I don't think that's the case at Cropredy for Fairport. Everybody spends the weekend drinking, but when Fairport come on people are listening.
The surprising thing about it is they drink an awful lot of beer and... well they ran out of cider this year, cider seems to be the way it's going. Simon Nicol only drinks cider now. He is Ciderman. But you don't get too many casualties at Cropredy, and historically there have been very few people that have actually missed the whole weekend. There was one guy I remember... when we used to do our own bootlegs, we did a double cassette called *The Boot.* We went to great trouble - well, we had a revox recorder on the desk! - it was all you could do at the time unless you recorded it all on multi-track which would have cost a fortune. So we taped the whole set, chucked out the crap stuff, and what was reasonably passable we used. It was like "if it isn't too bad, we'll use it!", that was the A&R decision, which was me and my dog. So we were looking for a sleeve and some sleeve

notes, and we got a letter from David somebody in Wellingborough. We get a lot of letters from Cropredy which is good, because you can't always tell what the majority of people thought about it because not everybody writes to you. We've got a great filing system now because whenever anybody writes a letter of complaint we just take 'em off the computer and they go off the mailing list! It's good because they won't have anything to moan about in future. We do get some nasty letters from time to time. But this guy had written complaining that he'd had rather a lot to drink and had fallen over at the bar and broken his glasses. He'd then wandered backstage - this was before we had any kind of security - and he met an Irishman who sympathised with him and shared a drink with him. The next thing the guy knew he was waking up, the next day, underneath the stage! He had missed the Fairport gig completely. He asked if we had any tapes of the show that we could send him. It was just as we had finished doing the double cassette so we used his letter on the back. We didn't mention his name, just initials. I was really pleased about this because it saved us having to write sleeve notes, and I thought, "The guy's gonna be so happy!", you know. I sent him this really nice letter, thanking him for saving me from having to think about writing sleeve notes, and included a copy of *The Boot*, and I got this really irate letter back from him. He was **really** pissed off about it. I suppose he thought his friends might realise who he was. We bootlegged our own stuff for three years. The second was *The Other Boot* and then we did *The Third Leg*. One of the best ones we did was *AT2*, which was from the show in '82, funnily enough! It was in the year of ET, and we nicked the ET poster design and put Swarbrick in the basket at the front of the bike, with Simon peddling him away.

[*Terry*] Have you any plans to record one of the Fairport acoustic gigs for a live album?
No, we haven't. The gigs are great fun to do, but we cover a lot of material that we would normally do with the full band. There are some other things which are very popular, like the Loudon Wainwright songs and some others. It is great fun, and it's much more relaxed than Fairport gigs... well last night it was like a pantomime, it was hilarious. It's a lot less serious than getting up with the band as a part of the tour, where you just want to play the music. Hopefully you entertain people and have fun as well, but the music is the most important thing. Some nights are so good that it would be nice to have something on tape, but it would also be nice to record a proper acoustic album, which would also involve Dave Mattacks. Then we would have something that we could go out and play at these little gigs, instead of just sticking your gear in the car, drawing up a set list in the pub ten minutes before you go on, and playing the gig just for the crack. It works well on this level, but it's not really representative of what we could do.

But Fairport are possibly unique in the sense that you could do that, press up 1,000 CDs of a gig, and sell them yourself. People would know exactly what they were buying wouldn't they?
Oh absolutely, we could do it. We have thought about it, but at the moment Dave Mattacks isn't involved in it, and it's a bit unfair. We are all loyal in that respect, so I think if it was the five of us, and we had something new, songs that people hadn't heard before, and we'd worked on it properly, then it would be viable to record a gig. But there are so many Fairport albums, and so many live things. When we used to do those Cropredy bootlegs it was the same stuff year in and year out, albeit played by different people. You'd have a version of *Sloth* with Gerry Donahue playing guitar, and the next year *Sloth* with Richard Thompson playing guitar, then next year the 14 minute version with both of them playing guitar! It's great, but.....

Well, if you're not selling it somebody else is selling it.
Well we don't mind people bootlegging stuff. It's not as bad as it is with Tull, where there are so many. I mean there are literally thousands of CD bootlegs. I was amazed when I went to that convention in Germany, all the stuff that's about. But it's great. I got a load of them, which were great gigs. They are nice things to have, and I can see why fans want them.

Frank Zappa had the right idea, sticking out his own official versions of his best bootlegs. At least the fans know they are getting a decent album then.
Well, tapes do the rounds. There are some good Fairport ones around, people send them to us. In fact we were selling one ourselves recently, some Italian thing, which was quite good. Nobody knew where they came from - but we were selling 'em!

Getting back to the Fairport Acoustic gigs, we last saw you a few months back in Birmingham and were amazed at how good it was. We thought afterwards that it really would have been better if Tull had done that, a straight, purely acoustic set, on the "Light Music" tour instead of the half acoustic, half electric set.
I thought so too. That was the original concept of it. I wanted it to be that way.

Jethro Tull could do it well.
The problem with Tull doing it is the audience, because again there is such a great variety of music, all those songs that Ian has written. The hard rock stuff, for a lot of Tull fans, is what they want, that's what they like. They arc not particularly up for a mandolin version of *Pussy Willow* or whatever. For them the band is *Aqualung* and *Thick As A Brick* etc. There are a lot of Tull fans like that.

But that was the time, surely, to say, "This is an acoustic gig, and we are going to play this stuff. If you don't want to hear it, don't come. Wait for the next normal Tull gig"?
Well, yes. As it turned out it wasn't really what it was supposed to be. It certainly could have been more acoustic. But it was great going out and playing all the little venues, we played in some fantastic halls. Musically we had some fabulous nights, and we could hear everything. I think Ian didn't enjoy the exposure of suddenly being able to hear everything that was going on.

On a musical level?
Yeah. Because it is quite scary, all of a sudden you can hear yourself. Most of those big gigs, it's just cacophony, it really is; it's absolute hell. It might sound OK out front to the fans, but when you are actually doing it some nights it can be murder. We play some halls... where was one particularly awful gig?... Swindon, that was it. Abysmal! There is no point in doing a sound check even. There are times when it does get on your nerves. It's a dreadful racket, and you get headaches. Well I do. Usually in the morning though! But when you are in bed at 3am and suddenly your ears start ringing you wonder, "What's it all about?", you know. It's the noise level - not so much on the stage, because it's quite quiet these days on stage - but it's the noise coming back off the hall. I enjoyed doing that semi acoustic thing, but I can see why some of the fans didn't enjoy it. Another great thing about it was it became very relaxed. Not musically, performance-wise, but it gave Ian a chance to talk to the punters; it was like playing in somebody's living room in some of the places we played. It was a very nice atmosphere to play music in, and Ian had some great nights, he was very, very amusing and entertaining. And he took the time to talk to the audience, which he doesn't normally do. He came up with great introductions and funny stories, which you can't normally do, especially in Germany or The States. You play the songs and that's it, there's no communication really. But in a smaller venue, where people can hear what you say, you can communicate. We couldn't do it all the time, but as a one-off tour it was great fun.

Are you looking forward to linking up with Tull again?
Oh yeah, I hope so. Ian has plans and projects, he's done his classical thing and he will be doing things to promote that. And he is moving house now, so he'll be setting up his studio, and then he'll be keen to start on a Tull album as well. I hope to be involved in it, but of course if he starts in January / February I can't do it because I'm out with Fairport on tour. But obviously I'd love to be involved.

Getting back to *Jewel In The Crown*, I see there's a song on there written by Rob Beattie. Is that the guy who writes for *Q* magazine?
It is indeed.

[*MW*] That's at least one good review then!
Well it isn't, because obviously he can't do the review now. It's a double edged sword. But I didn't know who had written the song, we got it from Beryl Marriot who is the Jerry Lee Lewis of the folk world - except that she drinks more than him! Rob had sent the song to her, and she passed it onto us. I wasn't that keen, it did nothing for me or Ric on first hearing, but Maart and Simon really wanted to do it. And I have to say it's turned out really well, it does sound great. But we got Rob to come up when we were mixing it, to see how it all works. He was there all day, and when we

finished in the evening we let him put a vocal on, so he has a tape of him singing with our backing track. But he only did it in one bloody take! He was brilliant, not at all nervous, and just got on the mic and did it right through. We were very impressed. Well we'd spent three bloody weeks recording it! But then afterwards I thought, "This is terrible! There goes our review in *Q* now. The only kind of friend we've got there and we can't send him the CD. But it doesn't actually work like that at *Q*, there's one guy who decides what gets reviewed and what doesn't, so we don't even know if *Q* will review it at all.

I think so. Fairport have gone the way Tull went haven't they? Both bands have been derided and laughed at, but you've stuck it out and stayed for so long that you've regained your credibility with the "critics".
Well I would like to think so but you can never do... I mean we still do exactly the same as we always did, we just kind of bollock on, following whatever direction we are going. There's no ultimate goal, we still enjoy playing music.

That's got to be the title of the next official bootleg hasn't it? *Bollock On*!

With that, Dave had to bollock off to play the gig. The Fairports were fab, as ever, and, as we write this in 2012, still are... Catch 'em if you can.

Chapter 27

ANDREW GIDDINGS

(Published in #47, January 1995)

DR had been trying for some time to meet up with Andrew Giddings for a chat about "all things Tull", with a specific eye on the forthcoming orchestral album by Ian Anderson [Divinities]. Andy had been rather busy, and at one stage the suggestion was that the interview could be conducted by fax to and from South Africa. But, after ten years of messing about with A New Day, *DR felt almost qualified to utilise at least a nuance of journalistic suss and professionalism, and came up with an elaborate, devilishly clever and deeply CUNNING PLAN. "Sod that for a lark, let's go down the pub". It transpired that it was Andy's kind of plan, so it came to pass that they met at a hotel in deepest, darkest Kent. After the traditional interview preparations [95 pints of Guinness and an excellent Chinese meal] they returned to the hotel bar to discuss everybody's favourite subject - Jethro Tull. Well, everybody except DR's wife, who took the opportunity to chat to Andy's then fianceé about dogs, cats, chipmunks, curtains, children and Parker, the legendary parrot of "untitled" Jethro Tull instrumentals fame. Meanwhile...*

What can you tell us about the "classical" album you have been recording with Ian?
Well, from start to finish... Roger Lewis, who is head of EMI UK's Classical Division, approached Ian, and they discussed the fact that, for whatever reason, you couldn't buy any classical music that wasn't already the heavy, established classical stuff or the traditional modern composers that everybody already knew about. Basically, why doesn't somebody come up with an alternative, a different slant on classical music? Although I have to say at the start, we are calling it classical out of convenience for ourselves in as much as it contains orchestral instruments. Whether or not that makes the music "classical", I don't know. A lot of people would find that term a bit frightening, or perhaps boring. They might simply prejudge it as not being their kind of thing. It is classical in as much as it has violins, violas, cellos, harp, oboes, clarinets etc

Is there a full orchestra, or a string quartet or something similar?
The *sound* of it is sometimes a full orchestra, sometimes.... not a quartet, but a scaled down orchestra. An orchestra that is not being quite so excited! It is all orchestral music.

A real orchestra or synthesized orchestra?
It's a little bit of a mixture, and one has to use one's imagination. Ian and I would get together in the studio and he would play me his ideas on some melodies. We kicked some chords about, played with some arrangements and came up with a rough version of a song. I then created, with samples, the sound of the orchestra. The idea was to do it all that way to make the demos, and then replace the synths with real instruments. We did a bit of that, but we found a lot of it worked as it was, so we didn't need to replace as much as we thought we would. There is a real violin, oboe, clarinet. We have Doane playing timpani and real percussion. Some of it is electronic, some of it is real, and I hope that it is hard to tell which is which. There is a healthy amount of both, and..... well, you decide. I'll play you a bit in a minute and you decide what is real and what is Memorex.

Ignorant slobs like me won't know the difference then?
Well, no, I would hope that lots of people won't know the difference. The idea wasn't to set out to deliberately trick people into thinking that this is a real orchestra, although to a large extent it is. There are real orchestral players, albeit possibly playing together with some synthetic sounds as well. But they are in there, real people have played it, and it hasn't all been sequenced and click tracked and all the rest of it. It was all played in real time, a lot of it just Ian and I playing together, and then Doane has come in and put some percussion on it.

Are these 'real' people just session players, or is there anybody we would know?
They are from The Royal Philharmonic Orchestra. Good players, obviously.

No rock musicians?
No, other than obviously the three of us, Doane, Ian and myself.

I think Doane's involvement will surprise a lot of people, because Ian said he definitely didn't want a traditional drum sound on the album.
Ah well, there is not a drum sound on it. Doane plays timpanis, crotales, and an arrangement of curious percussive instruments. Crotales are things that look like flying saucers; they start off at 8 inches, then 6 then 4 etc, and form a pyramid of these round, cymbally things, but they are really thick. You hit them and they go "dinggggg" forever! They make a really good sound. They are Japanese, I think.

Are they part of his standard kit, or did he get them just for this album?
Oh yeah, he had them already. We borrowed some timpanis for him, but he brought some other stuff himself. The timpanis were a bit awkward to use, because of the individual tuning of each one. When we did the demos it was easy, because I just emulated the sound on the keyboard, but when it came to recording them we had to go through the various tracks that used the same tunings, and then retune them all for the next thing. But it sounded great, and Doane was excellent! It was brilliant, and we had a great time doing it. Really good fun.

Is it all original material?
Yes, all original, all Ian's compositions. We all had some input, we co-arranged much of the stuff, but it is basically Ian Anderson material. We knocked them into shape together; I would come up with something and he'd say yes or no. We started from a melody on the flute and then thumped away at it until we arrived at the finished song. Once we had the melody and the basic chord arrangement I took it all home with me and put down what I thought the violins should do, the violas, the cellos etc. They all have to play their own part, it can't just be a wodge of chords. You have to think of it as all these individual people playing their own instrument, so that if and when we wanted to replace it with a real instrument it is a bone-fide part for them to play - they haven't just got to rip off somebody playing with ten fingers on a keyboard. It has to be more than that. So I'd knock it into shape, and Ian would listen to it the next day and say, "Yes, that's OK there, but after that we should do this," and then he'd come up with a whole, completely different, piece of music. So then we had to work that into the first piece. We just did it as we went, basically. We almost made it up as we went along, although he had it all in his head in the first place. He told me what he wanted and I had to convert his ideas into music, and then he decided whether it worked or not.

Is it an album of individual songs or tunes, or is it more of a concerto type piece?
No, it's.... you see that's the danger of calling it a classical album, because it might seem a bit heavy. Actually what it is is twelve GREAT tunes. Real tunes, tunes that you can sing along to and remember. There is a theme that runs all the way through the album. It sort of touches on religions of the world. Again, that might sound a bit heavy. It is called *Divinities*, which could sound a bit heavy or intimidating. Perhaps I shouldn't say that, because I don't want to piss people off who are religious who are maybe thinking "why is that intimidating?".

I was wondering about that. I had heard the title was *Twelve Dances With God*, which seemed strange to me because I don't think Ian is particularly, overtly concerned with religion.
No, it isn't that. It isn't a celebration of Ian's religious beliefs, whatever they may be. It is an acknowledgement of all the religions that are around. It is not aimed at religious people, it is not aimed at any one religious group, it just happens that the theme for the album is that of the various religions throughout the world. Different religions tend to stem from different continents, and from our point of view different continents all have their own kind of music. You can then link that music back to its respective religion. For instance there is a stark contrast to the Italian Catholic music and the Israeli Jewish kind of music. The musical

element is what was attractive to us, not the religion. It gave us at least twelve completely different styles of music that we could work into our own style, but retain some of that initial ingredient. Whether it be the Italian flavour, Jewish, African.... they've all got their own thing going, and they've all got their own music. That's not to say we've done an Italian piece and a Jewish piece and an African piece, we haven't made an album of "World Music", but there are elements, even if it's only a whisper, of those ethnic musical styles. But it is NOT a religious album, at all. It was just a good theme to use. It gives the album a definite feeling of continuity all the way through.

Is it brilliant??
Yes, it is! It is excellent, without a doubt. Absolutely superb!

Are there any vocals on it?
None that.... err, yes. Yes and no! There's not a great deal, very little, and nothing that is recognisable as anybody that anyone might know. There are no Ian Anderson vocals on it.

He mentioned that he might use a couple of "world musicians"....
Yeah, you could say that there are some voices on it, of unknown origin. Unknown to me and unknown to Ian.....

Ahh! We're talking sampled vocals. Not singing, as such.
Yes, samples. No actual singing. Voices, choirs, as instruments.

I gather there will be a tour, or rather "a few gigs", to promote the album.
Yeah, we will do a few in Europe and America, assuming that the promoters come back with the sort of venues that we want. We have to be careful about the venues we play, because it is obviously a completely different thing to Jethro Tull. It is in the classical vein, and slightly more formal. A little more reserved perhaps, a bit more dignified for most people. We are certainly going to do some dates. The whole idea of it was to do it with a view to live performance.

I get the impression that Ian is slightly concerned about Tull fans going to the performances purely because it is Ian Anderson.
Well obviously he wants Tull fans to go to the concerts.

Oh sure, but is he not worried that they might go just because it is him, and still expect, perversely, to see a Tull-like concert?
There will be people there because they are Ian Anderson fans, but whether they like it or not will depend on why they are his fans. If they like his flute playing they are gonna love it, because there's a lot of it, and very good stuff. I can't speak for Ian, but as far as I'm concerned I hope there are a lot of Tull/Ian Anderson fans there, and I'm sure they will appreciate the music. They know his musical background, a bit classical, a bit blues/jazz or whatever. This is Ian leaning much more towards the classical element. Staring it in the face. But we are hoping that other people who are perhaps more into the more serious classical music will give it a shot.

Do you think it will stand up? Will it be accepted as serious classical music? Or rather, serious orchestral music?
Yes, orchestral. Classical is the wrong word, orchestral is much better. In fact all the times I've said classical so far, go back and change it to orchestral when you type it up. [*I would do Andy, but I just can't be arsed! DR*] Yes, it will stand up as serious orchestral music, without a doubt. Here, listen to some of it now and see what you think.

[Andy passed his Walkman to me after selecting a suitable track on the tape. I can't deny that I felt a bit of a plonker sitting in a hotel bar at 2 in the morning with head phones on, but these things have to be done. So good was the music however, that I could easily have sat there for an hour listening to the whole thing. I did return to the tape several times before we

parted company at 4am, and there was not a moment on the tape that could not in all honestly be described as absolutely wonderful. I mean, really superb. I offered to look after the tape in case Andy lost it on the way home from the hotel, but sadly he declined my generous offer. DR]

What do you think Dave?

It is amazing. Brilliant stuff!
It is isn't it? We've taken a lot of trouble mixing it, and it will sound great if you have a surround-sound system. It sounds mega. And it will sound good on a mono transistor radio as well.

What, when they play it on Radio 1 you mean?
Err.... yeah, [*ironic smiles all round*]. But they might play it on Classic FM. I hope they go for it. The way the pieces are structured, with a start, an end, a "middle bit".... they are good, short tunes, it doesn't drag on into some endless concerto, but all good orchestral pieces, using all the aspects of a real orchestra.

It's odd that Ian, who has been drifting more and more towards the blues recently, which is after all the most basic form of popular music, can produce a work as complex as this on the back of it. I think a lot of Tull fans will be surprised... and possibly relieved.
It's a good thing for him to do. It is good music, and I'm hoping that because of the way we have approached it people who might normally pooh-pooh an orchestral record might give it a listen. Because it is Ian Anderson and he is playing flute that.... I mean, if you want to hear excellent flute playing, you will hear it on this, with the luxury of being backed by a full orchestral sound, with all the light and shade and sparkle of a beautiful, big orchestra.

Might this change the direction of Jethro Tull once more? Away from the blues and back towards more complex, "progressive" music?
No, I don't think so, although it has been an education for me, playing this kind of music. I sometimes write incidental music for films and television -I fool around with it really, it's not something I take too seriously - but I recently did a session using the full orchestral set up that I have at my disposal, the technology I have to recreate an orchestra, whereas before I may not have used that. It has opened my eyes to the fact that there is so much more than just piano and a bank of strings to make up orchestral music. There are all the other individual departments, the woodwind, the percussion, the first and second violins etc. So I have learnt an awful lot, so while it may not influence Jethro Tull musically, you may find in future that there is the odd string section in there somewhere. I mean there was in earlier Tull, so I guess they might well reappear.

I hope so. Personally, I love the blues, and if that's the direction Tull are heading still it would be fine by me, but I know that an awful lot of long time Tull fans are not so keen. Many yearn for Tull to return to the complex arrangements of the 70's stuff, strings 'n' all. This new stuff reminds me in parts of the best musical parts of "A Passion Play".
Yes. A Passion Play was unfortunately overlooked by a lot of people, and I think possibly it was ahead of it's time. Maybe it was a bit too complicated back then? But as I say, I don't suppose the next Tull album will be that kind of thing, but there may well be the extra embellishment of orchestral sounds on some tracks rather than the head-on bass, guitar, flute and organ. There might be some other little niceties.

And you start work on the next Tull album in January?
We do indeed. The songs are written, but I don't know too much about them at the moment.

Have you not heard any of them?
Well Ian and I made some demos a while ago, we just kicked around some songs, and they turned out very well but I don't know if they will actually be on the album. It was an exercise

in song writing. It is important for Ian, when he gets in that creative mood, to be able to translate it into music, so we got together and simply put his songs into some sort of rough shape, just to get them down. But he might not use them, and I've not heard any of the new ones, but I'm sure Ian has them all on "hard disc" [*points to his head*] and is waiting to pour them out on us as soon as we get together for rehearsals.

It's definitely happening soon then? No delays?
Absolutely. The schedule is booked.

I've heard that there are pretty firm plans right through to 1996....
1996, gig-wise, is looking like Australia and New Zealand. Early '96. Our schedule is the orchestral album in March which will be promoted in between finishing the Jethro Tull album and then going out to play that live. That in itself will take us through the year, because we won't start any big touring for the Tull album until after the summer. So we are probably looking at touring from August until early 1996. So the Tull album will be out in the summer.

Another busy year ahead then. Where are you going to find the time to record your solo album?
Ha! There is no time to record a solo album. And even if there was Dave, I have to ask myself "would anybody want to buy it if I made one?". I do write little things, I come up with bits and pieces all the time, but whether or not they would be of any interest to anybody else I don't know. And I wouldn't really want to make an album for the sake of it, just so I could say, "Look, I play for Jethro Tull so here is my album". That's no reason for anybody to want to buy it. OK, Martin has made an album, but he has got a lot more reason to make a solo album than I have. It's the same with Doane. He has various other projects on the go, and whether or not he'll use his Jethro Tull connection to promote it, I just don't know, but I strongly suspect he won't. It is nothing like Tull for a start. But it's more of a band thing, another band that he is involved with, whereas I just don't have the time to do that, and I haven't had the time for the last four years. I haven't got involved in anything else, because I've been happy getting involved with Jethro Tull and now this orchestral stuff.

You never sit at home in your studio trying to compose your own songs?
I do that, yes. My next thing on my list of priorities is an opening for me to produce an album's worth of incidental music, which is a polite term for library music. Stuff that might get picked for films and TV. There's an awful lot of it about, but I do have somebody who can look after me on that front. As soon as I get the time to sit down and come up with some bits and pieces then I might do that. But from that, some of it might turn into something that's worth putting on an album. But at this moment I haven't got a whole load of songs running around in my head. I have, as all musicians have, piles of tapes of ideas but I suspect we all prefer to keep them within the confines of our own house rather than embarrass ourselves by playing them to other people! If I thought for one minute that one person would buy an album of music that I'd made, then I might do it, but at this stage I've no reason to think that they would. And I'm not being falsely modest, and I don't want to sound pompous about anything, but I can't use the fact that I happen to play with a major rock band as an excuse to go and make a solo album. And as I say, I am very happy at the moment to be involved with Tull, and right now there just isn't time for anything else.

Basically you just can't be arsed, can you?
[*Laughing*] Yes, I loved that comment you made about Martin Webb in the last issue after he'd come up with some lame excuse for not taking pictures and you said basically he couldn't be arsed! Excellent! No, I can be arsed, but I've never got the time. I can never sit at home with my equipment any more because it is always in Ian's studio or in a truck or on its way somewhere for us to go and do something. Anyway, never mind that, listen to some more of the orchestral album.....

[*10 glorious minutes later*]
    ]

That is just bloody amazing! I think this will please people in both camps, the Tull fans and classical fans.
Yes, I hope so. And I hope they see it for what it is, rather than what they think it should be. Serious classical music conjures up a great long epic work of furious, moody classical music.

Do you listen to much classical music?
Not really. I've got the obligatory Planets, and a fair bit of Ravel and Debussy, but not a lot else. I'm certainly no expert on it.

What do you listen to? Who are your favourite artists at the moment?
Sting, of course. Brilliant. Top of my pyramid for sure.

Who is at the bottom, creeping upwards?
Ah, I know, there was a band... and I've been meaning to ask you this for ages...there was this really good band...

The King Earl Boogie Band???...
Ha! Not The King Earl Boogie Band, no, though I understand that they are indeed...

The dog's...?
Yeah, that's it, "The Dog's"! ....But there was a band called "Ya Ya" who sent me a tape a long time ago. They sent the tape with a view to me playing with them, and I'd be really interested to hear whatever happened to them.
Who else do I like? Crowded House, Def Leppard, Thomas Dolby, Pink Floyd, my favourite band of all time. Dave Gilmour is my guitar hero - after Martin of course! And I didn't get to one of their gigs, and I wish I had. Next time I will.

Did you see the gig on the TV recently?
Yes I did, and wasn't it mega?

Yes, wasn't it! I'd thought about going but couldn't get sufficiently interested, but watching the TV thing I really wished I had been there. I can't believe how well it came across.
It was brilliant. I would love to have seen that live.

Do you buy many CDs? What was the last one you bought?
Yes I do buy a lot. The last one I bought was actually Sting, his greatest hits thing. But I often browse through the racks, just to see what's about. I don't necessarily rush out and buy the latest offering from somebody, I buy a lot of old albums, just by chancing on them. Steely Dan and Ozric Tentacles were recent purchases. Great band, Ozric Tentacles. What else have I bought?

Err... The King Earl Boogie Band?
No I haven't yet Dave... but I WILL buy it, I promise!

It's OK Andy, it's not actually out yet. I was just checking. Do you like any of the newer bands. Suede? Blur?
No, I hate that. I hate Radio 1 bands. I hate the whole thing about Radio 1 and the stuff they play. They play next week's number 1 a week before it comes out, you know. It all seems to be worked out, they sort out the playlist and they know where it will be in the charts the week after. Maybe that's not the case, but it seems that way. I have no time for music that has to be seen to be fashionable. Of the current pop successes I can only think of Jimmy Nail; I perhaps wouldn't buy his music, but he is very talented. He writes well for TV and the music is always good too. But let's get to the BOTTOM of the pyramid, the stuff that I really haven't got the time for but who have always been around. REM, I just can't get into them, I don't know what the attraction is... although I seem to be just about the only person who doesn't like them!

What do you think of M People Andy? *[There <u>was</u> a reason for this apparently random question, but I just can't remember now what it was! DR]*
I refuse to talk about M People. I thought we were talking about music. What else can we talk about? I think that's just about it isn't it?

But we haven't talked about The Mechanics yet...
I don't really know much about them. I know them, I know people in The Mechanics. You probably know that I was in a group called The Chase with Steve Jackson, the Mechanics' drummer. He got me the job with Tull, indirectly. But you know more about them than I do. You tell me.....

Needless to say, DR did, but we won't go into that now... By then it was 4am, time and Guinness had taken its toll, and it was time to call it a day. Sadly, despite DR's valiant efforts to get Andy drunk and stupefied through endless boring questions, he still didn't fall for the old "swapping of Walkmans" trick. He escaped with the orchestral album intact, and DR had to go home and type up this interview. Sod it! But he was grateful to have had the chance to hear the tape, which promised to be the ALBUM OF THE YEAR. That and the Tull album of course. Oh, and not forgetting the King Earl B...

288

Chapter 28

MICK ABRAHAMS

(Published in #48, April 1995)

A New Day #48 *contained reviews of two new video releases. Mick Abrahams had filmed an instruction video for guitar, while Clive Bunker had done likewise for drums. Clearly, both ventures were of not inconsiderable interest for all Jethro Tull fans, and it was* A New Day's *bounden duty to find out more - hence a trip to deepest Dartford to take in a Blodwyn Pig gig. Unfortunately Clive wasn't able to make it on the night, but Mick was duly cornered in the dressing room before the gig. DR produced his Walkman, wired Mick up for sound - and promptly announced that he was off to the pub across the road! No matter. Talking to Mick Abrahams is hardly a chore - indeed, the only problem MW had was keeping the interview on the rails in the face of regular heckling from assorted Blods, coupled with Mick's own irrepressible humour. What follows is a severely edited version of an hour or so's conversation, with a bewildering array of jokes, funny voices, impressions and anecdotes too filthy even for* A New Day *sadly expurgated.*

So how did the video come about?
Simply through chatting with Robin Lumley, who I know from the old days when he used to work with Jack Lancaster. He also did that *Peter and the Wolf* thing that was released recently. Robin has formed a company with Mike Matthews, who used to work for HTV, called Masterfield, solely with the intention of putting out teaching videos. He asked me whether in principle I'd be up for doing a teaching video, because I've always had the piss taken out of me something alarming about the very stylistic and now legendary and very collectable and pricey *Have Fun Learning The Guitar With Mick Abrahams* LP. Somebody paid £120 for that LP, you know. What a c***!
So I said yes. I did a bit of market research first, and some of the guitar tuition videos we saw were just so far over the top... I mean, if it's quite clearly specified that this is an advanced teaching video for people who have a very good, clear working knowledge, then fine. But the one I've produced is for people who are somewhere between the stage of just starting and the intermediate stage. Basically I want to come in at the point at which people are getting bored and saying, "I can't do that," and to say, "Yes you can!" There are three separate videos of an hour each. The first one deals with very basic stuff and how you can expand and elaborate on it. It's elementary stuff, mainly in the key of E, the usual guitar player's favourite key. The second video deals with bottle-necks and chord sequences and so on, and the last hour deals with playing in a band situation. I created some backing tracks using my own equipment which sound fairly cred - given the equipment which I've got! - and which they actually used on the video. I also slowed some sections down, to help demonstrate things. There's nothing about written music, nothing about tab, no chord sheets and so on; but there are a lot of 'hands on' shots, which is what I feel people want to see and learn. The questions I ask when I'm watching another guitar player... I don't want to do exactly what he does, but it's nice to be able to do it so that I can then play it arse backwards and do it my own way; and that's what I've emphasised in the video. The video is actually called *From The Heart*, which the music is, certainly.

I haven't actually seen the video yet. Is it just electric guitar, or acoustic guitar as well?
It's all electric guitar. I do actually own an acoustic guitar now - 'Three Guitars Abrahams' they call me now! Maybe we could do an acoustic video later. Anyway, at the end of the video we've put down a few backing tracks so that people can play along to it. I've tried not to complicate the issue, not to do all this "whiddly-diddly-twiddly" stuff, where people just go, "How did he do that???" There are so many videos which are like that. There are a couple of little jokey moments too, and I think all in all the videos have worked out

quite well. It's funny watching yourself though, as it was as if I was talking to an imaginary person.

Did you have a script?
Some of it I scripted, some of it came straight from my head. There were some great out-takes.

Are they included?
I wish! But no, sadly. There were some wonderful wind-ups. At one point I was sitting at a table showing all the stuff I keep in my guitar case. There were a couple of moments where I screwed up, so I looked straight at the camera and went into a dirty routine. And once I'd got the cackles, I'd just gone, and I was rolling around the floor helpless. And Mike was just letting the camera roll and saying, "Carry on then, you just have some fun," and I was howling, "Switch it off, you bastard!" They did use one bit of me falling off the chair. And on the last day of filming we had a brilliant wind-up. Everyone was in on it apart from Mike. We had about an hour's worth of filming to do, of me playing some solos from the *Lies* album. All week I'd sown the seeds of destruction in Mike's mind, with everybody's help, saying that at lunchtime I was going down the docks to score a major deal. Of what, he had no idea, but obviously all sorts of things were going through his mind. I'd arranged with the make-up department for them to do me up as if I'd been in a fight. And they did a blinding job on me - I really did look like I'd been in a good old scrap, fake blood on me, torn shirt, everything. The scenario was that I'd gone down to do this mythical villainous deal and got into a scrape with some bad boys, and as a consequence I couldn't do the rest of the video. I sat in the office with my back to the door, and they went to tell Mike what had happened. As he walked in, someone was saying to me, "Oh, I think you'd better go to the hospital," and "The police are on the line; they want to talk to you," and so on. I turned round slowly and mumbled, "I'm sorry about this, Mike". And he just looked at me and said, "If you think a slap of make-up can fool somebody like me, who worked on *Minder* for 14 years, you're sadly mistaken. Get me another guitar player!" So of course everybody collapsed laughing. But the upshot was that we decided to do something with it, and I did a whole scene about fighting with the other band members in the dressing room after the gig.

And that's in the video?
Er, no, I'm afraid not! There was lots of bad language, which I know is difficult to imagine coming from me...

So is it a video which the average *A New Day* reader who doesn't particularly want to learn guitar can still enjoy?
Yes. I think that all teaching videos should have a certain entertainment value. I've played several live pieces, like *Gnatz, Billy The Kid, The Victim, Dead Man's Hill, Aby's Lean*, and some new things which people won't have heard. So there's enough music in there for it to be interesting on that basis, I hope. I made a comment at the beginning of the video, which perhaps didn't come over as well as it should have, where I said, "This is not about music, it is not about reading, it is not about tablature, you can throw all your books away". It wasn't meant to sound arrogant, I was just saying that this is the only way I know. If you can fathom something from the simple way I'm trying to present it, then please take it, shake it around and make it part of what you are - as, indeed, I've done with other people's music.

And do you cover a variety of styles, not just blues?
Yeah - rock, basically. *All Said And Done* for example, which I've done on the video, is straightforward FM rock really; and *Cat's Squirrel* includes some simple country blues finger picking.

Have you seen Clive's video?
I've seen some of it, and it's very good - excellent, in fact. Clive, of course, being Clive, won't agree. Clive is such a perfectionist, he's convinced he'll never get a thing right. Which in some ways can be a good attitude, but sometimes you have to let it go.

So what else have you been up to recently?
I've just done the music for *A Midsummer Night's Dream* for my youngest lad, Nick, who played Oberon, The Faerie Prince in Shakespeare's play. It was a school production at the Stantonbury Campus in Milton Keynes. My missus, who's a teacher at the same school that Nick goes to, asked me to do some music for it. So I did some stuff in the studio at home, eight songs and instrumentals in all.

So was it *Blues For A Midsummer's Night*??
Well, no - but it is kind of blues rock. It was on for three nights, and the school had sold about 30 tickets for each night. Then we went on Central TV News last Friday night, me, Nick and the headmistress, at about 6.20pm, and by 7pm they'd sold all the tickets for the Friday night. A local video company filmed it, and we're going to send a video to the Royal Shakespeare Theatre at Stratford-on-Avon, because although they do modern productions I don't think they've thought about the rock music angle. Even though I did it myself I have to say it worked well. Nick sang a song which I wrote called *Ill Met By Moonlight* where he meets Titania in the glade. There was also a song for Bottom, wonderfully well played by a lad called Edward White, called *What Do You See That I Don't?* about the part where Puck has turned his head into a donkey, and he spoke the song in a Welsh accent - it was great. There was *Puck's Dance*, and a Gregorian chant with my voices and a few effects. And there was a funny one called *The Burgermaster's Dance* for which I invented a musical instrument called a Yodelphonium - bits of junk kindly donated by Boosey and Hawkes, painted gold and green with leaves on, stirrup pumps, all sorts of medieval attachments - including part of my bloody shower! It was really fun doing it, and I felt so proud sitting there on the Saturday night thinking, "That's my boy down there!"
I'll ask the school if they'd agree to your printing an address of where to get the video. It's only a low-budget recording, with one camera - but a decent one, not a cheap camcorder - but for the collectors and train-spotters out there it will be the only opportunity to obtain some otherwise unrecorded and unreleased songs.

And what's planned for Blodwyn Pig? You've been talking about an acoustic blues album.
Yeah, although that's not Blodwyn Pig, that's me. I've had an offer to do a purely acoustic album, with maybe a bit of percussion, bass and acoustic piano, so if I can use some guys from the band, clearly I will. But with a Blodwyn Pig album imminent, it's probably best to keep the two things entirely separate. A new Blodwyn Pig album has been planned for about six months, but we're having trouble finding dates when everyone will be available at the same time to go into the studio. I've written about 30 new songs for Blodwyn Pig, of which we'll record about ten of the best, and about twelve new songs which I've written acoustically.

A devil's advocate question: what about a sax player for Blodwyn Pig? You always used to have one.
We did always have one, yeah. But I kind of feel in some ways with what I'm writing now that it would get in the way, apart from certain passages. I don't like having someone in the band if they're just going to be there to do the occasional "toot" or whatever. I like to give someone room to express themselves; like Gordon [*Murphy*] used to take solos all the time. I've always wanted to work with a complete brass section, to be quite honest, the way Gary Moore has. That really turns me on more than the idea of an individual sax player.

I hear you're involved in an Alexis Korner tribute?
Yes. Norman Shapiro is writing a biography of Alexis, and he got in touch with me, and we had lunch. The next day I happened to speak to Bobbi Korner, Alexis's widow, who I've always kept in touch with. And the next day I got a call from Norman Beaker, who asked if I would be interested in playing at a tribute concert to Alexis. Would I? Is the Pope a Catholic?? So that will be on 21 May at the Opera House in Buxton.

And you were involved in the Peter Green tribute album?

Yes. It was a privilege to do it. And it will be a privilege to get paid for it, too! It hasn't been released yet. Pete Brown is the bloke producing it, and I believe there is still some work to do. Ian Anderson did *Man Of The World*, as you know, and I believe people like Rory Gallagher and Gary Moore also did some stuff. I did *The Same Way* 'with Jim Leverton, Graham Walker and Dave Lennox, the one that goes [*singing*]: *"I wake up in the morning, get me breakfast in me bed; Lord, she's so good to me, I'll love her 'till I'm dead"*.

[*DR* (who has finally deigned to return from the pub)]: **But that's in the wrong tense. If it's a blues song, it should be "I woke up this morning..."**
We did it in the studio. We weren't in any tents...

Let's talk a bit about your public burying of the hatchet with Ian Anderson over the last twelve months or so. There was always a perception, I think wrongly, that you and Ian were daggers drawn for 20 years.
If you really look back on it, both of us were a pair of c***s. Ian's got his point of view, I've got mine. So what? Life goes on. I never had any malice towards Ian, and I've never wished him bad, and I'm sure he never has me, either. I was annoyed with him at the time, and it was my choice to leave the band. And I was particularly upset about [*Terry*] Ellis coming in and saying, "You can't leave - you're fired". That's just playground games. At the time I probably blamed Ian for that, but I now firmly believe it was not the case. I mean, Ian is as honest as the day is long; he's hard, but he's honest. It still cracks me up when Ian goes on about me being a part-timer; I think it's quite amusing.

[DR] And is it not true?
Well, given that Ian is a total workaholic, then no, it's not true. I'm certainly not lazy, or I wouldn't be out doing what I do. I do remember saying to him that I didn't want to be working eight nights a week all year; I'd like the occasional day off between good quality gigs. I think he got the impression that that was my way of saying I didn't really want to do any work, which it wasn't - I've never ducked work. But I didn't enjoy doing the silly shit gigs where you'd just about pay for the petrol, and you go on after the pubs have shut when nobody's interested, to play to a crowd of total dickheads. [*Laughing*] Like tomorrow! I mean, Blodwyn Pig have been known to do 12 or 13 nights on the trot, but then I need a break to rest the old Hobson's [*voice*]. But I can remember being very angry with Ian because of all that going on and, as I've told you before, I acted like a total arsehole on two occasions - totally unreasonable, totally stupid and totally childish, which I take full responsibility for. But I'd had enough pressure, and it was the only way I knew of making some kind of statement, albeit perhaps the wrong one. Ian was mad about that, and I think he was quite right to be, as well - but in the same way that I was quite right to be mad about the kind of curtain that suddenly came down on me. But it was all so stupid that if you hang on to something like that for years and years... well, there's never been that kind of thought in my mind.
The other thing to say is that I've had some laughs and good times with Ian. He's a witty bloke, he's very talented at everything he does, and he's straight. And from what I've seen, he's done some good for other people as well as for himself; and he's got my total undying respect for that.

How did it feel being back on a stage with Ian?
Great. It was good fun. It's strange, he seems to have come so much back to the blues, and he's doing now what I'd loved to have heard him do if I'd stayed with Jethro Tull! So it really was a treat to get up there and play with him. And I'll tell you, if it hadn't been Ian asking me to play *Move On Alone* at Clapham, nobody else would have got heaven and earth to move to get me to do that!
I'd like Ian to be on the acoustic blues album, but not playing flute. I'm thinking along the lines of another version of *Some Day The Sun Won't Shine For You*, and a hitherto unexplored Sonny Terry and Brownie McGhee number called, I think, *I'll Be Round Again*, which Ian used to sing in the van. I used to think we'd do it live one day, and he

always said how much he liked it. It was an odd one, almost like a pop song, except it wasn't.

[At this point, the arrival in the dressing room of Terry "Blond Bombshell" The Innocent to an only marginally undeserved barrage of friendly abuse from a bevy of Blods raises the Raucous-o-Meter to overload. "Woaah – wot 'ave you done to yer hair, mate??" chortled Mick, "You look like bleedin' Worzel Gummidge!!!" (So, not Robert Plant then, Terry...) Amidst the mayhem, Mick is somehow reminded of a repeatable story of The Mick Abrahams Band back in the seventies:]

We played a gig in Southampton, on the south coast. It was a nice day, so instead of travelling down with the rest of the band I put the leathers on and rode down on my old Honda 750 motorbike. I arrived about half-an-hour later than the others, and banged on the stage door. This heavy on the door goes, "Yeah?" I said, "I'm Mick". He said, "Mick who?" I said, "Mick Abrahams". He said, "He's in there". I said, "I'm not mucking you about mate, I'm not a ligger - I'm with the band." "He's already in there, I've told you," this bloke said. So I said, "Look mate, I'm not being troublesome, but would you mind getting the manager or someone - they'll recognise me." Eventually he agreed, slammed the door in my face, and came back about five minutes later with Ritchie Dharma [*the drummer*]. I said "Ritchie - thank God for that!" And Ritchie turned to the bouncer and said, "I don't know who that is mate, I've never seen him before." And the bloody door slams in my face again! If you could have seen Ritchie's face - he did exactly what I'd have done, the bastard! I was out there another half-an-hour, and got to the point of going to the box office to buy a ticket and getting a refund from the gig money!

Anyway getting back to the new Blodwyn Pig album, I think you'll find that there will be some pretty interesting stuff on there. There are two songs which I think are going to be blinders, and the main songs on the album, called *Fire In The Hole* and *Raining Again*.

Will you be playing some of it live?
Not until we've done the album. Then we'll change the set right around.

But if you play a song live for a few months before recording it, it often develops with the playing...
You're right. I think all the songs on *Lies* have got better as we've gone on, partly because the band's a lot tighter. But I've also learnt that you get to the point where you're playing a number... I mean, I've been playing *I Wonder Who* forever, and when I got to record it I thought, "Yeah, this will be cool" - and it was, it worked out a good version. But I still play a better version of it now, or at least in my head I do. It's more arranged, and yet more relaxed. So I agree with Ian Anderson entirely when he wrote on *This Was* that this was then; it's like a diary. It's like... whenever I'm a bit down I look at a Fawlty Towers tape, and I guarantee it will make me laugh. Even though I know exactly what's coming, it's still funny. And I bet you that, looking at the video, the people who made that show will think that they could have done bits of it better. Truth is, I don't think they could have; and that's why it is what it is.

[TtI] (*attempting to regain a modicum of credibility by progressing the interview*) **Are you very self-critical of the stuff you've recorded...**
... Yes, very...

... and when you listen to it afterwards, think "If only I'd done this, or that, it would have sounded better"?
Well, the rest of the lads in the band have been saying that all along - I just don't agree with them! But yes, I am very self-critical. But there's always a point where you have to give it up. You do the best you possibly can, and then you have the basic bones to work with, onto which you can put your vocals, overdubs and whatever. But it can always be better. I've never done anything I'm 100% satisfied with. The danger is that you can be too perfectionist.

Ian Anderson has always aimed for doing just one or two vocal takes in order to capture that initial passion or whatever.

Yes, there's a great sense in that. *I Wonder Who*, for example, was done in one vocal take. Clive, Andy and I played it live, and Bruce and Dick put piano and saxes on afterwards. But that was in one shot, I never even stopped for breath.

At this point, despite the efforts of the redoubtable Terry the Innocent, the interview disintegrated completely, and tracks were made for the bar prior to another blistering gig from The Pig. On reflection, perhaps it was as well that Clive Bunker wasn't there that night and sitting in on the interview. Mike Matthews had told MW that his greatest fear when filming the videos was that Mick and Clive would turn up together on the same day, because he knew that he would be faced with eight hours of larking about and have nothing sensible in the can by the end of it!

*As for the acoustic blues album Mick mentioned – Ian did play on it (harmonica **and** flute).The album was called simply "One", released on the A New Day label*

Chapter 29

CLIVE BUNKER

(Published in #48, April 1995)

Having spoken to Mick Abrahams about his guitar tuition 3-video set, MW then subjected Clive Bunker to a telephone interrogation about his own tuition 3-video set – about drumming, natch – entitled Out Of The Head.

How did you come to be involved in making your videos?
It was all my idea actually. Abrahams always gets in on my ideas later. It was about a year and a half ago, arising from some teaching I'd been doing with local chaps. I used to buy drum videos done by various people, just to keep up with what was happening, and I noticed that there wasn't anything for beginners. Some of the structures of the videos just weren't right. So I started working on this idea, and went to Robin Lumley, who's in the film business, and asked his advice. He thought it was a really good idea, and started a company with his cameraman mate Mike Matthews. Then they roped in Mick, Robin's done his own keyboard video, and I think The Moody Blues' Graeme Edge is going to do one about tropical fish.

Well, Mick told me that, but I thought he was joking!
Oh no, no, no, no, no! It's a question of someone knowing a subject - you could do one on anything really. Growing plants upside down in a tea-cup, perhaps...

So you see the video as being aimed very much at the beginner?
I only saw them for the first time myself last night! But yes, if you start on the first video, then you should be able to follow and count through what's in it. But, people being people, they'll probably buy the second or third one first! The second one's not too bad for beginners still, but the third one I wouldn't like a beginner to be put off by.

And are you happy with the overall results?
Yes. It's the same as everything, really. You try to make the best thing that's ever been done, and if you get somewhere close, you've got to feel a bit pleased about it. You'll always get those moments where you think, "Aah, if only I'd done that a bit differently..." But on the whole, I think it works. I'm a bit disappointed in the packaging, which I think looks a bit cheapish. And the photo they printed was of me playing a Gretsch kit with Zildjian cymbals.

Well, it's Graham Walker's kit! *[I took the photo at a Blodwyn Pig gig when Clive sat in for a few songs. MW]* **I did volunteer to pop down to the studio when you were filming to take a few photos, to which Masterfield said, "Great idea"; but then I never got the call.**
Oh, right. But the guys at Premier and Paiste are going to wonder what that's all about.

Mick suggested that you wouldn't be happy with the video, but simply because you're a perfectionist. Is that a fair accusation, if that's the right word?
Yeah, probably, yeah. I wouldn't say I'm a perfectionist. In some things I am, but in other things I like things to feel a little bit loose, to feel a little more 'grabbable' as it were, rather than too clinical.

I think that comes over in the video. It really is nice and chatty, and user friendly rather than intimidating. It's actually entertaining as well as being instructive.
Oh good. These are the things that I can't look at myself. All I see is this balding prat! It's hard to be objective like that.

Why the title *Out Of The Head*?

I was trying to come up with... initially, some of the exercises in the video, people didn't used to do. I would sit down at home to rehearse, and I'd wonder what to do. So I'd go through the count, playing it on a foot instead of a hand and whatever, and think about how to turn things upside down. And most of it just came 'out of the head'. If you start talking about music to people, they back off; but if you start talking about things coming out of the head or the heart, then, as we said before, it feels a bit more user friendly. Basically, I didn't want to make it sound druggy, I didn't want to make it sound as if I was stupid and going to lark about, and I didn't want to make it sound as if it was a college course. I didn't know what to do, and I'm still not sure if I did the right thing. I didn't want to put jokes in, but I wanted some things that were a bit humorous - hence the opening titles.

You told me in a previous *A New Day* interview that you were entirely self-taught, and that in the early days you were doing things like paradiddles without actually knowing what a paradiddle was. You've clearly amassed a great deal of technical and professional knowledge since. Did you just pick it up over the years, or have you ever studied music and percussion?
I was in every drummer's dream world, being in Jethro Tull, in that I was in a huge band, swanning around the world, [*laughing*] with no talent, and all my mates were some of the best drummers in the world! And you can't help but learn. You'd be sitting around somewhere, and they'd say, "Have you tried this?" And they'd show you it, or write it down, and then you'd ask what it was, and they'd explain it. Being on the front end of it there, the things that they were just starting to practice or had just heard of, I knew about instantly. So I was learning all the new tricks before I learnt what drumming was all about, if you know what I mean. Later, when I'd got my own studio, then I studied backwards as it were, to learn about jazz, and so on. I went for two or three lessons on reading music, and that's about it. The rest of it has been pretty hands on, with better drummers showing me what I should be doing.

To what extent would you say that somebody starting from scratch can 'learn to play' the drums, and to what extent does somebody have to have some innate natural talent?
I don't believe in this natural talent stuff. There are people who can just tap their foot along to music naturally, and be pretty much there. But when it comes to playing an instrument, nobody can just get up and blast away on a drum kit, or guitar, or keyboard. You have to learn it. It also depends how much you want to put into it. Treat it as a hobby and enjoy it, and if you want to get better, then that's the way to go. If you're thinking, "Well, if I put this amount of effort into it then in two years' time I'll probably be earning a million pounds," take up something else!

You mentioned that you've done teaching. Is that on a one-to-one basis, or just the drum clinics, and so on?
Oh, one-to-one, at my own house. I used to have no more than about nine pupils at a time - not at the same time! - and some of them would come round weekly, and others fortnightly, for an hour's tuition. They were all people who really wanted to do it. Some people who started did so just because it was me, and really didn't want to put the work and time in, and those sort of people I let go so that I could concentrate on those who really wanted to learn. A couple weren't even interested in being drummers in bands. There's a truck driver who has built an extension onto his garage so that he can practice on his massive double drum kit in there, and yet he never intends playing live, it's just his hobby. And he's very good!

Presumably that experience was useful in putting the video together, and scripting it?
Oh, yeah. I was bouncing things off them, and checking things out with them; very interesting. And it was good for me as well, as it keeps me going if I've got people I'm teaching.

When you listen to a record or a piece of music yourself, do you find yourself concentrating on the drums and mentally playing the parts, or can you appreciate the music as a whole, as it were?

It's the music as a whole first. In fact when I played recently with some mates in a covers band, someone asked me if I knew such-and-such a song, and I said yes - I could remember the whole tune. But as he was counting 'one, two, three, four' I thought, "Blimey, I don't actually know what the drum part is!" When you do listen back to and study some of these old tracks that you think you know, and then really listen to the drum track, there's lots in there that you haven't heard before at all. I mean, music is music to me. I like to enjoy the music, and then if there's something interesting in there, then I'll really listen to the drum track.

You mention in one of the videos that you are completely unfamiliar with the workings of TV studios, and so on. Was it fun doing the filming?
In all honesty, I've got to say no - although not because of the filming process itself. I was so over-prepared for the video - I had pages and pages of stuff - that I was having to do a fair bit of editing, trying to work out what to throw out in order to keep the flow, without there being big holes in the story. And it was all a bit of a rush, plus I was in the process of getting a divorce, so most evenings I would just go back to my hotel and feel really depressed. I'd be thinking oh shit, I've got to go back and stand in front of that camera again tomorrow. That's why I haven't watched it before now.

I was actually quite worried about watching it, in case I really was bored and didn't like it, but...
You don't want to be worried about it!

Yeah, but I've got to review the blooming thing for *A New Day*!
Well, just be honest. If you're honest with everything, then you can't offend anybody, can you? Nobody offends me being honest, anyway. And even if you gave it a slagging, you'd probably be less critical than I would be of my own stuff anyway.

On a wider front now, we were all disappointed that you couldn't make it to Clapham last year, when Mick and various others played with Tull...
Yeah, I heard it was a good night. That was when we were actually filming the video, so I was away in Cardiff unfortunately.

So what are you up to now, and what are your future plans?
I'm a bit in limbo, in all honesty. Manfred [Mann], who had told me that he would have an album out and be touring all this year, has now informed me that the album won't be finished this year, and that he won't be touring, so that's left me rather high and dry. I have got something else in the fire, which I can't mention yet, so I hope and pray that will come off, as it will mean a few months touring abroad. I'll let you know if it does happen. In the meantime I'm panelling my house! I've become the local joke; they're waiting for me to panel the windows and doors too. Half the Brazilian rainforests are now on my walls...

I think that's covered all the questions I wanted to ask. Is there anything else you wanted to say to *A New Day*?
Only keep up the bloody good work! [*MW blushes audibly.*] No, I mean it! I was actually telling someone the other day that you've got one of the most comprehensively and lovingly put together fanzines that I've ever seen.

Well, it is a labour of love. I mean, it's a two way thing really. The guys in Jethro Tull, and people like you and Mick, are very helpful to us, so I hope we can help you too.
And it is appreciated, y'know.

Well, you've just secured that good review!
Phew, and I thought I was going to have to put some money in an envelope!

And one final question – what can Doane Perry learn from this video?
How, in later life, to keep the top of your head from shining into cameras...

JETHRO TULL – THE A NEW DAY TAPES VOLUME 2

Planned publication early in 2013

Includes further interviews with

Ian Anderson
Martin Barre
Andrew Giddings
Mick Abrahams
Clive Bunker
Glenn Cornick
Dave Pegg

plus

Jon Noyce
Chris Leslie
John Carter
Dee Palmer
Kit Morgan
James Duncan Anderson
Lucia Micarelli
David Goodier
John O'Hara
Florian Opahle
Anna Phoebe
Anne Marie Calhoun

For news and updates check out
www.jethrotullnewdaybook.co.uk

A NEW DAY
The Jethro Tull Magazine

Published (very approximately) four times a year with news, reviews and of course exclusive interviews with Tull members past and present.

Subscriptions online at
www.anewdaymag.co.uk
also available on Kindle via Amazon

JETHRO TULL
"Minstrels In The Gallery"
by David Rees

First published in 1998. Now available on Kindle via Amazon

A NEW DAY RECORDS

Roster includes CDs by

The John Evan Band
Mick Abrahams
Blodwyn Pig
John Carter & Martin Barre
Maartin Allcock
Clive Bunker

and many guest appearances by Jethro Tull members

www.anewdayrecords.co.uk

With thanks to the following Jethro Tull fans and many others, for their help and support in the production of this book and A New Day magazine

A D Newport
A K Downing
A R Cole
A R Savage
A Robertson
A Samwell
A Savage
A Snewin
A Warner
A Watson
A Weymouth
A.N.Baldock
Adam Anderson
Adam Ewart
Adam Siviter
Ade Perry
Adin Clarke
Adrian Harrison
Adrian Wheeler
Alan Baldock
Alan Bell (NI Version)
Alan Gallimore
Alan Hartnell
Alan Hodgson
Alan John Smith
Alan Kent
Alan Lindabery
Alan RH Watson
Alan Rhind
Alan Robertson
Alan Samwell
Alan Sharp
Alan –The Maddhatter
Alan Weir
Alex Sackel
Alfred Tuescher
Alistair Mutch
Allen Graham
Amarpal Singh Gaind
Andrew Cliffe
Andrew Deards
Andrew Geake
Andrew Godden
Andrew Guthrie
Andrew Hinton
Andrew Morgan
Andrew Pierce
Andrew Quinn
Andrew Revell
Andrew Richards
Andy Turnbull
Angelo Colombo
Angie Robertson
Ann Turnbull

Anne Chilcott
Anthony Brooks
Anthony Ellett
Anthony Reynolds
Arne Bakka
Arthur Smith
B Drake
B Jones
B Kovacs
B Moore
B Navier
Barbara Kilsby
Barry & Angela Hawkins
Barry Grodsky
Barry Pegram
Barry Smith
Alan Smith
Janet Smith
Claire Smith
Bev Maynard
Big Jeff Gibson
June Gibson
Bill Campbell
Bill Cox
Bill Saunders
Bill Sullens
Bill Taylor
Billy Bignell
Bob Brooker
Bodo Kester
Brent Kasl
Brian Cooper
Brian Grimwood
Brian Navier
Brian Newman
Bryan Buckle
C M Swinbank
C Masey
C Noyes
C Oakes
C Orduz
C Puddephatt
C Silver
Carole Bersantie
Carl Bowditch
Carl Brabant
Carl Cheffins
Carl Partington
Carl Wolff
Carol Mohan
Caroline Callaghan
Caroline Hunt
Carsten Bergmann

Catherine Lloyd
Charles Silver
Chris Cox
Chris Hallsworth
Chris Honeywill
Chris Rowsell
Chris Shapland
Chris Symmonds
Chris Taberham
Christer Lindh
Christer Nilsson
Christine Roche
Christopher Taberham
Christopher Wiltshire
Claes Wollin
Claire Hunter
Clark Findlay
Clive Newbury
Clive W Noyes
Colin & Valerie Raynor
Colin Glendenning
Colin Kedward
Colin Kerr
Colin McCormack
Craig Hohman
Craig Welsh
D Brooks
D Cook
Derek Doel
D G J East
D Garner
D Johns
D McDonald
D McNeill
D Pegler
D R Clowser
D Stevenson
D Stratton
D Withers
D Wright
Dallas Seawright
Damian McNeill
Dan Duvall
Dan Podsobinski
Dai Haskins
Daniel A. Flynn
Daniel Lewis
Daphne Stanford
Darren Allen
Darren J Humble
Darren Lawbuary
Dave (Ratchy) Ratchford
Dave Bennett

Dave Brooks
Dave Brown
Dave Campbell
Dave Cantrill
Dave Gaylor
Dave Humble
Dave Mitchell
Dave Perrons
Dave Phillips
Dave Richardson
Dave Setchfield
Dave Snaith
Dave Stockley
Dave Walker
Dave Walters
Dave Wilcoxon
Dave Wright
David Bersantie
David Carole
David Carss
David Cork
David Cranch
David Djuric
David Gauler
David Gorse
David & Karen Koon
David J Koukol
David Jipps
David Leeks
David Longford
David Newboult
David Nisbet
David Pegler
David Phillips
David Pickering
David Pitts
David Purdy
David Ratchford
David Smith
David Snaith
David Swift
David White
David.T.Gray
Davy Russel
Dawn Palmer
Debz Lewis
Dennis Jones
Dennis Stratton
Derek Hubbard
Derek Laing
Diarmuid Mallon
Dominic Keating
Don Foss
Don Stewart

Doug Pybus
Doug Turnbull
Doug Walker
Dr. Greg Walker
Dr. Jonathan Heath
Duncan Cresswell
Ed Donnelly
Edward Booth
Edward Harrigan
Edward Scully
Elfed Wynne
Eliana Campi
Emma Flowerday
Emyr Lewis
Enric Martí
Eric Stewart
Ernst C. Zach
Ethan Foskett
Evelyn Leydon
Federica Traina
Fergal Woods
Florian Tanty
Frank Kremer
Frank The Snowman
G Bailey
G Briggs
G Carey
G Dean
G Francis
G Mason
G Oxford
G Pound
G Scarrott
G Smith
G Thompson
G Watson
Gary Burke
Gary Cole
Gary Michael Pollard
Gary Pannell
Gary Parker
Gary Pollard
Geoff Bell
Geoff Brown
Geoff Hunt
Geoff White
George Broadwell
George Marple
George Mina
Gerard Van De
Langkruis
Gerrit De Geus
Gill & Mike Sierens
Gina Bersantie
Glenn Picking
Glynn Calvert
Graeme Cowe
Graham Douglas

Graham Jenkins
Graham Maisey
Graham Smith
Graham Taylor
Graham Thompson
Graham Whitelaw
Greg Peters
Greg Walker
Guy Peskin
H Twiddle
Halford Peter Stone
Hans-Jürgen Beck
Harold Dawson
Harold Norcott
Herbert & Karin
Schmiedl
Howard Mason
Howard Whitfield
I Herrmann
I Langford
I Smethurst
Iain Hathorn
Ian Bailey
Ian Benger
Ian Booth
Ian Gordon
Ian Hicks
Ian Kirby
Ian Littler
Ian Mcmillan
Ian Probert
Ian Reeves
Ian Sleigh
Ian Thomas
Ian Van Ryne
Isabel King
Ivan Simpson
Ivy Palmer
J C Farr
J Fullerton
J Goodall
J Goodhand
J Green
J Gregory
J Grubb
J Hilton
J Holyome
J Jelley
J Lungan
J Lyon
J McGregor
J Orton
J Roberts
J Robinson
Jack Watson
Jacques Arsenault
Jacqui & Frank Hill
Jacqui Smith

James King
James Oeming
James Palace
James Tucker
James Wainwright
Jamie Crawford
Jamie Pipe
Jan Werkhoven
Jan Wojtowicz
Jane Westing
Jean Margerison
Jean Norris
Jean-Jacques Haultier
Jean-Pierre Del Vecchio
Jeff Hemmerling
Jeff Platts
Jeff Wrack
Jennie Brooks
Jenny Bailey
Jens Dossing
Jeremy Cook
Jill Lightley
Jim Bruner
Jim Crick
Jim Geckle
Jim Mcneill
Jim Rice
Jim Shorter
Jim Tucker
Jim Whitton
Jo Beyer
Joe Chadwin
Joe Orton
Joe Ransby
Joerg "Whistling
Catfish" Neumann
John (Rabbie) Burns
John B Telfer
John Beetham
John Belville
John Blaise
John Bullock
John Burrell
John Chapman
John Cleaveley
John Connett
John Davies
John Dawson
John Dean Hudspith
John Dedman
John Fullerton
John Gibaut
John Green
John Hester
John Holyome
John K Mallis
John Kimber
John Lee

John Lester
John Mallis
John McCrory
John Porter
John Purcell
John Radford & Linda
Radford
John Raftery
John Sherwood
John Taylor
John Thompson
John Tichborne
John Tierney
John Uriel
John Vesey
John Walmsley
John Winning
Jol Bartle
Jonathan Jago
Jonathan Porter
Jorge J Tovar
Josef Langwieser
Jouni Hämäläinen
Julia and Bill Gristwood
Julian Goodhand
Juliet Beale
June Gibson
June McLenaghan
K Bainton
K Clark
K Cooper
K March
K Mills
K Patterson
K Smart
K Turner
K Wood
K Woodsford
Karen McIntyre
Karin & Werner Fiebig
Karl Shaw
Karsten Kupillas
Katie Czohara
Keith Booth
Keith Burchett
Keith Evans
Keith Hood
Keith Main
Keith Murray Main
Keith Pipe
Keith Rule
Keith Stewart
Kelvin Watson
Ken Brown
Ken Cripps
Ken Ebbens
Ken Lamb
Ken Morris

Ken Woodsford
Kenny Matheson
Kevin Jones
Kevin Leary
Kevin Murray
Kevin Smith
Kevin Wakefield
Kevin Wilkinson
Indiana
Kristy Connolly
L Bridge
L M Withers
L Tait
L Wellman
L.J.Britton
Lars Hegndal
Laurent Béost
Lawrence McBride
Andrew James McBride
Heather Joan Gordon
Lawrence Paulauskas
Lee Jessup
Len Bridge
Len Manley
Les Baker-Smith
Lesley Boswell
Leslie Pattison
Libor Mysliveček
Linda Bottomley
Linda Cameron
Linda Ritchie
Luis M Bueno
Lutz Meissner
M D Wright
M Davenport
M Flavell
M Francis
M French
M Gilmore
M Hales
M Hammett
M Herrington
M Hurst
M J Menhenitt
M J O'Rourke
M J Reed
M Jessop
M Langwieser
M Mahoney
M McCloud
M Morris
M P Hinchliffe
M Post
M Roach
M T Janaway
M Thundercliffe
M Wilson
M.Allsopp

M.Bradley
Macdara Woods
Malcolm Sims
Manfred Zimmermann
Manuel Ángel García Teixeiro
Marcel Paton
Marco (Laufi) Laufenberg
Margaret Kendall
Marion Donaldson
Mark Bengeochea
Mark Brooks
Mark Collins
Mark Hammett
Mark Holborough
Mark Horbowsky
Mark Paul Murphy
Mark Rogers
Mark Smith
Mark Snowden
Mark Stuart
Mark Thundercliffe
Mark Ward
Martin (The Minstrel)
James Willgrass
Martin Driver
Martin Ewart
Martin Foskett
Martin Futoma
Martin Mueller
Martin Rees
Martin Richard Paterson
Martin Robinson
Martin Thompson
Martin Wiemann
Martin Willgrass
Matt Cox
Matthew Hales
Matthew Kean
Matthew Sims
Maurizio " kallarma" Traina
Melvin Cockerill
Michael A Jackson
Michael Billington
Michael Edgeworth
Michael Geeves
Michael Hurst
Michael Kurzman
Michael Langwieser
Michael Lawrence
Michael Lees
Michael Nauber
Michael Papke
Michael Stanway
Michel Birrell

Mick Comerford
Mick Hutchinson
Mike (4-Days-On-A-Bus) Taylor
Mike Ashman
Mike Chavez
Mike Crane
Mike Dixon
Mike Evans
Mike Goswell
Mike Hance
Mike Herrington
Mike Hutchinson
Mike Kelly
Mike Larking
Siobhan Larking
Mike Lockyer
Mike Menhenitt
Mike Nightingale
Mike Smart
Mike Winter
Mike.Batty
Mikko Uusi-Oukari
Mrs J Hill
Mrs L Thompson
Mrs S Pritchard
Mrs Sheila Robinson
N Cotterell
N J Lewis
N Larcombe-Williams
N Linfield
N Oreton
N Timms
Neil Barham
Neil Durbin
Neil J Oreton
Neil McSheffrey
Neil Williams
Nene Bailey
Nick & Diane Steel
Nick Bayley
Nick Chadwin
Nick Harrison
Nick Naddell
Nick Roll
Nick Skilton
Nick Steel
Nigel & Jeanie Duffin
Nigel Cochrane
Nigel Cooper
Nigel J Evans
Nigel Robinson
Nigel Sheppard
Nigel Watt
Niko Ottowitz
Nils-Olov Andersson
Noel McGough
Noel O'Brien

Norman Carreck
Norman Fisher
Øystein Skottun Lyngdal
Oz Hardwick
P A Wojtusciszyn
P Chalmers
P Colledge
P Dean
P Godfrey
P J Cox
P Lynn
P Missing
P Neaber
P Needham
P Scanlan
P Simpson
P Snow
P Tyrrell
P Wray
Pat Kent
Pat McGuckin
Pat Ryan
Patrice Nicod
Patricia Storey
Patrick Rowbottom
Paul Bone
Paul Brash
Paul Chalmers
Paul Chapman
Paul Davison
Paul DeGuglielmo
Paul Frame
Paul Gray
Paul Hammond
Paul Hooper
Paul Johnson
Paul Kennedy
Paul Lewis
Paul Linn
Paul Marsh
Paul Reed
Paul Slowgrove
Paul Snowden
Paul Stacey
Paul Swarbrook
Paul Thompson
Paul Torrance
Paul Tremble
Paul Vizard
Paul Welsby
Paul Willis
Paul Wrightson
Per Ekström
Pete Dennis
Pete Hallam
Pete Rawlings
Pete Simpson

303

Pete Tyrrell
Pete Williamson
Peter Blomeley
Peter Canty
Peter Cowley
Peter Matazinskas
Peter O'Neill
Peter Paul Blomeley
Peter Ryder
Peter Snow
Peter Spratt
Peter Vines
Peter Wood
Phil Bambrick
Phil Calvert
Phil Hill
Phil Kelcey
Phil Panto
Phil Perry
Phil Worrall
Philip Brown
Philip Moss
Philip Woodruff
Pippa Mahoney
R Bell
R Birbeck
R Dandy
R Dubey
R G Gascoyne
R Lyford-Smith
R Maxfield
R Mcilveen
R Milne
R Nunn
R R H Van Den Brom
R Richardson
R Waghorne
R Whincup
R Wiggins
R Williams
R Winfield
Rainer Opiela
Ray Bonington
Ray Ford
Ray Judd
Ray Waters
Raymond Graves
Raymond Hutchinson
Rebecca Carter
Rebecca Costin
Sanchez
Reinhold Polster
Renée Spizz
Revd Garry Whittaker
Revd Tony Kinnersley
Richard Connell
Richard & Julia
Gascoyne

Richard Drake
Richard Glinn
Richard Grainger
Richard Houdmont
Richard Hutchins
Richard Jackson
Richard Kennedy
Richard Knowles
Richard Lord
Richard McKone
Richard Morton
Richard Rolfe
Richard Samways
Richard Smith
Richard Sutton
Richard Taylor
Rick Bailey
Rick Dodderidge
Rick Drake
Rob Chard
Rob Chitty
Rob Lovett
Rob Mcadam
Rob Moss
Robbie Harrison
Robert Blaisdell
Robert Graves
Robert Hay
Robert Richardson
Robert Rodie
Robert Studnicki
Rockit Roy Powell
Rod Ward
Rogan Ashton
Roger Cove
Ros Palmer
Russ Pinnegar
Russell Tarvid
S A Saunders
S Baldwin
S D King
S Davies
S Duckett
S Flower
S Forrest
S Franklin
S Gough
S Green
S Henshall
S Horner
S J Hall
S J Maidment
S J Miller
S Johnson
S Loveday
S Matthews
S Narey
S R Lock

S Robinson
Sally Carter
Sallyann Stones
Sara Frances Morgan
Sarah Dengel
Sarah Dixon
Sarah Robinson
Savva Christofides
Sean Eaton
Sean Gough
Selwyn Rhys Morgan
Sheila Robinson
Siân Williams
Simon Biggs
Simon Chavasse
Simon Clarke
Simon Hall
Simon Riley
Simon Stringfellow
Ste Greenall
Stein Arne Ystheim
Stephen Bush
Stephen Langwieser
Stephen McLean
Buchan
Stephen Rogers
& Julie Rogers
Stephen Spence
Stephen Waters
Steve Brook
Steve Cant
Steve Connolley
Steve Davies
Steve Evans
Steve Greenall
Steve Halligan
Steve Hanks
Steve Harrison
Steve Henshall
Steve Kehoe
Steve Parkhouse
Steve Pitt
Steve Rowlands
Steve Saunders
Steve Spann
Steve Taylor
Steven Flowerday
Steven Marcus
Steven Rees
Steven Walker
Stewart McMinn
Stu Higgins
Stuart Hornby
Stuart Murdoch
Stuart Robinson
Sue Bishop
Susan Wilkinson
Indiana

Svein-Magne Forsgren
T Wilkinson
Tanya Graves
Ted Capstick
Terry Bennett
Terry "The Innocent"
Coates
Terry Osborn
Theresa Mitton
Thibault, Marilyne
and Ian Vogt
Thierry Vogt
Tim Cross
Tim Hilton
Tim Jones
Tim Kay
Tim McGuinness
Tim Short
Tim Taylor
Tim Williams
Tina Langwieser
Tom Nelson
Tony (Jack) Warner
Tony Armitage
Tony Downing
Tony Honour
Tony Marsh
Tony Tortorella
Tony Warner
Tony Wood
Tor Sandberg
Torbjörn Onegård
Trevor Dickerson
Trevor Hill
Trevor Kirby
Trevor Puttergill
Trish Storey
Tyler James Elias
Indiana
Ulla Hilger
W Talbott
Wade Goertz
Wayne Gatward
Wayne Rowland
William Cowie
William Harrison
William McKay
William Munro
William Nugent
Xavier Riera i Valenti

In memory of our
good friends
Dave Hall
Andy Faux
Michael Veith

304